AF594647

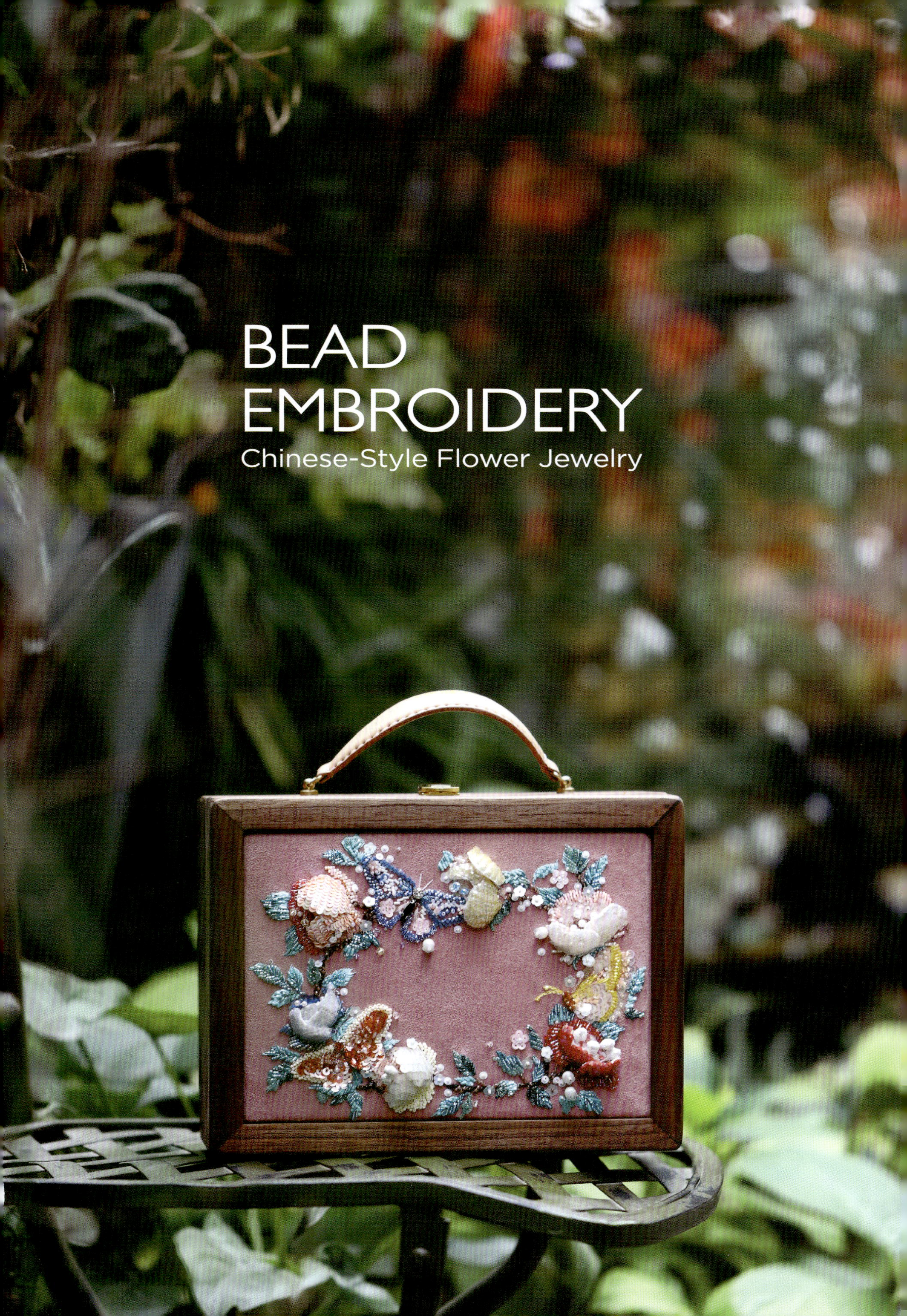
BEAD
EMBROIDERY
Chinese-Style Flower Jewelry

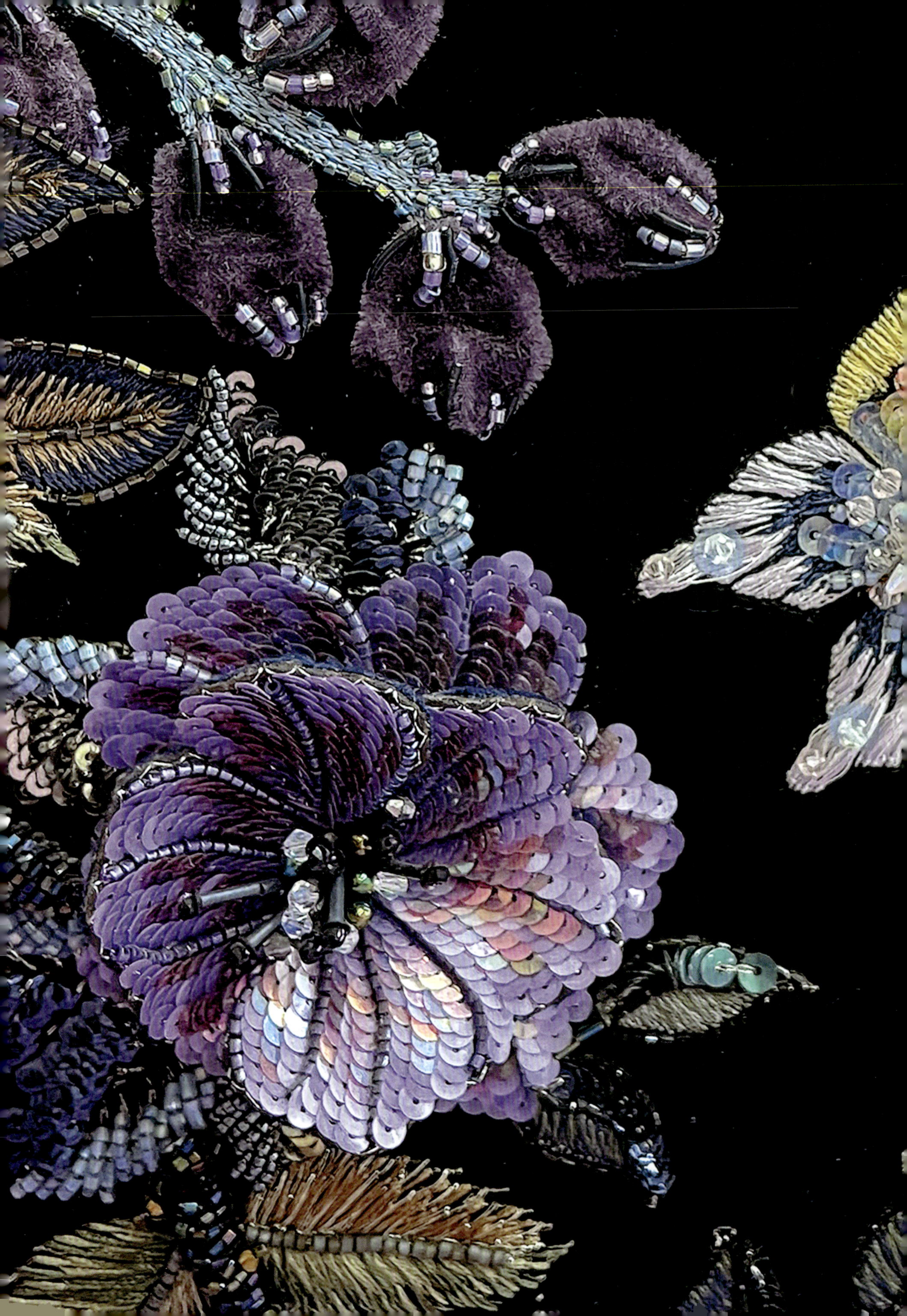

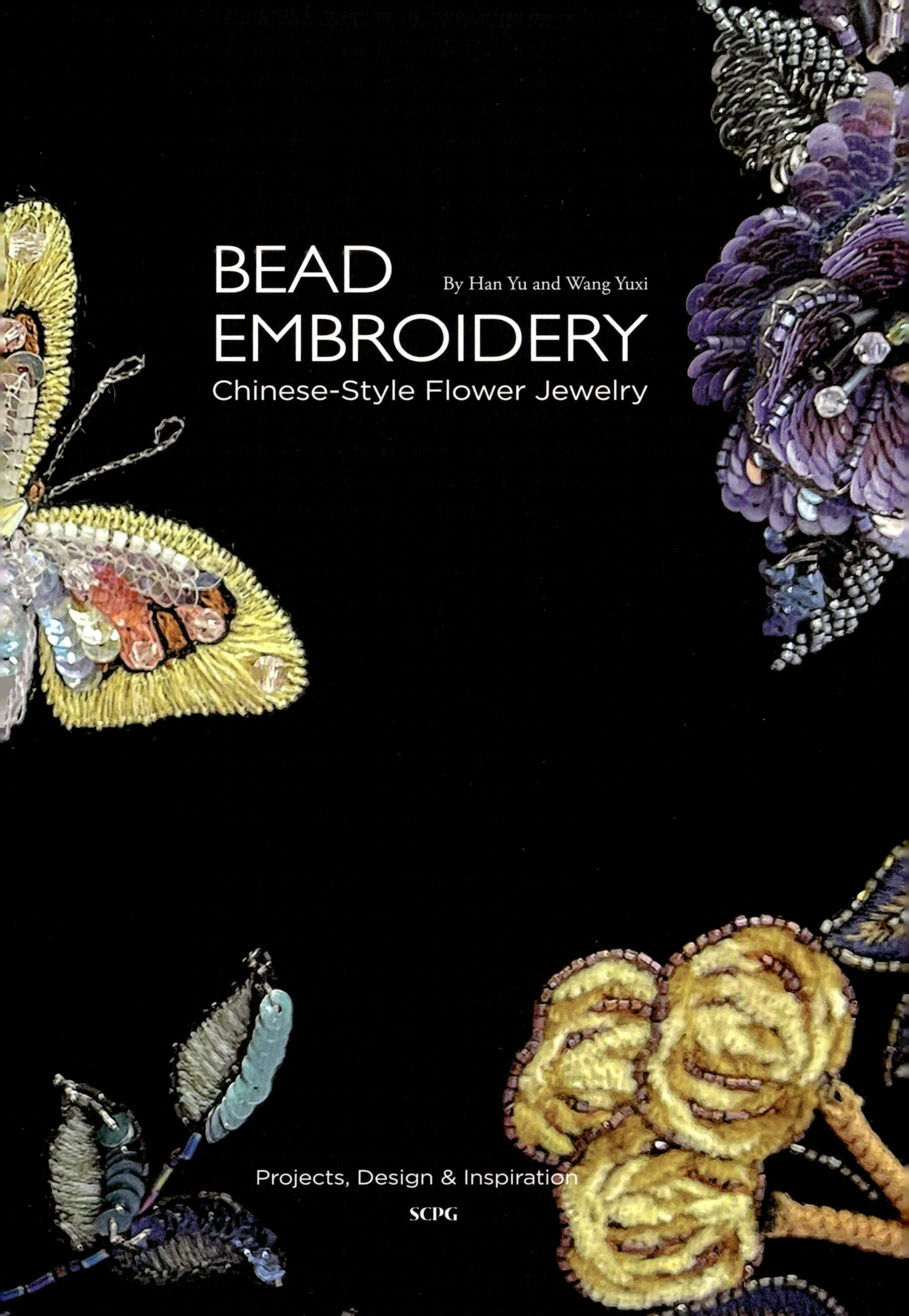

BEAD EMBROIDERY

Chinese-Style Flower Jewelry

By Han Yu and Wang Yuxi

Projects, Design & Inspiration

SCPG

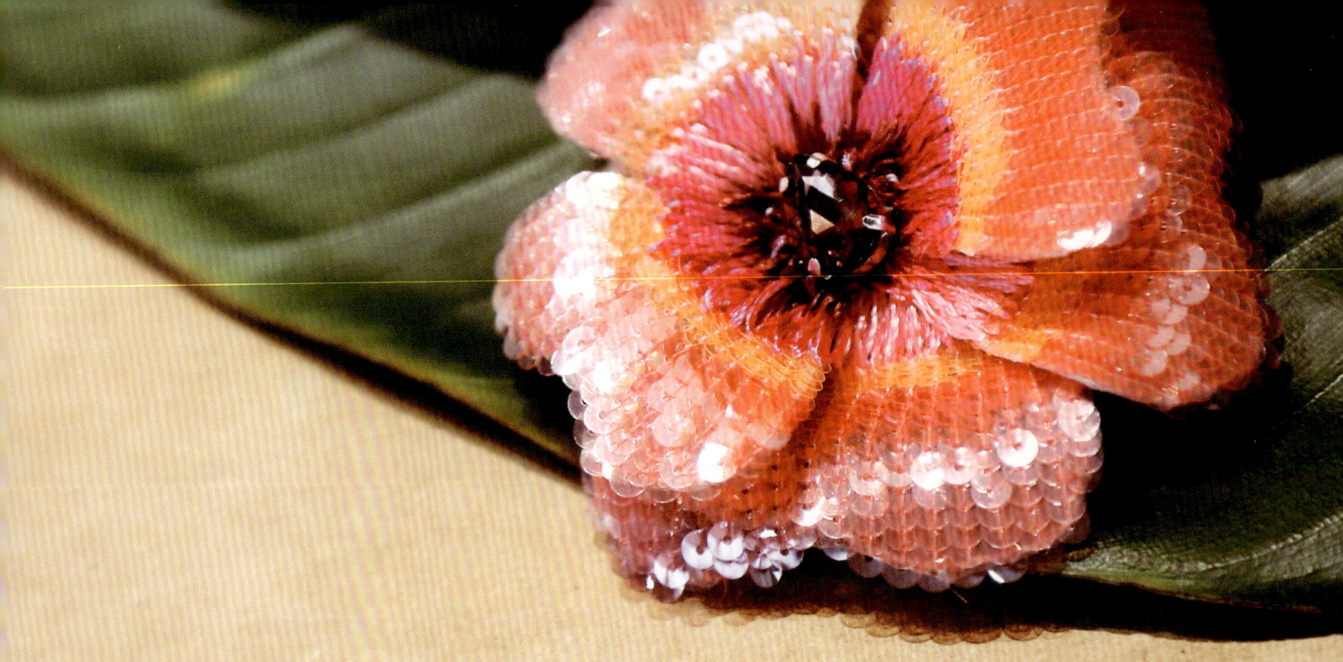

Text: Han Yu, Wang Yuxi
Jewelry Design: Bao Shuang
Embroidery Steps: Song Yujie, Xu Meng, Li Jie, Sun Yijing, He Yuan, Kuai Leran, Wang Zhangwen
Photographs: He Haili, Peng Dongmei
Digital Drawing: Song Yujie

Translation: Shelly Bryant
Cover Design: Wang Wei
Interior Design: Hu Bin, Li Jing (Yuan Yinchang Design Studio)

Editor: Cao Yue

ISBN: 978-1-93836-881-3

Address any comments about *Bead Embroidery: Chinese-Style Flower Jewelry* to:

SCPG
401 Broadway, Ste. 1000
New York, NY 10013
USA

or

Shanghai Press and Publishing Development Co., Ltd.
Floor 5, 390 Fuzhou Road, Shanghai, China (200001)
Email: sppdbook@163.com

Printed in China by Shanghai Donnelley Printing Co., Ltd.

1 3 5 7 9 10 8 6 4 2

On page 1
Fig. 1 *Butterflies Chasing Flowers*
This combination of beaded embroidery and luggage is robust yet soft, and exudes luxury and personality. The piece depicts colorful butterflies dancing among flowers in a sea of dreamy colors using beads and sequins.

On pages 2–3
Fig. 2 *Purple Flower and Butterfly*
A colorful butterfly is lingering over the fragrance of a secret garden. This is detail from the embroidery of a handbag.

Above
Fig. 3 *Wild Pansy*
Here, beaded embroidery is used to create a three-dimensional wild pansy, comprising warm red, bright orange, and delicate pink colors in graduating layers. The overall tone is warm and bright.

CONTENTS

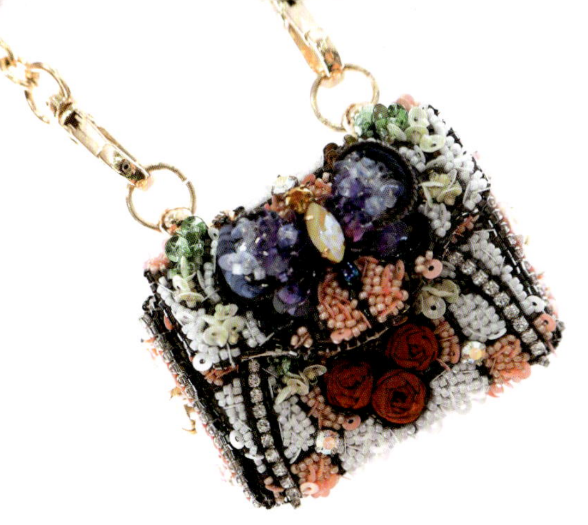

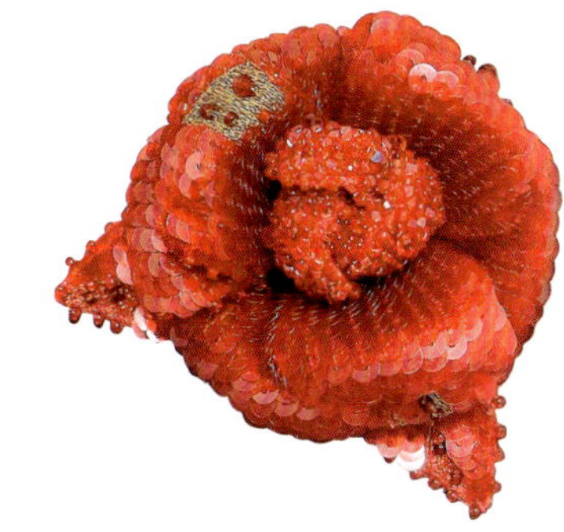

Fig. 4 *Mini Rose Bag*
Colorful beads surround three lively roses made of red fabric—perfect for dates.

Fig. 5 *Red Camellia*
The enduringly popular red camellia is a classical Chinese flower. It has a long history, inspiring a myriad of camellia-themed works in various domains, including literature, painting, and utensils.

CONTENTS

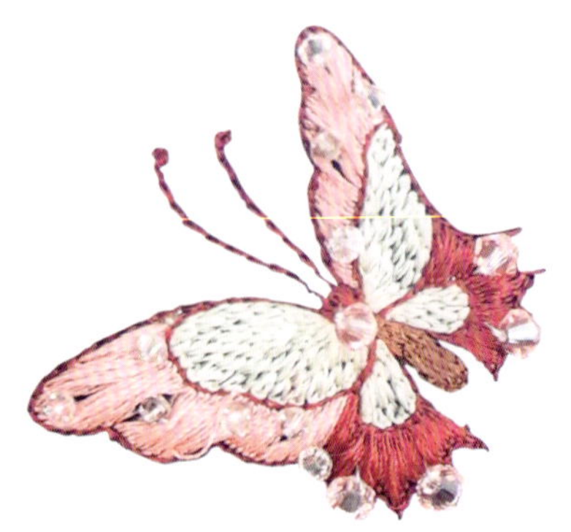

CONTENTS

On facing page
Fig. 6 *Pink Butterfly*
In China, butterflies symbolize freedom and beauty, and appear in tales such as *The Butterfly Lovers*—one of the four major love stories of Chinese folklore. This beaded work features pink crystals interspersed between threads, depicting a beautiful butterfly in flight.

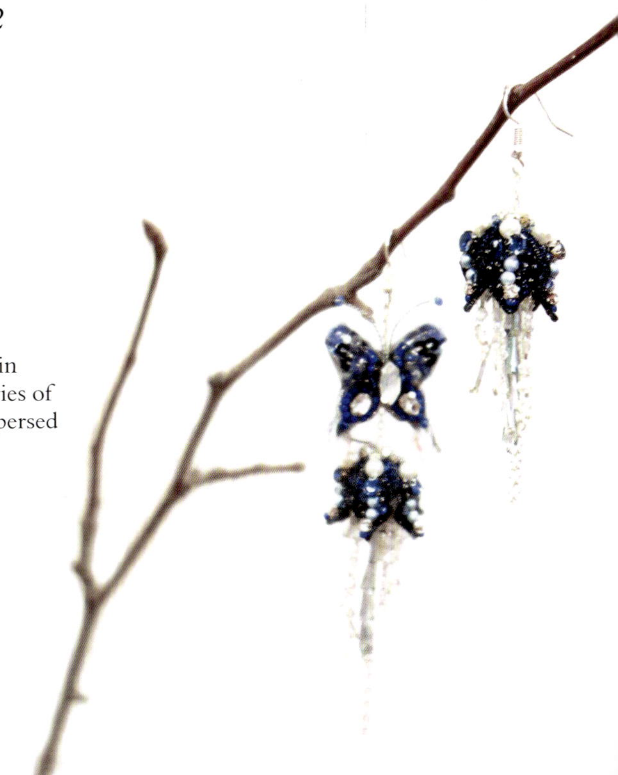

Right
Fig. 7 *Balloon Flower Earrings*
See page 108 for the production process.

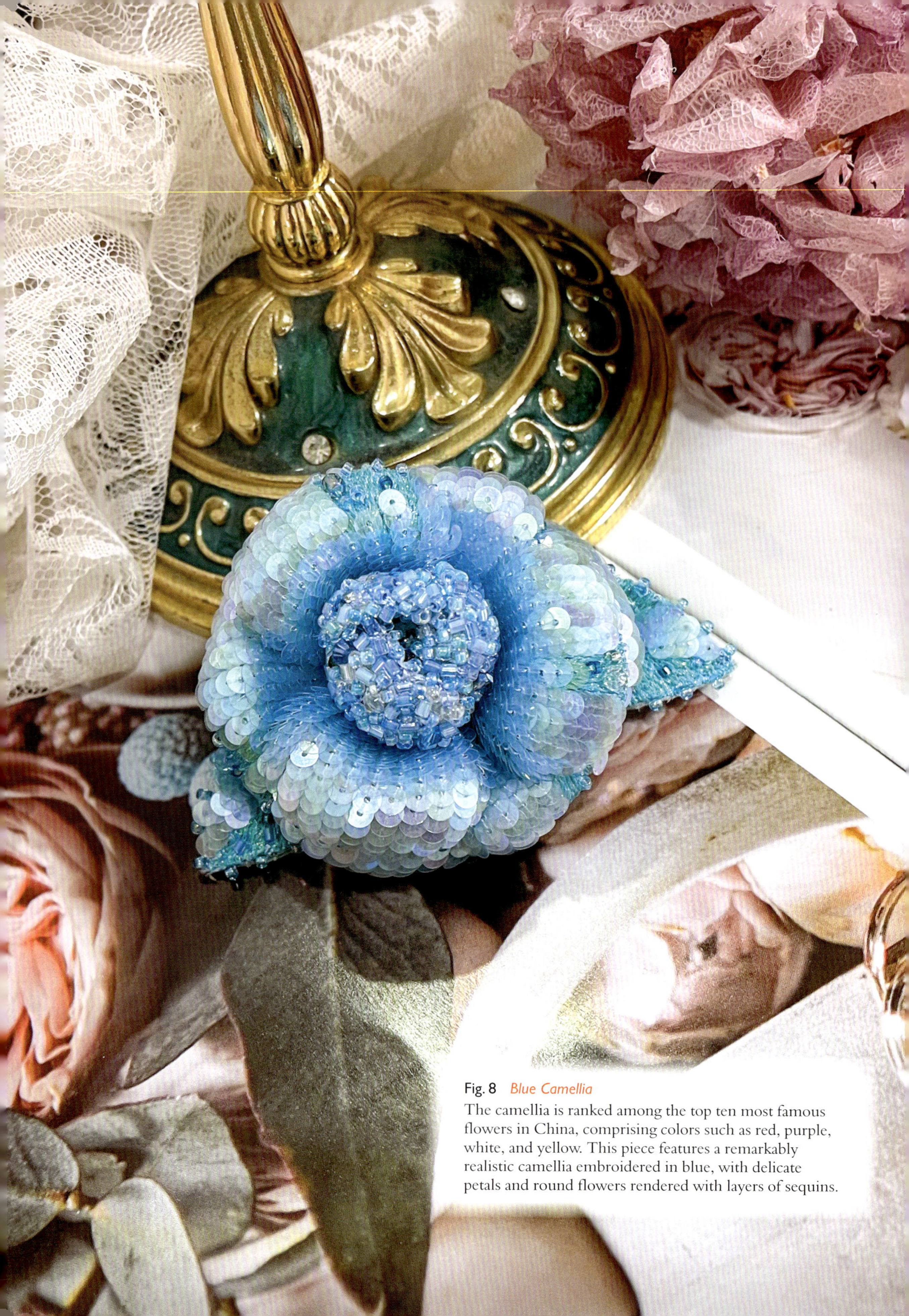

Fig. 8 *Blue Camellia*

The camellia is ranked among the top ten most famous flowers in China, comprising colors such as red, purple, white, and yellow. This piece features a remarkably realistic camellia embroidered in blue, with delicate petals and round flowers rendered with layers of sequins.

Preface

When a woman is still a child, she has a fantasy world all of her own, which is constructed while watching fairytales and cartoons. When I was a child, I loved observing flowers and birds. The gorgeous feathers and petals filled me with curiosity and whimsical thoughts about nature.

Many years ago, I happened to see an haute couture sunflower dress on the Internet. Its skillful color matching and use of different materials captivated me. I wanted to know what the fluffy materials were, and the reasons for the plastic sheet's ability to stand on its own.

With these questions in mind, I read many books and articles, and learned that the bead embroidery industry was established a long time ago in Xiamen, China, where glass beads were embroidered onto bags and shoes. The roots of this art form can be traced back to the Tang dynasty (618–907). With support from my family, I went to France to take embroidery courses, and became acquainted with a dazzling array of seed beads, sequins, and threads. The answers to my questions were revealed, which gave me a great sense of satisfaction.

When I returned to China, I combined the knowledge and techniques I'd picked up overseas with the traditional embroidery techniques I learned in China. I kept attempting to express the silhouettes of these beautiful flowers in my mind, using a needle and thread to depict the floral world that I'd begun imagining when I was a child. Delicate herbaceous peonies, fresh and elegant narcissi, and lovely roses ...

I began with a natural style of design, and continued incorporating the artistic modes of other cultures. Chinese culture had a significant influence on me, so I tried integrating traditional Chinese embroidery with techniques such as French bead embroidery to express a Chinese-style floral theme. China encompasses a vast territory and a wide variety of flowers, which has brought about a wide-ranging and profound floral culture over thousands of years. As a result, my embroidery work pursues not just aesthetics but also my aspirations, which you will be able to appreciate in this book.

I hope that our creations will give you inspiration to create your own imaginary garden.

Han Yu

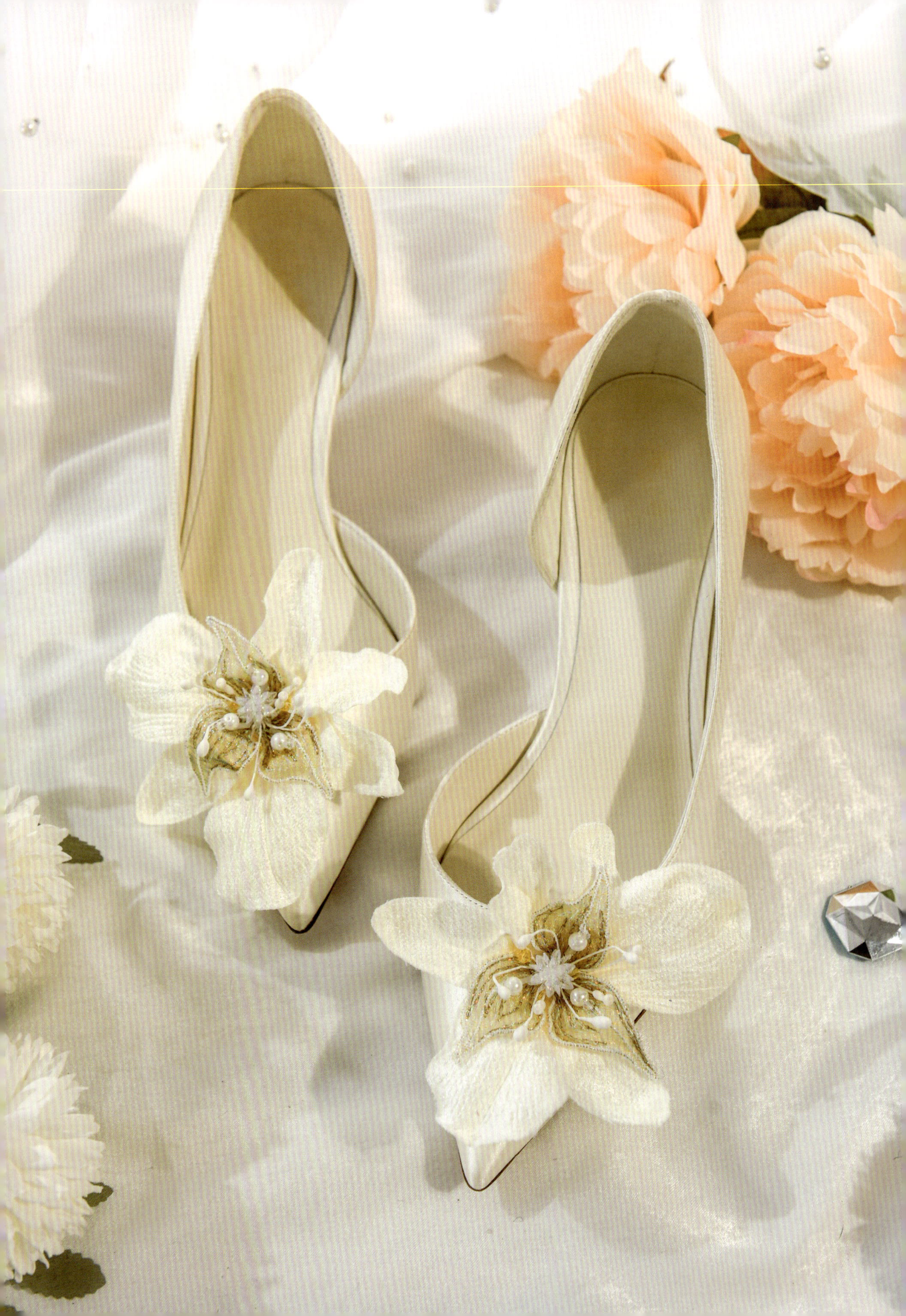

Preface

My handicraft story began when I sneaked a look inside my grandmother's bag of rags as a child. That bag was my favorite toy during my childhood, and using the rags to make handicraft items was my hobby throughout that period. When I grew up, I majored in Fashion, and became a lecturer in Fashion Design at a university. Everything seemed to fall into place. My passion for handicraft continued in the fashion and design industries, where I have been working for more than 10 years. It has become part of my career and everyday life. The use and creation of bead embroidery materials and techniques play a pivotal role in my profession, especially when I make haute couture dresses. In addition, I acquired the techniques of traditional Chinese embroidery, Japanese-style flower making, French-style flower making, three-dimensional embroidery, and Indian bullion wire embroidery techniques. I am devoted to the integration of modern design and traditional Chinese embroidery, participating in the design and production of haute couture clothing for fashion brands and fashion weeks. Looking back, I have completed a lot of pieces, and have taught many courses. I can easily obtain materials for my creations these days, and no longer need to sneak into my grandmother's bag of rags, but that was the starting point of my little dream.

My design philosophy for bead embroidery is to strike a perfect balance in terms of aesthetics. For instance, during a university lecture I once gave, I spoke about one of my pieces, which featured a small bee. For materials, I primarily used Indian gold wire, Japanese seed beads, and embroidery thread. Particular attention was paid to how each material was matched. For example, Indian bullion wires create a three-dimensional effect, while traditional embroidery thread can realize flat layers, forming a balance between three-dimensional and flat aesthetics. In terms of presentation, the bee—which is the main element—is accentuated with sleek textured leaves, while the main body is made of gold to symbolize the harvest, creating the effect of a decorative painting. The bee is detachable, and can be made into everyday

On facing page

Fig. 9 *Lilies*

These lovely beaded lilies, studded on the front part of the shoes, exude elegance and intellectuality. In Chinese, it carries the auspicious meaning of "one hundred years of harmony."

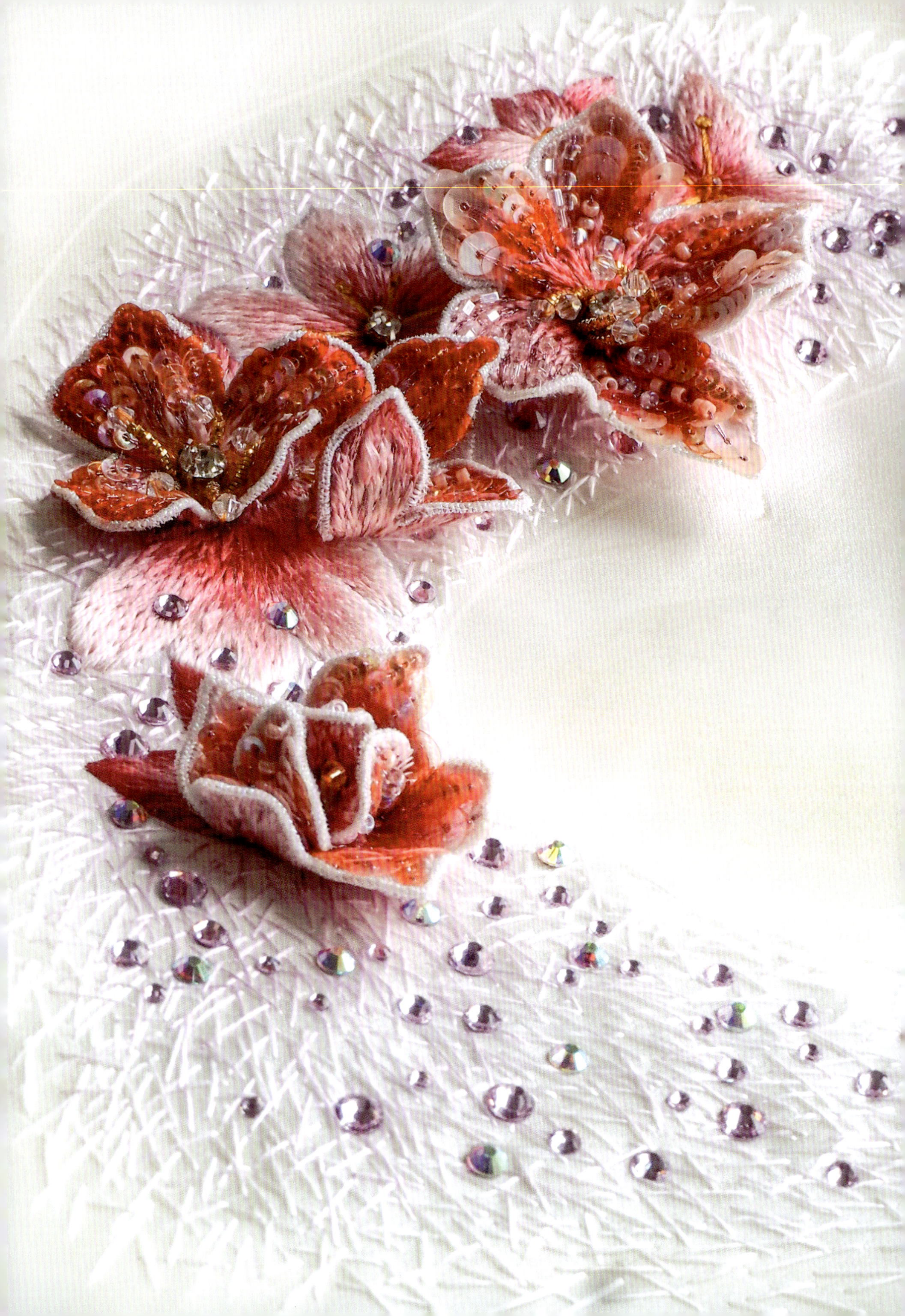

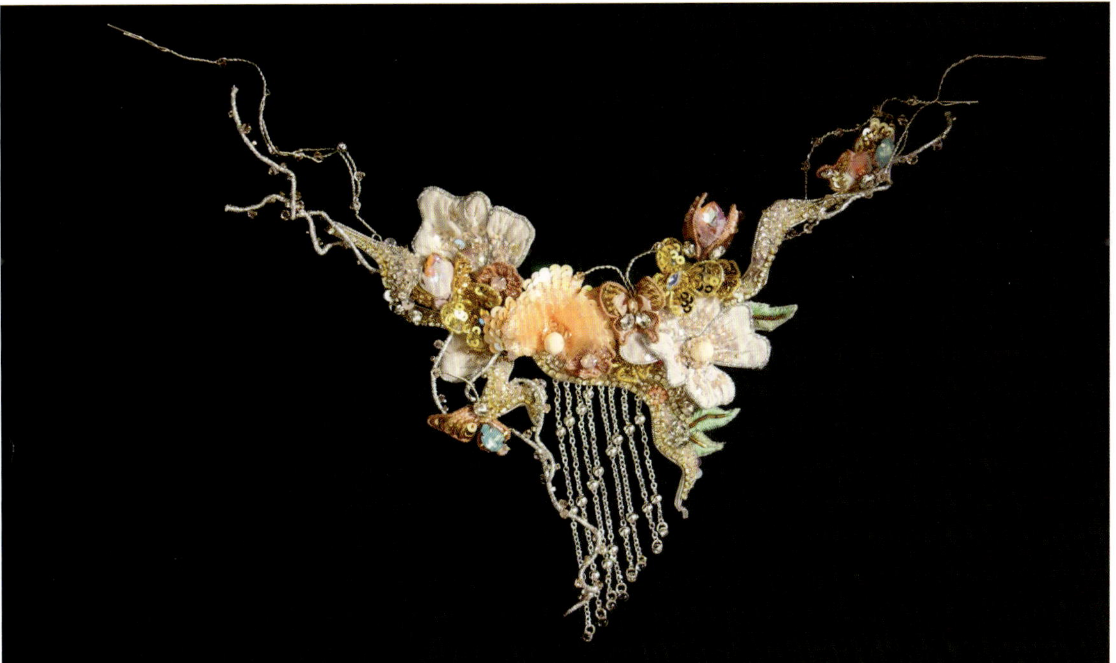

Fig. 10 *Flower Necklace*
This necklace is a combination of bead-embroidered flowers, buds, and butterflies. It will go well with an evening gown.

accessories such as brooches and pendants, striking a balance between artistry and practicality.

This is the second bead embroidery book that I have worked on with Han Yu. The beautifully decorated and practical jewelry made in this book revolves around the theme of flowers. The appendix contains all the patterns of the sixteen pieces of work. You may copy them directly on the tracing paper or scan and enlarge them to a proper size before tracing. You can also modify the patterns to create your own design.

I hope this book will convey the joy of bead embroidery and aesthetic pleasure.

Wang Yuxi

On facing page
Fig. 11 *Peach Blossoms*
In Chinese culture, peach blossom symbolizes perfect love. This embroidery piece is for decoration on shoes.

Right
Fig. 12 *Silk Tree Flower Brooch*
See page 136 for the production process.

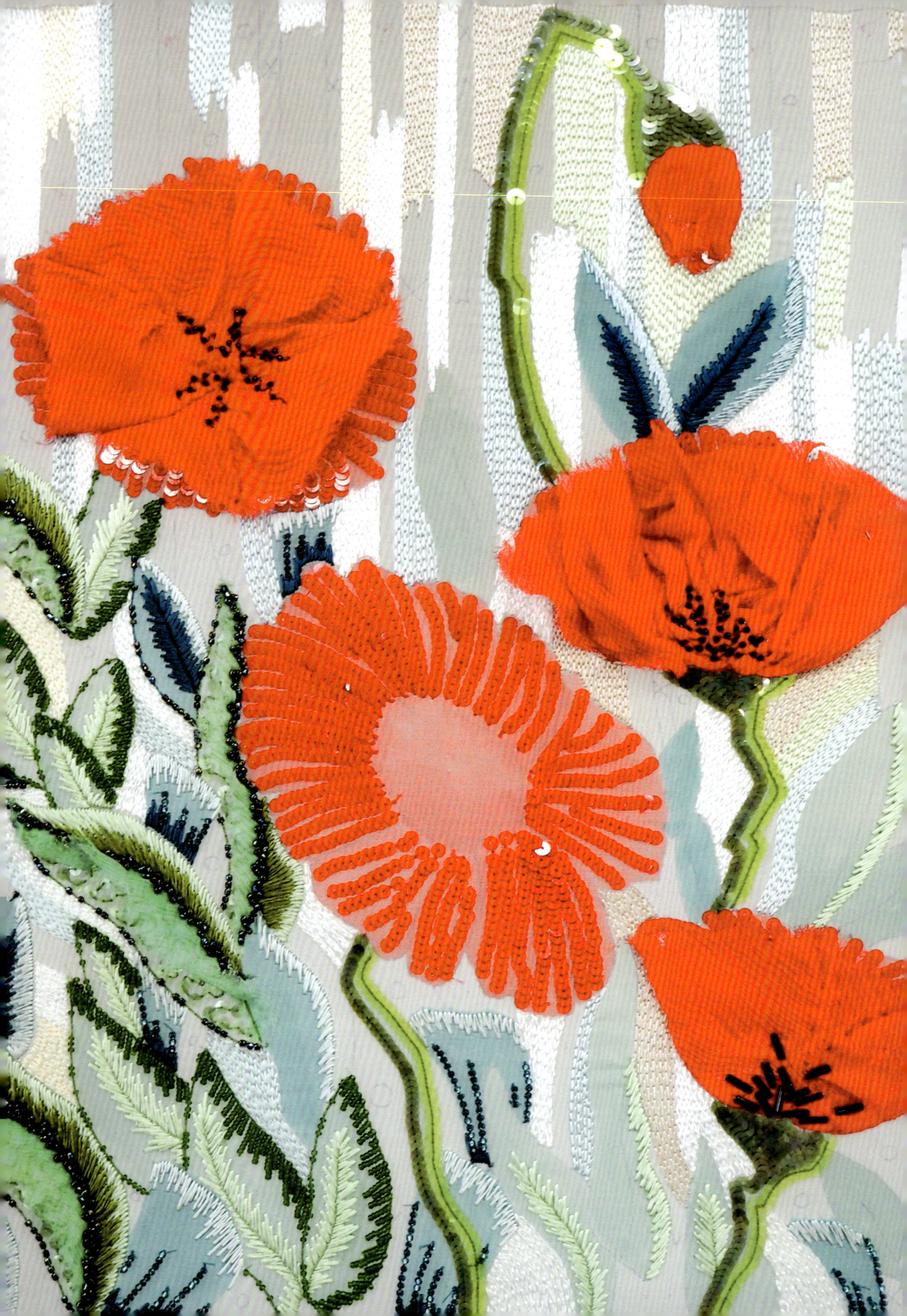

Embroidered Flowers Reimagined for Modern Stitchers

Chinese culture has traditionally placed great emphasis on careful observations of nature, which are viewed as the basis for art, aesthetics, and creativity. However, the beauty of nature cannot transform spontaneously into art. It requires artists to internalize it through the integration and transformation of emotions and personal experiences in order to produce their work, aligning with the idea that "art comes from life." Nature has given us an abundance of breathtaking scenes, and the past 5,000 years of Chinese culture are an inexhaustible treasure trove of aesthetic value. The combination of observations of nature with the essence of Chinese culture creates a perpetual stream of artistic inspiration, which forms the basis of this book.

Flowers have been symbols of beauty since ancient times. We have sung their praises with poetry, depicted their beauty with ink and brushes, and recreated their intricacies with needles and thread. The way flowers are appreciated within Chinese culture is also unique. Chinese people admire not just the color, fragrance, and posture, but also the appeal of flowers—a characteristic that is bestowed upon them and integrated with their spiritual symbolism. Chinese flower lovers believe that it is difficult to enter a high artistic realm without knowledge of the appeal of flowers. For example, plum blossoms are revered by the Chinese not only because they are as colorful and fragrant as they are delicate and lovely, and they are able to blossom even in the harshest weather conditions, ushering in spring. Therefore, it has earned a reputation for nobility, tenacity, and humility both internally and externally. The lotus is also appreciated in Chinese culture, as depicted in the poem, for the beauty of "its multiple densely-layered leaves, which sprawl to the horizon. The flower takes on a distinctive red hue as it basks in the sunlight." More importantly, the lotus stays pure and untainted as it grows out of the mud, imbuing it with the meanings of self-love and an untainted

On facing page

Fig. 13 *Corn Poppies*

In China, corn poppy is also called Beauty Yu, as the flower is said to be a personification of Yu Ji, a beauty of the Qin dynasty (221–206 BC). This piece of work features bright red corn poppies embroidered with red sequins and fabrics.

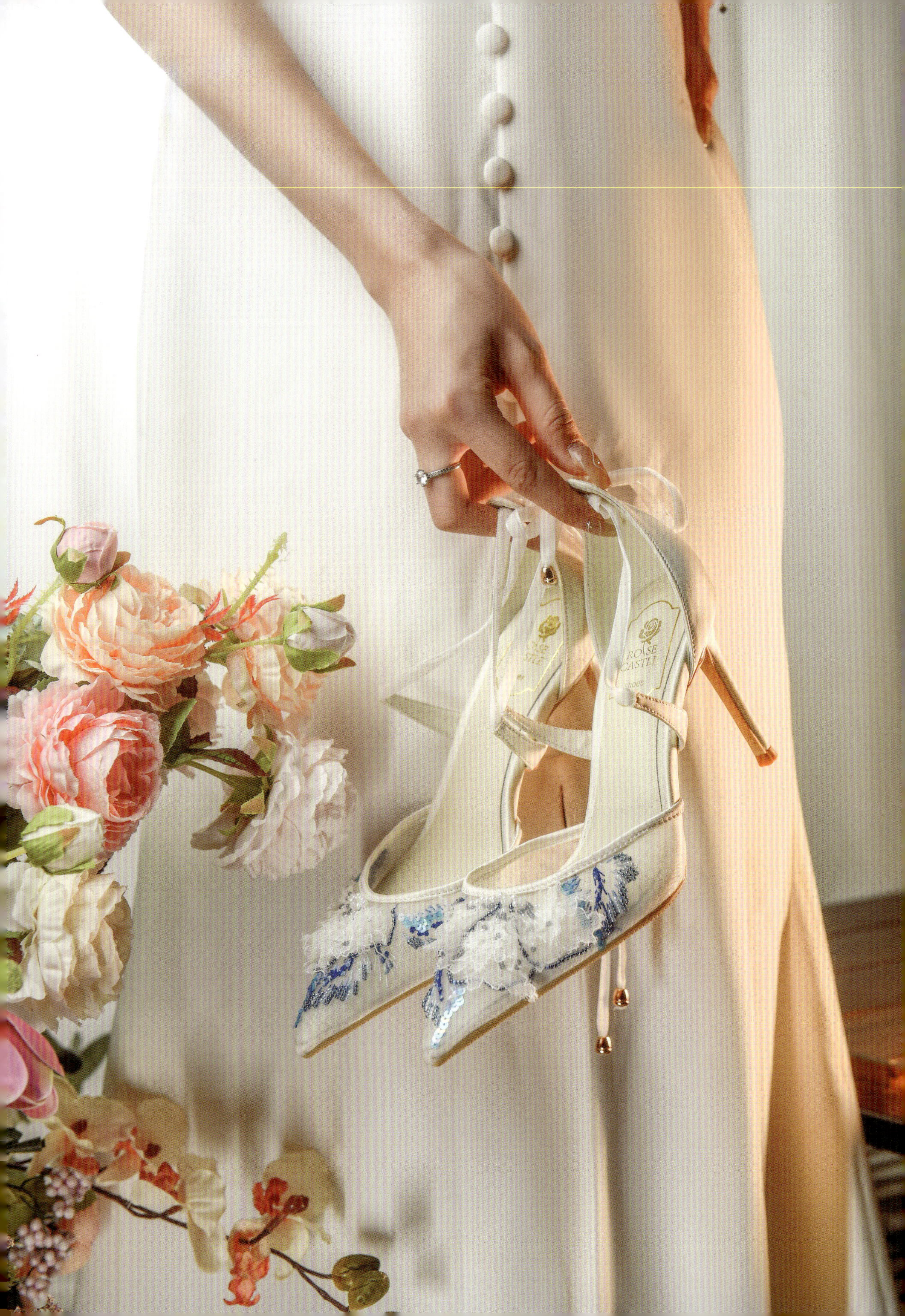
ROSE
CASTLE
shoes

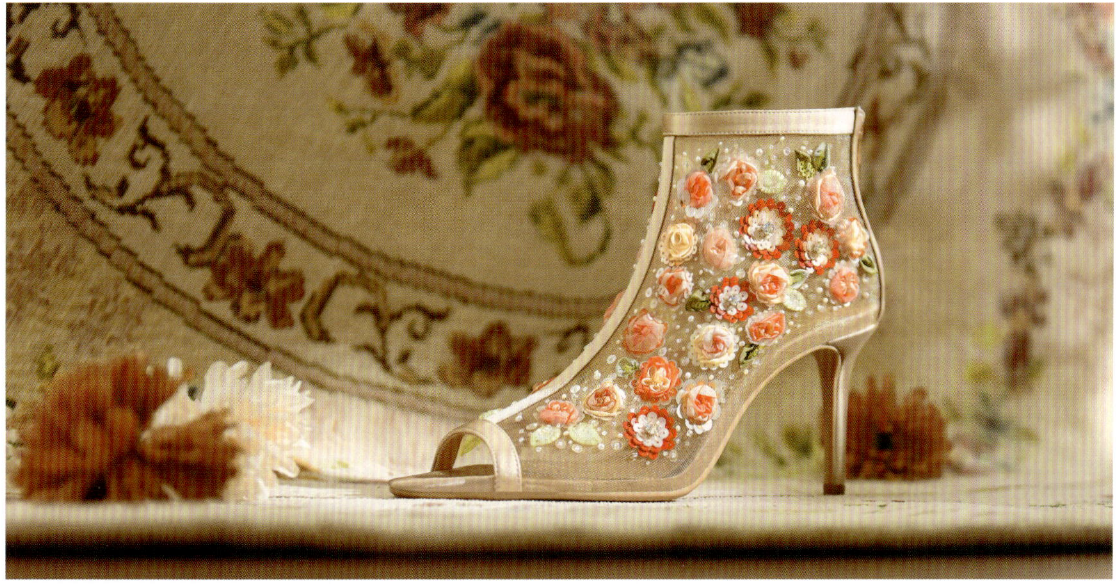

Fig. 14 *Rose High Heels*
Ribbons and sequins are combined to embroider orange-pink roses all over the shoe, giving the wearer an air of a fairy among the flowers.

character. Cultural exchanges between China and the rest of the world have spread knowledge about flowers and their symbolism. For example, the role of carnations as the "flower of mothers" has long been known and accepted across cultures.

Flowers are depicted using bead embroidery, combining artists' perceptions of their color, fragrance, posture, and appeal after making nature-based observations and using creativity to represent them. It is also an attempt by the author to integrate French embroidery techniques with Chinese flora aesthetics. In this book you will find a series of creative beadwork projects including pansies dancing like butterflies, Baroque-style iris flowers, fluffy white dandelions, romantic twin lotus, crabapple flowers blooming like ballerinas, and feather-light silk tree flowers. The various blooms represent and bring good wishes for love, freedom, friendship, strength, and good luck. The fusion of Chinese and Western aesthetic culture is a feast for the senses, conferring a unique allure onto beautiful hair accessories, rings, brooches, bags, bracelets, and earrings.

Creativity has no fixed form, and takes on the shape of its surroundings. Through this book, you will discover the joy of bead embroidery and find a new understanding and appreciation of the flowers that make the world a livelier and more beautiful place.

On facing page
Fig. 15 *Blue and White Flower High Heels*
White lace, and blue thread and beads are combined to embroider flower patterns on the shoes.

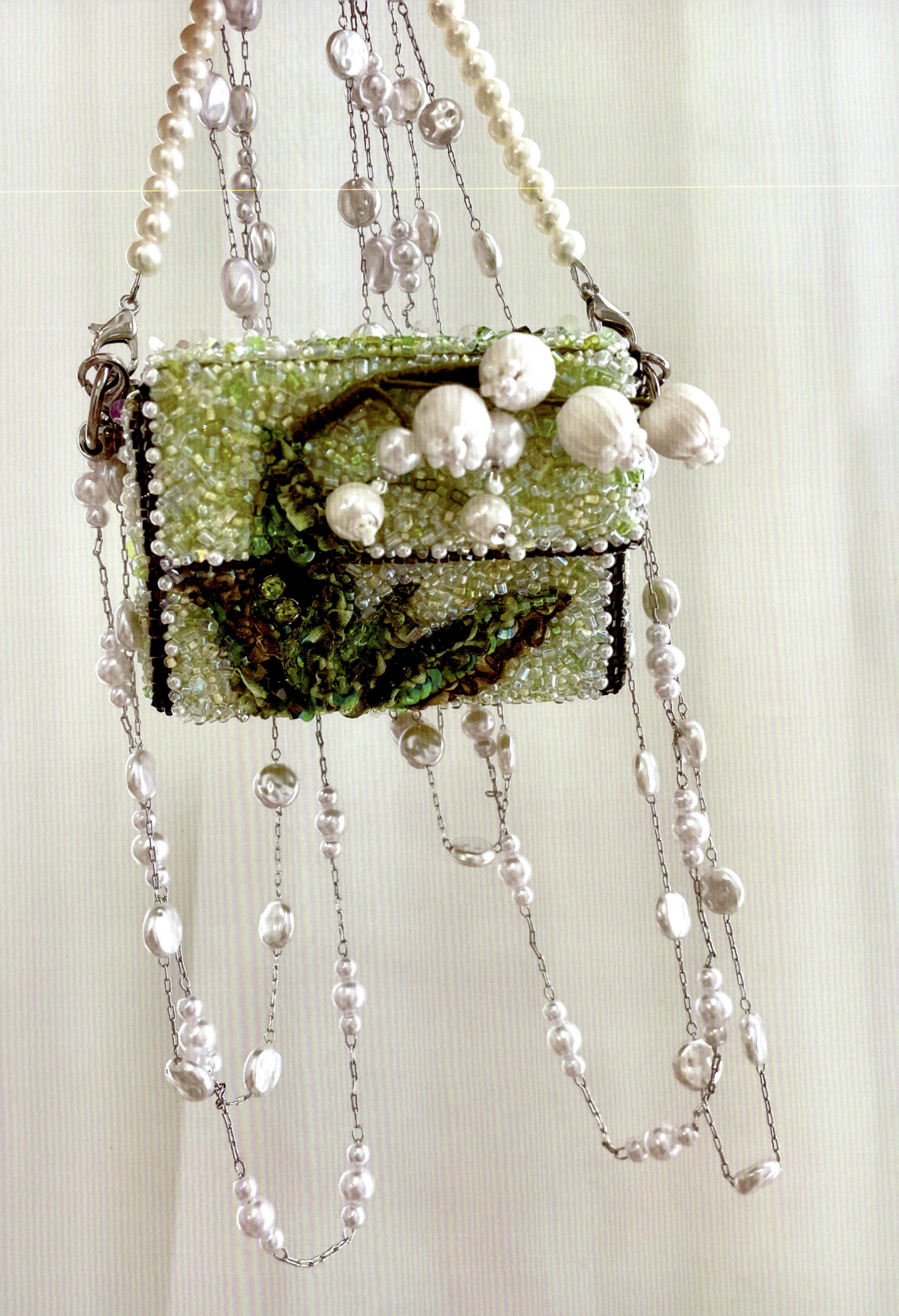

Getting Started

The appeal of bead embroidery lies in its colorful beads, sequins, threads, and fabrics. The colors of beads and sequins can be categorized into monochrome, colored, transparent, and iridescent, while the materials include matte, glossy, and metallic. They also come in a variety of shapes, including round, square, tubular, water droplet-shaped, flower-shaped, and horse eye-shaped. The combinations of beads, sequins, and threads are limited only by your imagination. The materials used in this book's tutorials are not fixed; you are free to change them according to your preferences, and create your own unique work.

This chapter will introduce you to the most commonly used beads, sequins, threads, fabrics, and tools. However, in the world of bead embroidery, there are far too many materials for them all to be listed in this book. You can explore more interesting materials in handicraft shops or on the Internet.

1. Tools

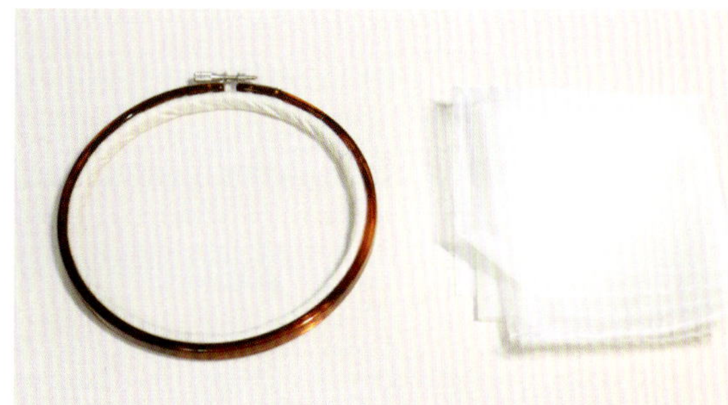

Embroidery hoop (left) and organza (right): The picture shows a small round embroidery hoop. When embroidering, the fabric is stretched directly onto the small round hoop.

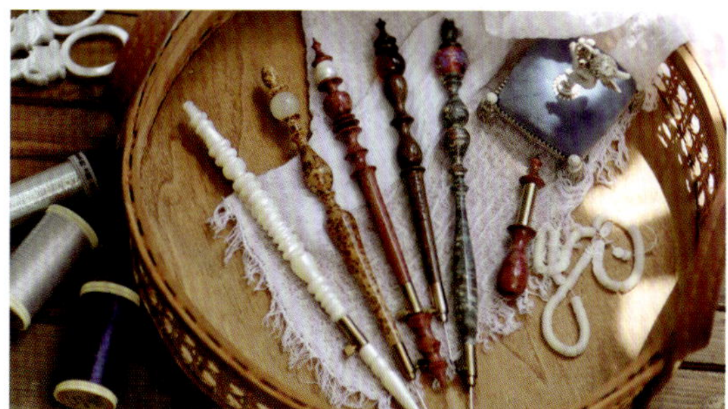

Tambour hook: Comprising a needle head, which is generally divided into model numbers 70–140 (with diameters between 0.7 mm–1.4 mm) and a handle made of wood or other materials.

On facing page

Fig. 16 *Lily of the Valley Mini Bag*

The lily of the valley is a reclusive flower that exudes a faint fragrance all of its own. The body of this bag is embroidered with green beads. White beads and ribbons are used to create three-dimensional lily of the valley flowers. It is decorated with pearls of various shapes, giving a fresh, elegant feel.

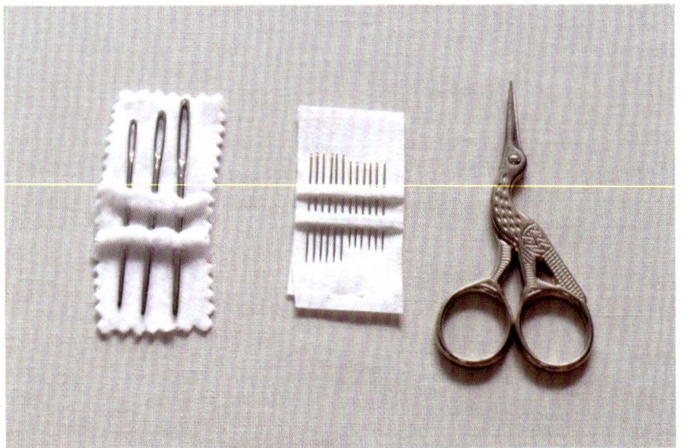

Hand sewing needles: There are differences between the holes and lengths of hand sewing needles. Generally, the appropriate hand sewing needle is selected according to the thickness of the thread.

Scissors: Scissors are usually used to cut threads, metal wires, and fabrics, and are selected based on the object to be cut. The image shows the type of scissors used for thread cutting.

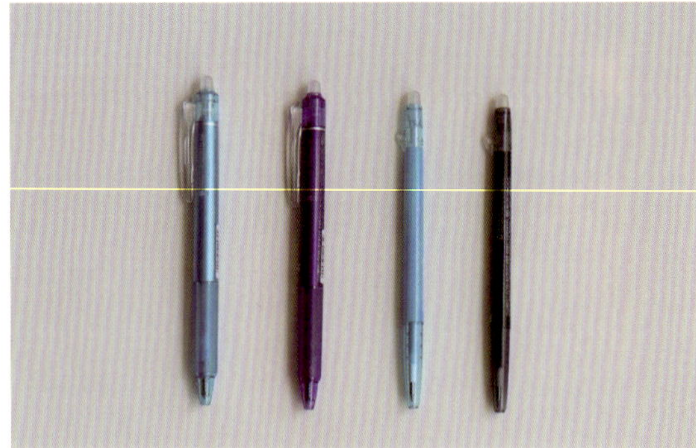

Heat erasable marker: An erasable marking pen used when tracing. The handwriting will disappear when it has been ironed at a high temperature.

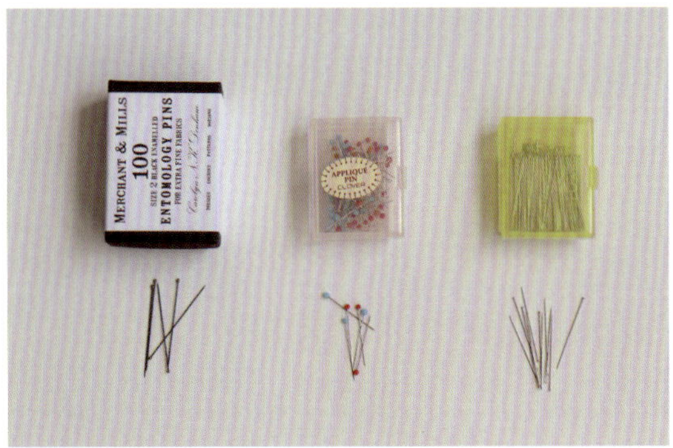

Pins: They are used to fix fabrics or drawings. Fine pins are generally used to fix thinner fabrics such as silk and chiffon, while pins of an ordinary thickness are used to fix thicker fabrics.

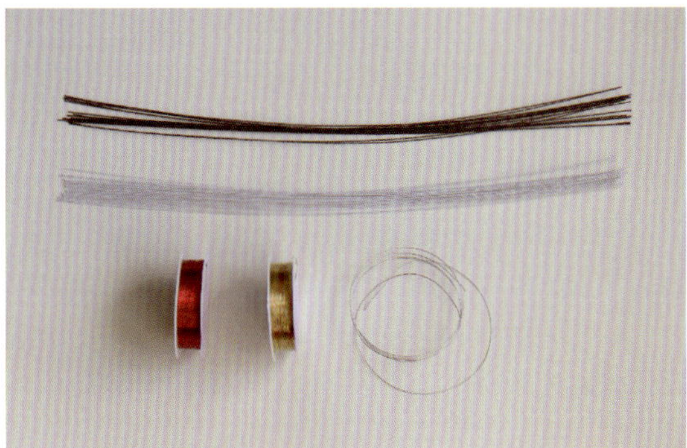

Iron wire and copper wire: These wires are of a certain hardness, and are used to make three-dimensional shapes, such as flower poles and petals.

2. Beads

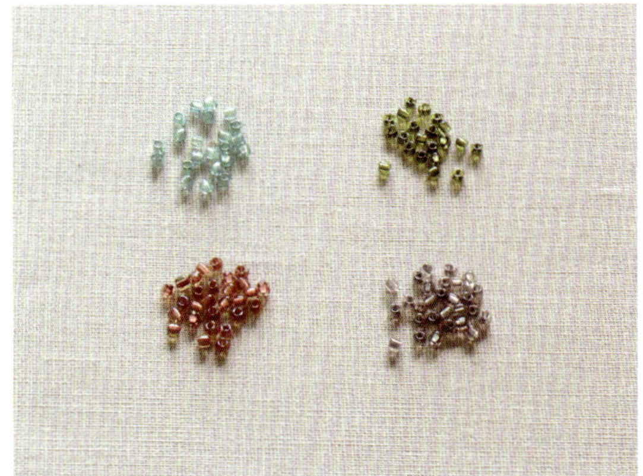

Seed beads: These are the most frequently used beads in this book, and are available in a variety of colors.

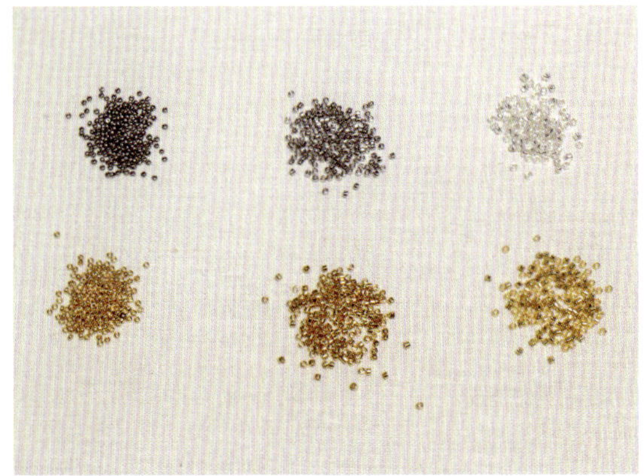

Metallic beads: Beads with a metallic look.

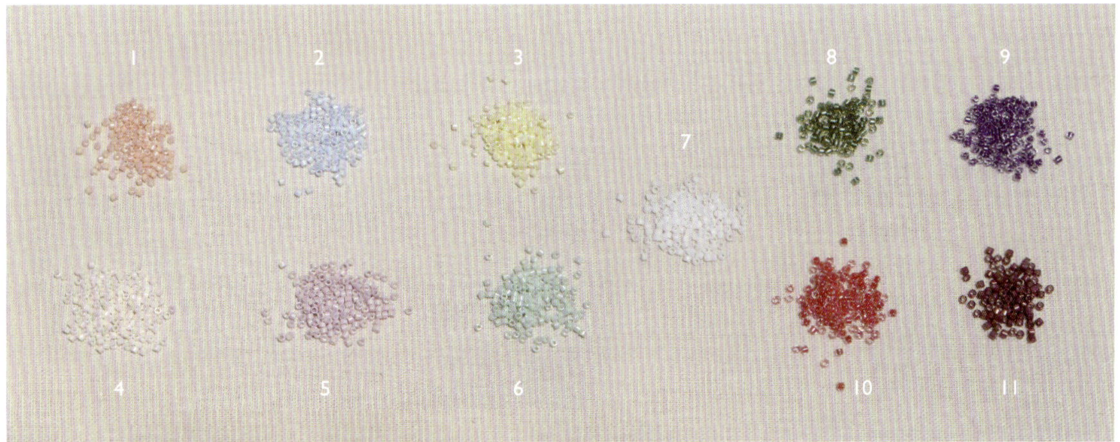

Antique beads: Figures 1–6 show pearlescent antique beads made of glass from the 1.6 mm cream color series. Figure 7 shows white antique beads. Figures 8–10 show color-lined antique beads. Figure 11 shows antique beads with a metallic texture.

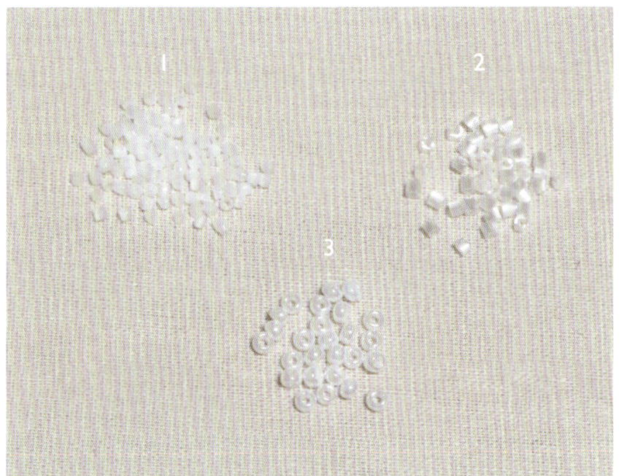

Figures 1, 2, and 3 show **French cat's-eye beads**, 2 mm **hexagonal tube beads**, and **round beads** respectively. The cat's-eye beads have irregular facets, while the tube beads are hexagonal in cross-section.

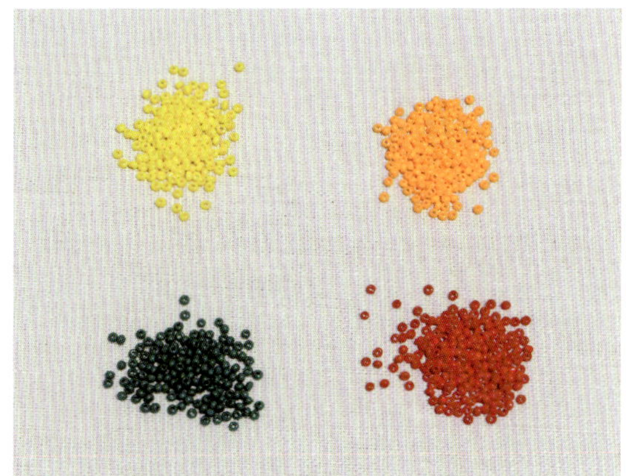

Mini seed beads.

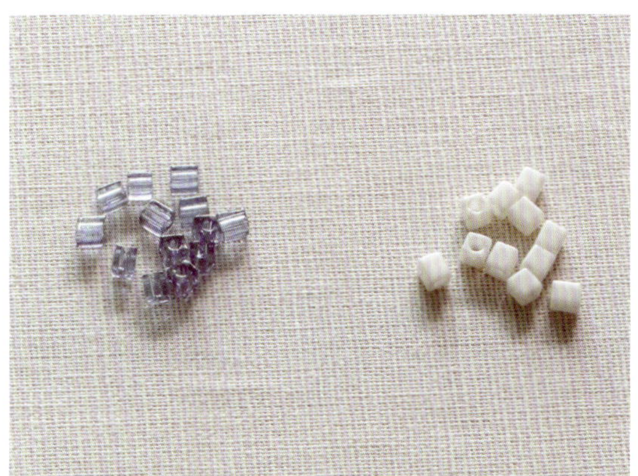

Square beads: These beads are square-shaped, with 1.8 mm, 3 mm, 4 mm being the most commonly used sizes. They come in many colors. The image shows transparent and solid color square beads.

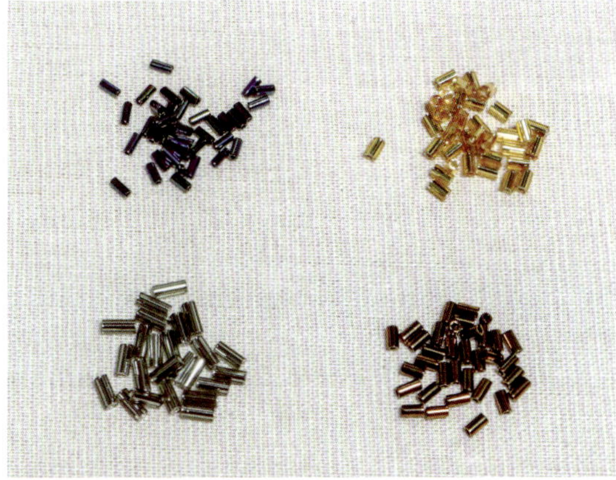

Tube beads: With a length between 2 mm–16 mm, tube beads come in transparent, metallic, and silver-lined of varying colors and textures.

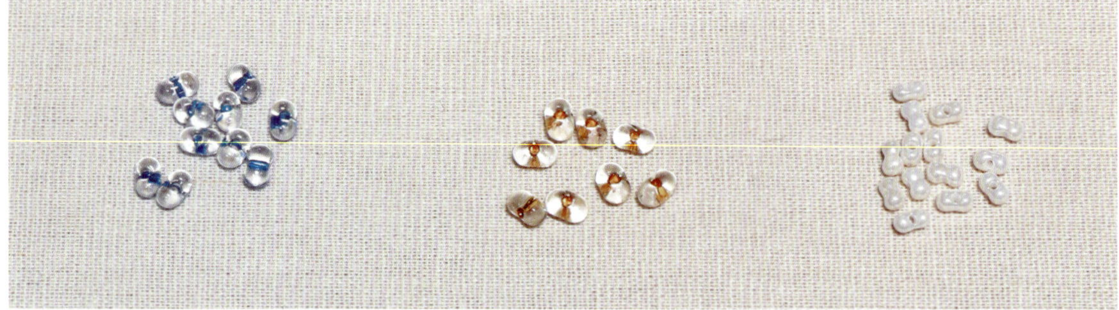

Peanut beads: Peanut-shaped beads with a hole in the center.

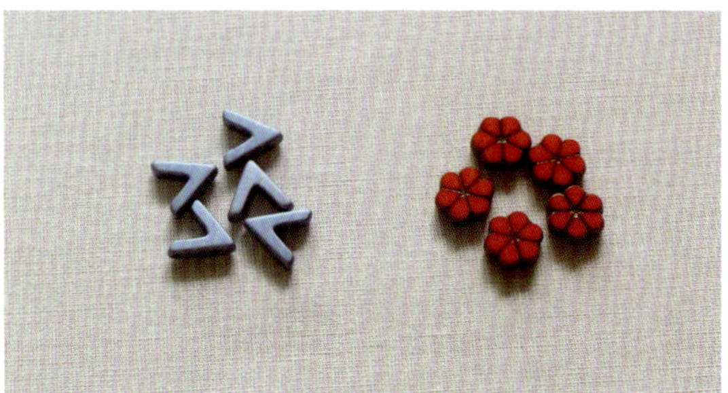

Odd-shaped beads: V-shaped beads on the left, and flower shaped beads on the right.

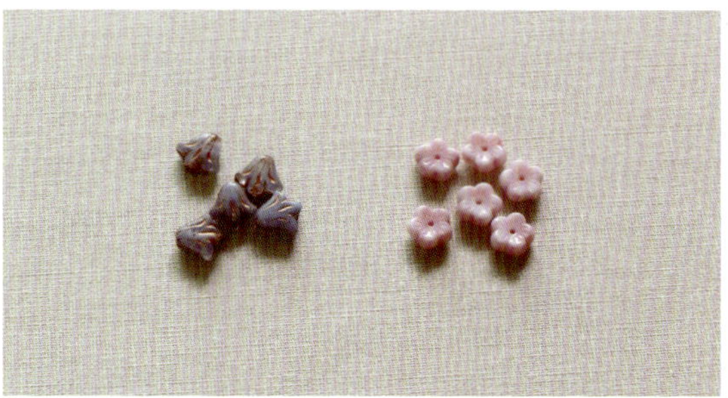

Czech glass beads: Lily of the valley-shaped beads on the left, and five-petal flower-shaped beads on the right.

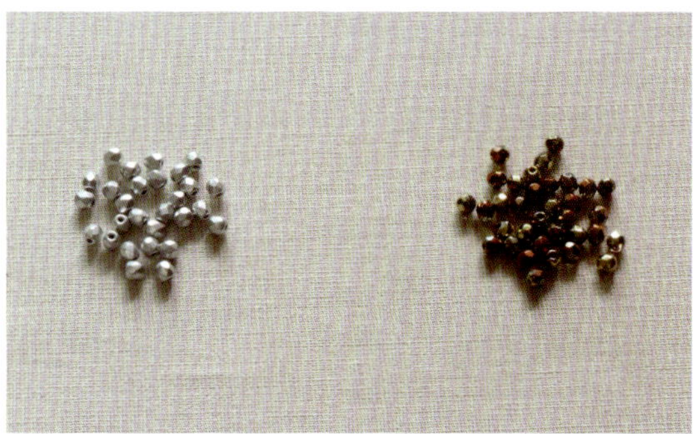

Czech faceted beads: Their surfaces present multiple diamond-shaped facets.

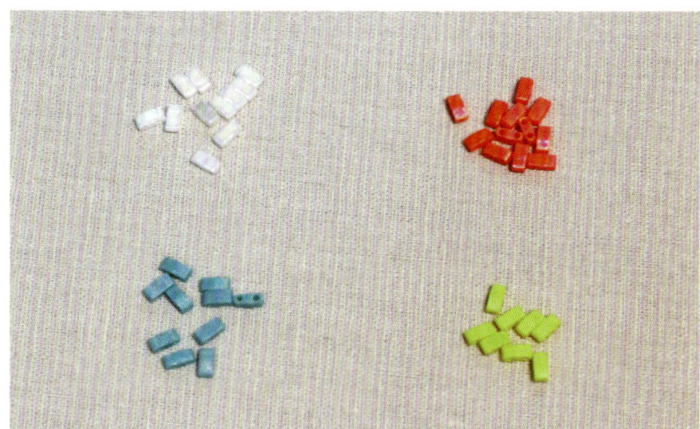

Tila beads: Flat and oblong with two holes.

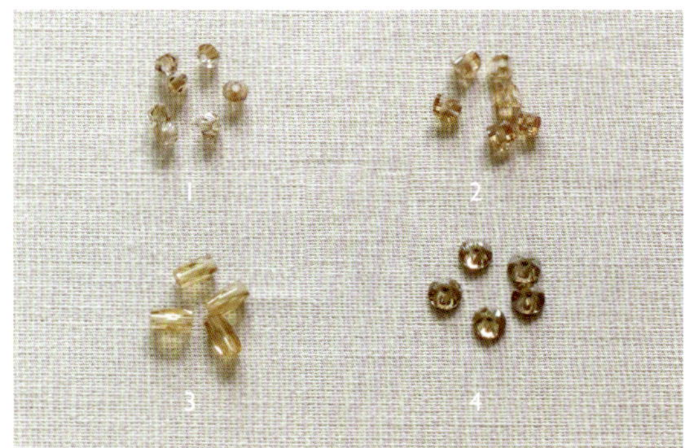

Items 1, 2, 3 in the figure are **transparent crystals** of various shapes. Number 4 is a **flatback rhinestone**, with a flat bottom on its back and a hole in its center.

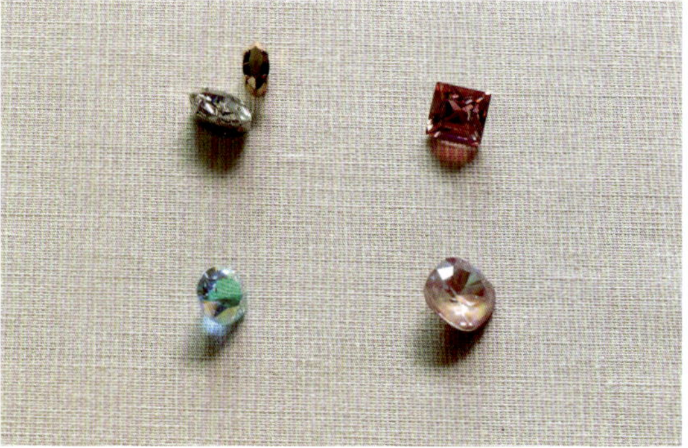

Sew-on rhinestones: The image shows sew-on rhinestones of varying shapes, including round, square, and teardrop. The four holes on the back are presented in a cross-distribution.

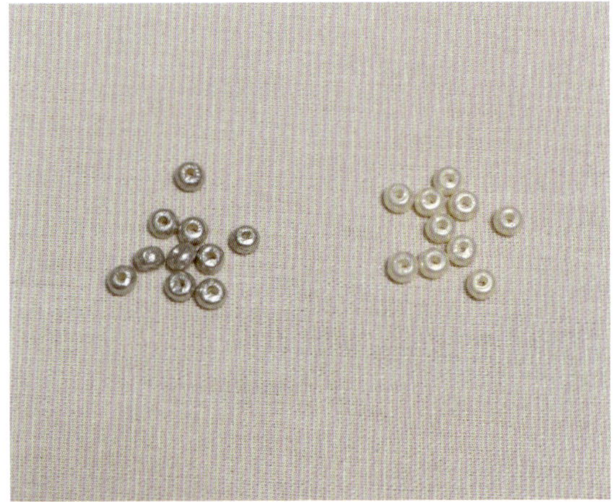

Cotton pearls: Artificial pearls made using beads pressed with cotton.

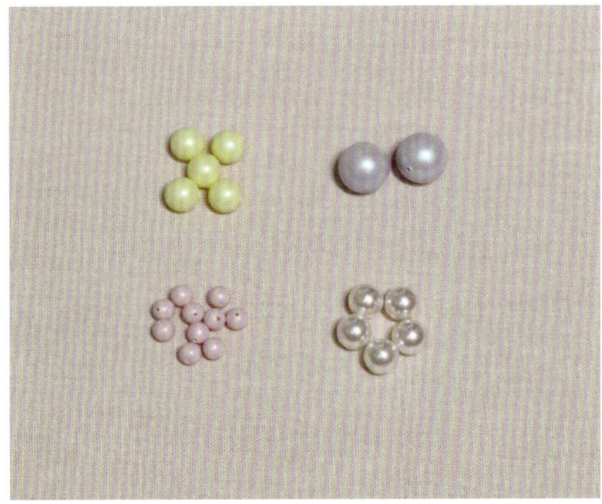

Pearls: Round with a variety of colors.

3. Sequins

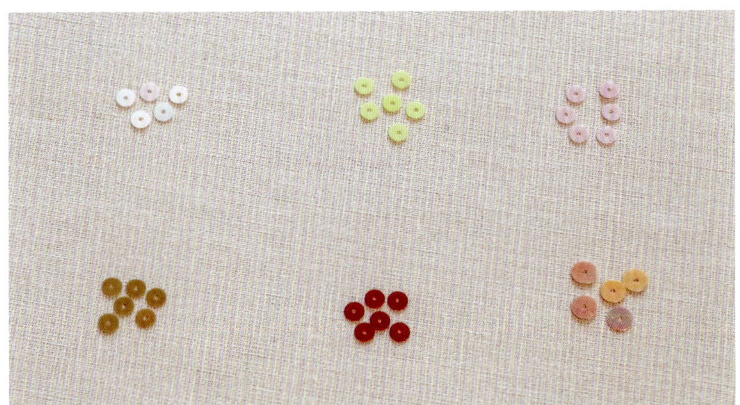

Flat sequins: Flat surfaces, with a hole in the middle. Their diameters range from 2 mm to over 20 mm.

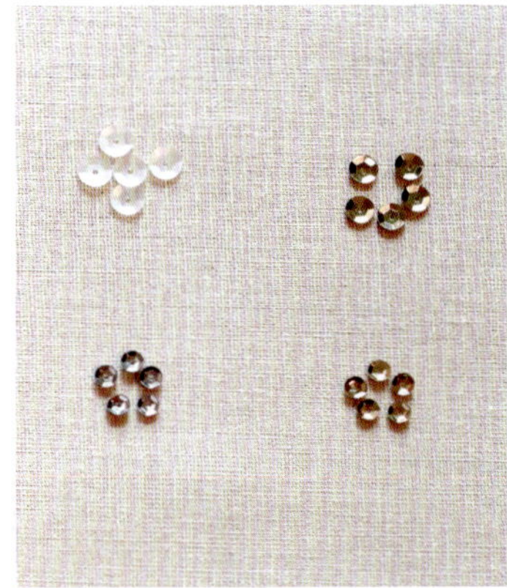

Cup sequins: A concave bowl with a hole in the center.

Edge-hole sequins: The holes are on the edge, which can create a hanging effect.

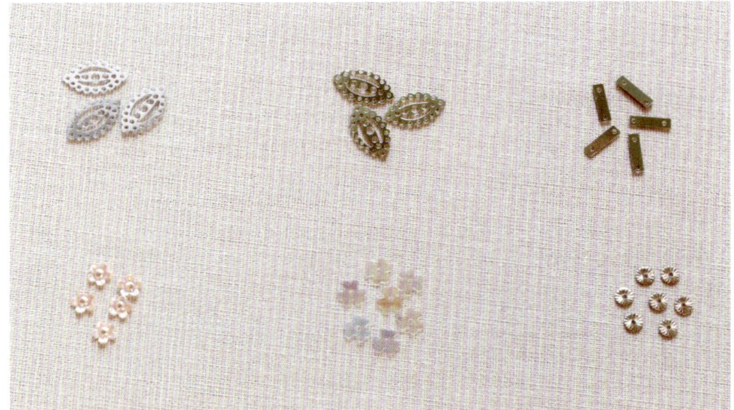

Special-shaped sequins: (clockwise) silver horse eye-shaped sequins, gold horse eye-shaped sequins, bar-shaped sequins, embossing plum-shaped sequins, clover-shaped transparent AB sequins, and embossing wheel-shaped sequins.

4. Threads

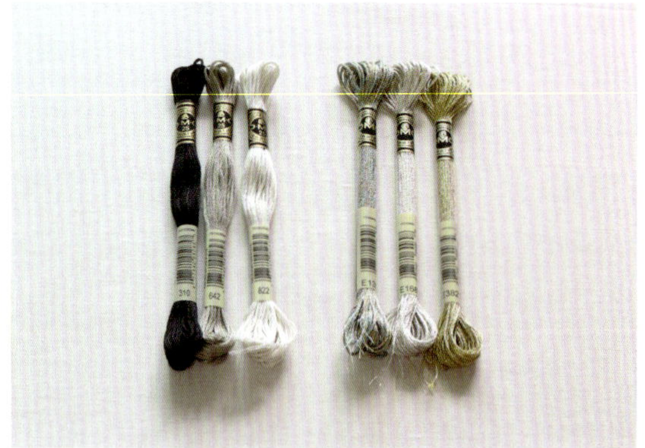

On the left is **cotton embroidery thread**, and on the right is **metallic embroidery thread**.

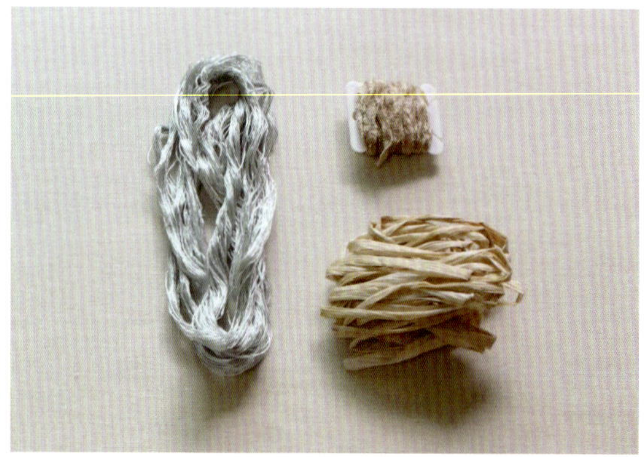

Clockwise: **Silk**, **wool**, and **rapha**.

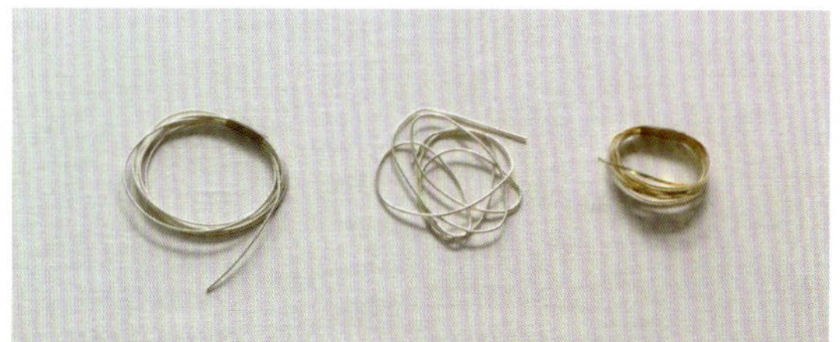

Bullion wire: (from left to right) hard bullion wire, soft bullion wire, and flat bullion wire.

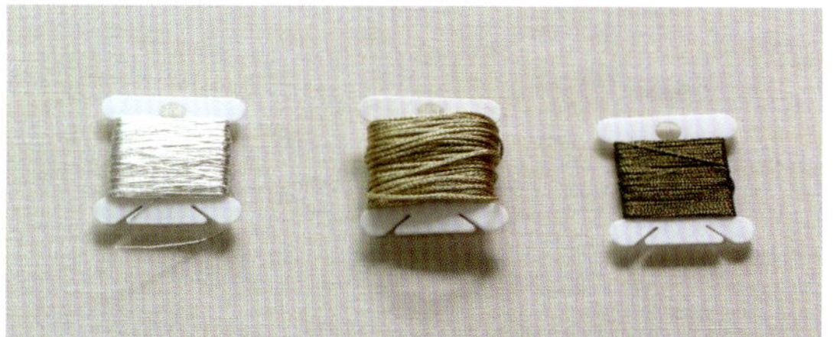

Silver embroidered thread (left), and **metallic wires** of varying patterns (middle and right).

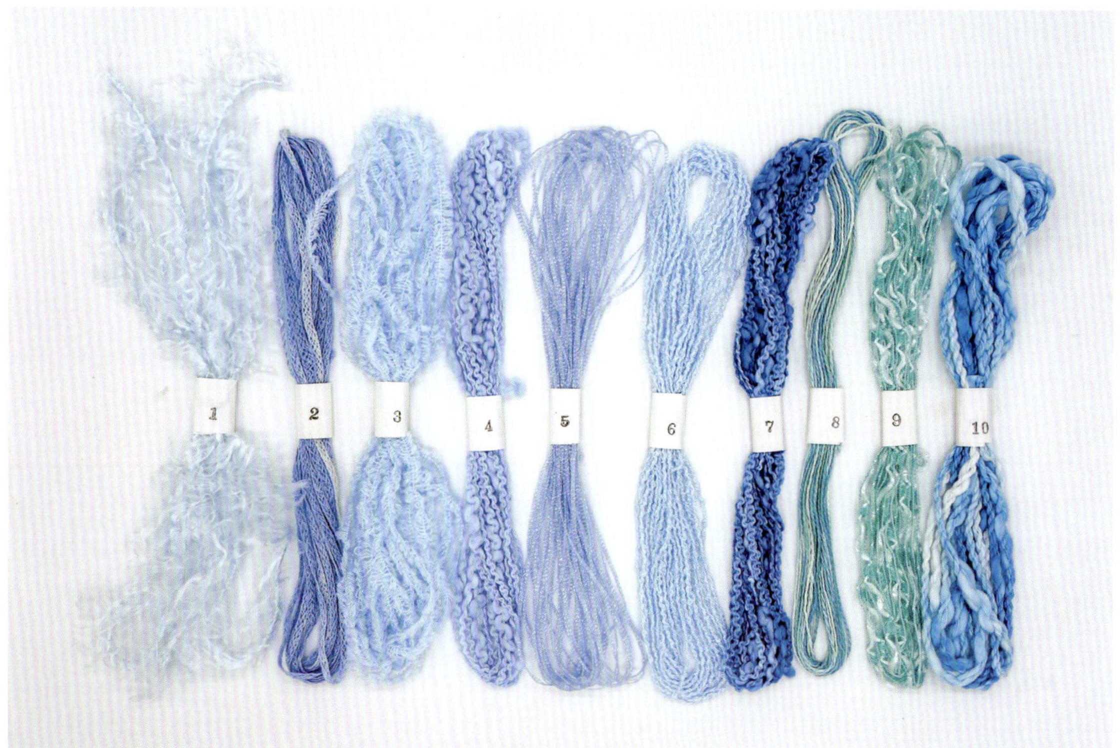

Flower Yarn: A type of yarn for decorative purposes, in various forms.

5. Fabrics

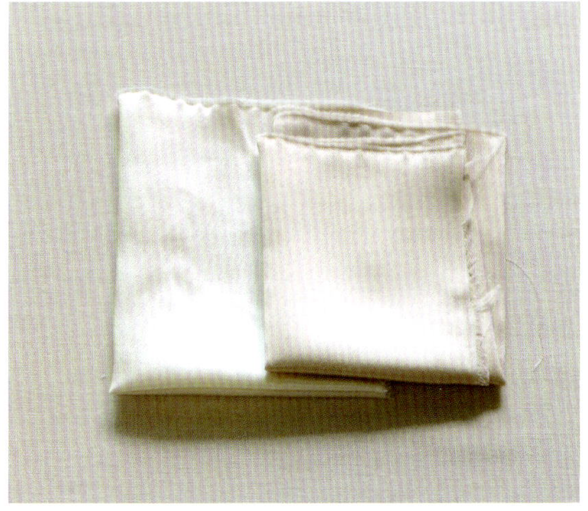

100% silk.

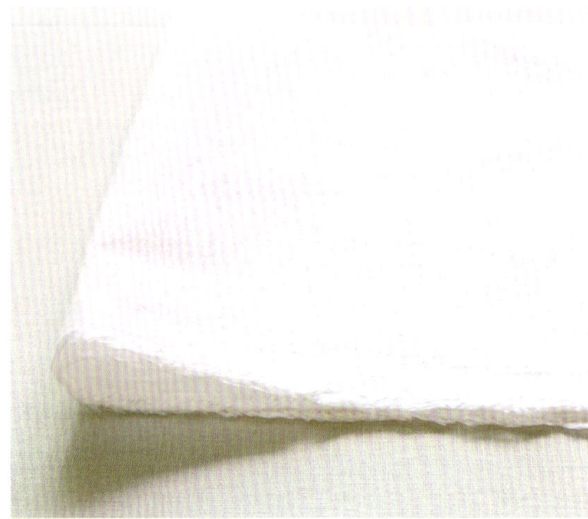

Glitter fabric.

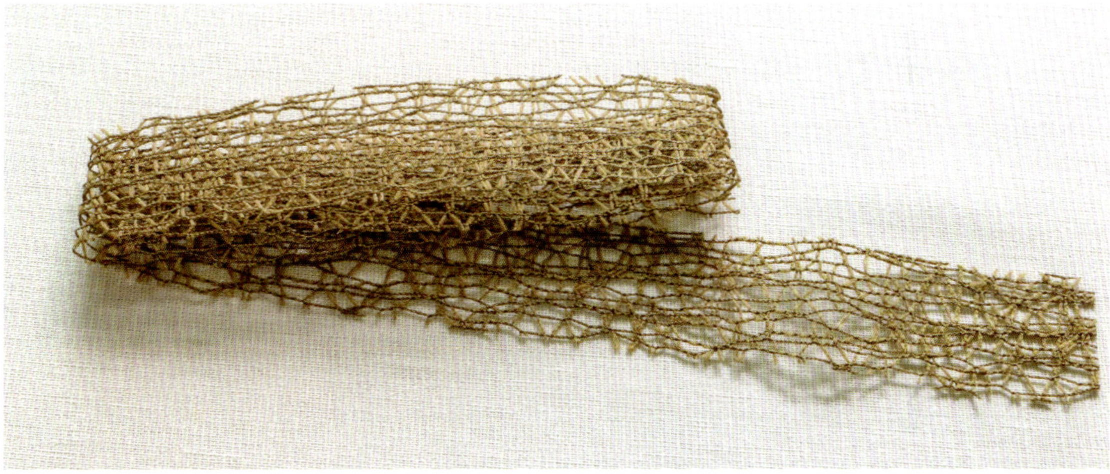

Floral cut-out ruffle textured lace ribbon.

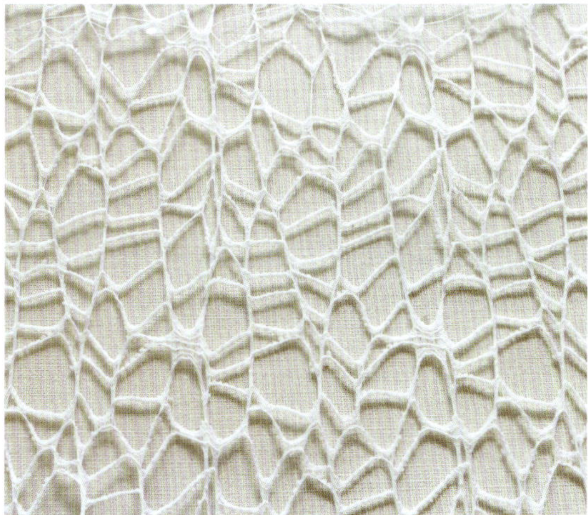

Textured mesh.

Iridescent irregular hollowed-out mesh.

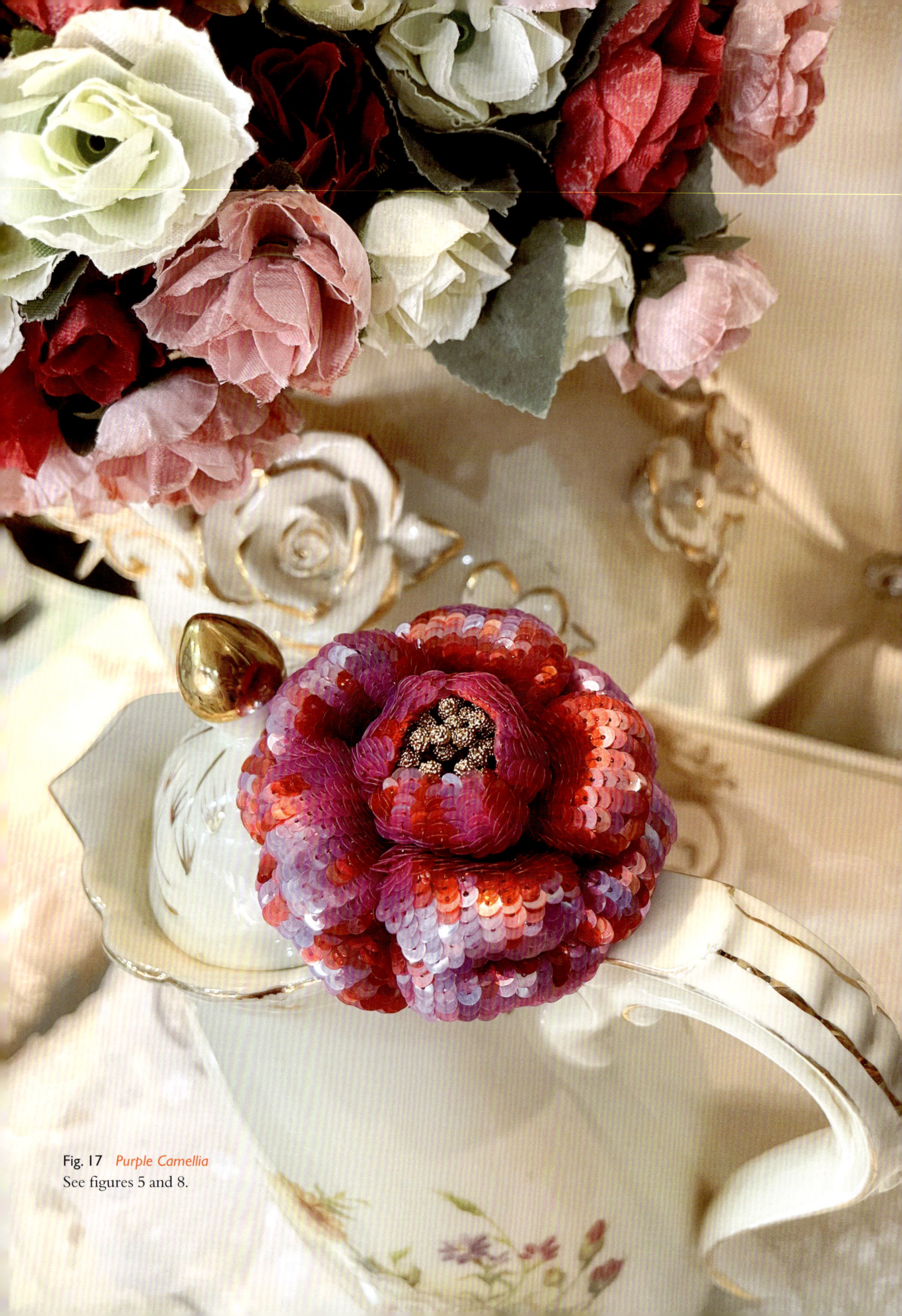

Fig. 17 *Purple Camellia*
See figures 5 and 8.

Gallery of Stitches

The examples in this book are an amalgamation of traditional Chinese and French embroidery, designed to create more varied pieces. Traditional Chinese embroidery primarily uses a hand sewing needle, while French embroidery employs a hook needle. This chapter will explain both hand sewing and hook needle techniques. After acquiring these basic techniques, you will be well-placed to start creating your own bead embroidery.

In this chapter, threads of varying colors are used to enable readers to see different stitches while narrating more complex ones. When you're actually embroidering, there is no need to change threads.

1. Techniques for Hand Sewing Needle

Thread the Needle & Tie a Knot

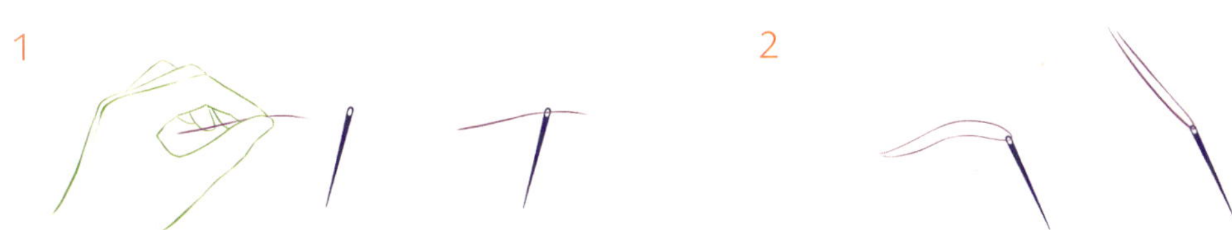

1 Cut a length of thread you need and thread it through the eye of the needle.

2 Align both ends of the thread and pull the thread straight.

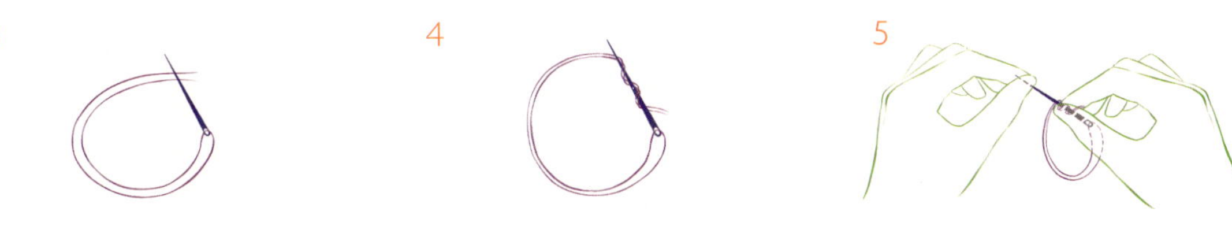

3 Hold the needle in your right hand (if you are right-handed). Let your left hand pass the tail of the thread under the needle, making sure the thread crosses the needle.

4 With your right thumb pressing the end of thread, your left hand winds the thread twice around the needle and pull it so it is tightly wound around the needle.

5 With your right thumb and forefinger pinching the wound thread on the needle, your left hand holds the upper part of the needle and your right hand pushes the wound thread forcefully towards the end of the needle until it reaches the tail of the thread.

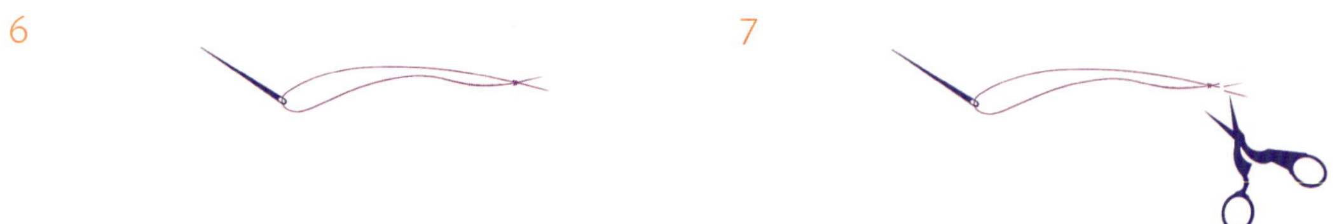

6

When it reaches the end of the thread, it becomes a knot.

7

Trim the tail of the thread, leaving a length of 5 mm beyond the knot. This completes the threading of the needle.

Starting Stitch

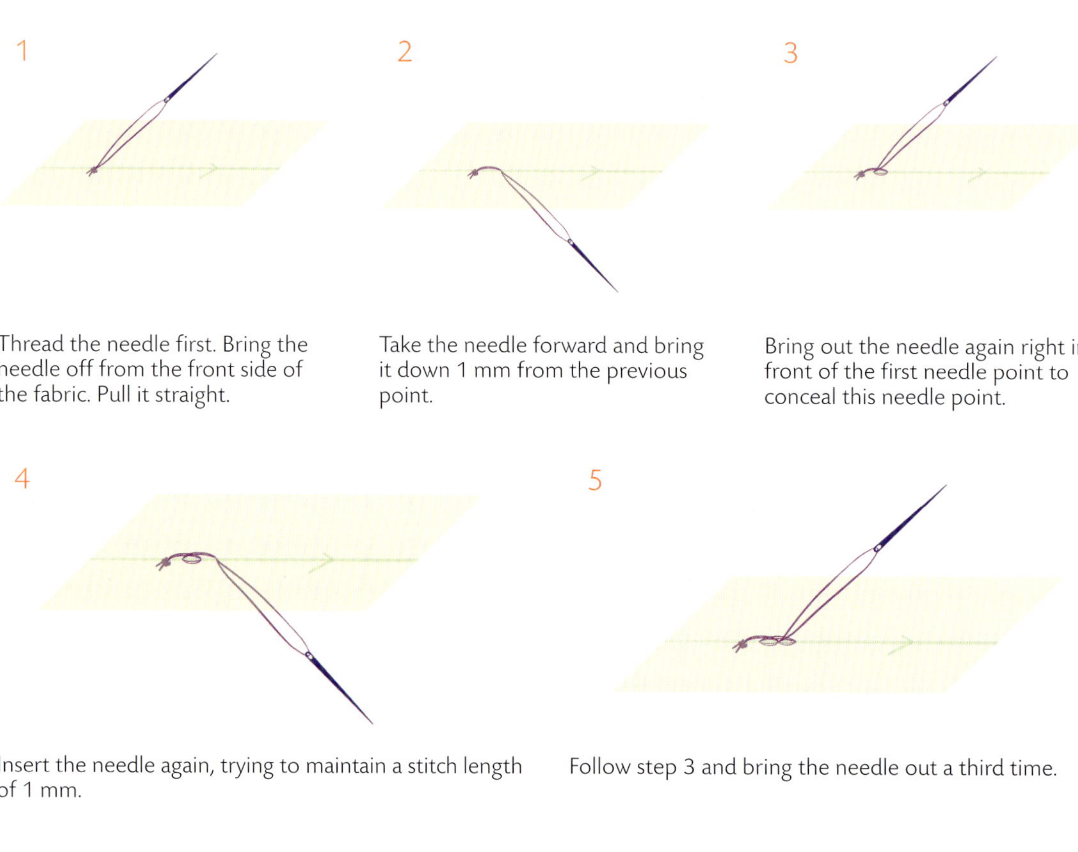

1

Thread the needle first. Bring the needle off from the front side of the fabric. Pull it straight.

2

Take the needle forward and bring it down 1 mm from the previous point.

3

Bring out the needle again right in front of the first needle point to conceal this needle point.

4

Insert the needle again, trying to maintain a stitch length of 1 mm.

5

Follow step 3 and bring the needle out a third time.

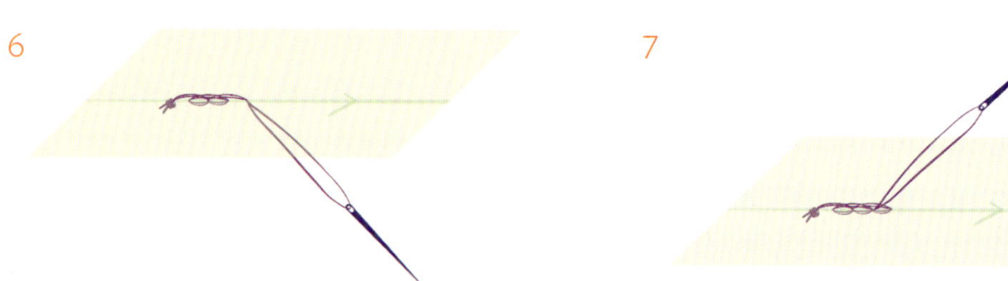

6

Take the needle down 1 mm away from the previous point.

7

Follow step 3 and pull the needle out the fourth time. After these three small stitches (the needle out four times and in three times) are secured, the starting stitch is complete. Now the thread is secure in place on the fabric, and you can start your embroidery.

Ending Stitch

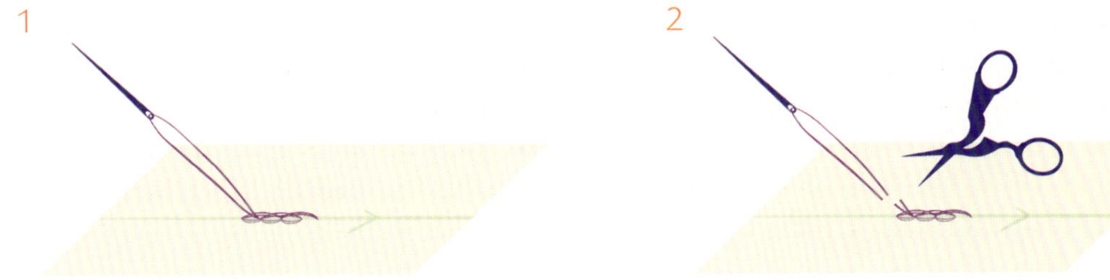

1. After finishing the embroidery, bring your needle back against the orientation of the embroidery to do three small stitches as you did when you began the stitches.

2. After you are done with the three small stitches, leave a length of 5 mm of thread and remove the rest. Properly conceal the tail of the thread.

Straight Stitch

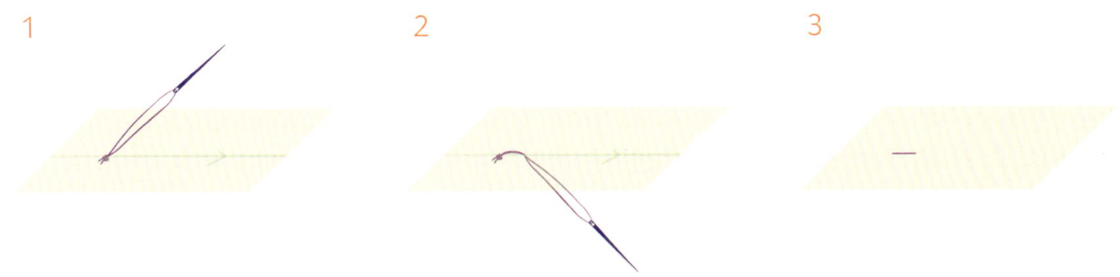

1. Work the starting stitches.

2. Bring the needle down at a point of your choice.

3. A straight stitch is done. Straight stitch is the most basic embroidery stitch. You can adjust the length of your stitch as you need. Continuous straight stitches make running stitch.

Back Stitch

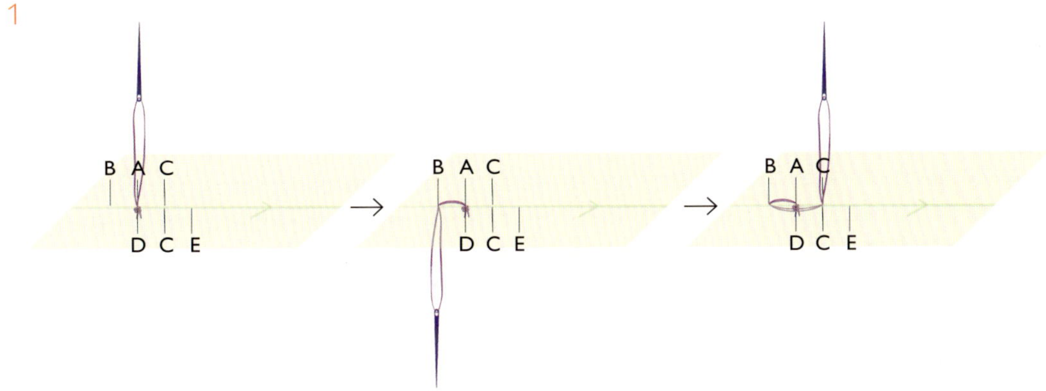

Bring the needle up through the fabric at A (midpoint between B and C), and then take the needle down at B and pull it out at the back side of the fabric and then bring the needle up at C.

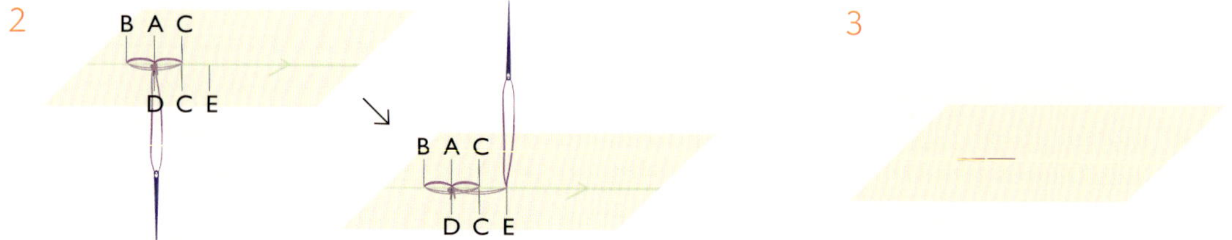

Bring the needle from C (midpoint between D and E) and back down at D (i.e. A in step 1) and bring the needle up at E.

Repeat the previous steps and go forward a stitch length in front and then backward two stitch lengths. Make sure the length of each stitch is even.

Random Stitch (with Thread)

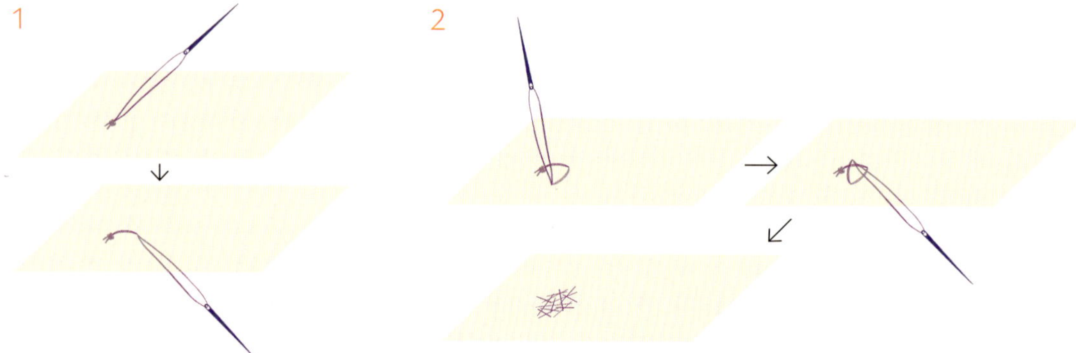

After the starting stitches, pull the needle up the fabric and then bring it down at a point of your choice.

Then choose a point of your choice to bring the needle up the fabric again and take it down at a point of your choice. The stitches can overlap one another. Repeat the process for more random stitches as you want.

Satin Stitch

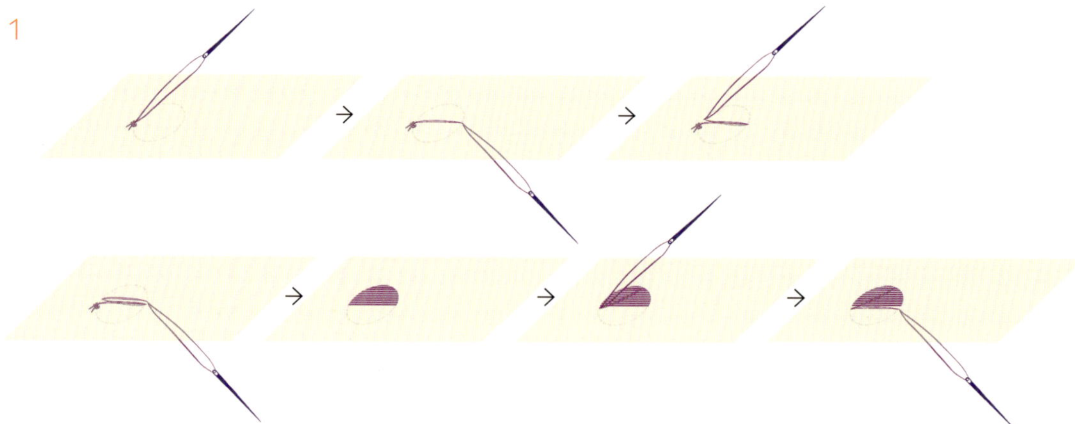

Satin stitch is used to fill areas of a design with stitches. The needle comes out one end of the design and down the other end. Then bring the needle right out next to the first stitch, and take it down right next to the previous stitch, so the two stitches are parallel. Repeat this process until you fill the whole area (as shown in the illustration, it is only half filled). You may also start in the center of the area and work outwards in two stages. After finishing the first half, you move to the next half. This can help keep the stitches even and smooth.

2

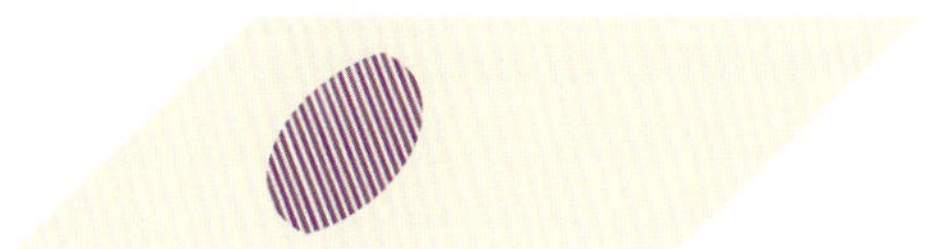

You can also adjust the angle of the parallel stitches uniformly, to fill the required area diagonally. One characteristic of a satin stitch is that it is flat and creates a smooth, delicate effect.

Long and Short Stitch

1

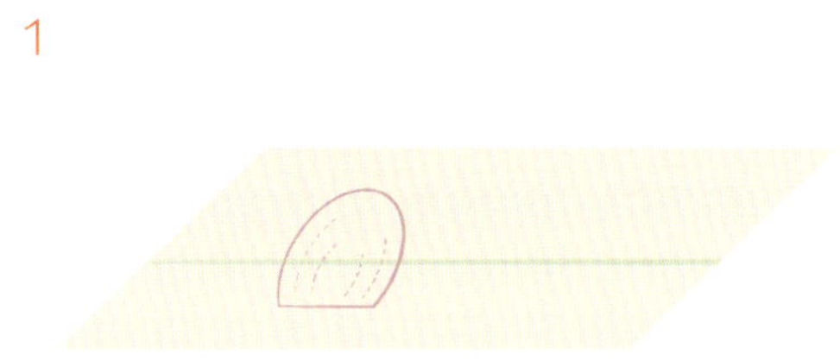

Long and short stitches are often used to embroider flower petals and give them depth and dimension. Use a water erasable marker to draw the contour of a flower petal first.

2

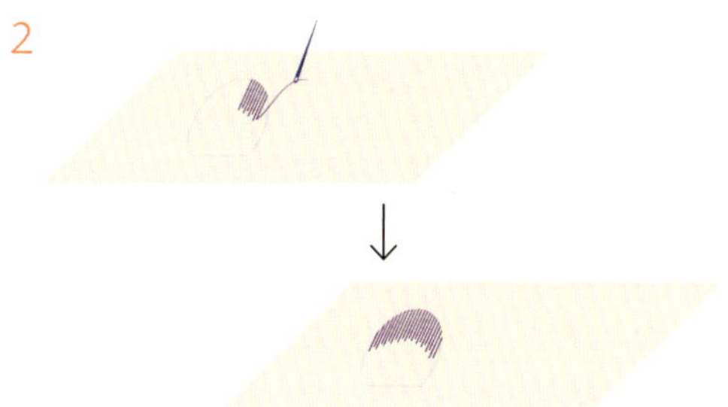

As shown in the illustration, work a long stitch and then a short one next to it. The stitches should be parallel. Repeat the process until the petal is filled. You can also start in the center and work outward in two stages: first one half and then the other half. This can help keep the stitches more parallel and even.

3

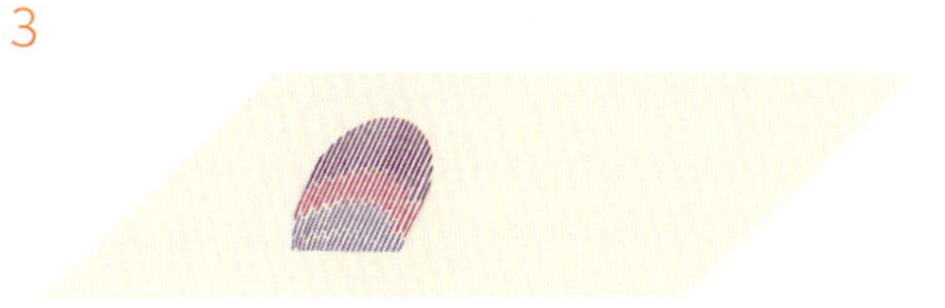

When you have stitched the top layer, continue with the layer underneath using the same method, which is a long stitch followed by a short stich. Repeat this process for the third layer. The stitches between the layers should be tight. You can divide it into many layers as you wish, and stitch using threads of the same color shades to create a gradient effect.

Stem Stitch

1

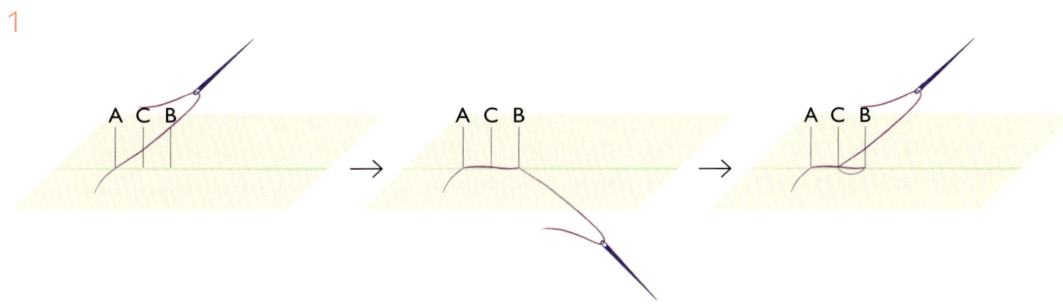

Working from left to right, bring the needle and the thread up through the fabric at A and take the needle down a stitch length at B to the back of the fabric. Then bring the needle up through the fabric just above the center of the first stitch at C (midpoint between A and B). Make sure that the stitch length between A and B is not too long.

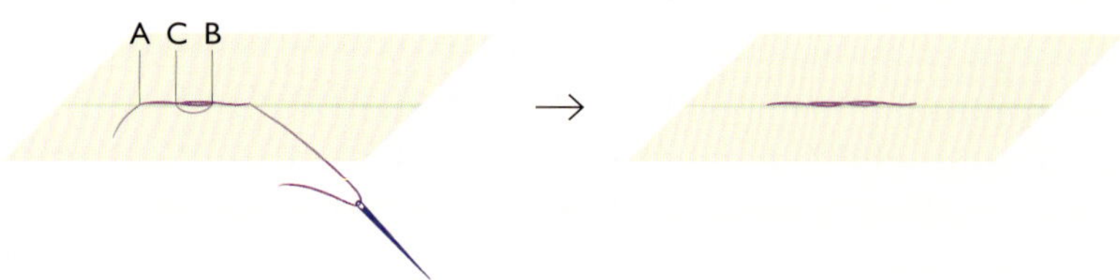

Work one stitch and bring the needle down half way back the previous stitch and repeat the process. Make sure that every stitch is of equal length and the latter stitch comes out just above the center of the previous stitch. The stitches should be close together and parallel, with no gaps between them. Both stem stitch and back stitch can be used to embroider continuous lines, but the former has tighter stitches.

French Knot

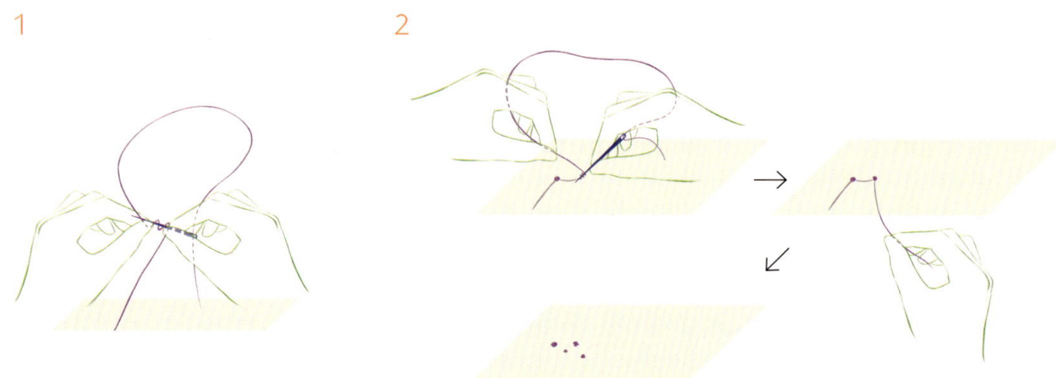

Bring the needle up through the fabric at the position of the knot, hold it with your right hand, wind the thread around it twice. You may wind it once or thrice depending on how big you want the knot to be. The more times you wind it, the bigger the knot is.

Hold the thread taut in your left hand and your right hand brings the needle down but still keep the wound thread on the needle taut. Pull the needle and the thread out to the back side of the fabric, leaving a knot on the surface of the fabric.

Edging Stitch

Edging stitch is often used to secure a metal wire (or thread hoop, bullion wire) onto the fabric. As shown in the illustration, the needle comes out of the fabric at A on the left of the wire and then go a little bit forward and down at B.

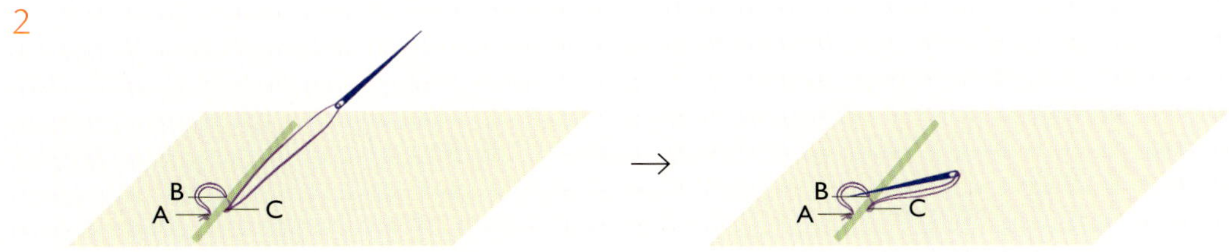

Pull the needle and the thread out next to the wire at C on the right but do not pull the thread tight, thread the needle back into the loop on the left of the wire.

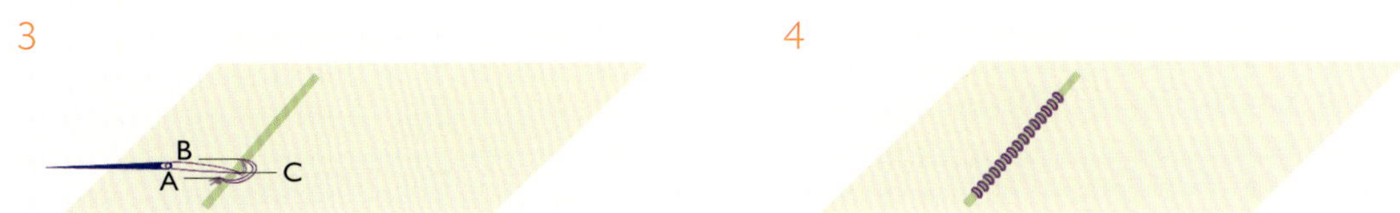

Then pull the thread tight.

Repeat steps 1 through 3 along the wire to secure the wire in place. The illustration shows what it looks like after a length of wire is secured.

Embroidering a Single Bead

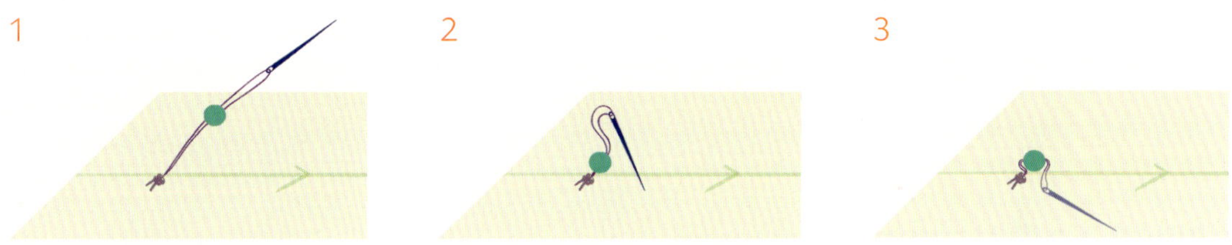

Start with beginning stitches and then slide a bead down the thread.

Bring the needle forward and then down where the width of the bead ends.

This completes the embroidery of a single bead.

Embroidering Multiple Beads

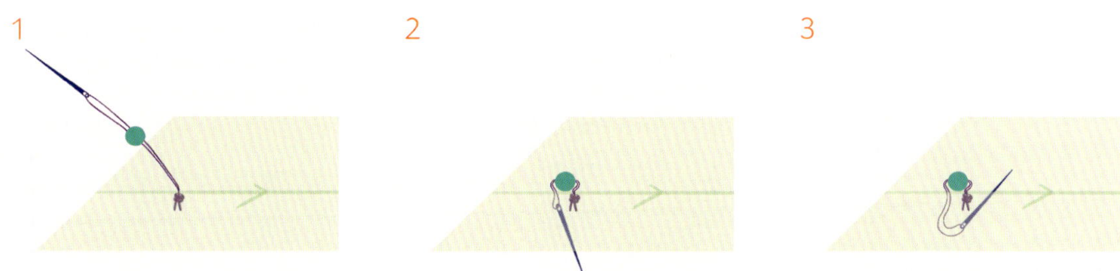

Begin with starting stitches and then slide a bead down the thread.

Bring the needle back against the orientation of the embroidery work and take it down where the width of the bead ends.

Bring the needle out at some distance ahead of the previous one.

4

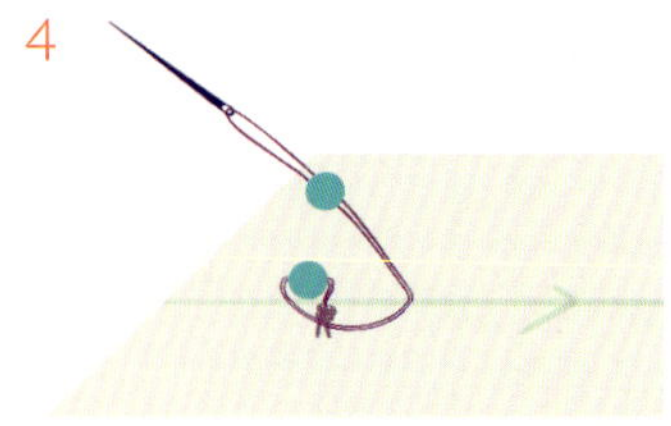

When the needle comes out, slide a bead down the thread.

5

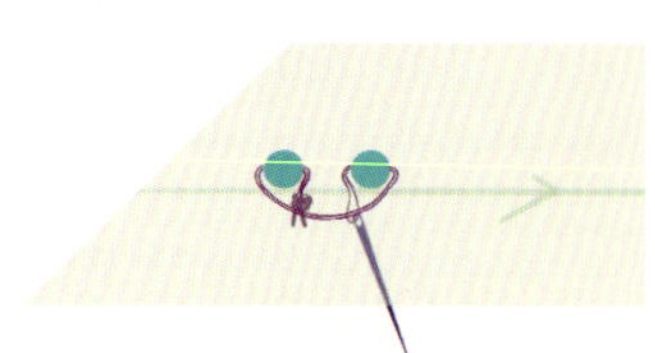

Bring the needle backward and take it down where the width of the bead ends.

6

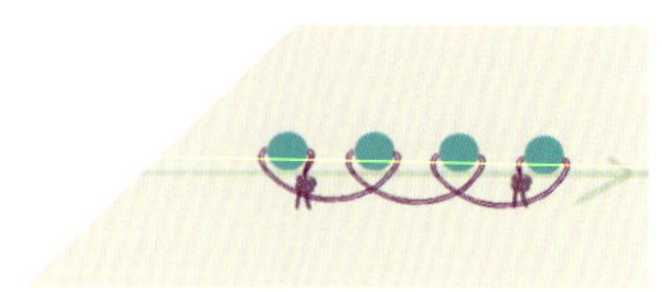

Repeat the previous steps if more beads are needed.

Embroidering Bead Groups

1

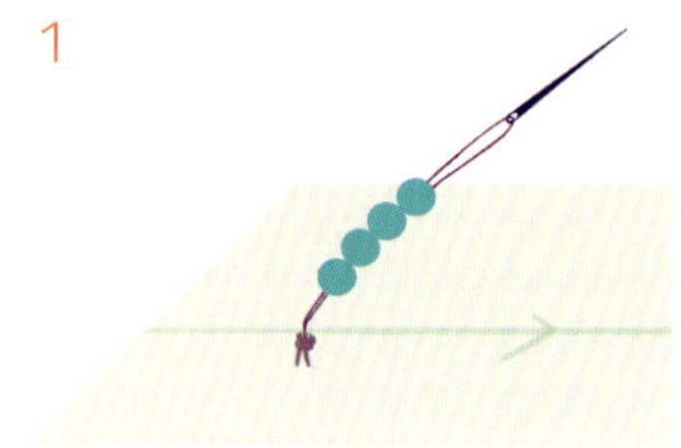

The needle comes out of the surface and pick up four beads.

2

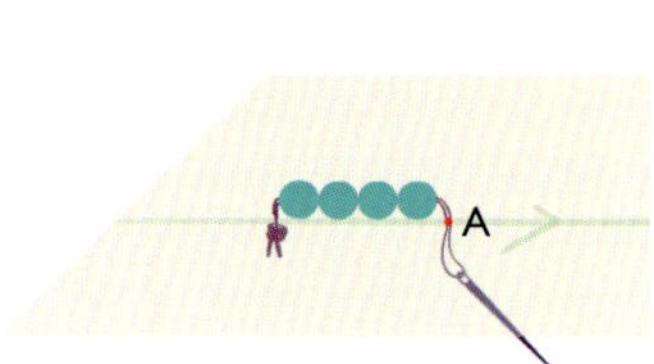

Take the needle down where the length of the four beads ends (point A).

3

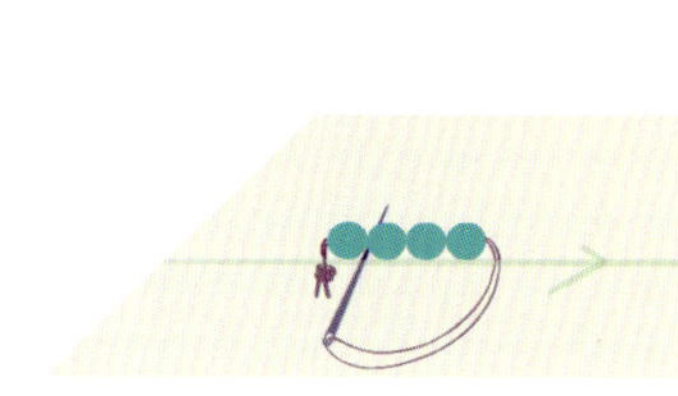

The needle comes out between the first and the second beads.

4

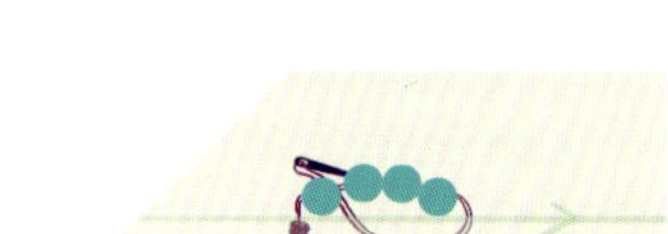

Insert the needle into the hole of the last three beads. Pull the needle out and reinsert it into the point where the needle is first inserted, which is point A of step 2.

5

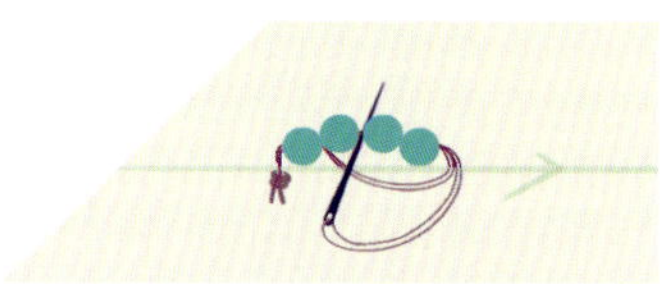

The needle comes out between the second and the third beads.

6

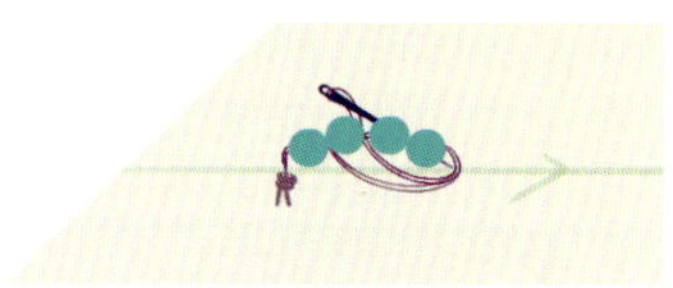

Thread the needle through the remaining two beads and pull the needle out. Take the needle down where it first went down (point A).

7

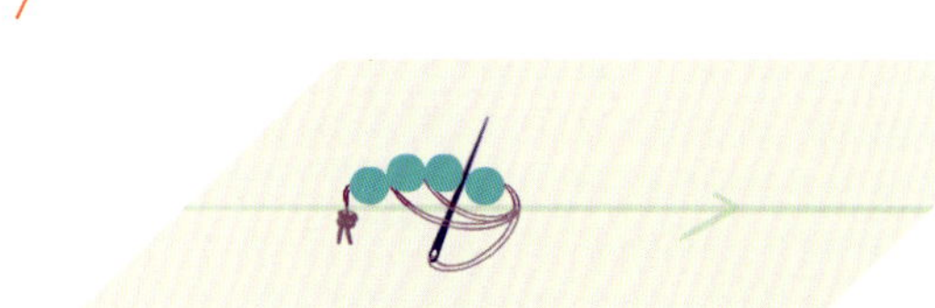

The needle comes out between the third and fourth beads.

8

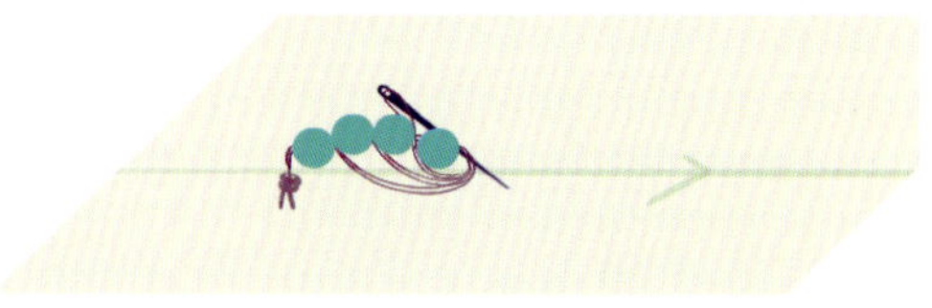

Thread the needle through the last bead.

9

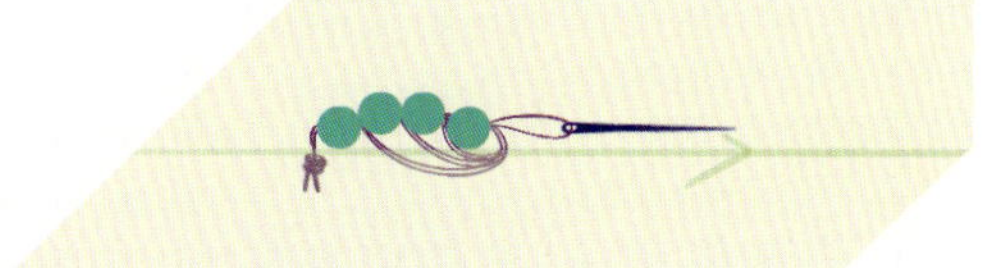

Pull the needle out and straighten the thread.

10

This completes the sewing of a group of beads.

Embroidering Bead Clusters for Additional Dimension

1

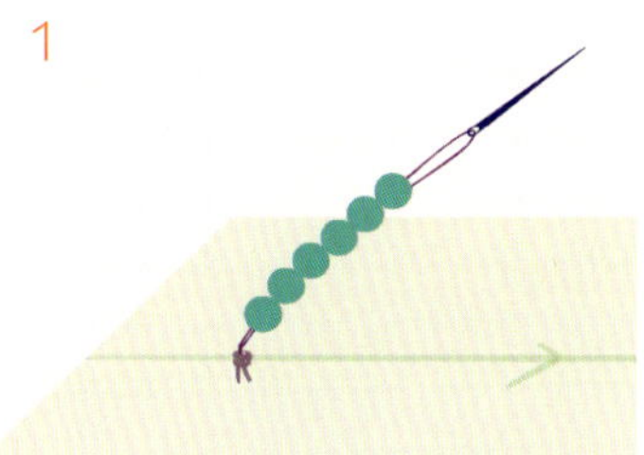

String multiple beads (even number) through the needle.

2

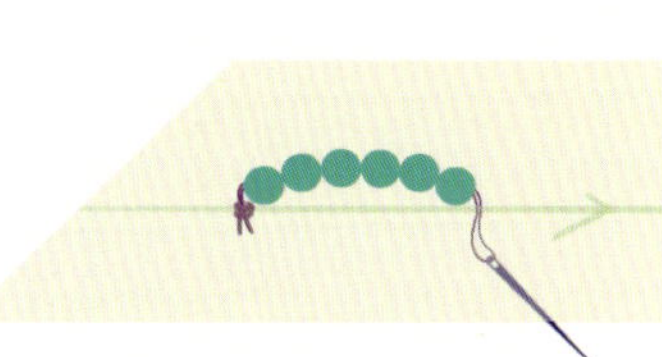

Bring the needle down where the length of the beads ends.

3

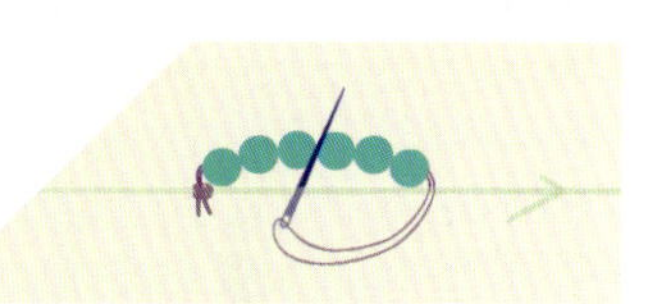

Take the needle back up and bring it out in the middle of the beads.

4

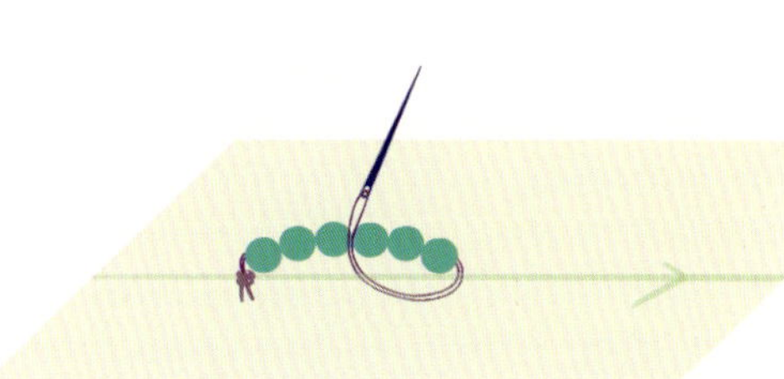

Bring the needle off the fabric and pull the thread straight.

5

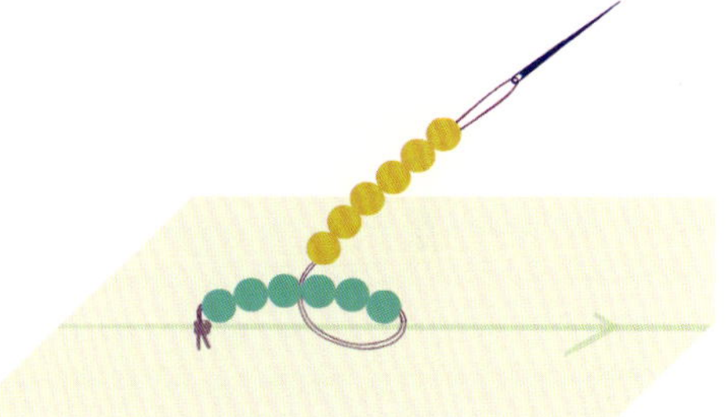

String same number of beads through the needle.

6

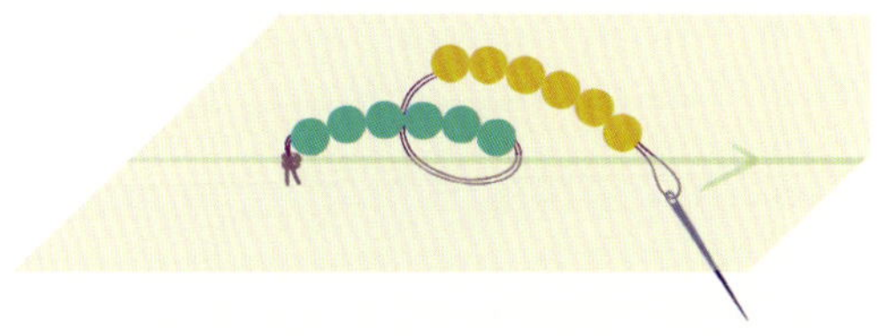

Bring the needle down where the length of the yellow beads ends.

7

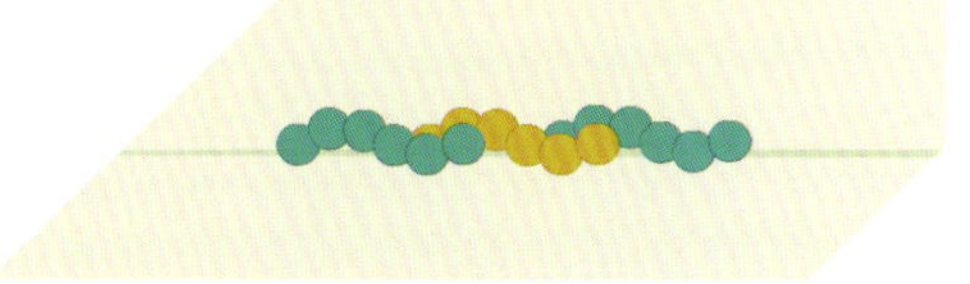

Repeat steps 3 through 6 so the three rows of beads tangle creating an extra dimension.

Random Stitch (with Beads)

1

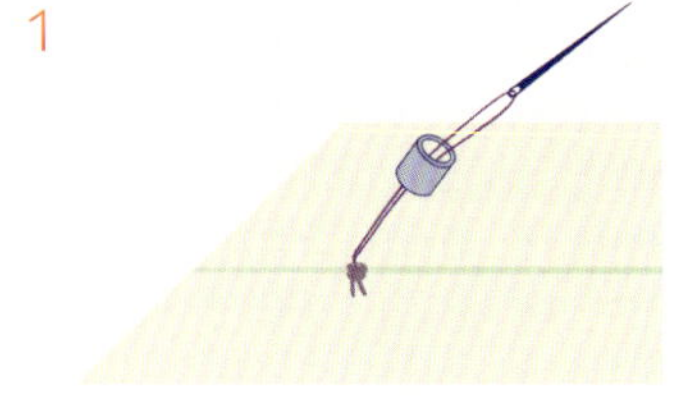

Bring the needle off the fabric and thread a bead through the needle.

2

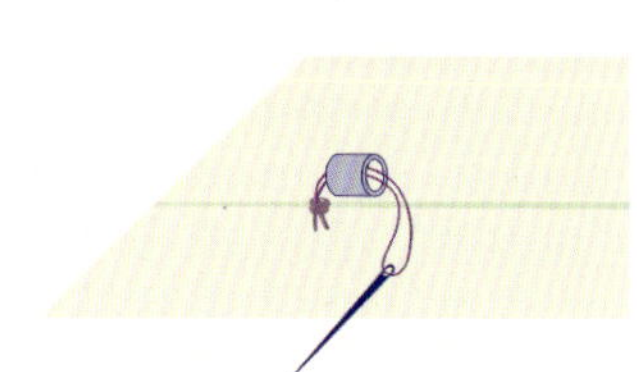

Take the needle down where the length of the bead ends.

3

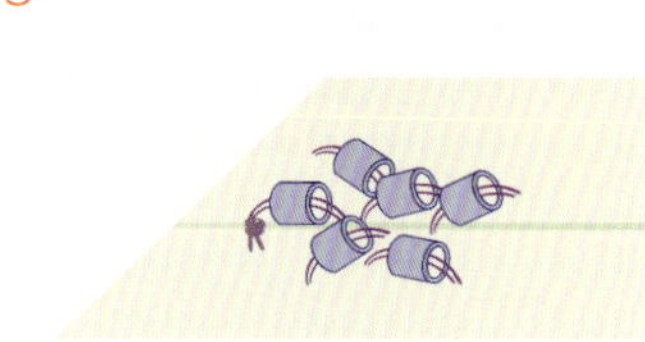

Stitch more beads anywhere around the previous bead and spread them irregularly on the fabric.

Embroidering Sequins by Securing Both Sides

1

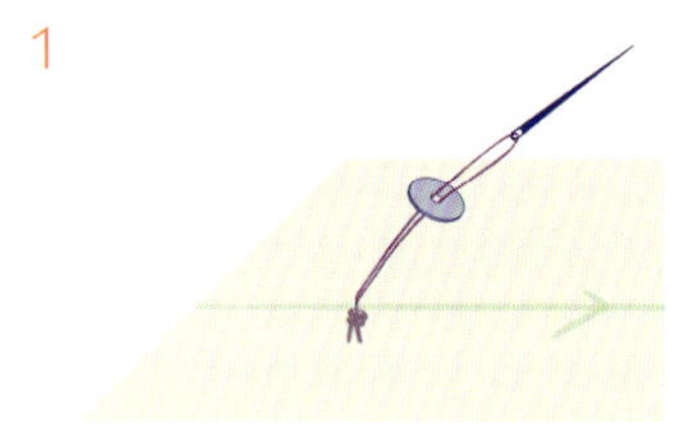

Bring the needle off the fabric and thread a sequin on the needle.

2

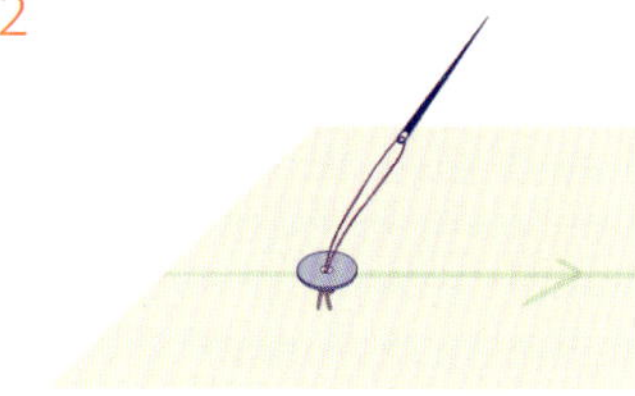

Push the sequin to the end of the thread and pull the thread straight.

3

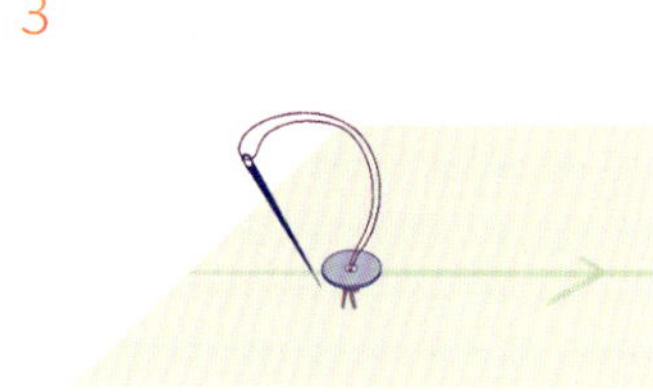

Insert the needle close to the edge of the sequin. The securing on one side is complete.

4

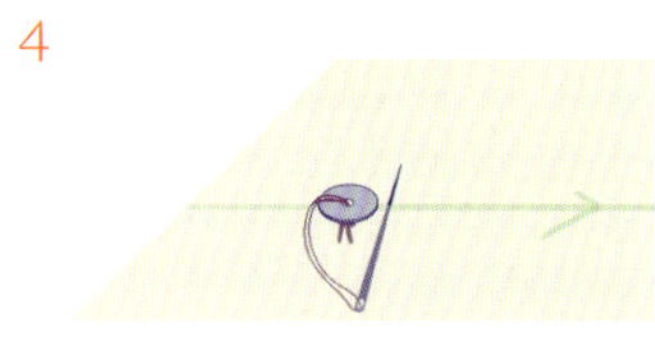

Pull the needle across the diameter of the sequin from the back of the fabric and bring the needle up at the edge on the other side.

5

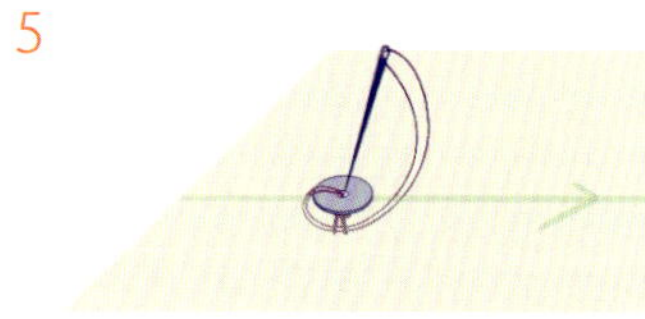

Then bring the needle down the hole in the middle of the sequin.

6

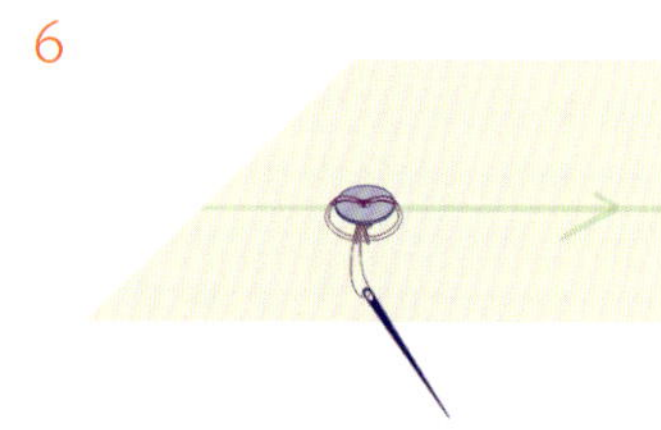

Both sides are now secured in place.

7

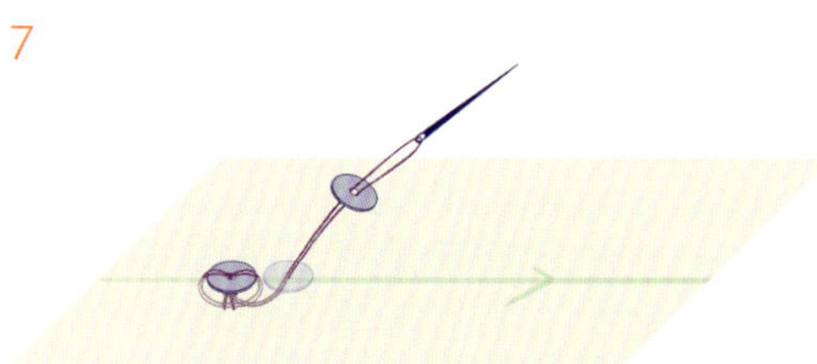

Bring the needle up at the radius of the next sequin (the hole in the middle), thread a sequin on the needle and secure both sides of this sequin.

8

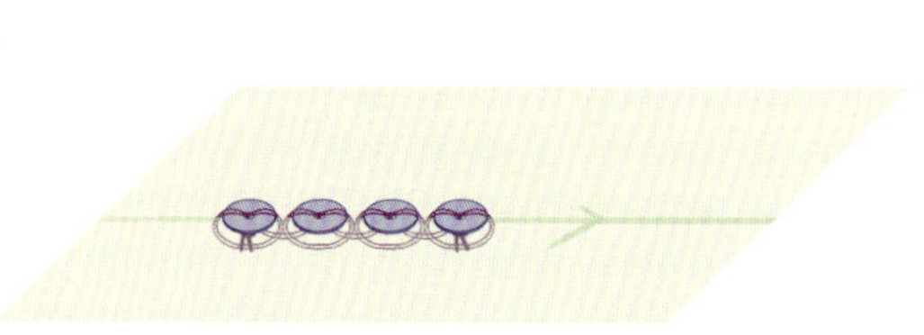

Repeat the previous steps if more sequins are needed.

Embroidering Sequins that Are Overlapped

1

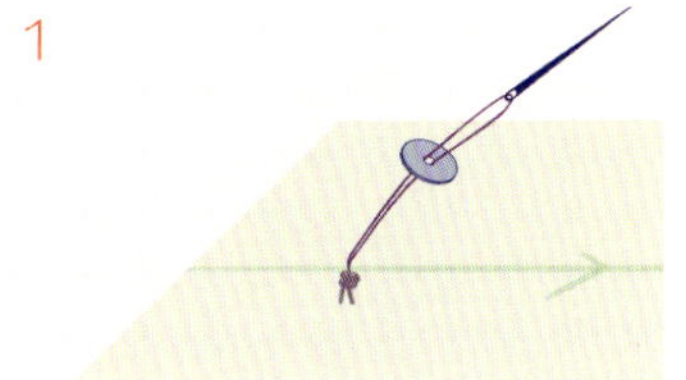

Work the starting stitches and then pick up a sequin with the needle.

2

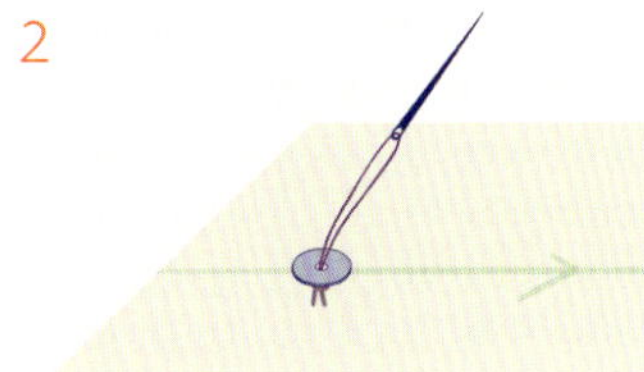

Push the sequin down to the bottom of the thread and straighten the thread.

3

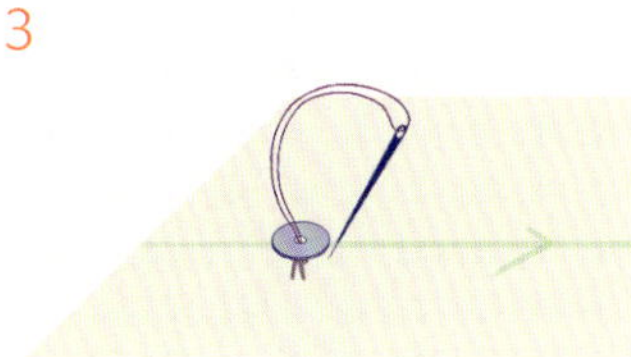

Bring the needle down right next to the edge of the sequin to the back.

4

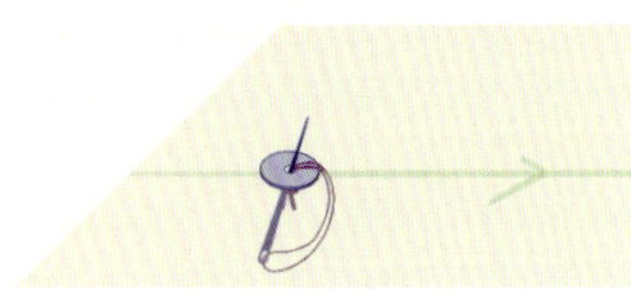

The needle comes out from the hole of the sequin in the middle.

5

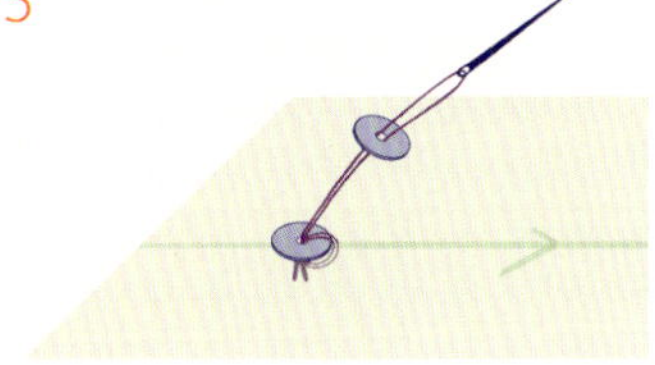

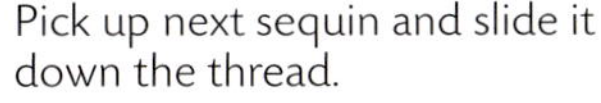

Pick up next sequin and slide it down the thread.

6

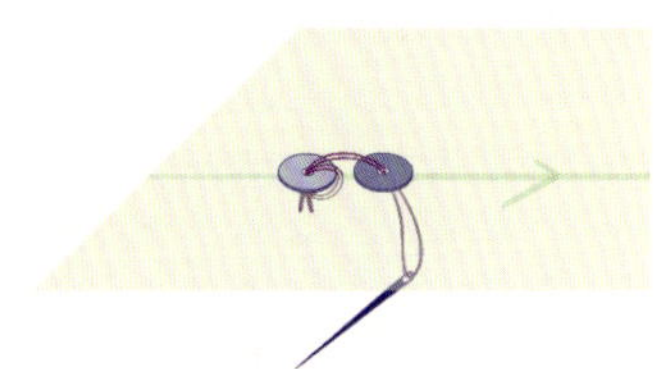

Bring the needle down at the radius of the sequin to the back.

7

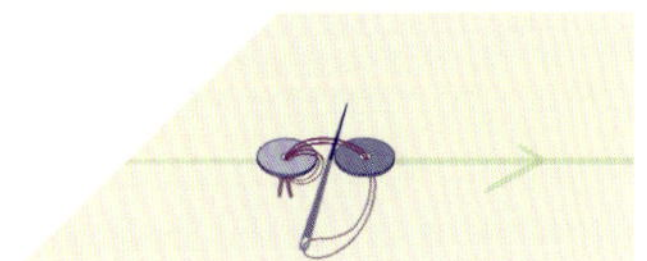

The needle comes to the surface from between the two sequins.

8

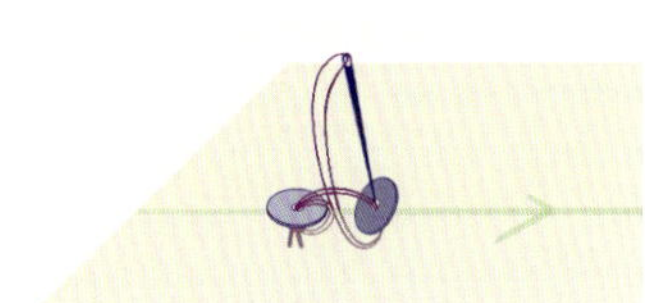

Then slide in the hole of the second sequin from its back side.

9

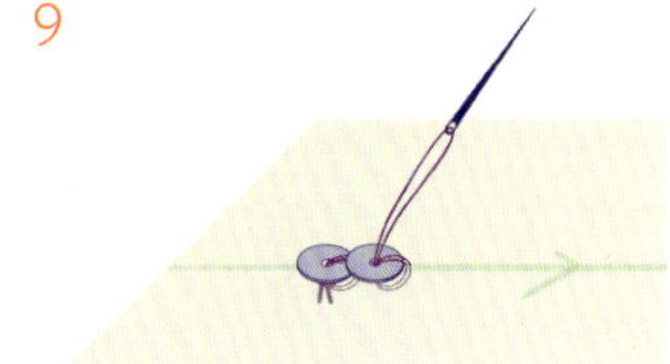

Take the needle out and flip the sequin back to its surface side, overlapping half of the previous sequin.

10

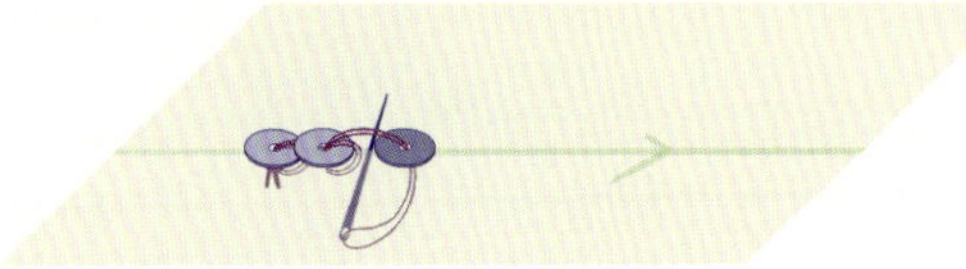

Repeat steps 1 through 9 if additional sequins are needed.

11

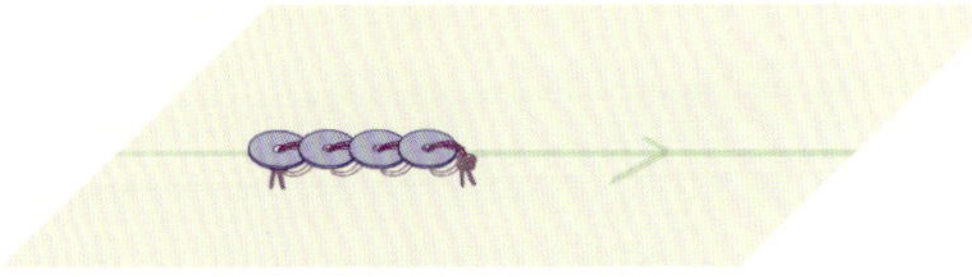

The illustration shows what it looks like when the sequins are sewn overlapping one another.

Embroidering a Bead on Top of a Sequin (or a Tube)

1

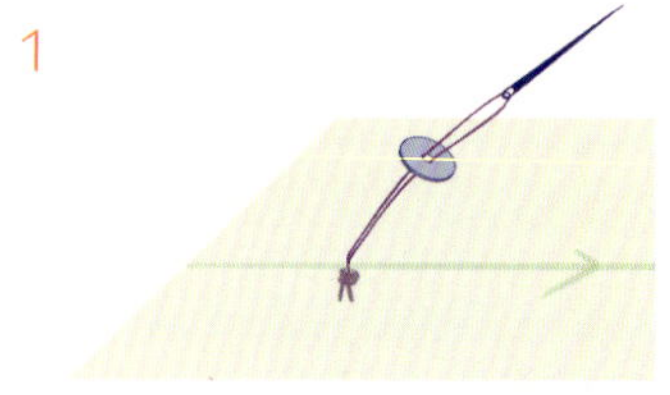

Begin with starting stitches and then thread a sequin on the needle.

2

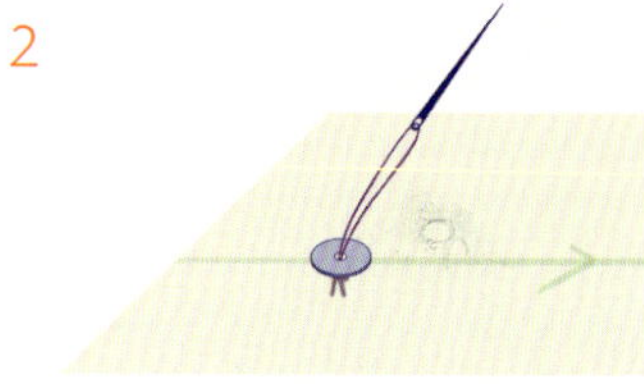

Push the sequin to the bottom and pull the thread tight.

3

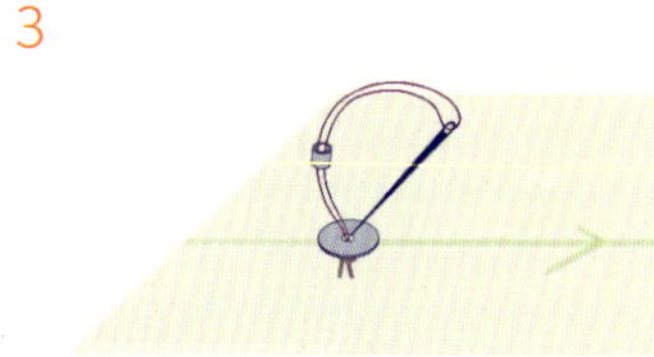

Slide a bead down the thread and bring the needle back into the hole in the sequin all the way through to the back side of the fabric.

4

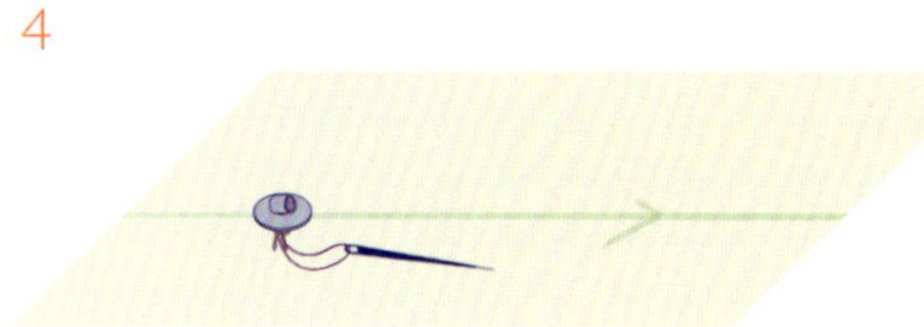

Tighten the thread and the bead is attached on top of the sequin.

5

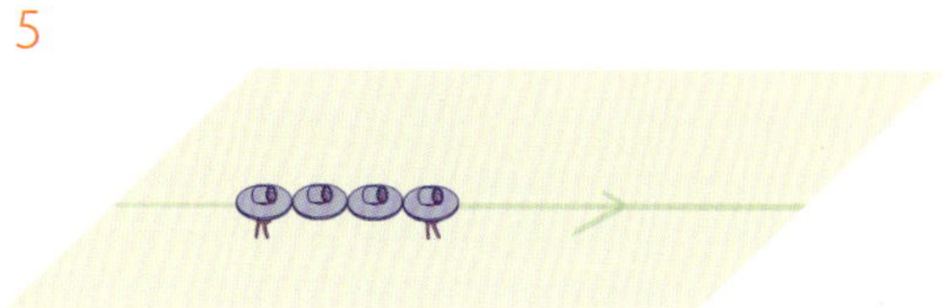

Repeat the previous steps if more is needed. The picture here shows what it looks like when you embroider a series of them.

Embroidering Sew-on Rhinestones

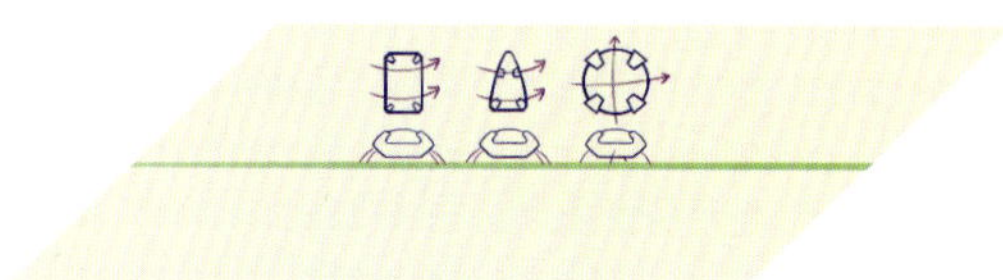

Square sew-on rhinestone: Pass two embroidery threads parallel through the four holes on both sides to secure the rhinestone.

Drop sew-on rhinestone: Pass two embroidery threads parallel through the four holes on both sides to secure the rhinestone.

Round sew-on rhinestone: Pass two embroidery threads crossing each other through the four holes along the side to secure the rhinestone.

Fixing Rhinestone Chain

1

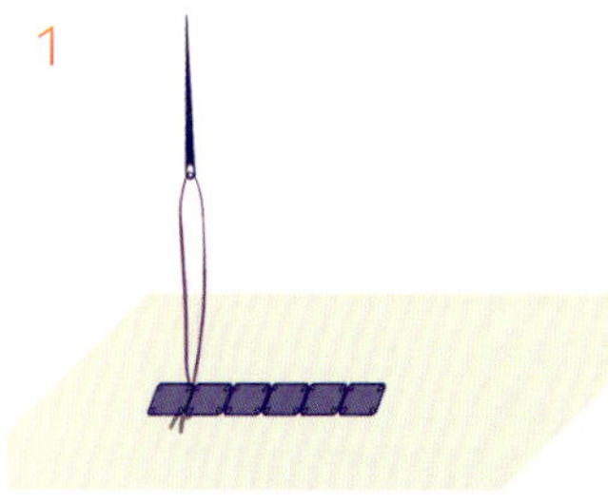

Place the rhinestone chain on the fabric. Start the stitch and lift the needle from the fabric at the edge of the connection point between two rhinestones.

2

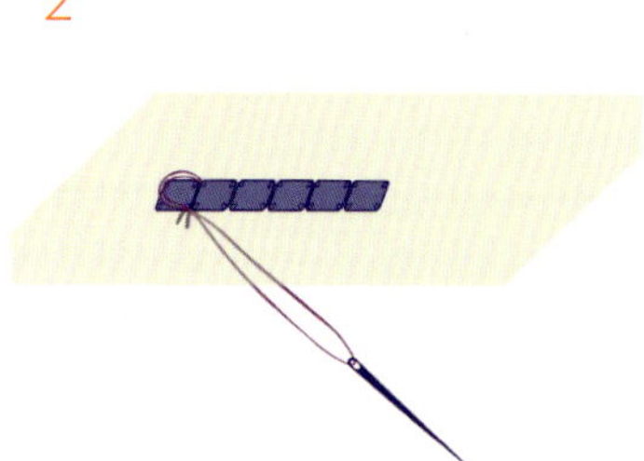

Insert the needle from the opposite of where the connection point of two rhinestones is until it reaches the back of the fabric.

3

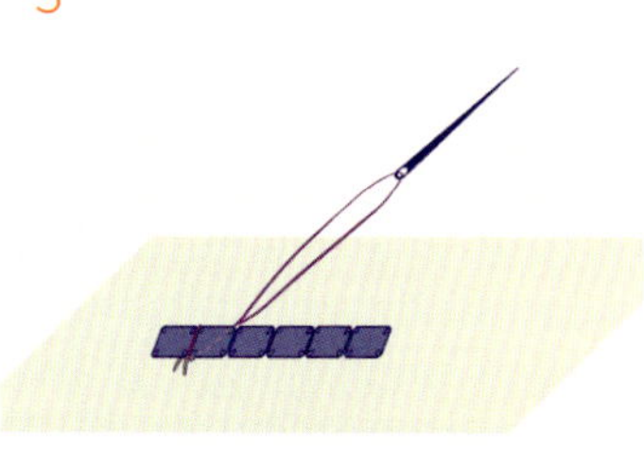

Lift the needle from the next connection point of two rhinestones.

4

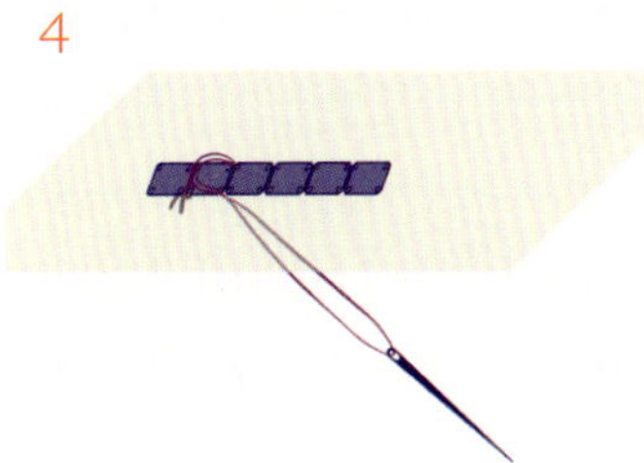

Next, insert the needle at the opposite of this connection point. When inserting and lifting the needle, make sure that it is kept close to the edge of the rhinestone chain.

5

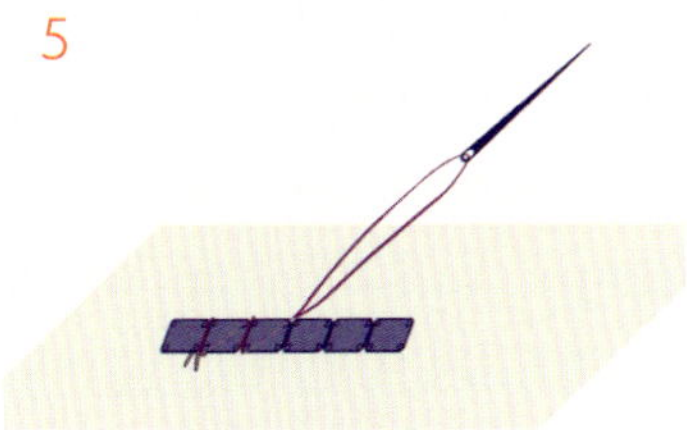

Use this method to fix the connection point for every two rhinestones.

6

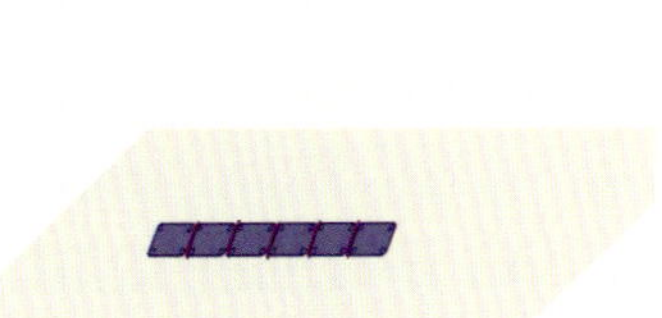

When every connection has been fixed, it is complete.

Fixing Cotton Thread

1

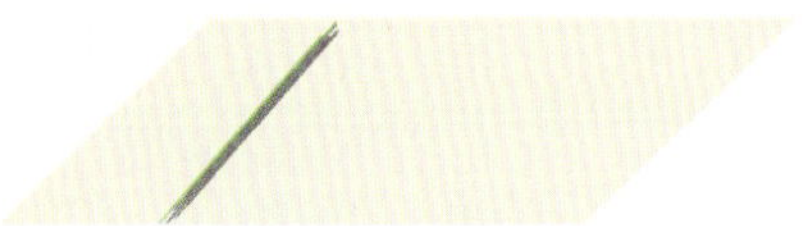

Prepare a length of multi-strand cotton thread (the number of threads is typically dependent on the width and thickness required for the finished effect).

2

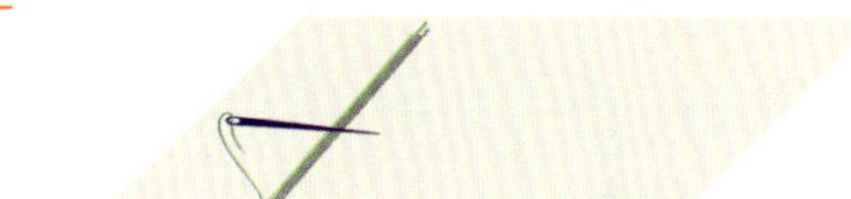

Take a thread of a similar color to the cotton thread, and thread it into your hand sewing needle. Start the stitch on one side, and continue in the direction of the cotton thread. Next, fix the stitch on the other side of the cotton thread.

3

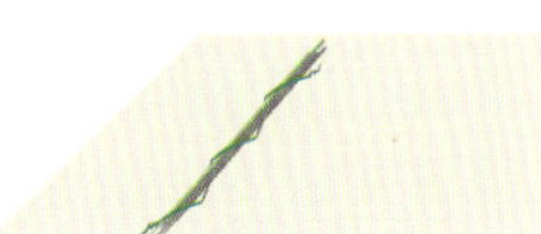

Repeat the steps above to fix the cotton thread on the fabric.

4

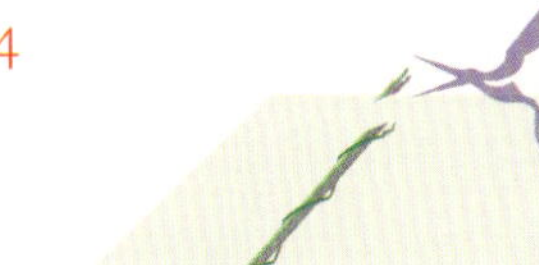

Trim both ends of the cotton thread at an oblique angle to enable a smooth transition between the cotton thread and the fabric.

5

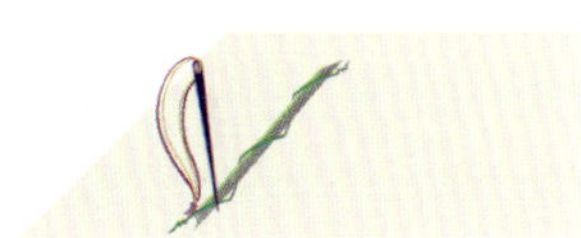

Take another piece of thread (usually 2 or 4 strands) and thread it on the hand sewing needle. Start the stitch next to the edge of the cotton thread.

6

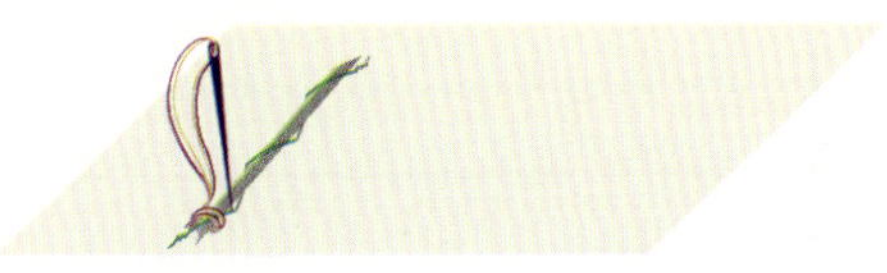

Begin stitching across the cotton thread. The position should remain close to the edge of the cotton thread, ensuring that the stitch is perpendicular to the cotton thread.

7

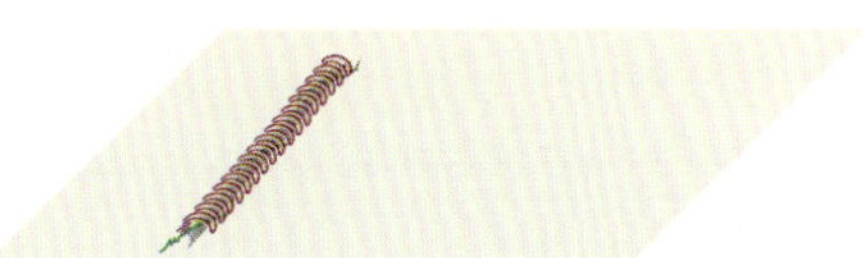

Repeat steps 5–6. Each stitch is next to the previous stitch, with the stitches parallel to each other. Wrap the entire cotton thread, and try not to expose it.

Fixing Folded Ribbon

1

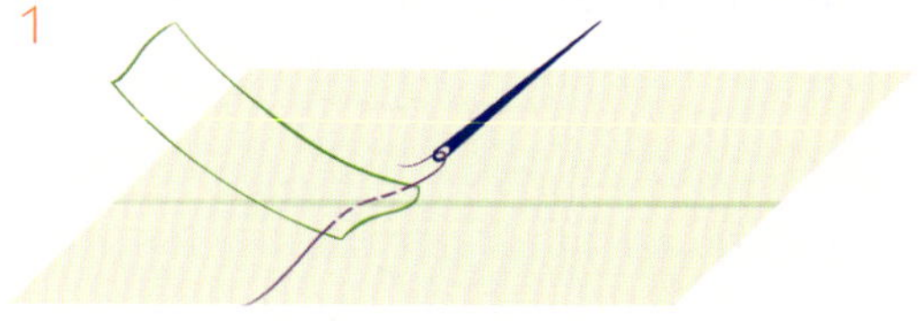

Thread your needle and run straight stitches at one end of the ribbon.

2

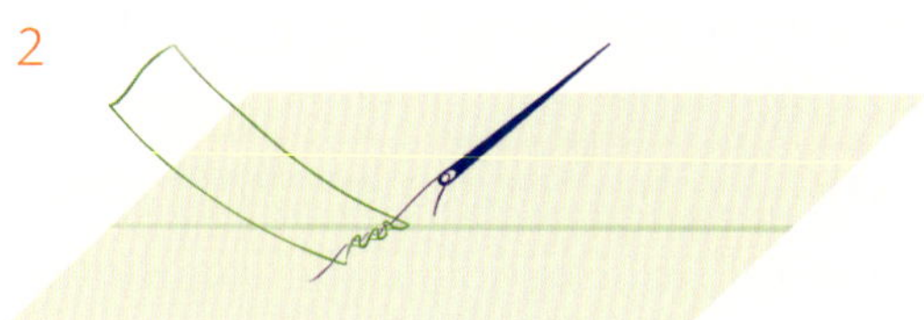

After finishing the straight stitches, tighten the thread to form a pleated effect. Next, fix it onto the fabric.

2. Techniques for Hook Needle

Starting Stitch

1

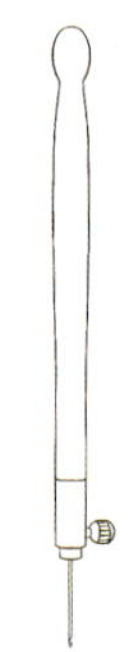

A hook needle consists of two parts: the upper part is the handle and the lower part is a needle with a small, bent tip.

2

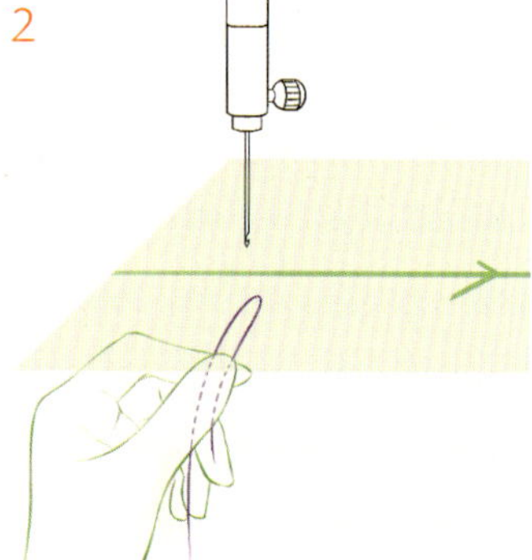

Hold the needle in your right hand and the thread in your left. The hook faces the orientation of your embroidery.

3

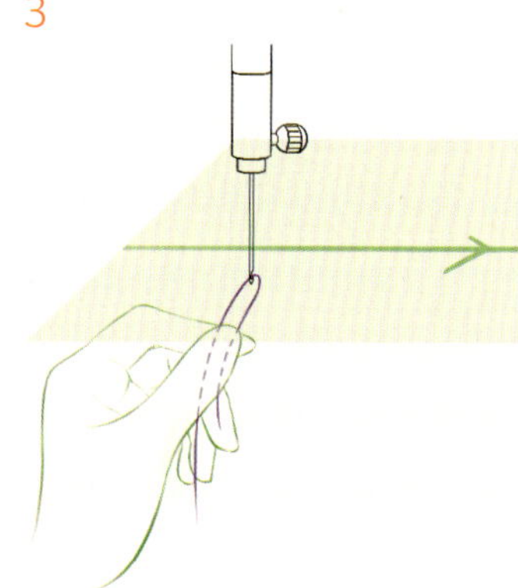

Take the needle down the fabric and catch the thread in the hook on the back of the fabric.

4

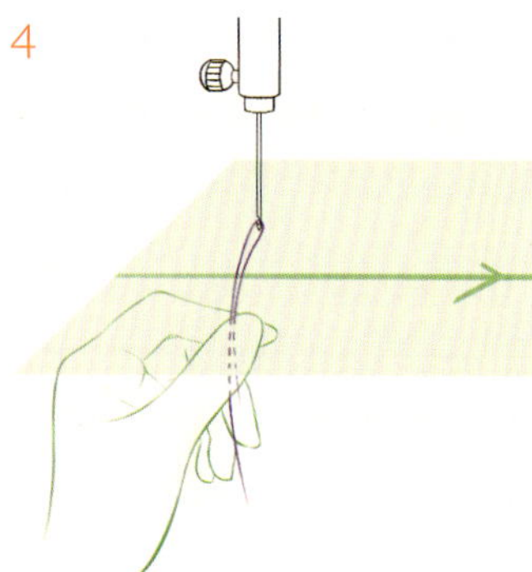

Turn the hook 180 degrees and pull it up the fabric.

5

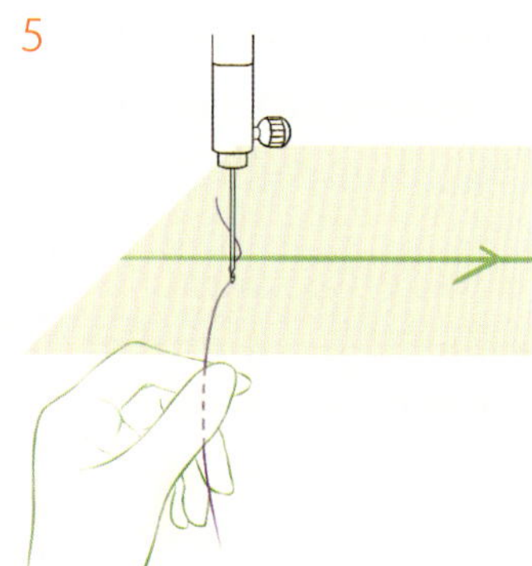

Then turn the hook needle 180 degrees again and bring it down 0.5 mm away from the previous point against the orientation of the embroidery and catch the thread on the hook.

6

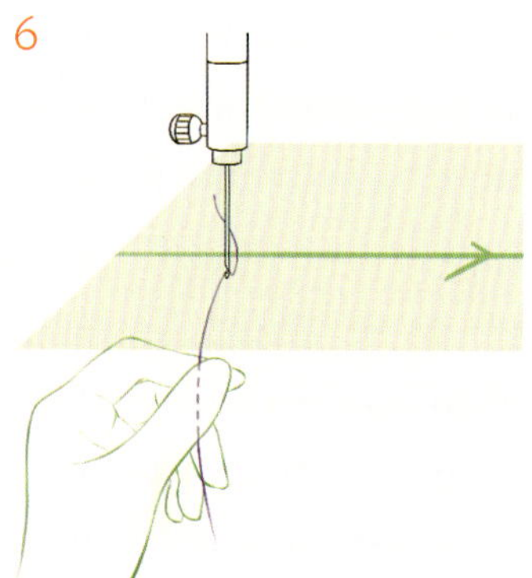

Turn the hook needle 180 degrees.

7

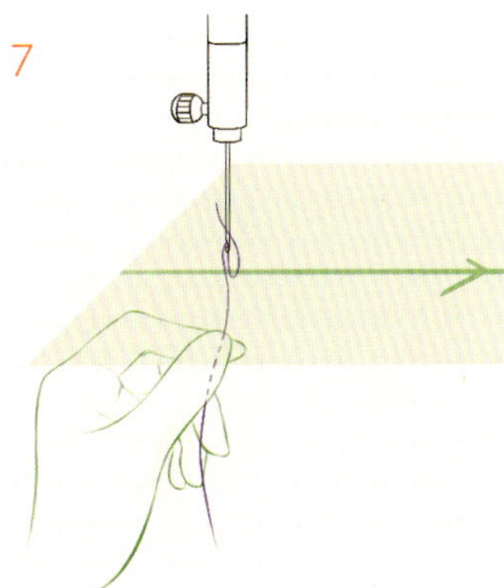

Pull the needle and the thread up the fabric.

8

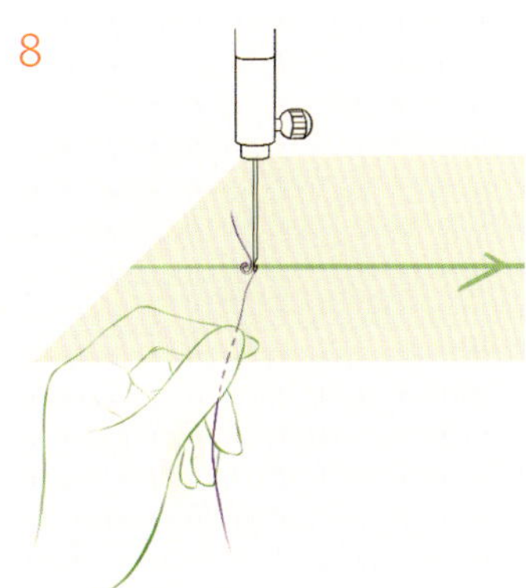

Then turn the needle 180 degrees and bring the needle forward and down 0.5 mm from the previous stitch point.

9

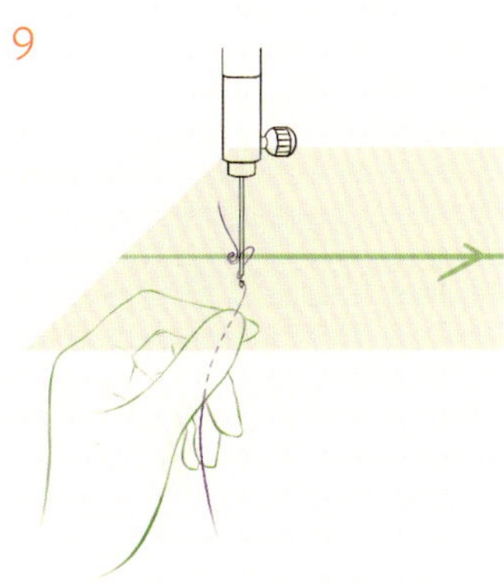

Wind the thread around the hook.

10

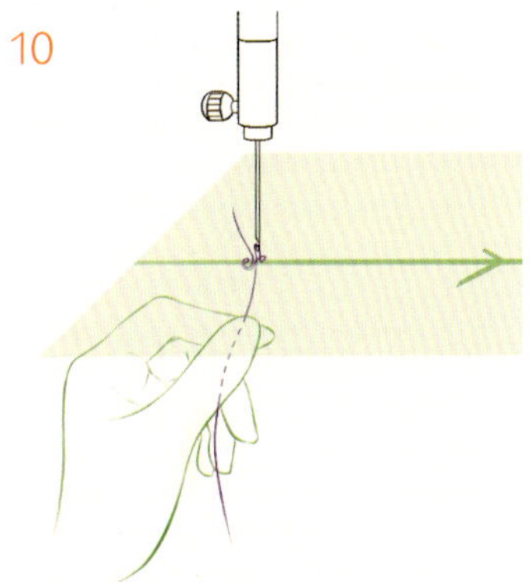

Turn the needle 180 degree and pull it up the fabric.

11

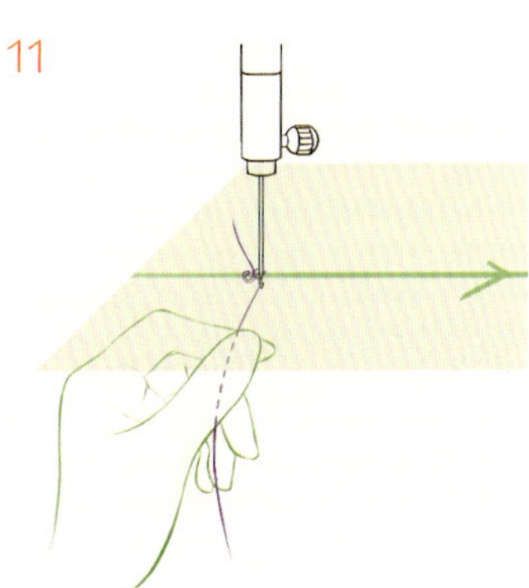

Then bring the needle forward and down 0.5 mm from the previous stitch point.

12

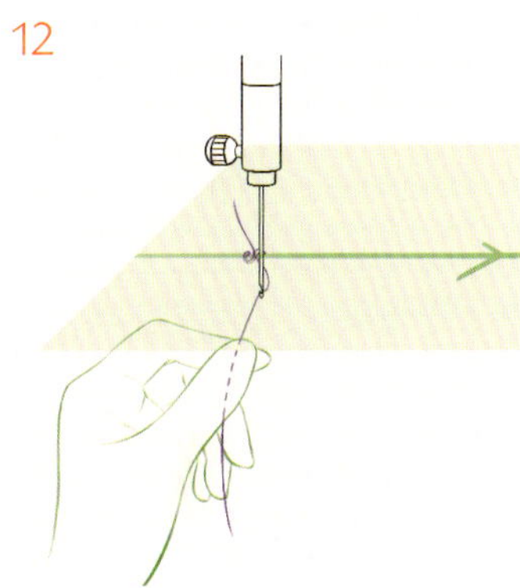

Wind the thread around the hook and pull it up the fabric. Now you are good to start the embroidery.

13

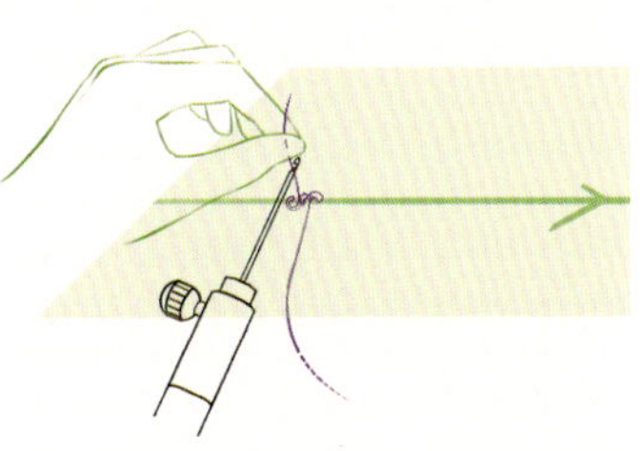

After working the starting stitches, cut short the excess thread left on the fabric. Then hold the thread in your left hand and the needle in your right, use the hook to catch the excess thread and send it to the back of the fabric.

14

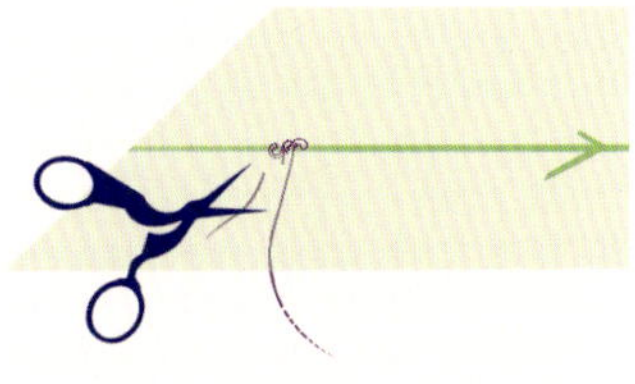

Remove the excess thread.

15

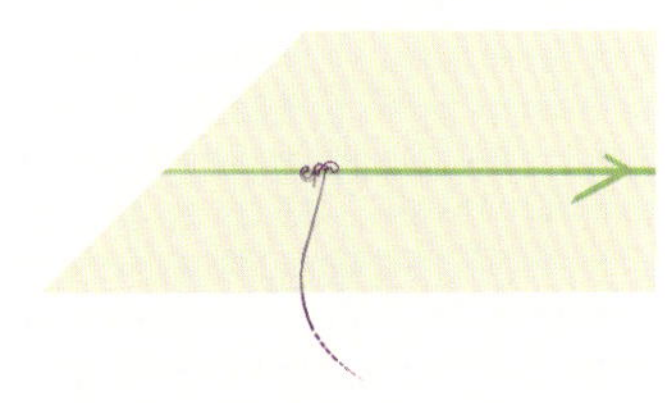

The fabric is clean and free of unwanted thread tail.

Chain Stitch

1

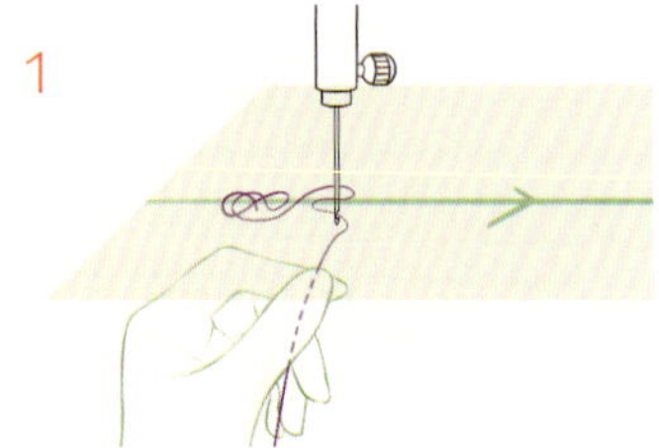

After working the starting stitches, take the needle down a point following the orientation of the embroidery and then wind the thread around the needle once.

2

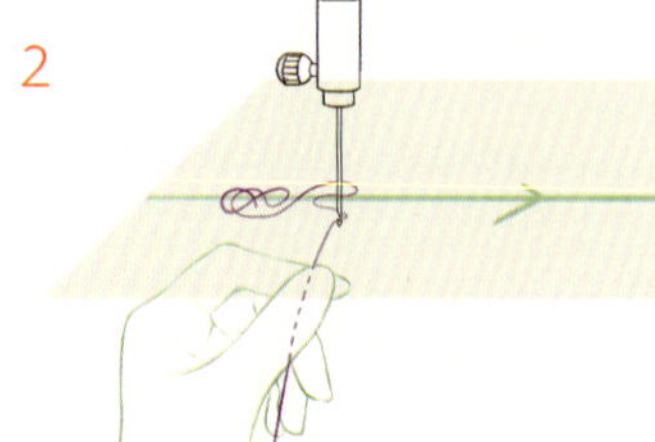

Turn the needle 180 degrees.

3

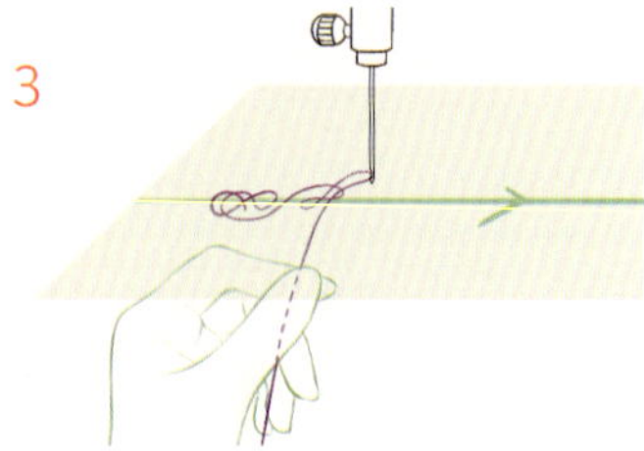

Pull the needle and the thread up the fabric.

4

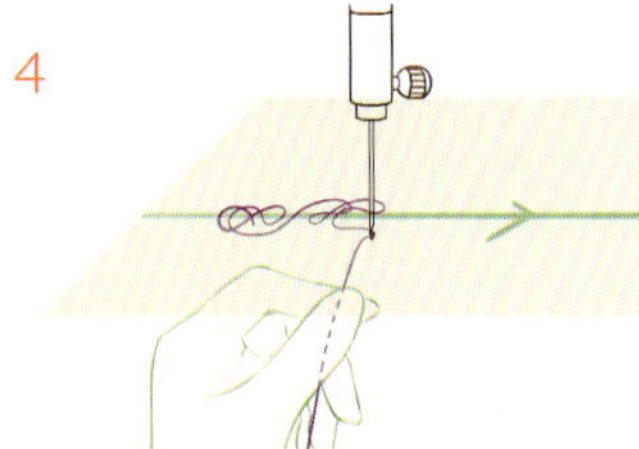

Move forward, turn the needle 180 degrees and take the needle down again in the same stitch length as the previous one, and wind the thread on the needle.

5

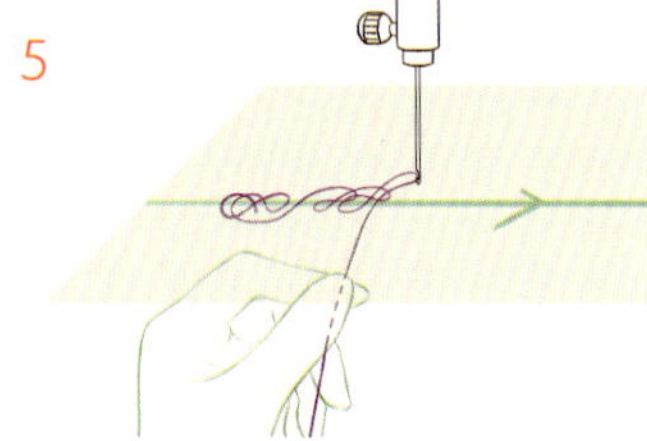

Turn the needle 180 degrees and pull it up the fabric. Repeat the same process, and you will get a chain-like line of stitches on the fabric.

6

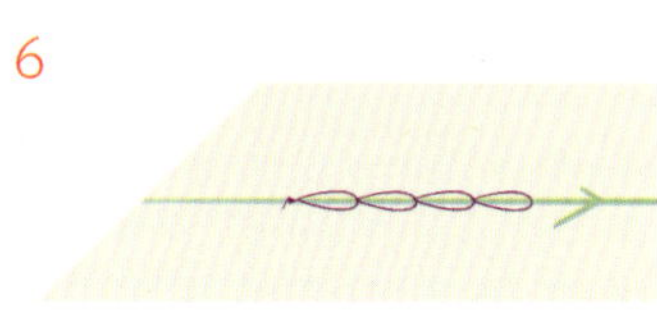

The illustration shows what it looks like when the chain stitches are complete.

Ending Stitch

1

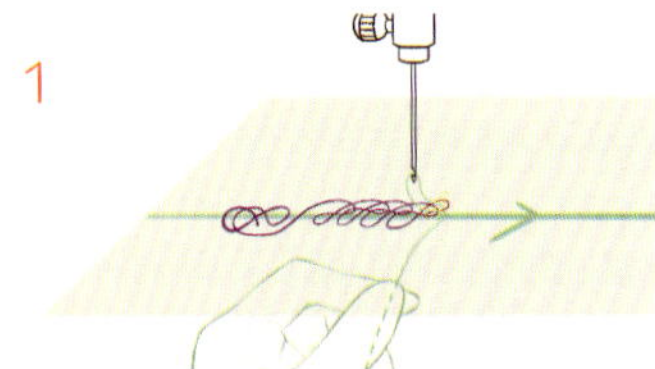

Before the ending stitch, perform three short-distance chain stitches to fix the thread (represented by three colors—red, green, and yellow). Pull the thread up the fabric after you have finished embroidering.

2

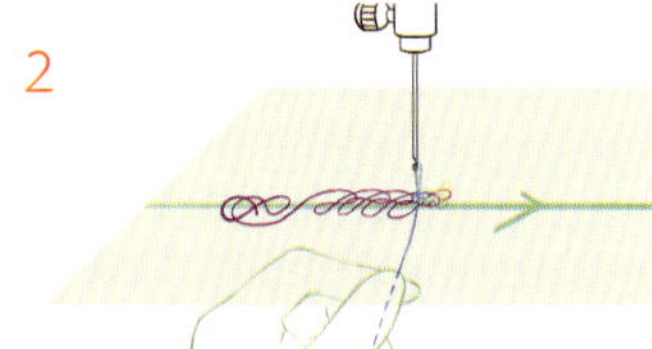

Bring the needle down to the left of the previous stitch point. Repeat steps 1 and 2 to work two more chain stitches (represented by blue). Please note that every stitch is very close to one another.

3

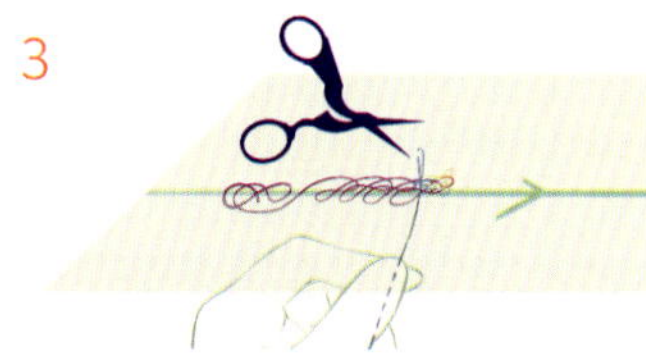

After the short chain stitches are done, remove the excess thread on the fabric.

4

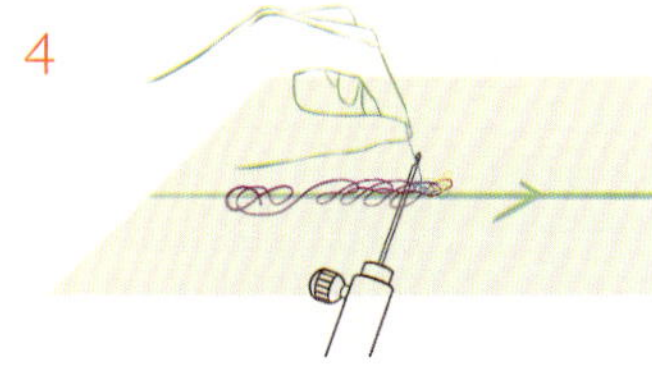

Hold the thread in your left hand and the needle in your right, catch the thread on the hook and take the needle down to the back of the fabric.

5

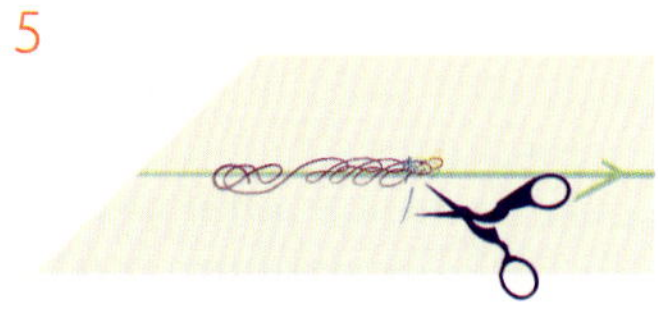

After taking the thread down the back of the fabric, remove the excess thread.

6

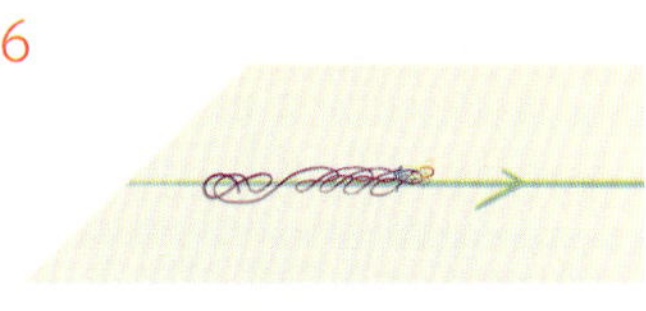

The ending stitches are done.

Edging Stitch

1

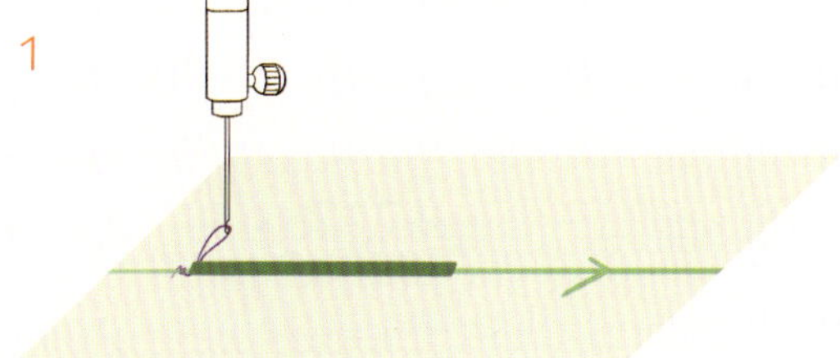

Edging stitch is often used to secure a metal wire (or wire hoop, bullion wire) onto the fabric. As shown in the illustration, the horizontal line is a length of metal wire. Work the starting stitches and then pull the needle up the fabric.

2

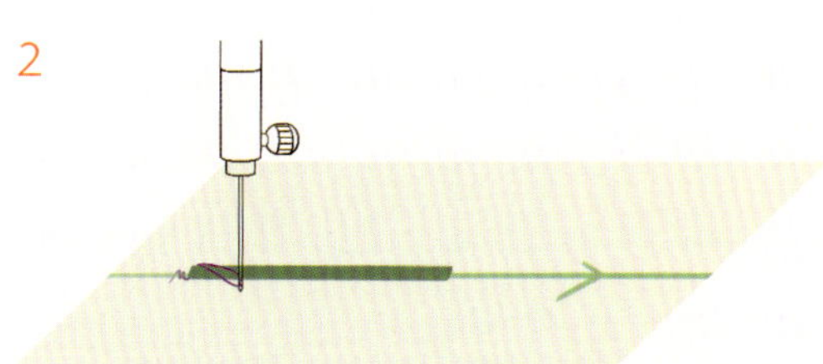

Bring the needle forward along the wire a stitch length (of your choice) and then take it down the fabric on the other side of the wire.

3

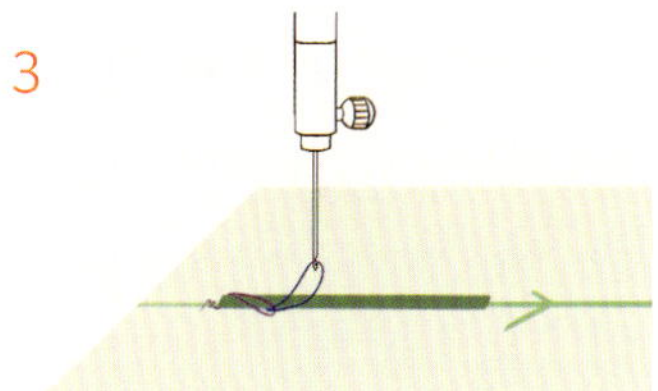

Apply the method of a chain stitch and pull the needle up the fabric.

4

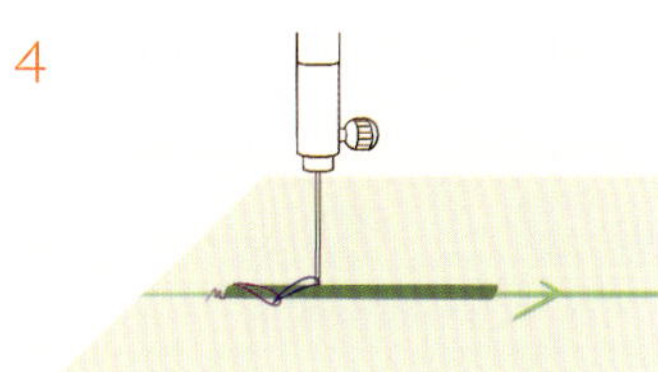

Bring the needle forward along the wire a stitch length and take it down the fabric on the other side of the metal wire.

5

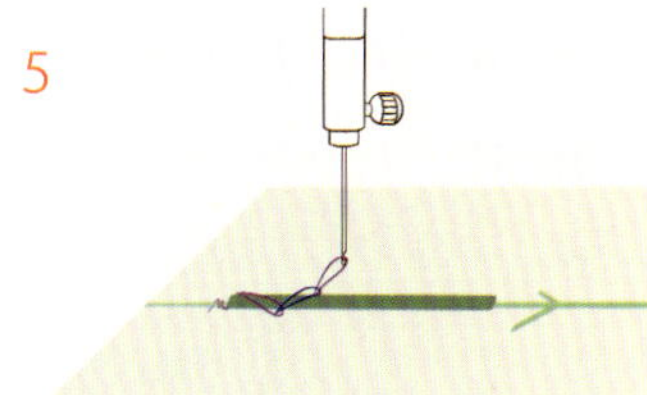

Repeat the process for more stitches.

6

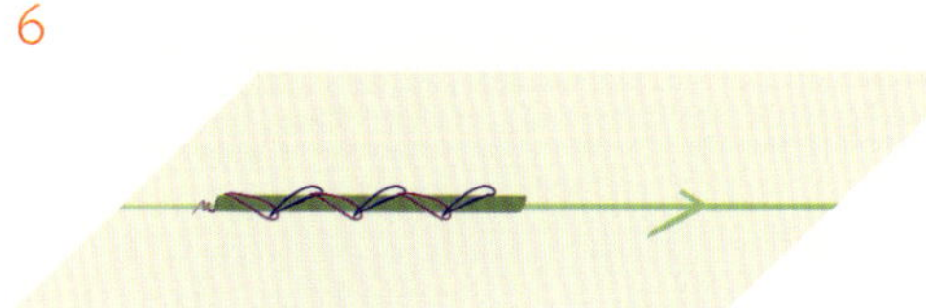

The illustration shows what it looks like after the metal wire has been held securely in place.

7

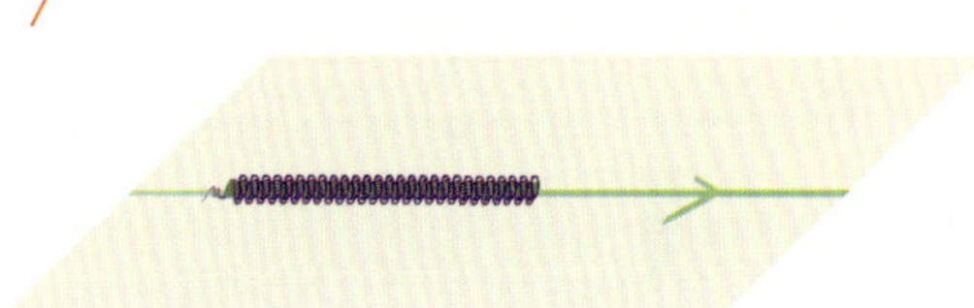

The longer the stitch length, the more exposed the metal wire is. The smaller the stitch length, the less exposed the metal wire is (as shown in the figure).

Pulling Stitch

1

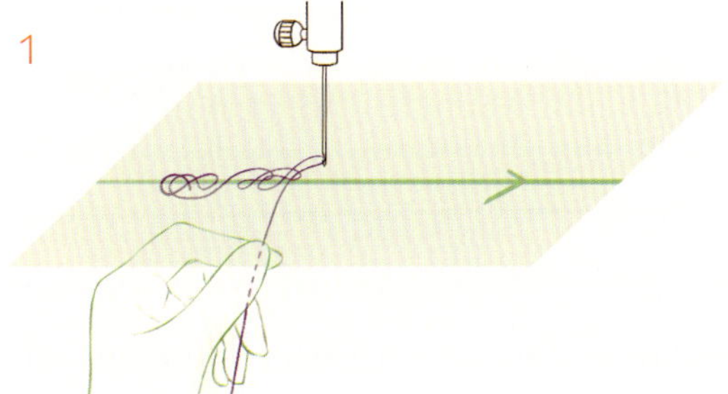

Pull the needle and the thread loop up the fabric for a certain distance.

2

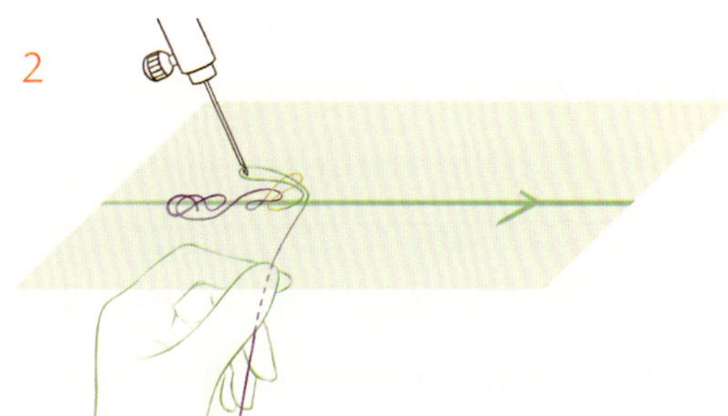

After fixing the stitch within a suitable distance, pull the needle and the thread loop backwards.

3

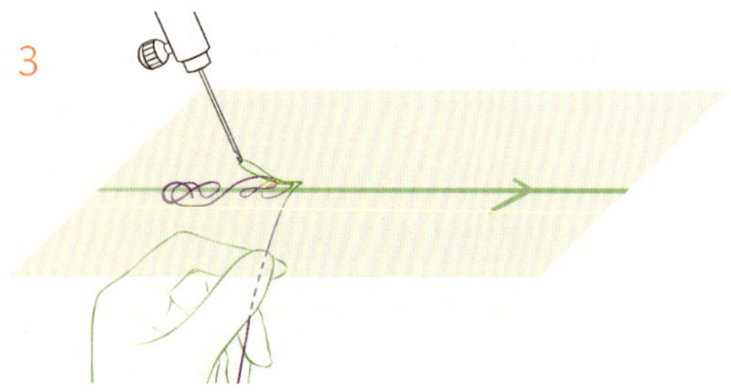

Pull the thread loop to the point near the starting stitch, and tighten the thread with your left hand at the same time.

4

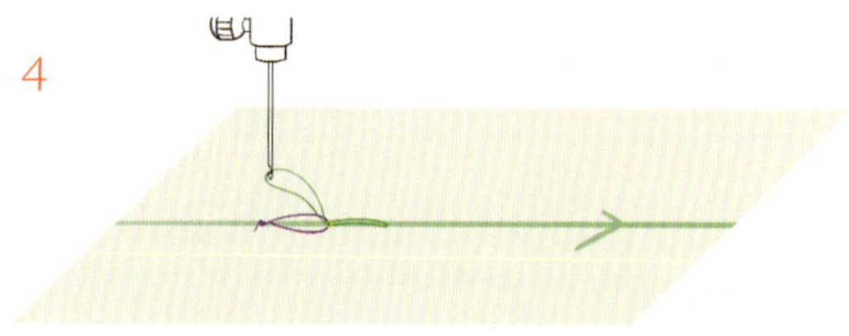

After fixing a stitch near the starting stitch, pull out the needle again and move towards the preferred point. Repeat steps 1–4. You can pull the thread to any position you like on the fabric.

Long and Short Stitch

1

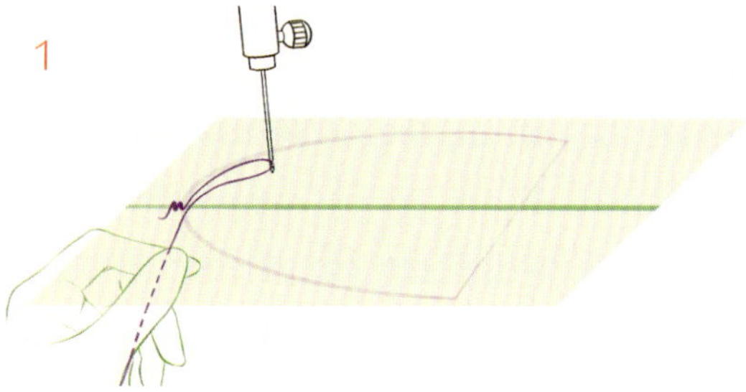

Set a semicircular area within the pink outline on the fabric as the area for embroidering long and short stitches. After the starting stitches, pull the thread loop up the fabric.

2

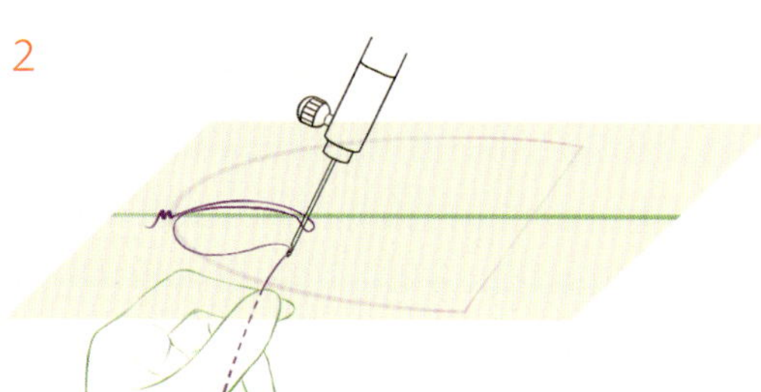

Fix the stitch after going a certain length.

3

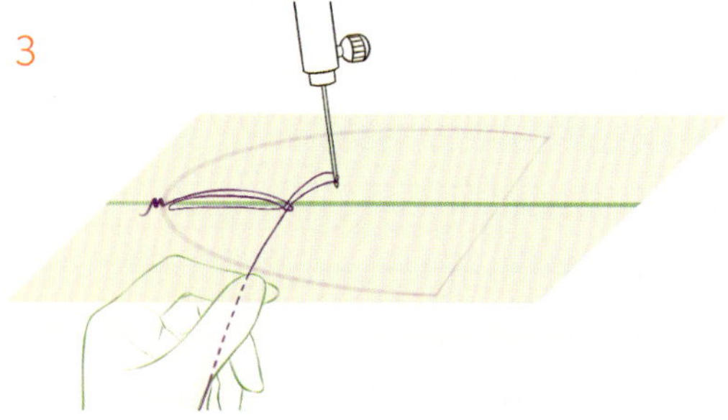

Pull the thread loop up the fabric and continue going forward.

4

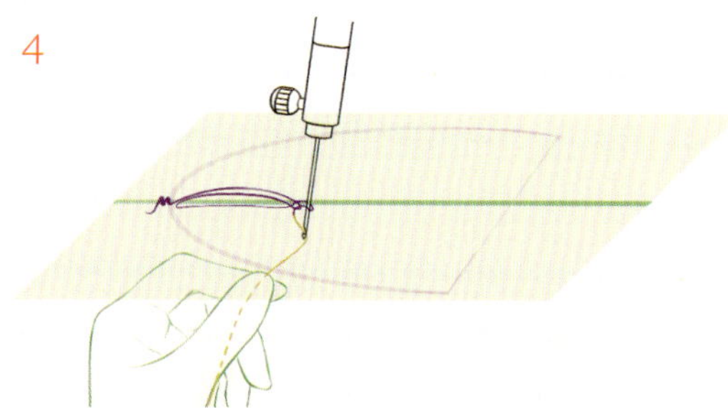

Go forward about 1 mm, and fix the stitch.

5

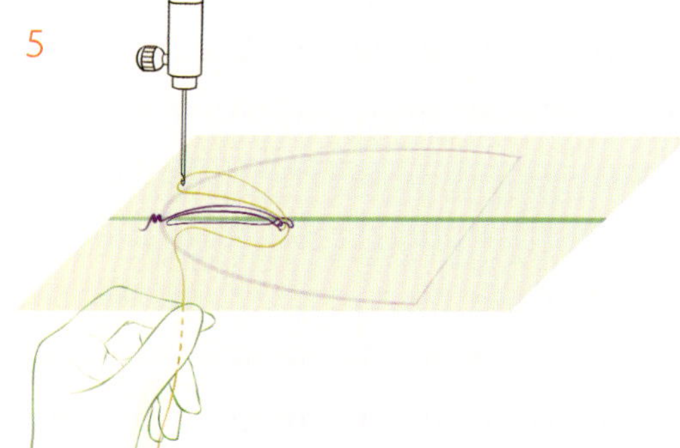

Pull the thread loop back close to the outline.

6

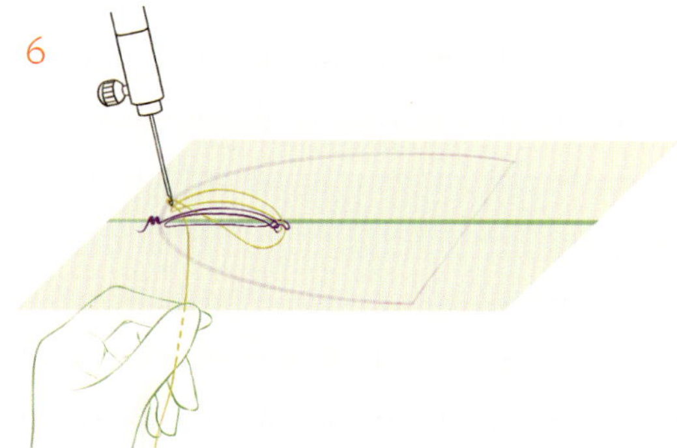

Fix the stitch near to the outline.

7

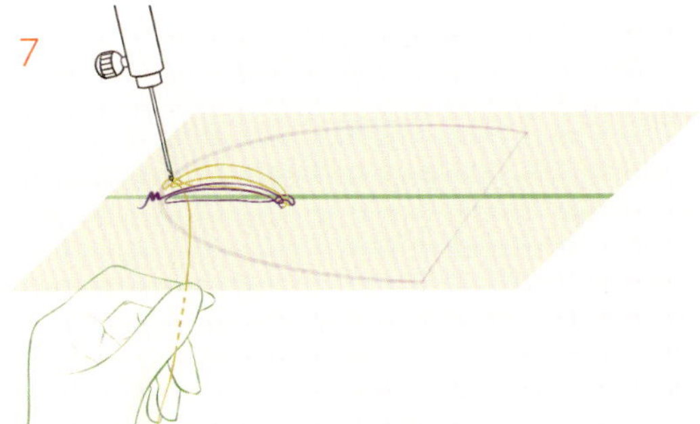

Go forward about 1 mm from the previous stitch. Fix another stitch.

8

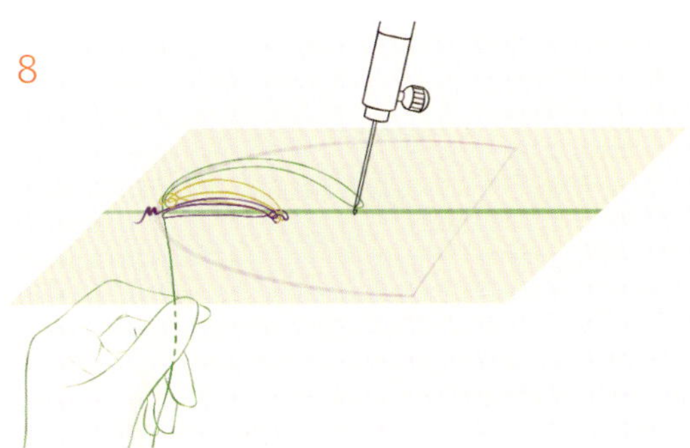

Pull out the loop. Fix a stitch again after going a certain length.

9

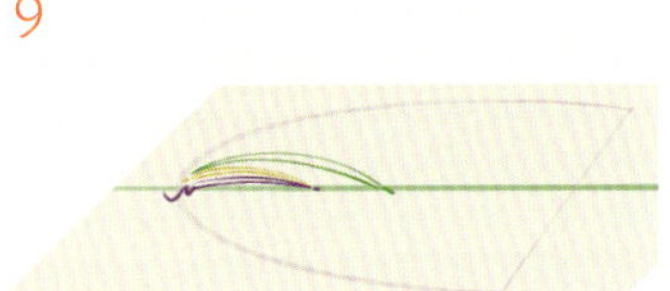

Continue fixing the thread in the semicircle area using the method above.

10

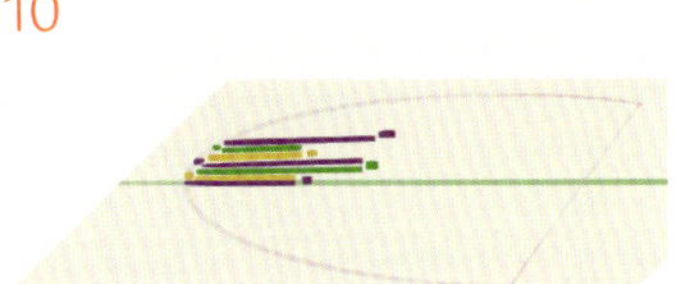

The length of each stitch is different, which is a convenient way of filling more patterns.

11

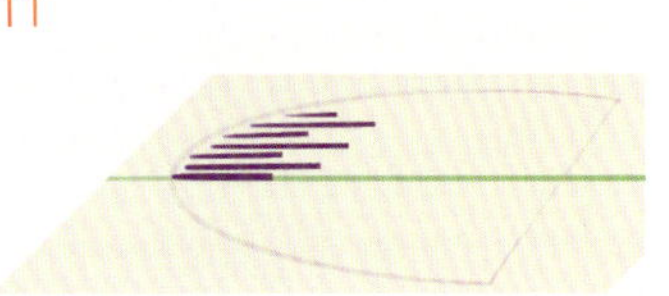

You can also apply the hand sewing long and short stitch technique (refer to page 31) to layer the pattern, and use different threads to create a gradient effect.

Stitching Sequins (or Beads) from the Front Side of the Fabric

1

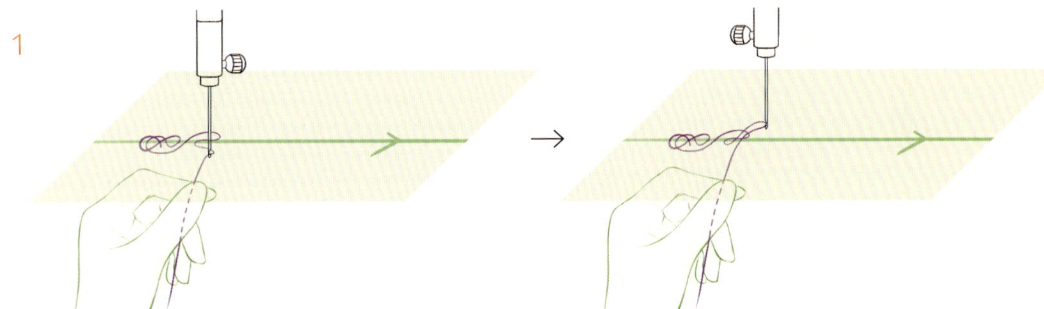

Work the starting stitches. Pull the needle with thread up the fabric.

2

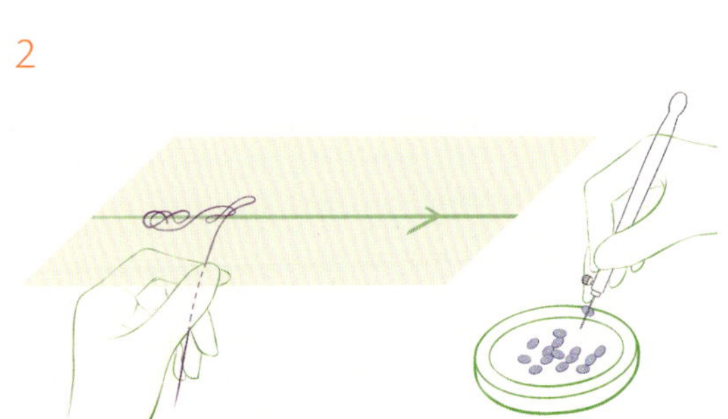

Release the needle from the loop, pick up a sequin (or a bead) and use your middle finger to hold it.

3

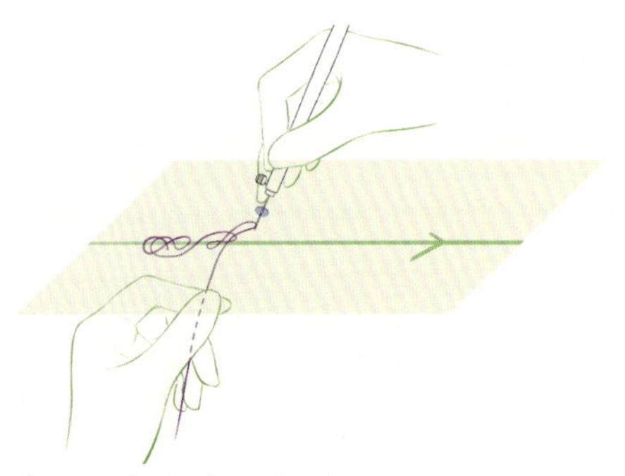

Bring the needle back to the loop.

4

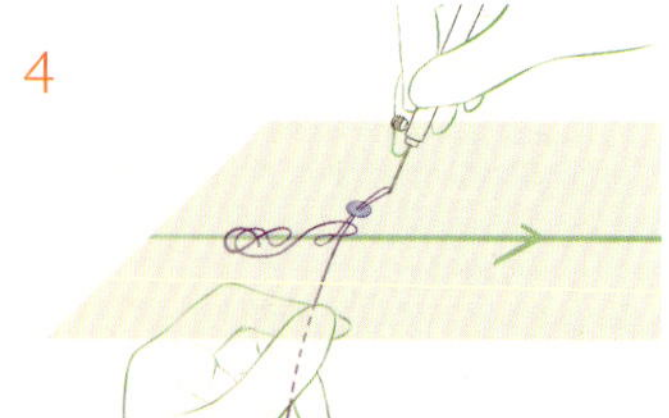

Push the sequin to the thread loop and straight down so it lies flat on the fabric.

5

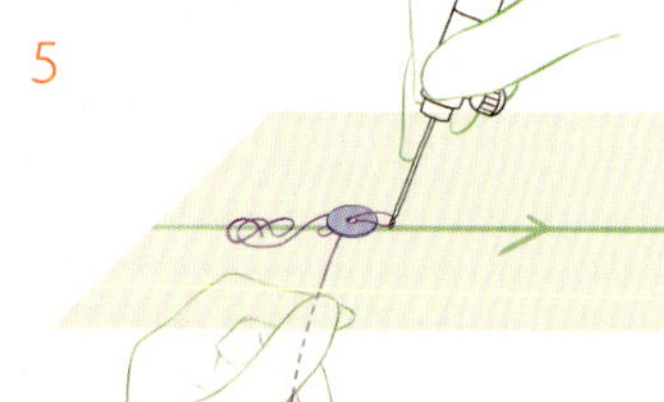

Bring the needle down right next to the edge of the sequin.

6

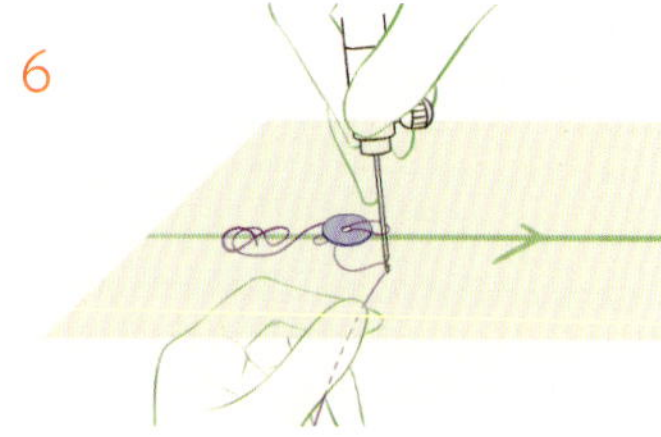

Wind the thread round the needle.

7

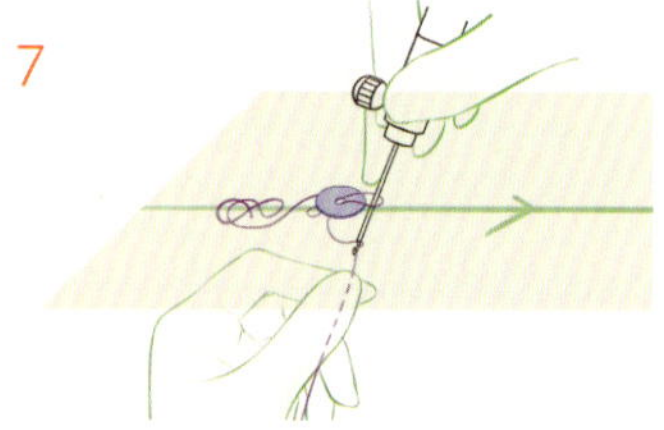

Turn the needle 180 degrees.

8

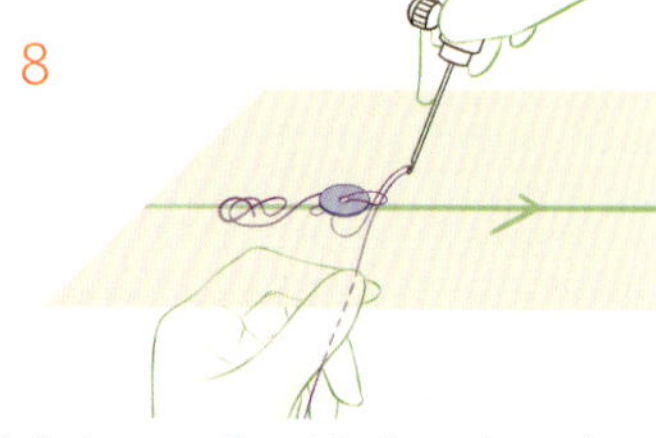

Pull the needle with thread up the fabric.

9

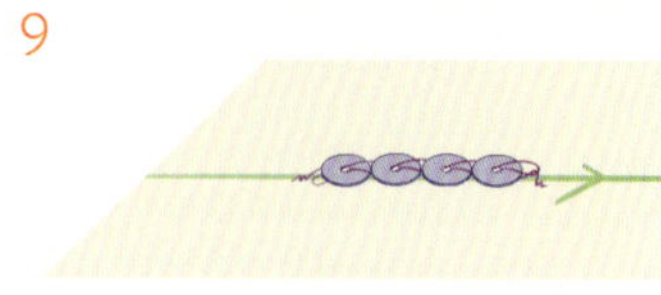

Repeat the previous process for additional sequins (or beads). The illustration is what it looks like when the sequins are stitched.

Stitching Beads (or Sequins) from the Back Side of the Fabric

1

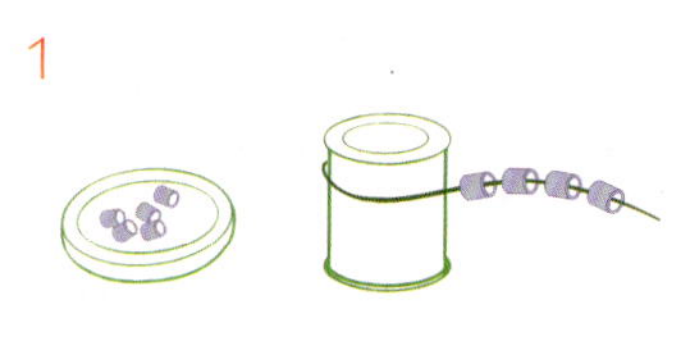

String a group of beads (or sequins) on the thread from a spool.

2

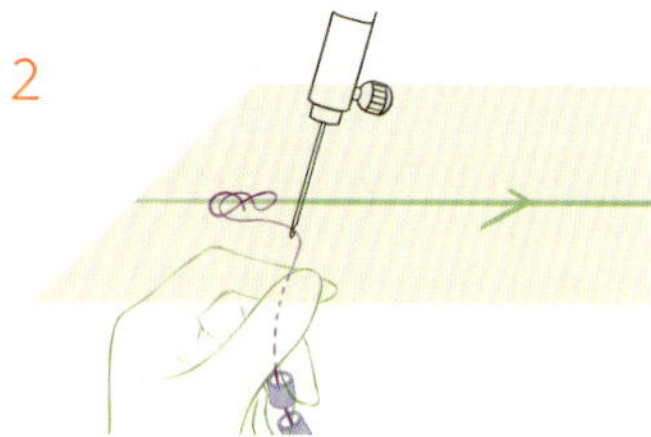

Work the starting stitches. Place the embroidery hoop face down. Hold the thread in your left hand and the needle in your right. Wind the thread round the hook.

3

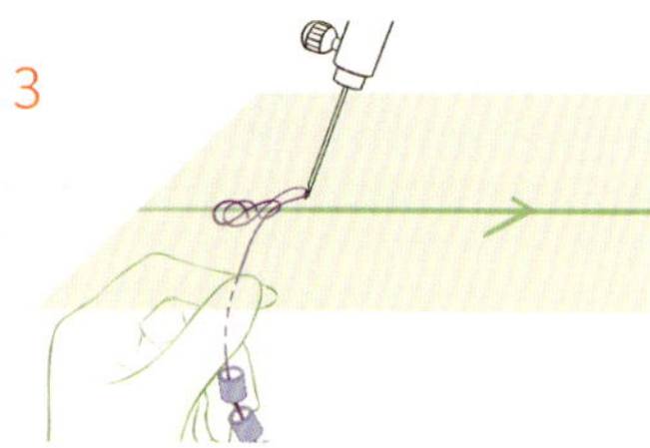

Pull the needle with thread up the fabric.

4

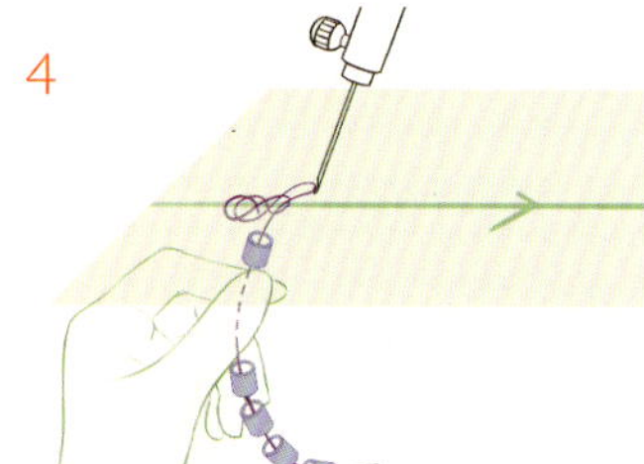

Then use your left hand to push a bead up.

5

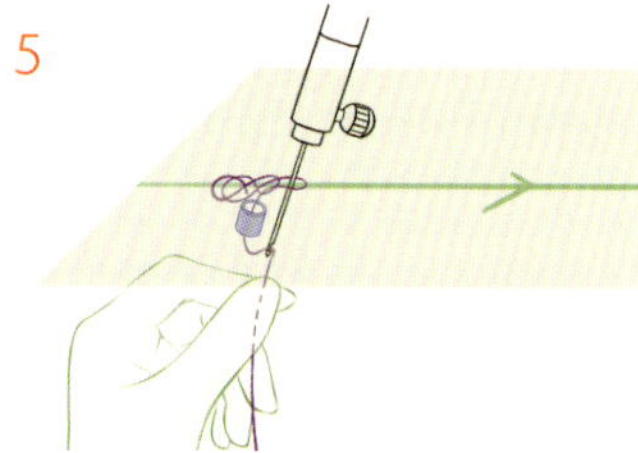

Bring the needle forward along the orientation of the embroidery and down where the length of the bead ends (if it is a sequin, the stitch length is the radius of the sequin). When the needle is down the back of the fabric, push with your left hand the bead closer to the fabric but between the hook and the fabric. Wind the thread around the needle.

6

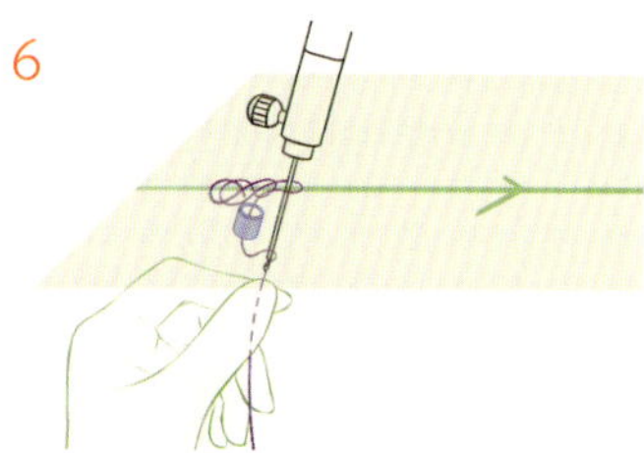

Turn the needle 180 degrees so the hook faces against the orientation of the embroidery.

7

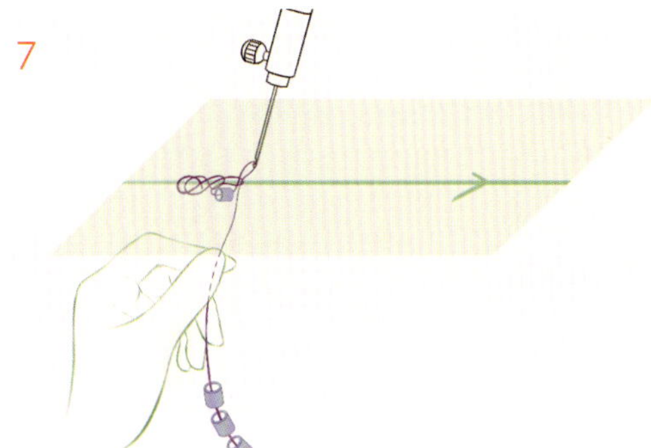

Pull the needle up the fabric and the bead is held securely in place on the back of the fabric.

8

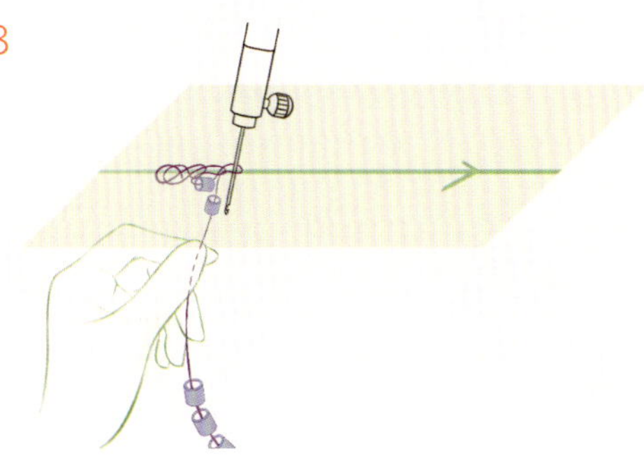

Bring the needle forward following the orientation and take it down where the length of the bead ends (if it is a sequin, the stitch length is the radius of the sequin).

9

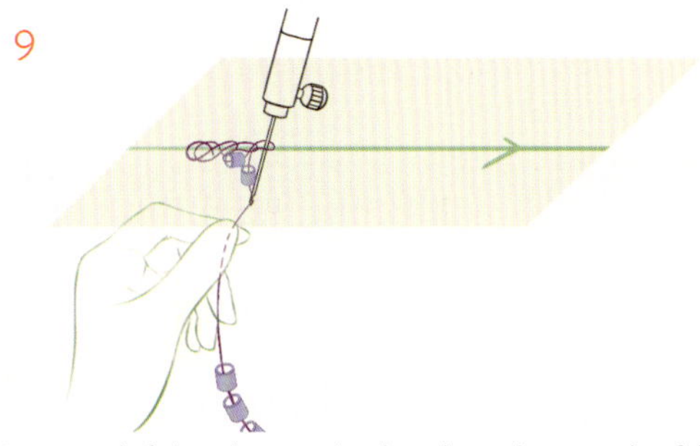

Use your left hand to push a bead up close to the fabric and wind the thread around the hook.

10

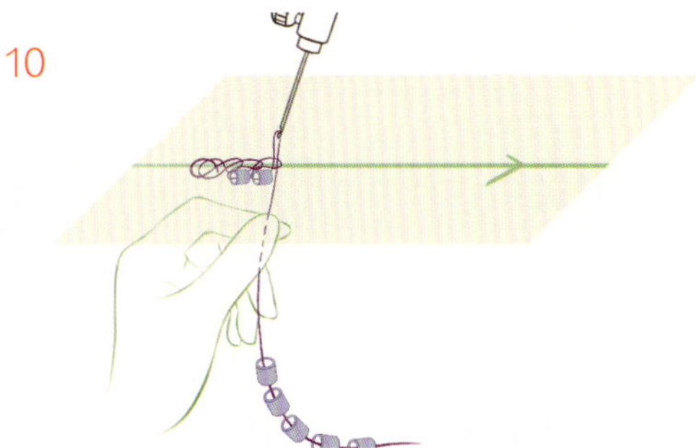

Then turn the needle 180 degrees and pull it up the fabric. The second bead is held securely in place.

11

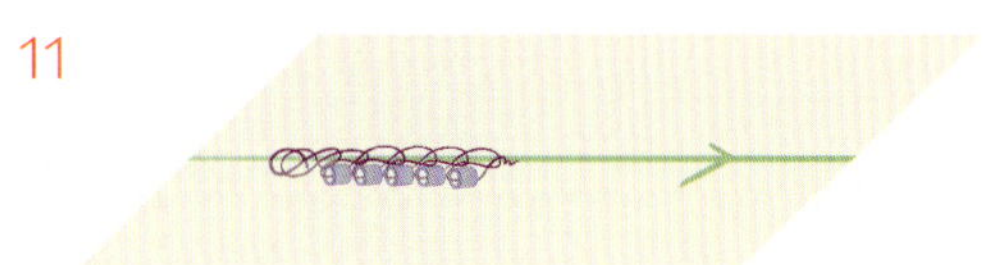

Repeat the previous process for additional beads (or sequins). Make sure the space between the beads is adequate. The illustration shows what it looks like when a series of beads are sewed securely in place.

12

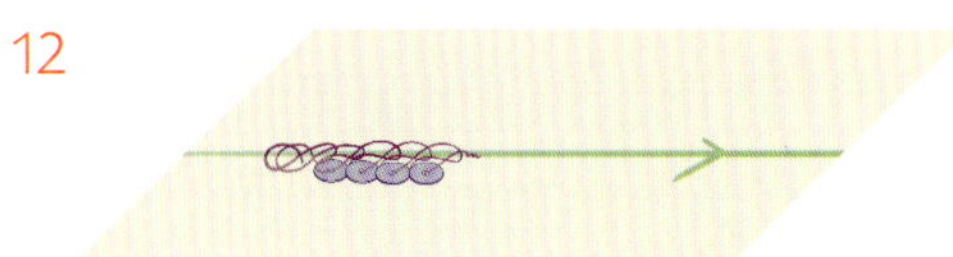

When stitching sequins from the back side of the fabric, apply the same method. The stitch length is the radius of a sequin. Subsequent sequin overlaps the previous one. Try to reveal as little as possible the hole in the sequin when having them overlap one another.

Stitching Multiple Beads from the Front Side of the Fabric

1

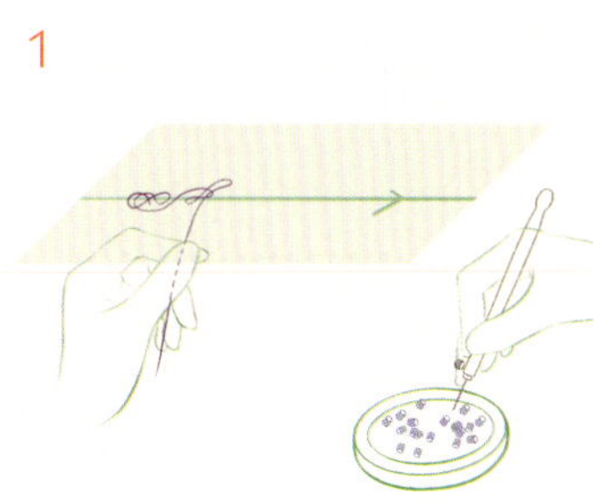

After the starting stitches, take the needle out of the loop.

2

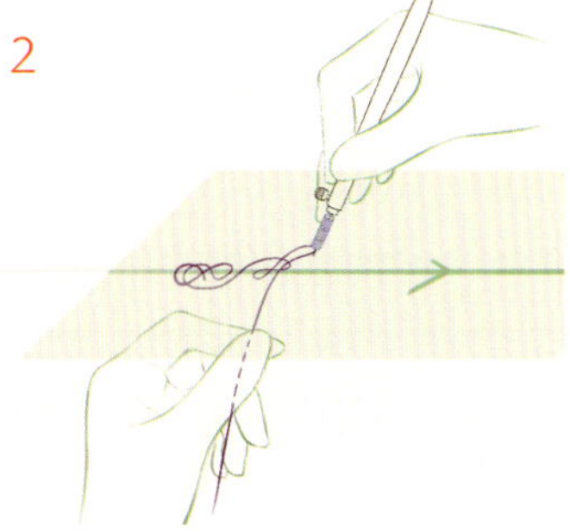

Thread multiple beads onto the needle and catch the thread in the hook.

3

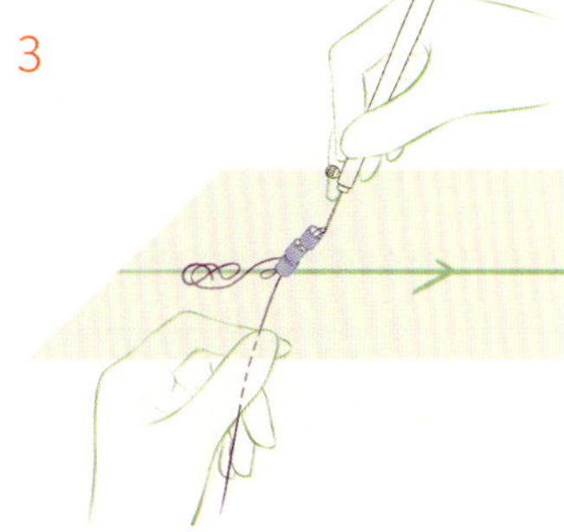

Push the beads towards the loop. Tighten and pull them onto the surface of the fabric.

4

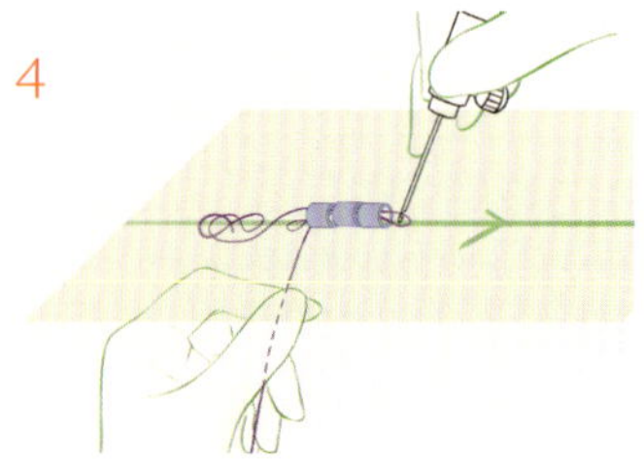

Insert the needle from the edge of the last bead to the back of the fabric.

5

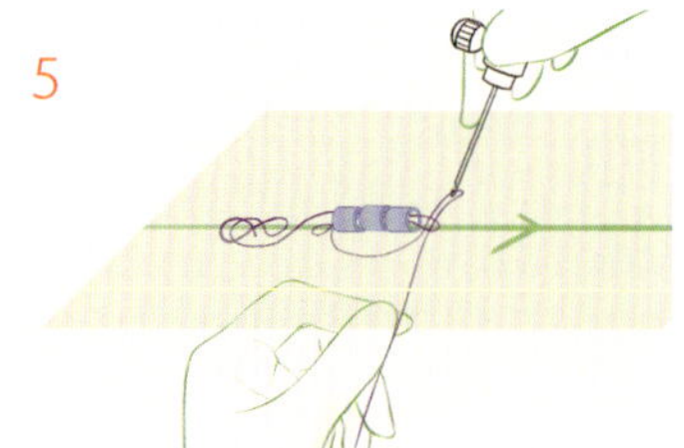

Wrap the thread around the needle. Turn the needle 180 degrees, then lift the thread and needle from the fabric.

6

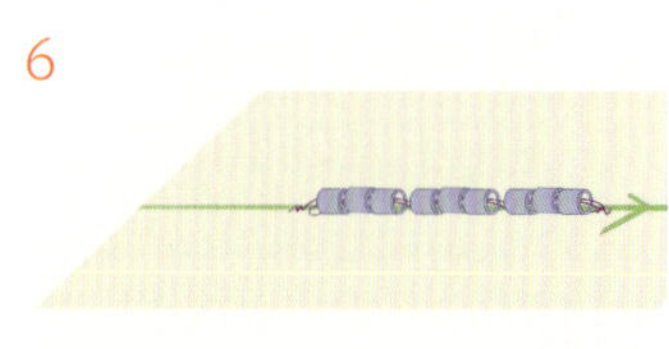

Repeat the steps above. The image is the end-product of embroidery comprising three groups of beads.

Stitching Beads Irregularly from the Front Side of the Fabric

1

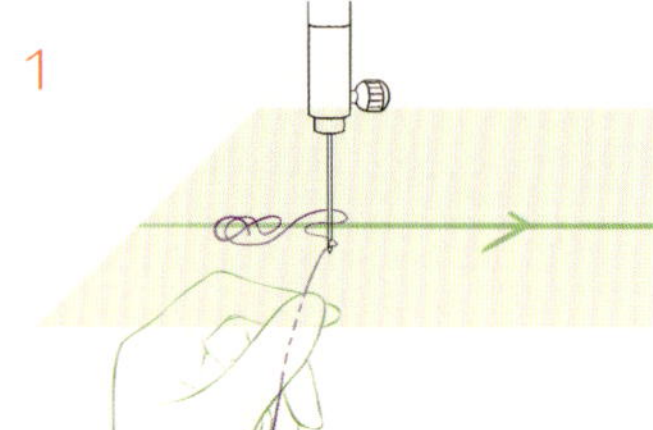

Start the stitches.

2

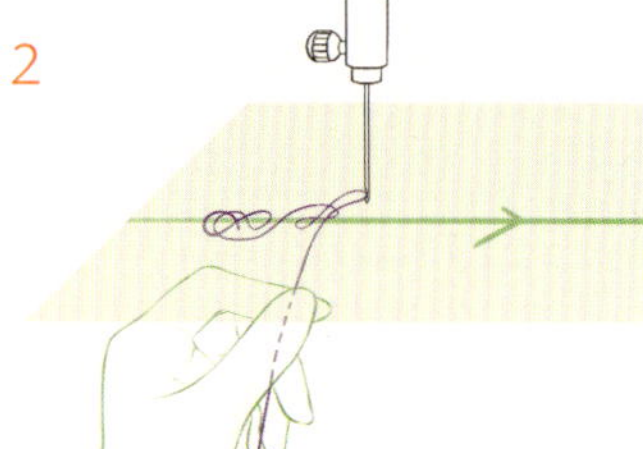

Pull the hook up the fabric.

3

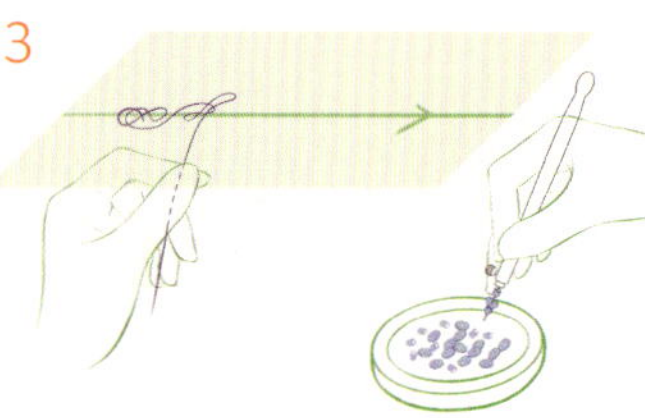

Thread the materials required on the needle, such as a bead, multiple beads, a sequin, or a combination of beads and sequins. (In this example, a combination of beads and sequins is used, with a bead, a sequin and another bead threaded in this sequence.)

4

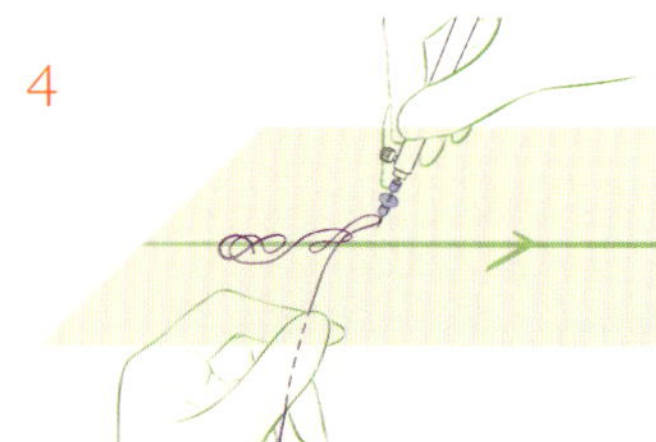

Catch the loop in the hook.

5

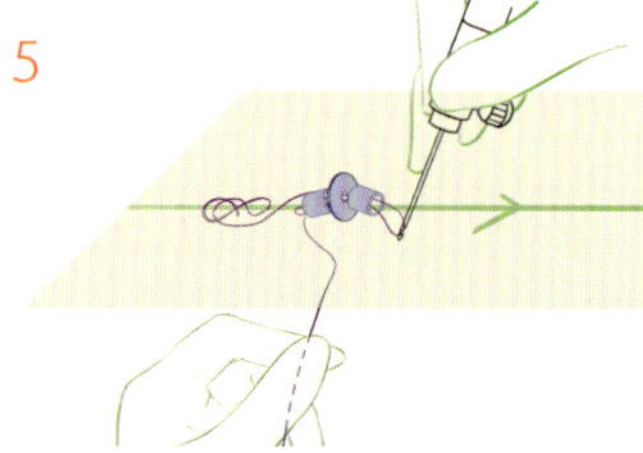

Push the materials onto the loop and take the needle down the fabric at the edge of the last bead.

6

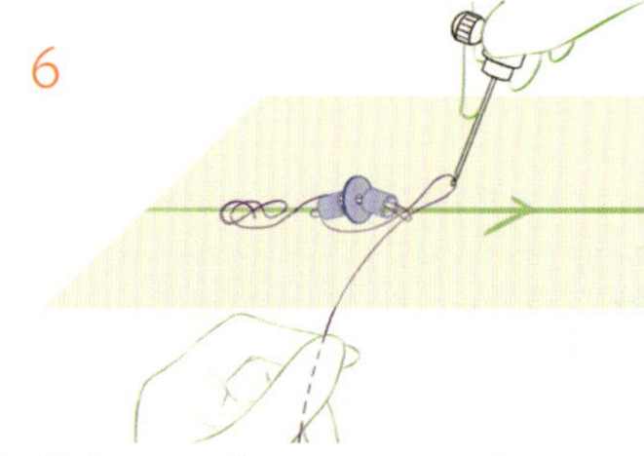

Pull the needle outwards after fixing a set of beads/sequins.

7

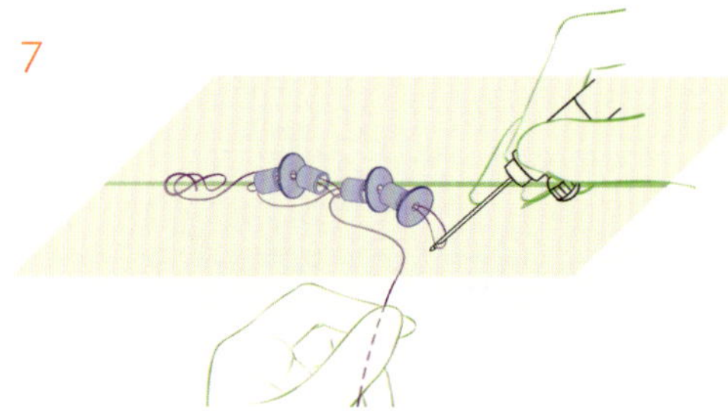

Continue to select a mixture of beads/sequins. Catch the thread in the hook and insert the needle at a random point that is near to the first group.

8

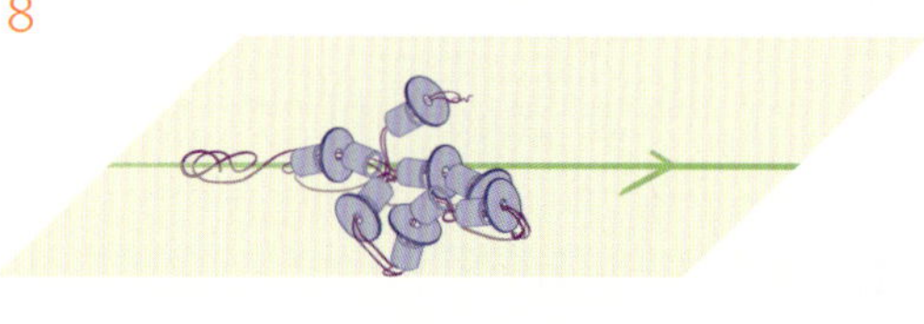

Repeat the steps above. The points where you insert the needle should be at a random point near to the previous group of beads, resulting in an irregular distribution of beads and sequins until the pre-determined area is filled.

Stitching Beads Irregularly from the Back Side of the Fabric

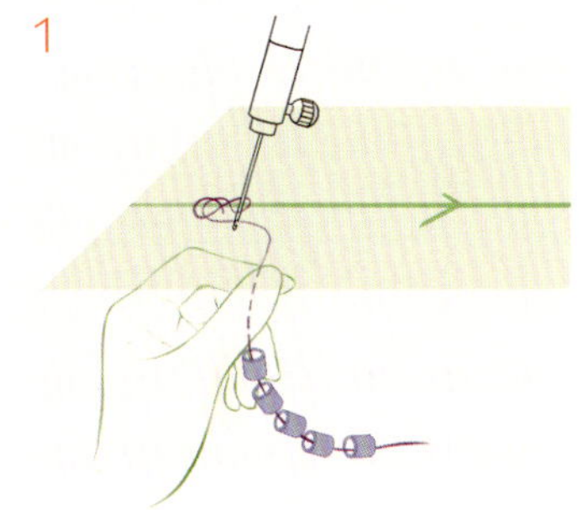

Place the embroidery hoop face down and start the stitch. Your left hand should be holding the thread below the fabric, while your right hand above the fabric is holding the needle. Wrap the thread around the hook under the fabric.

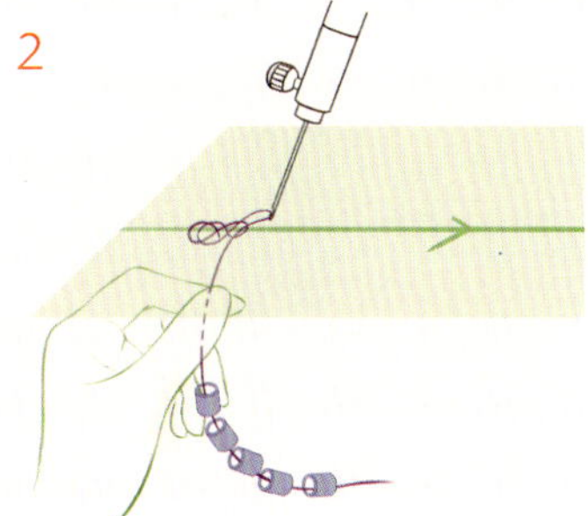

Pull the thread up the fabric.

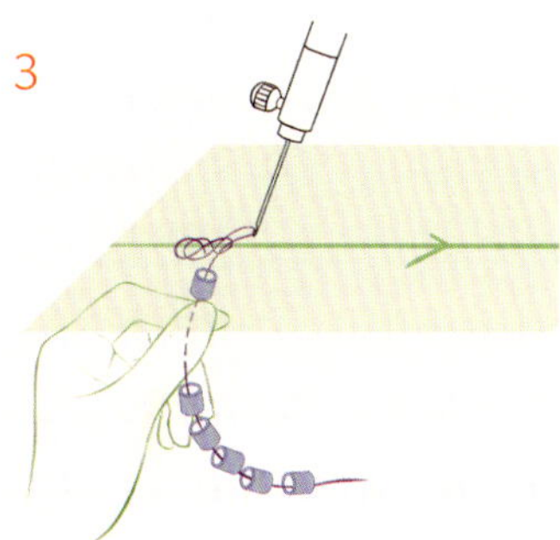

Use your left hand to push a bead upwards.

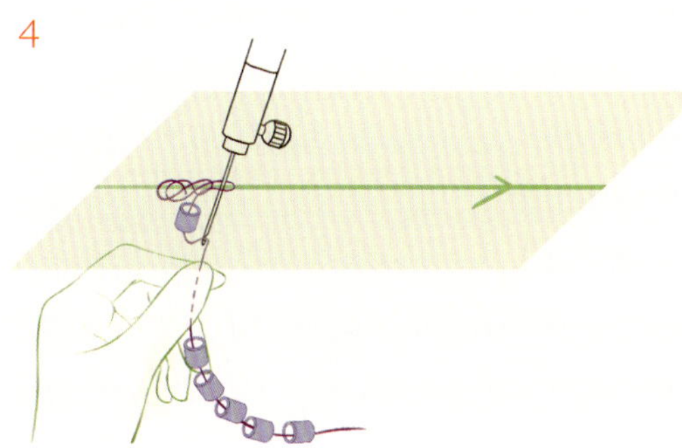

Take the needle down a point following the orientation of the embroidery. The distance between a stitch and its previous stitches is equal to the diameter of a bead (if it is a sequin, the distance should be halved). After taking down the needle, push the bead towards the fabric using your left hand to a point that is between the needle head and the fabric surface. Wind the thread around the needle.

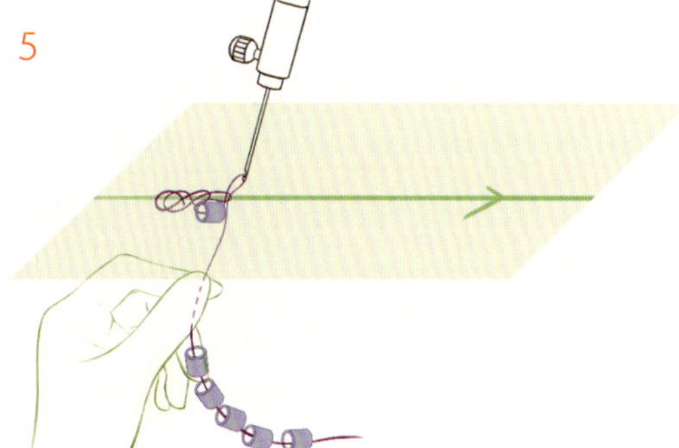

Lift the needle and thread up the fabric to fix a bead.

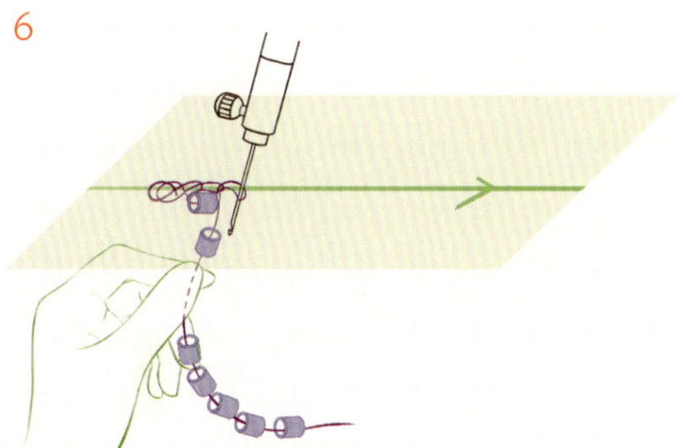

Take the needle down again at a random point at a distance from the last stitch that is equivalent to the diameter of the bead (if it is a sequin, the distance should be halved), and fix a bead.

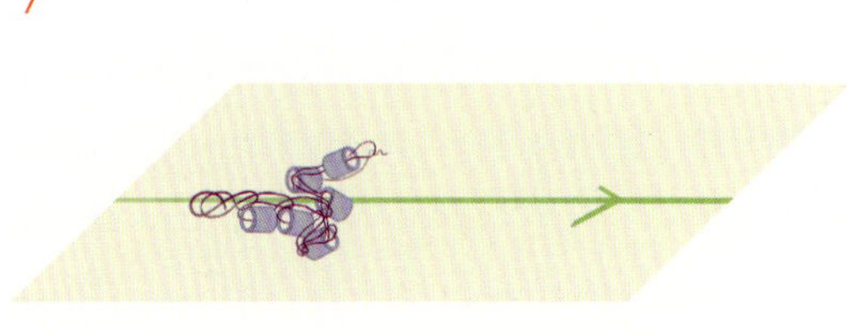

Repeat the steps above to fix each bead in different directions, and fill the pre-determined area.

Stitching Beads/Sequins Discontinuously from the Front Side of the Fabric

1

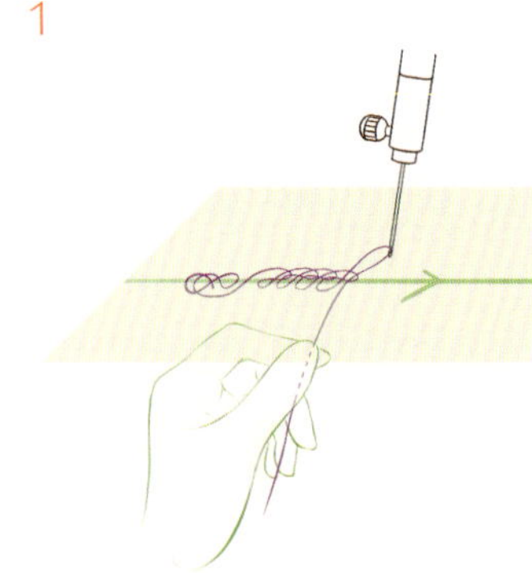

After the starting stitch, pull the needle and thread loop up the fabric.

2

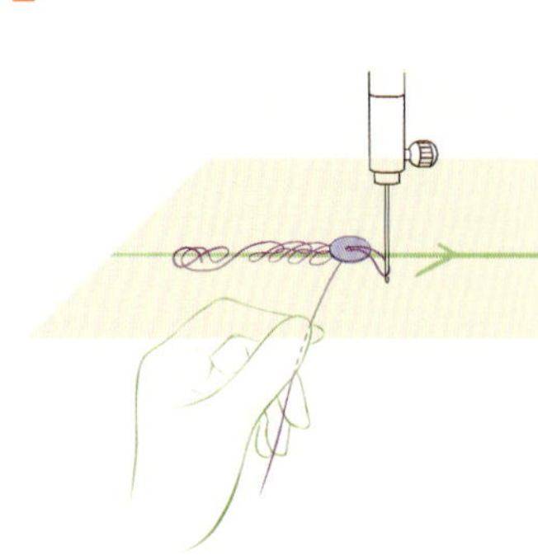

Thread a bead/sequin onto the loop, push it and let it lie flat on the fabric.

3

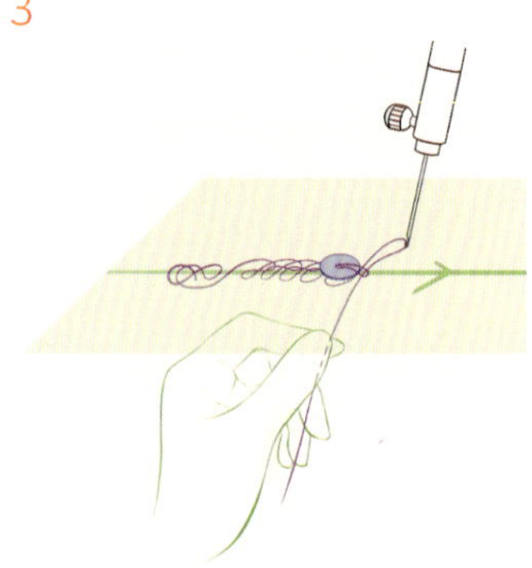

Fix a stitch following the orientation of the embroidery (the distance should be the diameter of a bead or the radius of a sequin).

4

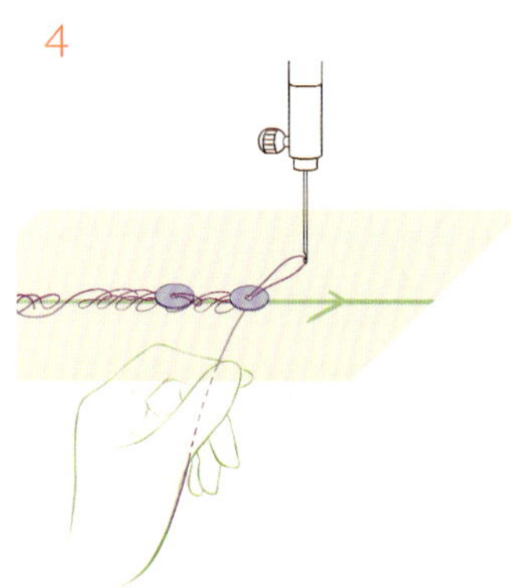

Stitch one or several chain stitches following the orientation of the embroidery, and then fix a bead/sequin again.

5

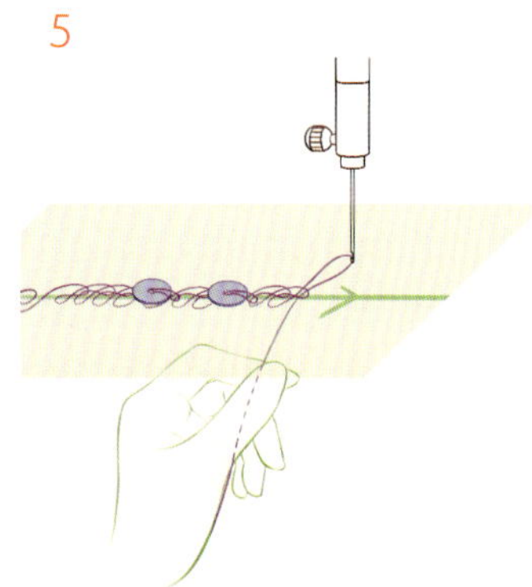

Continue one or several chain stitches following the orientation of the embroidery.

6

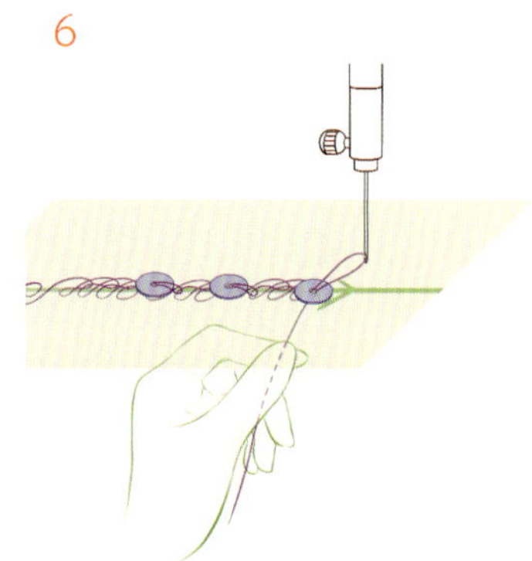

Insert another bead/sequin.

7

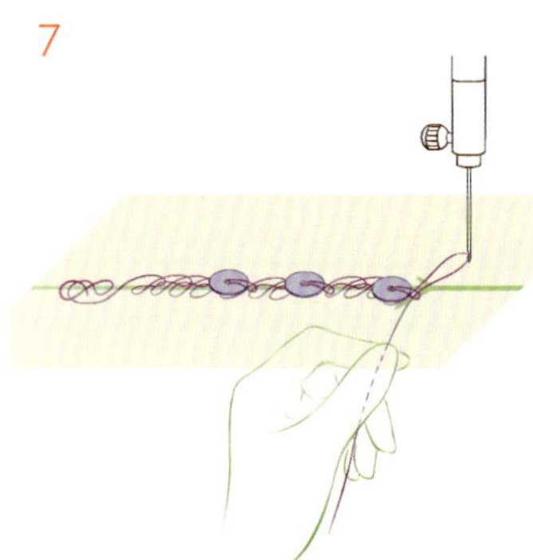

Fix the bead/sequin following the orientation of the embroidery.

8

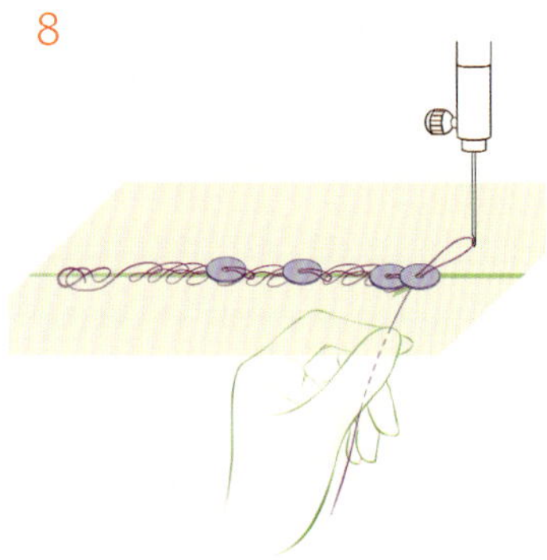

At this point, you can also continue to thread a bead/sequin and fix it.

9

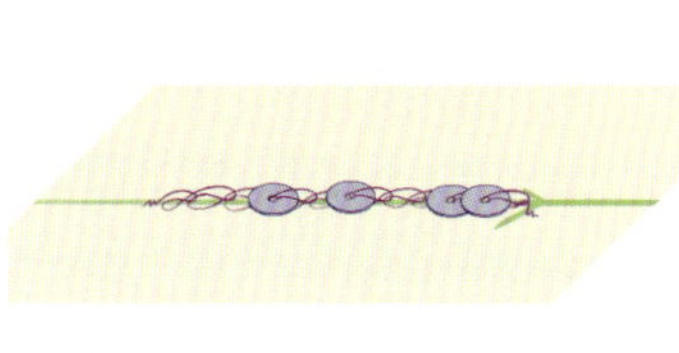

Continue stitching by following the foregoing steps. You can adjust the distance and quantity of the beads/sequins as you wish, to form irregular lines.

Embroidering Bead Clusters for Additional Dimension

1

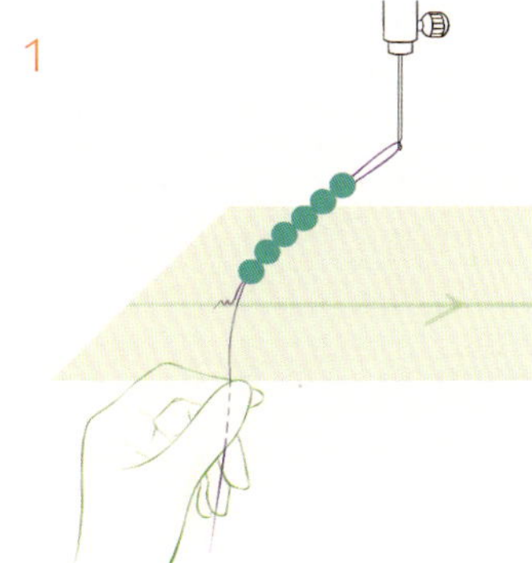

After the starting stitch, use hook needle to take multiple beads before catching the thread loop on the hook, and push the beads onto the loop.

2

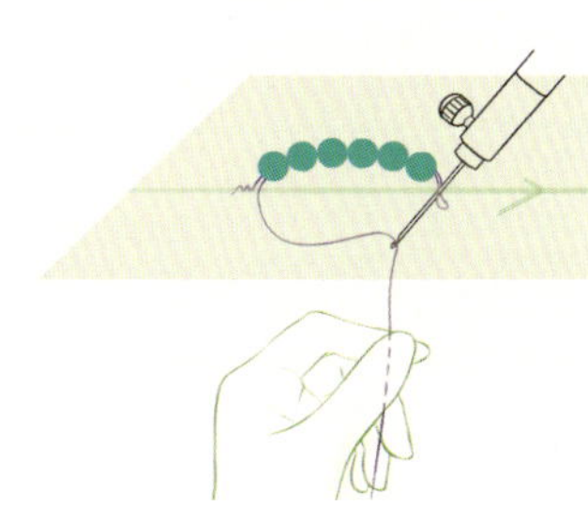

At a point that is slightly shorter than the overall diameter of the beads, insert the needle to make the beads arch slightly to form a three-dimensional effect. Next, catch the thread on the hook under the fabric.

3

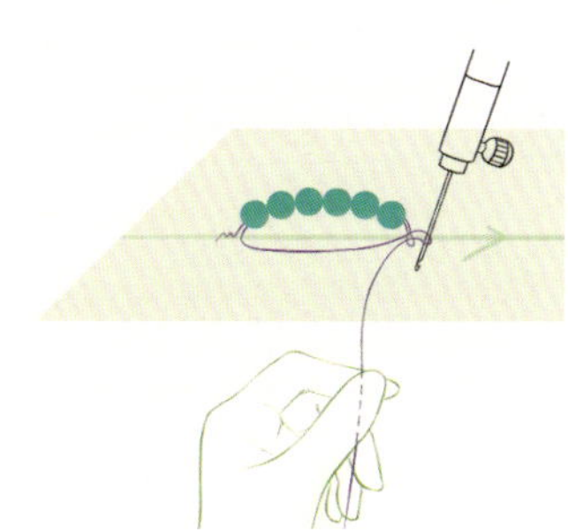

Pull the thread up the fabric.

4

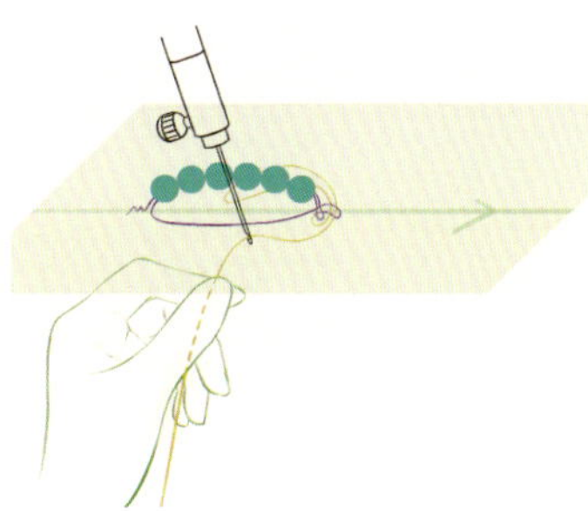

Pull the loop back to the middle point of the blue beads. Insert the needle down through the side above the beads and try to align it with the starting stitch.

5

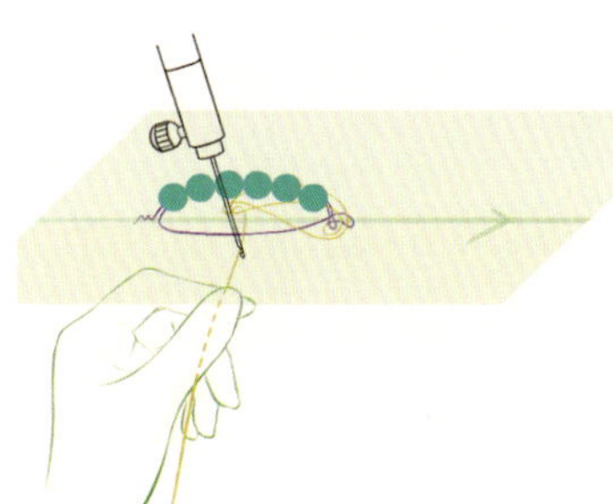

Fix the loop in a determined point.

6

After the thread is pulled up the fabric, take the same number of beads and push them into the loop.

7

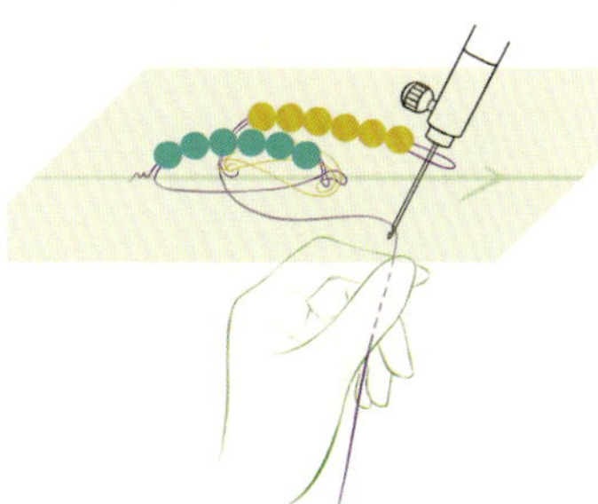

The distance where the stitch is fixed is the same as last group of beads, and the stitch is aligned with the starting stitch.

8

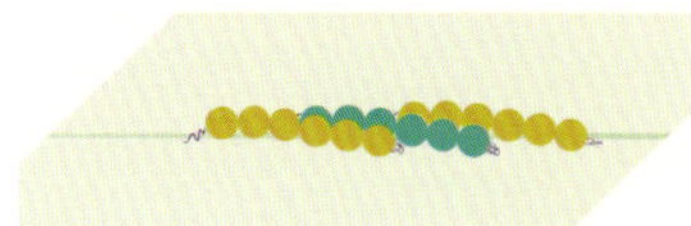

Repeat the steps above to form a three-dimensional effect comprising multiple beads.

9

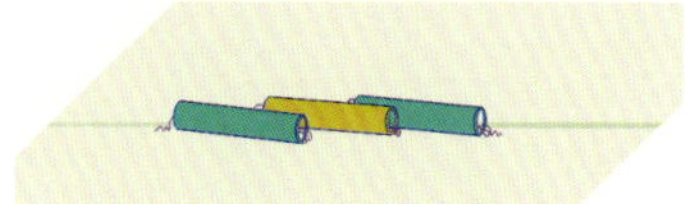

If you replace multiple beads in this technique with single tube beads, this is known as the outline stitch of the tube beads.

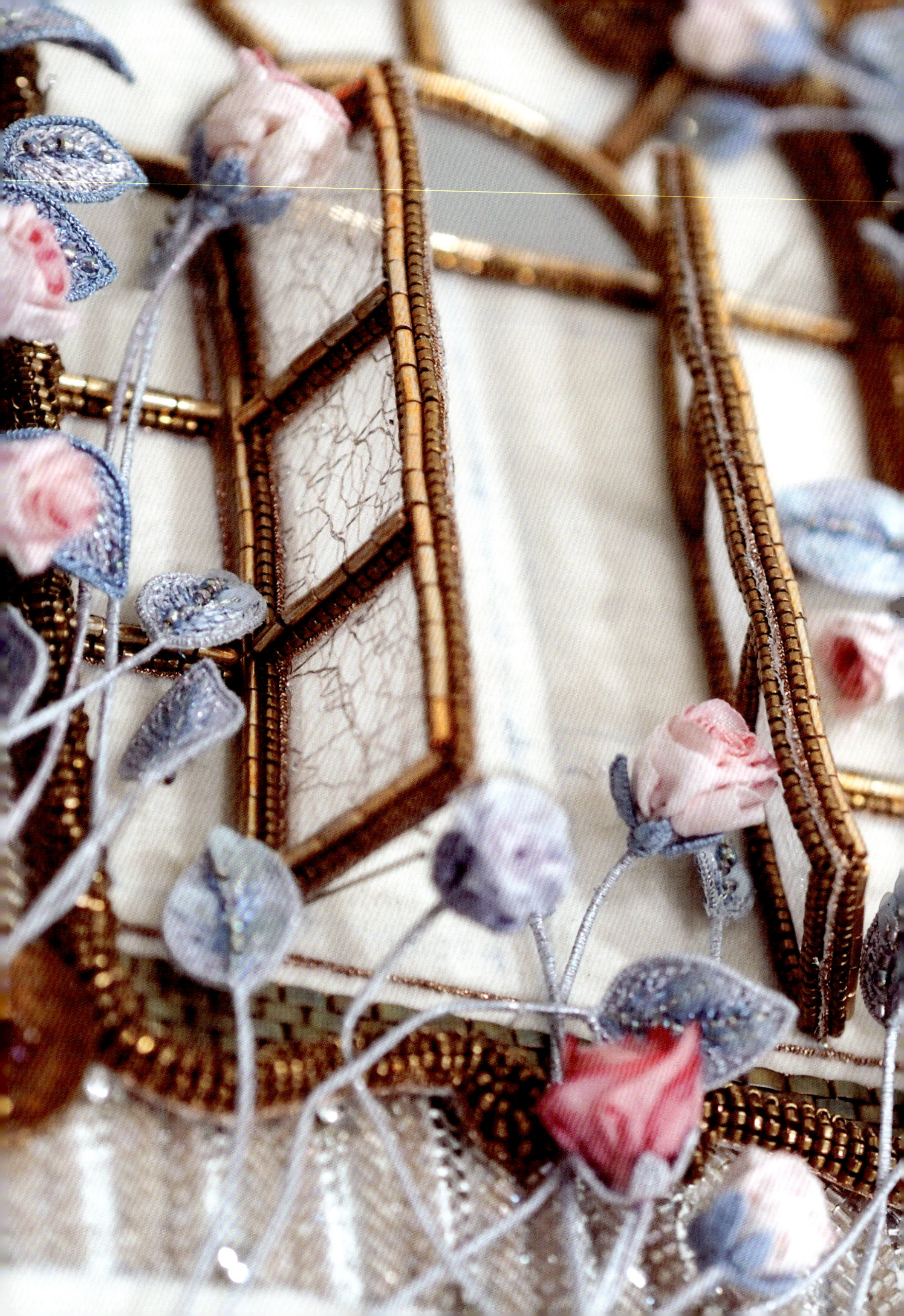

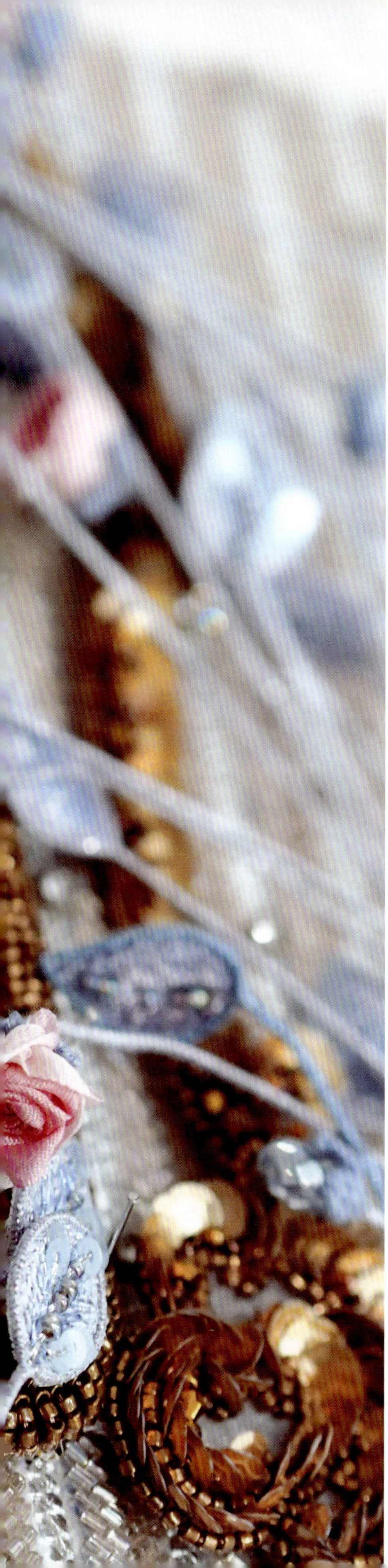

Projects

In previous chapters, you learned about materials and beading techniques. Now it's time to pick up a needle and thread, and follow the steps to make beautiful rings, hair accessories, brooches, bracelets, earrings, bags, belts, and cuffs, which will add color and character to your everyday outfits. You can also combine the materials from the lessons to make your own creative beaded jewelry—the perfect gift for any occasion.

Left

Fig. 18 *Flower Window*

The window is outlined using gold beads. Blue thread and sequins are used to create leaves and vines, and pink ribbons are crafted to look like flowers. The golden window frame is concealed by flowers, as if a fairytale princess is about to peek out.

Fig. 19 *Bauhinia Ring*

See page 60 for the production process.

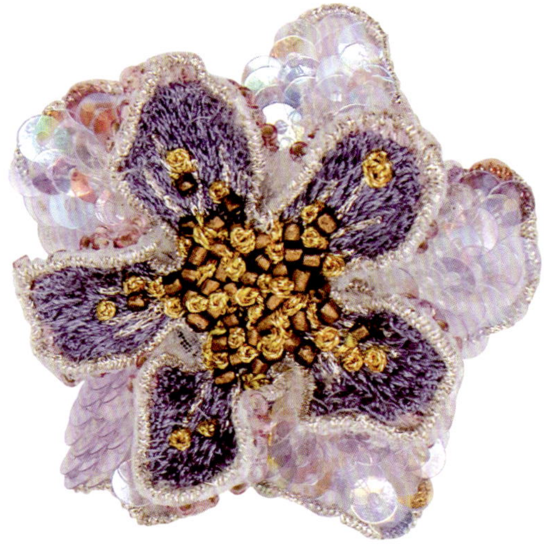

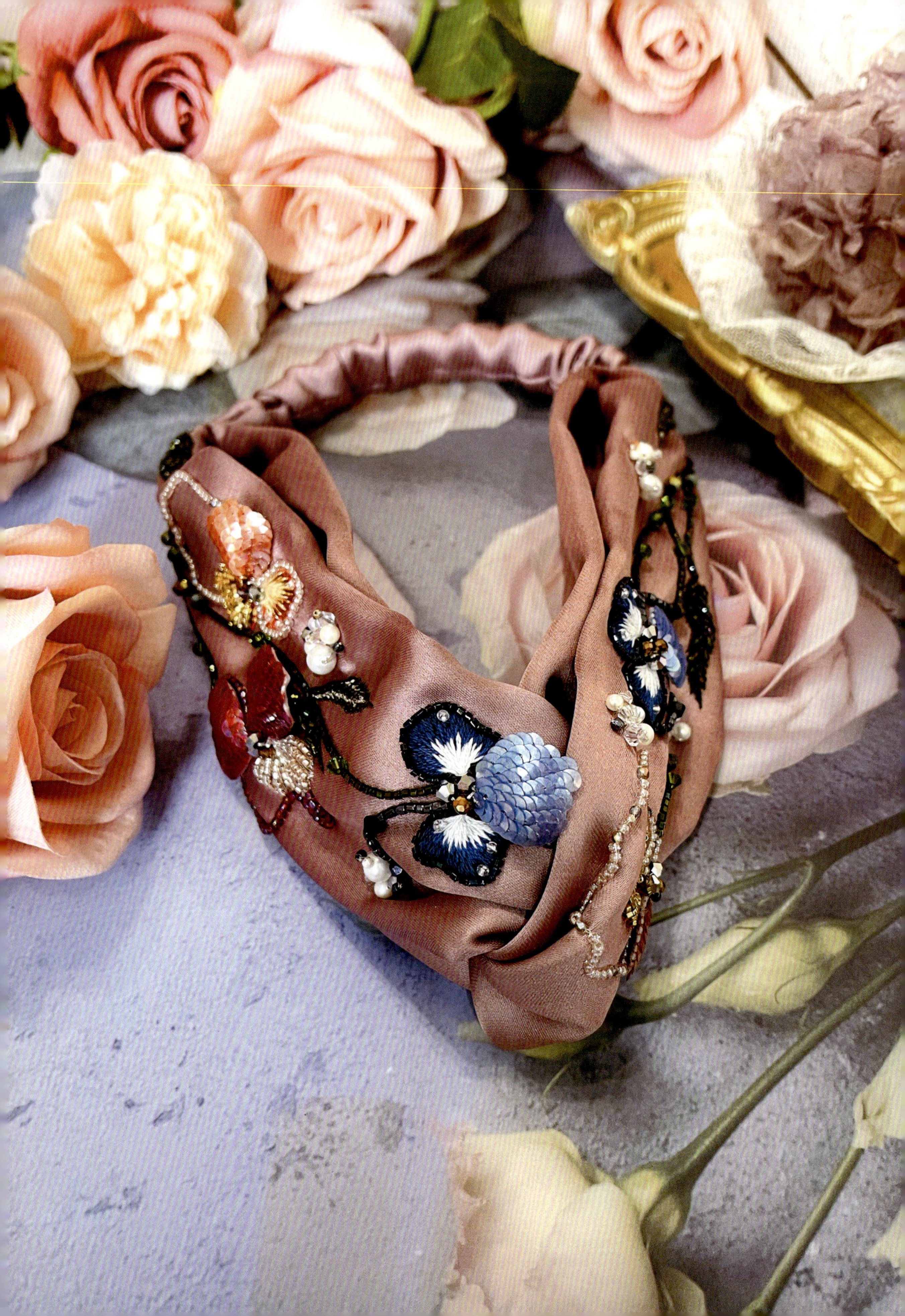

1. Wild Pansy Headband

The wild pansy, which is usually purple, yellow, and white, is widely planted as an ornamental flower in China. It is commonly known as the "butterfly flower," as it resembles a butterfly. In Chinese culture, butterflies symbolize freedom, love, and auspiciousness. This pattern uses colorful beads, crystals, and pearls to represent flowers in a variety of positions, akin to colorful butterflies dancing on the branches.

You Will Need

Threads	embroidery thread	silver, gold, dark blue, light blue, white, dark green
	metallic thread	orange
Beads	seed beads	1.6 mm gold, 1.6 mm silver, 1.6 mm dark blue, 1.6 mm purple, 1.6 mm transparent orange, 1.6 mm dark green, 2 mm transparent, 3 mm dark blue
	cup sequins	4 mm blue, 4 mm orange
	flat sequins	4 mm purple
	crystals	3 mm iridescent, 3 mm gold, 4 mm green, 4 mm dark blue, 4 mm white, 4 mm gray
	pearls	4 mm white, 6 mm white
Fabrics	pinkish purple satin, organza	
Tools	white iron wire, glue, embroidery frame, 10 cm embroidery hoop, 70# hook needle, heat erasable marker, hand sewing needle, scissors, fabric glue	

Embroidery Steps

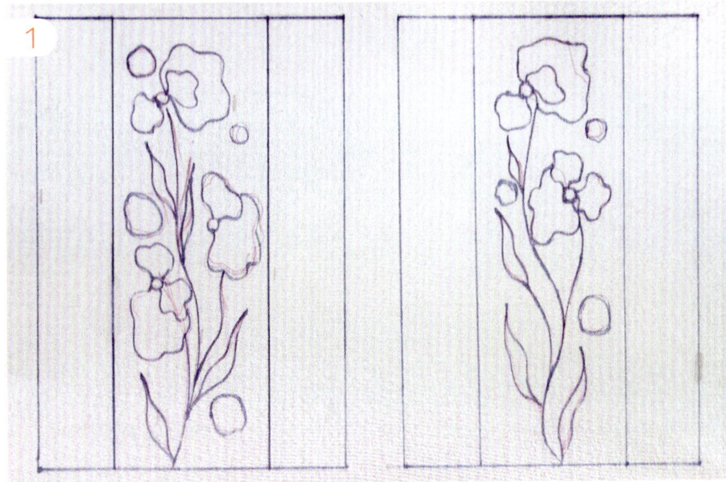

1 Trace the pattern (see page 162) on the pinkish purple satin with heat erasable marker.

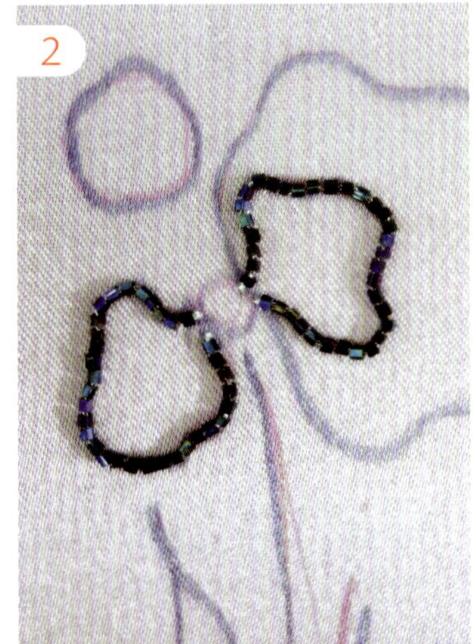

2 Apply the technique of stitching beads from the front side of the fabric to form the outer contours of the blue flowers on the left with a hook needle, silver embroidery thread, and 1.6 mm dark blue seed beads.

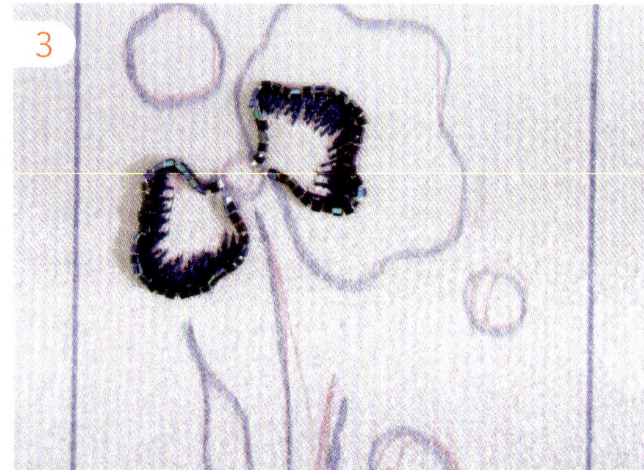

Use the long and short stitch technique with a hand sewing needle and dark blue embroidery thread. Continue along the inner side of the blue flower to sew about 1/3 of the petals.

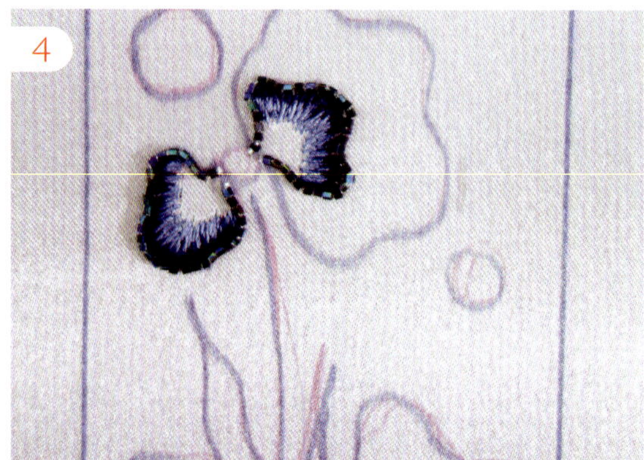

Use the long and short stitch technique with a hand sewing needle and light blue embroidery thread. Continue along the inner side of the dark blue embroidery thread to sew approximately 1/3 of the petals.

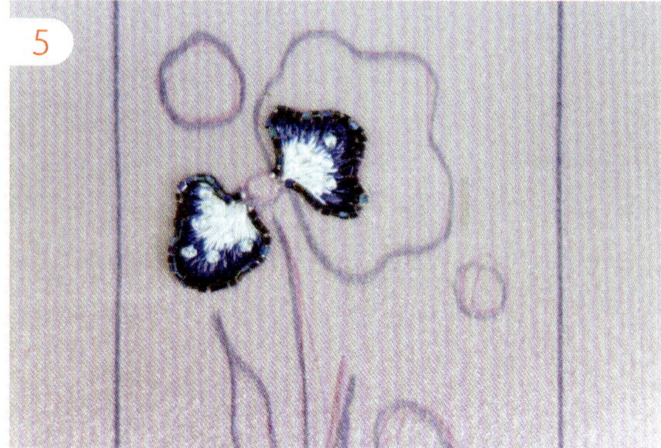

Use the long and short stitch technique to stitch the flower petals with a hand sewing needle and white thread, and continue along the inner side of the light blue embroidery thread to complete the flower petals. Use 2 mm transparent seed beads to decorate the entire petal in an irregular fashion.

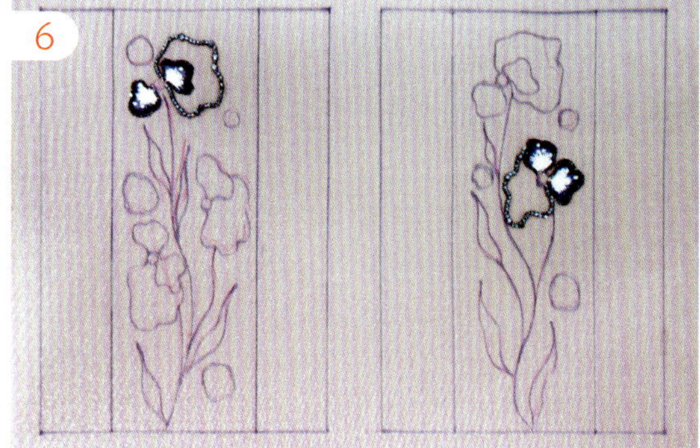

Apply the technique of stitching beads from the front side of the fabric to stitch the outer contour of the blue flower with a hook needle, silver embroidery thread, 3 mm dark blue seed beads, and 4 mm dark blue crystals. Use the same techniques from steps 2–6 to complete the blue flower on the right.

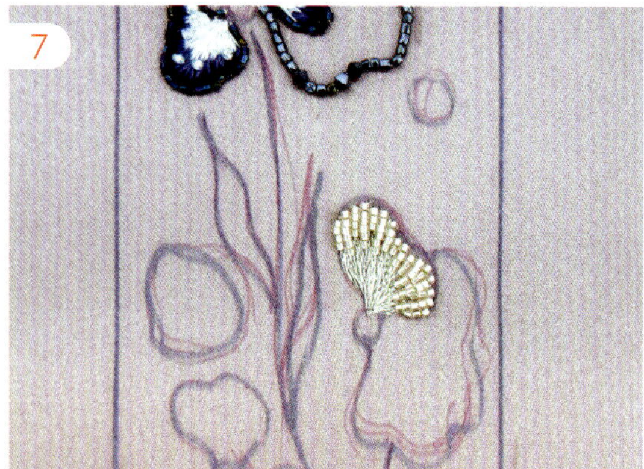

Use the techniques of embroidering bead clusters for additional dimension and pulling stitch with a hook needle, 1.6 mm silver seed beads, and silver embroidery thread to stitch the petal of the purple flower petals.

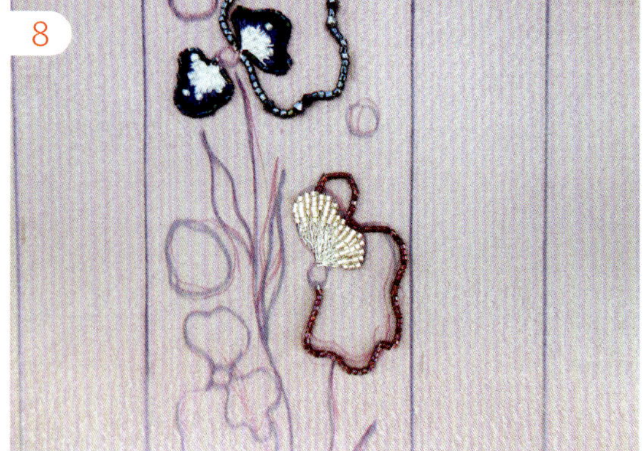

Use the technique of stitching beads from the front side of the fabric to stitch the outer contour of the purple flower with a hook needle, silver embroidery thread, and 1.6 mm purple seed beads.

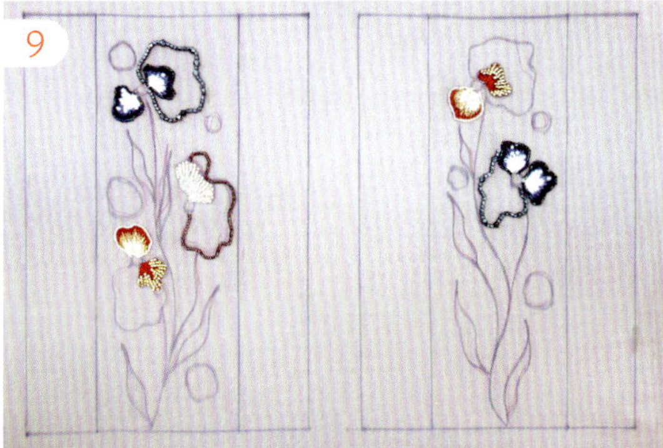

Apply the same techniques for making blue and purple flower petals to complete the orange flower petals, using both hook needle and hand sewing needle, alongside 1.6 mm gold seed beads, 1.6 mm transparent orange seed beads, orange metallic thread, and gold and white embroidery thread.

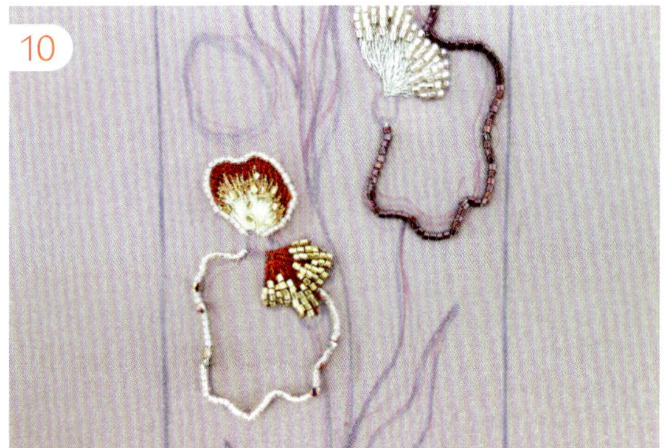

Stitch beads continuously from the front side of the fabric to form the outer contour of the orange flowers with a hook needle, 1.6 mm transparent orange seed beads, and 3 mm iridescent crystals.

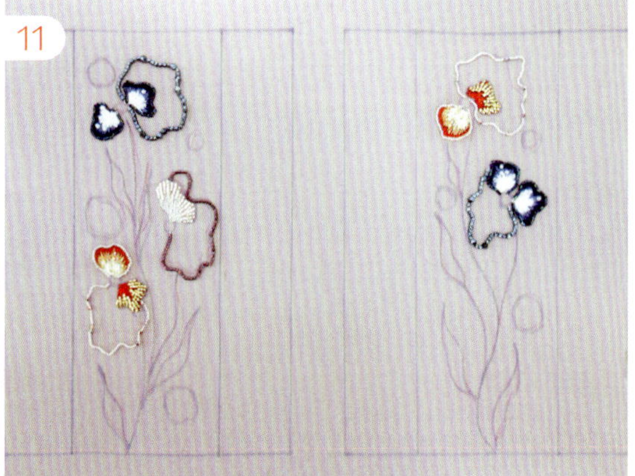

The portion where the flowers lie flat is now complete.

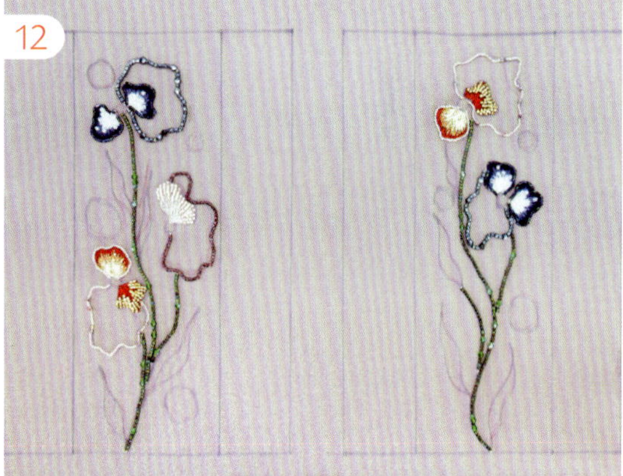

Stitch beads continuously from the front side of the fabric with a hook needle, dark green embroidery thread, 1.6 mm dark green seed beads, and 4 mm green crystals to form the flower stems.

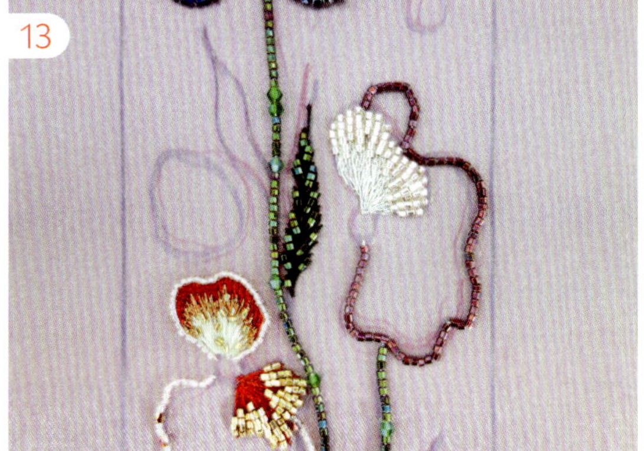

Apply the techniques of stitching multiple beads from the front side of the fabric and long and short stitch with a hook needle, dark green embroidery thread, and 1.6 mm dark green seed beads to sew a leaf on the right side of the flower stem.

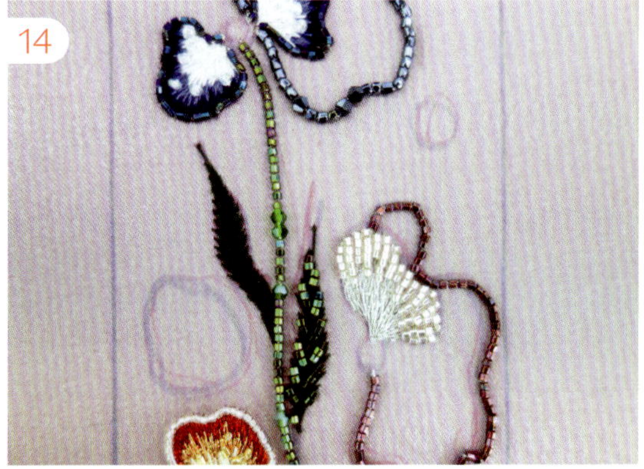

Use the long and short stitch technique with a hook needle and dark green embroidery thread to sew a leaf on the left side of the flower stem.

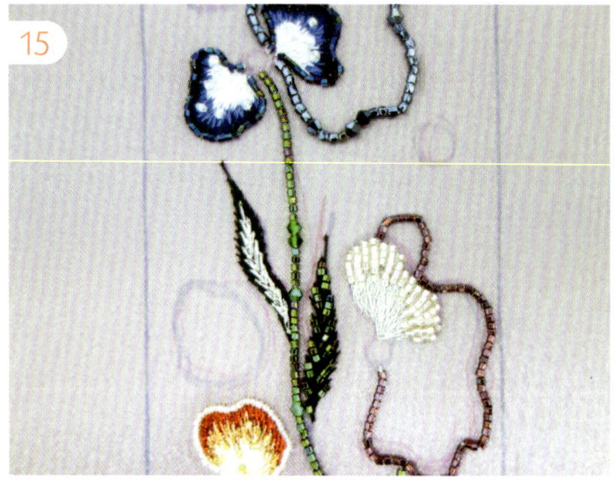

15 Use the long and short stitch technique with a hook needle and silver embroidery thread to sew the internal of the leaf in step 14.

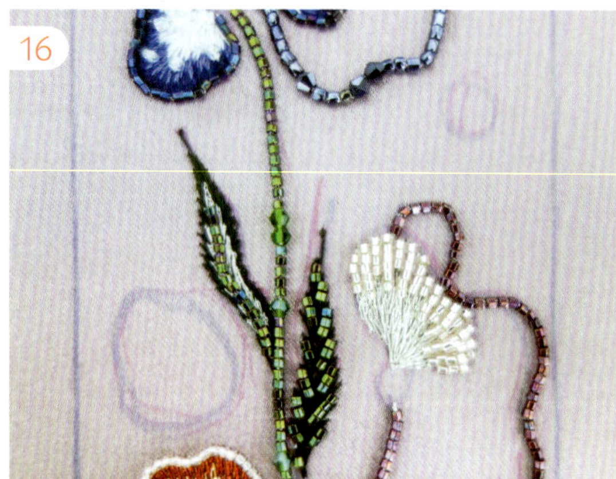

16 Stitch beads continuously from the front side of the fabric with a hook needle and dark green embroidery thread to sew a row of 1.6 mm dark green seed beads in the middle of the leaf.

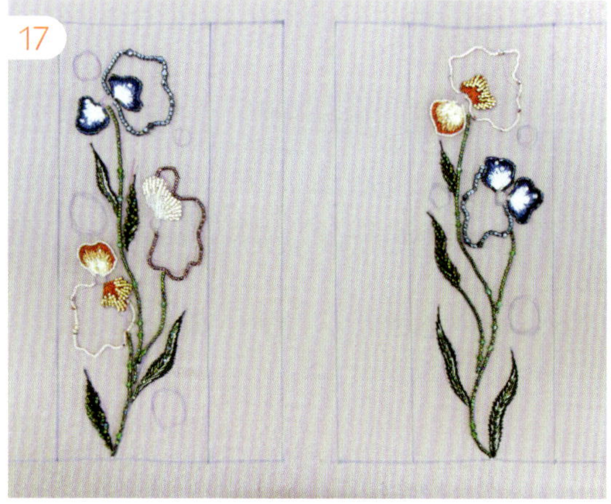

17 Use the same techniques in steps 13–16 to complete all the leaves.

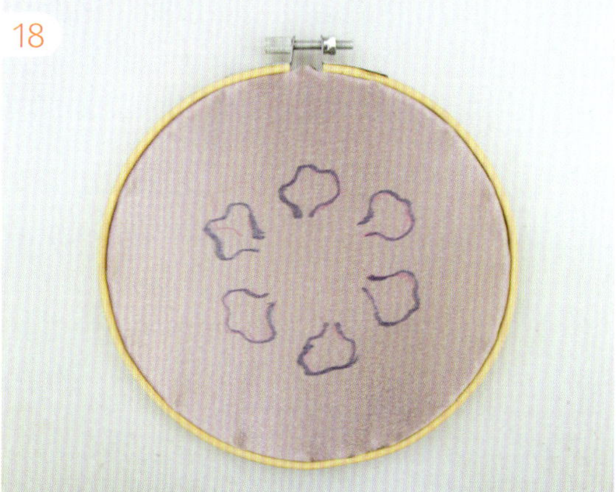

18 Take another piece of fabric (or organza) and stretch it on an embroidery hoop. Draw separate petals (see page 162) with a heat erasable marker.

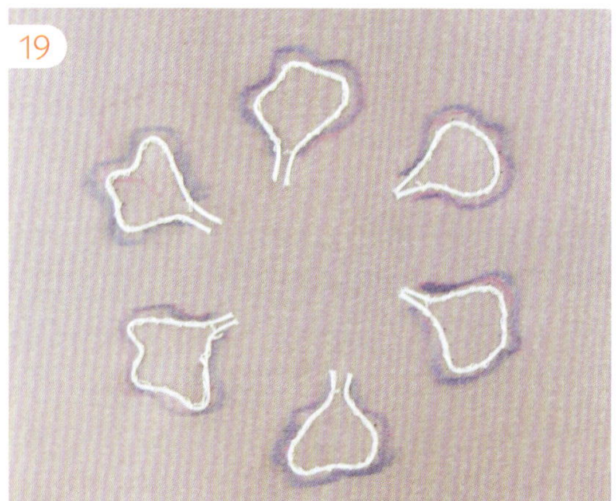

19 Use a hook needle and silver embroidery thread to fix the white iron wire at approximately 1 mm along the inner side of the contour of the petals with edging stitch.

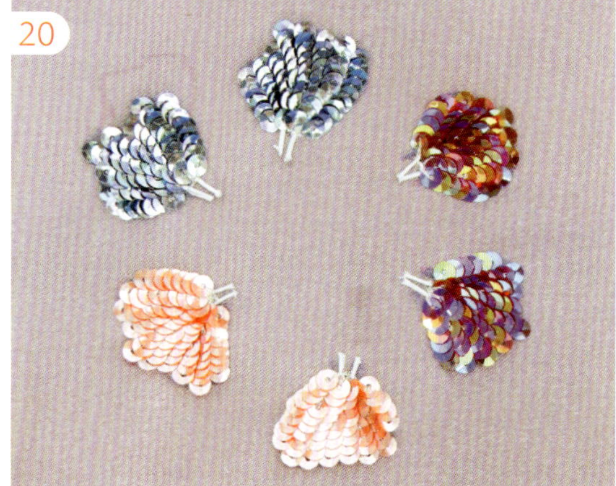

20 Stitch sequins continuously from the front side of the fabric with 4 mm blue cup sequins, 4 mm orange cup sequins, and 4 mm purple flat sequins to sew the petals.

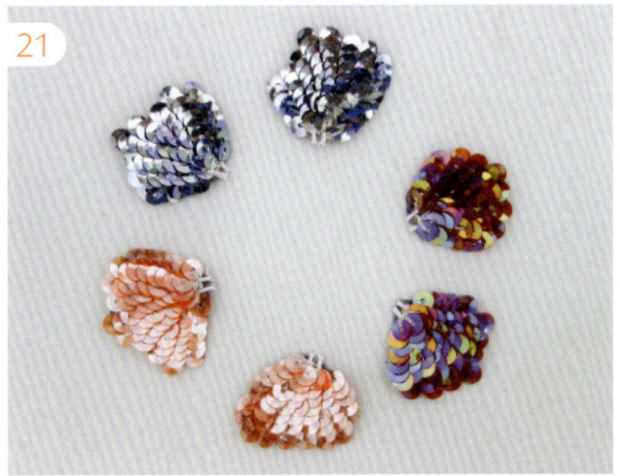

Use fabric glue to the back of the sequins and fix the petals on the embroidered cloth to prevent the sequins from becoming unstitched. Cut the petals after the glue has dried.

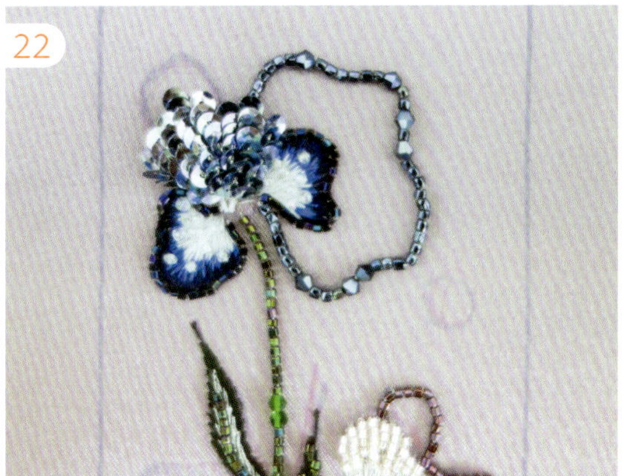

Use a hand sewing needle to fix the petal as shown in the figure. You can also sew a 6 mm pearl under the petals for a more three-dimensional effect.

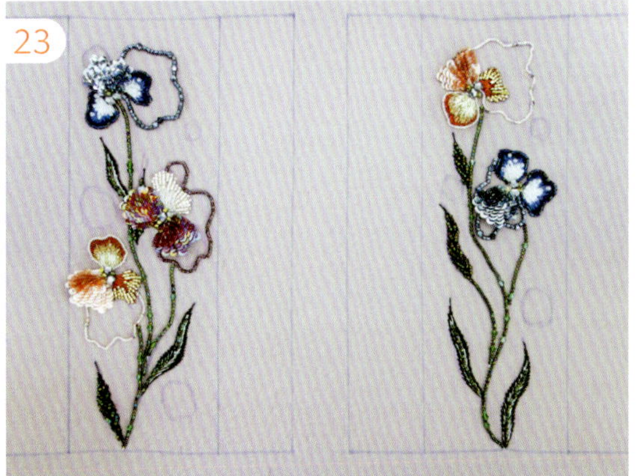

Use the same technique to sew the remaining petals, and sew three crystals at the center of each flower. Match the 3 mm gold crystals and 4 mm gray crystals according to your preference.

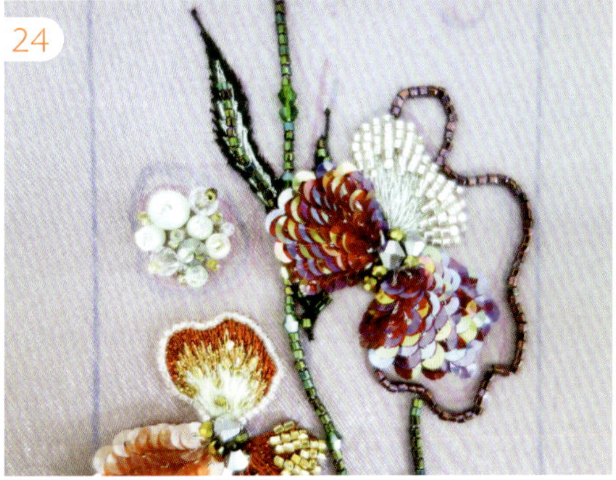

Use hand sewing needle and the technique of embroidering a bead on top of a tube with transparent or white pearls, crystals, seed beads, and other materials of various sizes to fill the circles in the pattern.

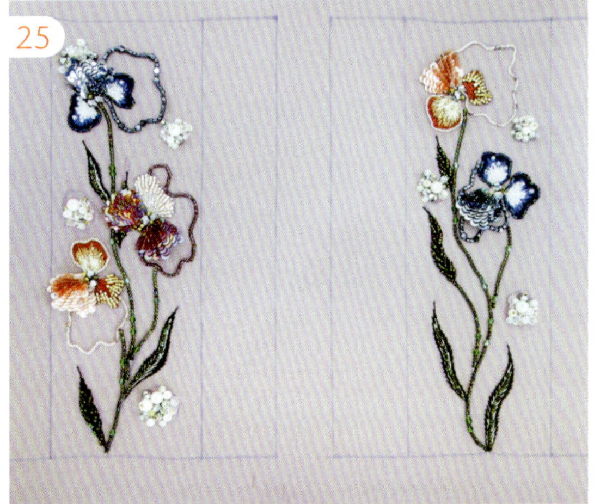

The pattern is now complete.

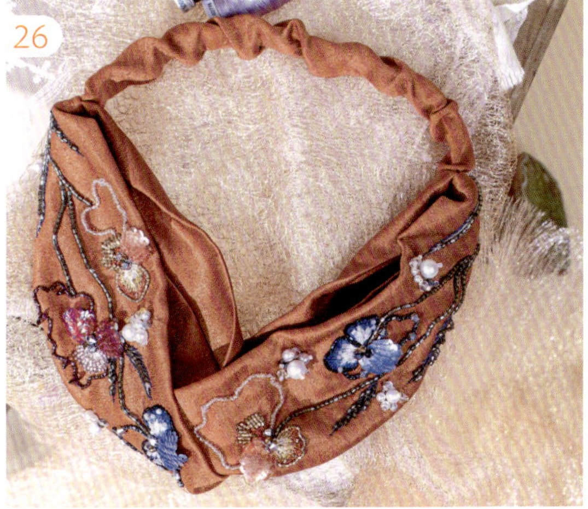

Sew the embroidered piece onto a hair band. It is now complete.

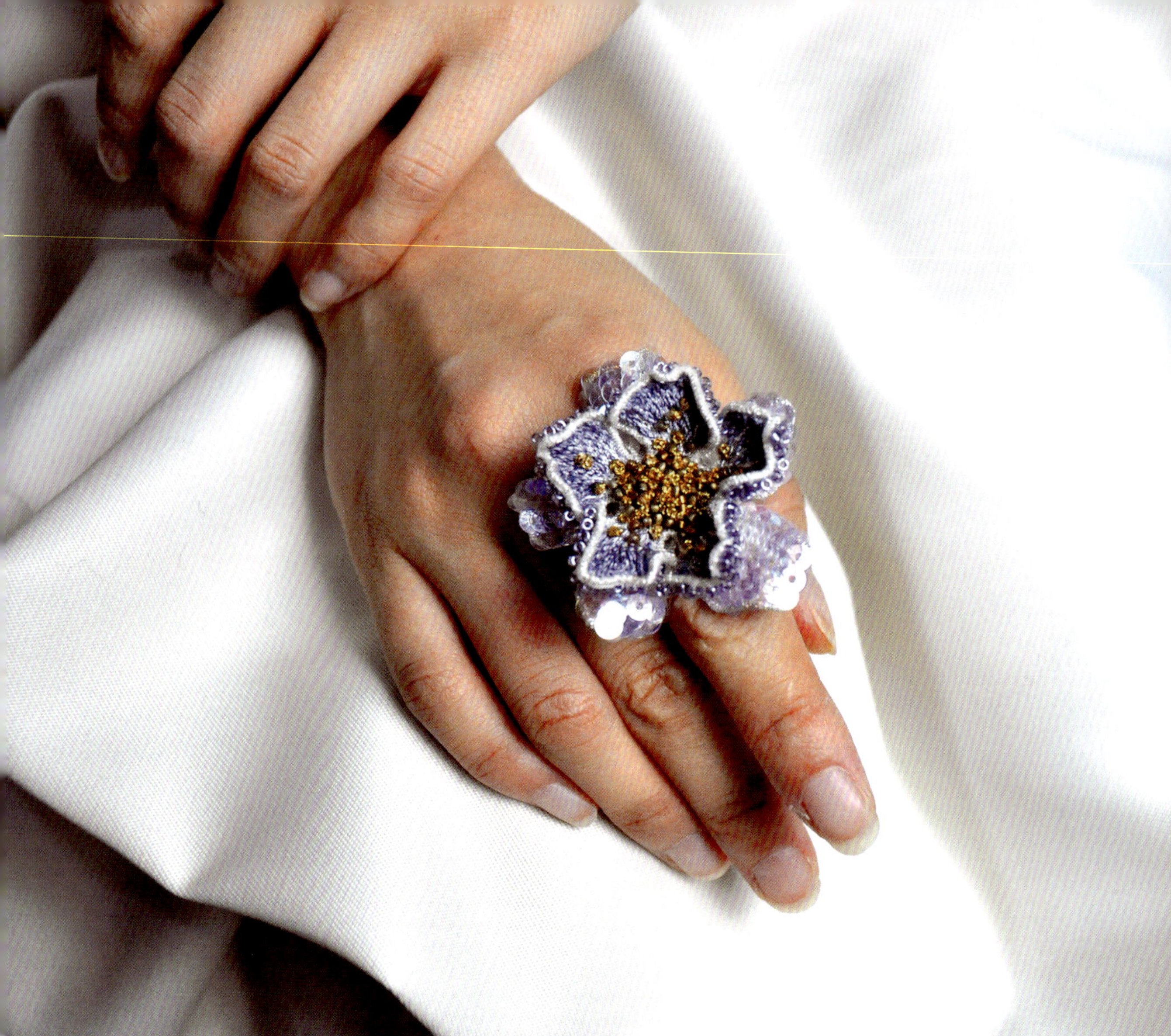

2. Bauhinia Ring

The bauhinia has five purple petals, which are elegant in shape. In China, it is said that three brothers in the Eastern Han dynasty (25–220) divided their family property after the death of their parents. They even wanted to divide a bauhinia tree into three sections. When they went to cut the tree the next day, they found that it had withered, and its flowers had fallen. From that moment, they no longer harbored thoughts of going their separate ways, and lived happily together. The tree sprung back to life. As a result of this incident, the bauhinia became a symbol of kinship and harmony. This piece uses petals made of purple sequins to complement the surroundings of the five main petals, creating a dreamy atmosphere.

You Will Need

Threads	embroidery thread	silver, invisible, purple, dark golden
Beads	seed beads	2 mm purple, 2 mm golden
	sequins	3 mm clear, 4 mm purple
Fabrics	white organza, gold leather, wool felt	
Tools	embroidery hoop, 70# hook needle, hand sewing needle, scissors, fabric glue, heat erasable marker, ring setting, 0.4 mm iron wire	

Embroidery Steps

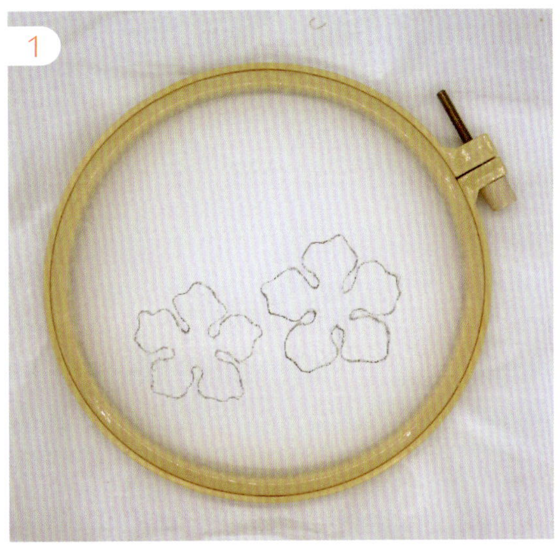

Stretch the white organza on the embroidery hoop. Draw two flowers, one large and one small (see page 165), on the fabric with a heat erasable marker.

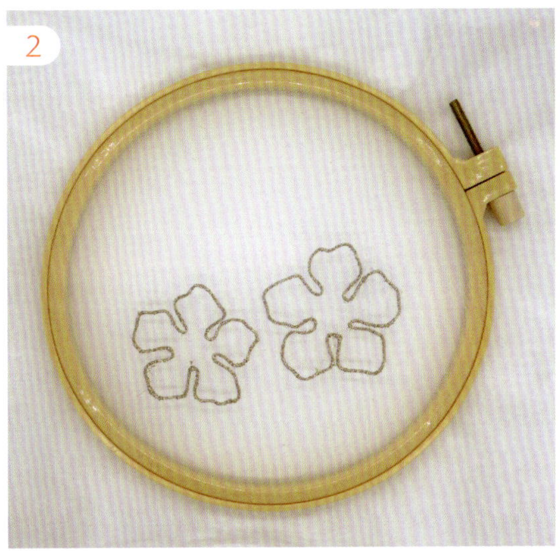

Apply edging stitch with a hook needle and silver thread to overlock 0.4 mm iron wire to create the outline.

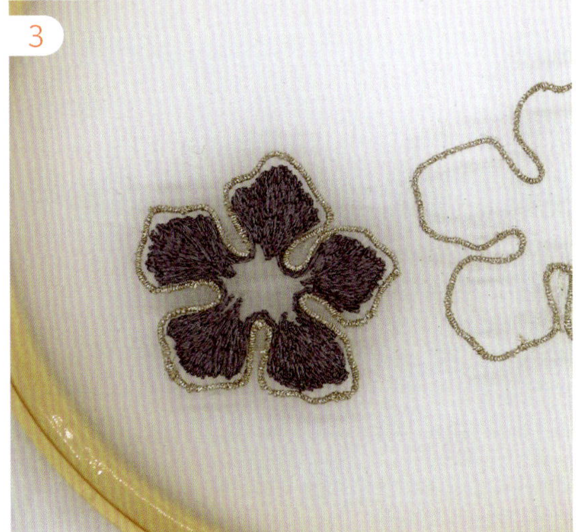

Use the chain stitch technique with a hook needle and purple thread to fill the petals of the smaller flower.

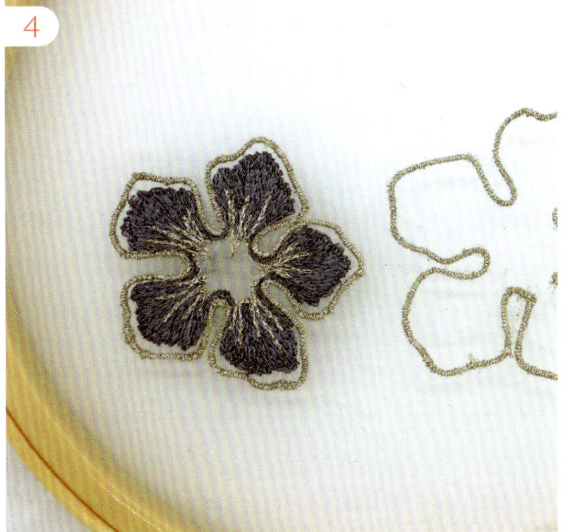

Use the chain stitch technique with a hook needle and silver thread to decorate the lower part of the petals, leaving out the flower center.

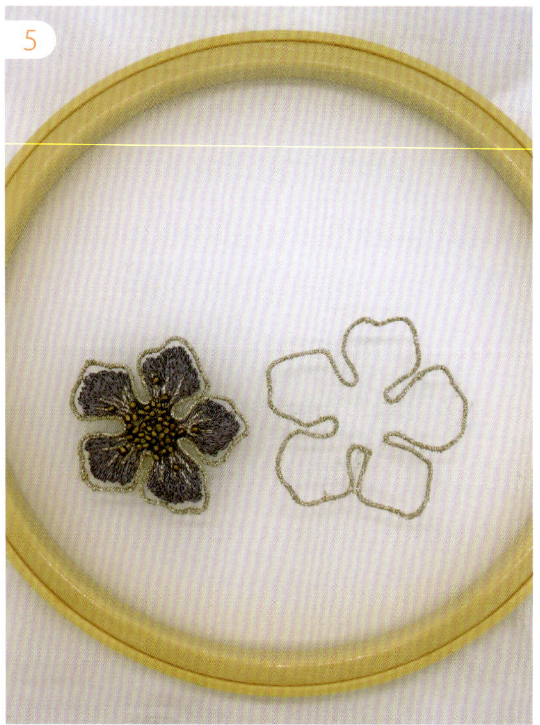

Use a hand sewing needle and invisible thread to fix the 2 mm golden seed beads in the center of the flower in an irregular fashion.

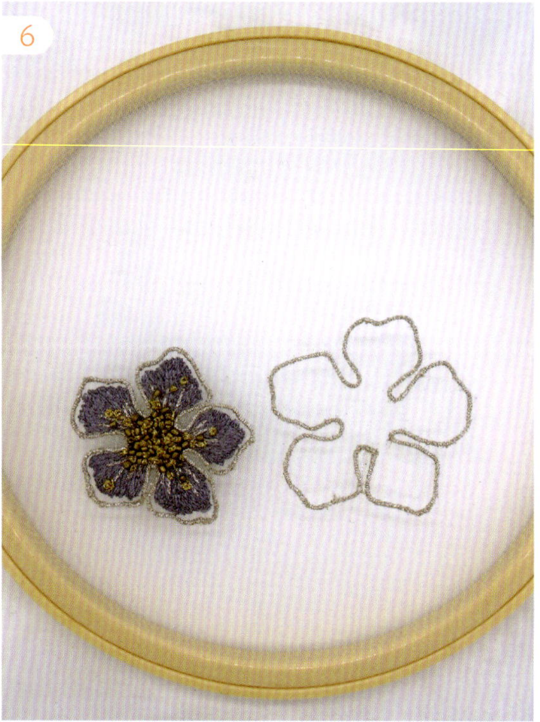

Use the French knot technique with a hand sewing needle and dark golden thread to sew the stamens in the center area of the flower in an irregular fashion.

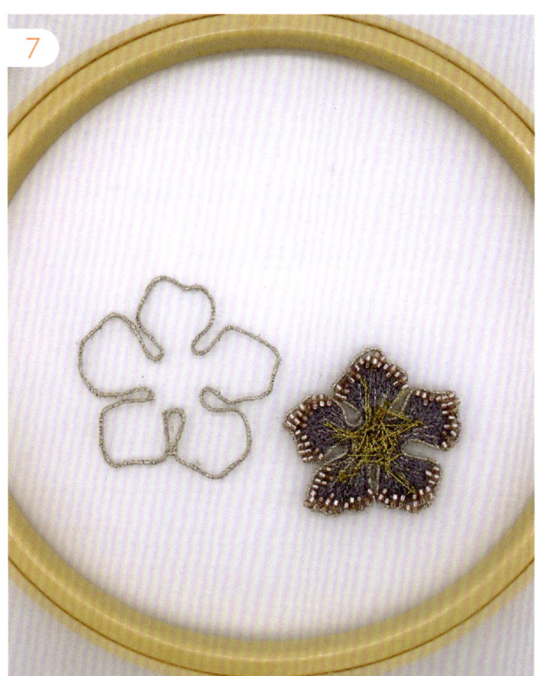

Turn the embroidery hoop over. Apply the technique of stitching multiple beads from the front side of the fabric using a hook needle, invisible thread, and 2 mm purple seed beads to fill the parts of the flower's petals close to the outer contour.

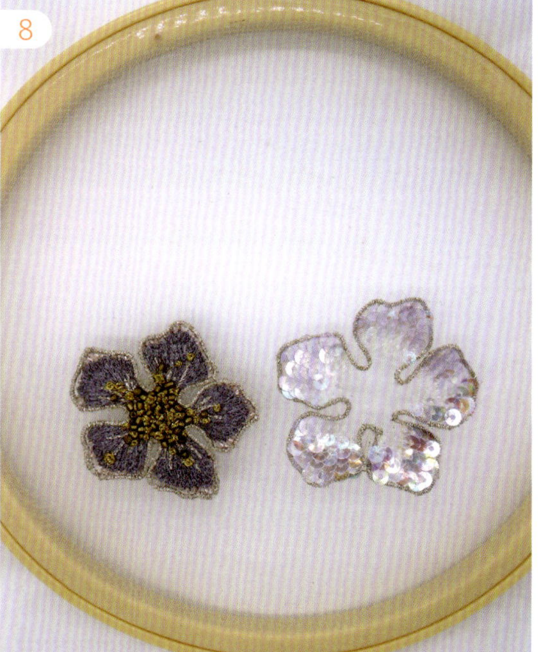

Turn the embroidery hoop over again. Apply the technique of stitching sequins from the front side of the fabric using a hook needle, invisible thread, 3 mm clear sequins, and 4 mm purple sequins to sew the petals of the bigger flower.

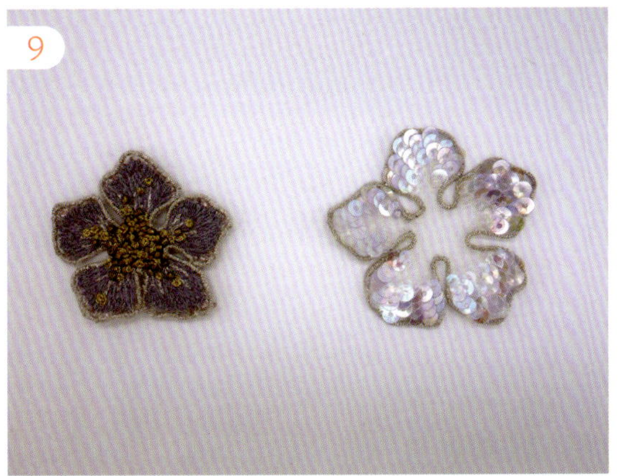

Cut the embroidered patterns along the outer contour.

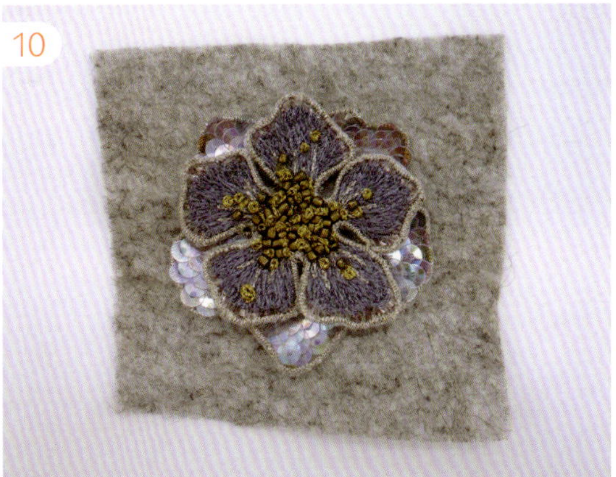

Take a piece of wool felt. Use a hand sewing needle and invisible thread to fix the two flowers. Be mindful that the petals of the two flowers are to be staggered and overlapping one another.

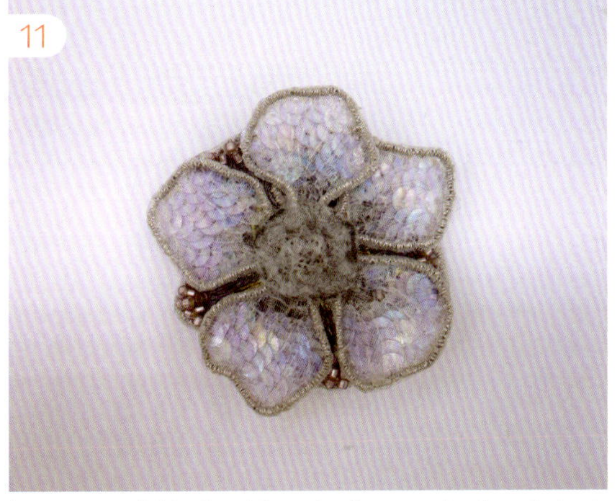

Leave a wool felt disc 1.5 cm in diameter in the stitched part, and trim off the excess.

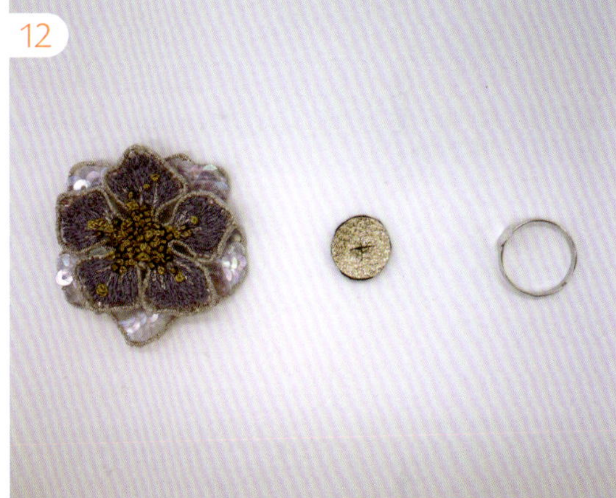

Prepare the ring setting and a gold leather disc of the same diameter (1.5 cm). Use a pair of scissors to cut a cross in the middle of the gold leather disc.

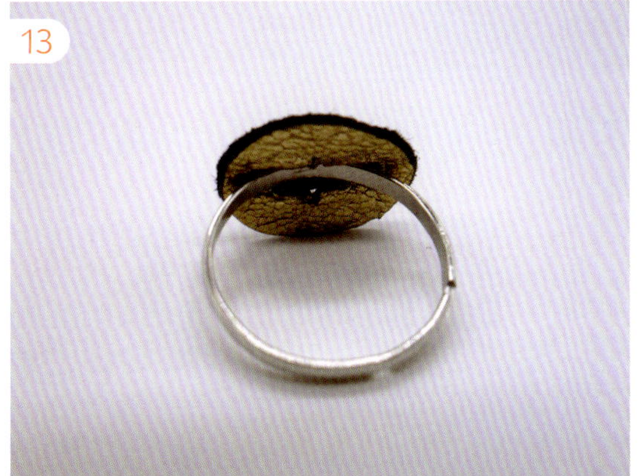

Insert the ring setting into the cross on the gold leather, and apply a little fabric glue to fix it in place.

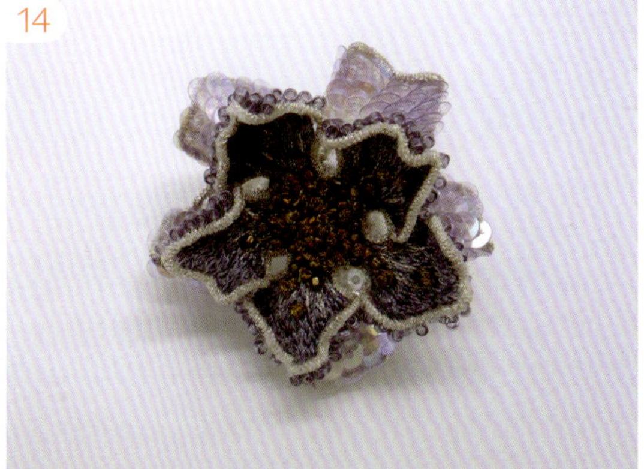

Apply fabric glue to the ring setting and gold leather and fix them to the back of the wool felt. Allow the glue to dry, then arrange the flowers. The ring is now complete.

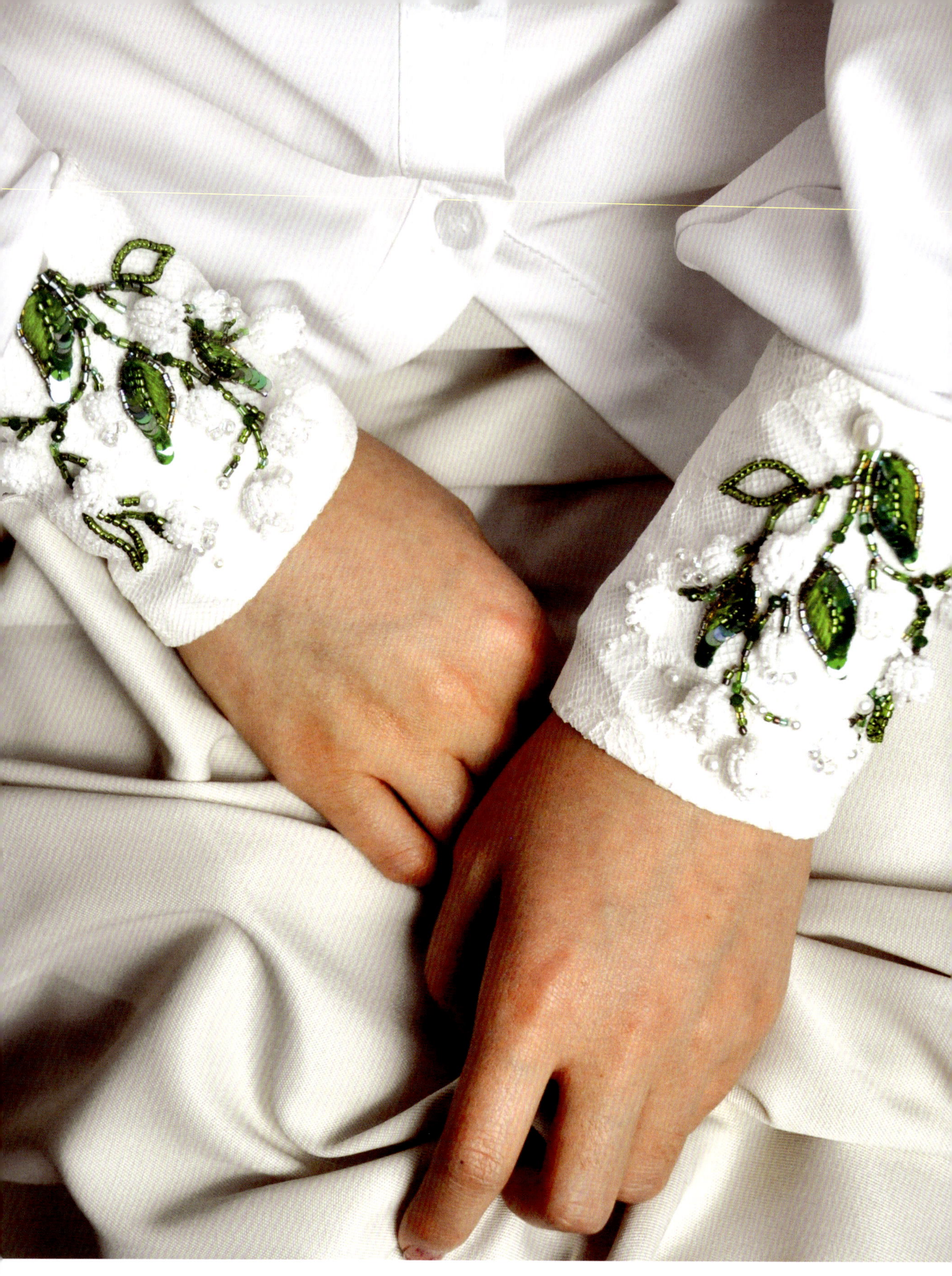

3. Lily of the Valley Cuff Bracelets

The beautiful white lily of the valley has flowers that bend downwards in full bloom, akin to a string of delicate little bells. In China, it is also known as *jun ying cao* because it often grows in dark and humid environments within deep mountains. It blooms alone, giving off a gorgeous fragrance, but never attempting to please others. Hence, the Chinese liken it to a gentleman who stays true to his heart. This beadwork accessory takes the lily of the valley as its theme, and can be used as a cuff decoration to add a fresh and artistic appeal to a plain shirt. You can also embroider it directly onto your clothes wherever you like.

You Will Need

Threads	embroidery thread	green, invisible, white
	wool	green
Beads	seed beads	1.5 mm white, 2 mm green shades (3–4 colors can be matched as you wish)
	crystals	3 mm green, 3 mm white
	pearls	3 mm white, 4 mm white, 5 × 8 mm oval white
	sequins	4 mm green
	drop-shaped beads	3 mm transparent
Fabrics	white satin, white lace, 35 mm wide white ribbon	
Tools	embroidery frame, hook needle, hand sewing needle, scissors, heat erasable marker, tracing paper, sewing pins, 7 mm transparent sew-on buttons	

Embroidery Steps

◆ Three-Dimensional Lily of the Valley

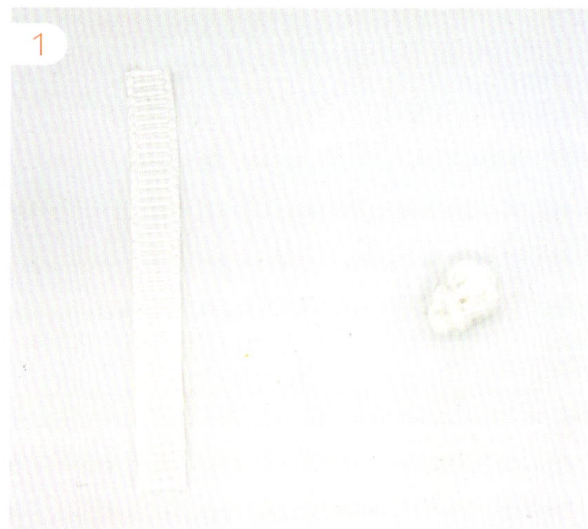

Cut a white ribbon about 6 mm in length. Form it into a ball and fix it using a hand sewing needle and white thread.

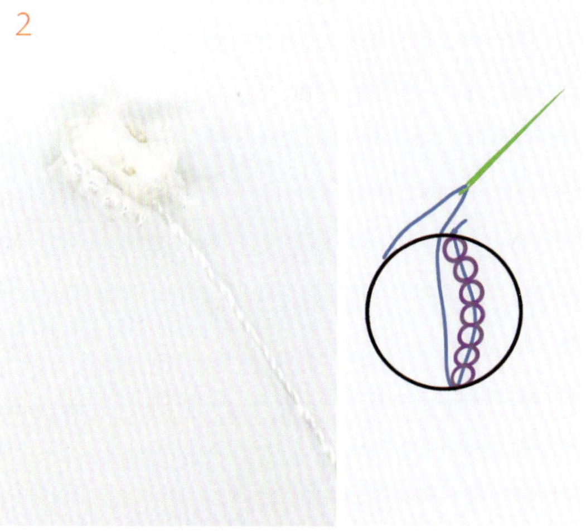

Pass the thread through the diameter of the ball. Use a hand sewing needle and white thread to fix six to eight 1.5 mm white seed beads onto the ball's surface.

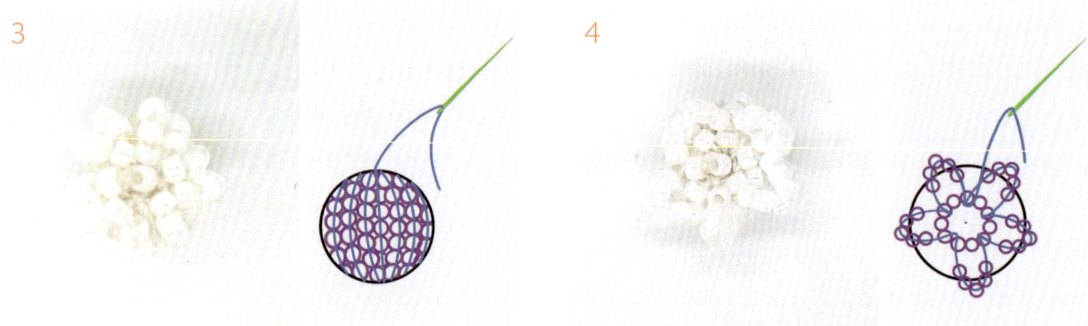

Apply the same technique as step 2 to cover the spherical surface with 1.5 mm white seed beads.

Using a hand sewing needle and white thread to fix five groups of 1.5 mm white seed beads on the upper end, at about 1/5 of the ball surface. Each group consists of 5–7 seed beads, forming a three-dimensional effect (refer to the top view picture on the right).

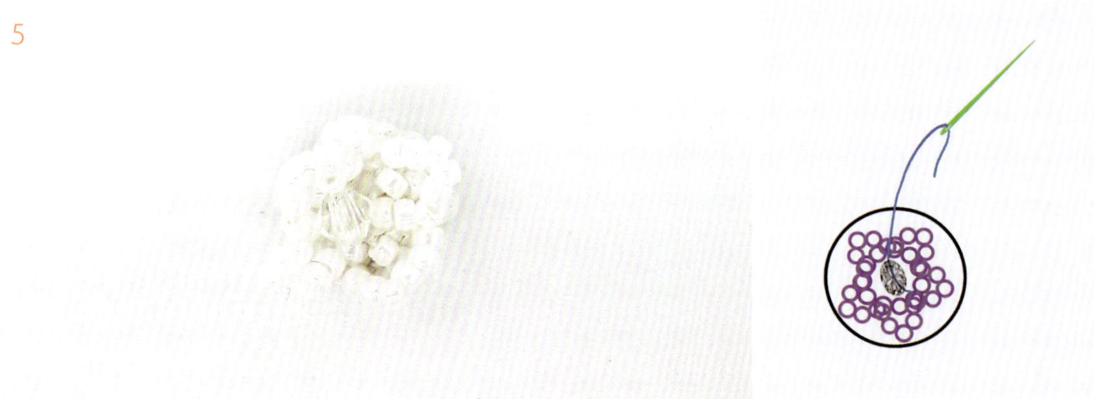

Tighten the embroidery thread. Next, use a hand sewing needle and white thread to fix a 3 mm white crystal into the center of the circle enclosed in step 4 as the center of the flower. A three-dimensional lily of the valley flower is now complete. Then create 11 identical lily of the valley flowers using the same method.

◆ Plane Embroidery

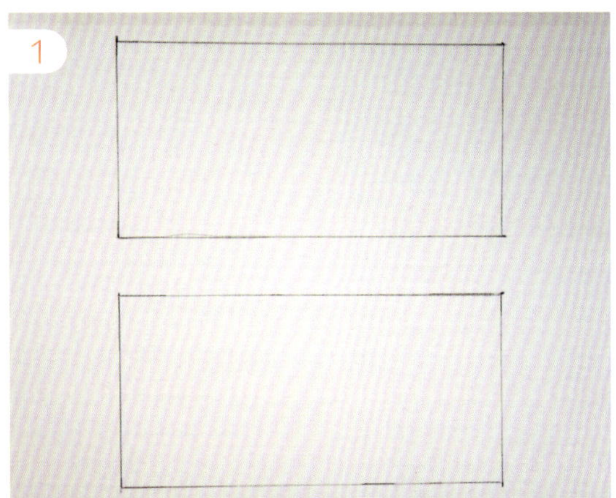

Stretch the white satin onto the embroidery frame and draw two 20 × 10 cm rectangles with a heat erasable marker. The space between the two rectangles should be at least 2 cm.

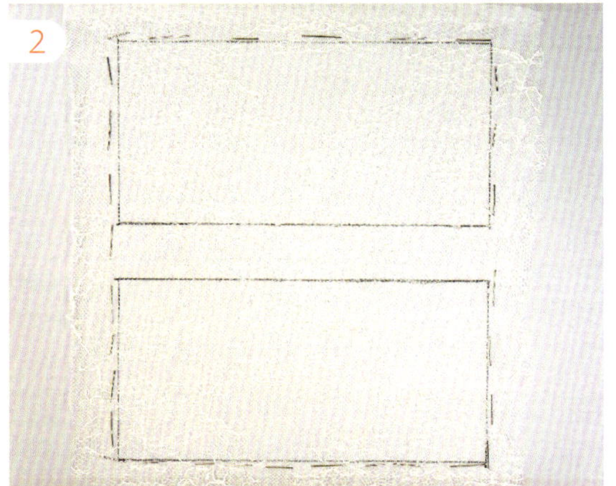

Lay the white lace flat on the rectangles on the white satin, and use sewing pins to fix the lace fabric along the outer edge of the outline.

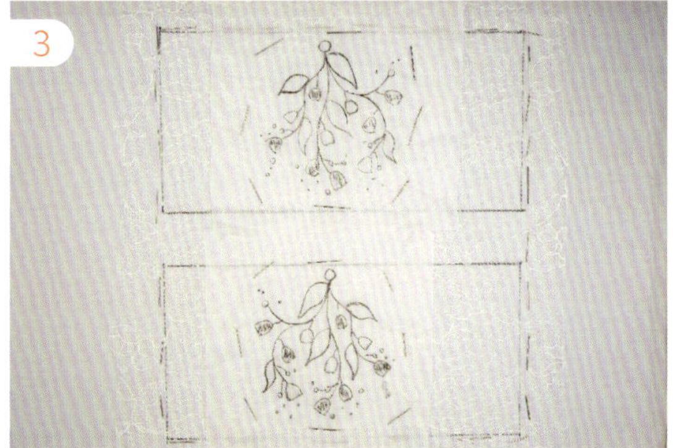

Trace the embroidery pattern (see page 163) onto the tracing paper, and use sewing pins to fix the two pieces of tracing paper in the middle of the two rectangles along the outer edges of the pattern. These two patterns are the same, and are just mirrored.

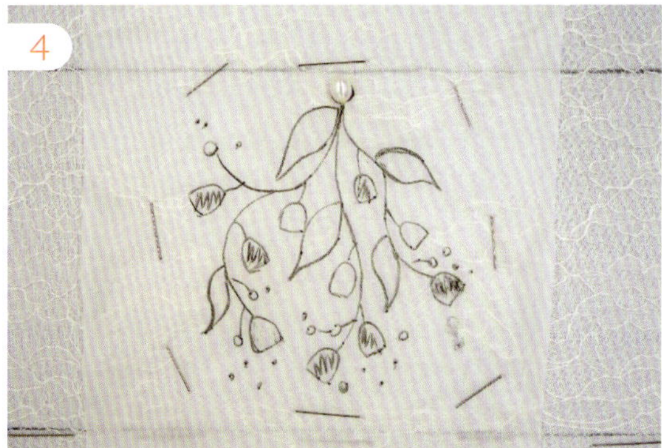

The following steps uses the embroidery pattern at the bottom of step 3 as an example to describe the embroidery process. Apply the technique of stitching beads from the front side of the fabric, using a hook needle and invisible thread, to fix a 5 × 8 mm oval white pearl in the position, as shown in the image.

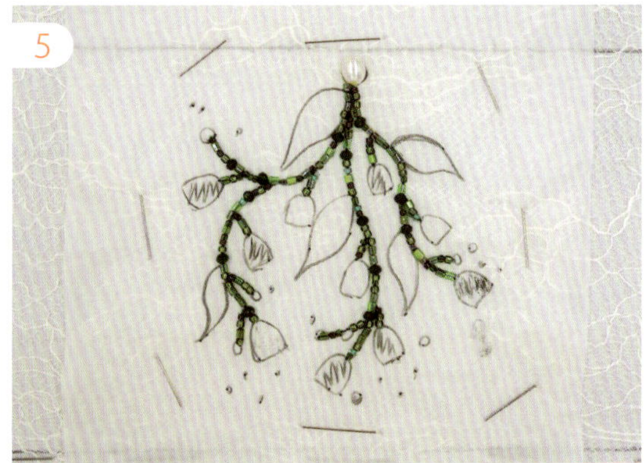

Apply the technique of stitching beads from the front side of the fabric, using a hook needle, green thread, 2 mm green shades seed beads, and 3 mm green crystals to sew stems. The order in which the beads are embroidered is up to you.

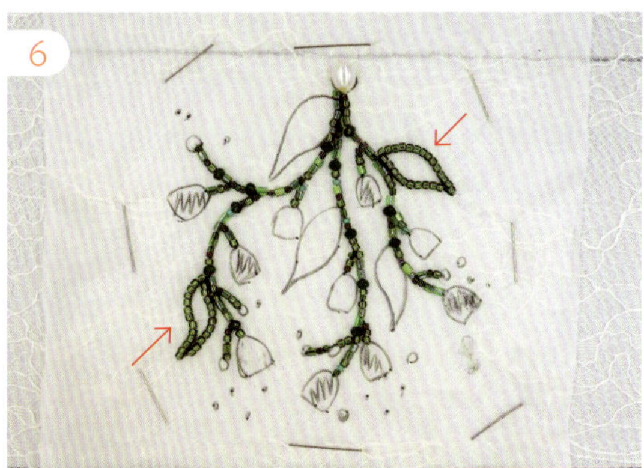

Apply the technique of stitching beads from the front side of the fabric, using a hook needle and green thread, to sew the outer contours of the two leaves. The color of the leaves can be selected from the 2 mm green shades seed bead.

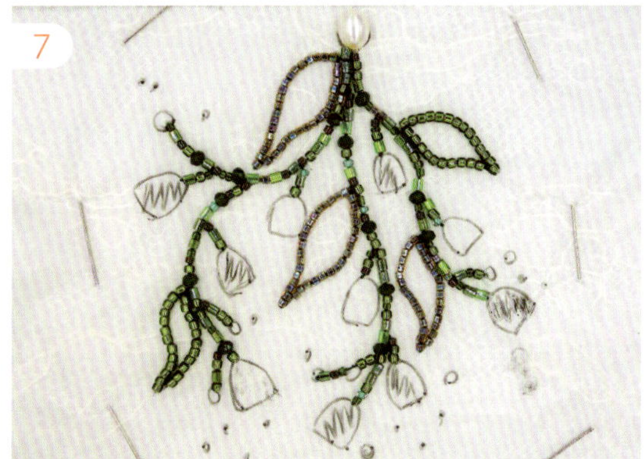

Apply the technique of stitching beads from the front side of the fabric, using a hook needle and green thread, to sew the outer contours of the remaining three leaves. You can select another color from the 2 mm green shades seed bead for these leaves.

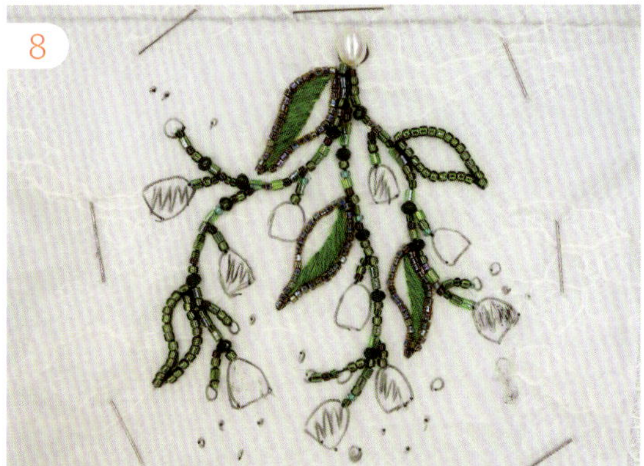

Apply the satin stitch technique using a hand sewing needle and green wool to fill half of the three leaves.

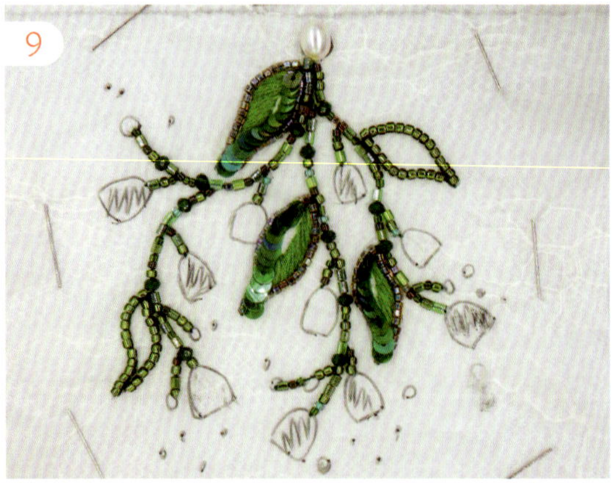

Apply the technique of stitching sequins from the front side of the fabric, using a hook needle and green thread, to sew a row of 4 mm green sequins along the outer edge of the remaining parts of the three leaves.

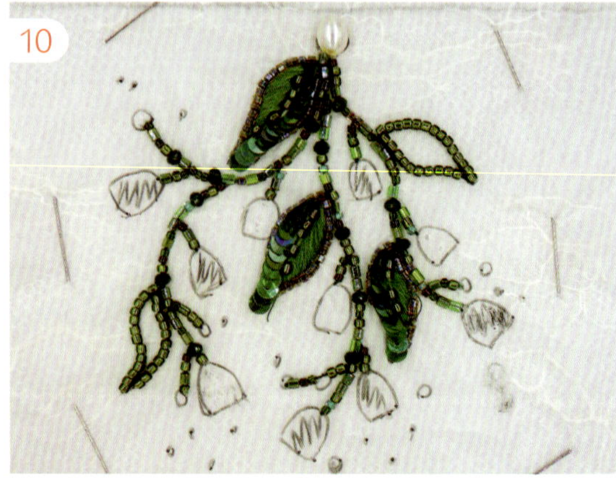

Apply the technique of stitching beads irregularly from the front side of the fabric, using a hook needle, green thread, and green shades seed beads, to sew the veins of the three leaves.

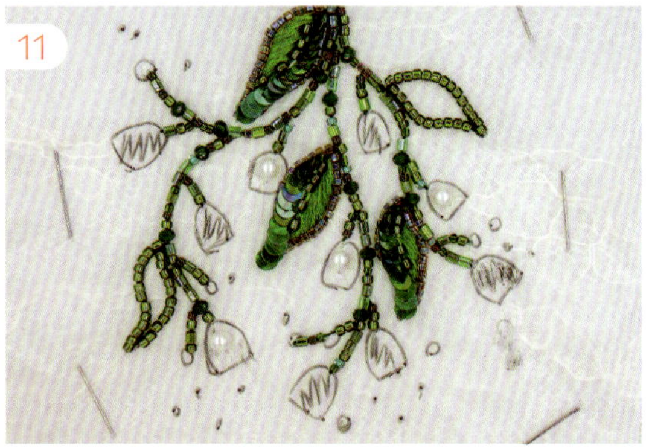

Apply the technique of stitching beads from the front side of the fabric, using a hook needle and invisible thread, to sew a 4 mm white pearl in the four flowers as shown in the picture.

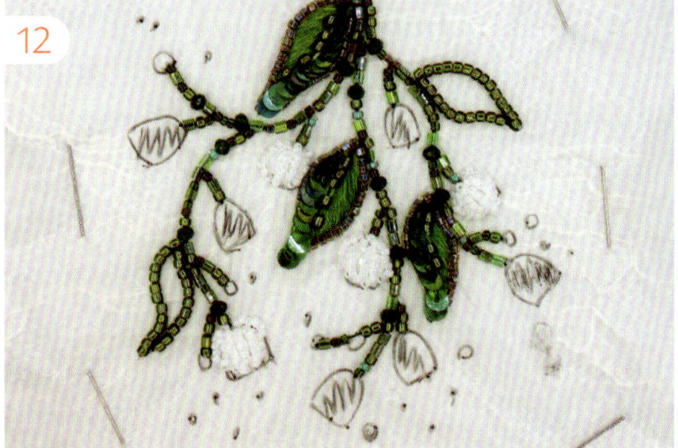

Apply the technique of stitching multiple beads from the front side of the fabric, using a hook needle, invisible thread, and 1.5 mm white seed beads, to fill the four flowers. Allow the white seed beads to cover the white pearls from step 11 to form a semi-stereoscopic effect.

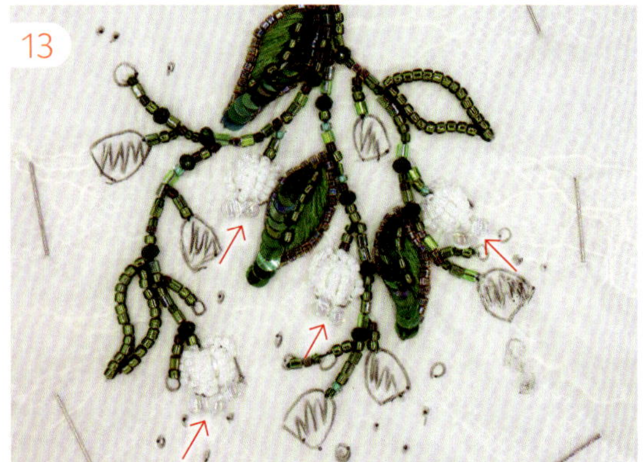

Apply the technique of stitching beads from the front side of the fabric, using a hook needle and invisible thread to sew two to three 3 mm transparent drop-shaped beads on the top of the four flowers (positions indicated by the arrows) as stamens.

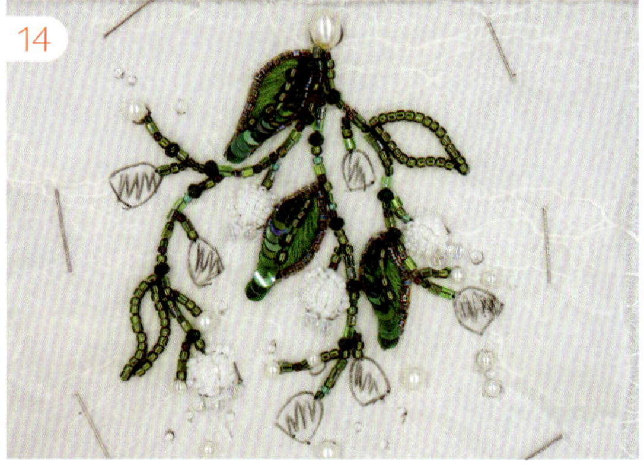

Apply the technique of embroidering a single bead, using a hand sewing needle, invisible thread, 1.5 mm white seed beads, 3 mm white pearls, and 4 mm white pearls, to decorate around the flowers.

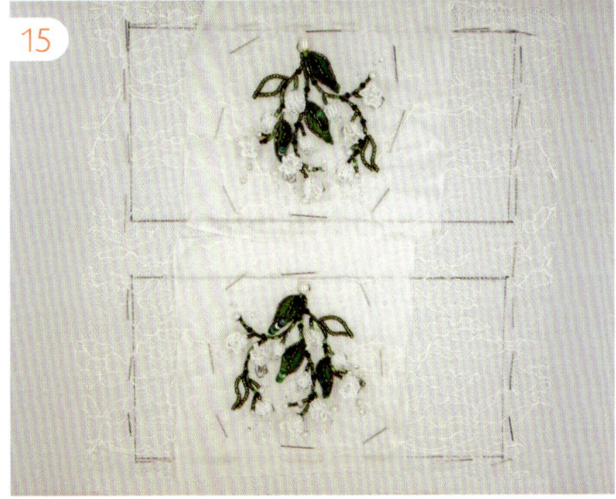

Apply the same method to embroider the upper portion of the pattern in step 3, and use a hand sewing needle and white thread to fix the 12 three-dimensional lily of the valley flowers completed in step 5 on page 66 on the patterns of the remaining flowers. The embroidered part of the cuffs is now complete.

◆ Making the Cuffs

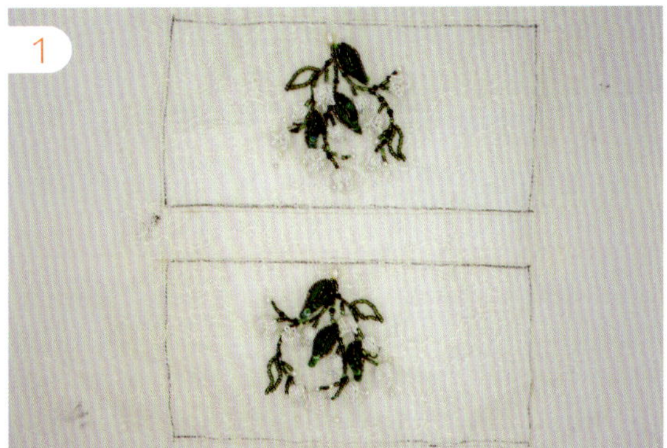

Remove the piece from the embroidery frame and tear off the tracing paper. Use a hand sewing needle or a sewing machine and white thread, to sew along about 1 mm outside the contour of the two rectangles, and fasten the white satin and lace together.

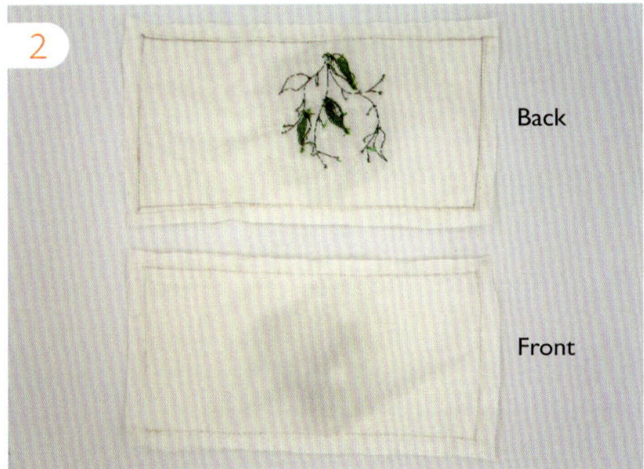

Take two pieces of white satin that are 1 cm larger than the whole rectangle as the lining, and align the front of the embroidery piece (one side of the embroidery) with the white satin. Sew along the rectangle, leaving an opening of about 3 cm at your preferred position, then cut along the white satin and trim the edges.

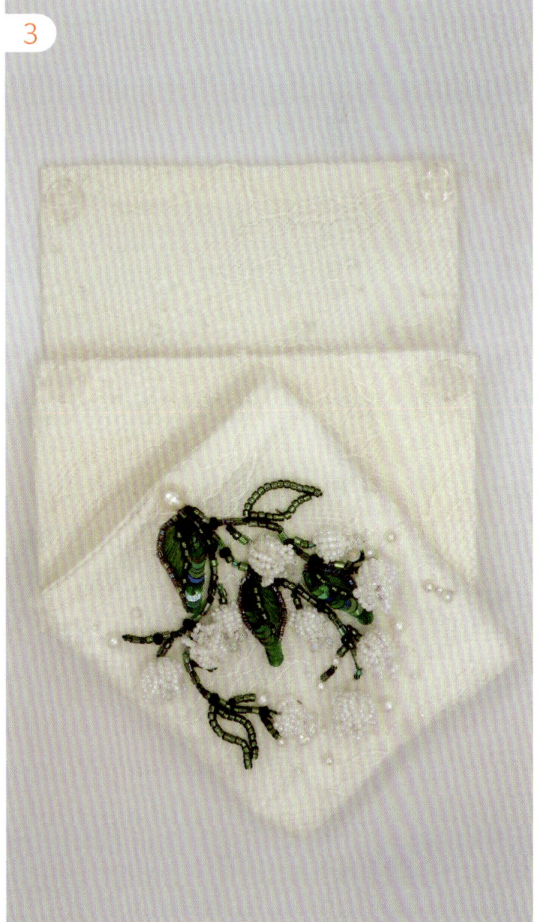

Flip the fabric through the opening to the front, and sew up the opening. Install 7 mm transparent sew-on buttons on the four corners (note the front and back directions of the buttons). The cuff is now complete.

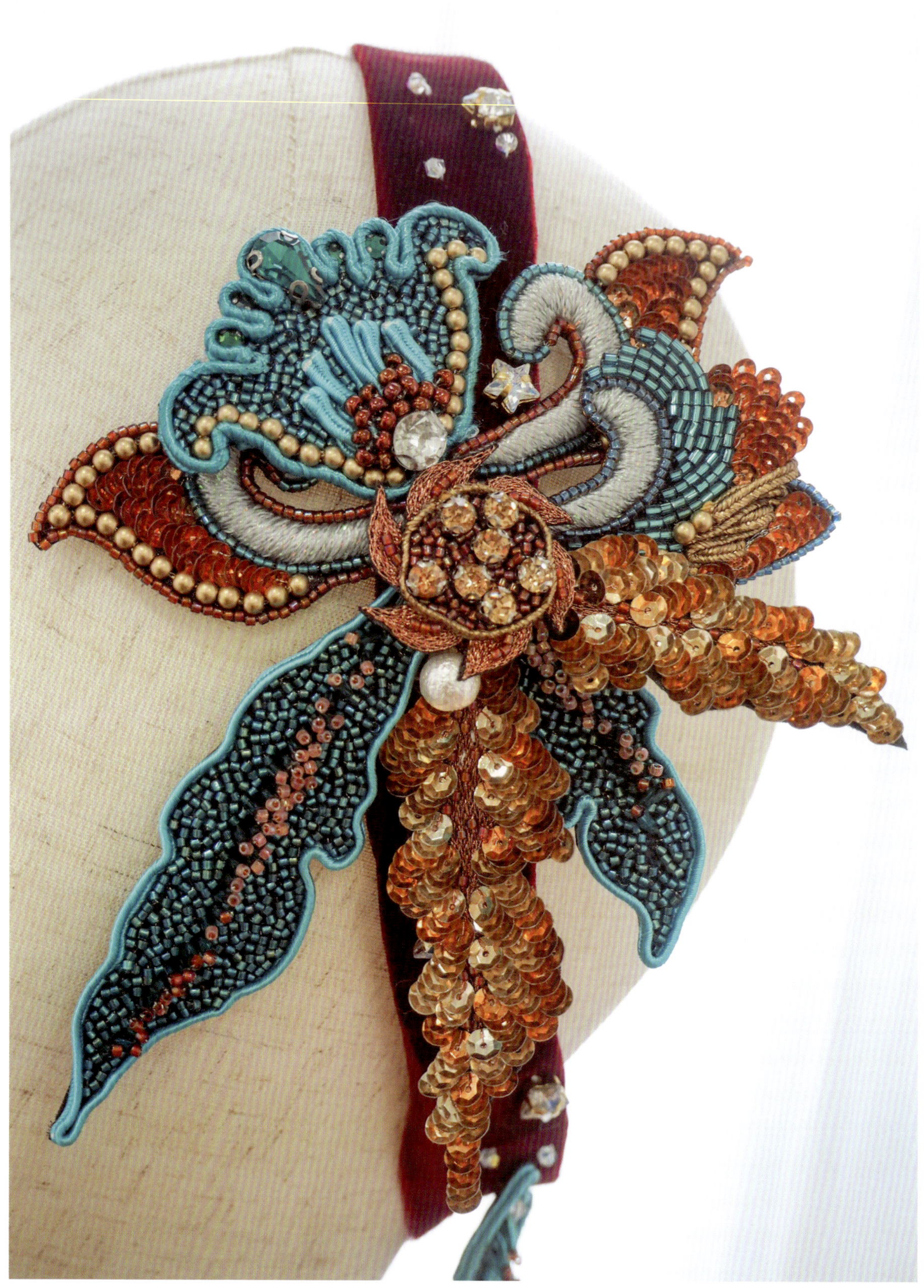

4. Iris Hair Accessory

When the iris is in full bloom, its long petals stretch out like a bird's tail. In Chinese culture, iris symbolizes love and friendship, and implies a bright future ahead. In this pattern, golden leaf blades complement a blue and purple iris. It uses simple and natural colors, creating a hair accessory that exudes elegance and nobility.

You Will Need

Threads	embroidery thread	silver, blue-green
	hand sewing thread	beige gold, beige
	metallic thread	brown
Beads	seed beads	1.6 mm blue-green, 1.6 mm brown, 1.6 mm flesh-colored, 3 mm brown
	cup sequins	3 mm brown, 5 mm gold
	tube beads	3 mm blue-green, 6 mm blue-green
	rhinestones	4 mm gold, 3 mm green, 6 mm silver, 6 mm green tear-shaped
	pearls	4 mm gold
Fabrics	black organza, black velvet, 2 mm blue-green embellishment cords, 2 mm gold embellishment cords	
Tools	embroidery hoop, 70# hook needle, hand sewing needle, scissors, fabric glue, heat erasable marker	

Embroidery Steps

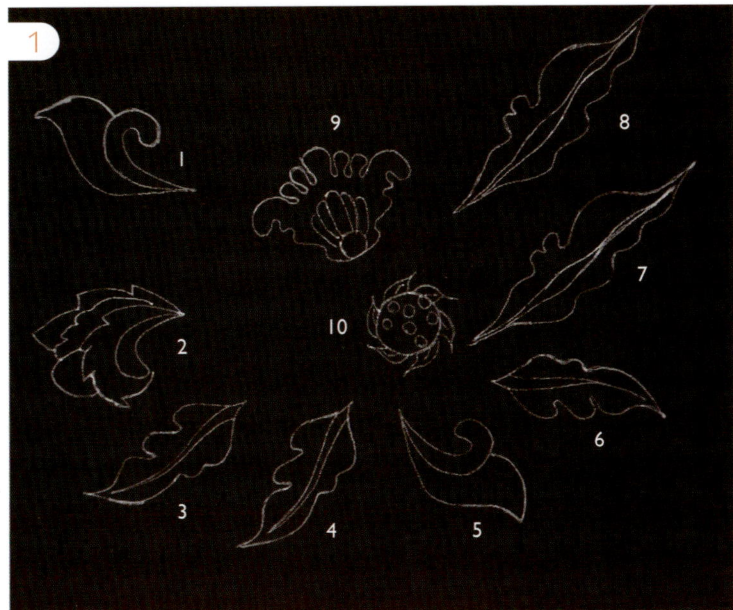

Stretch the black organza onto the embroidery frame, and trace the patterns (see page 164) onto the organza with a heat erasable marker.

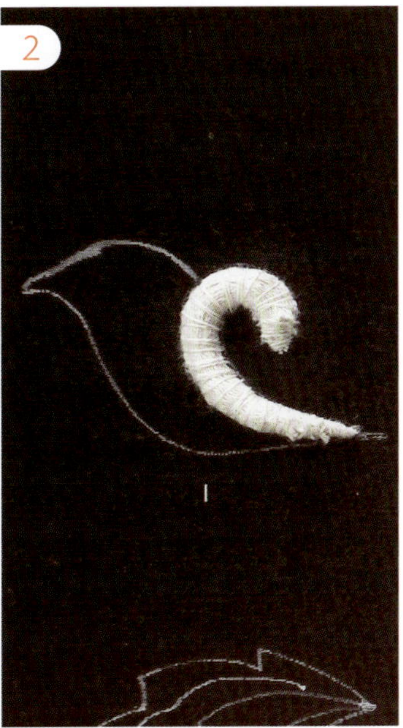

Use the technique of fixing cotton thread to fix the beige hand sewing thread on pattern 1.

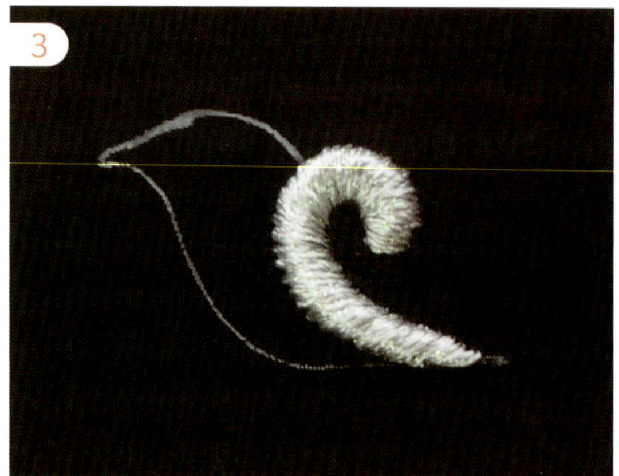

Use the satin stitch technique with beige gold hand sewing thread (note: fine gold wire is wrapped around the beige thread) to carefully cover pattern 1.

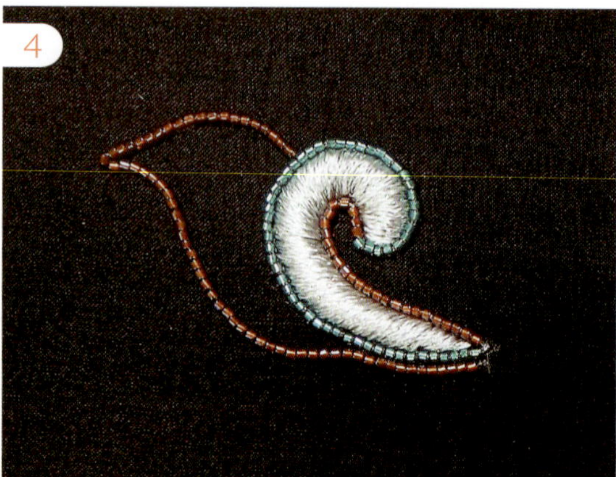

Stitch beads continuously from the front side of the fabric with a hook needle, silver embroidery thread, and 1.6 mm blue-green and brown seed beads to sew the contour of pattern 1.

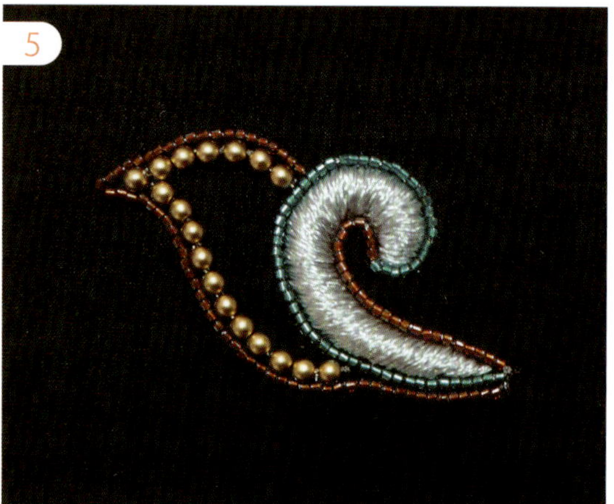

Use a hook needle and silver embroidery thread to stitch 4 mm gold pearls along the inside of the outline of pattern 1.

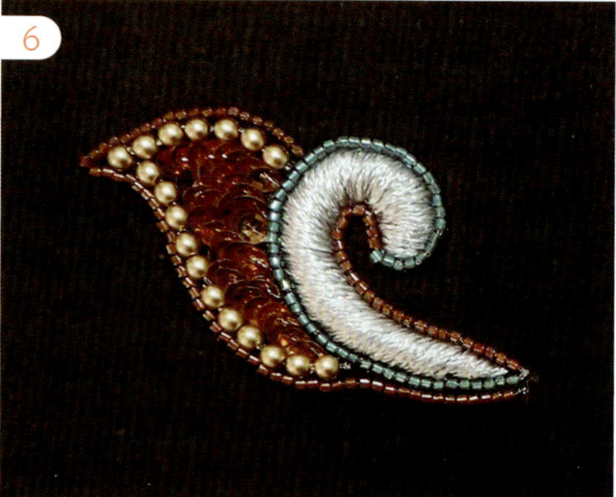

Stitch sequins continuously from the front side of the fabric with a hook needle, silver embroidery thread, and 3 mm brown cup sequins to fill the inside of pattern 1.

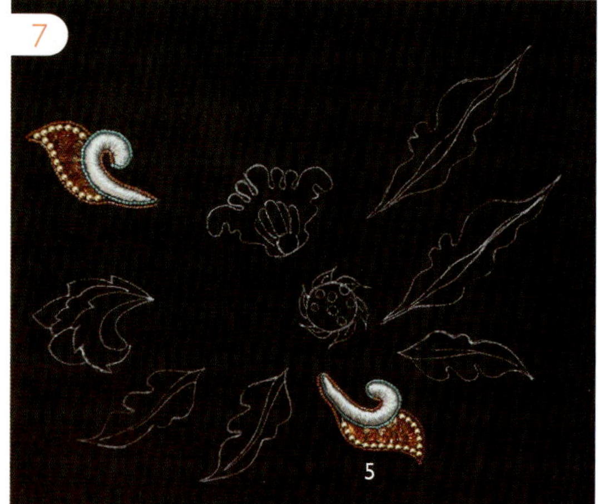

Use the same materials and techniques of steps 2–6 to complete pattern 5.

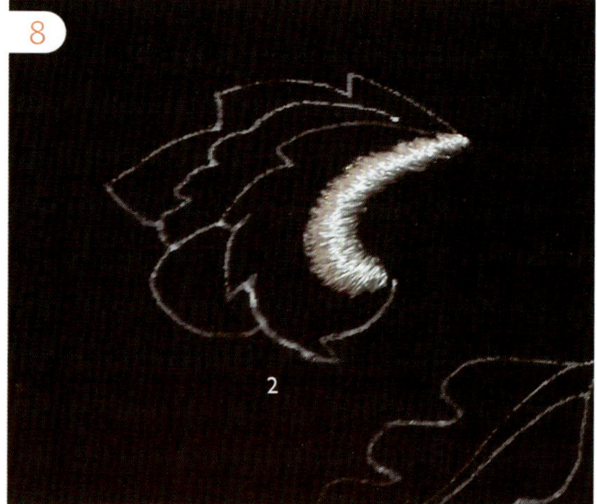

Repeat steps 2 and 3 to complete fixing the cotton thread in pattern 2.

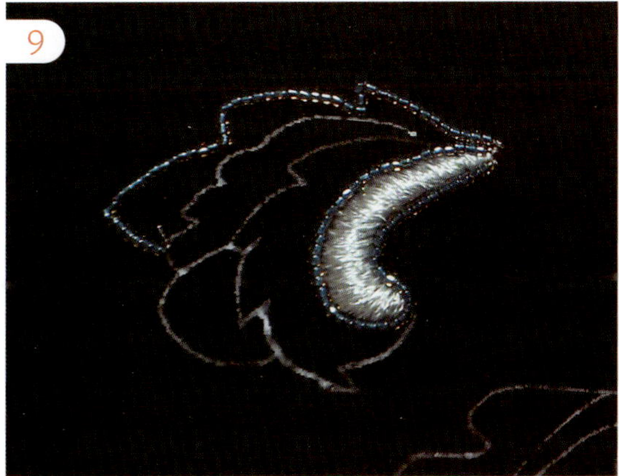

Stitch beads continuously from the front side of the fabric with a hook needle, silver embroidery thread, and 1.6 mm blue-green seed beads to sew part of the outline of pattern 2.

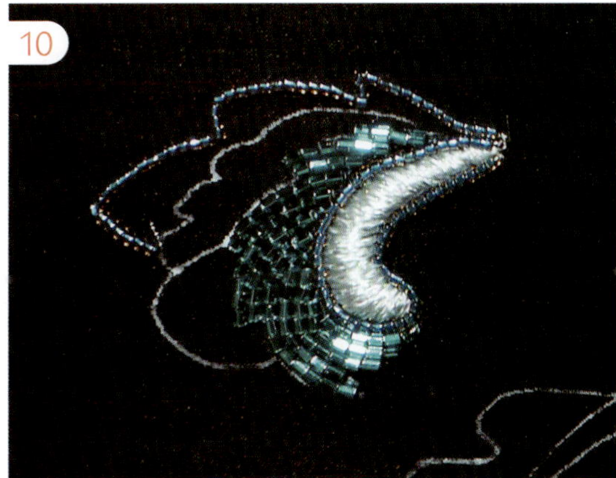

Stitch beads continuously from the front side of the fabric with a hook needle, silver embroidery thread, and 3 mm blue-green tube beads to partially fill pattern 2. Ensure that the beads are neatly sewn.

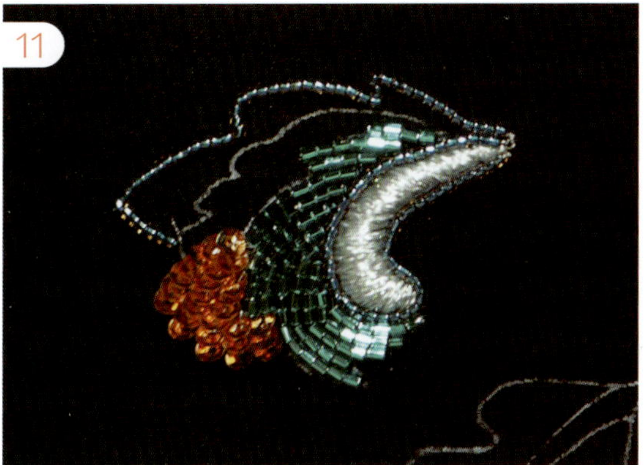

Stitch sequins continuously from the front side of the fabric with a hook needle, silver embroidery thread, and 3 mm brown cup sequins to complete the portion shown in pattern 2.

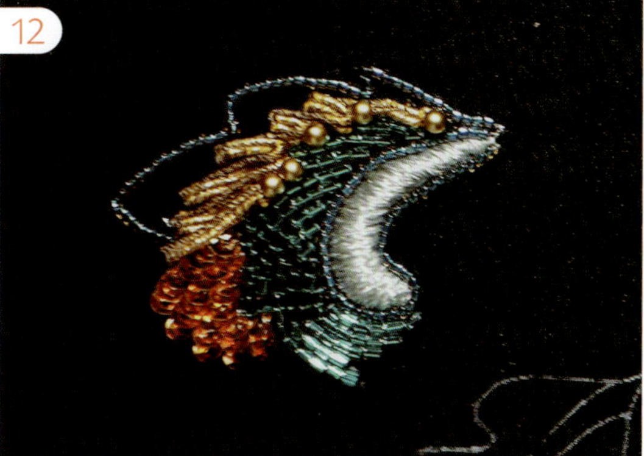

Use a hand sewing needle and silver embroidery thread to fix the 2 mm gold embellishment cords on the corresponding position of pattern 2 in zigzagging shape. Parts of the exposed creases can be covered and decorated with 4 mm gold pearls.

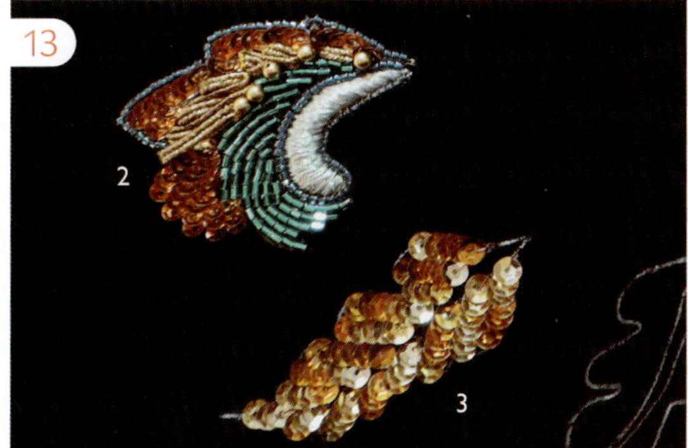

Stitch sequins continuously from the front side of the fabric with a hook needle, silver embroidery thread, and 3 mm brown cup sequins to fill up the remaining area of pattern 2. Next, apply the same technique using a hook needle, silver embroidery thread, and 5 mm gold cup sequins to sew the leaf blades for pattern 3.

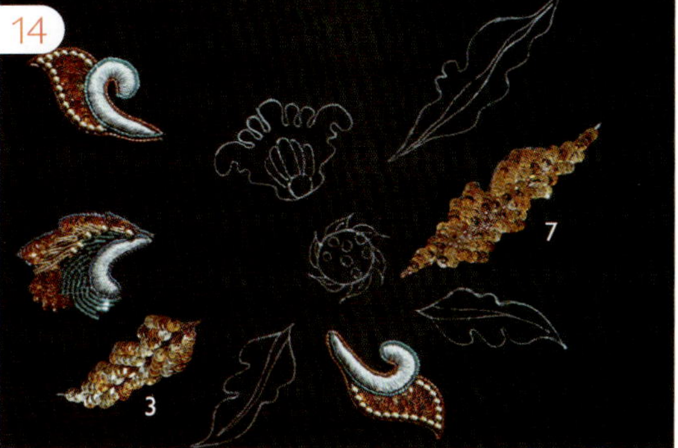

Use a hook needle and brown metallic thread to sew the veins in the middle of the leaf blade, and decorate it with 1.6 mm brown seed beads, leaving no blank space. Use the same materials and techniques as the leaf blade in pattern 3 to complete pattern 7.

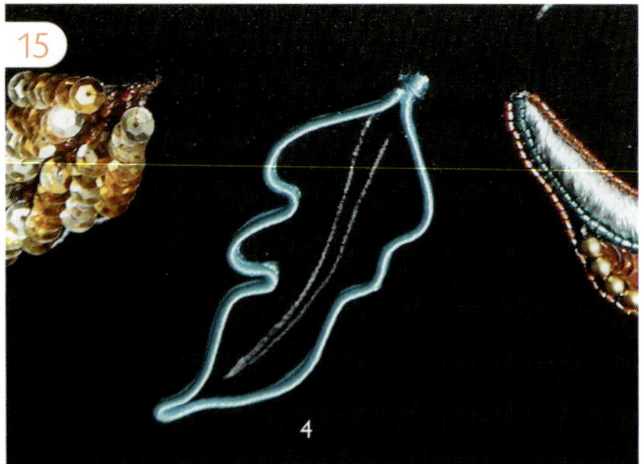

Use a hand sewing needle, blue-green embroidery thread, and 2 mm blue-green embellishment cords to align the cord 90 degrees to the embroidery surface, and sew the outer contour of the leaf blade in pattern 4.

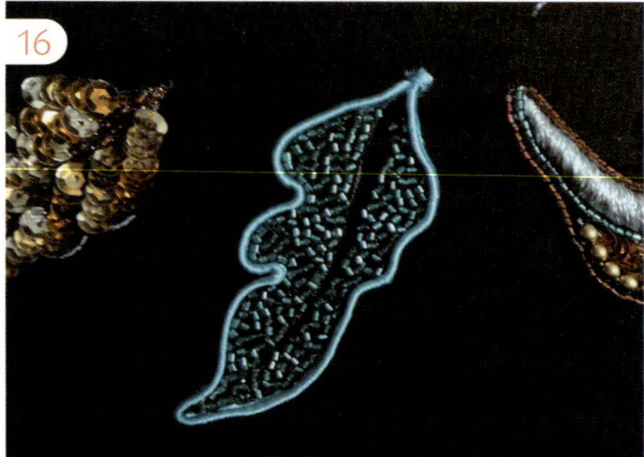

Stitch beads from the front side of the fabric with a hook needle, blue-green embroidery thread, and 1.6 mm blue-green seed beads to fill the inside of the leaf blade. Keep a lookout for the position of the leaf's central vein.

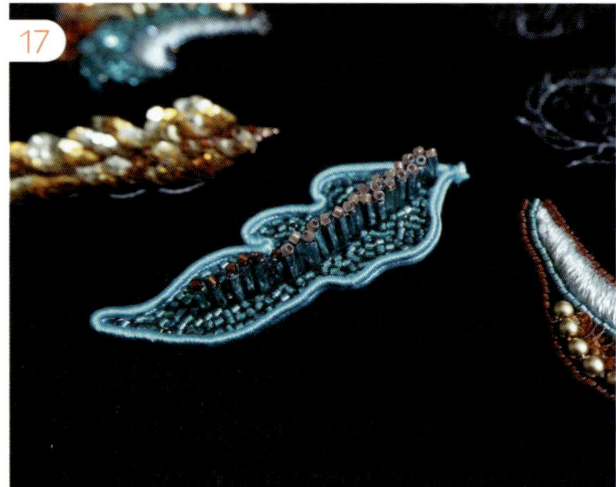

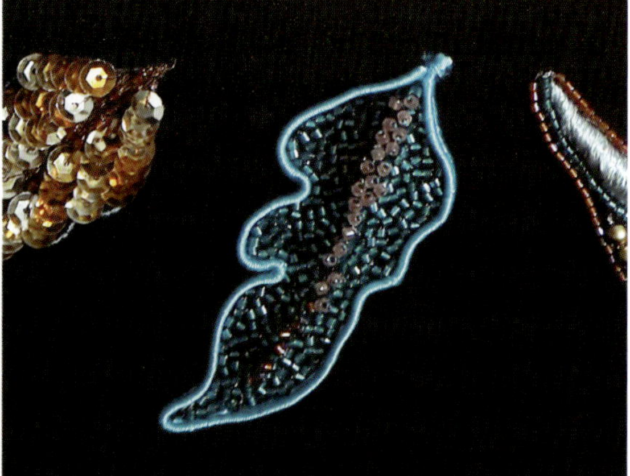

Use the technique of embroidering a bead on top of a tube with a hand sewing needle, blue-green embroidery thread, 6 mm blue-green tubes, and 1.6 mm brown and flesh-colored seed beads to fill the leaf's central vein. Note that each tube should be in an upright position.

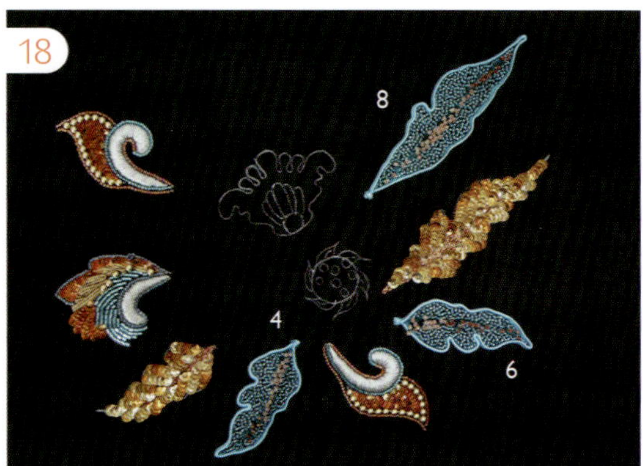

Use the techniques from pattern 4 to complete patterns 6 and 8.

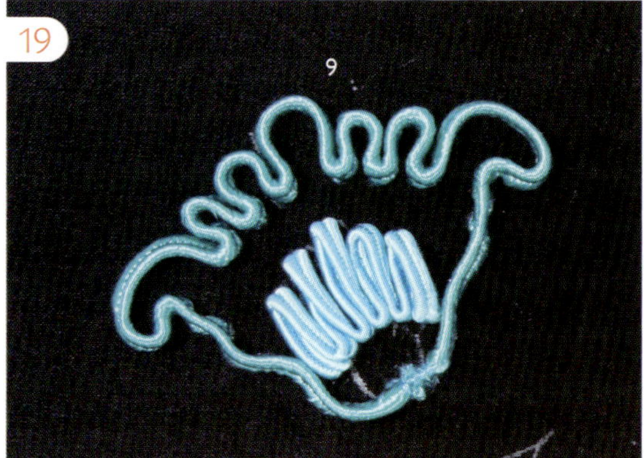

Use a hand sewing needle, blue-green embroidery thread, and blue-green embellishment cords to align the cord at 90 degrees to the embroidery surface. Sew the outer contour of pattern 9, and bend the cord to sew the central area.

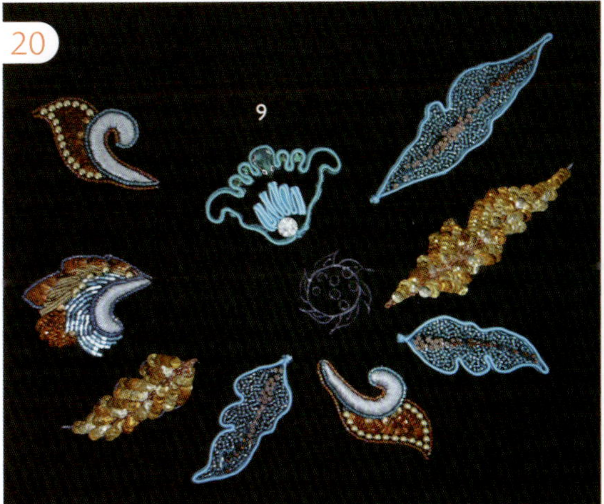

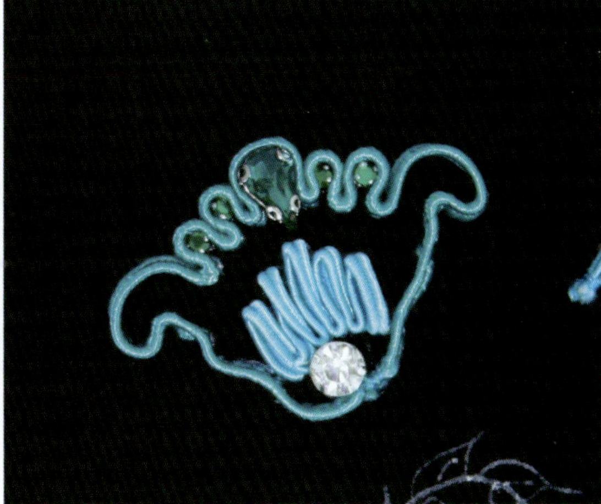

Decorate the gaps in pattern 9 using silver embroidery thread, four 3 mm green rhinestones, one 6 mm green tear-shaped rhinestone, and one 6 mm silver rhinestone as shown in the picture.

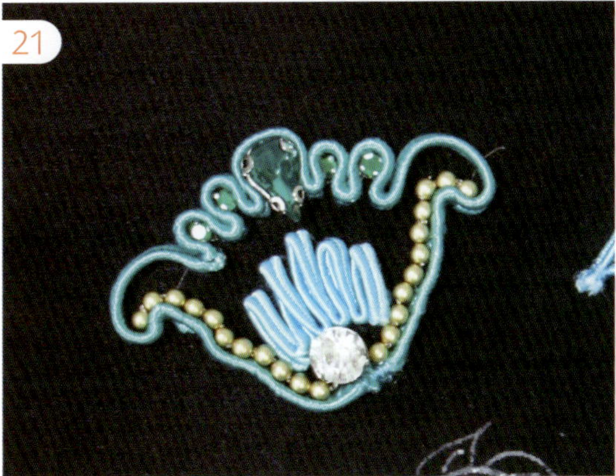

Decorate the inner contour of pattern 9 using a hook needle, silver embroidery thread, and 4 mm gold pearls stitched continuously from the front side of the fabric.

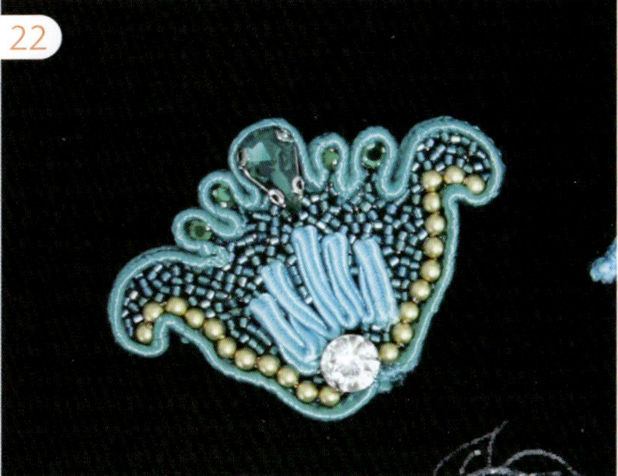

Fill the remaining parts of pattern 9 by stitching the beads from the front side of the fabric using a hook needle, blue-green embroidery thread, and 1.6 mm blue-green seed beads.

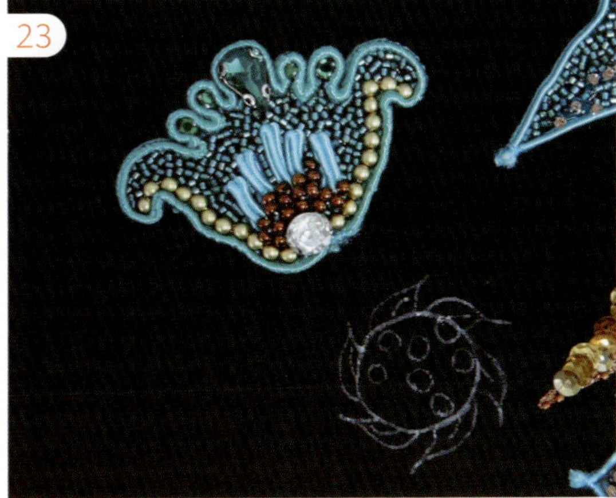

Use a hand sewing needle, silver embroidery thread, and 3 mm brown seed beads to decorate the upper portion of the silver rhinestone to create the effect of stamens.

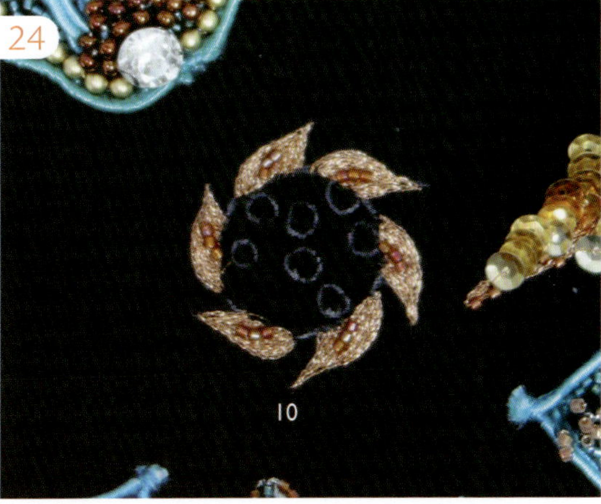

Stitch beads from the front side of the fabric using a hook needle, brown metallic thread, and 1.6 mm brown seed beads to sew the outer ring of pattern 10.

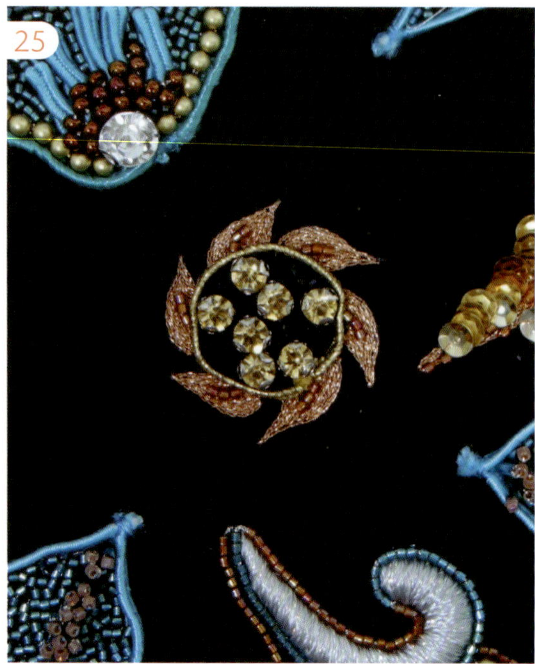

Use a hand sewing needle and silver embroidery thread to decorate the inner ring of pattern 10 with 4 mm gold rhinestones.

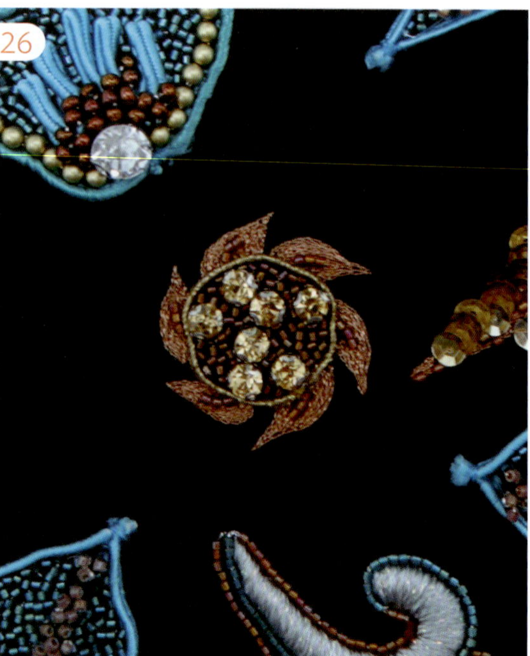

Stitch beads from the front side of the fabric using a hook needle, silver embroidery thread, and 1.6 mm brown seed beads to fill the empty portion of the inner circle of pattern 10. Use fabric glue to paste the black velvet on the back of each pattern, and cut them separately.

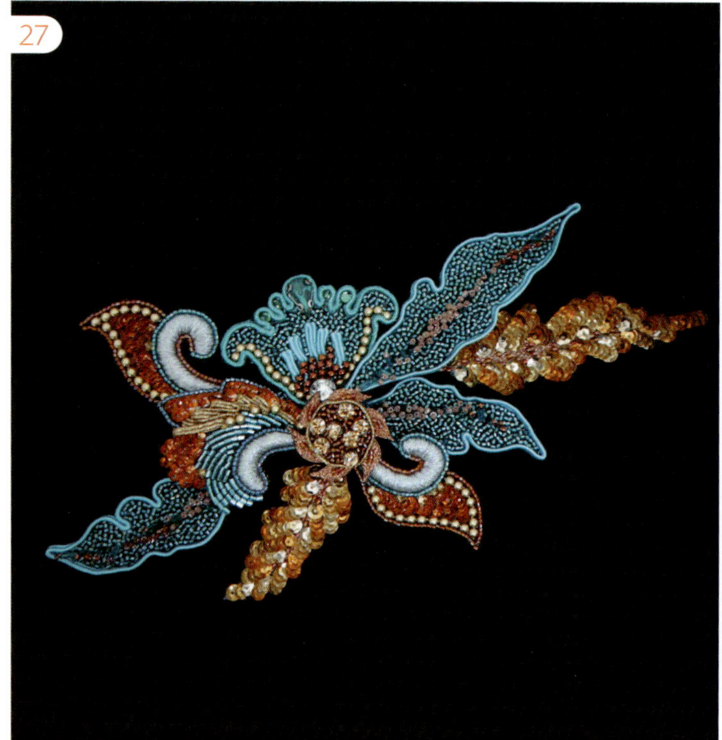

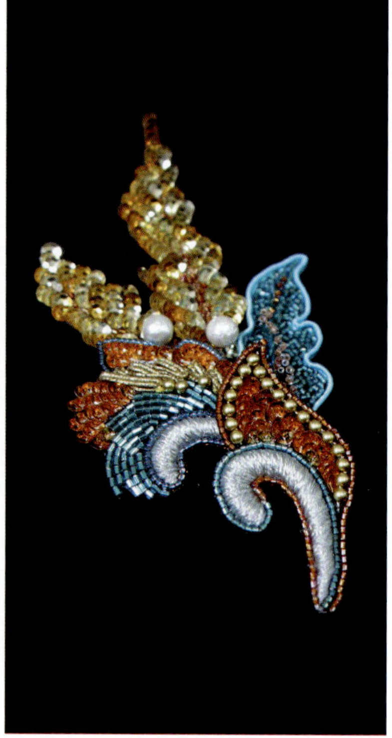

Each part can be matched as you wish, and sewn onto the hair hoop to create a personalized accessory.

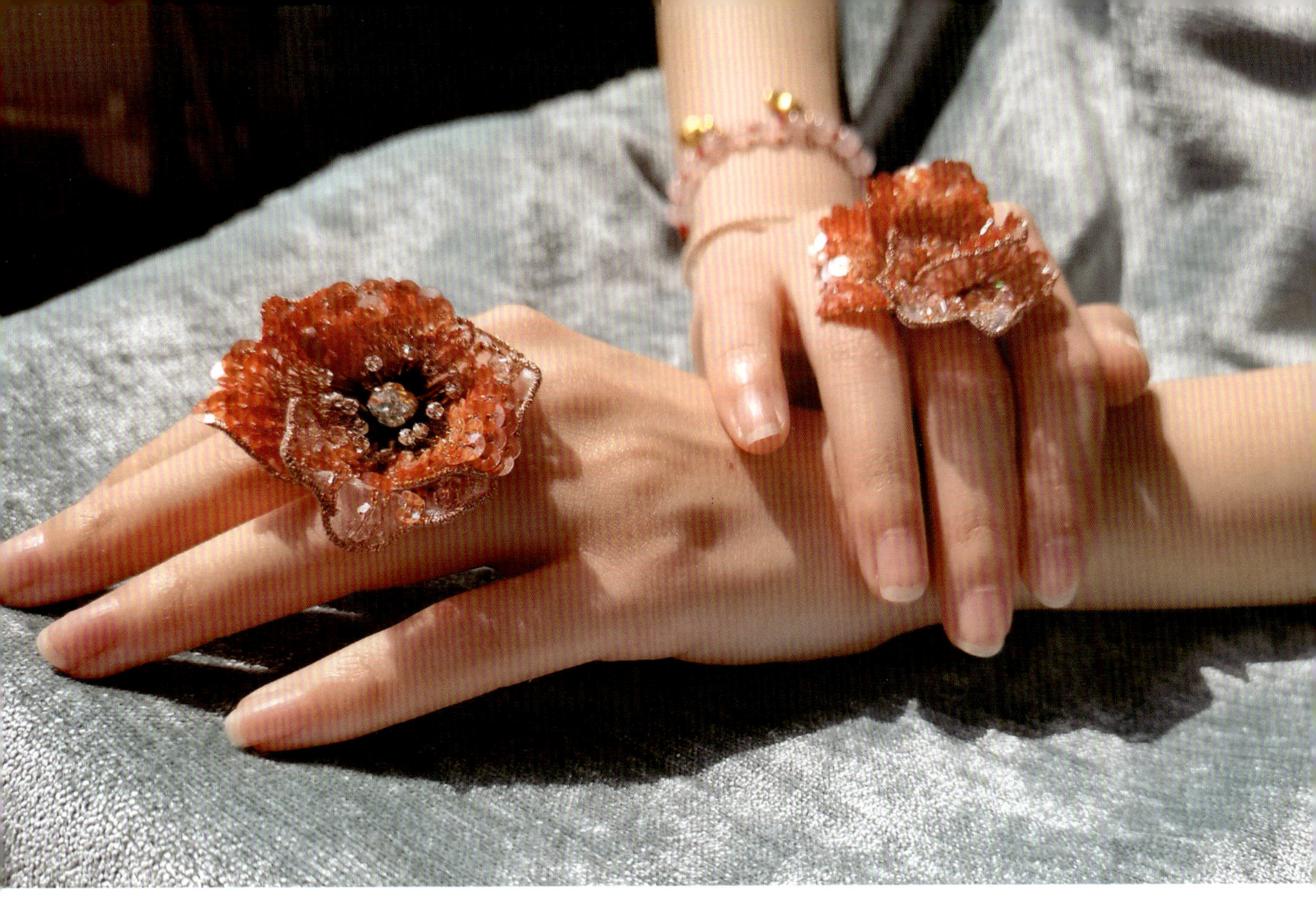

5. Chinese Flowering Crabapple Ring

The Chinese flowering crabapple is a unique and highly celebrated plant in China. Also known as the Goddess of Flowers, the crabapple flower has been admired by literary scholars since ancient times, and has been used as the subject of poetry, either as a metaphor for beauty or as a symbol of goodwill. The crabapple flower is also used as a metaphor for hardiness and resilience due to its ability to resist the cold. Use bead embroidery to frame this simple yet charming flower, and let it bloom between your fingers.

You Will Need

Threads	metallic thread	orange
	seed beads	1.5 mm orange, 2 mm orange
	sequins	3 mm orange, 4 mm orange
Beads	crystals	3 mm pink
	sew-on rhinestones	6 mm white
	tube beads	6 mm silver
Fabrics	white organza, wool felt, golden leather	
Tools	embroidery hoop, 70# hook needle, hand sewing needle, scissors, fabric glue, heat erasable marker, 0.4 mm iron wire, a ring setting	

Embroidery Steps

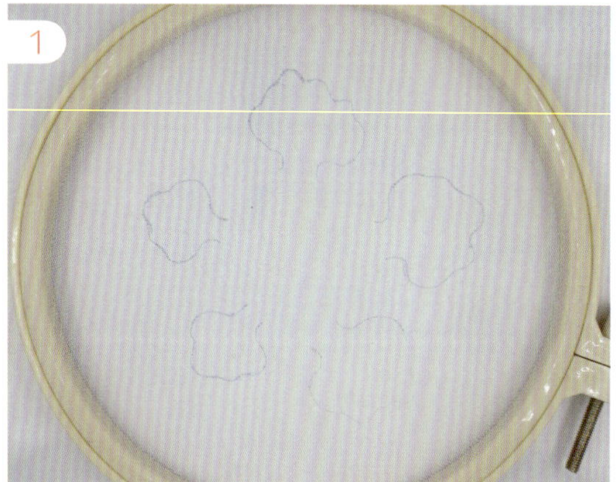

Stretch the white organza on the embroidery hoop, and trace the pattern (see page 164) on the fabric with a heat erasable marker.

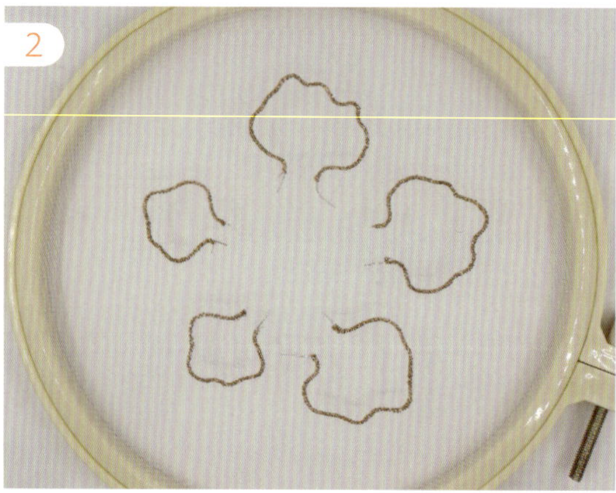

Apply the edging stitch technique with a hook needle to sew the flower petal outlines with orange metallic thread and 0.4 mm iron wire.

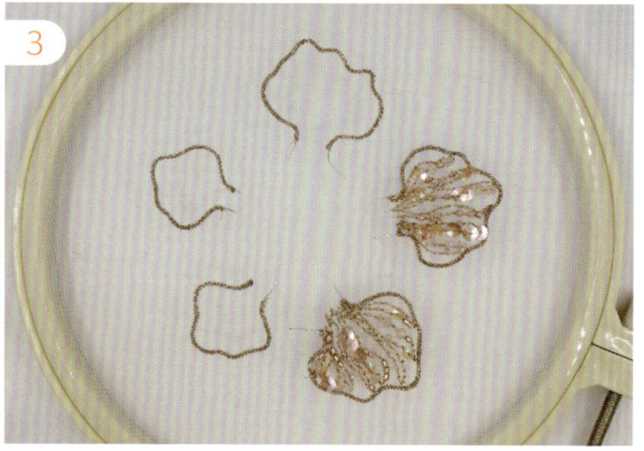

Apply the technique of stitching beads discontinuously from the front side of the fabric with a hook needle, 2 mm orange seed beads, 3 mm pink crystals, and 4 mm orange sequins to sew irregular lines in the two petals.

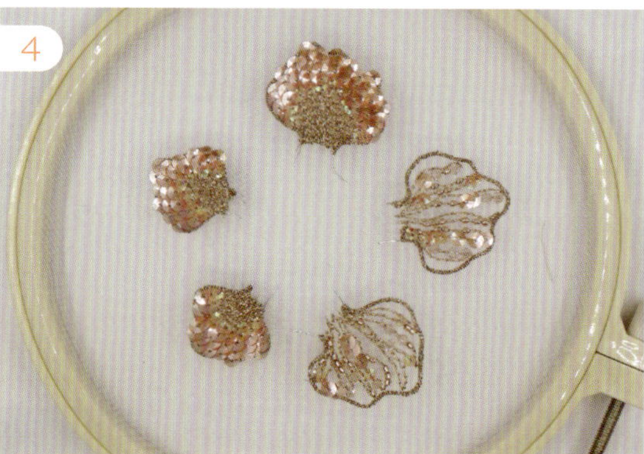

Apply the techniques of stitching sequins from the front side of the fabric and chain stitch with a hook needle, orange metallic thread, 3 mm orange sequins, and 4 mm orange sequins to fill the remaining three petals—two small and one large.

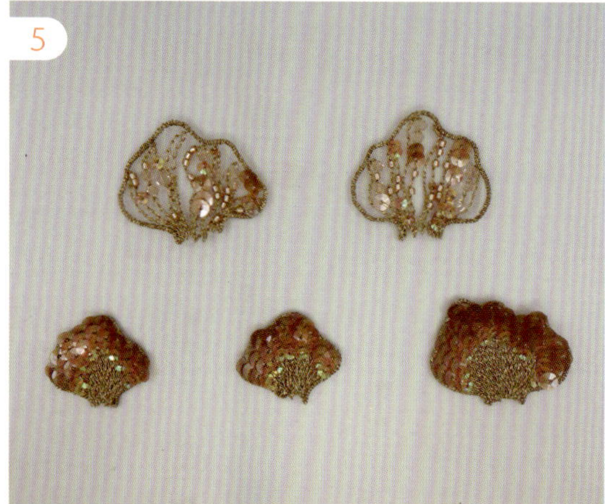

Cut out the embroidered patterns.

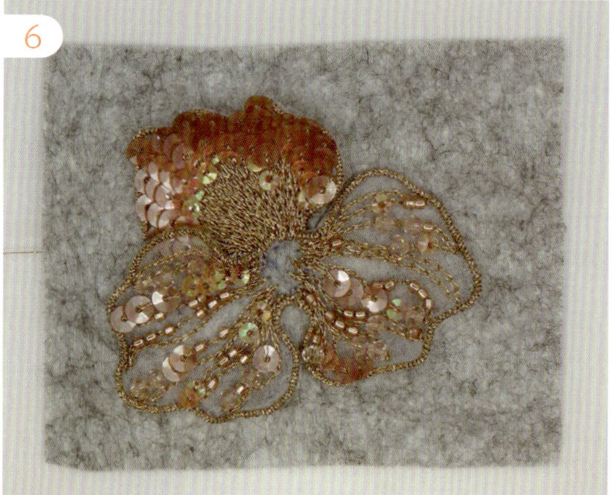

Sew the three larger petals onto the wool felt one at a time. Leave the center of the flower empty.

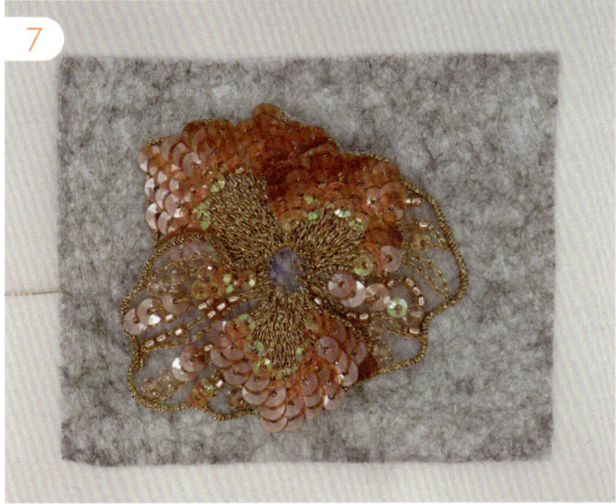

Sew the two smaller petals onto the upper layer of the larger petals, paying close attention to the flower's shape. Leave the area at the center of the flower empty.

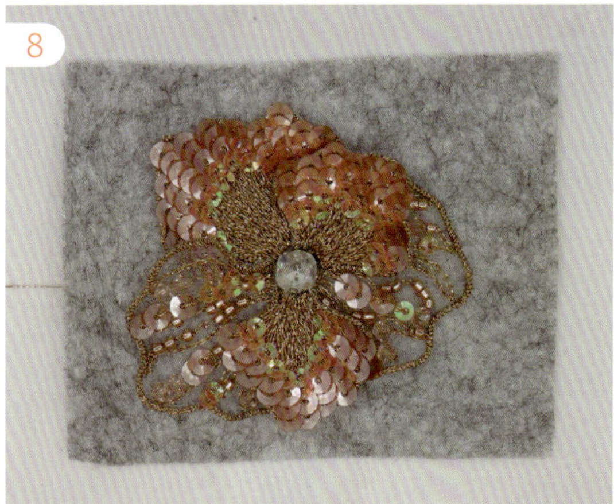

Fix the 6 mm white sew-on rhinestone at the center of the flower with a hand sewing needle.

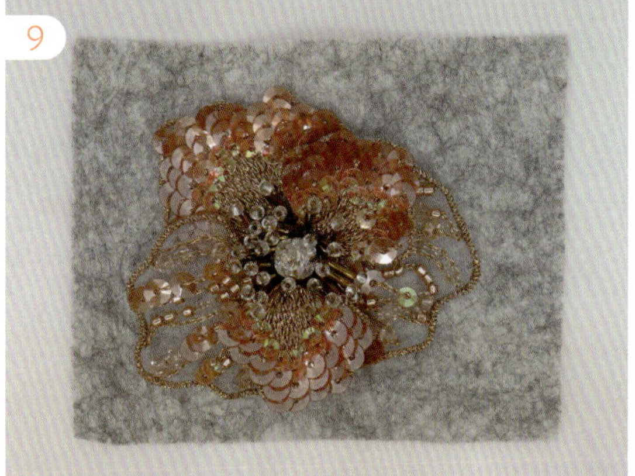

Applying the technique of embroidering a bead on top of a tube using a hand sewing needle, 1.5 mm orange seed beads, and 6 mm silver tube beads to decorate around the rhinestone, forming stamens.

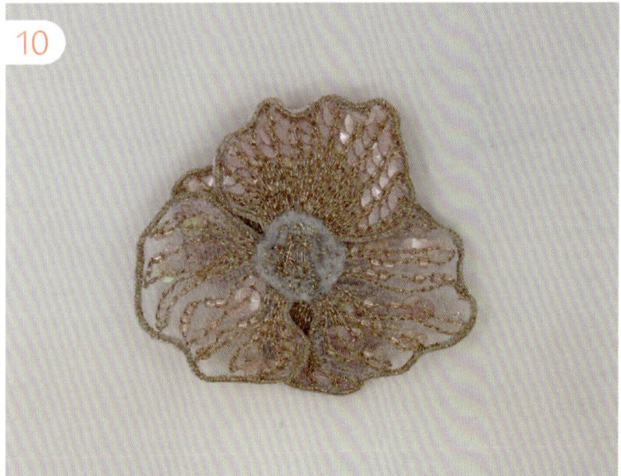

Leave a 1.5 cm diameter wool felt disc in the stitched part, and trim off the excess wool felt.

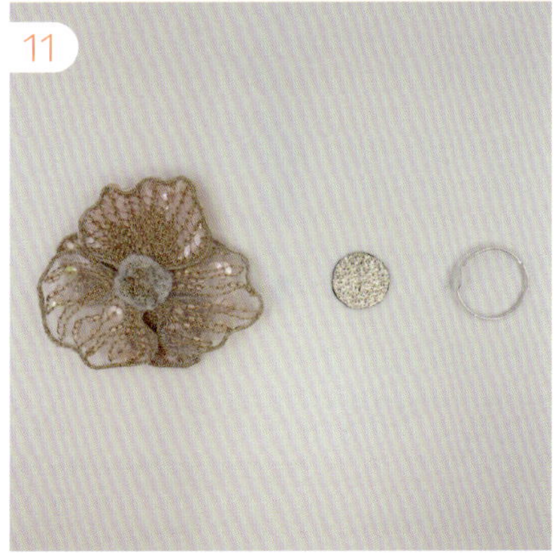

Prepare a ring setting and a golden leather disc of the same diameter (1.5 cm) and cut a cross in the middle of the disc.

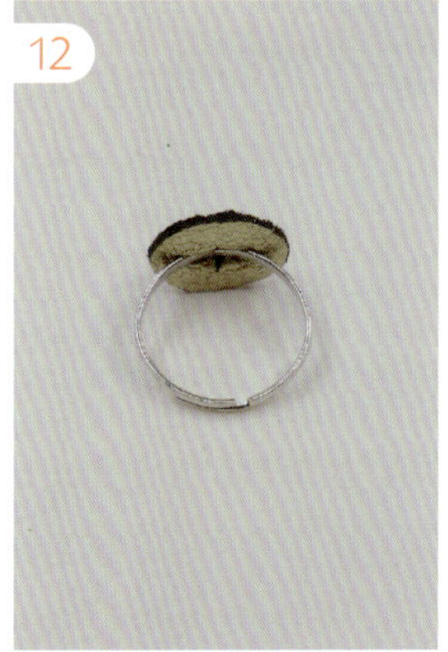

Insert the ring setting into the cross on the golden leather disc, and apply a little fabric glue to fix it.

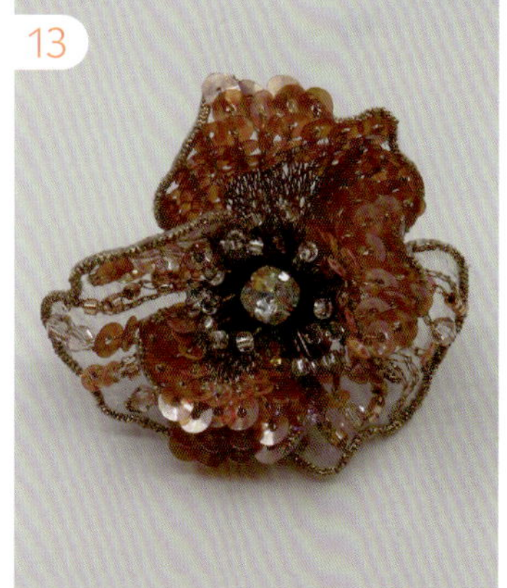

Use fabric glue to fix the ring setting and golden leather disc to the back of the wool felt. The ring is now complete.

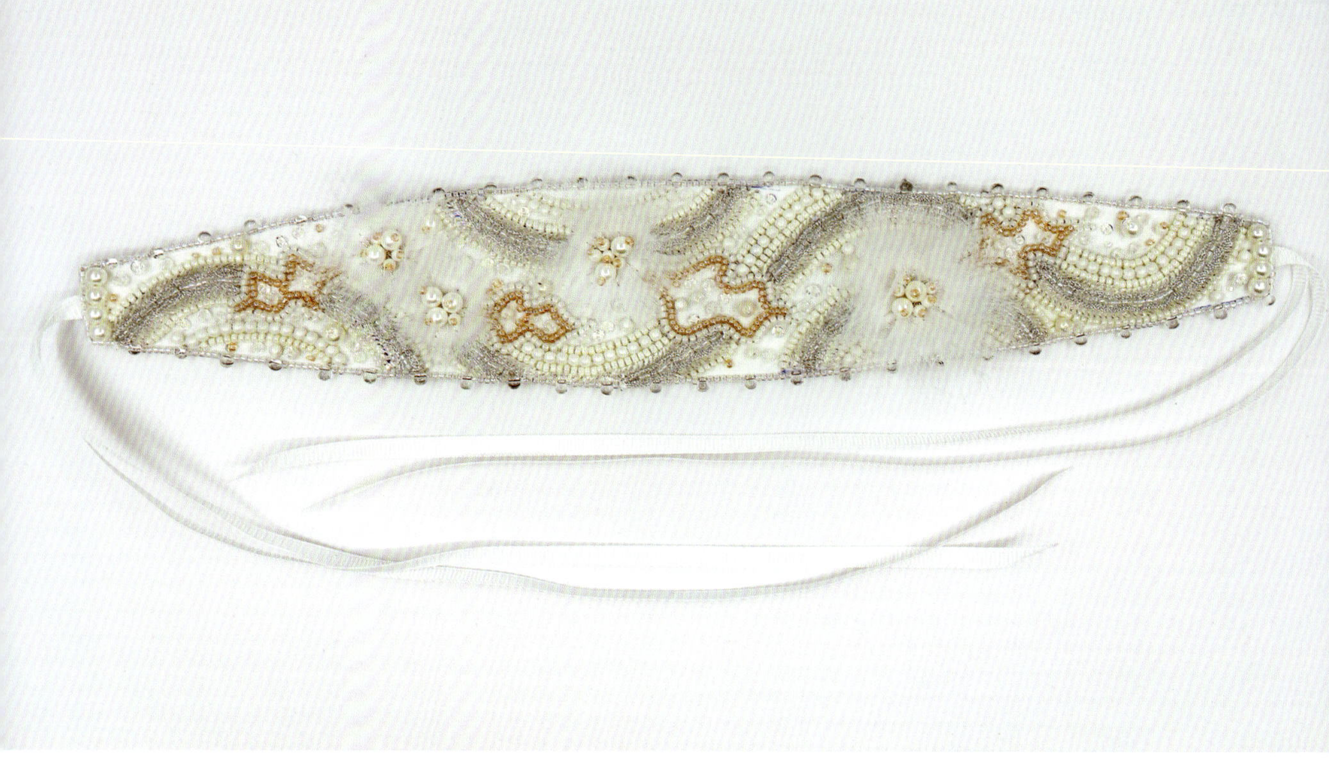

6. Dandelion Bridal Hair Ornament

The dandelion is a small, hairy wildflower. After it has bloomed, it flutters in the wind like white feathers all over the mountains, symbolizing tenacity and vitality. As well as being attractive in appearance, this flower is also a common medicinal herb in traditional Chinese medicine. This bridal hair ornament skillfully uses white organza as petals to reflect the light texture of dandelion flowers, and is supplemented by a large number of pearls, complementing the bride's elegance.

You Will Need

Threads	embroidery thread	silver
Beads	seed beads	1.5 mm transparent, 1.6 mm transparent, 2 mm white, 2 mm creamy white, 2 mm transparent flesh-colored
	cup sequins	3 mm silver
	drop beads	3 mm transparent
	crystals	3 mm transparent
	pearls	3 mm white, 4 mm white, 5 mm white
Fabrics	5 mm white grosgrain ribbon, 8 mm silver pattern ribbon, white satin, velvet, organza	
Tools	embroidery frame, 70# hook needle, hand sewing needle, scissors, fabric glue, heat erasable marker, iron, small steel comb, ball head pins	

Embroidery Steps

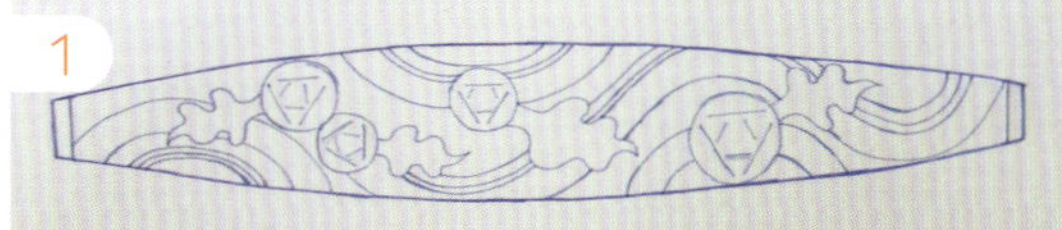

Stretch the white satin on the embroidery frame, and trace the pattern (see page 169) onto it with a heat erasable marker.

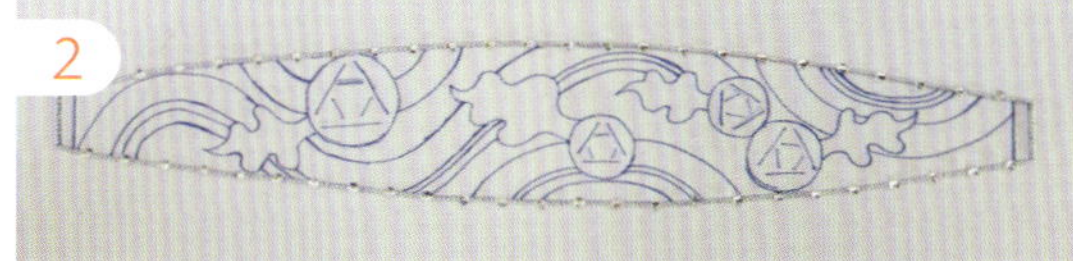

Stitch beads continuously from the front side of the fabric using a hook needle, 1.6 mm transparent seed beads, and 3 mm transparent drop beads to sew the outer contour. Note that the drop beads need to be evenly interspersed between the seed beads.

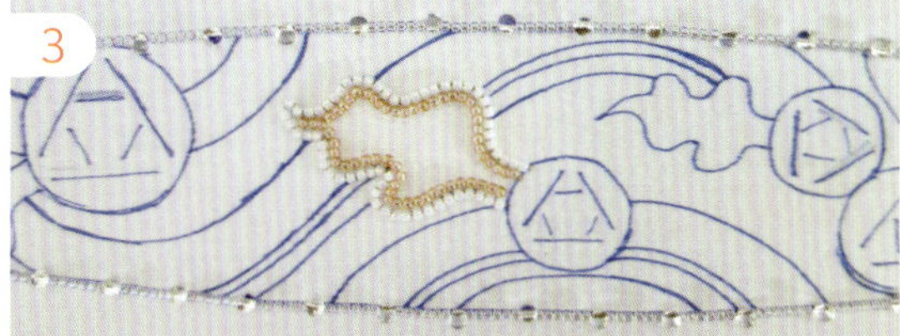

Stitch beads continuously from the front side of the fabric with a hook needle, as well as 2 mm white and transparent flesh-colored seed beads, to sew the two-layer contour of the leaf blade from the outside to the inside.

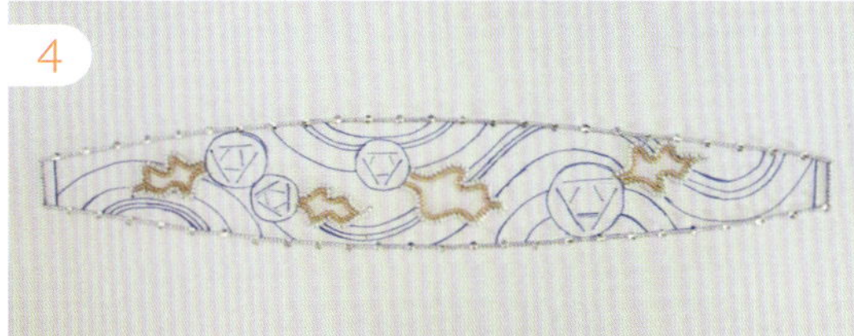

Use the same materials and techniques as step 3 to complete all the leaf blades.

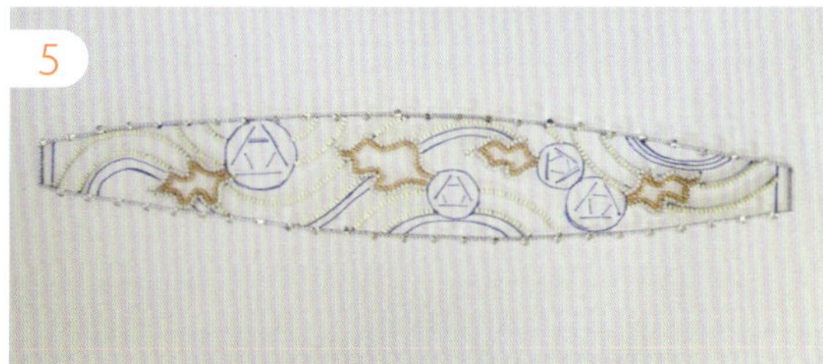

Stitch beads continuously from the front side of the fabric using a hook needle and 2 mm creamy white seed beads to complete the main arc lines in the pattern, as shown in the figure.

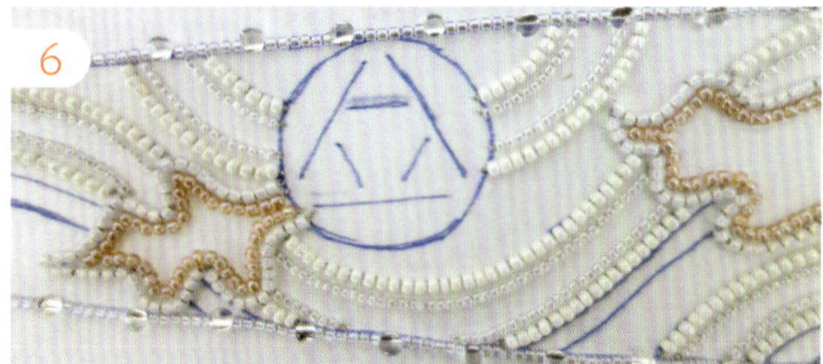

Stitch beads continuously from the front side of the fabric with a hook needle and 1.5 mm transparent seed beads to mark the second layer of lines at a distance of approximately 1 mm from the inner side of the lines marked in step 5.

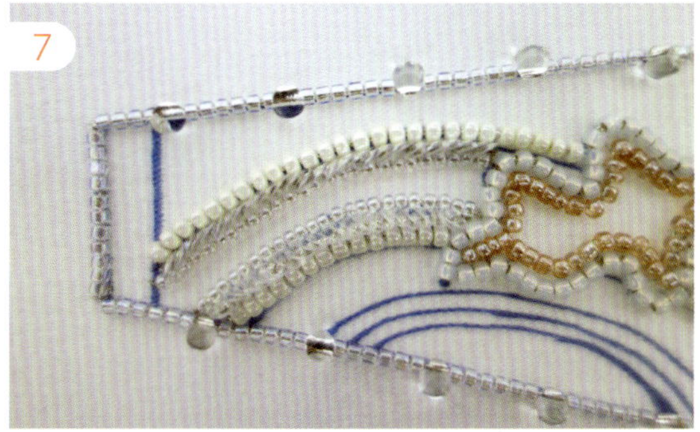

Stitch sequins continuously from the front side of the fabric with a hook needle and 3 mm silver cup sequins to fill up the area between the lines marked in steps 5 and 6. The cup sequins should be neatly arranged at approximately 70 degrees to the embroidered surface to form a three-dimensional effect.

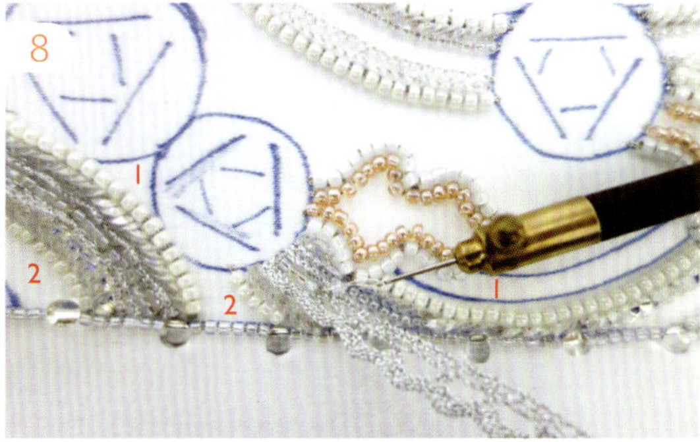

Stitch beads continuously from the front side of the fabric with a hook needle, 1.5 mm transparent seed beads, and 8 mm silver pattern ribbon to fill up the the empty portions between the main lines 1 and 2. When stitching the beads, press the ribbon downwards with the seed beads, and stitch them normally and continuously thereafter.

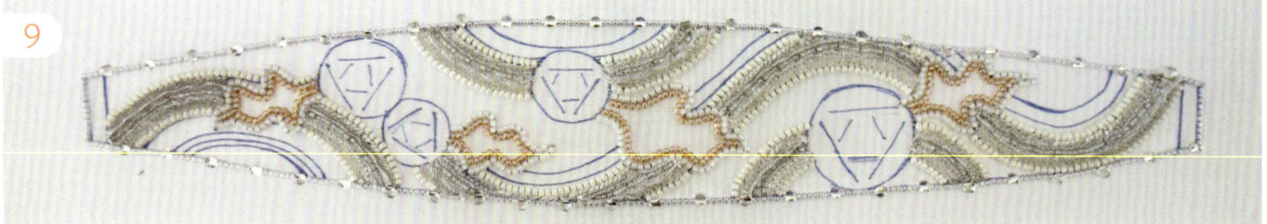

9

The overall effect is shown in the figure.

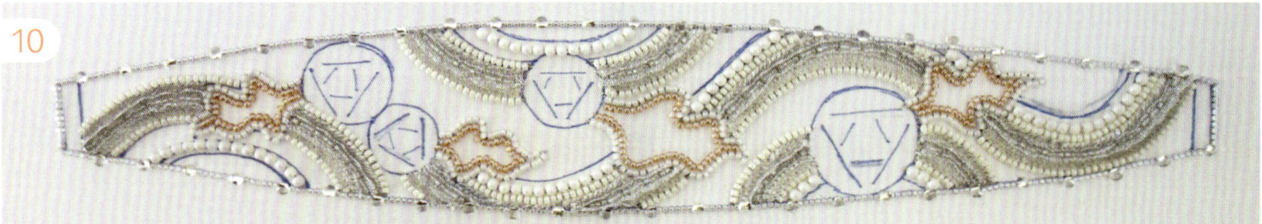

10

Stitch beads continuously from the front side of the fabric with a hook needle, 2 mm creamy white seed beads, and 3 mm white pearls to finish the remaining lines.

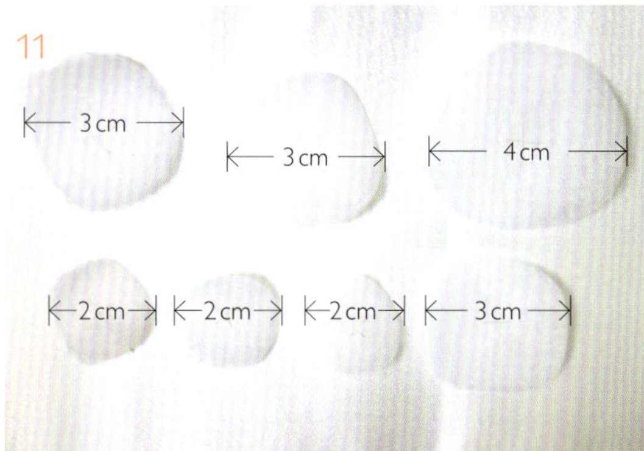

Fold the organza in half twice, and cut round shapes with diameters of 4 cm, 3 cm, and 2 cm respectively. Make one set of 4 cm shapes, three sets of 3 cm, and 2 cm. Each set should have four pieces. Sew a cross in the center of each shape with a hand sewing needle.

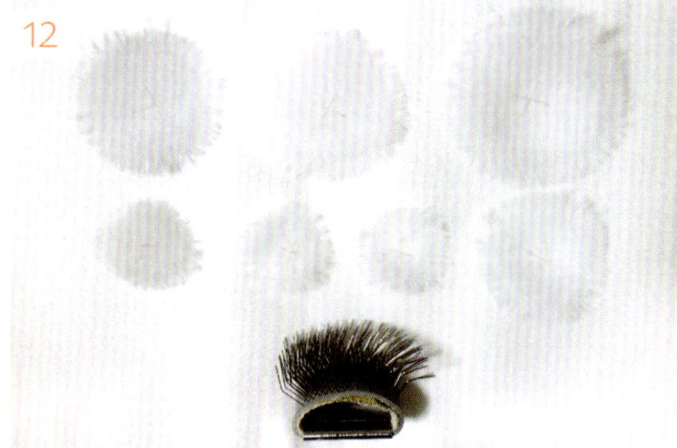

12

Brush the edges (about 5 mm) of the cut fabric circles with a small steel comb. If you do not have a small steel comb, rub the edges with your fingers.

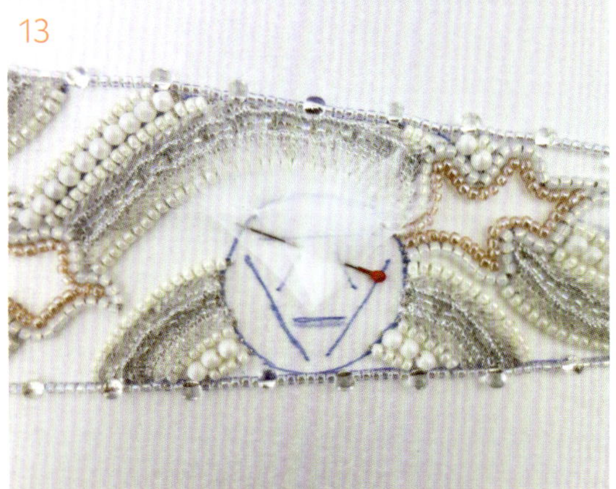

13

Remove the crossing thread in the center of the fabric. Take a piece of 4 cm organza, fold it in half twice, and fix it on the largest flower pattern with a ball head pin.

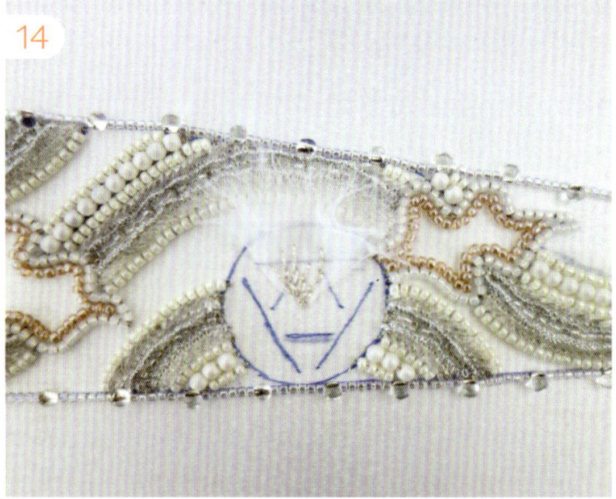

14

Use the pulling stitch technique with a hook needle and silver embroidery thread to sew the fabric in a fixed position, which forms a petal.

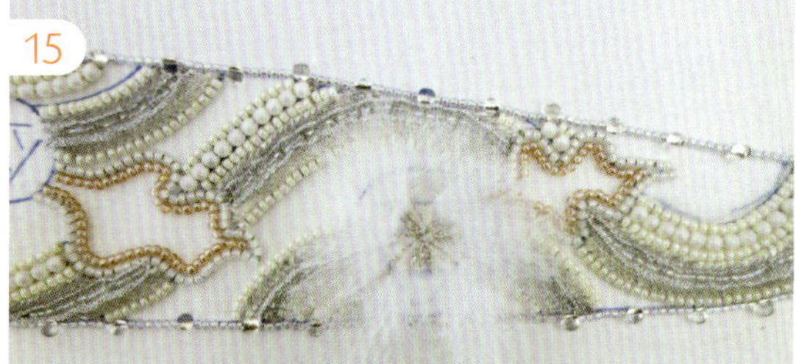

Use the same techniques and materials in steps 13 and 14 to sew petals of a flower, of which three 4 cm round organza shapes form the first layer, with three 3 cm round organza shapes superimposed on that layer.

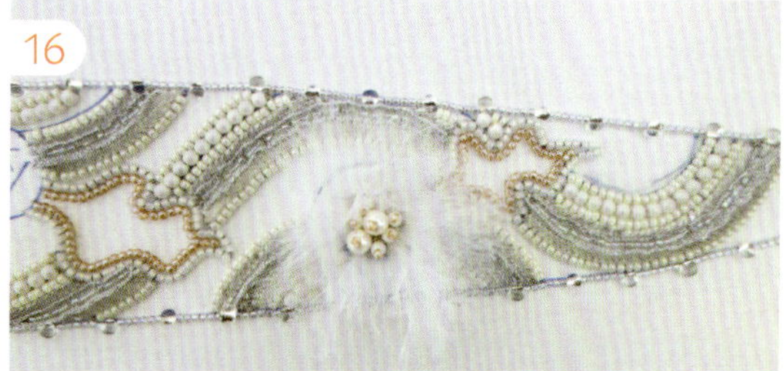

Use the technique of embroidering a bead on top of a pearl with a hand sewing needle, 3 mm and 5 mm white pearls, and 2 mm transparent flesh-colored seed beads to sew the stamen. The number and specific position of the pearls can be designed according to your preference.

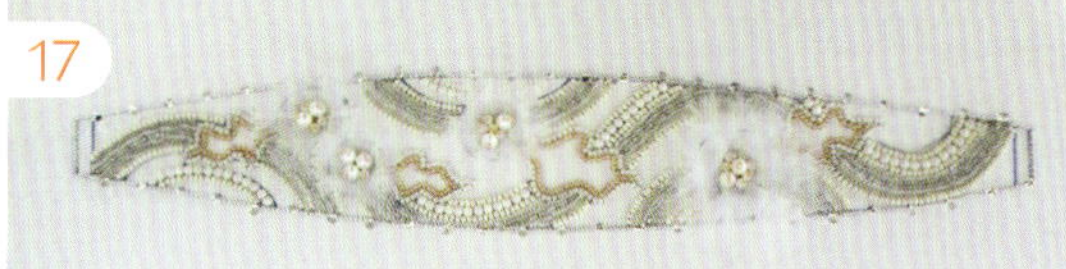

Use the same techniques and materials as the first flower in steps 13 to 16, coupled with 3 cm and 2 cm round organza, to complete the other three flowers.

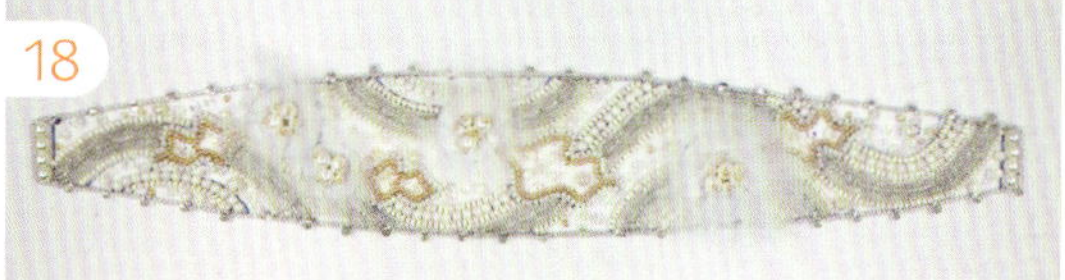

With a hand sewing needle, stitch 1.6 mm transparent seed beads, 2 mm transparent flesh-colored seed beads, 3 mm transparent crystals, 3 mm silver cup sequins, and 3 mm white pearls to fill the remaining spaces of the pattern, for instance, the flower edges and middle of the leaves. Then, sew four 4 mm white pearls side by side at the left and right ends.

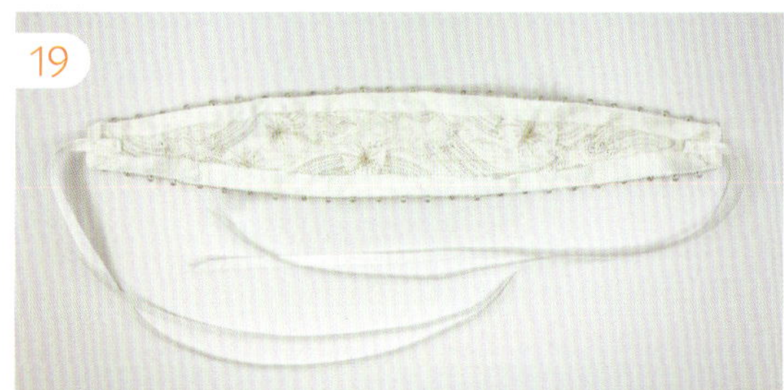

Cut the embroidery piece along the outer contour with a seam allowance of 1 cm, and press the seam allowance inward with an iron. Fix a white grosgrain ribbon with a folded length of approximately 20 cm on both sides with a hand sewing needle.

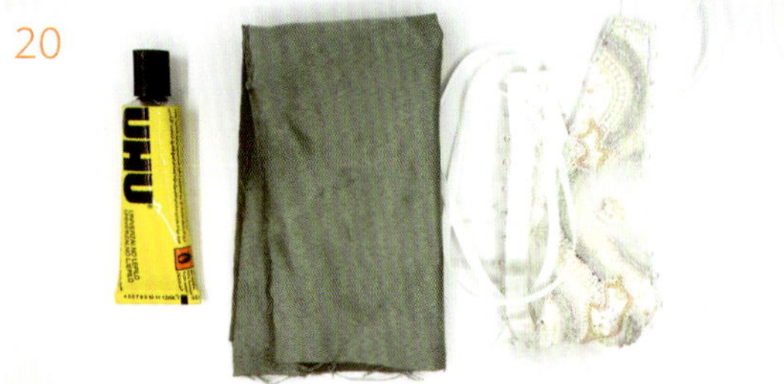

Prepare the fabric glue and velvet. Next, glue the velvet on the back of the embroidery piece and cut it along the embroidery piece. Then, trim the edges.

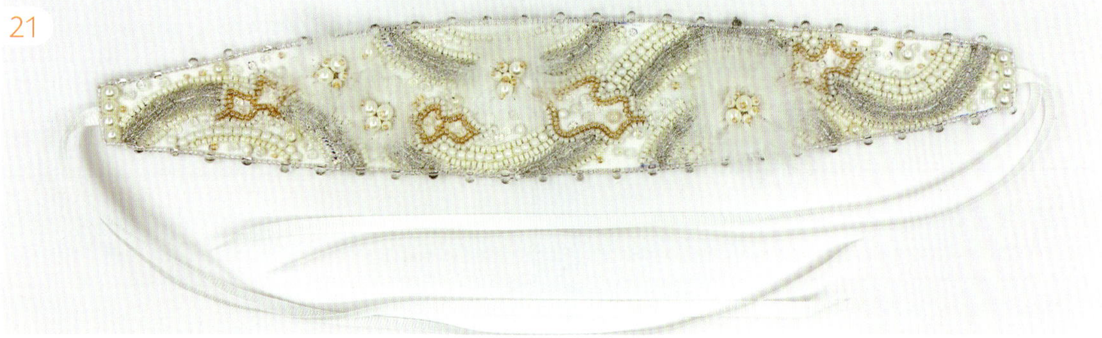

Allow the glue to dry. The hair accessory is now complete.

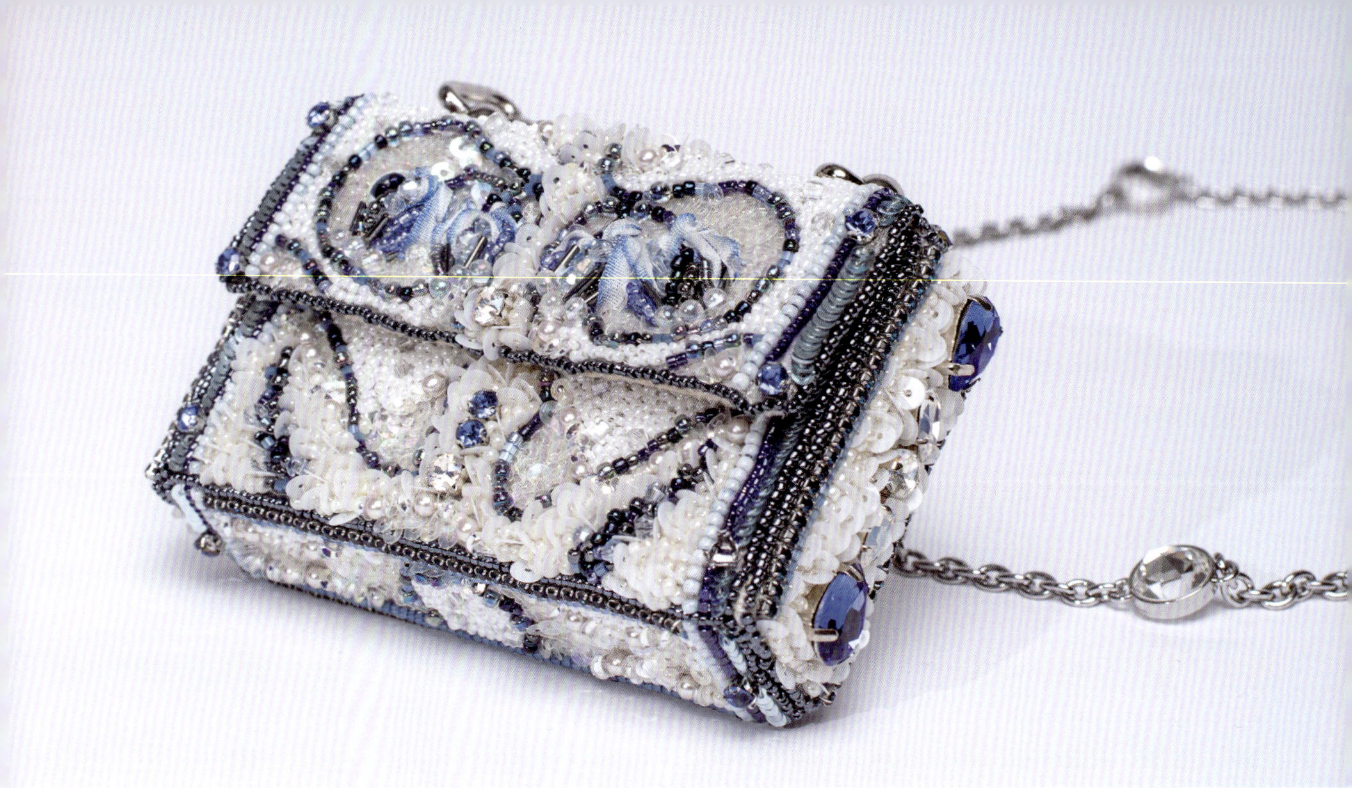

7. Mini Chinese Enkianthus Bag

Chinese enkianthus (fuchsia hybrida) have a distinctive shape, resembling lanterns hanging upside down, usually in red, purple, or white. When in full bloom, the petals cascade as if they were dancers attending a banquet in full costume, dancing freely on the branches with lively enthusiasm. In Chinese culture, lanterns are hung during auspicious events, as they represent peace and luck. Chinese enkianthus in turn have positive connotations. This project creatively combines flower patterns with blue and white porcelain colors to create a traditional but stylish mini bag.

Embroidery Steps

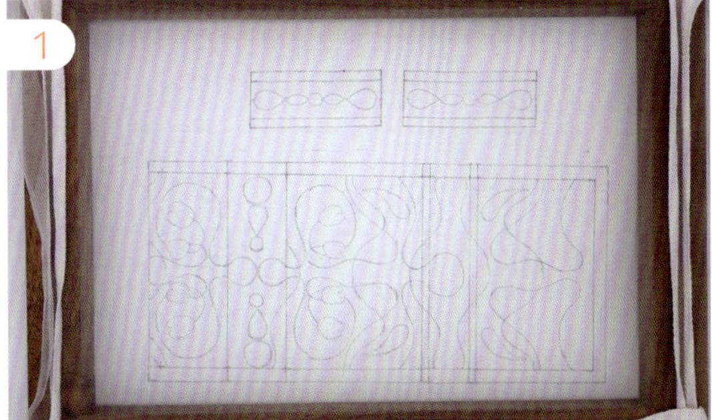

1 Stretch the white organza on the embroidery frame and draw patterns (see page 165) on it using a heat erasable marker.

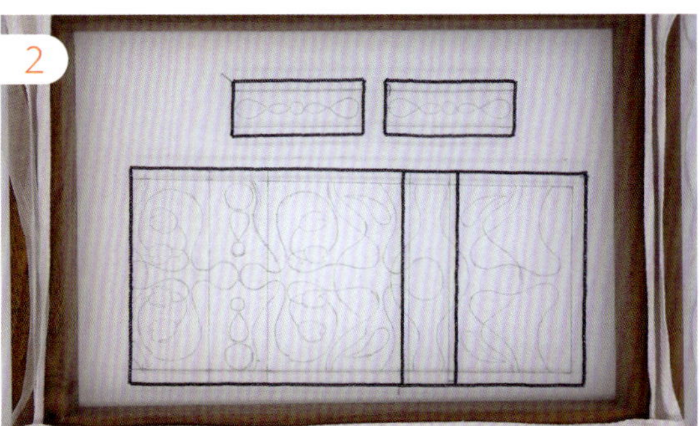

2 Apply the technique of stitching beads from the back side of the fabric using a hook needle, dark blue embroidery thread, and 1.5 mm dark blue seed beads to mark the outlines.

You Will Need

Threads	embroidery thread	dark blue, silver, beige
Beads	seed beads	1.5 mm white, 1.5 mm purple, 1.5 mm dark blue, 2 mm light blue, 2 mm dark blue, 2 mm medium blue, 2 mm gray, 2 mm beige, 3 mm dark blue, 3 mm white
	sequins	3 mm light blue, 3 mm silver and white, 3 mm transparent AB color, 4 mm beige
	crystals	3 mm light blue, 3 mm white
	rhinestone chains	2 mm blue
	drop beads	4 mm transparent
	tube beads	6 mm gray
	sew-on rhinestones	4 mm round blue, 5 mm round white, 8 mm round blue, 9 × 15 mm AB colored shield shape, 10 × 15 mm blue drop shape, 5 × 10 mm egg white horse eye shape
	pearls	4 mm white
Fabrics	4 mm blue gradient ribbon, white organza, gray self-adhesive velvet, beige velvet	
Tools	embroidery frame, 70# hook needle, hand sewing needle, scissors, fabric glue, heat erasable marker, utility knife, iron, ball head pins, 15 × 2 mm magnets, cardboard, 12 mm silver D ring stud screw ball post head buttons, bag chains	

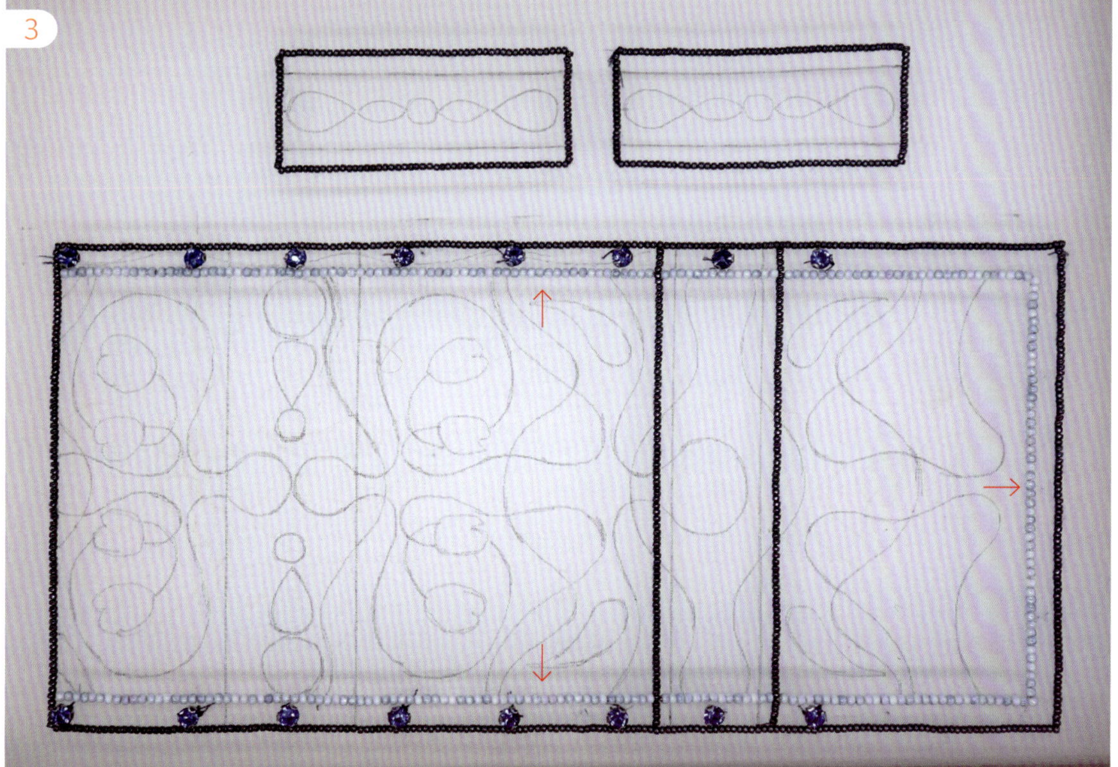

Apply the technique of stitching beads from the back side of the fabric using a hook needle, silver embroidery thread, and 2 mm light blue seed beads to mark the lines shown by red arrows in the figure.

Use a hand sewing needle and dark blue embroidery thread to fix the 4 mm round blue sew-on rhinestones in the position shown in the figure.

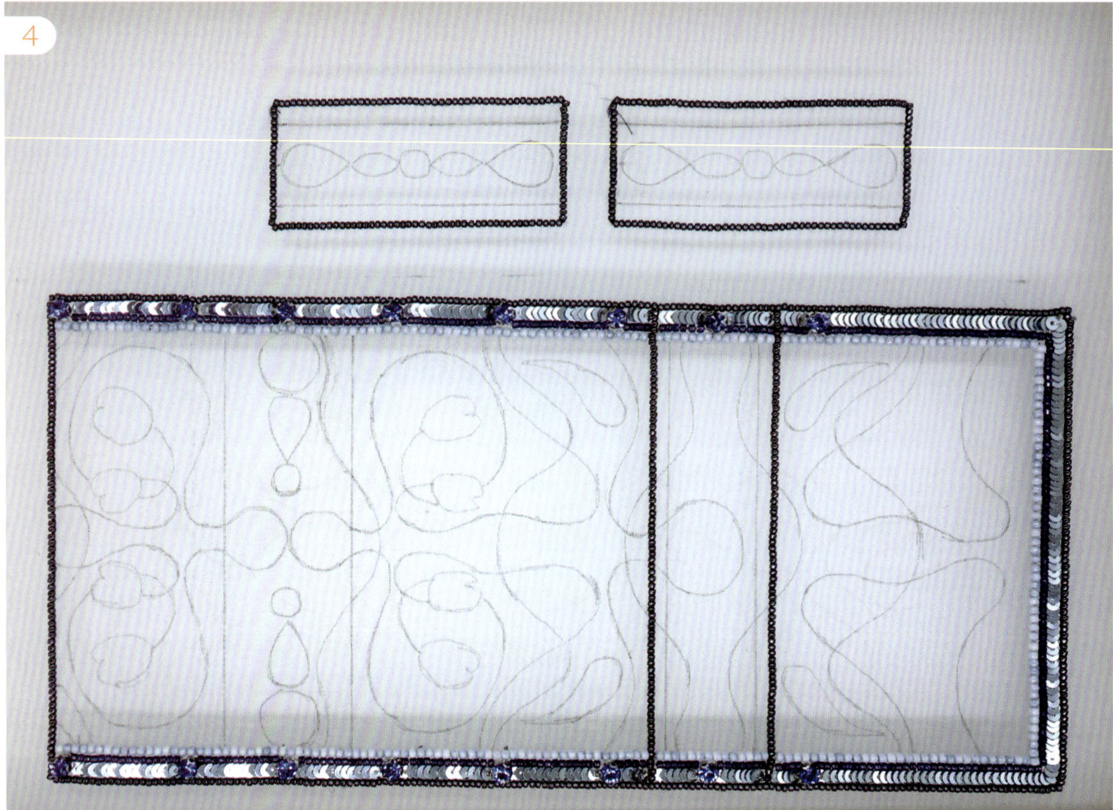

Apply the technique of stitching sequins from the back side of the fabric using a hook needle, silver embroidery thread, and 3 mm light blue sequins along the outer outline to mark the upper, lower, and right sides of the inner ring.

Apply the technique of stitching beads from the back side of the fabric using a hook needle, dark blue embroidery thread, and 1.5 mm purple seed beads to fill the gap between the light blue seed beads and light blue sequins.

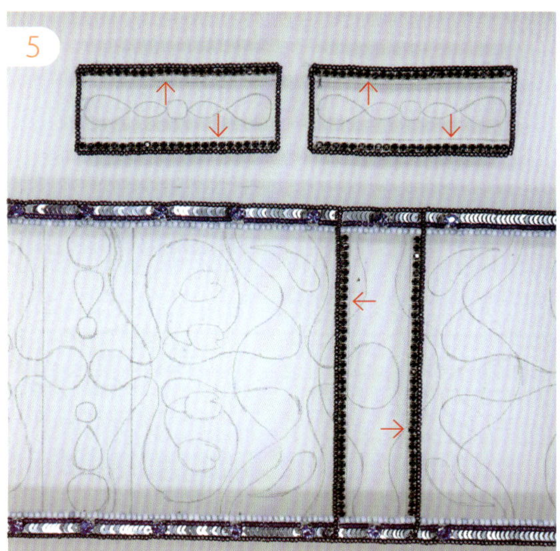

Fix the 2 mm blue rhinestone chains with a hand sewing needle and silver embroidery thread to sew the lines shown by arrows in the figure.

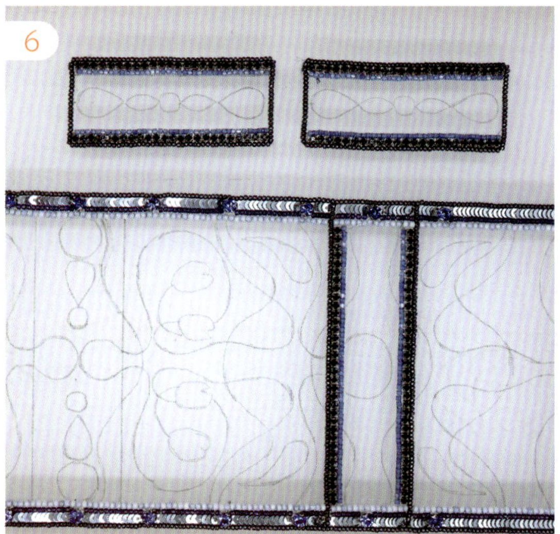

Apply the technique of stitching beads from the back side of the fabric using a hook needle, silver embroidery thread, and 2 mm medium blue seed beads to sew along the rhinestone chains from the previous step.

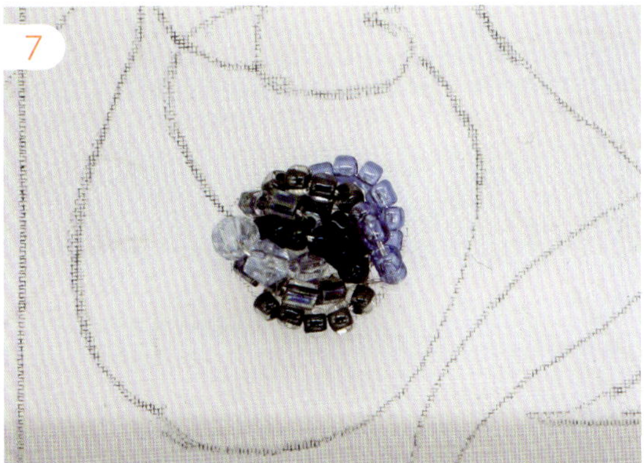

Apply the technique of embroidering beads groups using a hand sewing needle, silver embroidery thread, 3 mm light blue crystals, 2 mm dark blue seed beads, 2 mm medium blue seed beads, and 2 mm gray seed beads to sew the flower.

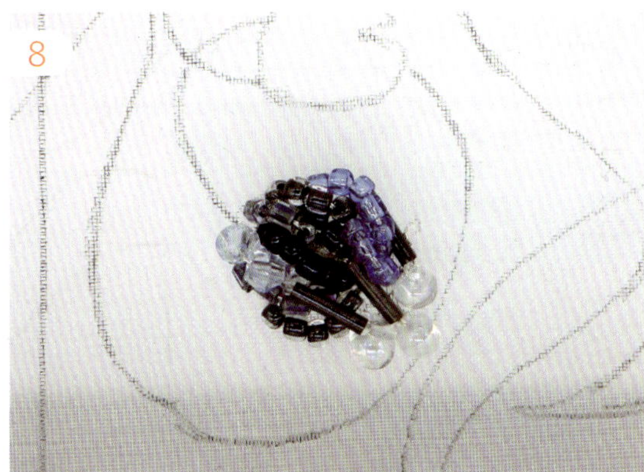

Apply the technique of embroidering a single bead using a hand sewing needle, silver embroidery thread, 6 mm gray tube beads, and 4 mm transparent drop beads to sew the stamen.

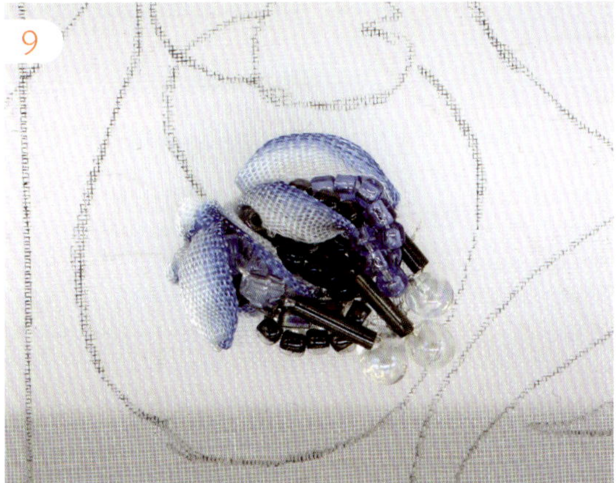

Sew the petals with the hand sewing needle and blue gradient ribbon.

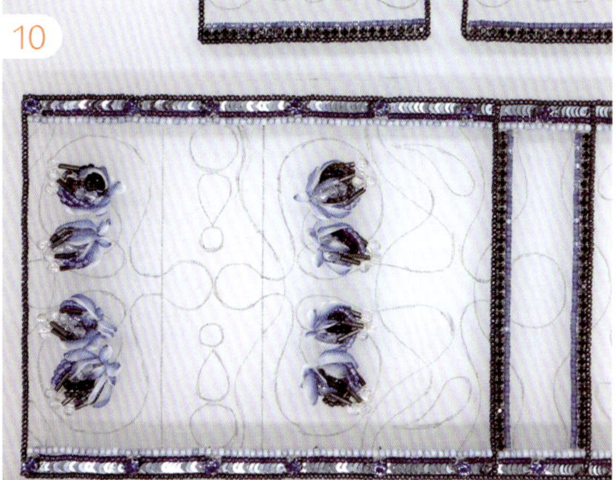

Repeat the techniques shown in steps 7 to 9 to sew the remaining flowers.

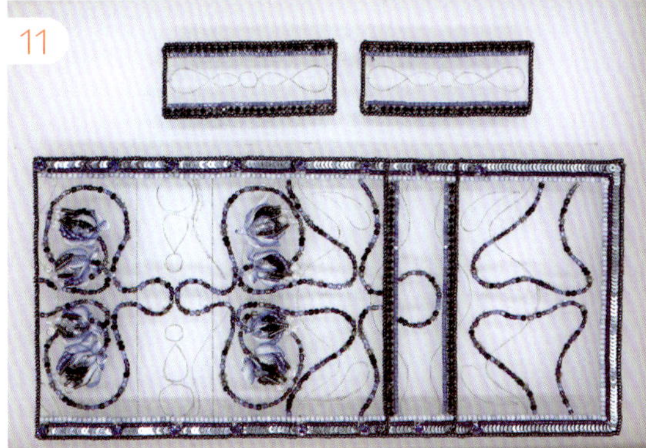

Apply the technique of stitching beads from the front side of the fabric using a hook needle, dark blue embroidery thread, 1.5 mm purple seed beads, 2 mm light blue seed beads, 2 mm medium blue seed beads, 2 mm dark blue seed beads, and 3 mm dark blue seed beads placed in an irregular order to sew the lines shown in the figure.

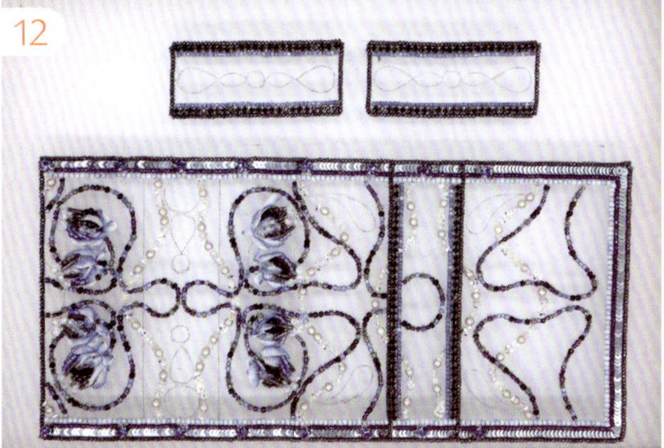

Apply the technique of stitching beads from the front side of the fabric using a hook needle, silver embroidery thread, 2 mm beige seed beads, 3 mm silver and white sequins, and 4 mm white pearls placed in an irregular order to sew the lines shown in the figure.

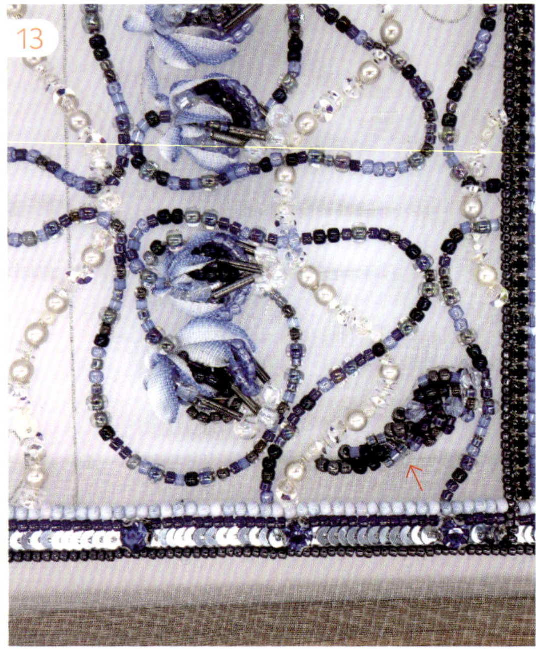

Apply the technique of embroidering beads groups from the front side of the fabric using a hook needle, dark blue embroidery threads, 2 mm light blue seed beads, 2 mm medium blue seed beads, 2 mm dark blue seed beads, and 3 mm dark blue seed beads placed in an irregular order to sew the leaf.

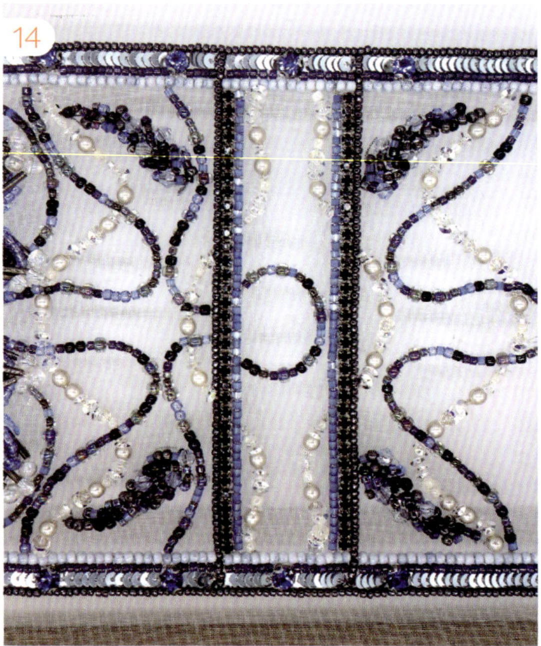

Apply the technique shown in step 13 to sew the remaining three leaves.

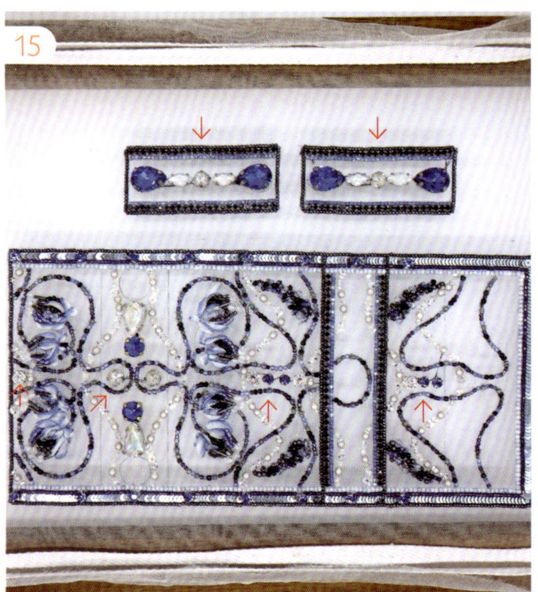

Apply the technique of fixing sew-on rhinestones with a hand sewing needle, and stitch the 4 mm round blue rhinestones, 5 mm round white rhinestones, 8 mm round blue rhinestones, 9 × 15 mm AB colored shield shape rhinestones, 10 × 15 mm blue drop rhinestones, and 5 × 10 mm egg white horse eye shape rhinestones with the beige embroidery thread to fix them in the positions shown by the arrows.

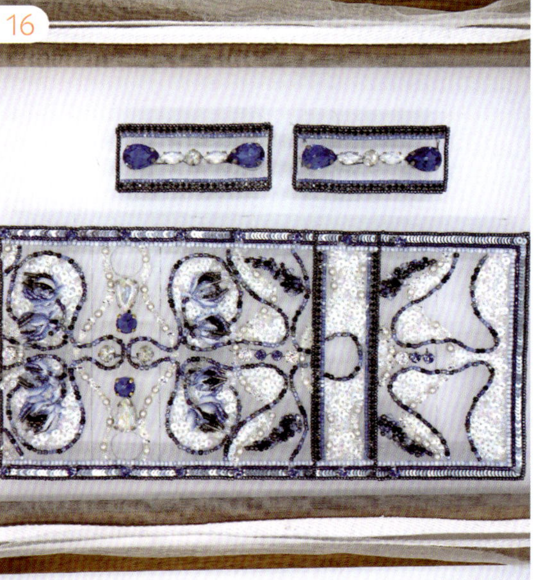

Apply the technique of stitching beads irregularly from the back side of the fabric using a hook needle, silver embroidery thread, and 3 mm transparent AB color sequins to fill the areas shown in the figure.

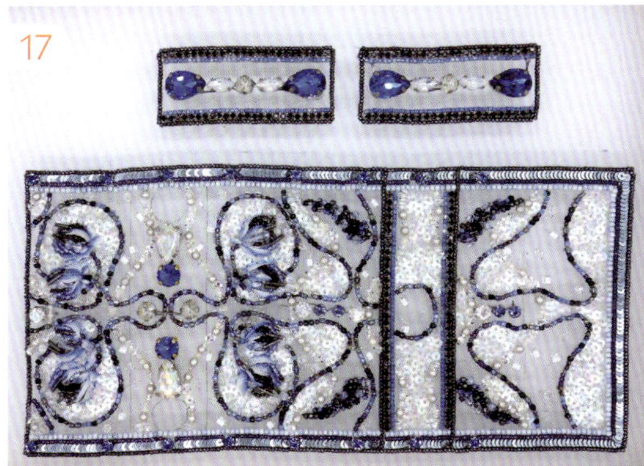

Apply the technique of stitching beads from the front side of the fabric using a hook needle and silver embroidery thread to sew the 3 mm white seed beads and 3 mm white crystals in the areas indicated in the figure.

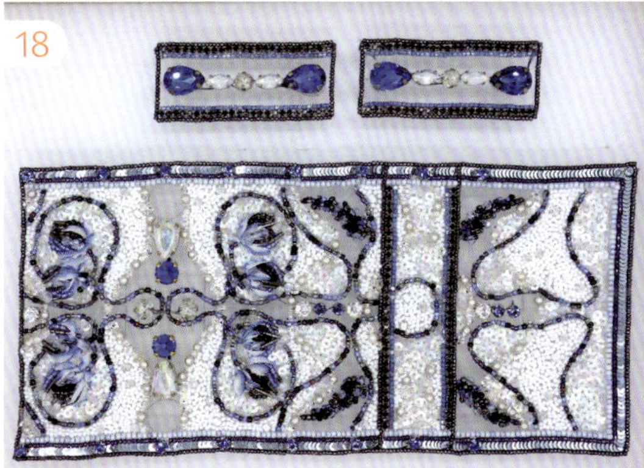

Apply the technique of stitching beads irregularly from the back side of the fabric using a hook needle, silver embroidery thread, and 1.5 mm white seed beads to fill the areas decorated in step 17.

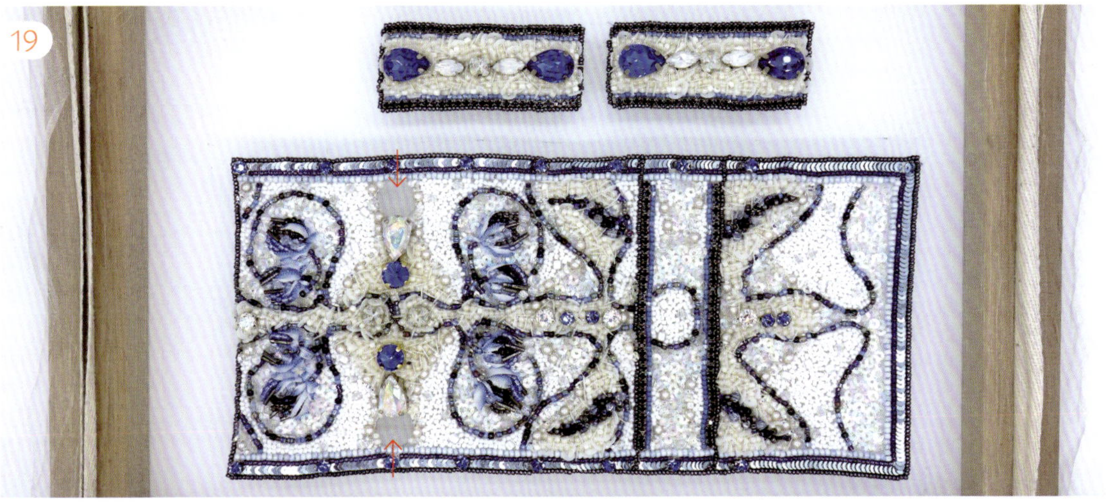

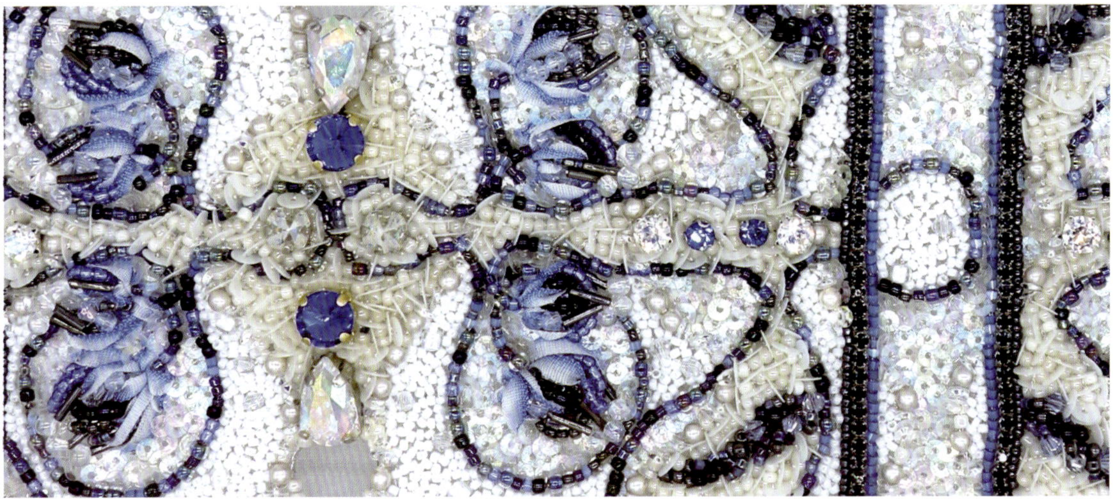

19

Apply the technique of stitching beads irregularly from the back side of the fabric using a hook needle, silver embroidery thread, and 2 mm beige beads to fill the remaining areas, excluding the two circular areas indicated by the arrows. Next, apply the technique of securing a sequin using a hand sewing needle and silver embroidery thread to fix the 4 mm beige sequins vertically in the gaps between the seed beads.

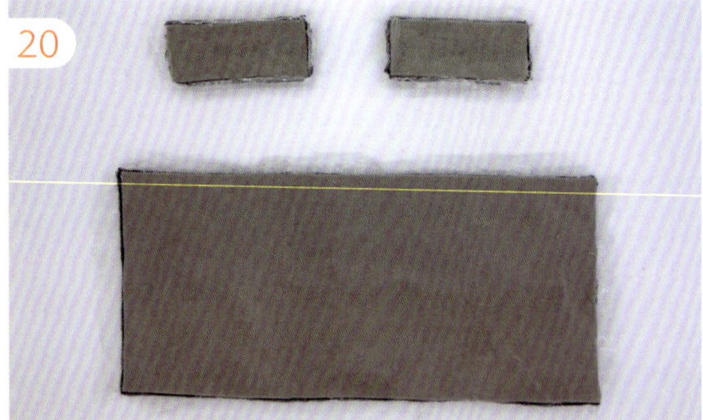

Paste the gray self-adhesive velvet on the back of the embroidery pieces and cut them, leaving a margin of about 5 mm.

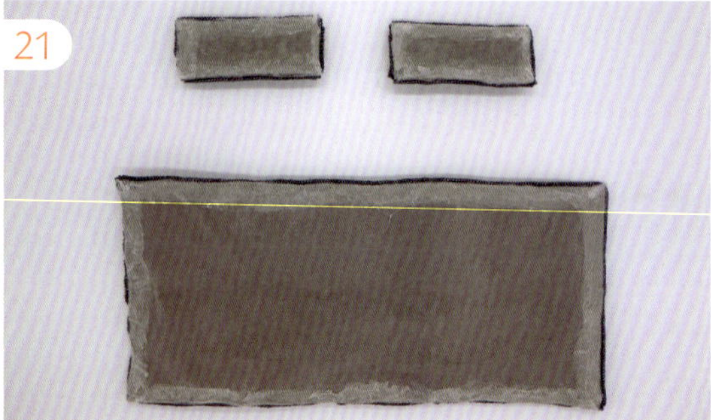

Fold the remaining parts of the organza inward, and stick it on the gray velvet using fabric glue.

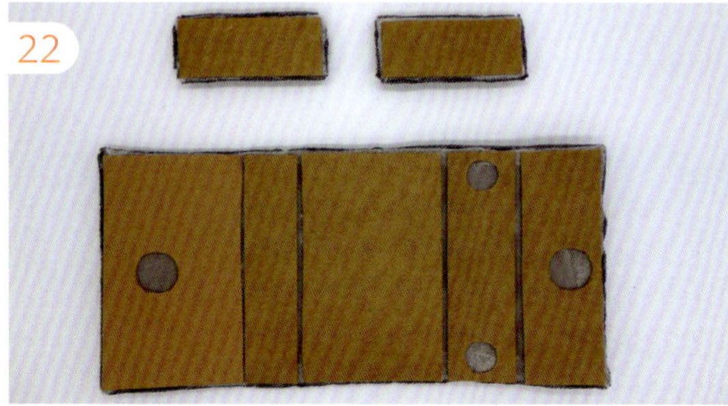

Cut the cardboard into areas. Cut four circles with a utility knife, and stick the cardboard pieces onto the corresponding positions of the embroidery pieces using fabric glue.

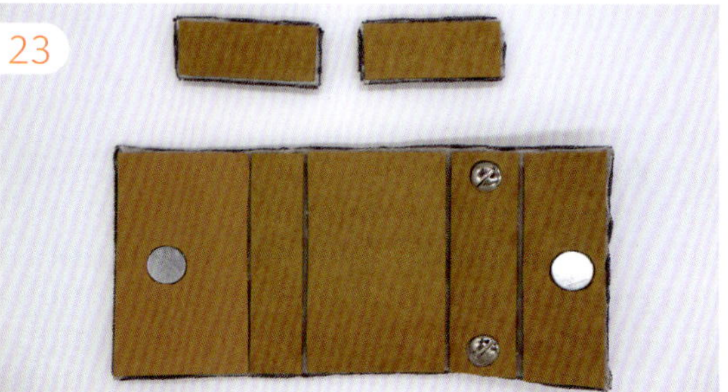

Place the 12 mm silver D ring stud screw ball post head buttons on the upper and lower parts of the cardboard (second piece from the right) and use fabric glue to stick the 15 × 2 mm magnets on the leftmost and rightmost cardboards where the blanks are reserved. Be mindful of where the positive and negative poles of these magnets are.

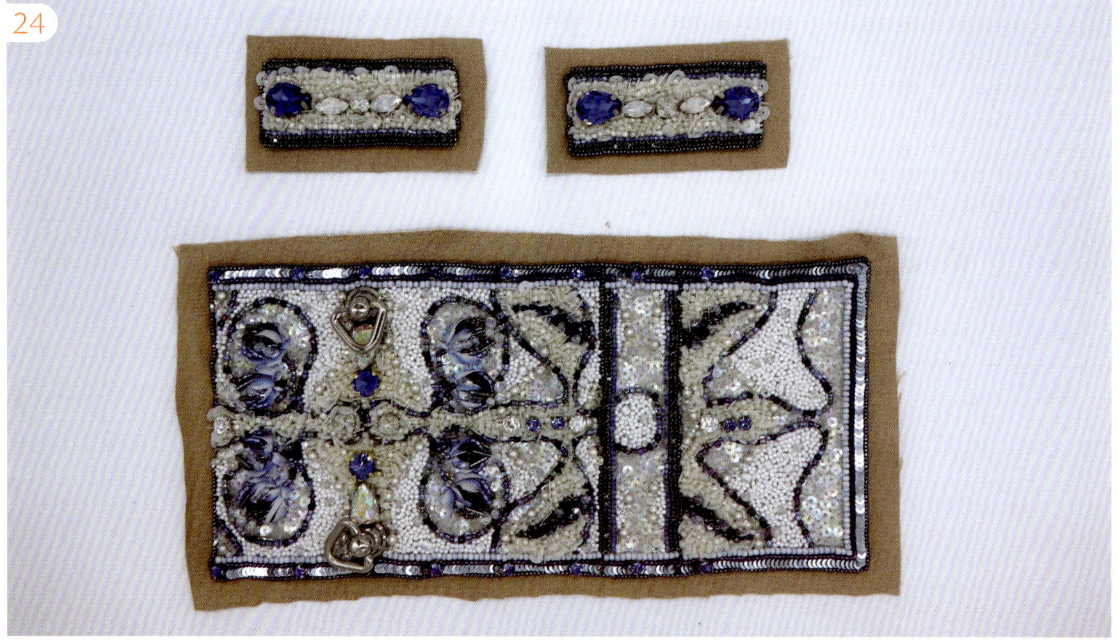

Cut beige velvet of appropriate sizes, and leave a margin about 5 mm bigger than the embroidered pieces.

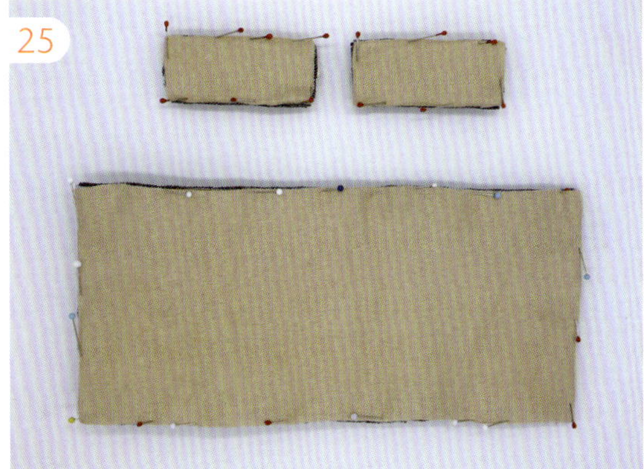

Fold the velvet margin inward to hide it. Ensure that the fabric is flat, and fix them with ball head pins.

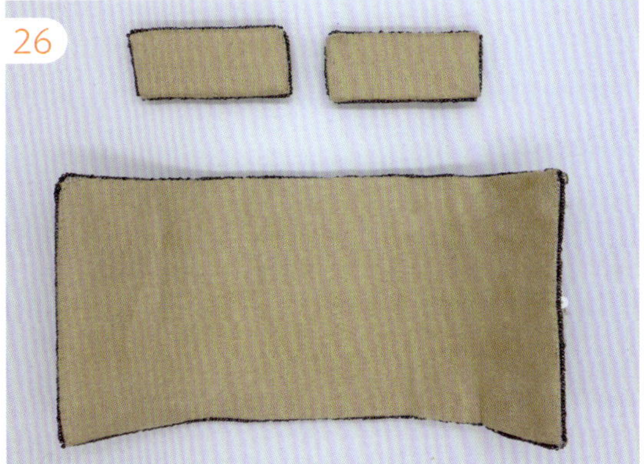

Sew the velvet to the embroidery pieces using a hand sewing needle and beige embroidery thread, ensuring that the fabric is flat.

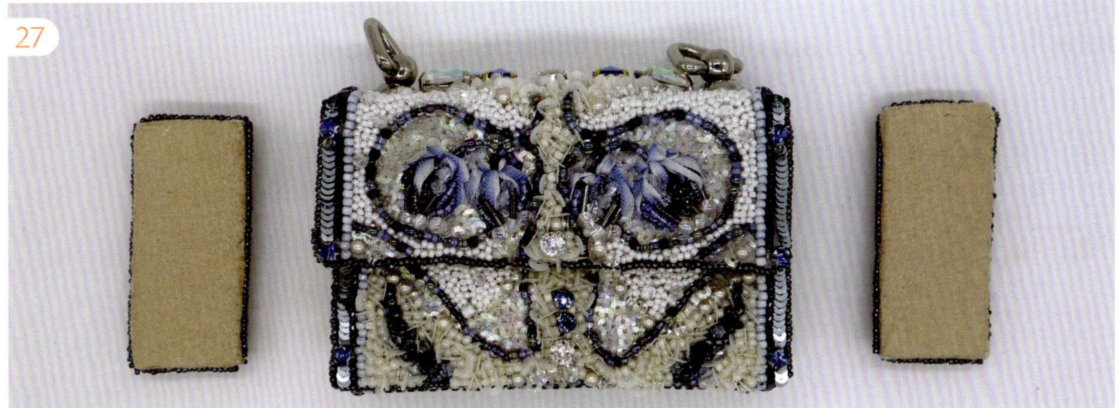

Sew the two small embroidery pieces onto the two sides to the main body using a hand sewing needle and beige embroidery thread.

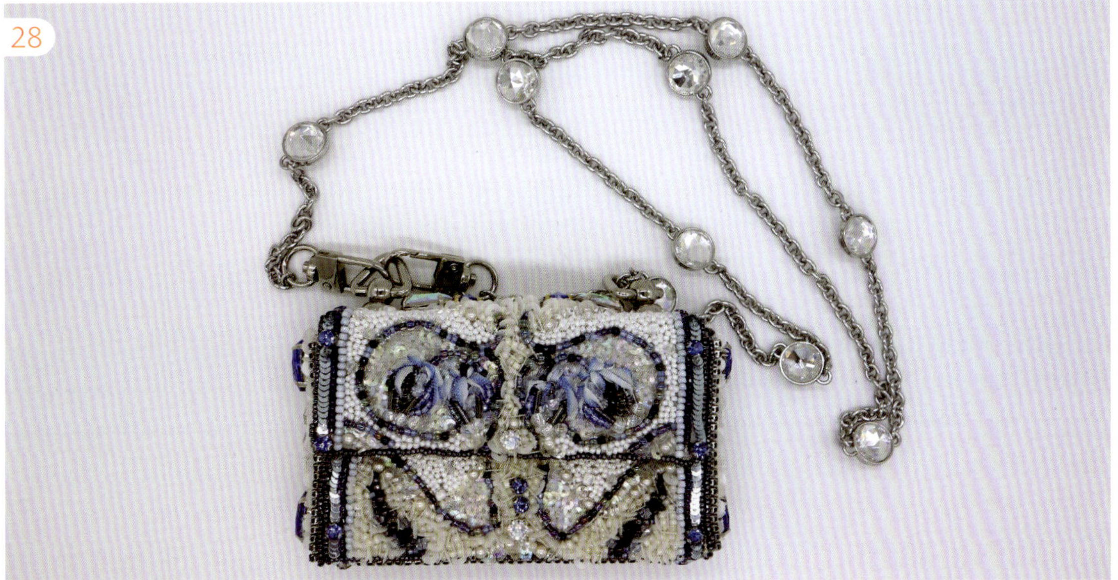

Attach the bag chain. The work is now complete.

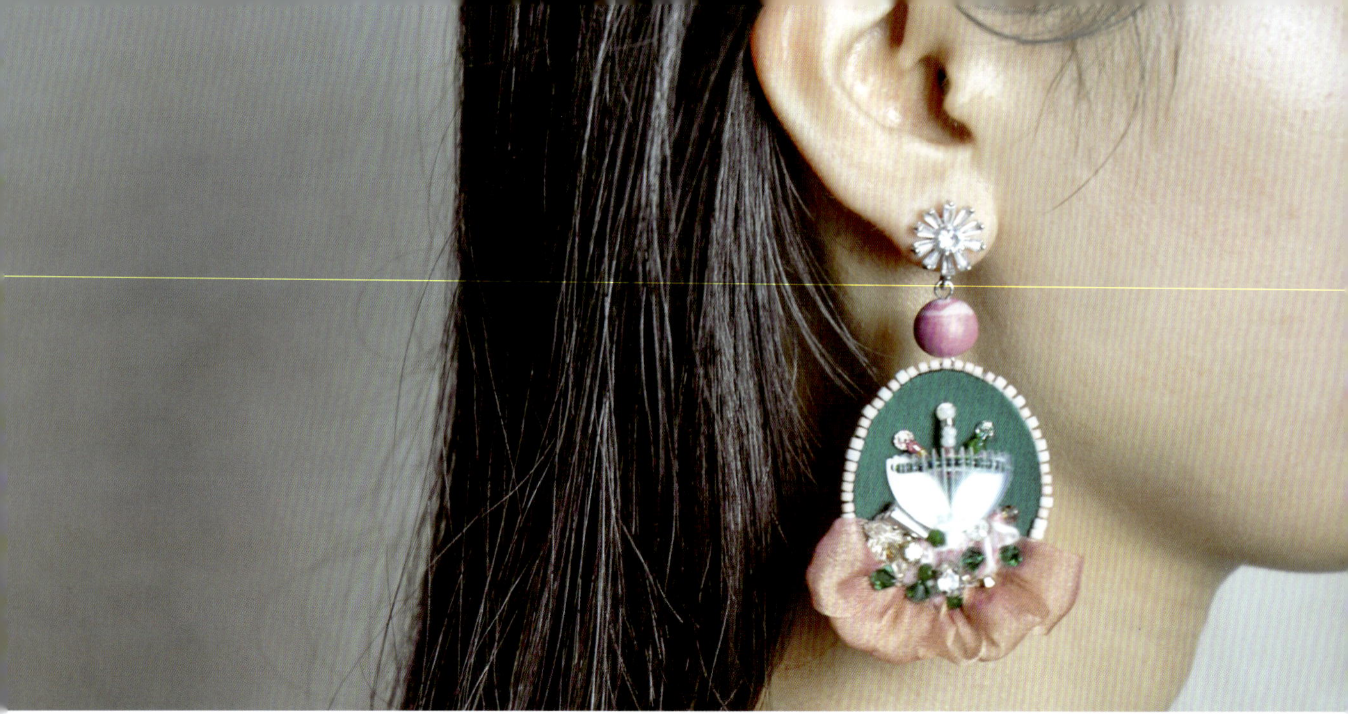

8. Canterbury Bells Earrings

When Canterbury bells hang from their stems, they look like a string of bells swaying in the wind. They have a bountiful variation of colors, comprising mainly blue, purple, and peach, and symbolize the warmth and gentleness of love. This piece uses clear horse eye sequins to simulate the light and breathable texture of the Canterbury bells' petals, while the embellished ribbons depict the movements of dancers.

You Will Need

Threads	embroidery thread	invisible
	ribbon	15 mm orange
	yarn	champagne silver, pink gradient
Beads	seed beads	1.5 mm pink, 1.5 mm orange, 2 mm white, 2 mm silver, 2 mm peach, 2 mm dark green
	tube beads	2 mm green
	crystals	3 mm brown, 3 mm dark green, 4 mm dark green, 4 × 8 mm silver trapezoidal
	lochrosen rhinestones	3 mm white, 4 mm white
	sew-on rhinestones	4 × 6 mm drop shape, 3 mm white
	sequins	5 × 12 mm clear horse eye shape
	pearls	10 mm pink gradient
Fabrics	green satin, white organza, 8 mm regenerated leather	
Tools	embroidery hoop, 70# hook needle, hand sewing needle, scissors, fabric glue, heat erasable marker, pliers, silver eye pins, daisy stud earrings	

Embroidery Steps

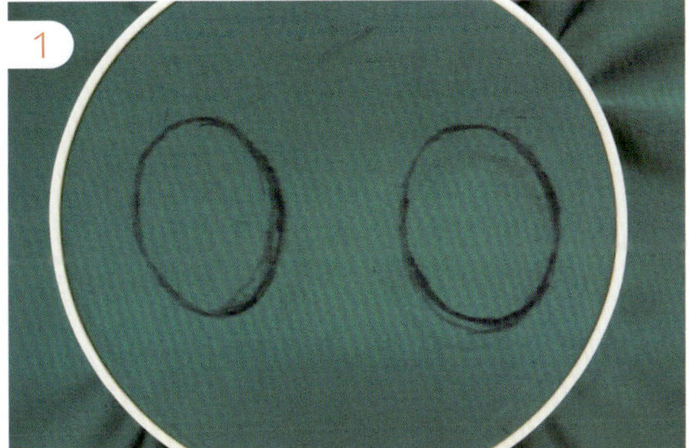

Stretch the green satin on the embroidery hoop and draw the patterns (see page 166) with a heat erasable marker.

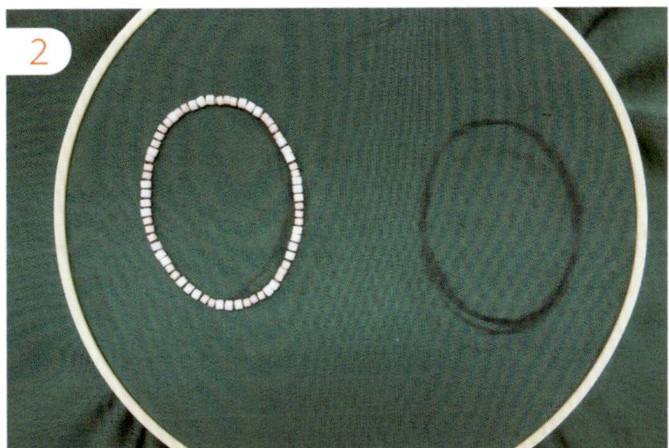

Apply the technique of stitching beads from the front side of the fabric using a hook needle, invisible thread, 1.5 mm pink seed beads, and 2 mm white seed beads to sew the outline along the pattern in an irregular order.

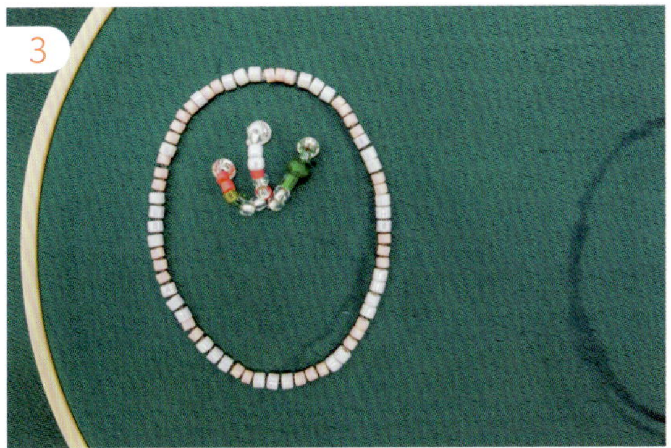

Use a hand sewing needle and invisible thread to fix 1.5 mm orange seed beads, 2 mm white seed beads, 2 mm silver seed beads, 2 mm peach seed beads, 2 mm dark green seed beads, 3 mm white lochrosen rhinestones, and 3 mm dark green crystals in three rows. The color and positions of the beads can be arranged according to your preference.

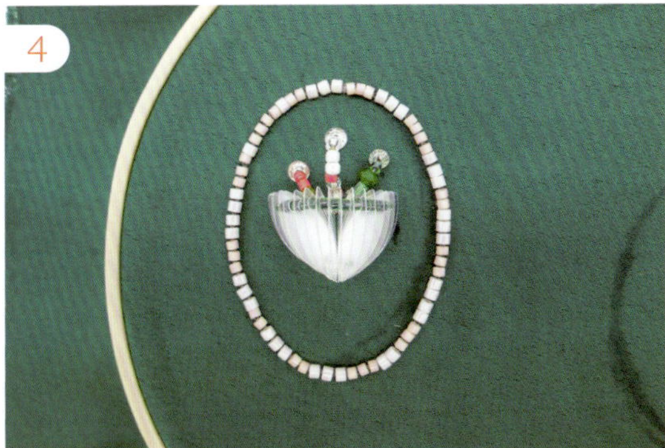

Use a hand sewing needle and invisible thread to fix seventeen 5 × 12 mm clear horse eye sequins at the position as shown in the picture. Use 2 mm dark green seed beads in an alternating fashion at the upper end of the sequins, and fix the lower ends with invisible thread.

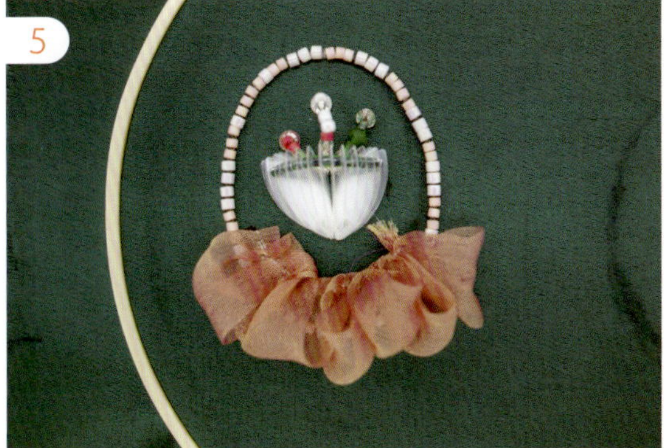

Fix the 15 mm orange ribbon in pleats just below the pattern. The ribbon should cover about a third of the circumference of the pattern's outline.

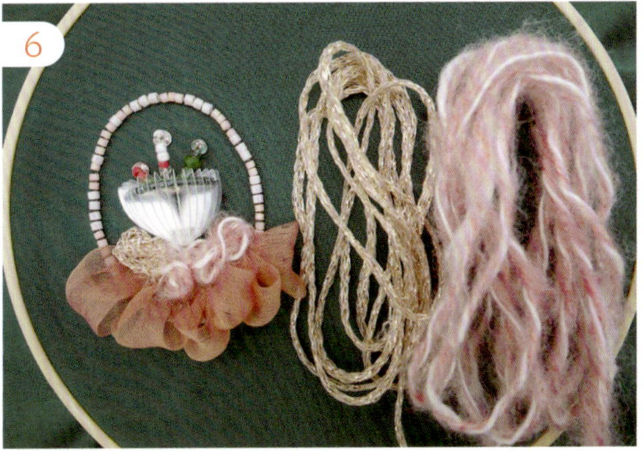

Use a hand sewing needle and invisible thread to fix the champagne silver yarn and pink gradient yarn in the gap between the horse eye sequins and ribbon in an irregular fashion. Make sure to cover the stitches of the ribbon.

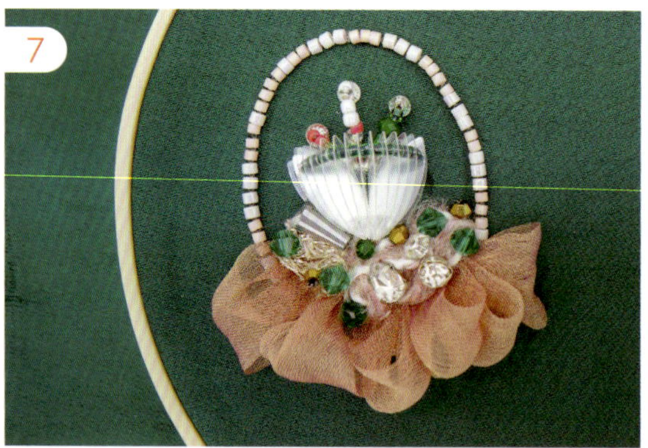

Use a hand sewing needle and invisible thread to fix the 4 mm white lochrosen rhinestones, 4 × 6 mm drop sew-on rhinestones, 3 mm white sew-on rhinestones, 3 mm dark green crystals, 3 mm brown crystals, 4 × 8 mm silver trapezoidal crystals, and 4 mm dark green crystals irregularly around the stitches of both yarns.

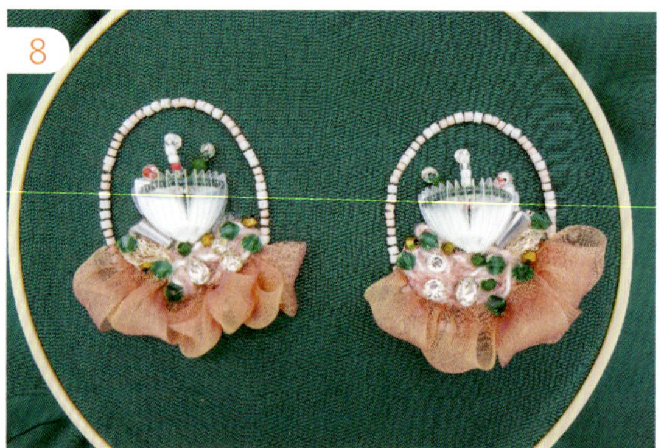

Use the same materials and techniques in steps 2–7 to complete another pattern.

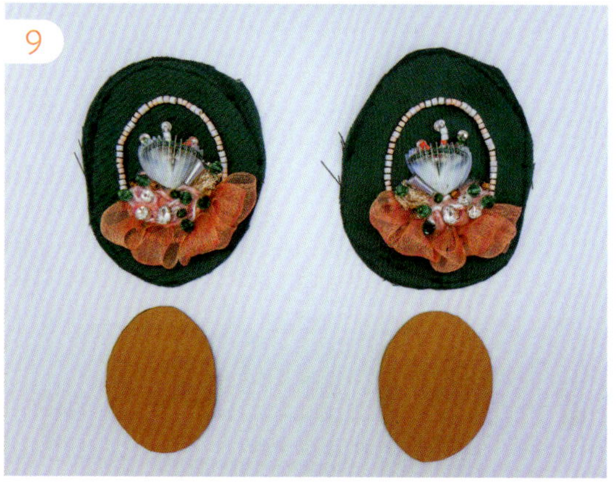

Cut out the embroidered pieces, leaving an allowance of about 10 mm, and prepare two pieces of 8 mm thick regenerated leather.

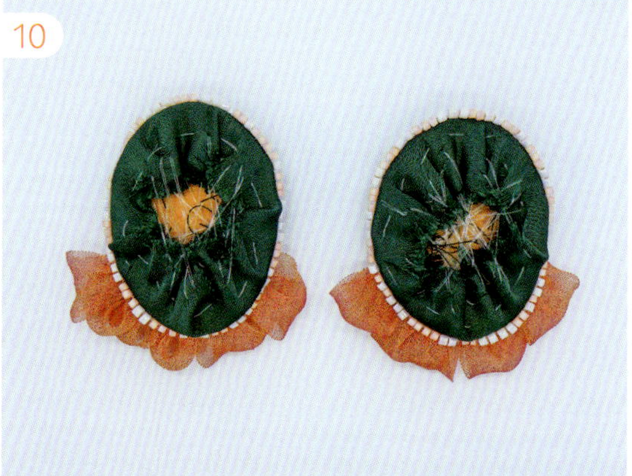

Place the 8 mm regenerated leather on the back of the embroidery pieces. Use a hand sewing needle and invisible thread to sew the 10 mm fabric allowance and wrap the regenerated leather.

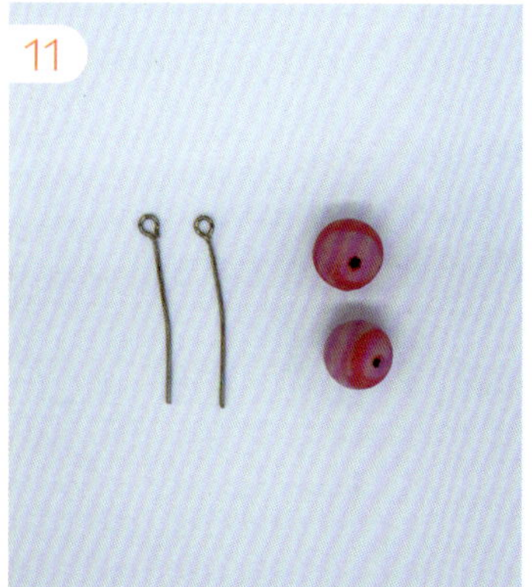

Prepare two eye pins and two 10 mm pink gradient pearls.

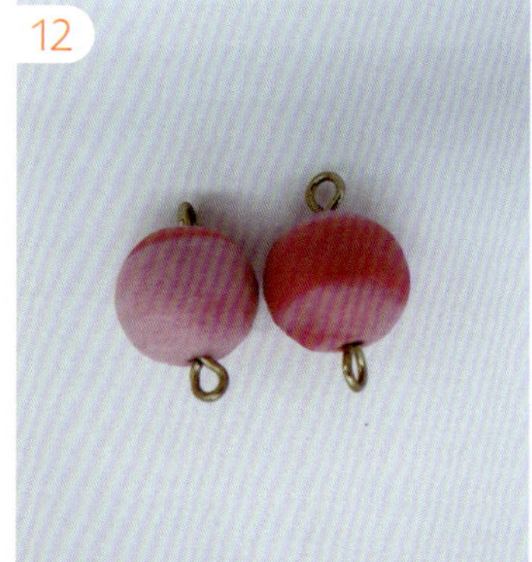

Thread the eye pins through the pink gradient pearls, and use pliers to form circles on the other side of the pearls to fix them.

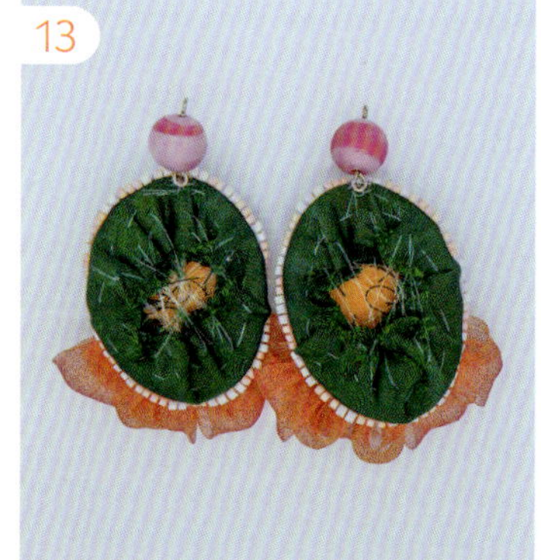

Use a hand sewing needle and invisible thread to fix the small ring of the pink gradient pearls directly above the back of the embroidery pieces.

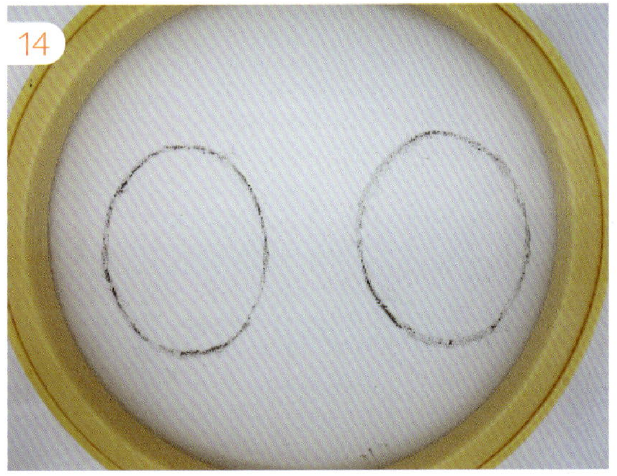

Start sewing the pieces on the back of the embroidery. Stretch another piece of white organza and draw patterns that are the same size as the back of the overall embroidery pieces with a heat erasable marker.

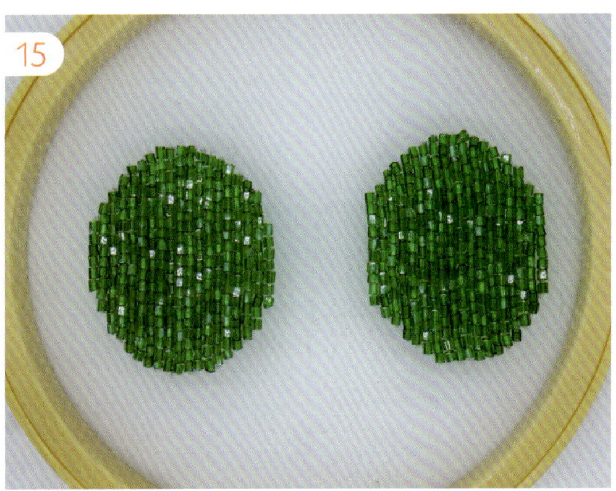

Apply the technique of stitching beads from the back side of the fabric using a hook needle, invisible thread, and 2 mm green tube beads to fill the patterns lengthwise.

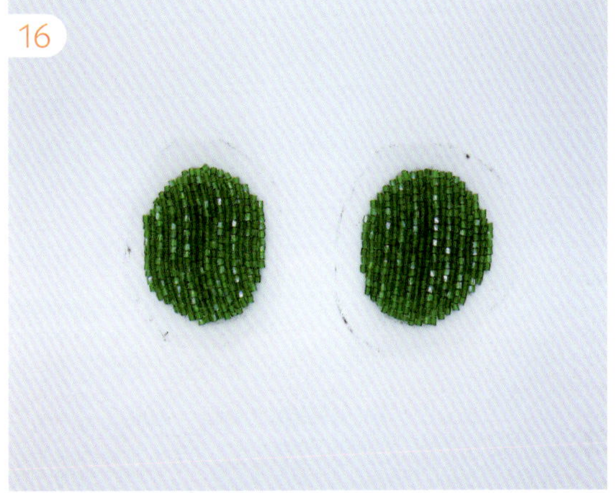

Cut out the embroidered patterns, leaving an allowance of about 5–8 mm around the edge.

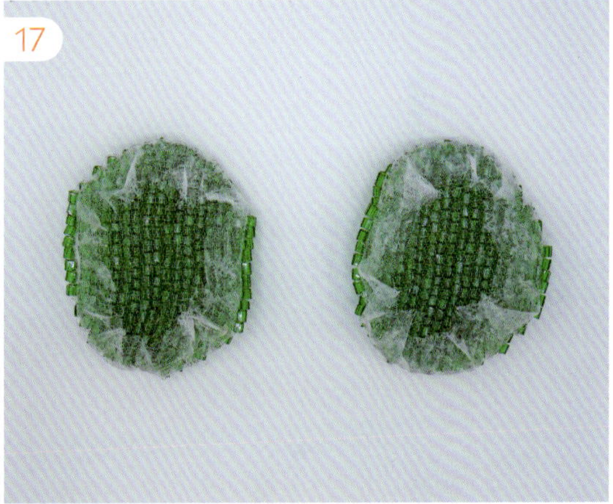

Apply some fabric glue on the edges of the back of the pieces. Fold and paste the remaining fabric allowance inwards, and let it dry for later use.

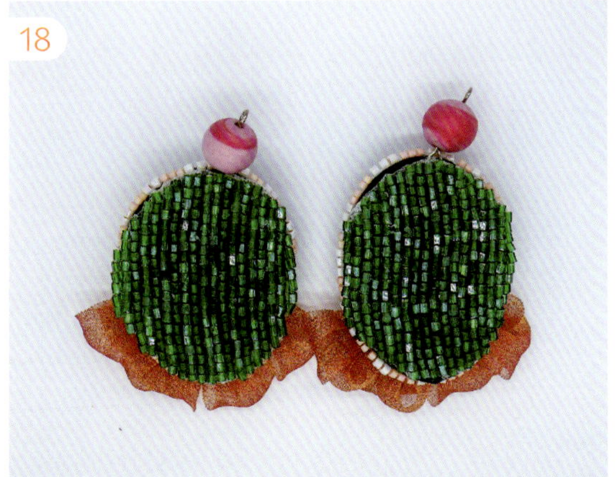

Apply some fabric glue to the back of the embroidery pieces, and paste the pieces completed in the previous step.

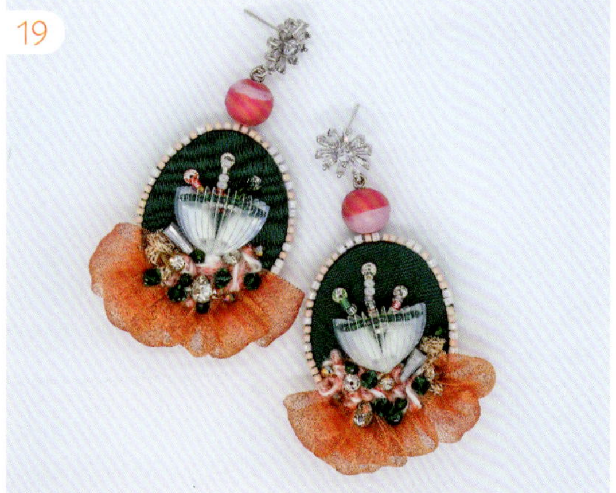

Allow the glue to dry. Use pliers to fix the daisy stud earrings above the pink gradient pearls. The piece is now complete.

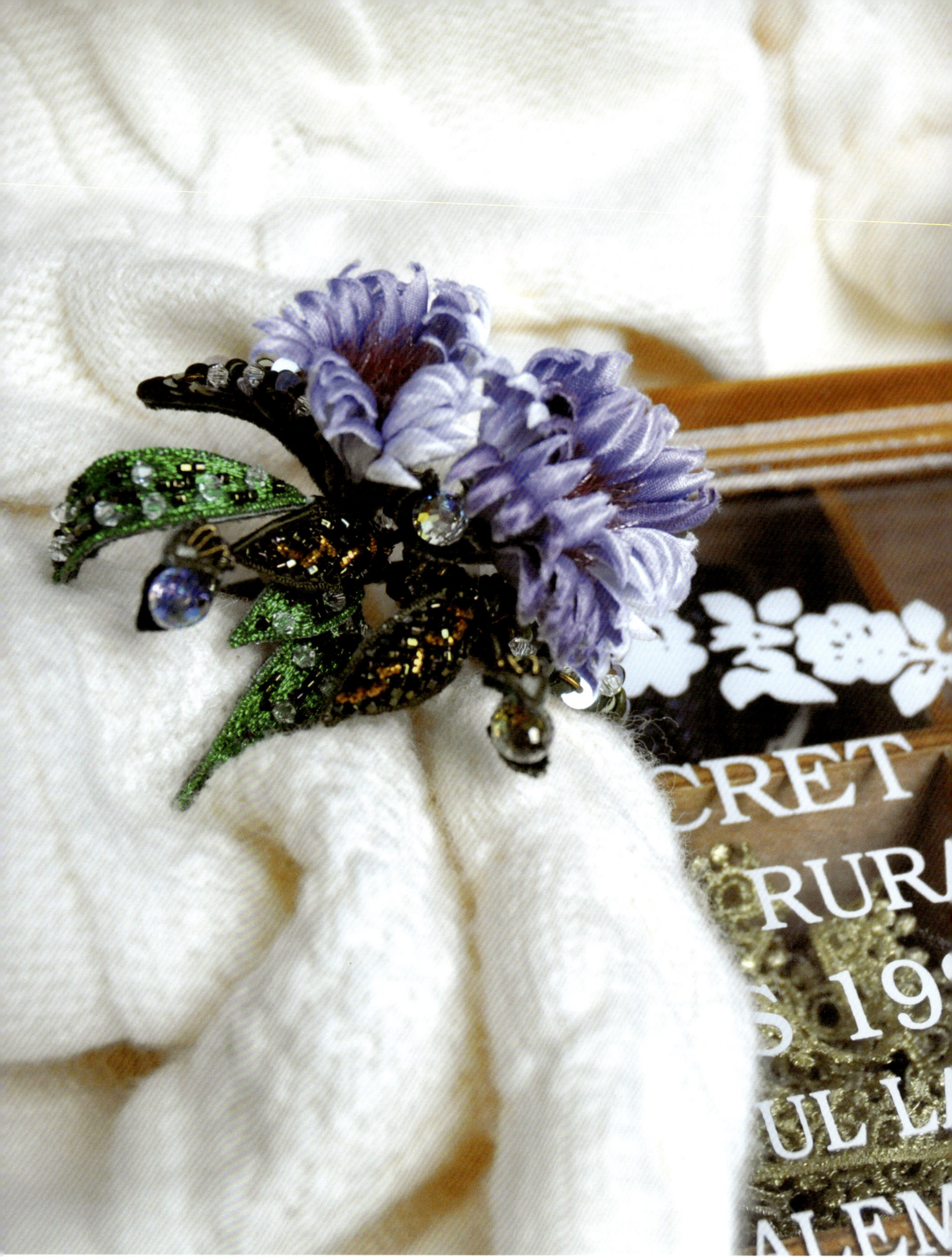
CRET
RURA
S 19
UL L
ALEM

9. Twin Lotus Brooch

In Chinese culture, the lotus symbolizes purity, as it grows out of the mud without being stained. The twin lotus—regarded as the best of the flowers—has two blossoms bursting from a single stalk. It symbolizes love and happiness between a husband and wife, and has been associated with good luck and festive occasions since ancient times. This brooch takes the shape of a beautiful twin lotus, and will add a touch of artistry to any outfit.

You Will Need

Threads	embroidery thread	dark green, light green, medium green
	metallic thread	green
	bullion wires	coffee color
Beads	seed beads	2 mm dark green
	sequins	3 mm light green, 4 mm dark green, 5 mm clear
	crystals	3 mm white, 6 mm brown, 6 mm drop shape
Fabrics	fuchsia fringe trim lace, purple gradient flower petals, white organza	
Tools	embroidery frame, 70# hook needle, hand sewing needle, scissors, fabric glue, heat erasable marker, 0.4 mm iron wire, 26# iron wire, bar pin	

Embroidery Steps

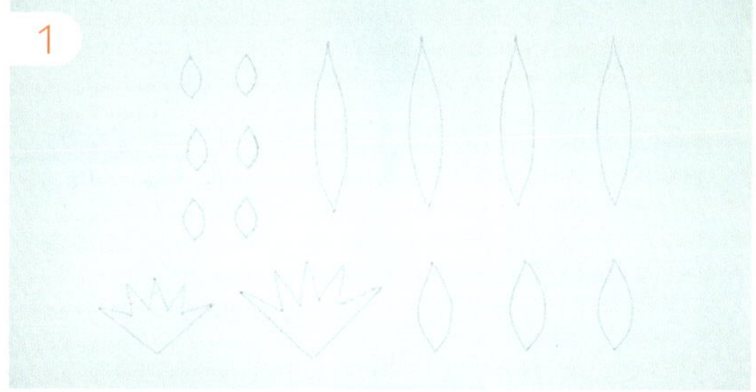

Stretch the white organza on the embroidery frame, and draw the patterns (see page 166) on the fabric with a heat erasable marker.

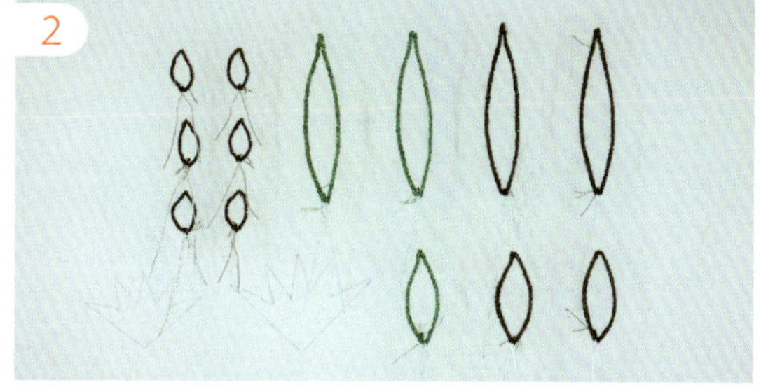

Apply the edging stitch technique using a hook needle, dark green thread, green metallic thread, and 0.4 mm iron wire to overlock the outlines of the leaves.

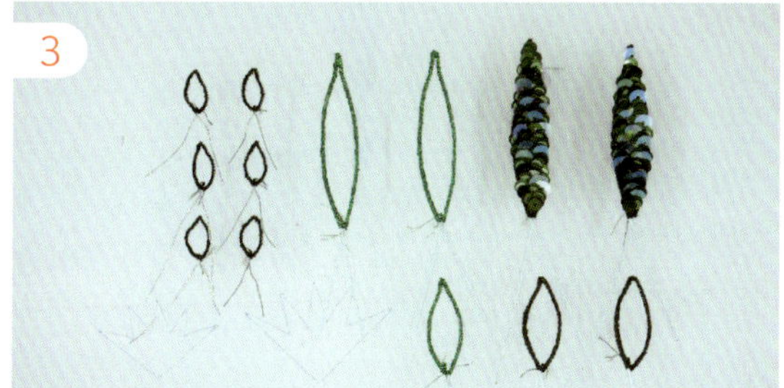

Apply the technique of embroidering sequins using a hand sewing needle, dark green thread, 3 mm light green sequins, 4 mm dark green sequins, and 5 mm clear sequins to fill two leaves.

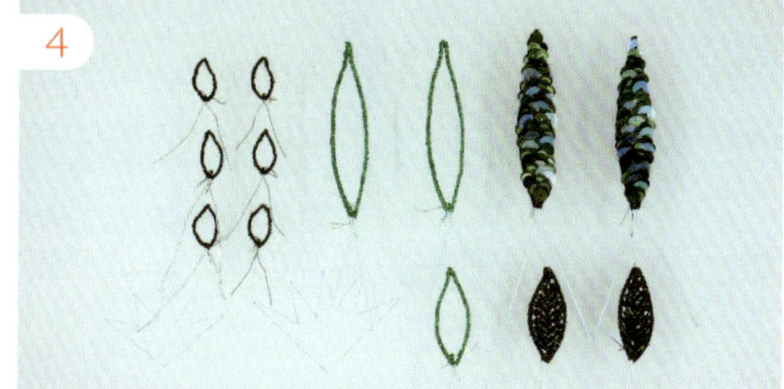

Apply the technique of stitching multiple beads from the front side of the fabric using a hook needle, dark green thread, and 2 mm dark green seed beads to fill two small leaves.

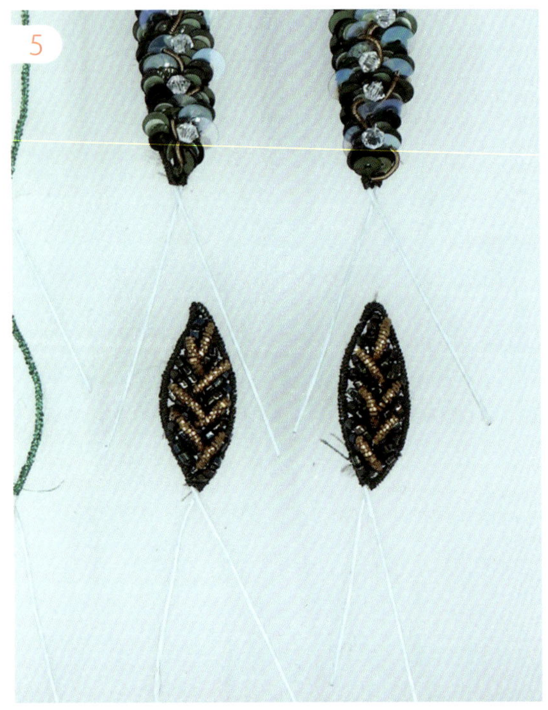

Use a hand sewing needle and coffee color bullion wires to sew the veins of the leaves embroidered in step 4.

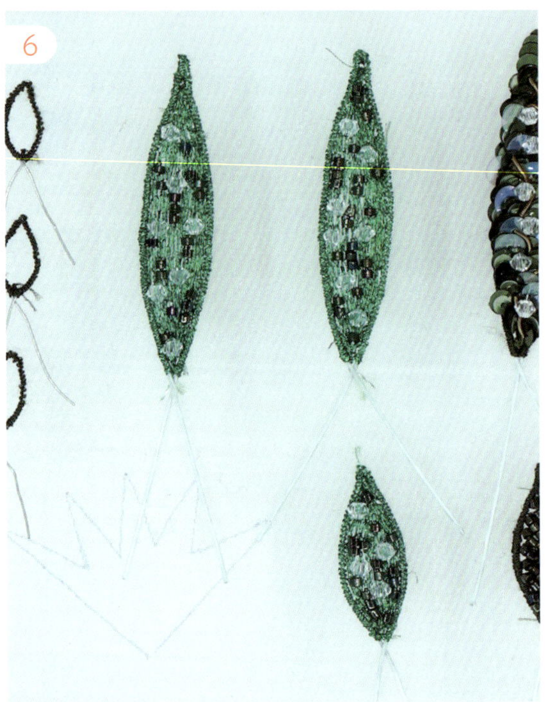

Apply the technique of stitching beads discontinuously from the front side of the fabric using a hook needle, green metallic thread, 2 mm dark green seed beads, and 3 mm white crystals to fill the three green leaves.

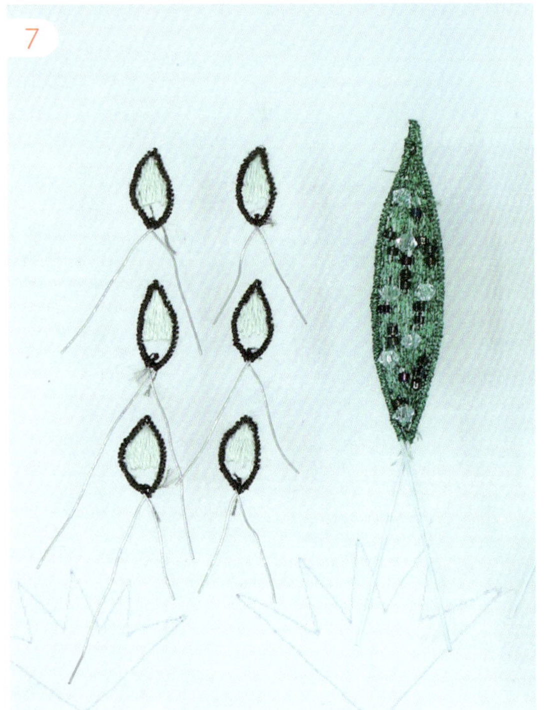

Apply the long and short stitch technique using a hand sewing needle and light green thread to fill up the upper half of the remaining six leaves.

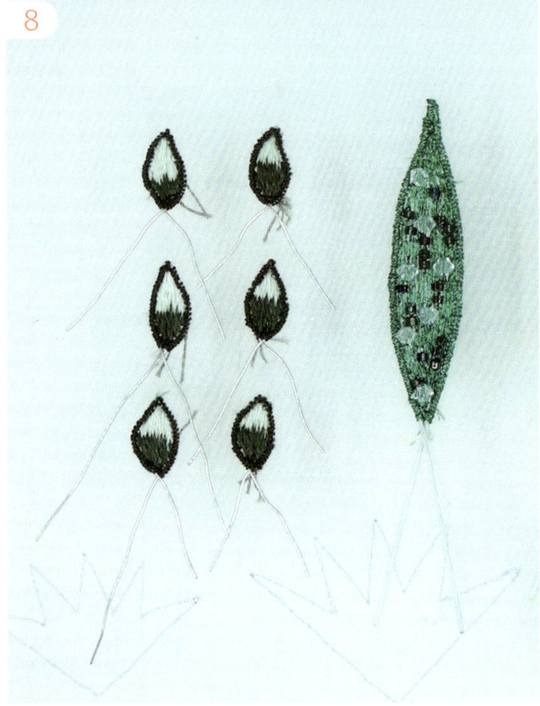

Apply the long and short stitch technique using a hand sewing needle and dark green thread to fill up the lower half of the remaining six leaves.

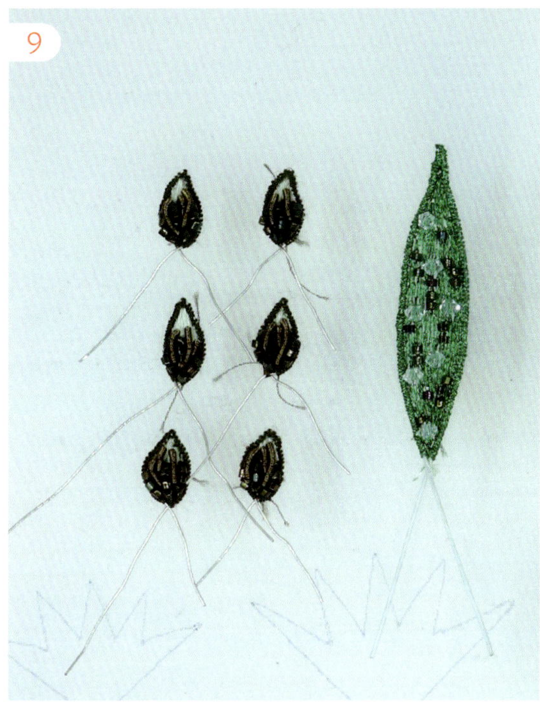

Apply the technique of embroidering multiple beads using a hand sewing needle, coffee color bullion wires, and 2 mm dark green seed beads to decorate the stitch in step 8.

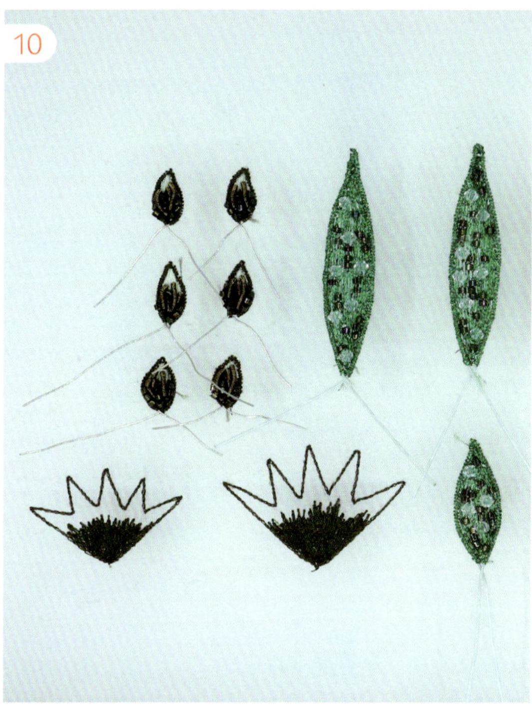

Apply the chain stitch technique using a hook needle and dark green thread to sew the outlines and fill up the lower half of the two calyxes as shown in lower left corner of the figure.

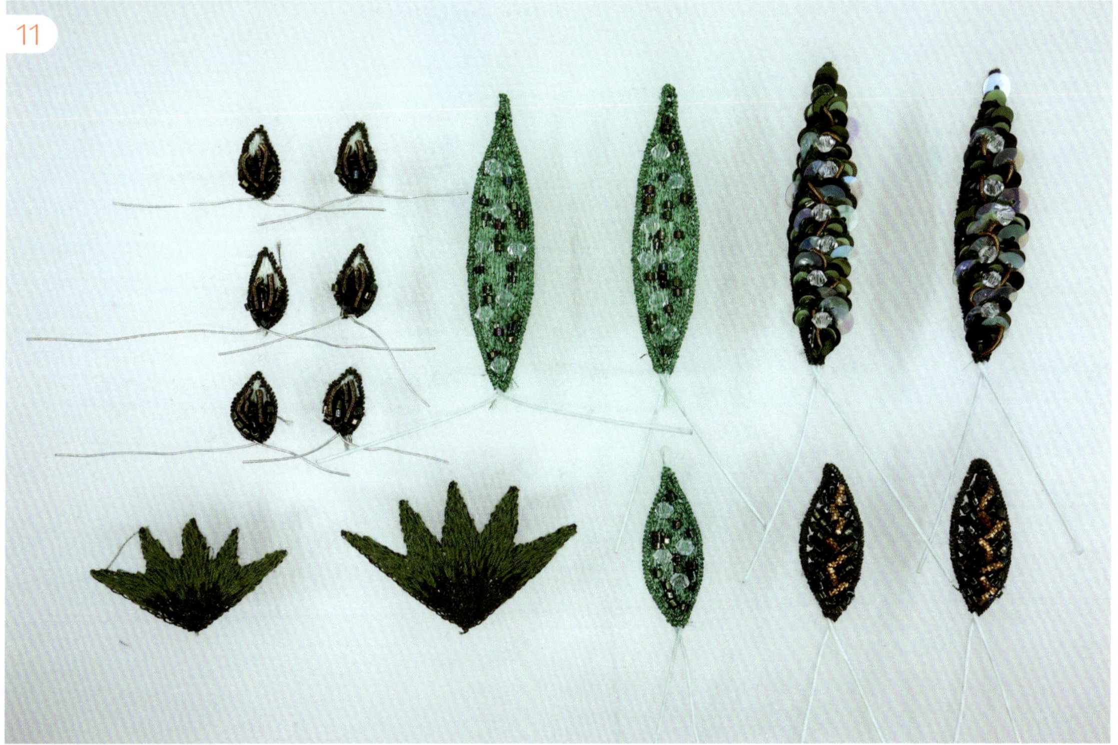

Apply the chain stitch technique using a hook needle and medium green thread to fill up the remaining parts of the calyxes. Cut out the embroidered patterns to use later.

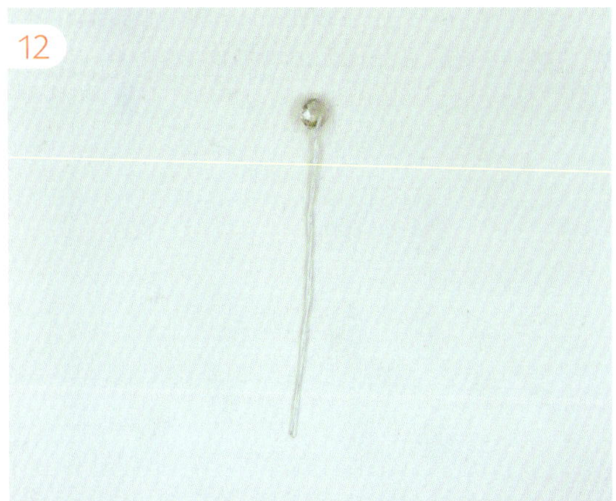

Take a 26# iron wire and fix a 6 mm brown crystal in the center. Then, twist and tighten the wire.

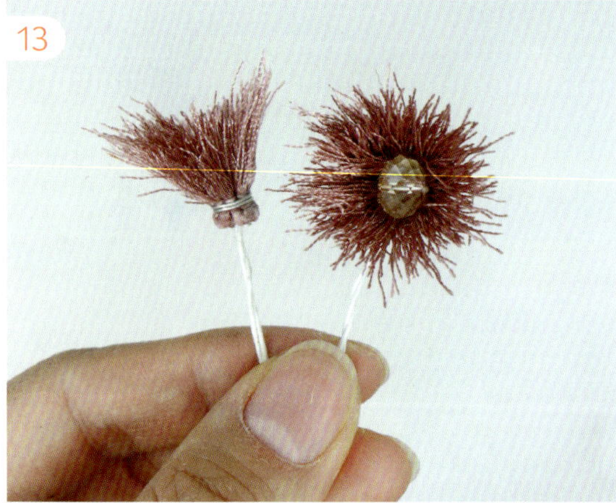

Stick the fuchsia fringe trim lace around the crystals with fabric glue. Tie and fix the root of the fringe with 0.4 mm iron wire to form the center of a flower.

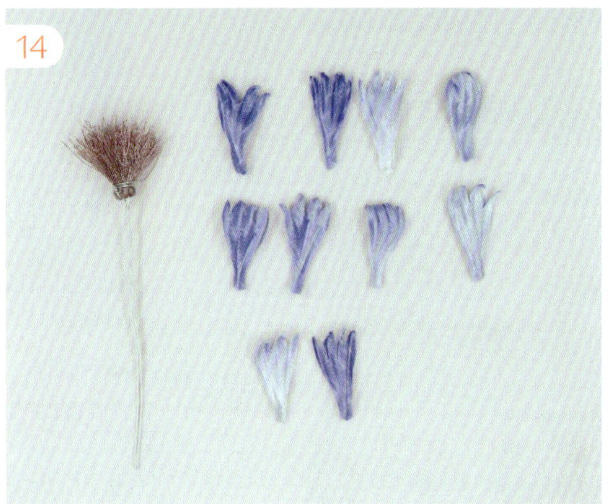

Prepare 8 to 12 purple gradient flower petals.

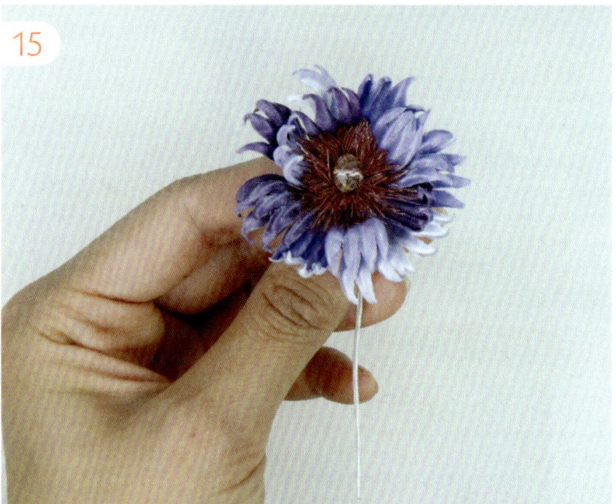

Apply fabric glue on the purple petal pieces and stick them around the center of the completed flower center. Let it dry.

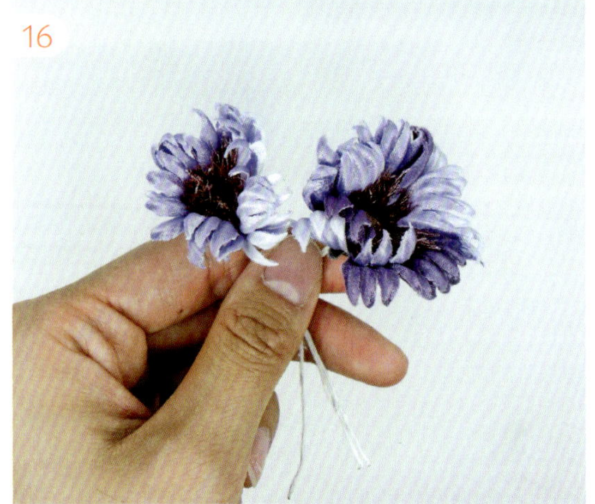

Apply the same techniques used in steps 13–16 to create another flower.

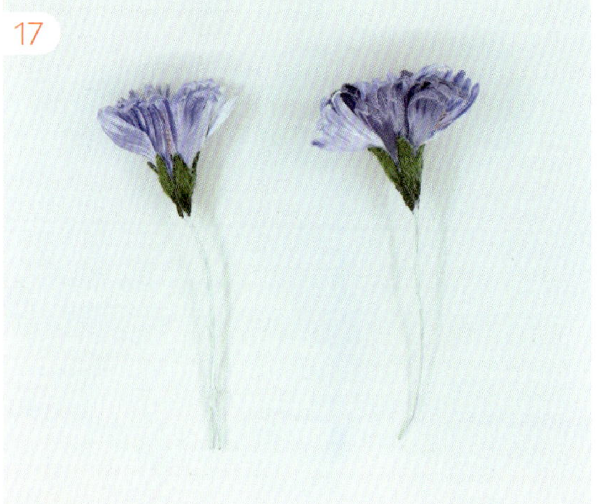

Stick the embroidered calyxes at the bottom of the two flowers with fabric glue.

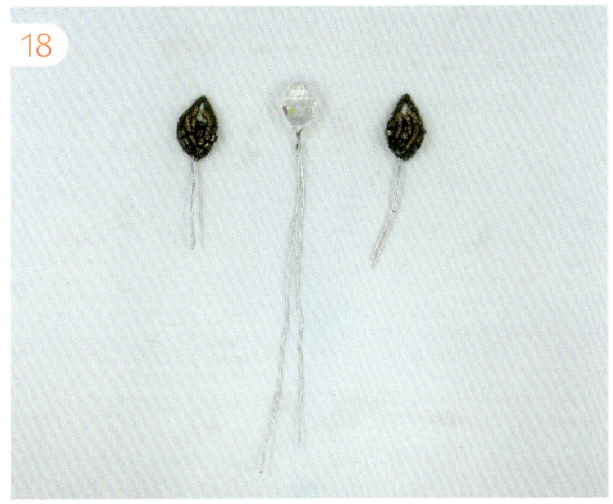

Use a wire to fix a 6 mm drop crystal. Prepare two bud leaves completed in step 11.

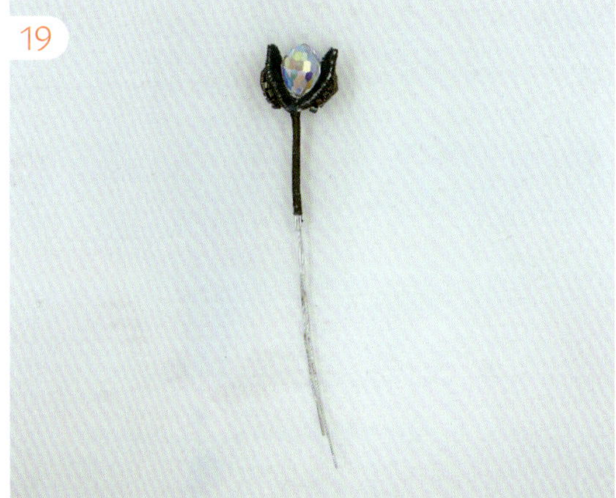

Use dark green thread to twist the fixed crystal and two bud leaves. Then, tie a knot on the thread and apply some fabric glue to fix it.

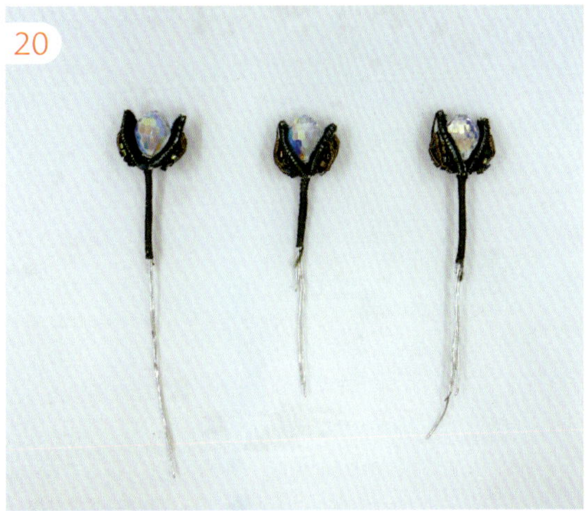

Apply the same method used for steps 18–19 to complete the three buds.

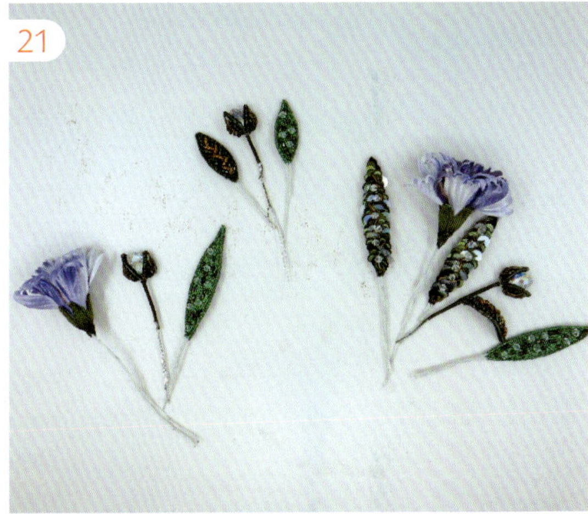

Divide all the parts into three groups in preparation for assembly.

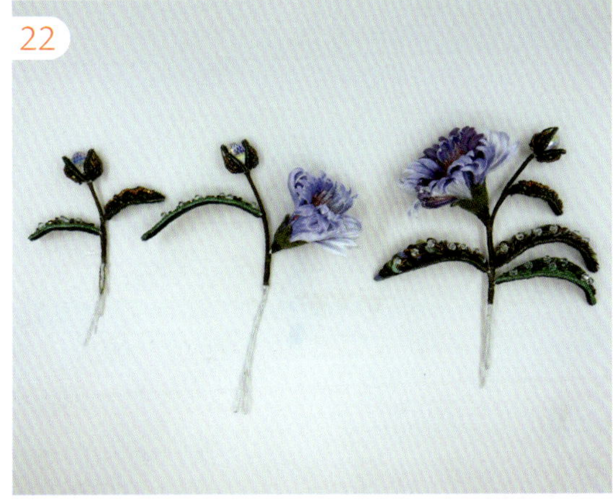

Use dark green thread to twist and fix the iron wire parts of the leaves and flowers to form three groups of flowers.

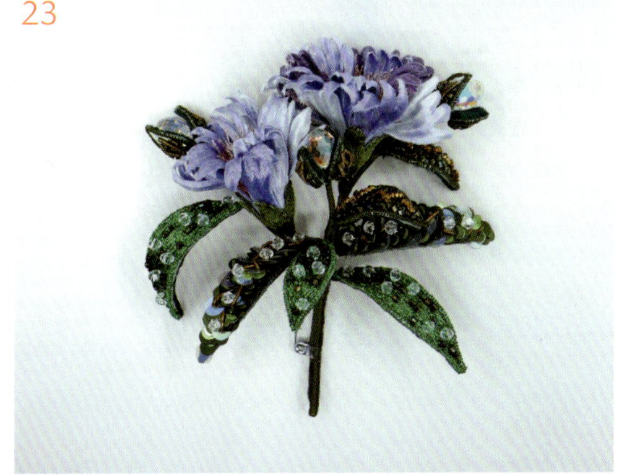

Use dark green thread to wrap three groups of flowers together, then wrap a bar pin behind. The piece is now complete.

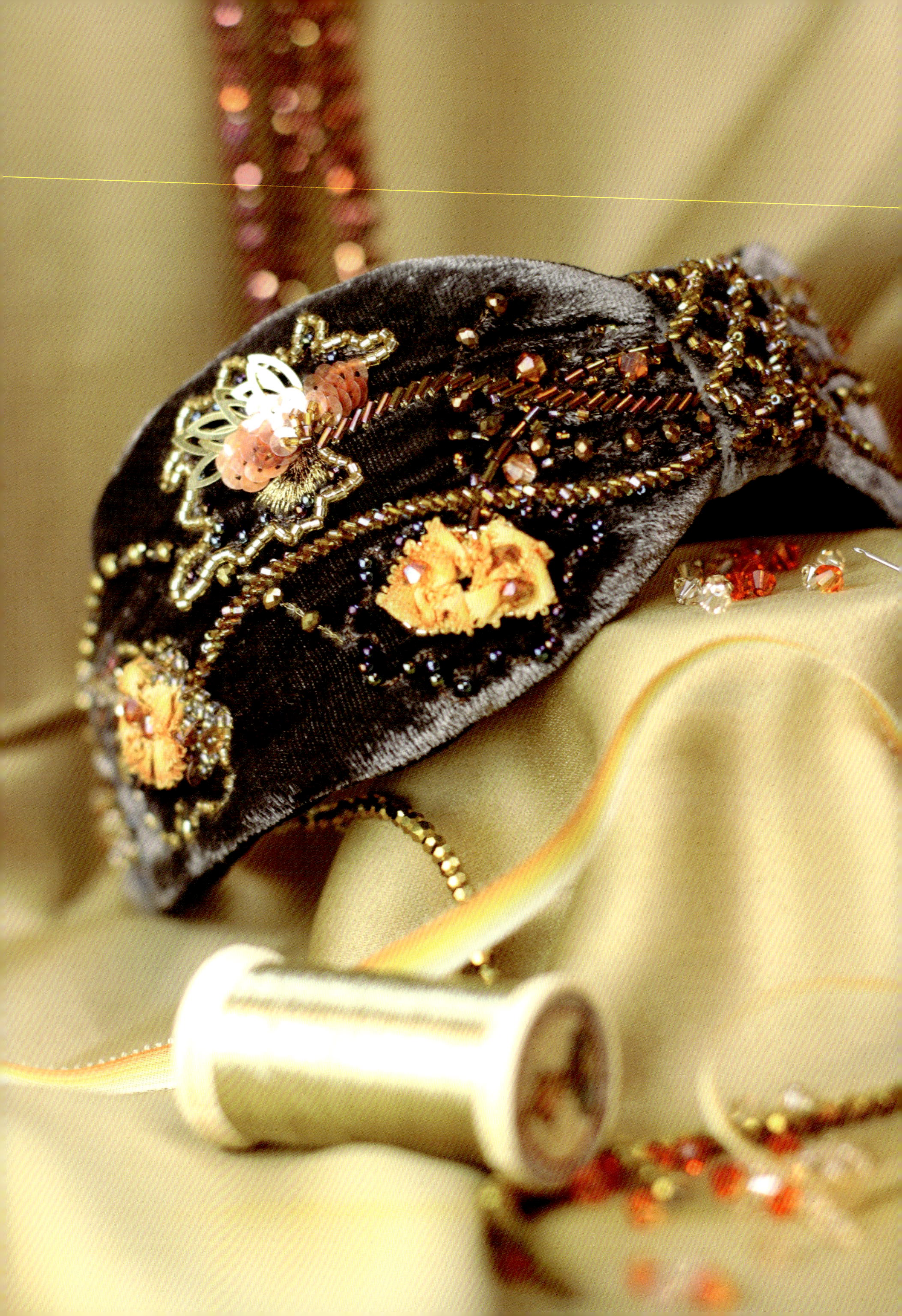

10. Peacock Flower Hair Band

The petals of a peacock flower are orange red, or yellow, with slender filaments. When it is in full bloom, it is beautifully delicate, like a peacock spreading its feathers, hence its name. In Chinese culture, the opening of the peacock tail symbolizes good luck. In ancient times, peacocks often appeared on official attire, so it also signifies a bright future. The freehand design of the work outlines the peacock flower's graceful posture, and the crystal-clear colored beads frolicking among the golden flower branches gives the hair band a charming elegance.

You Will Need

Threads	embroidery thread	gold, brown
Beads	seed beads	1.6 mm brown, 1.6 mm gold, 1.6 mm orange, 2 mm gold, 2 mm orange, 2 mm brown
	cup sequins	4 mm orange
	flat sequins	4 mm gold
	horse eye sequins	gold
	tubes	5 mm brown
	crystals	4 mm gold, 4 mm tawny
	pearls	4 mm gold
Fabrics	gray velvet, 6 mm orange ribbon	
Tools	embroidery frame, 70# hook needle, hand sewing needle, scissors, heat erasable marker	

Embroidery Steps

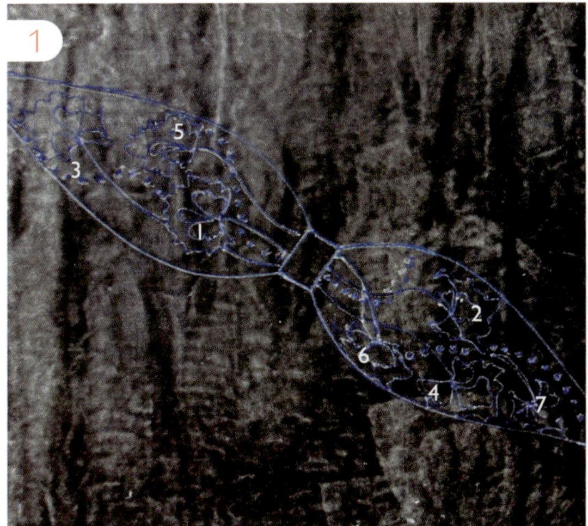

Trace the pattern (see page 168) onto the velvet fabric with a heat erasable marker.

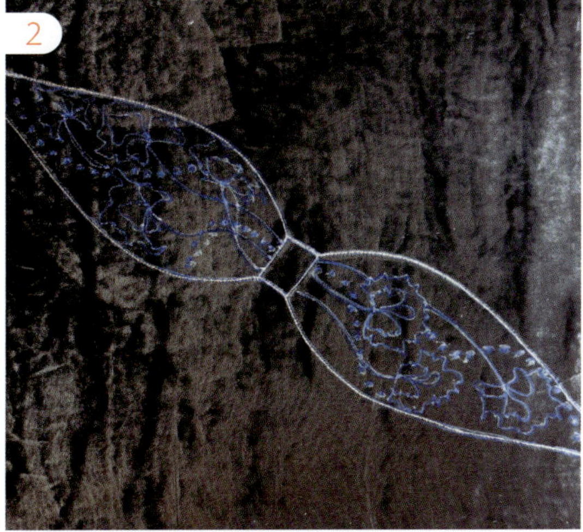

Apply chain stitch from the front side of the fabric, and use a hook needle and gold embroidery thread to form the outer contour of the hair band.

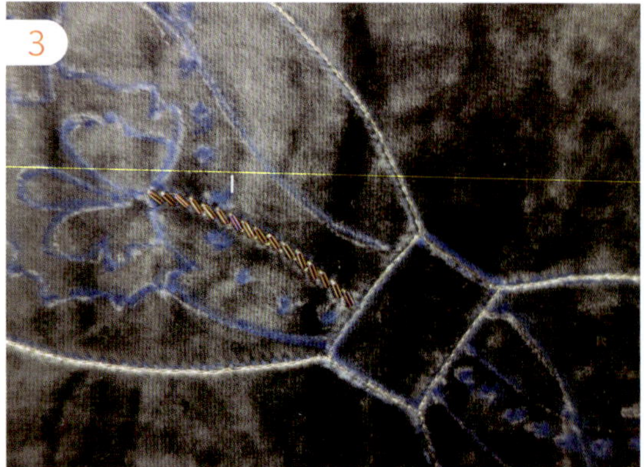

Use the outline stitch technique to sew the branch of Flower 1 with a hook needle, gold embroidery thread, and 5 mm brown tubes.

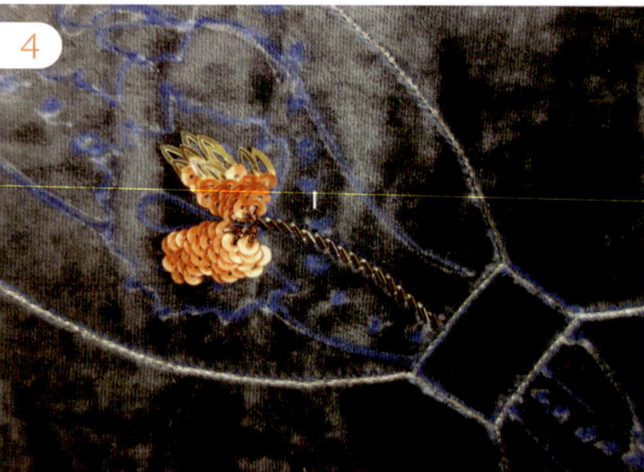

Use the technique of embroidering sequins that are overlapped to sew the stamen of Flower 1 with a hand sewing needle, gold embroidery thread, 4 mm orange cup sequins, gold horse eye sequins, and 1.6 mm brown seed beads.

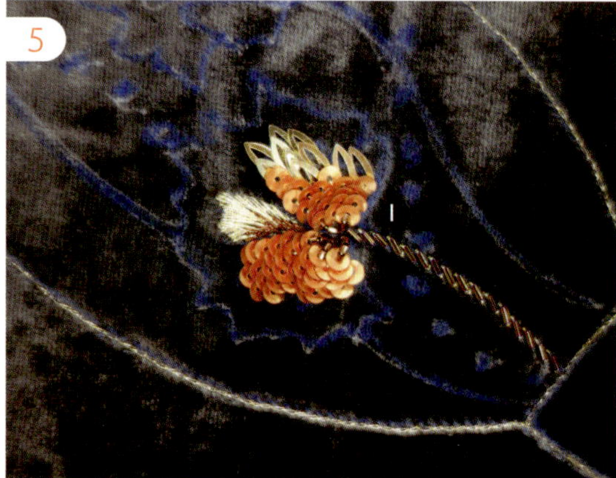

Use the satin stitch technique to sew the remaining part of the stamen of Flower 1 with a hand sewing needle, as well as gold and brown embroidery threads.

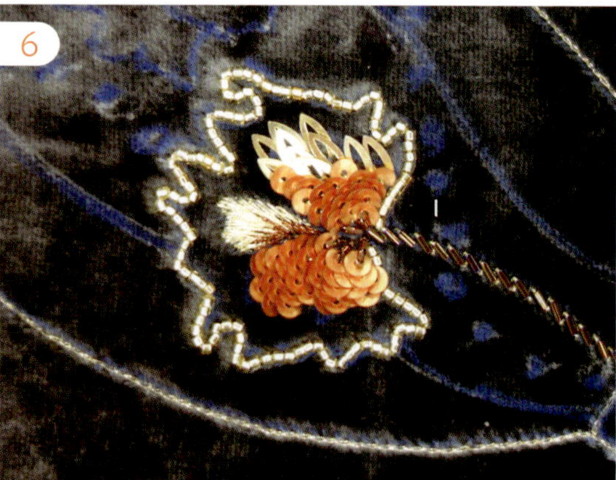

Stitch beads continuously from the front side of the fabric to sew the outer contour of Flower 1 with a hook needle, gold embroidery thread, and 1.6 mm gold seed beads.

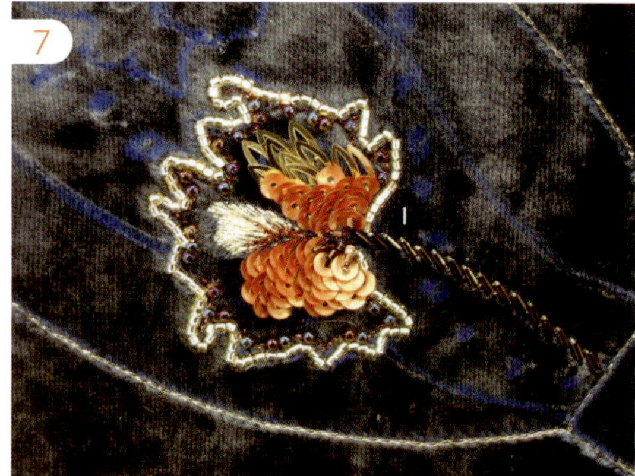

Stitch beads from the front side of the fabric discontinuously using a hook needle, gold embroidery thread, and 2 mm brown seed beads to sew along the inner side of the outer contour of Flower 1.

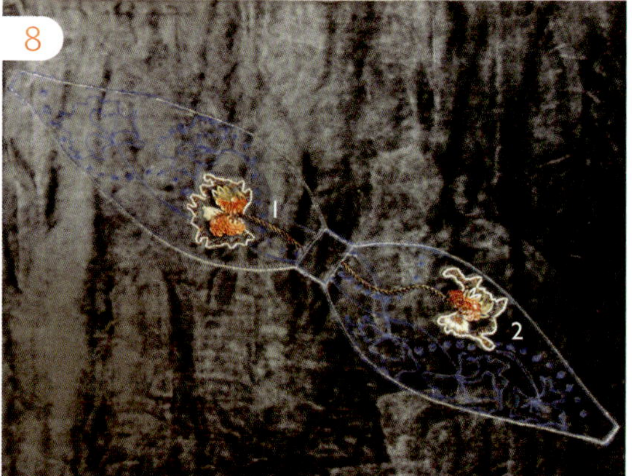

Use the same technique as Flower 1 to complete Flower 2.

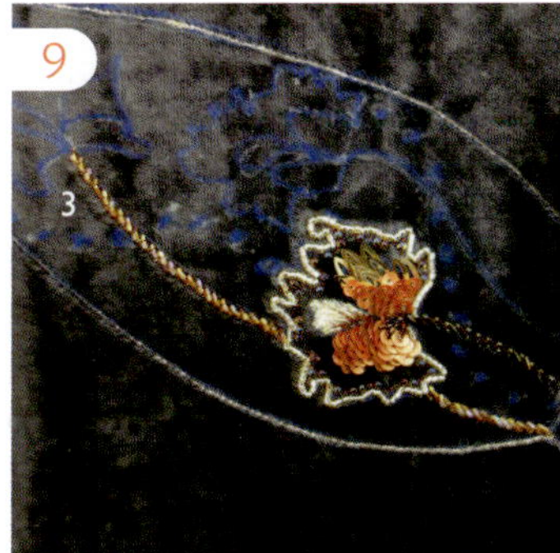

Apply the technique of embroidering bead clusters for additional dimension with a hook needle, gold embroidery thread, and 1.6 mm brown seed beads to stitch the branch of Flower 3.

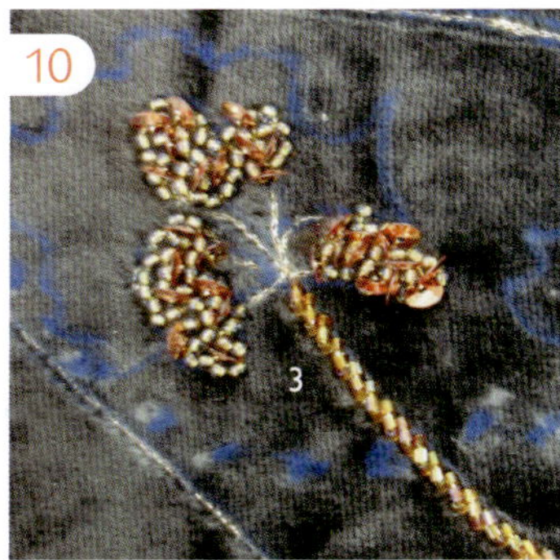

Stitch beads from the front side of the fabric with a hook needle, gold embroidery threads, 4 mm gold sequins, and 2 mm gold seed beads to fill the petals of Flower 3 as you like.

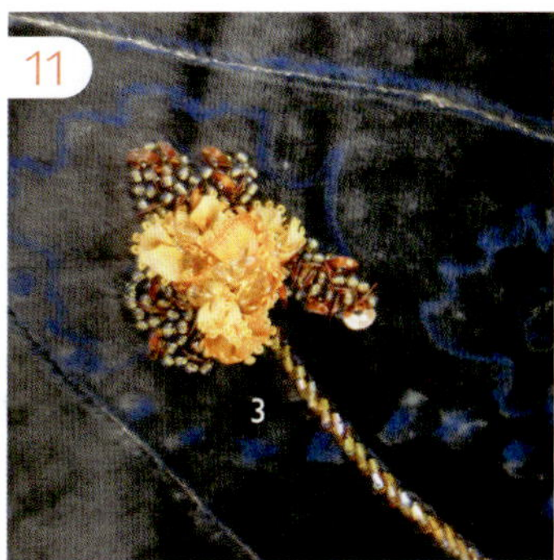

Use the technique of fixing folded ribbon with a hand sewing needle and gold embroidery threads to fix the 6 mm orange ribbon onto the stamen of Flower 3. Then sew some 4 mm tawny crystals to decorate it.

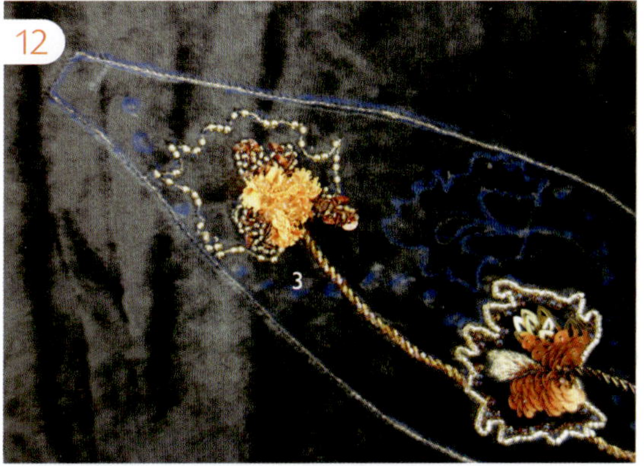

Stitch beads from the front side of the fabric discontinuously with a hook needle, gold embroidery thread, and 2 mm gold seed beads to sew the outer contour of Flower 3. The spacing between the seed beads does not need to be uniform. Flower 3 is now complete.

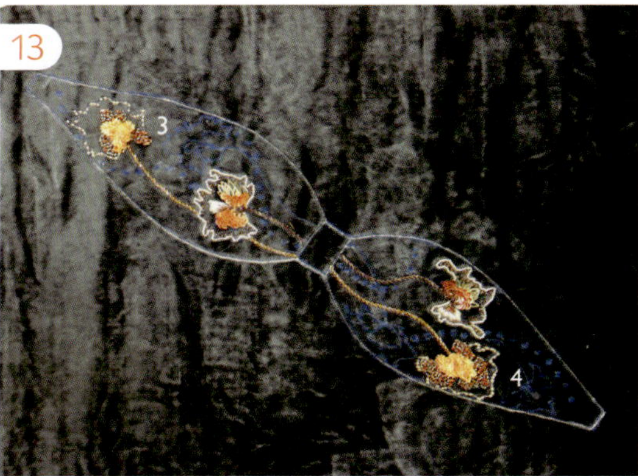

Use the same technique as Flower 3 to complete Flower 4.

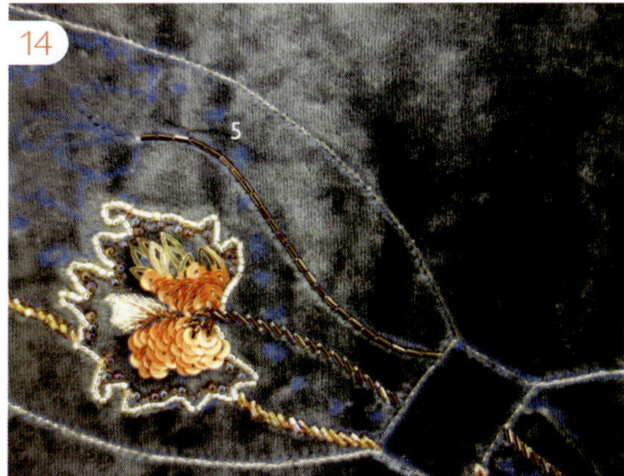

Stitch 5 mm brown tubes continuously from the front side of the fabric with a hook needle and gold embroidery thread to complete the branch of Flower 5.

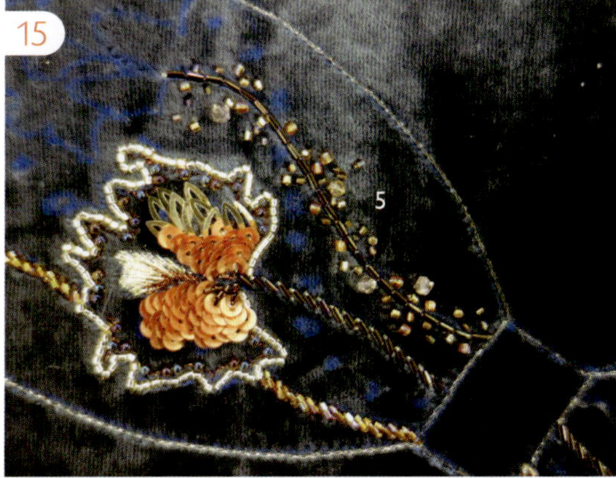

Embroider single beads with a hand sewing needle, gold embroidery thread, 1.6 mm orange and brown seed beads, and 4 mm tawny crystals to decorate the branch of Flower 5.

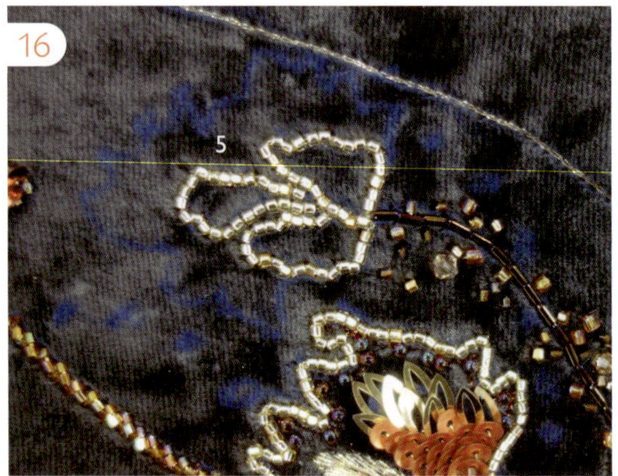

Stitch beads continuously from the front side of the fabric with a hook needle, gold embroidery thread, and 1.6 mm gold seed beads to sew the petals of Flower 5.

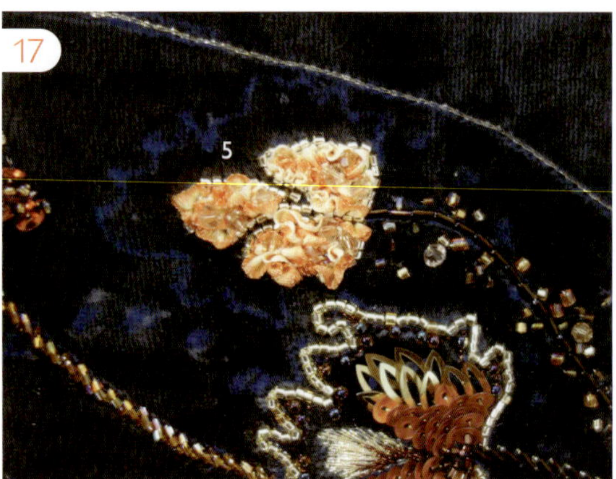

Use the technique of fixing folded ribbon with a hand sewing needle and gold embroidery threads to fix the 6 mm orange ribbon on the stamen of Flower 5. Sew some 4 mm tawny crystals to decorate it.

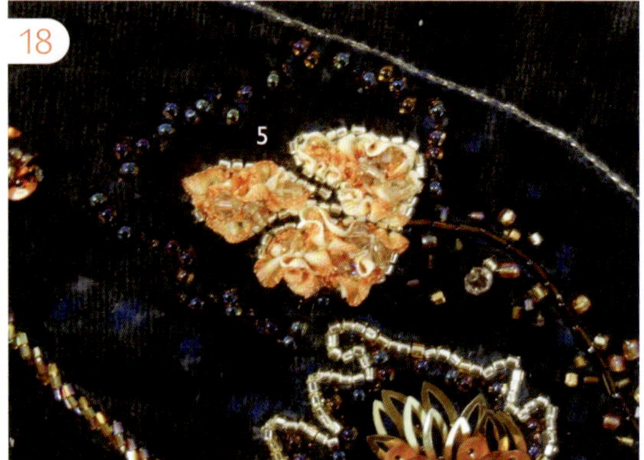

Stitch beads from the front side of the fabric discontinuously with a hook needle, gold embroidery thread, and 2 mm brown seed beads, to irregularly sew the outer contour of Flower 5. Flower 5 is now complete.

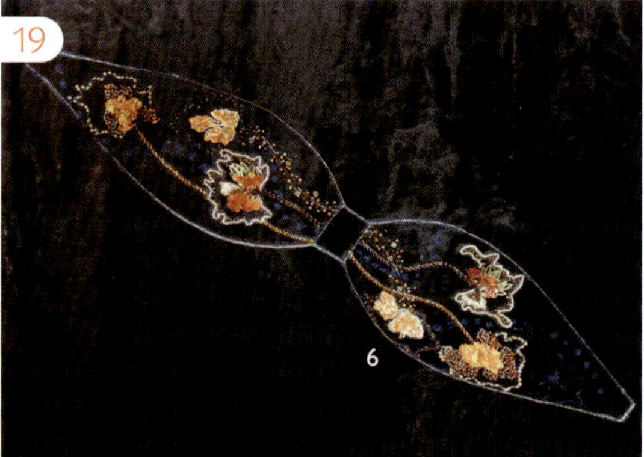

Use the same technique as Flower 5 to complete Flower 6.

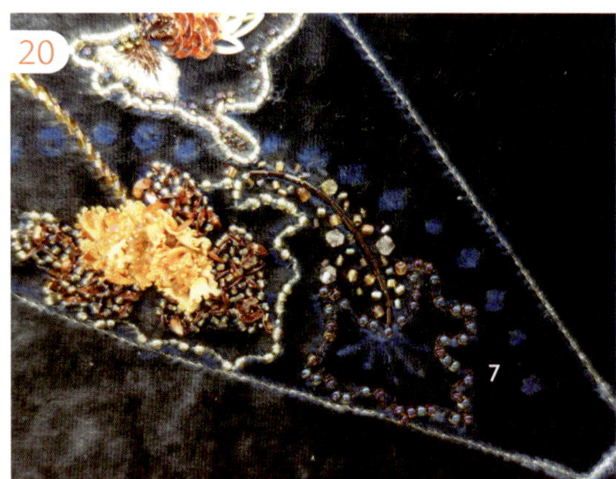

Use the same technique as Flower 5 to complete the branch and contour of Flower 7.

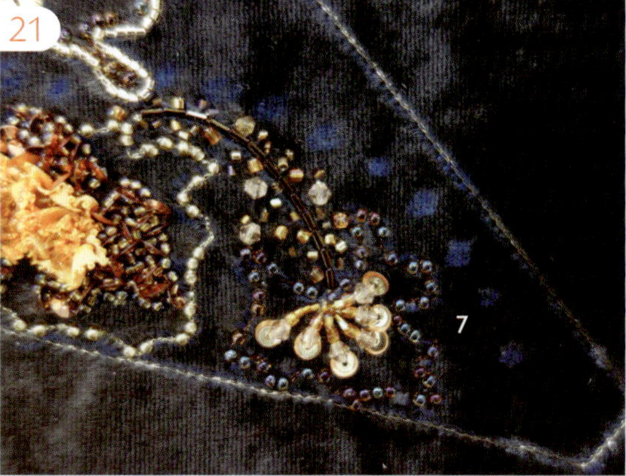

Use a hand sewing needle, gold embroidery thread, 1.6 mm orange seed beads, 2 mm orange seed beads, 4 mm tawny crystals, and 4 mm orange cup sequins to sew the stamens of Flower 7.

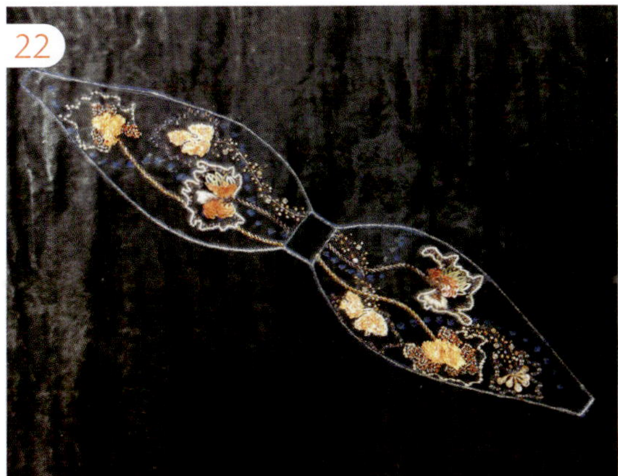

The embroidery of main flower patterns on the hair band is complete.

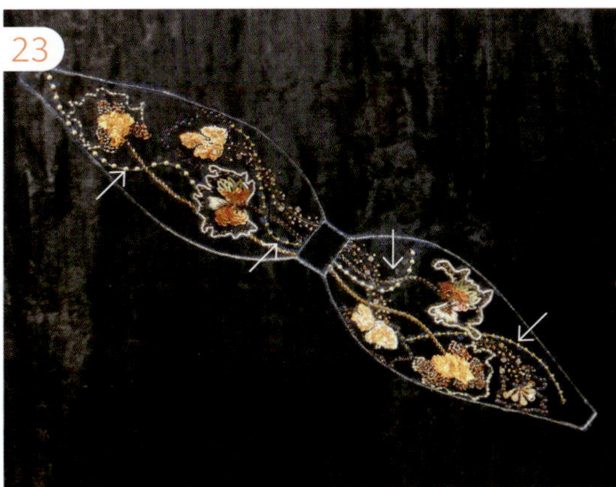

Use the technique of embroidering beads discontinuously with a hook needle, gold embroidery thread, 4 mm gold crystals, and 4 mm gold pearls to form the decorative lines of the hair band.

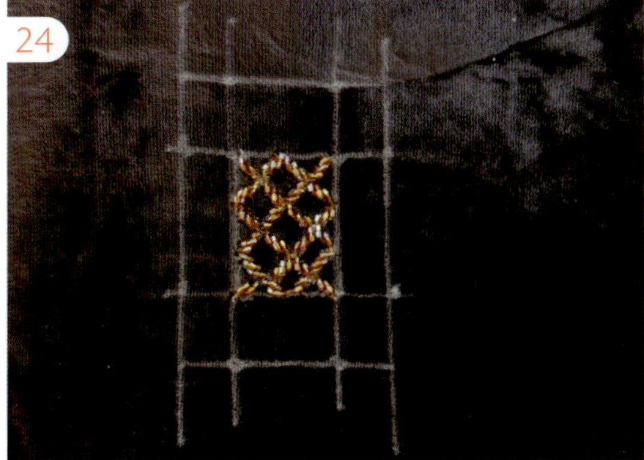

Draw the button at the middle of the hair band (see page 168) onto the blank portion of the fabric, and apply the technique of embroidering bead clusters for additional dimension to form the rhombic pattern with a hook needle, gold embroidery thread, and 1.6 mm brown seed beads.

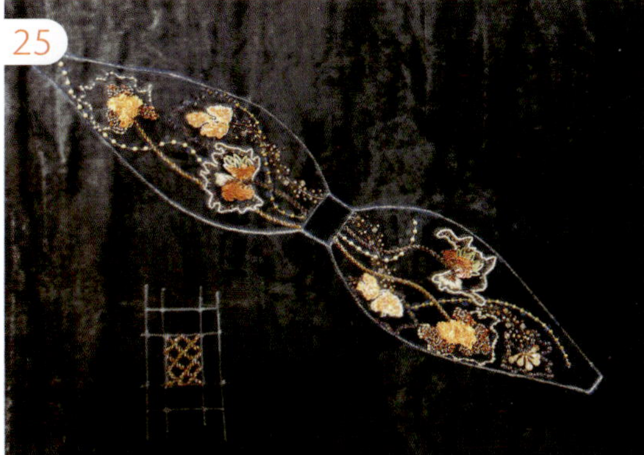

The embroidery portion of the hair band is complete.

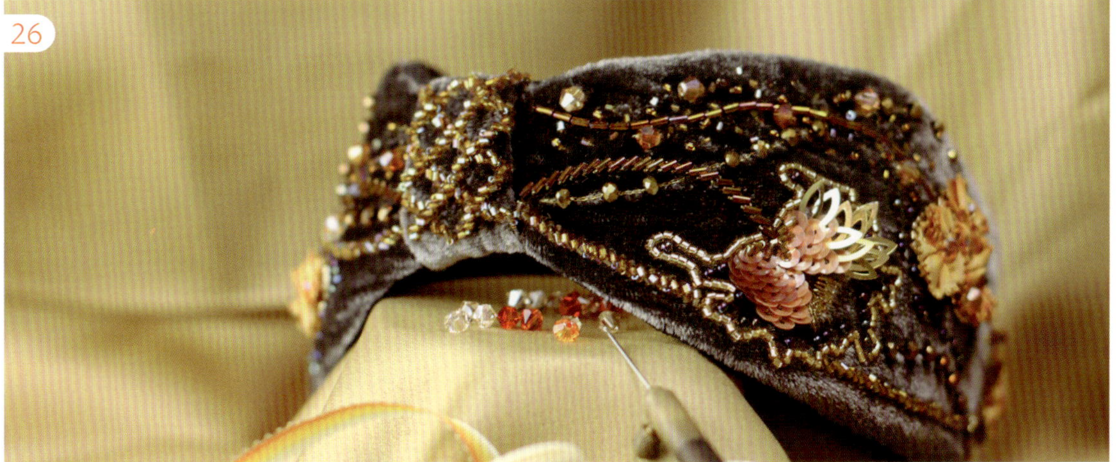

Cut out the embroidered pieces and assemble them into a hair band. It is now done.

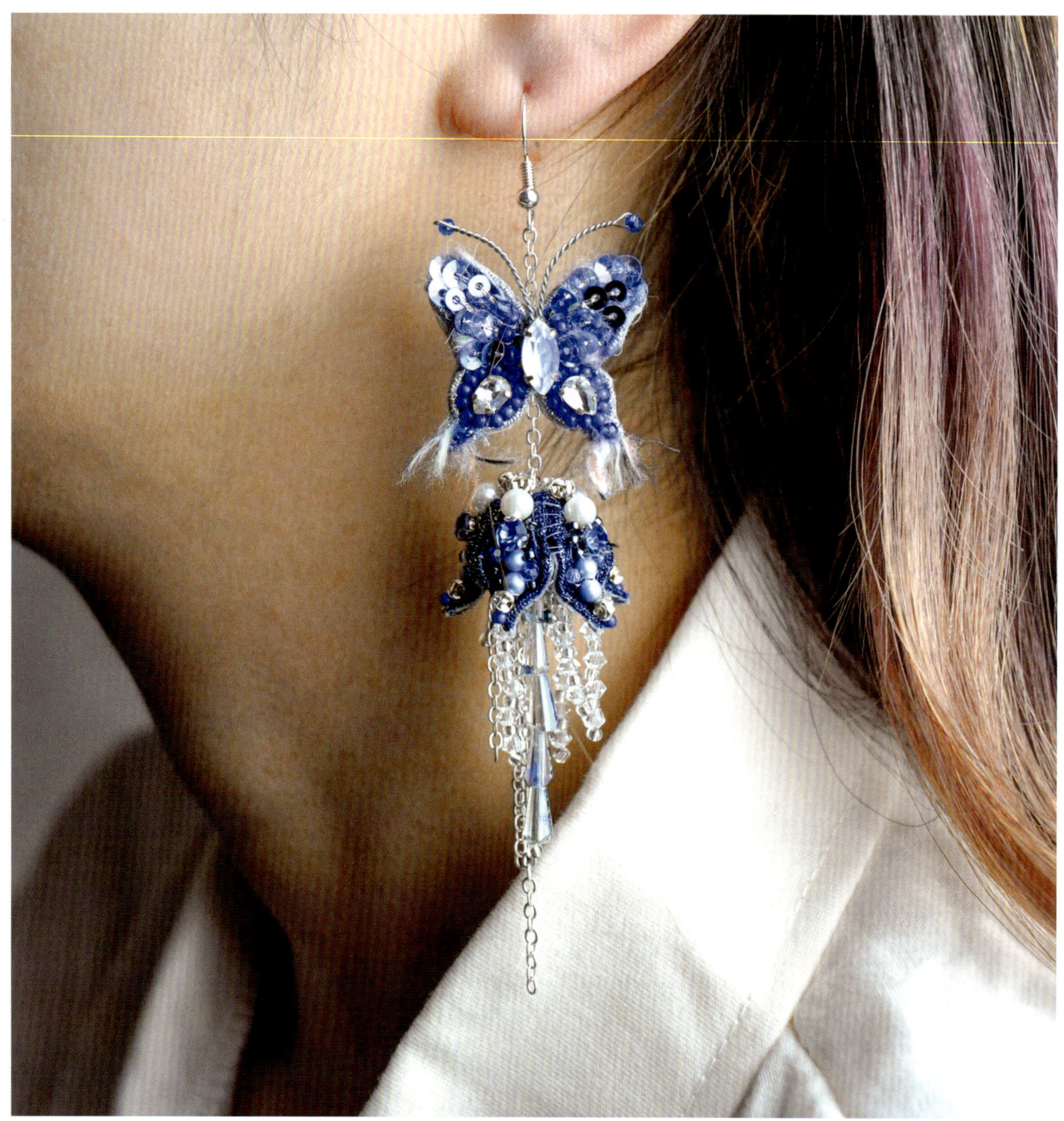

11. Balloon Flower Earrings

The balloon flower, which is native to China, is blue-purple and has five petals. It is shaped like a star when it blooms, and its roots are commonly used in traditional Chinese medicine. It exudes an air of tranquility and elegance, earning it the characteristic of being indifferent to wealth and fame. Inspired by balloon flowers, this piece uses iron wires and sequins to create the three-dimensional effect of flowers, and is matched with a butterfly of the same color, which represents simplicity and elegance.

You Will Need

Threads	embroidery thread	dark blue, silver, invisible
	metallic thread	dark blue
	wool	blue gradient
Beads	seed beads	1.5 mm dark blue, 2 mm blue, 2 mm silver
	crystals	3 mm blue, 3 mm white, 5 × 10 mm egg white, 4 × 6 mm white drop shape, 4 × 8 mm blue trapezoidal
	sequins	3 mm dark blue, 4 mm light blue
	pearls	3 mm blue, 4 mm white
	sew-on rhinestones	3 mm white, 4 mm blue
	tube beads	6 mm silver
Fabrics	white organza, blue leather	
Tools	embroidery hoop, 70# hook needle, hand sewing needle, scissors, fabric glue, heat erasable marker, silver ear hook, 2 mm wide silver chains, 0.4 mm iron wire	

Embroidery Steps

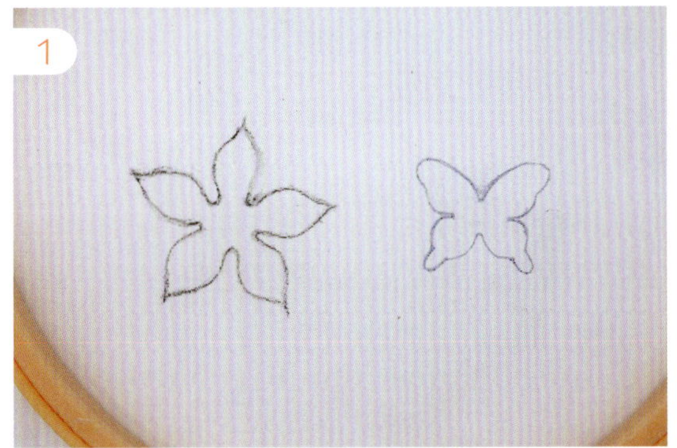

Stretch the white organza onto the embroidery hoop, and draw the pattern (see page 166) onto the fabric with a heat erasable marker.

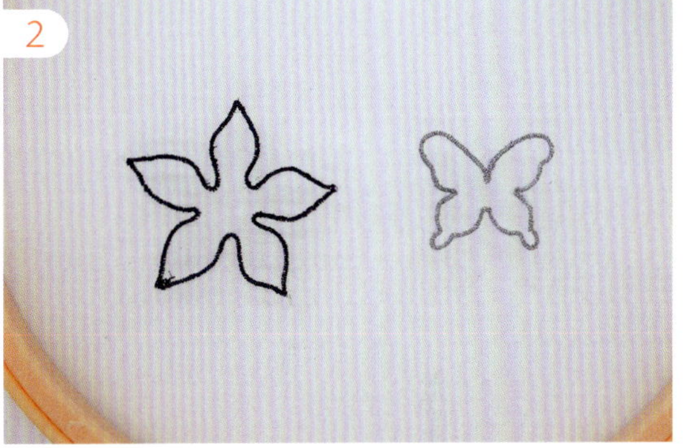

Apply the edging stitch technique using a hook needle, iron wire, dark blue metallic thread, and silver thread to sew the outer contours of the flower and butterfly patterns respectively.

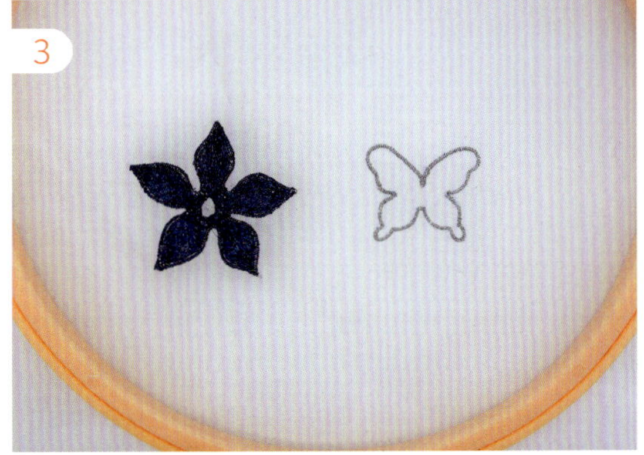

Apply the chain stitch technique using a hook needle and dark blue thread to fill the interior of the flower, leaving a circular gap with a diameter of about 5 mm at its center.

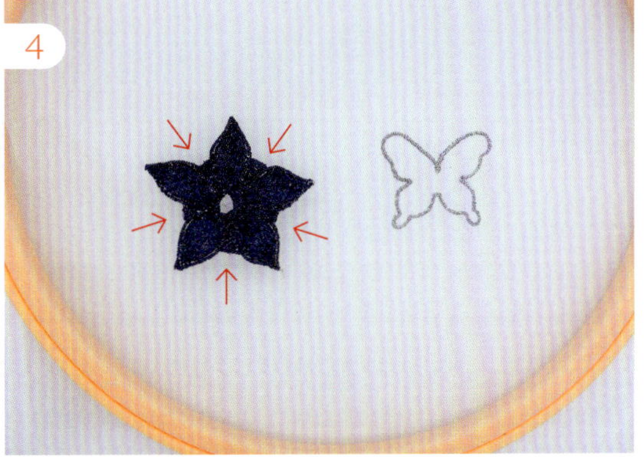

Apply the chain stitch technique using a hook needle and dark blue metallic thread to fill the gaps between the petals.

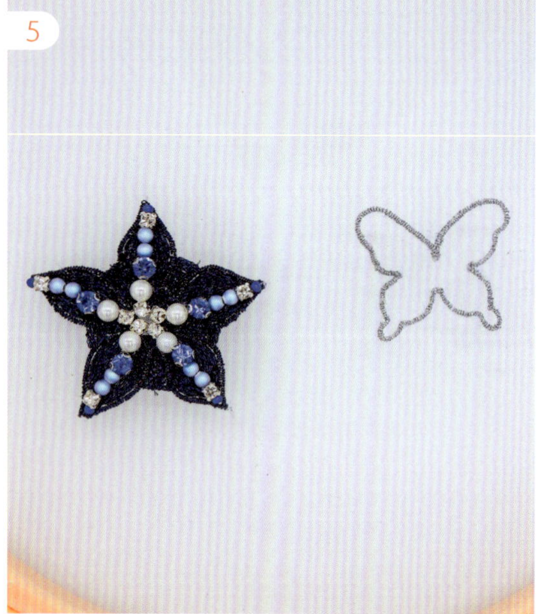

Apply the techniques of embroidering sew-on rhinestones and embroidering a single bead with a hand sewing needle and dark blue metallic thread outside-in on each petal with a 2 mm blue seed bead, 3 mm white sew-on rhinestones, two 3 mm blue pearls, 4 mm blue sew-on rhinestone, 4 mm white pearl, and 3 mm white sew-on rhinestone.

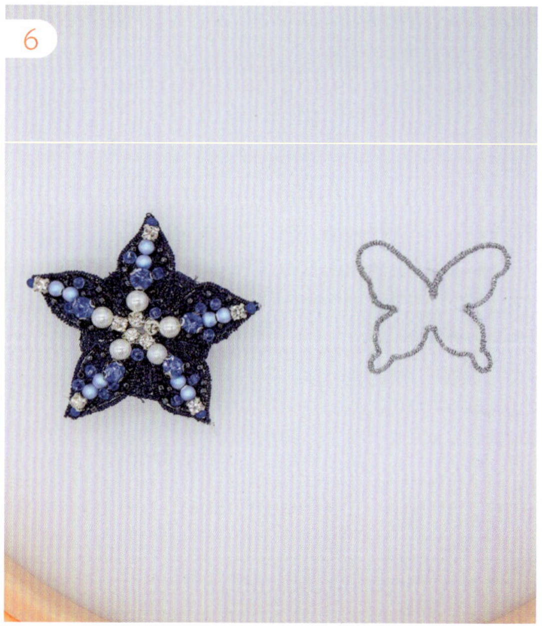

Apply the technique of embroidering a single bead using a hand sewing needle and dark blue metallic thread to embellish 1.5 mm dark blue seed beads and 3 mm blue crystals in the empty spaces on the petals.

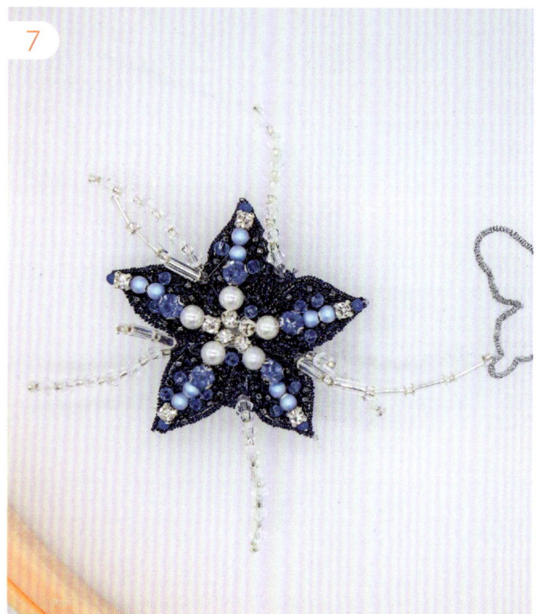

Apply the technique of embroidering a bead on top of a sequin (or a tube) using a hand sewing needle, invisible thread, 6 mm silver tube beads, 2 mm silver seed beads, and 3 mm white crystals to sew 1–2 fringes in the space between each petal.

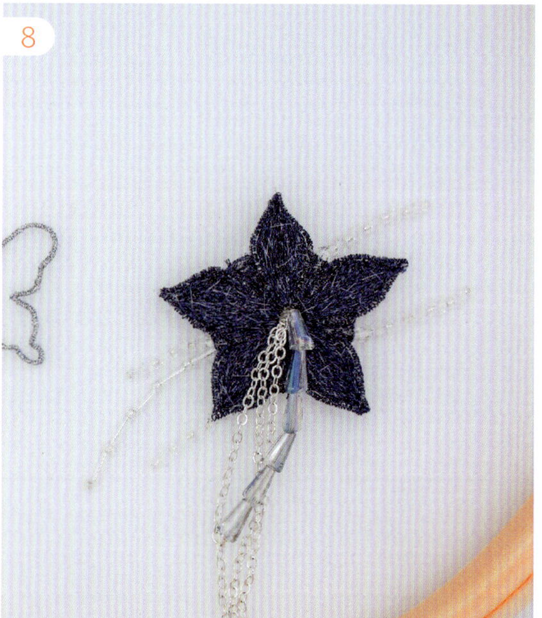

Flip the embroidery hoop to the back. Apply the technique of embroidering a bead on top of a sequin (or a tube) using a hand sewing needle and invisible thread to sew a string of 4 × 8 mm blue trapezoidal crystals in the center of the flower and a 2 mm silver seed bead at the bottom. Then fix three 2 mm wide silver chains.

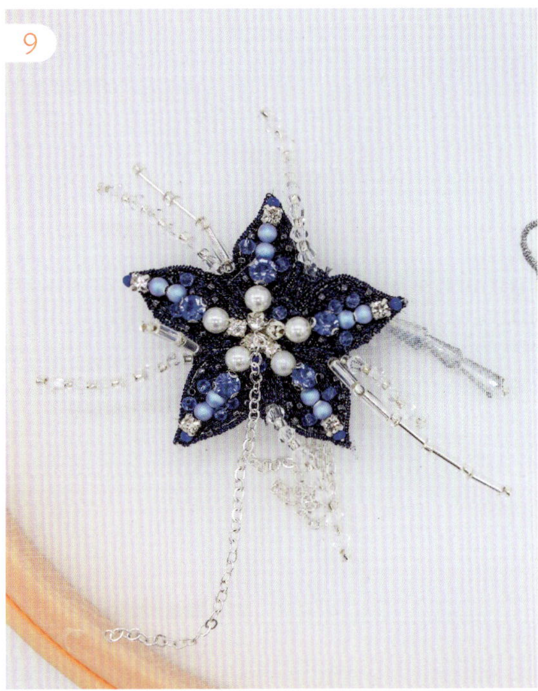

Fix the embroidery hoop to the front. Use a hand sewing needle and invisible thread to fix a 2 mm wide silver chain at the center of the flower.

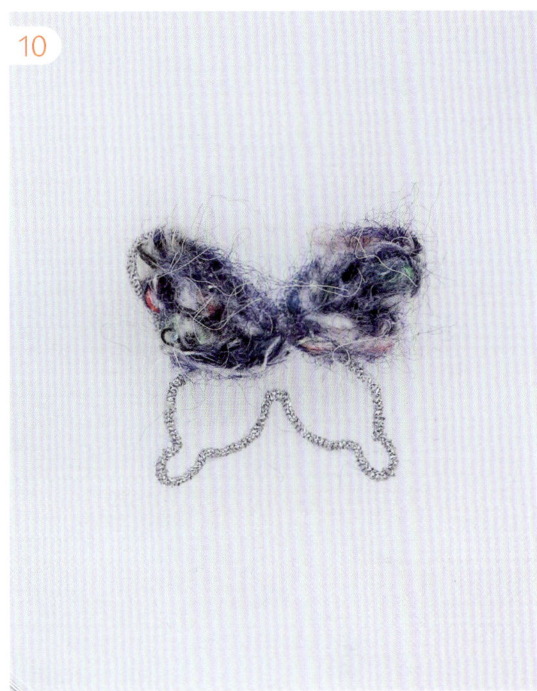

Use a hand sewing needle and blue gradient wool to fill in the butterfly's forewings.

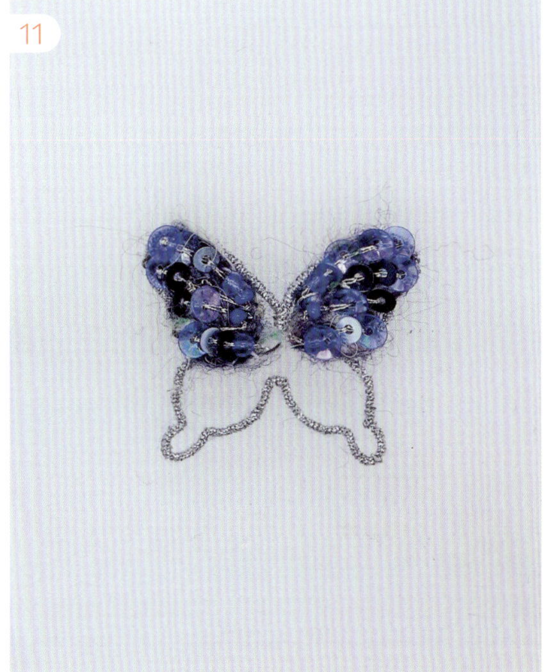

Apply the technique of stitching beads from the front side of the fabric using a hook needle, silver thread, 4 mm light blue sequins, 3 mm dark blue sequins, 3 mm blue crystals, and 2 mm blue seed beads on the blue gradient wool in an irregular fashion to sew the stripy patterns one after another.

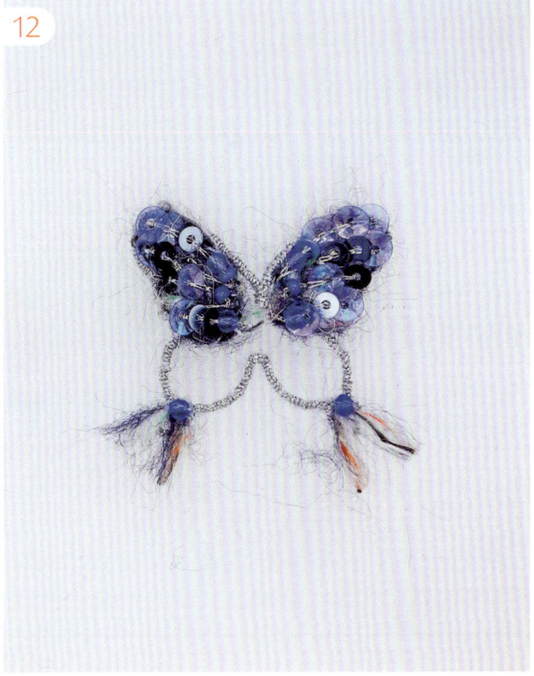

Use a hand sewing needle and invisible thread to fix a piece of blue gradient wool on the tail end of the butterfly's hindwings, and sew a 2 mm blue seed bead on top of it.

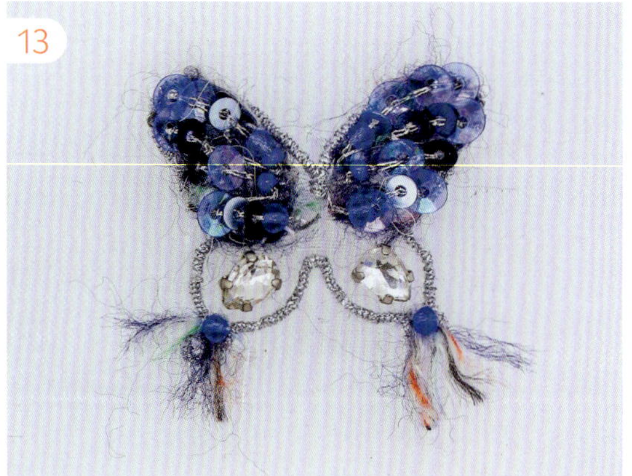

Use a hand sewing needle and silver embroidery thread to fix two 4 × 6 mm white drop shape crystals on the butterfly's hindwings.

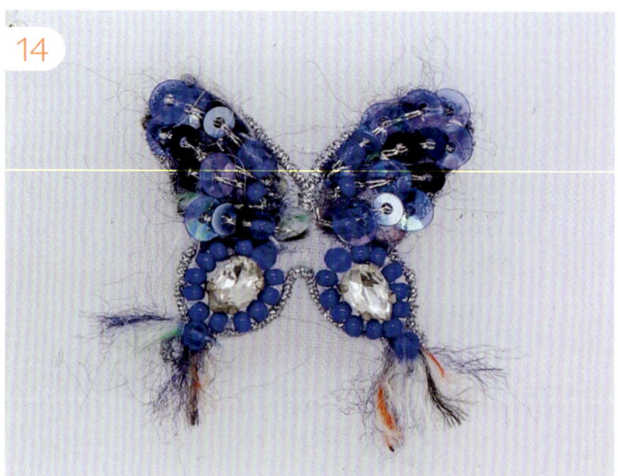

Apply the technique of stitching beads from the front side of the fabric using a hook needle and dark blue thread to sew a circle of 2 mm blue seed beads around the 4 × 6 mm white drop shape crystals.

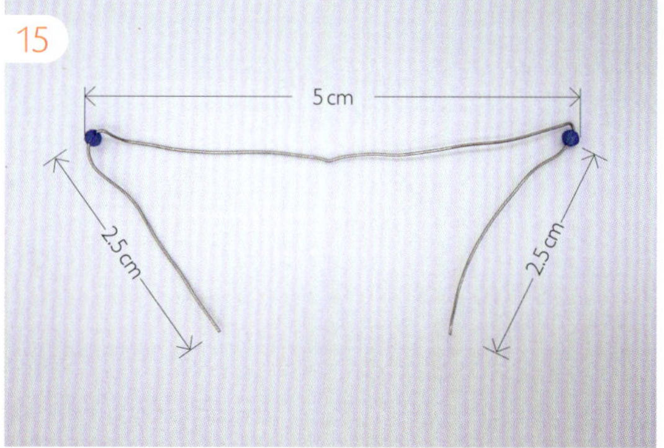

Take a piece of iron wire and thread two 3 mm blue crystals onto it.

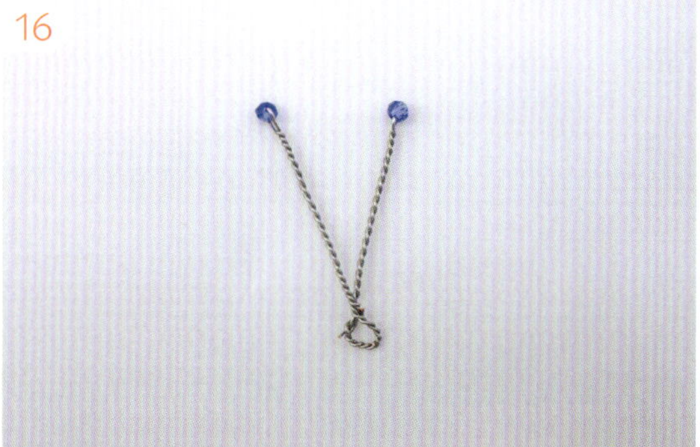

Twist the wire. Hold one of the beads with one hand. With the other hand, hold the wire on both sides of the bead and twist it quickly and consistently in a clockwise direction. Repeat for the other bead. After twisting the two pieces of iron wire, fold them into half, and cross the bottom ends to form a circle and create antennae.

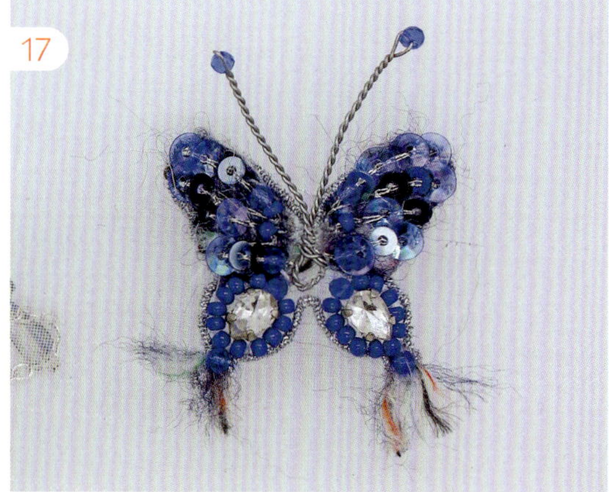

Use a hand sewing needle and invisible thread to fix the antennae to the center of the butterfly's body.

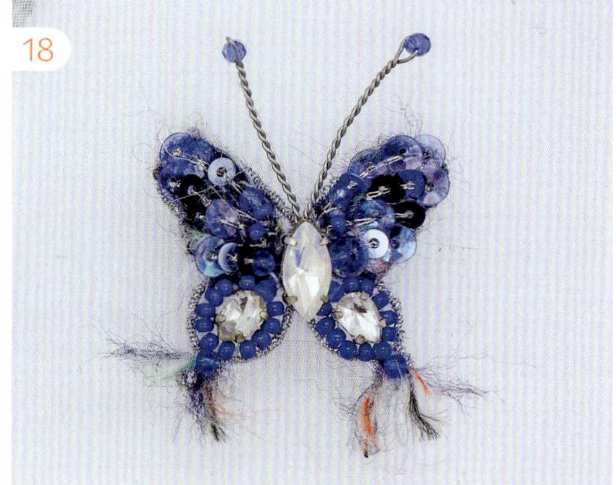

Use a hand sewing needle and invisible thread to sew a 5 × 10 mm egg white crystal onto the center of the butterfly's body.

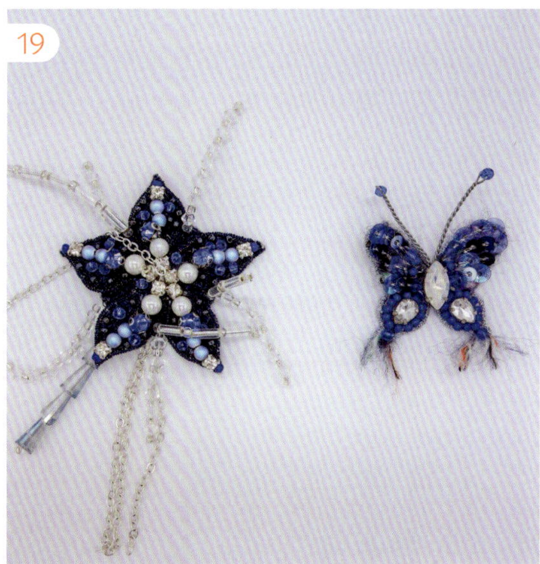

Cut out the embroidered pieces along the outer contours.

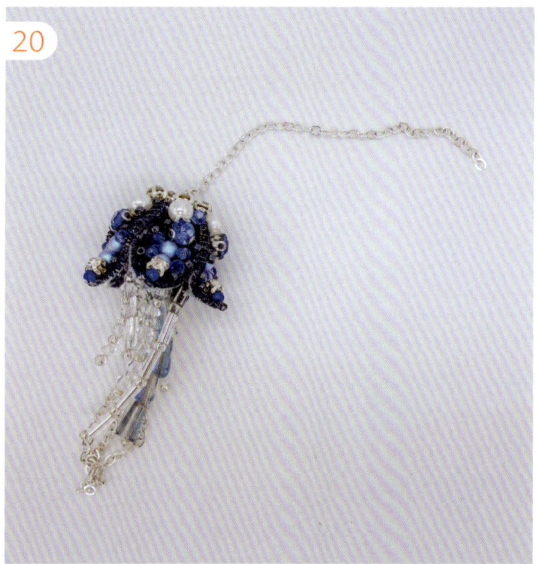

Use invisible thread to sew all the petals in pairs, i.e., sew the iron wire contour of the petals together. Next, fold the petals and the fringe inside the petals to create a three-dimensional effect.

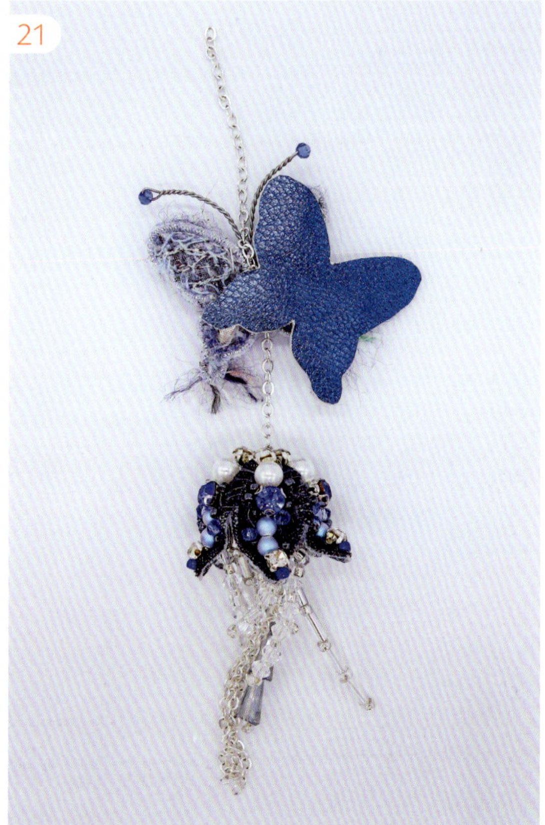

Cut a piece of blue leather that is the same size as the embroidered butterfly. Fix the back of the embroidered butterfly to the back of the leather and place the chain of the flower in between.

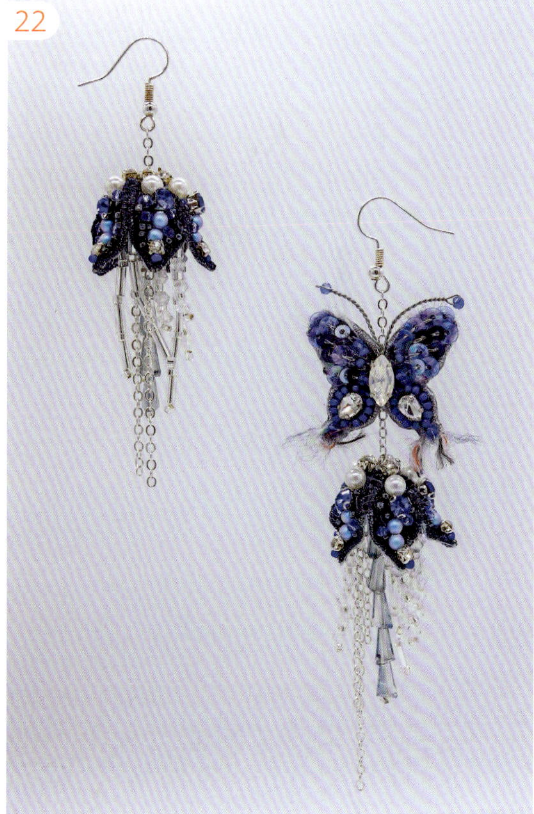

Affix silver ear hooks. The piece is now complete. You can also make another flower or butterfly-shaped pendant in the same way to form asymmetric earrings.

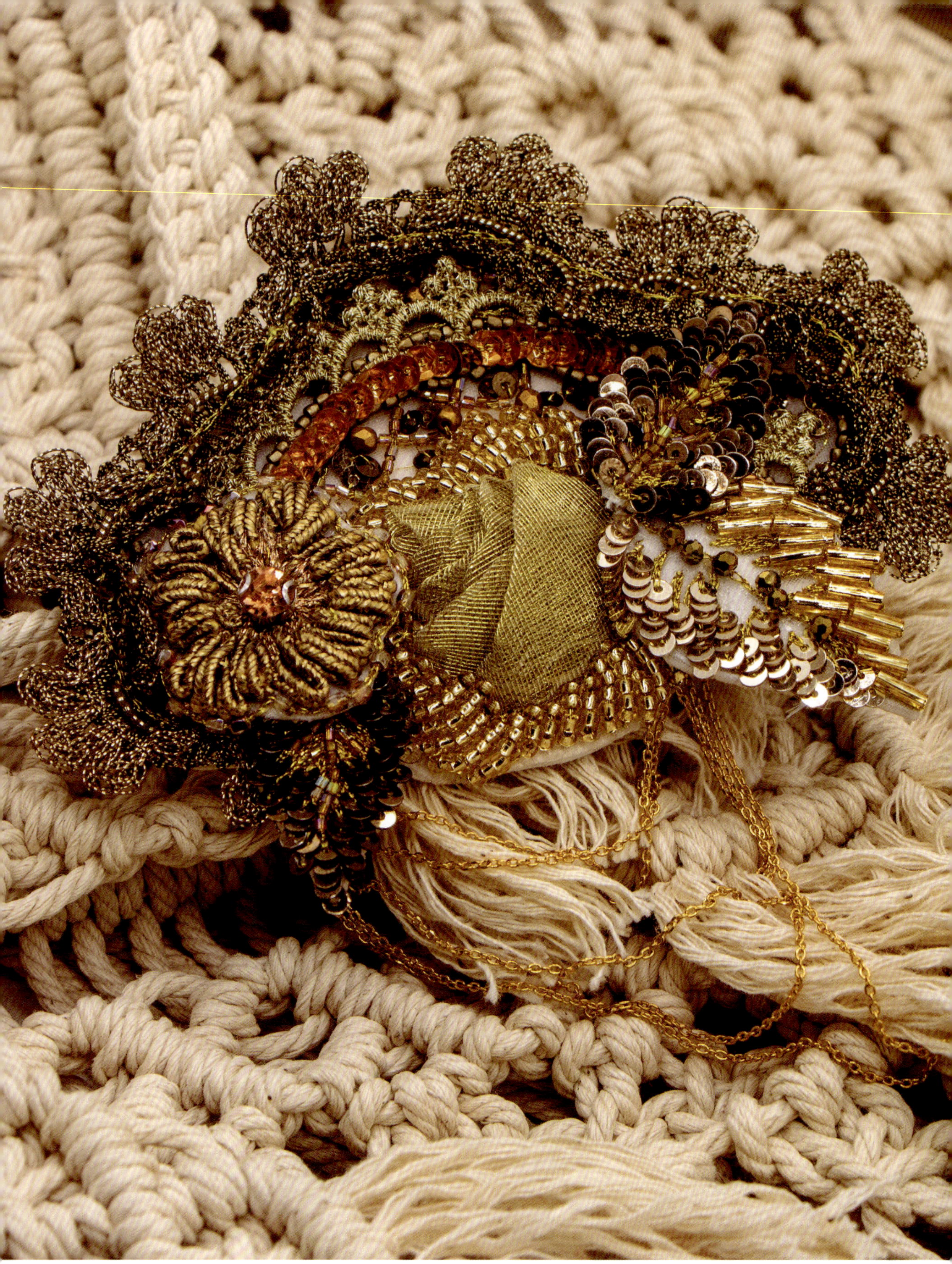

12. Rose Brooch

Throughout history, the rose has occupied a place of love and fascination around the world. With its intricate cascade of petals, it has been a token of affection between lovers in both the East and West. In China, roses have been cultivated for thousands of years. This brooch, with its gorgeous gold details, is a blend of vintage style and sophistication.

You Will Need

Threads	embroidery thread	golden
	metallic thread	orange
Beads	seed beads	1.5 mm orange, 2 mm golden, 2 mm dark golden
	Czech beads	3 mm colorful
	sequins	3 mm golden, 3 mm coffee, 3 mm dark gray, 5 mm orange
	oval beads	3 mm orange
	tube beads	1.5 mm orange, 6 mm golden
	crystals	3 mm brown
	sew-on rhinestones	4 mm pink
Fabrics	3 mm golden satin ribbon, 5 mm golden pattern ribbon, 20 mm golden vintage pattern ribbon, organza, golden Indian tulle, velvet, leather, felt	
Tools	embroidery frame, 70# hook needle, hand sewing needle, scissors, fabric glue, heat erasable marker, iron wires, ball head pins, golden metal chains, bar pin	

Embroidery Steps

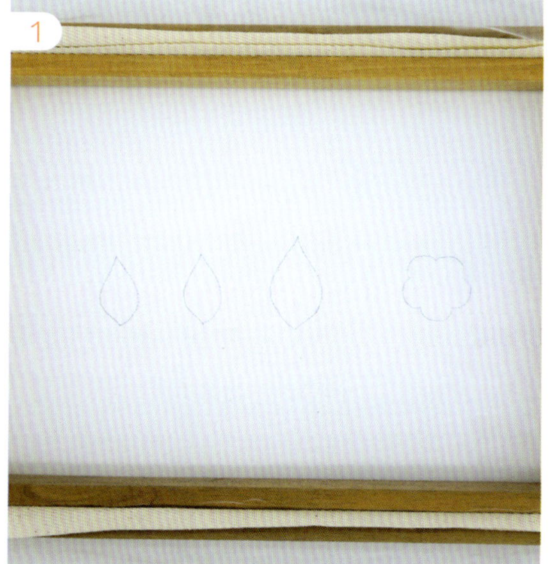

1 Stretch the organza on the embroidery frame. Use a heat erasable marker to trace flower and leaves (see page 167, 1 large leaf, 2 small leaves, and 1 flower) on the organza.

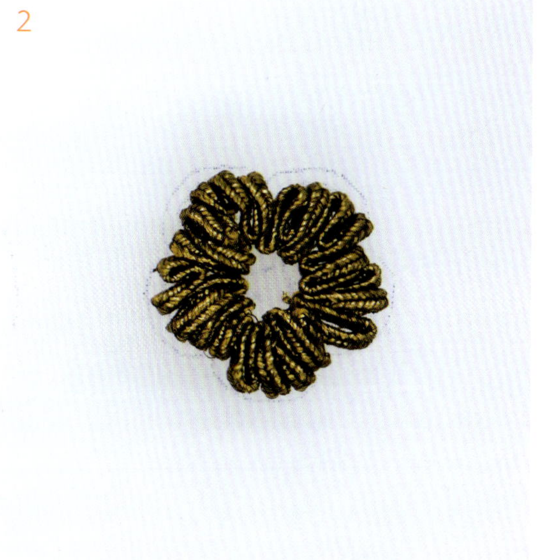

2 Use a hand sewing needle and golden thread to fix the 3 mm golden satin ribbon in a curved fashion where the flower is positioned.

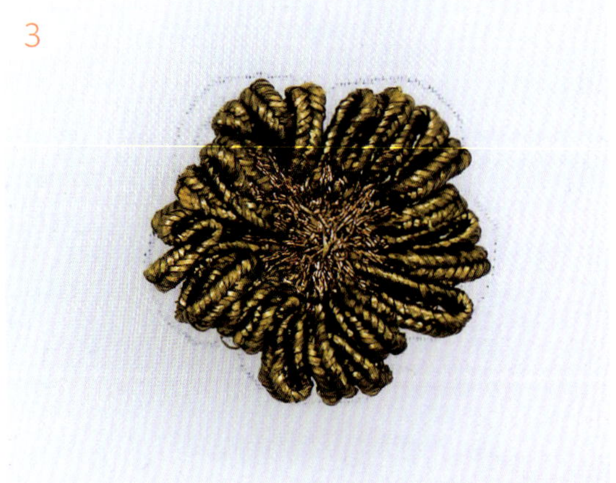

Apply the chain stitch technique from the front side of the fabric using a hook needle and orange metallic thread to fill the center of the flower.

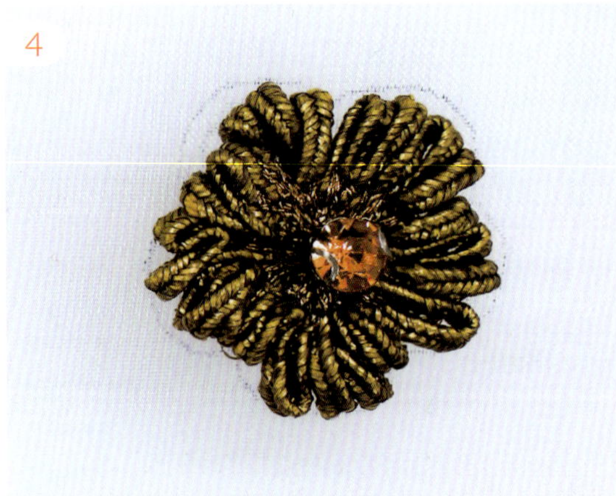

Use a hand sewing needle to fix a 4 mm pink sew-on rhinestone in the middle of the flower as pistil.

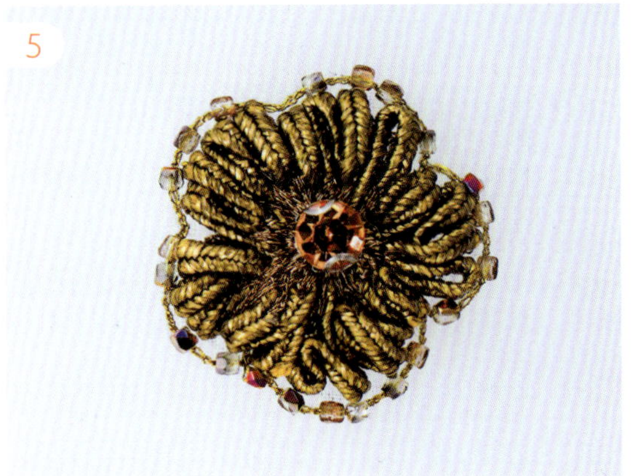

Apply the technique of stitching beads discontinuously from the front side of the fabric using a hook needle, golden thread, and 3 mm colorful Czech beads to outline the flower's contour.

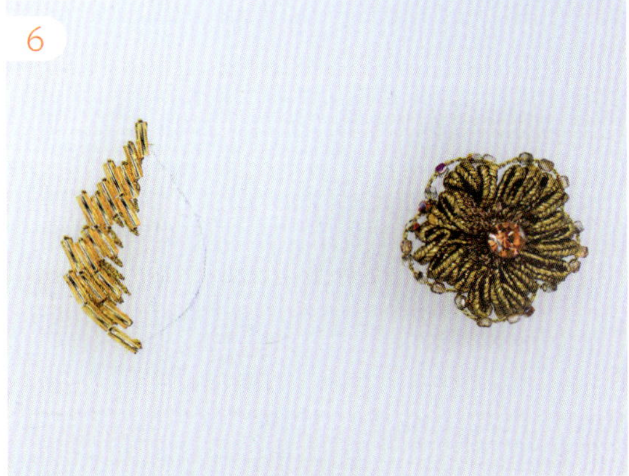

Apply the technique of stitching beads from the front side of the fabric using a hook needle, golden thread, and 6 mm golden tube beads to outline the left half of the large leaf.

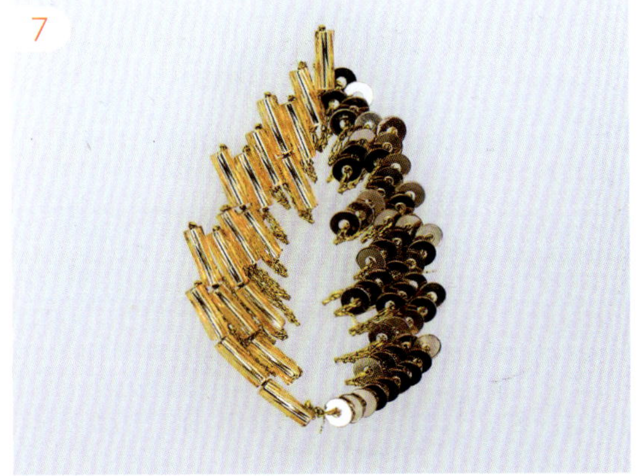

Apply the technique of stitching sequins from the front side of the fabric using a hook needle, golden thread, and 3 mm golden sequins to outline the right half of the large leaf.

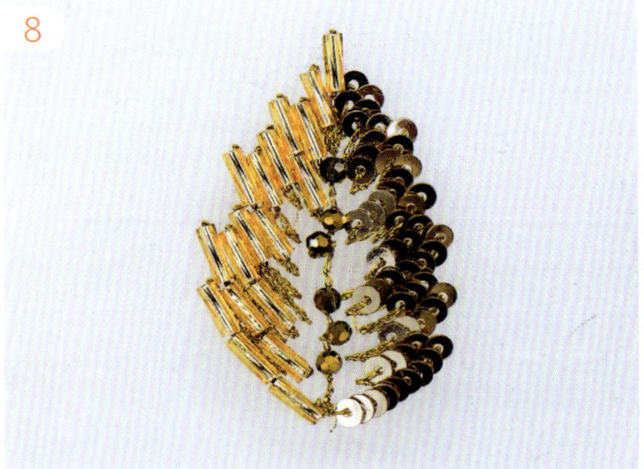

Apply the technique of stitching beads discontinuously from the front side of the fabric using a hook needle, golden thread, and 3 mm brown crystals to outline the vein of the leaf.

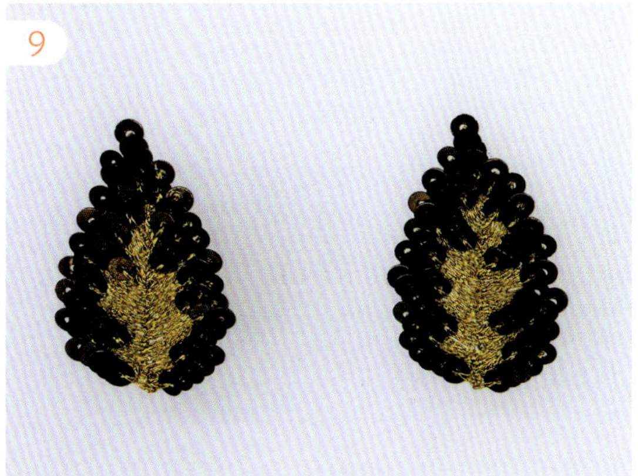

Apply the techniques of stitching sequins from the front side of the fabric and pulling stitch using a hook needle, golden thread, and 3 mm coffee color sequins to fill the two small leaves.

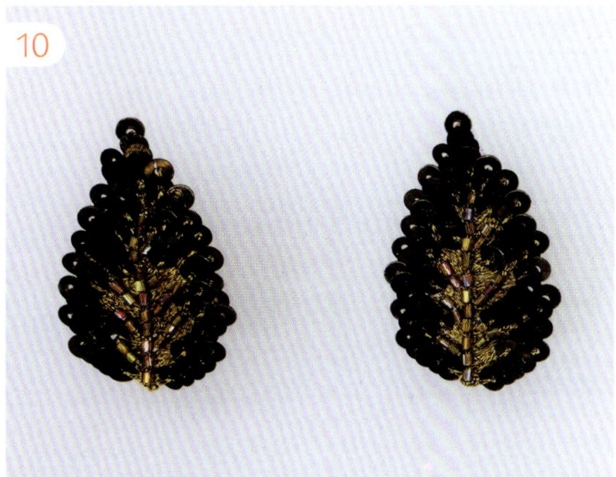

Apply the technique of stitching beads from the front side of the fabric using a hook needle, golden thread, and 1.5 mm orange tube beads to outline the veins of the two small leaves.

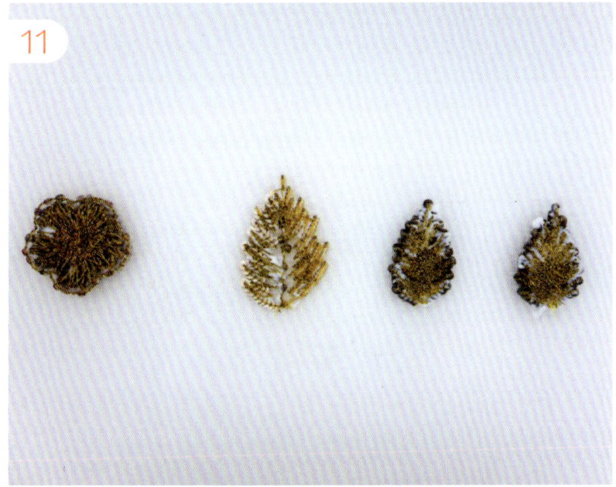

Cut out all the embroidered parts and leave a 5–8 mm margin on the edge of the embroidery pieces.

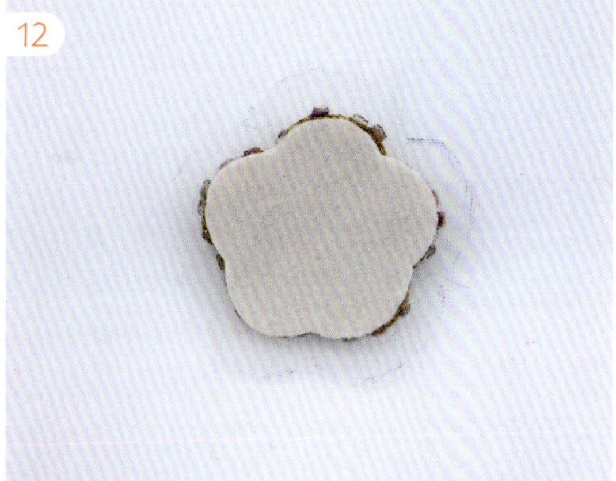

Cut out the velvet according to the shape of the flower, and stick it on the back of the flower using fabric glue.

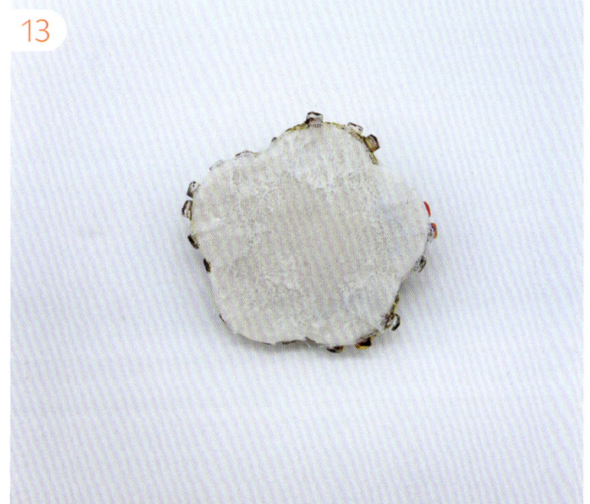

Use fabric glue to fold the edges of the organza inwards, and fit it to the velvet on the back of the flower.

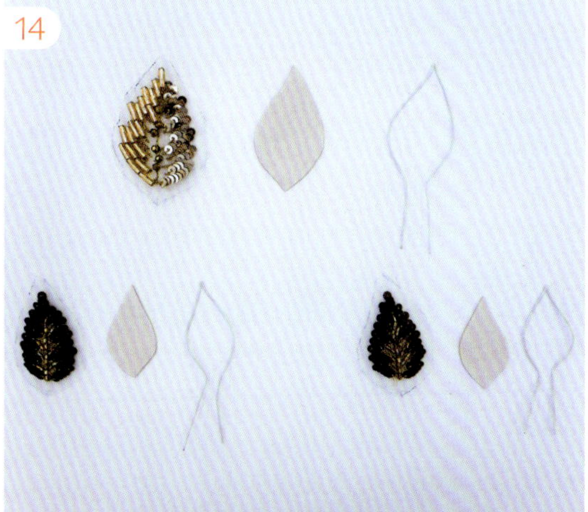

Cut out the velvet fabric according to the shape of the leaves, and bend the wires into the corresponding shapes.

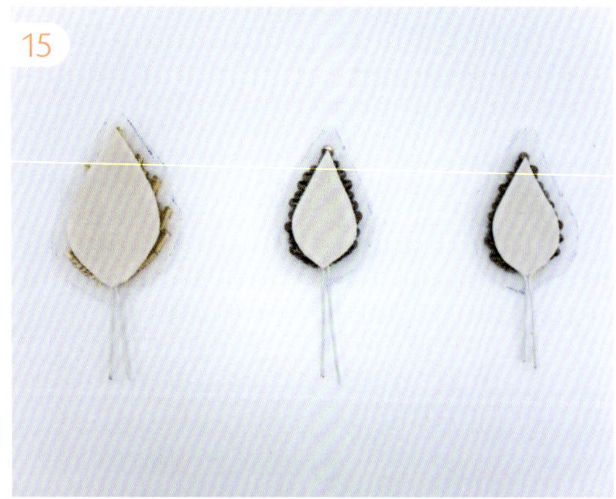

Use fabric glue to stick the back of the leaves, iron wires, and velvet fabric in turn.

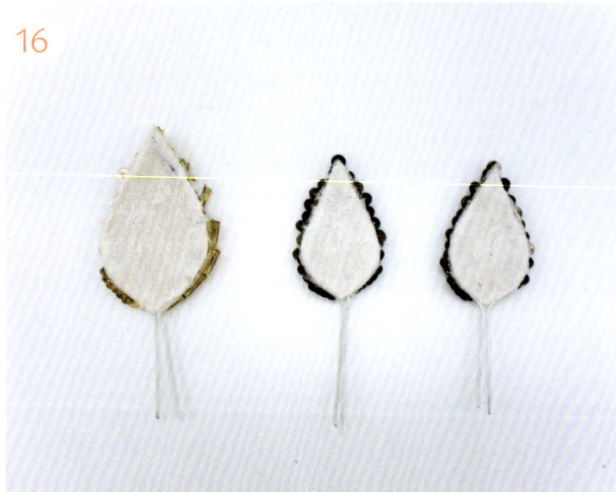

Use fabric glue to fold the organza on the edge of the leaves inwards, and fit it to the velvet on the back of the leaves.

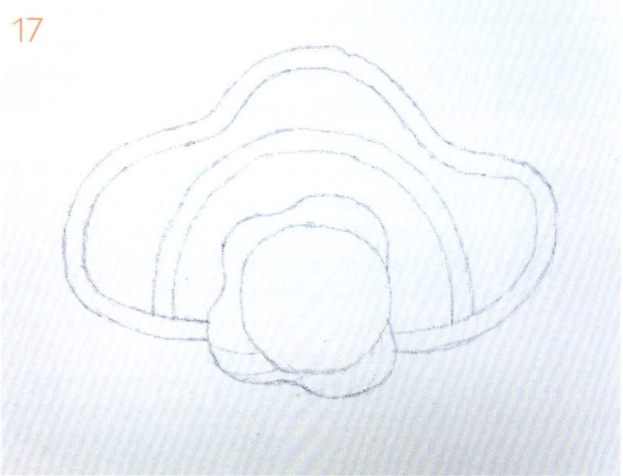

Take a new piece of organza and stretch it on the embroidery frame. Trace the lines of the pattern (see page 167) on the organza with a heat erasable marker.

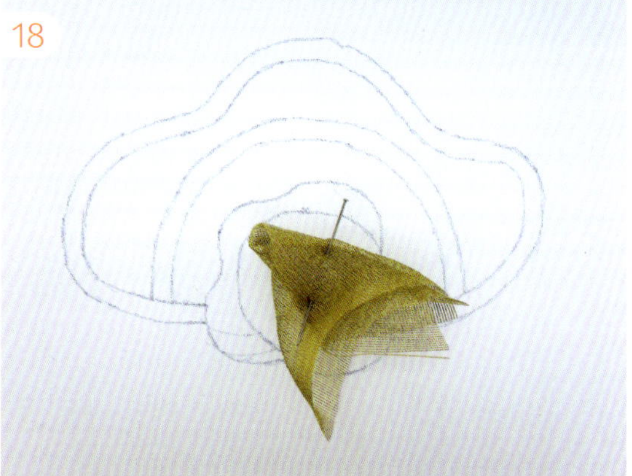

Take a square piece of golden Indian tulle, fold it along the diagonal direction twice to create the center of the flower, and fix it on the sketched pattern with a ball head pin.

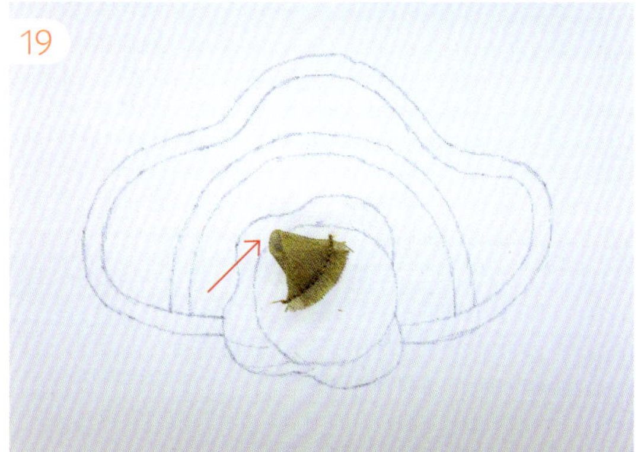

Apply chain stitch from the front side of the fabric using a hook needle and golden thread at a distance of about 1.5 cm from the top (arrowed position) to form a curved line and fix the golden Indian tulle, and then trim off the excess fabric, leaving a margin of about 2 mm.

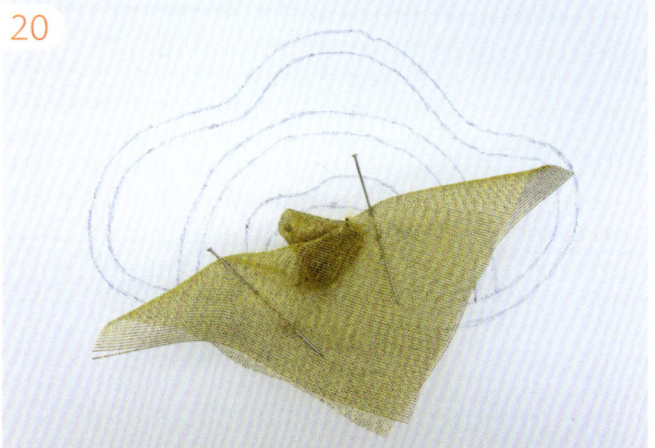

Take another square piece of golden Indian tulle, fold it along the diagonal, and fix it diagonally on the center of the flower that was completed in the previous step with ball head pins. Make sure to cover the previous stitches.

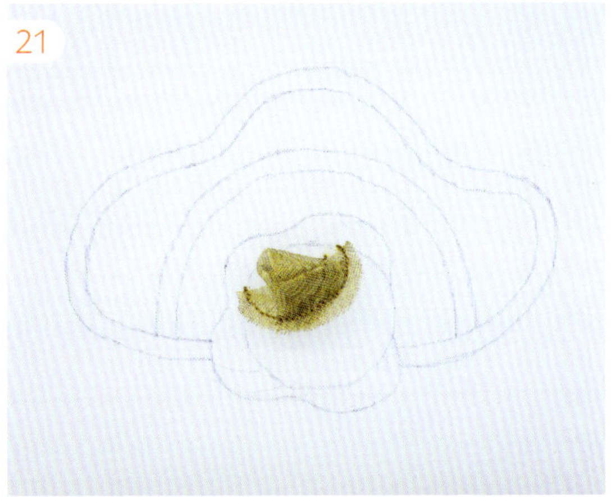

Apply chain stitch from the front side of the fabric using a hook needle and golden thread to sew a petal. Trim off the excess fabric, leaving a margin of about 2 mm.

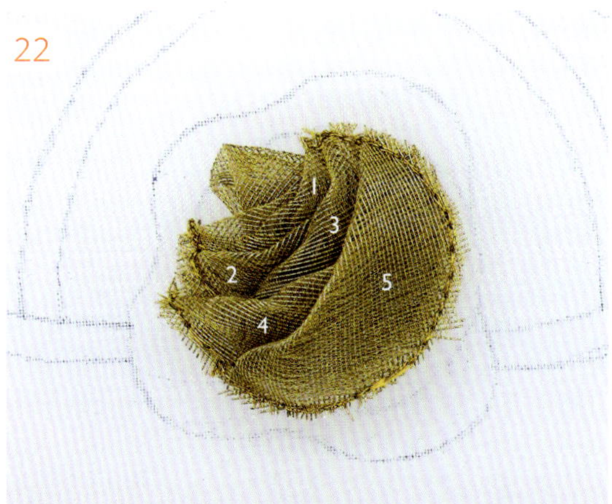

Sew the other five petals using the same techniques shown in steps 20–21. Take note of the positions of the petals in the figure.

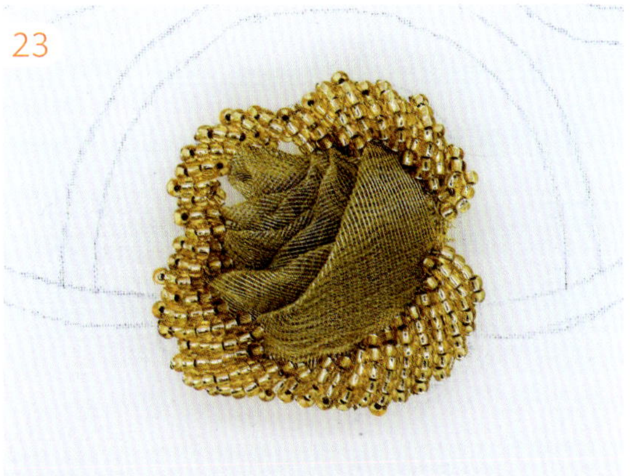

Apply the technique of stitching multiple beads from the front side of the fabric using a hook needle, golden thread, and 2 mm golden seed beads to outline the area along the periphery of the flower.

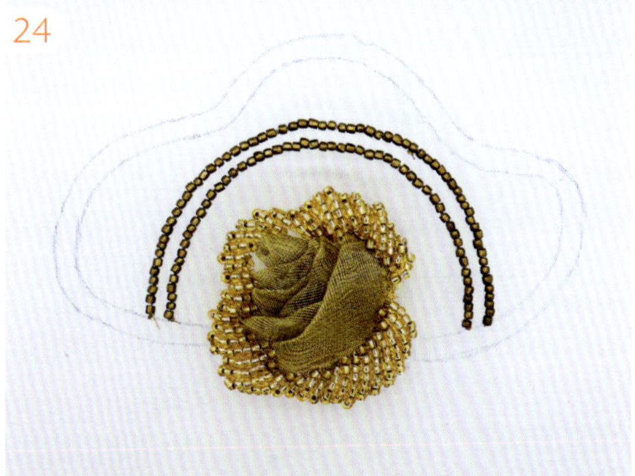

Stitch beads from the back side of the fabric continuously, using a hook needle, golden thread, and 2 mm dark golden seed beads to outline the two curves.

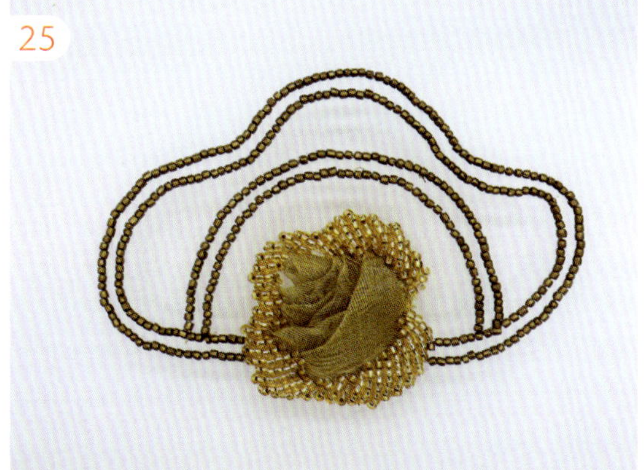

Stitch beads from the back side of the fabric continuously, using a hook needle, golden thread, and 2 mm dark golden seed beads to outline the other two curves.

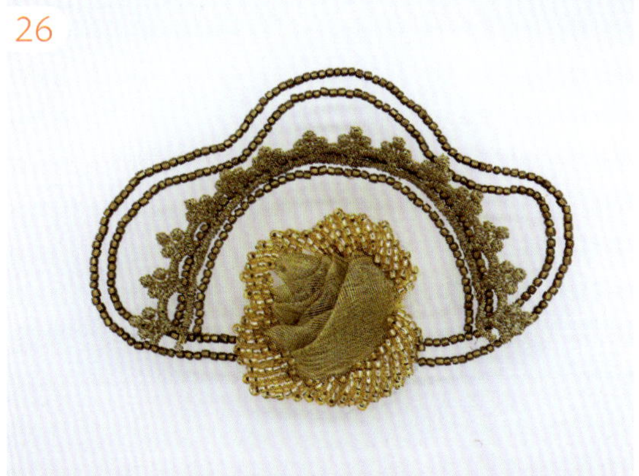

Use a hand sewing needle and golden thread to fix the 5 mm golden pattern ribbon on the inner side of the beads near the outer ring that was completed in step 24.

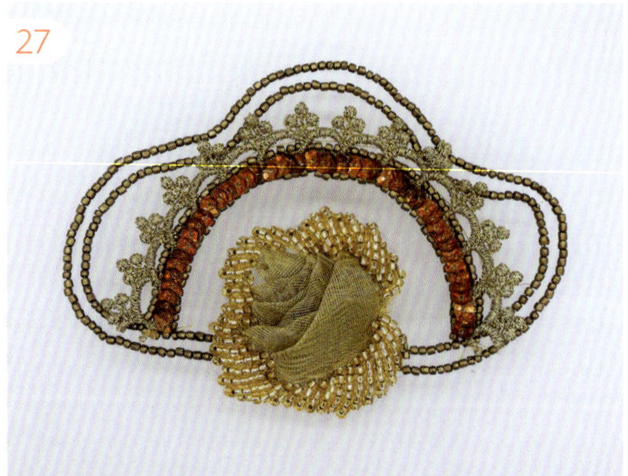

Stitch sequins from the front side of the fabric continuously using a hook needle, golden thread, and 5 mm orange sequins to fill the gap between the two curves, as shown in the figure.

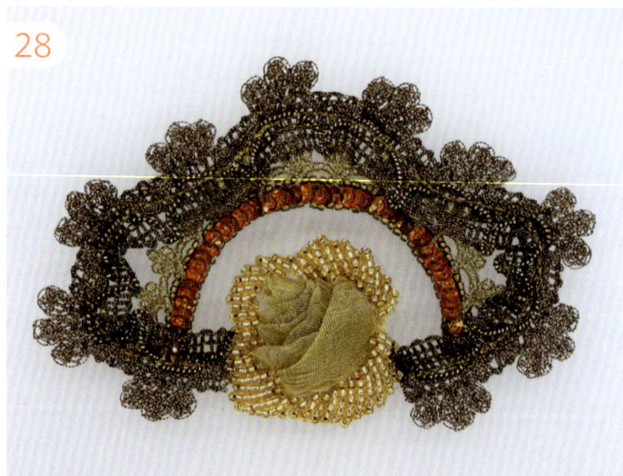

Use a hand sewing needle and golden thread to fix the 20 mm golden vintage pattern ribbon between the two curves completed in step 25.

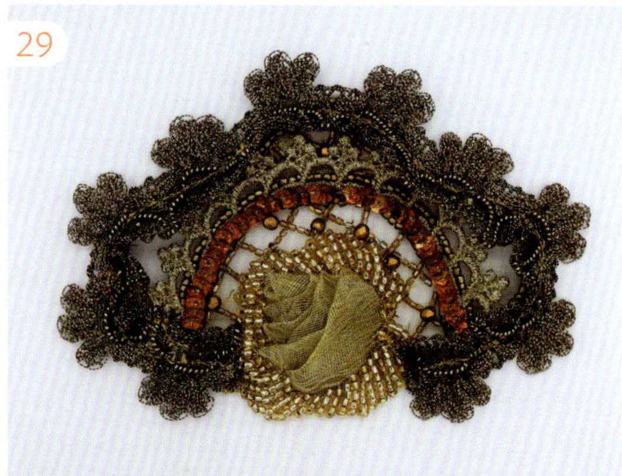

Stitch beads from the front side of the fabric continuously using a hook needle, golden thread, 1.5 mm orange seed beads, and 3 mm orange oval beads to create a grid effect at the position shown in the figure.

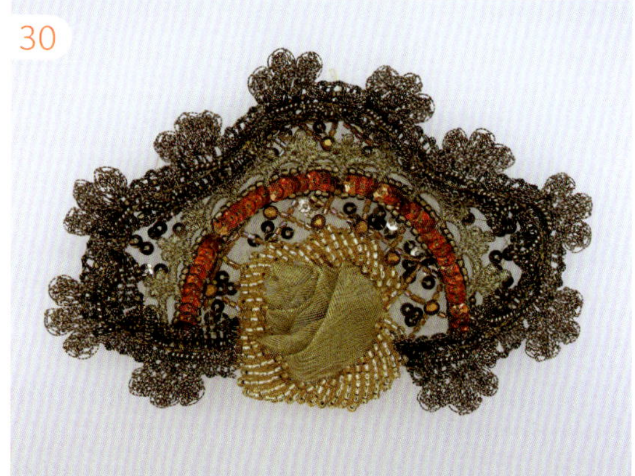

Apply the technique of embroidering sequins using a hand-sewing needle, golden thread, and 3 mm dark gray sequins to fill the interior of the grid in an irregular fashion.

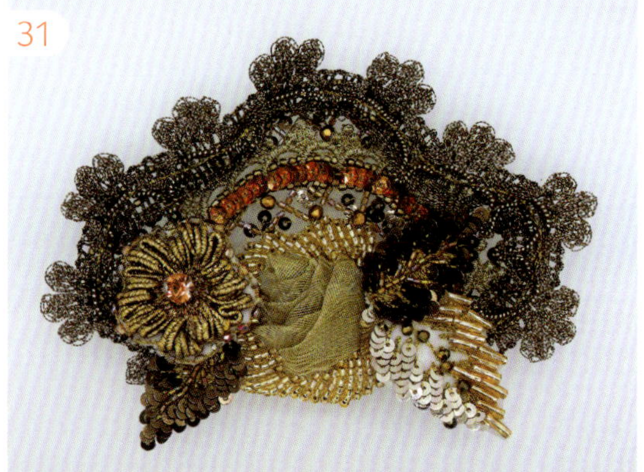

Use a hand sewing needle and golden thread to fix the flower and three leaves to the main body.

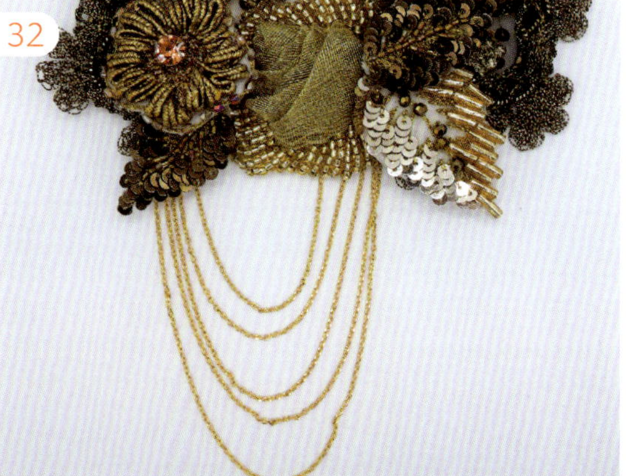

Use a hand sewing needle and golden thread to sew the golden metal chains in a suitable position to form arcs of varying sizes.

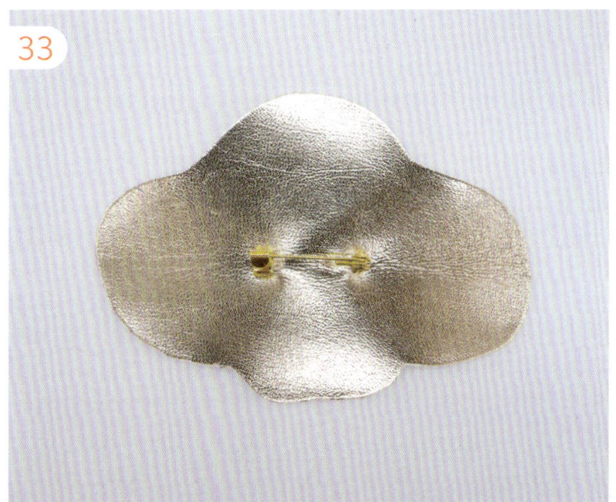

Cut out a piece of leather that is of the same shape as the embroidered piece to serve as the base of the brooch, and insert a bar pin in the center.

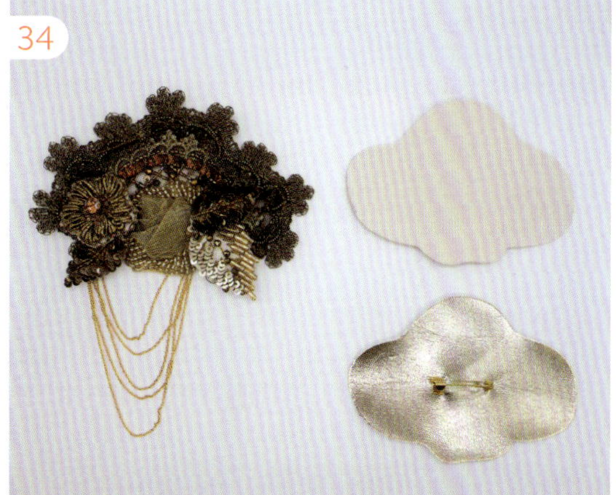

Glue the finished embroidery piece, a piece of same sized felt, and the leather brooch base together to form the final product.

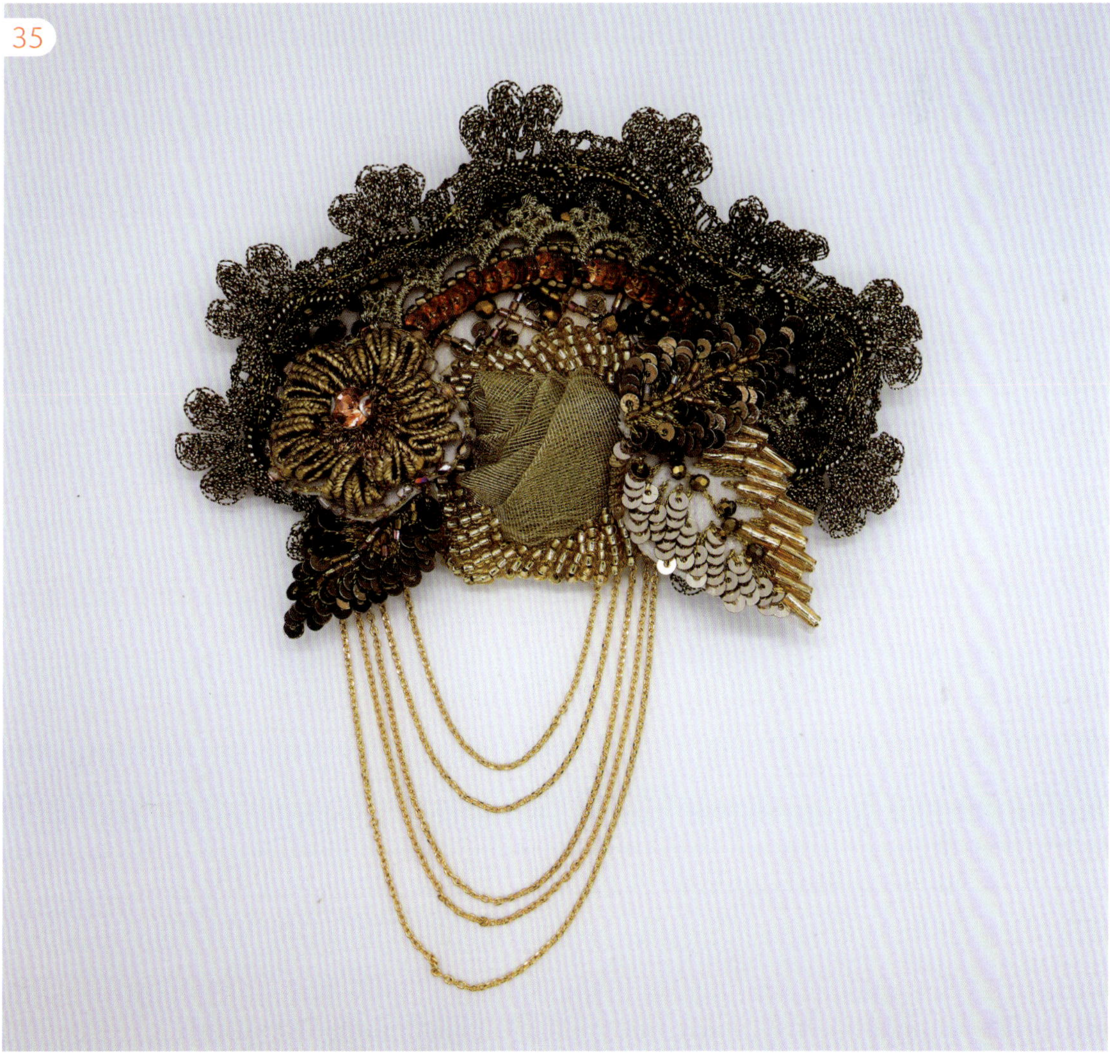

35

Allow the glue to dry. The piece is now complete.

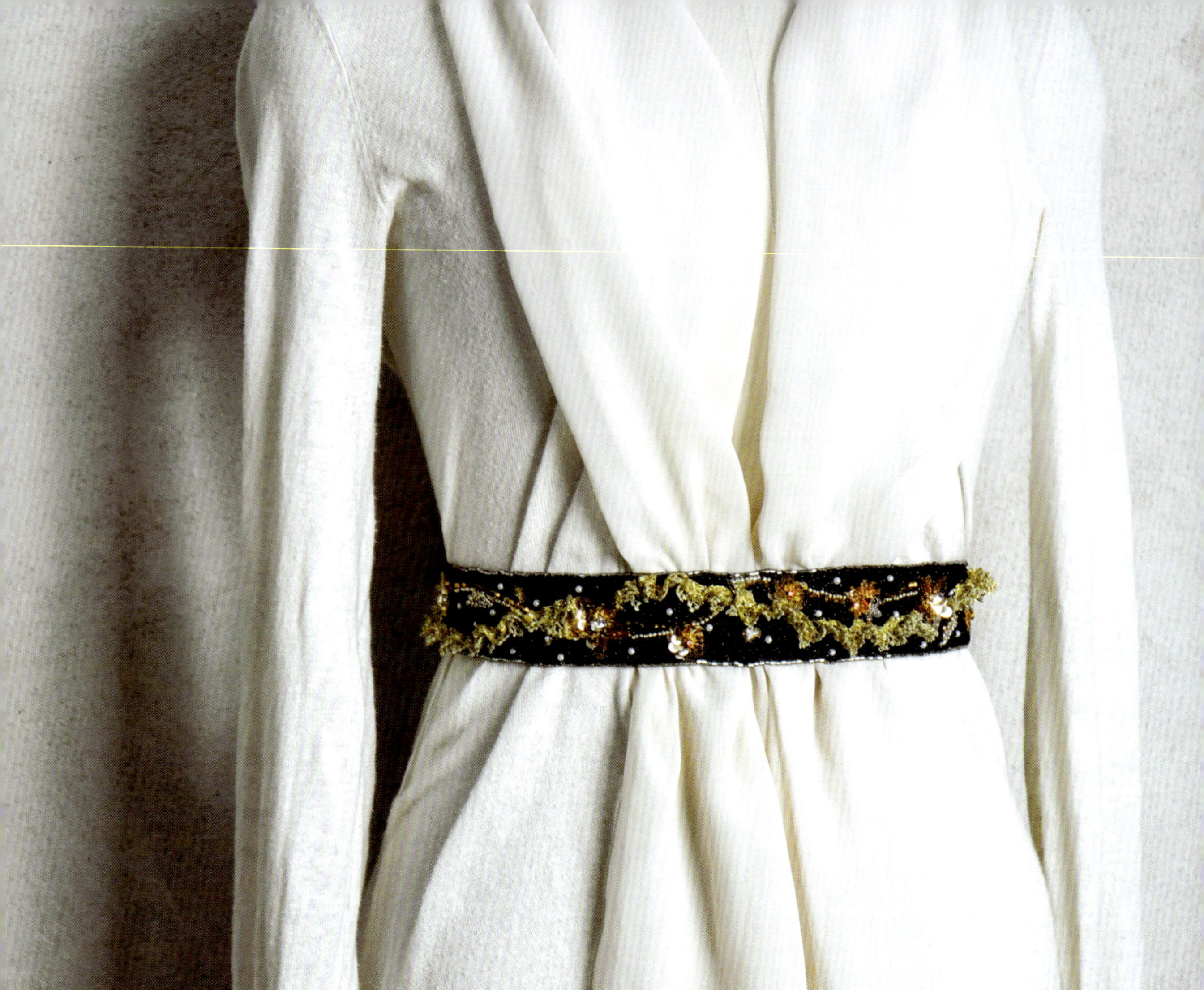

13. Plum Blossom Belt

The plum blossom exudes elegance, calmness, nobility, and dignity, and top the list of China's ten most famous flowers. It blooms even in the harshest weather, while other flowers wither. Hence, Chinese literati and writers across dynasties have appreciated its unrelenting character and its ability to carve out periods of solitude, and have devoted countless works to its beauty. The most famous calssical work inspired by the plum blossom is by Song dynasty (960–1279) poet Lin Bu (967–1028), depicting the calming fragrance of plum blossoms in hazy moonlight. The accessory we are working on in this section is inspired by this scene. Plum blossoms in various positions are represented by gold beads and sequins, akin to a plum garden shrouded in moonlight and a dream within a quiet night.

You Will Need

Threads	embroidery thread	silver, golden, black
Beads	seed beads	2 mm black, 2 mm gold, 2 mm silver, 2 mm white
	tube beads	3 mm gray
	crystals	3 mm dark golden diamond shape
	pearls	3 mm white
	sequins	3 mm golden, 4 mm golden, 4 mm light golden
	sew-on rhinestones	4 mm brown round, 5 mm golden round, 6 mm yellow round
Fabrics	white organza, scrap leather sheet, black self-adhesive velvet, black velvet, 6 mm golden floral lace trim webbing	
Tools	embroidery frame, 70# hook needle, hand sewing needle, scissors, fabric glue, heat erasable marker, 40 mm black belt buckles	

Embroidery Steps

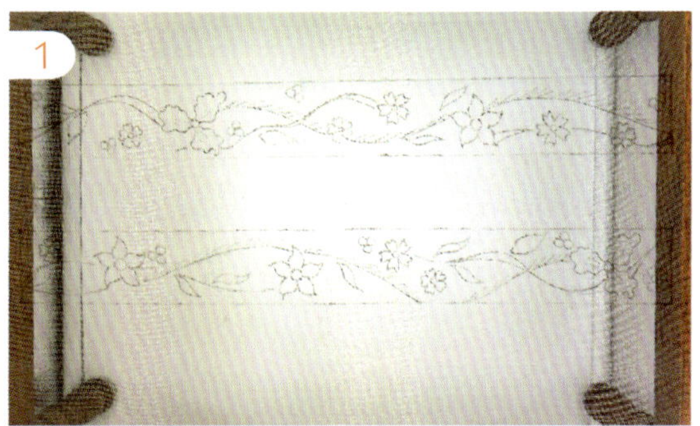

Stretch the white organza onto the embroidery frame and trace the pattern (see page 169) on the fabric in two sections with a heat erasable marker.

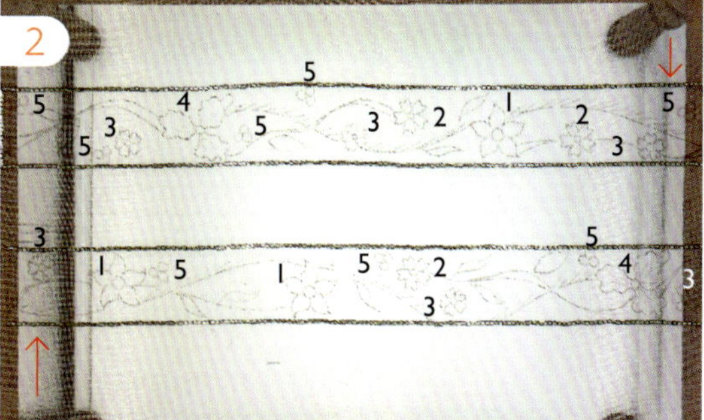

Apply the technique of stitching beads from the back side of the fabric using a hook needle, black thread, and 3 mm gray tube beads to embroider the outline of the pattern. Please note that the connecting section (position indicated by the arrows) between the two parts need not be sewn. (For the convenience of subsequent embroidery, the flowers in the picture are represented by different serial numbers.)

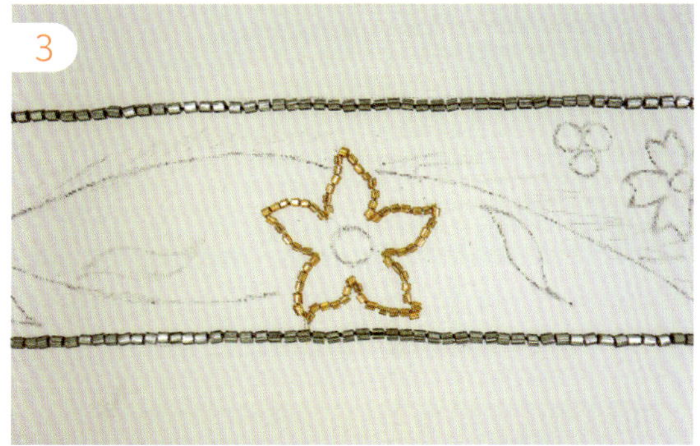

Apply the technique of stitching beads from the back side of the fabric using a hook needle, golden thread, and 2 mm golden seed beads to embroider the outline of Flower 1.

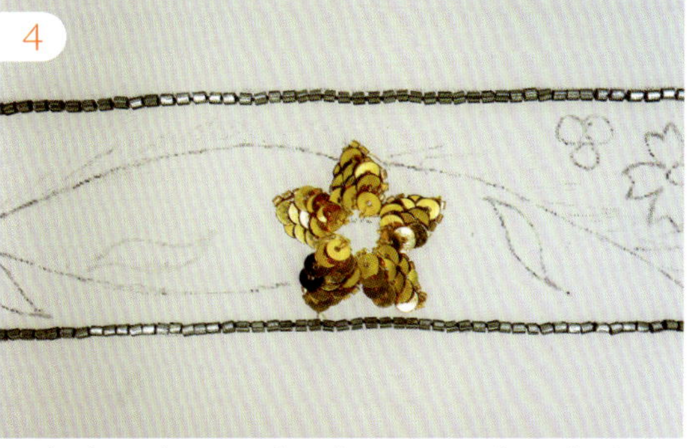

Apply the technique of stitching sequins from the front side of the fabric using a hook needle, golden thread, and 4 mm golden sequins to fill the petals of Flower 1.

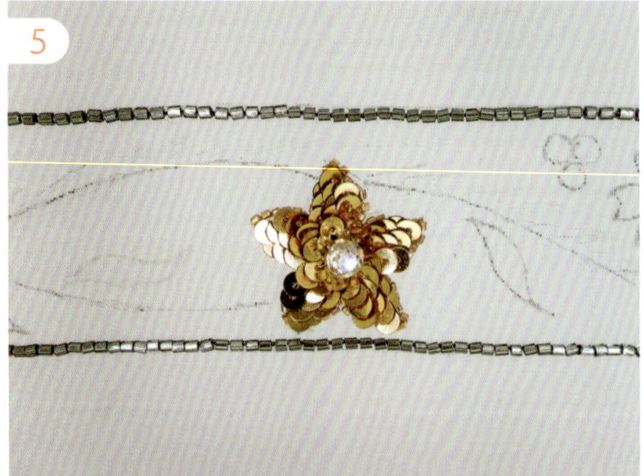

Use a hand sewing needle and golden thread to sew a 5 mm golden round sew-on rhinestone in the center of Flower 1.

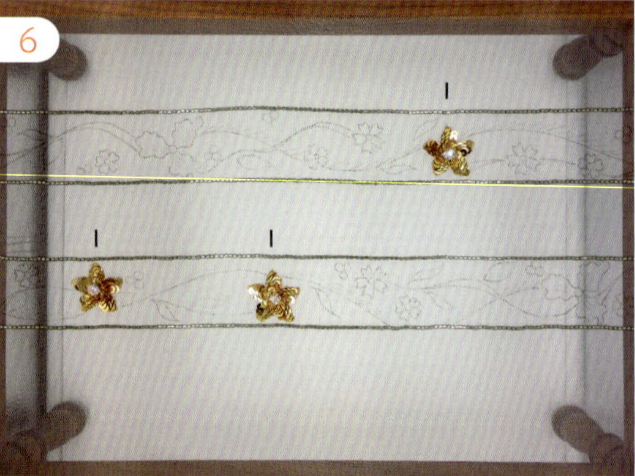

Apply the same techniques and materials in steps 3–5 to sew the other two identical flowers.

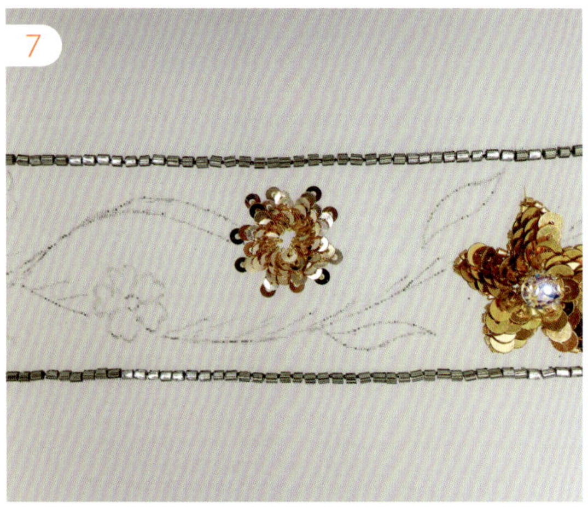

Apply the technique of stitching sequins from the back side of the fabric using a hook needle, golden thread, and 3 mm golden sequins to complete the sewing of the petals of Flower 2.

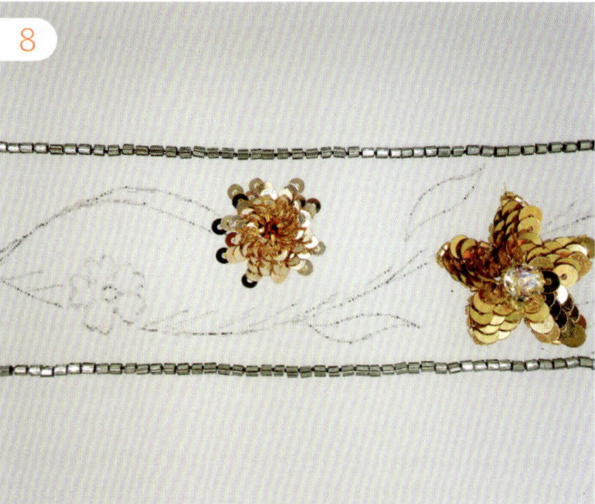

Use a hand sewing needle and golden thread to sew a 4 mm brown round sew-on rhinestone in the center of Flower 2.

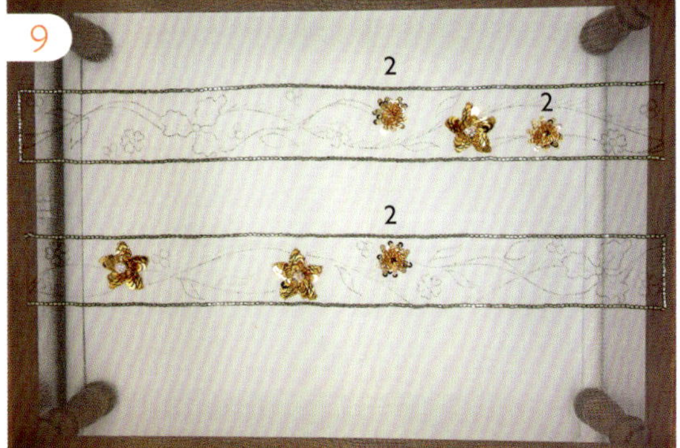

Apply the same techniques and materials in steps 7–8 to sew the other two identical flowers.

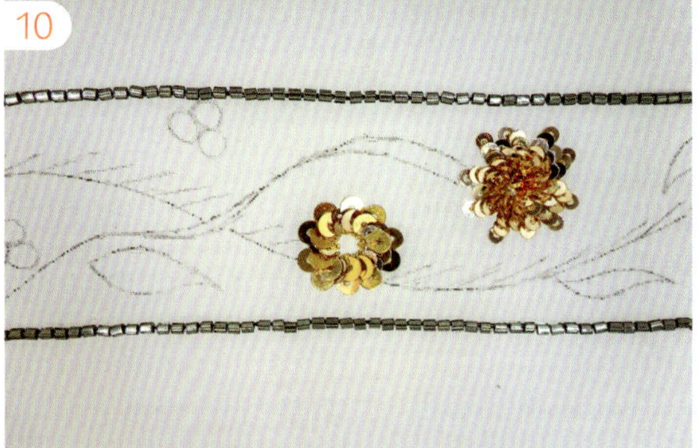

Apply the technique of stitching sequins from the front side of the fabric using a hook needle and golden thread, with two sequins in a row and each petal comprising a row of 4 mm golden sequins, a row of 3 mm golden sequins, and a row of 4 mm light golden sequins, to fill the five petals of Flower 3.

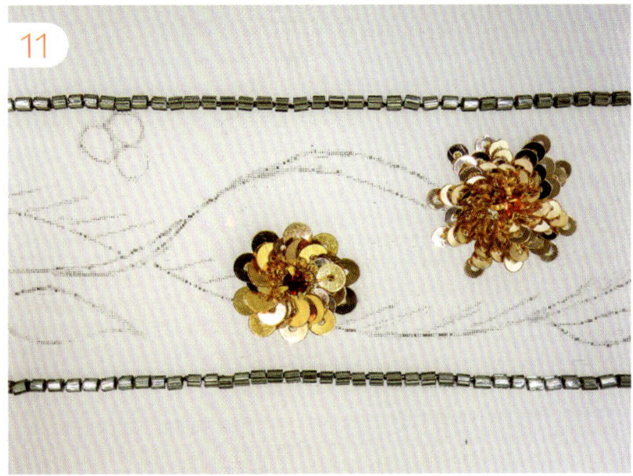

Use a hand sewing needle and golden thread to sew a 4 mm brown round sew-on rhinestone in the center of Flower 3.

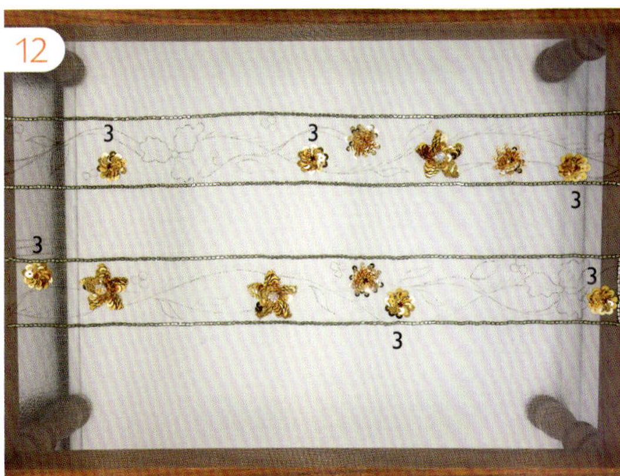

Apply the same techniques and materials in steps 10–11 to sew the other five identical flowers.

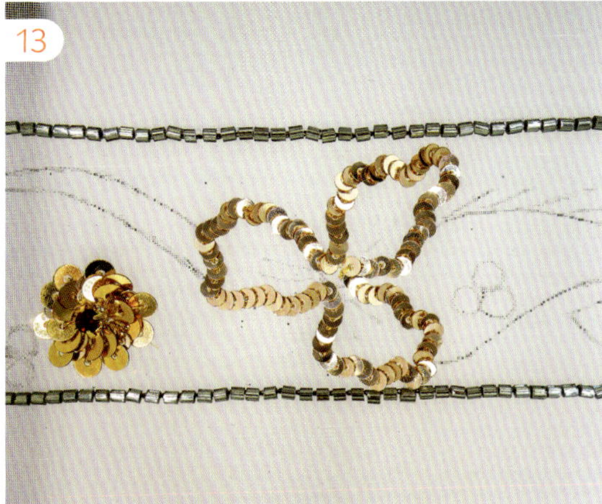

Apply the technique of stitching sequins from the back side of the fabric using a hook needle, golden thread, and 4 mm golden sequins to outline the outer contour of Flower 4.

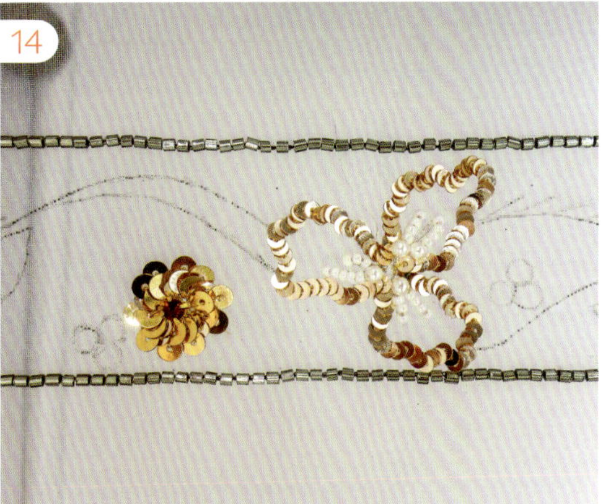

Apply the technique of stitching beads from the front side of the fabric using a hook needle, silver thread, 2 mm white seed beads, and 3 mm white pearls to outline the inner lines of Flower 4.

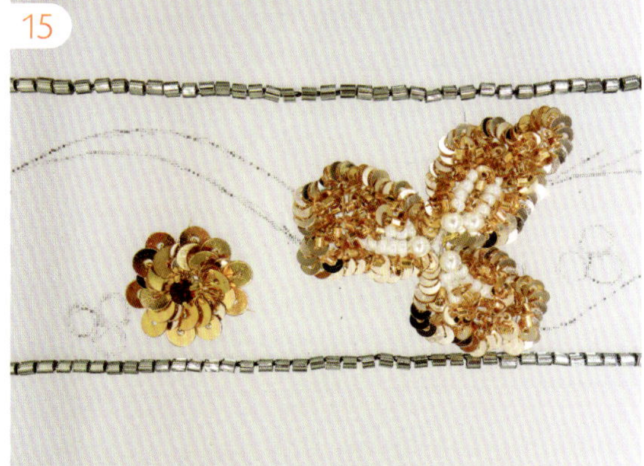

Apply the technique of stitching beads irregularly from the front side of the fabric using a hook needle, golden thread, 2 mm golden seed beads, and 4 mm golden sequins to fill the remaining parts of the inside of Flower 4.

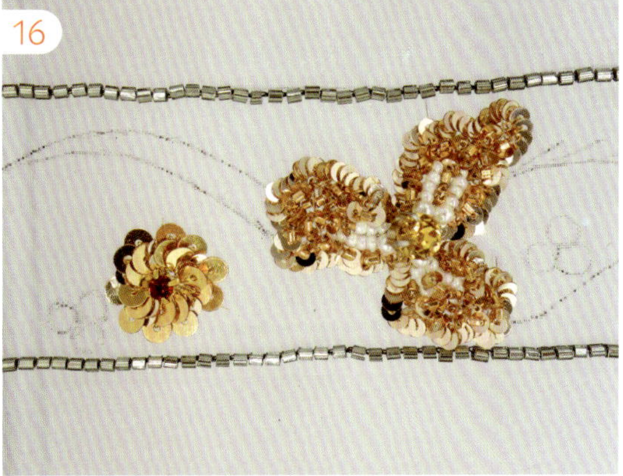

Use a hand sewing needle and golden thread to fix a 6 mm yellow round sew-on rhinestone to the center of Flower 4.

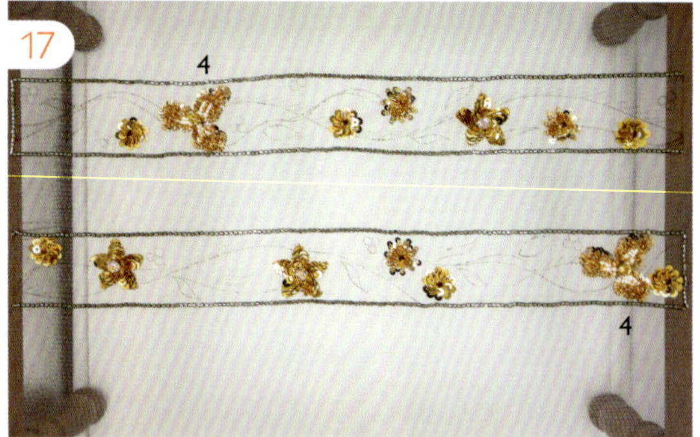

Apply the same techniques and materials in steps 13–16 to sew the other identical flower.

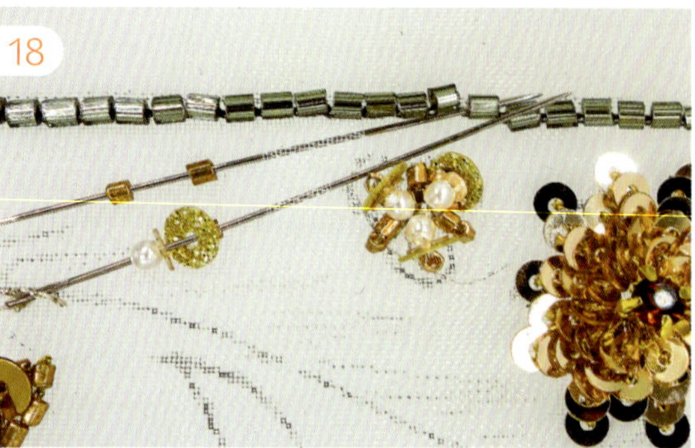

Apply the hand sewing technique of embroidering beads groups to string in turn 3 mm white pearls, 3 mm golden sequins, 4 mm golden sequins, and 2 mm golden seed beads onto the needle, followed by sewing the three petals of Flower 5. Thereafter, string two 2 mm golden seed beads onto the needle and sew among the three petals in intervals.

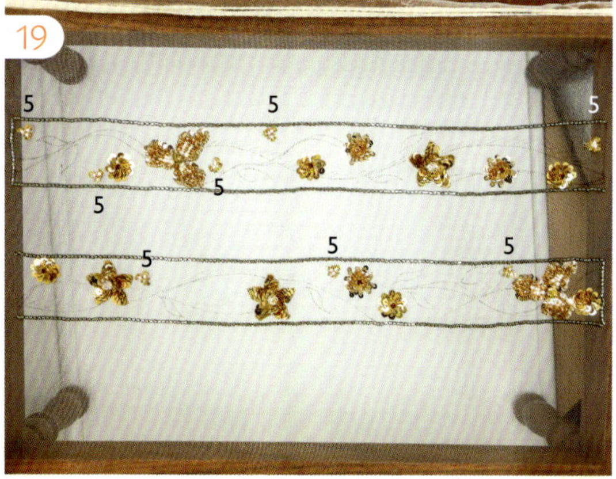

Apply the same techniques and materials in step 18 to complete the sewing of all Flower 5.

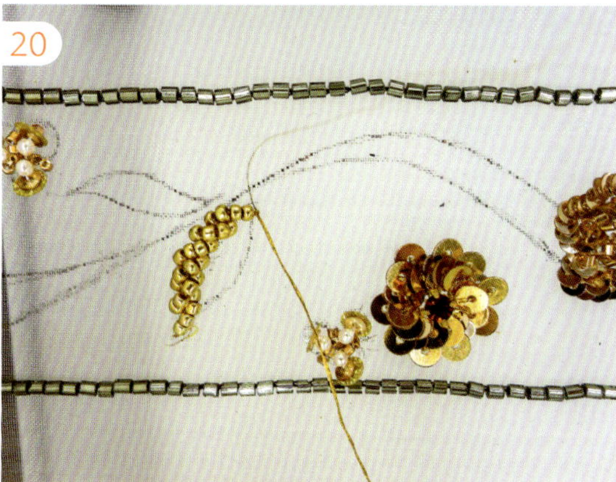

Apply the technique of stitching multiple beads from the front side of the fabric using a hook needle, golden thread, and 2 mm golden seed beads to sew the left half of the leaf, as shown in the image.

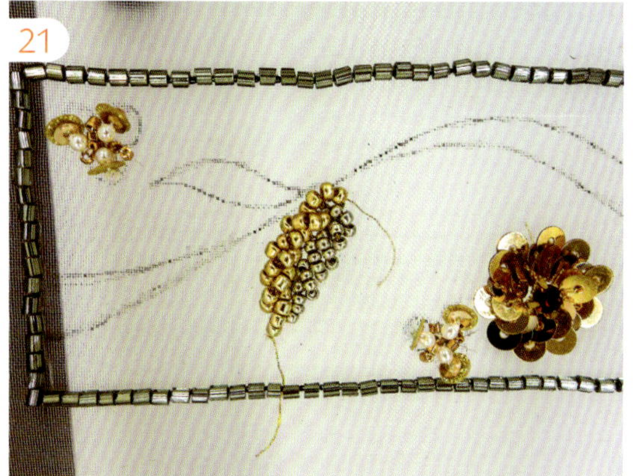

Apply the technique of stitching multiple beads from the front side of the fabric using a hook needle, golden thread, and 2 mm silver seed beads to sew the right half of the leaf.

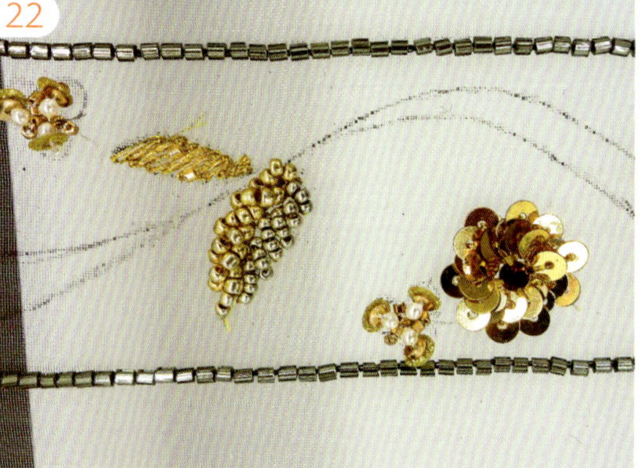

Apply the technique of stitching beads discontinuously from the front side of the fabric using a hook needle, golden thread, and 2 mm golden seed beads to fill the leaf, as shown in the image.

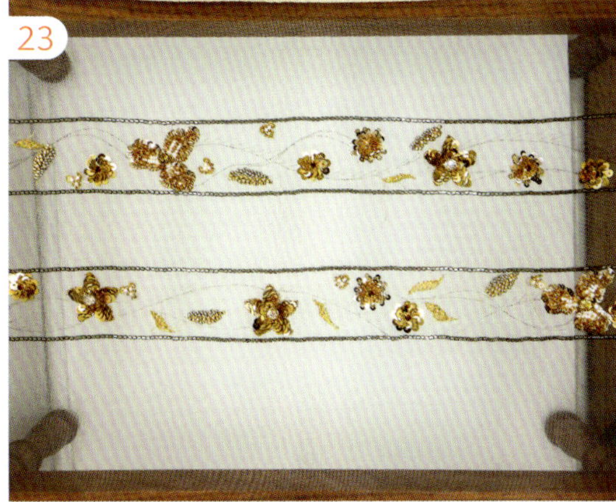

Apply the same materials and techniques in steps 20–22 to match and complete the sewing of the remaining leaves.

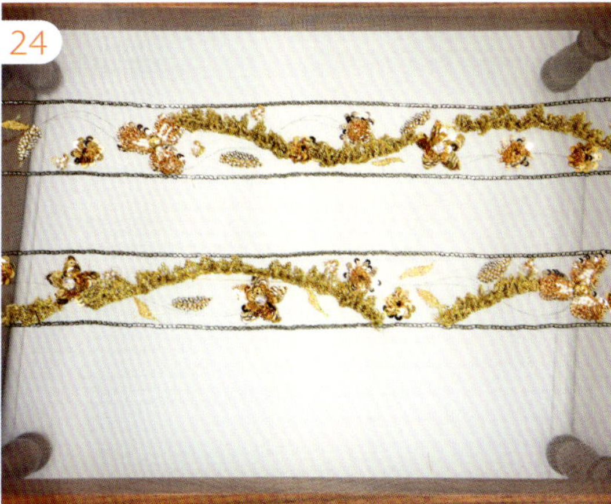

Apply the technique of fixing folded ribben to sew a 6 mm wide golden floral lace trim webbing on the lines as shown in the image.

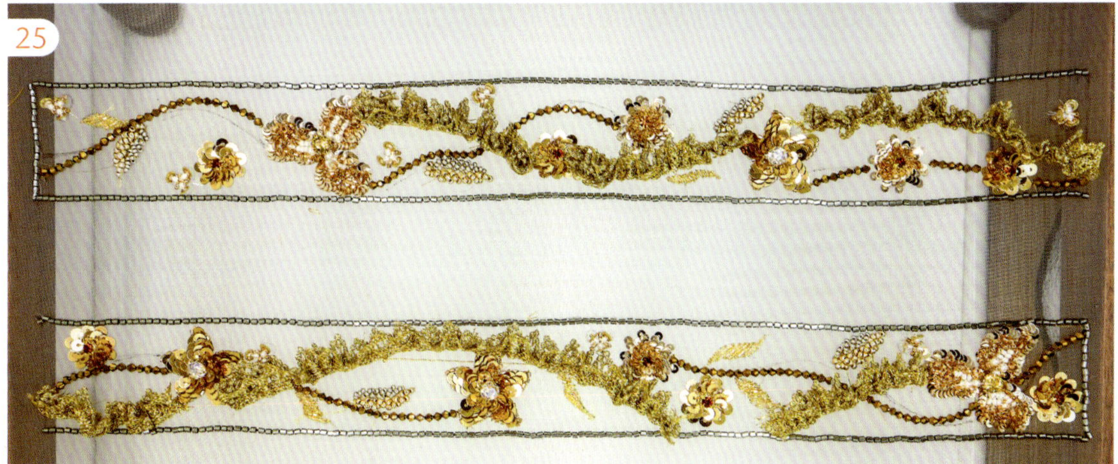

Apply the technique of stitching beads from the back side of the fabric using a hook needle, golden thread, and 3 mm dark golden diamond shape crystals to outline the lines as shown in the image.

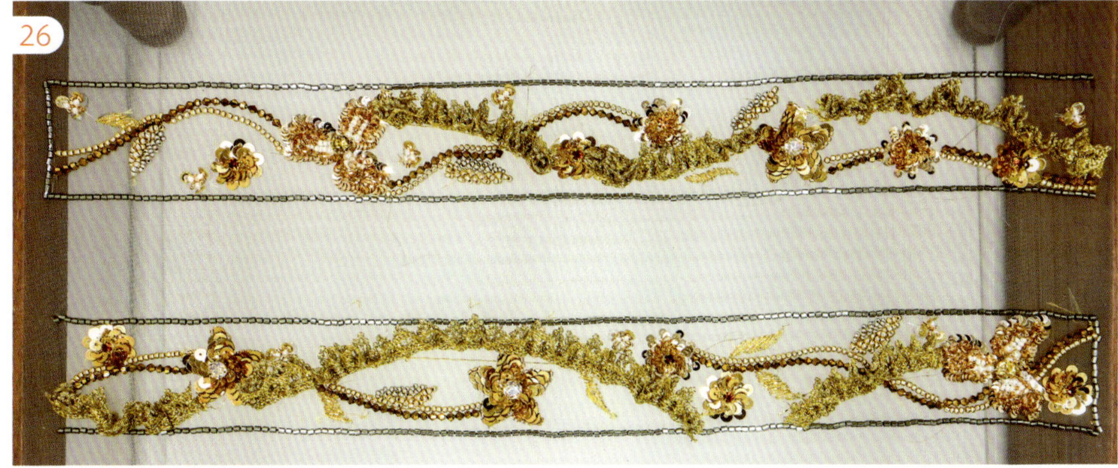

Apply the technique of stitching beads from the back side of the fabric using a hook needle, golden thread, and 2 mm golden seed beads to outline a row of beads near the lines in step 25.

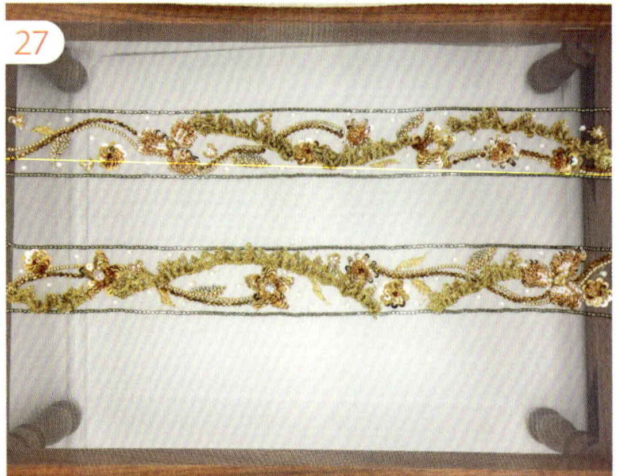

27

Apply the technique of stitching beads from the front side of the fabric using a hook needle and silver thread to fix a few 3 mm white pearls irregularly in the blank part of the pattern.

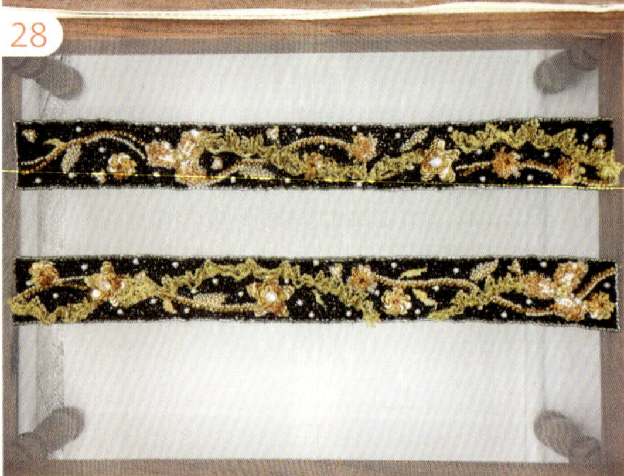

28

Apply the technique of stitching beads irregularly from the back side of the fabric using a hook needle, black thread, and 2 mm black seed beads to fill the rest of the belt.

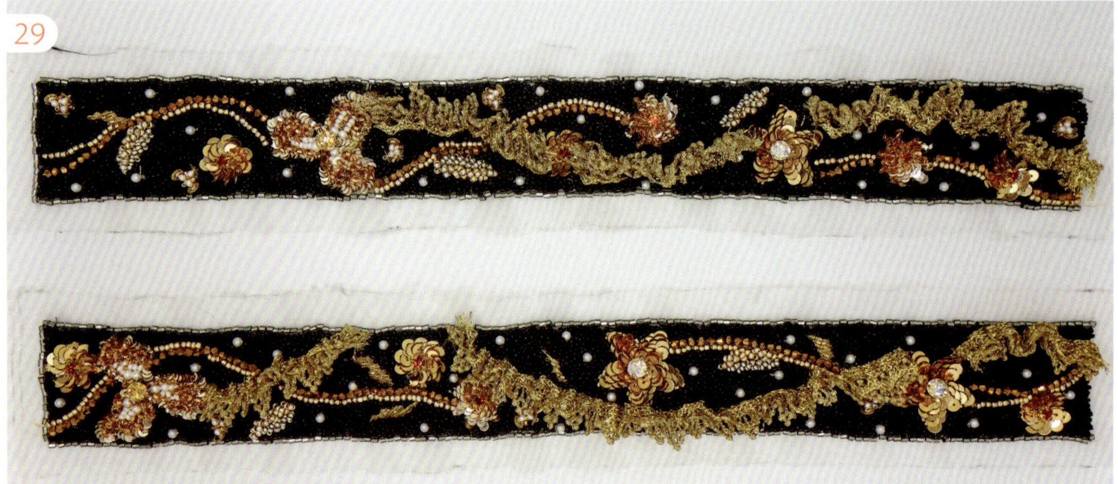

29

Leave a margin of 5–8 mm on the edge of the embroidery pieces, and cut the remaining parts.

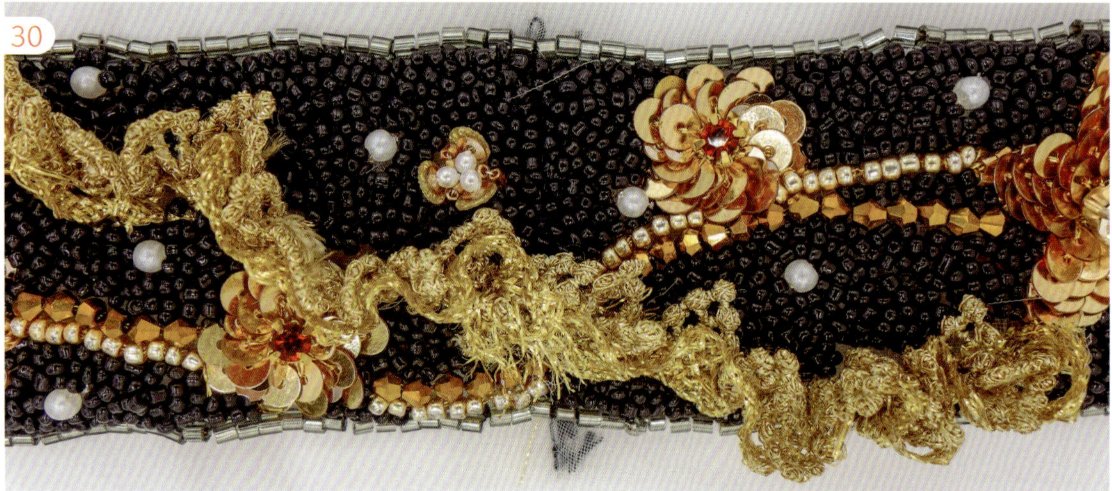

30

Use a hand sewing needle and black thread to sew the two parts of the embroidery piece together.

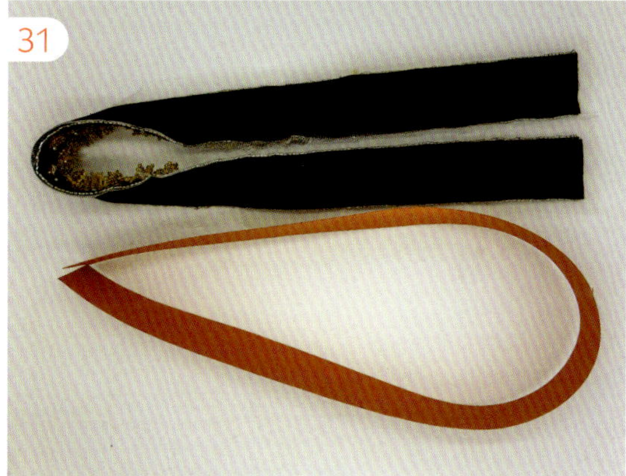

Stick the black self-adhesive velvet, which is the same size as the belt, on the back of the embroidery piece. At the same time, prepare a piece of scrap leather the same size as the back of the embroidery piece.

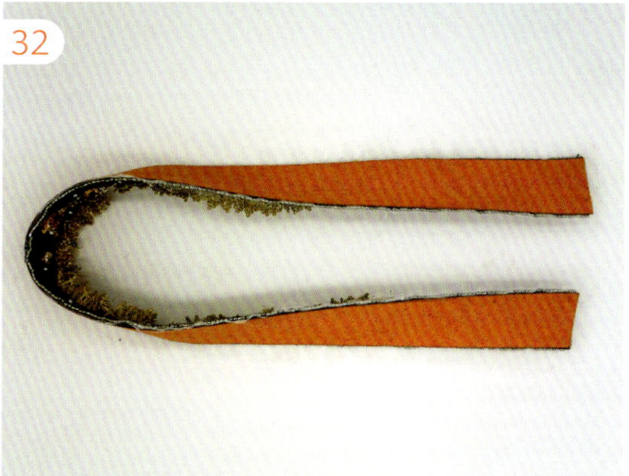

Use fabric glue to stick the scrap leather piece onto the black self-adhesive velvet.

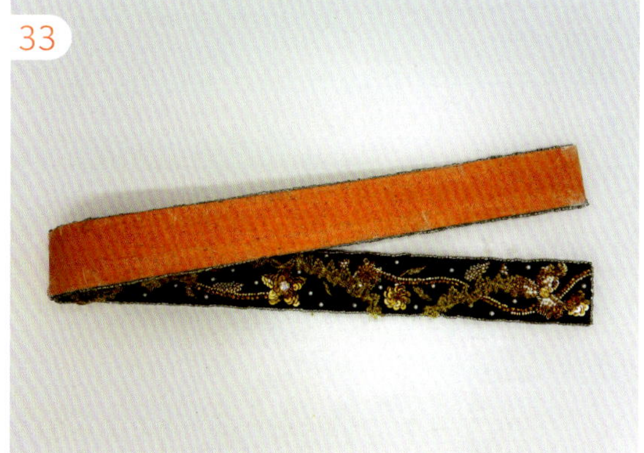

Fold the fabric margin on the edge of the embroidery piece inwards. Next, glue it to the scrap leather with fabric glue.

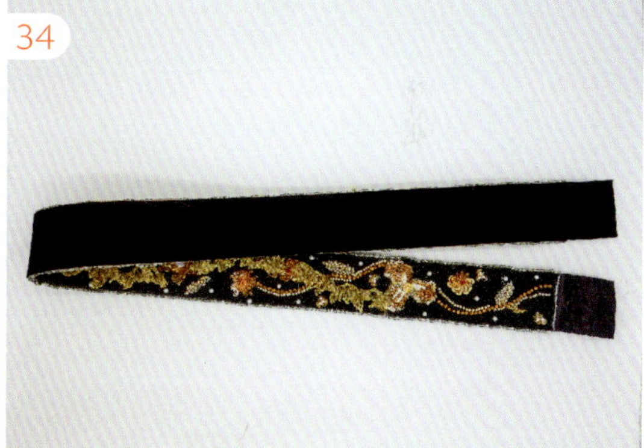

Prepare a piece of black velvet the same width as the embroidery piece and about 6 mm longer than it. Next, paste it onto the back of the embroidery, i.e., the scrap leather in step 33, leaving a margin of 3 mm at each end.

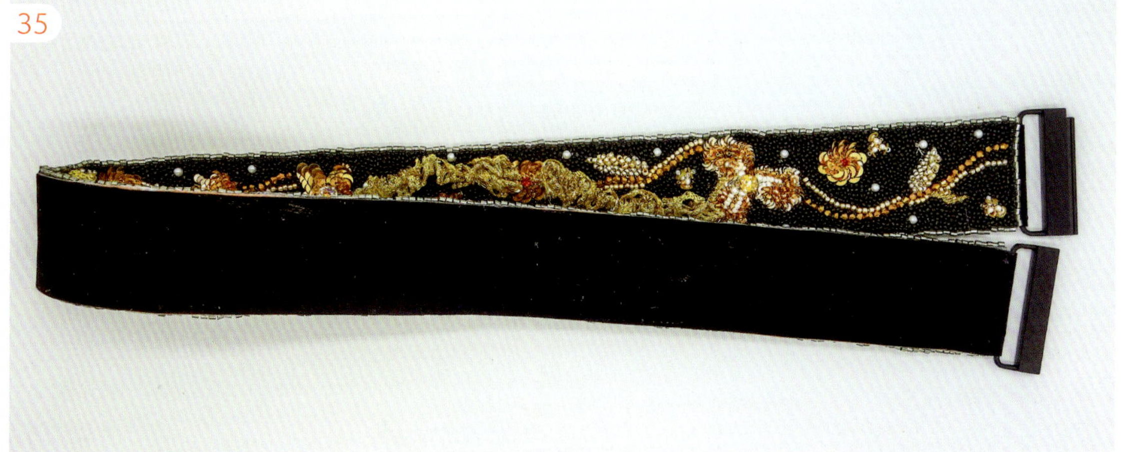

Pass the black belt buckles through the 3 mm margin of the black velvet at both ends. Next, use a hand sewing needle and black thread to sew the margin to the back of the embroidered piece. The belt is now complete.

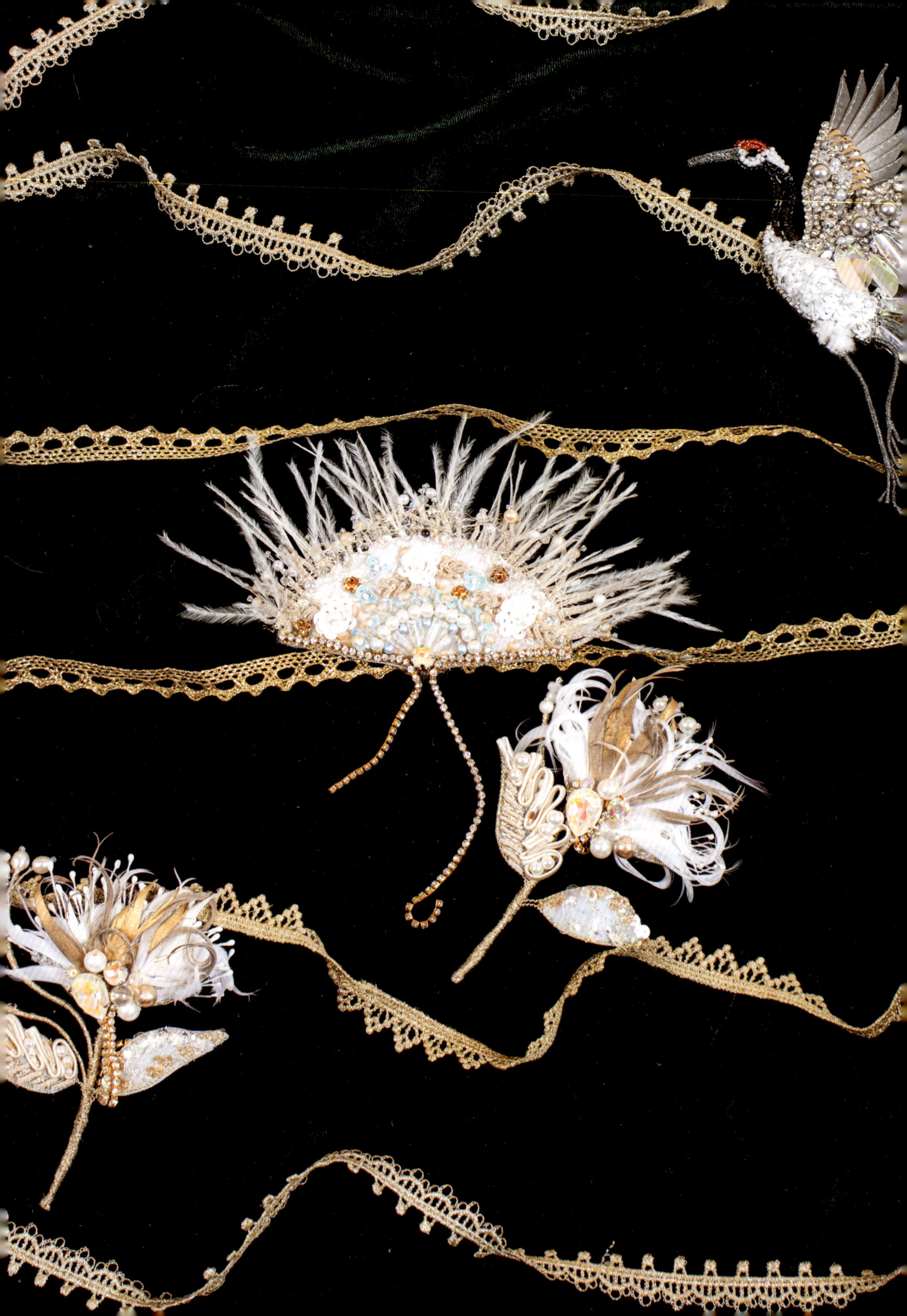

14. Silk Tree Flower Brooches

The flower of the silk tree is fluffy, resembling a fan made of feathers. Silk tree flowers are usually pink in color. When they come into bloom, the trees are full of "little fans" that flutter in the wind. Silk tree flowers are auspicious flowers in China, signifying harmony, unity, and friendship. In ancient times, couples or friends gave silk tree flowers to each other after a quarrel to make peace. This bead embroidery project reproduces the fluffy texture of the silk tree flower with ostrich feathers. With some finishing touches, the flower looks as if it is wearing an opulent dress at a masquerade ball.

Brooch 1

You Will Need

Threads	bullion wires	golden hard, light golden
	embroidery thread	golden, white, silver
Beads	seed beads	2 mm white, 2 mm silver
	pearls	3 mm white, 3 mm light blue, 4 mm white, 5 mm brown
	crystals	3 mm brown, 3 mm coffee color, 3 mm white, 3 mm white drop shape, 3 mm egg white gradient, 5 × 10 mm white trapezoidal, 6 mm yellow square
	sequins	4 mm light blue, 4 mm white
	rhinestone chains	2 mm white
Fabrics	glitter fabric, golden mesh, white organza, leather, white ostrich feathers trim fringe	
Tools	embroidery hoop, 70# hook needle, hand sewing needle, scissors, fabric glue, heat erasable marker, hot glue gun, bar pin, 0.4 mm iron wire	

Embroidery Steps

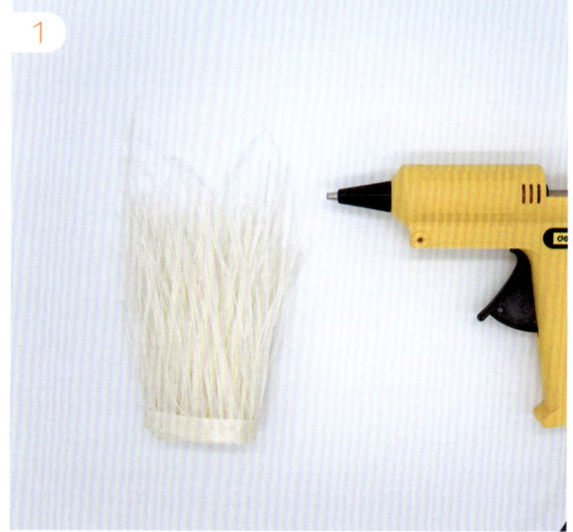

1 Prepare the white ostrich feathers trim fringe. Switch on the hot glue gun and wait for it to heat up.

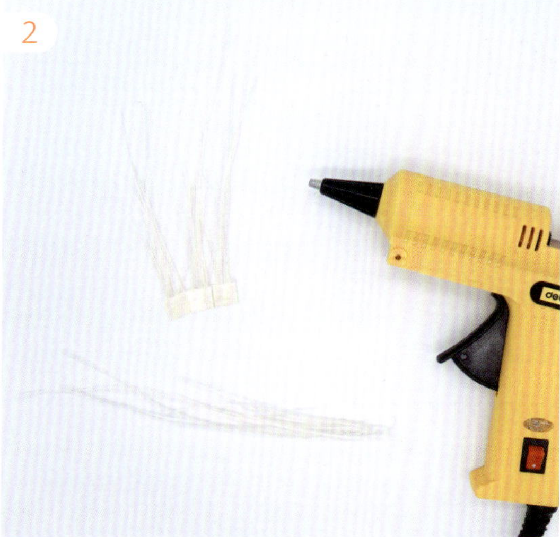

2 Cut out every white ostrich feather on the ribbon.

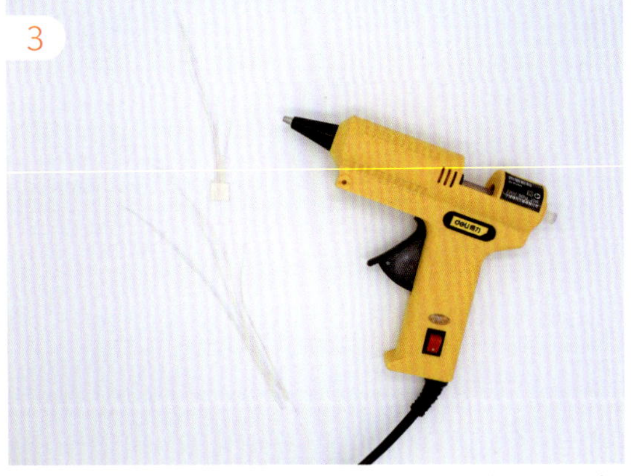
3

Use a hot glue gun to fix the roots of 5–8 white ostrich feathers to form a bundle. The height of every ostrich feather should not be the same.

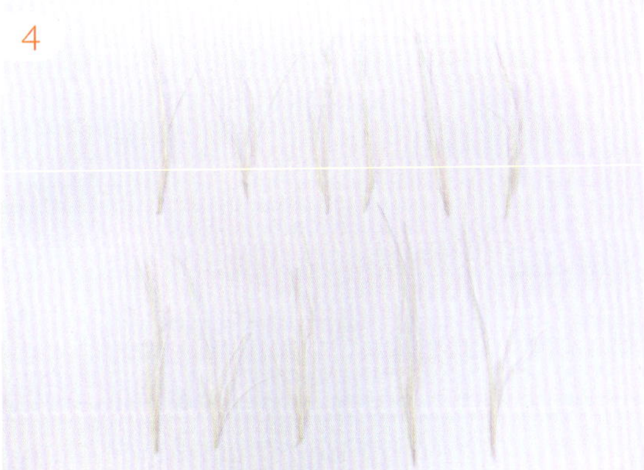
4

Repeat steps 2–3 to make 11 bundles of ostrich feathers of different lengths.

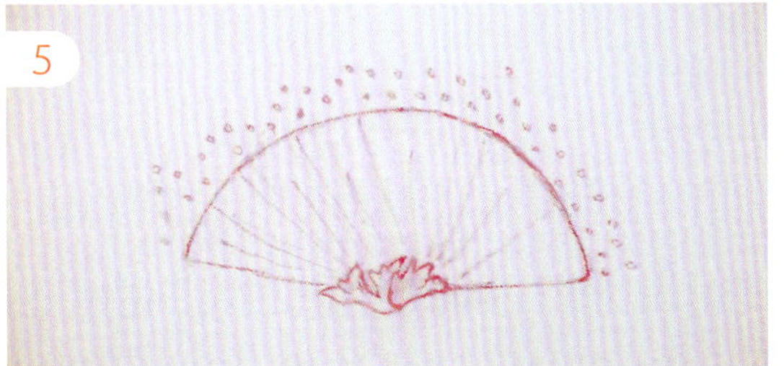
5

Stretch a piece of white organza on the embroidery hoop, and outline the pattern (see page 167) with a heat erasable marker, as shown in the figure.

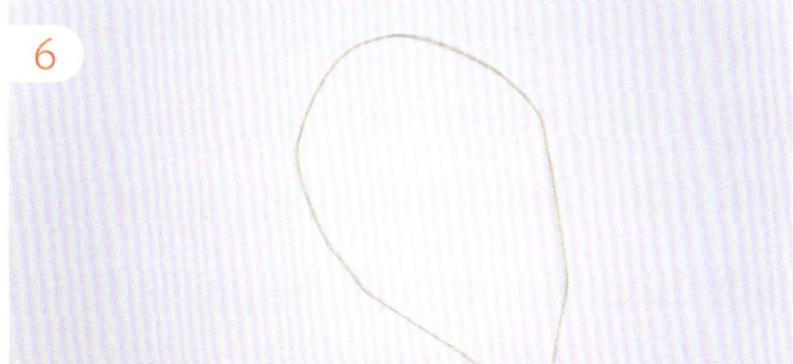
6

Take a piece of golden hard bullion wire and stretch it slightly.

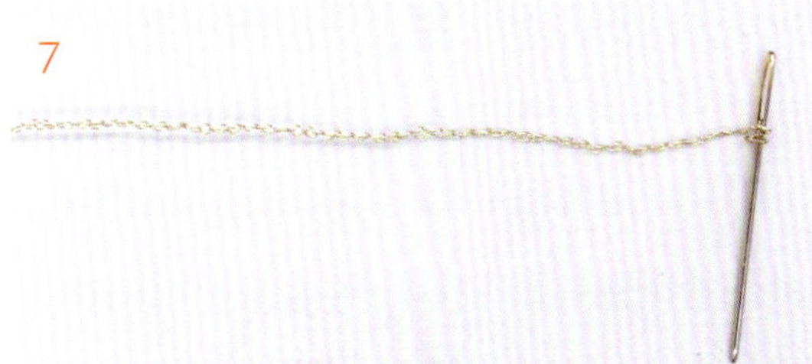
7

Fold the stretched bullion wire in half. Place a hand sewing needle at the midpoint and turn it to twist the bullion wire into two strands.

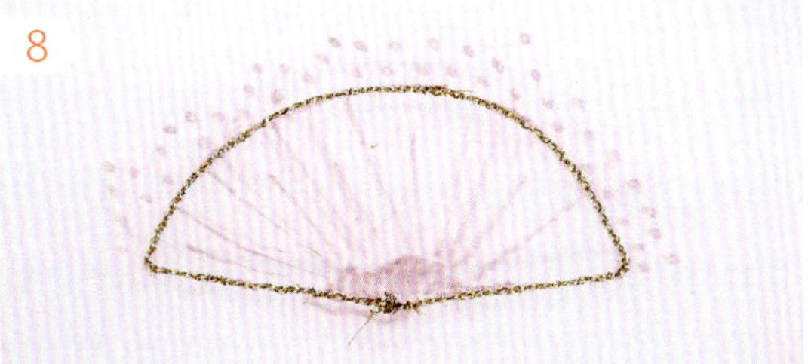
8

Use a hand sewing needle and golden thread to sew the two strands of bullion wire onto the fan-shaped outline as shown in the figure.

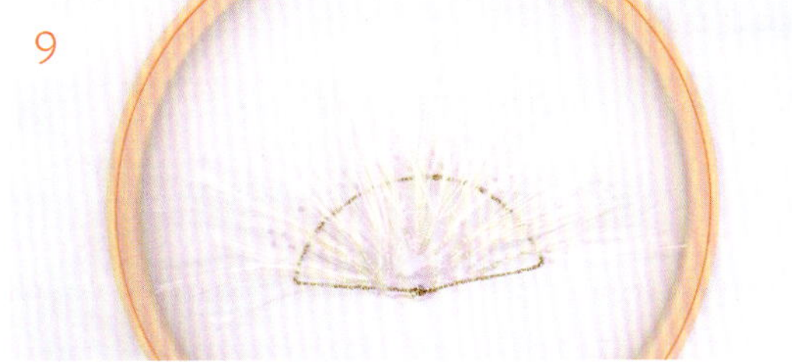
9

Use a hand sewing needle and white thread to sew the ostrich feather accessories, which were completed in step 4, in the position shown in the figure.

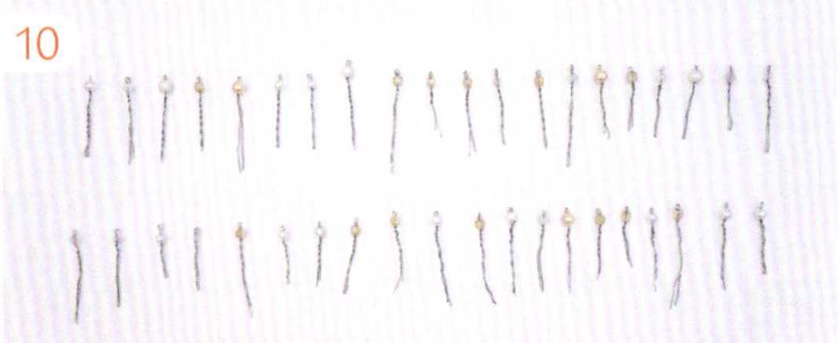
10

Take pieces of 0.4 mm iron wire and fold them in half. Insert a 4 mm white pearl, a 3 mm white pearl, a 2 mm silver seed bead, a 3 mm brown crystal, a 5 mm brown pearl, or a 3 mm white crystal into each iron wire randomly to make about 40 pieces.

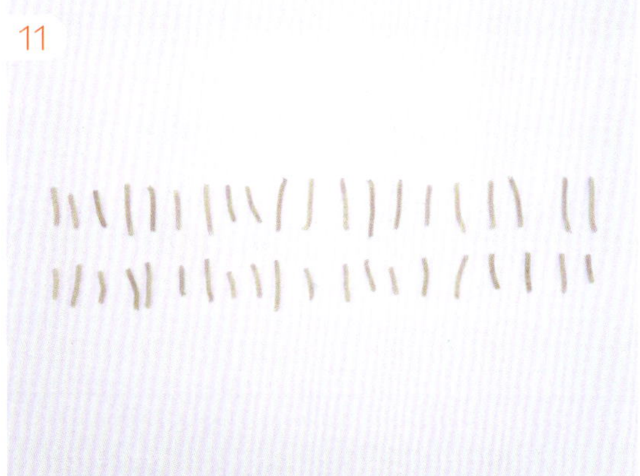

Cut the light golden bullion wires into different lengths (6–15 mm). The quantity should be the same as the number of pieces completed in step 10.

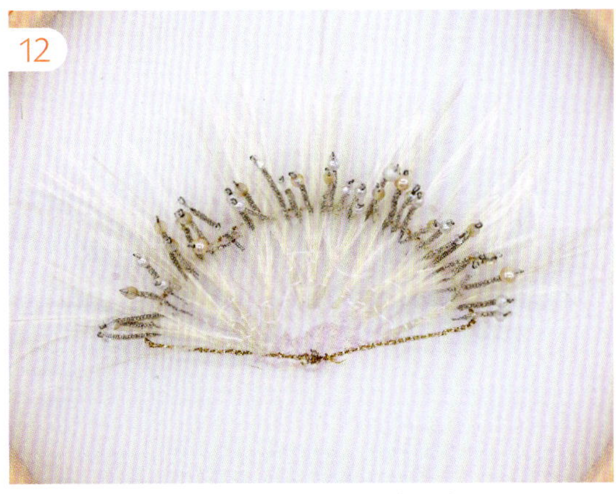

Insert every piece of iron wire completed in step 10 into one of the bullion wires prepared in step 11. Next, insert the iron wire at about 2 mm within the outline of the fan-shaped pattern.

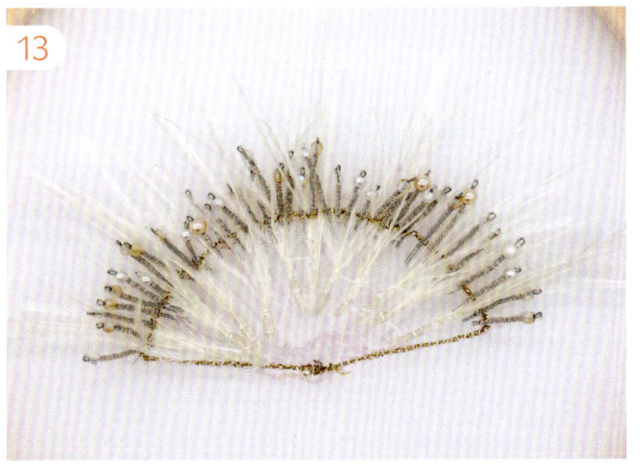

Use a hand sewing needle and golden thread to fix all of the pieces of bullion wires, which were completed in the previous step, onto the fabric. The stitches should overlap with the hard bullion wires on the fan-shaped outline.

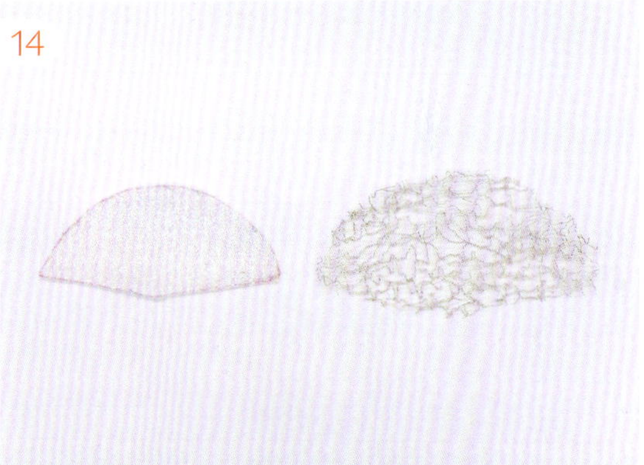

Cut out a piece of glitter fabric of the same size as the outer contour of the embroidery piece, as well as a piece of golden mesh that is slightly larger than the embroidery piece.

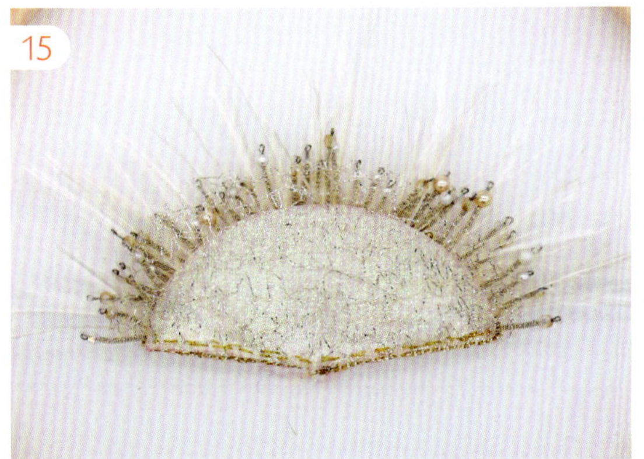

Use a hand sewing needle and golden thread to fix the glitter fabric and golden mesh on the pattern (i.e. the golden mesh on the glitter fabric). Trim off the lower part of the fabric neatly according to the outline of the hard bullion wire.

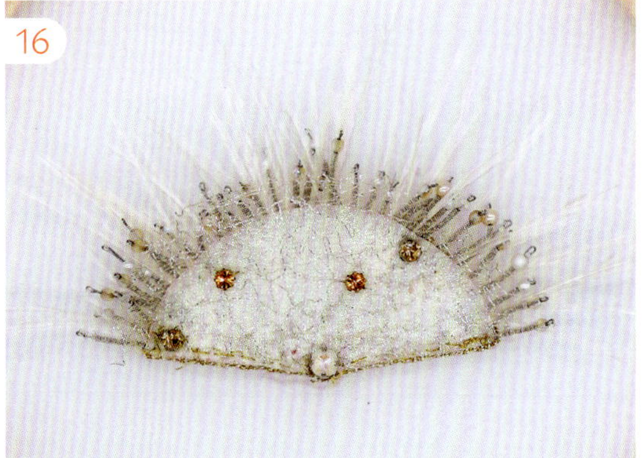

Use a hand sewing needle and golden thread to fix the 6 mm yellow square crystals and 3 mm coffee color crystals in their corresponding positions.

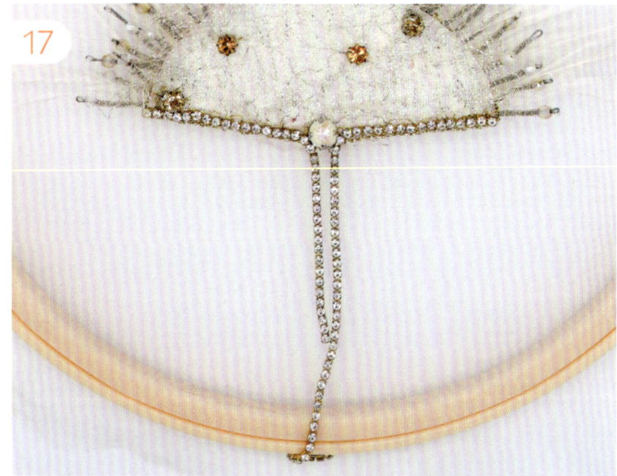

Sew two pieces of white rhinestone chains on the left and right at the lower outline of the pattern, leaving a margin of about 5 cm length unstitched at the lower part as a dangling decoration.

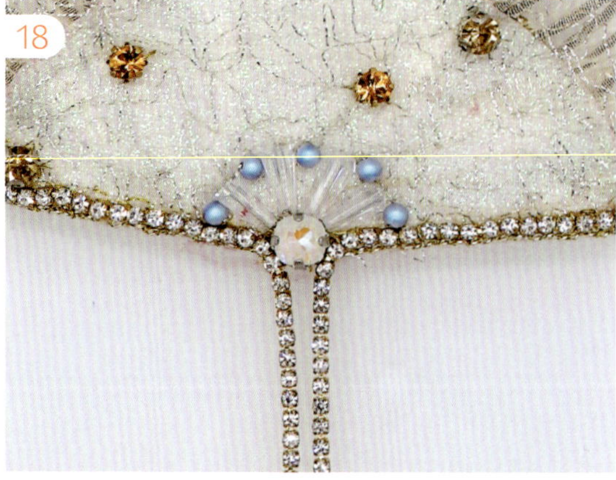

Use a hand sewing needle and silver thread to fix four 5 × 10 mm white trapezoidal crystals above the 6 mm yellow square crystal, and fix five 3 mm light blue pearls between the trapezoidal crystals.

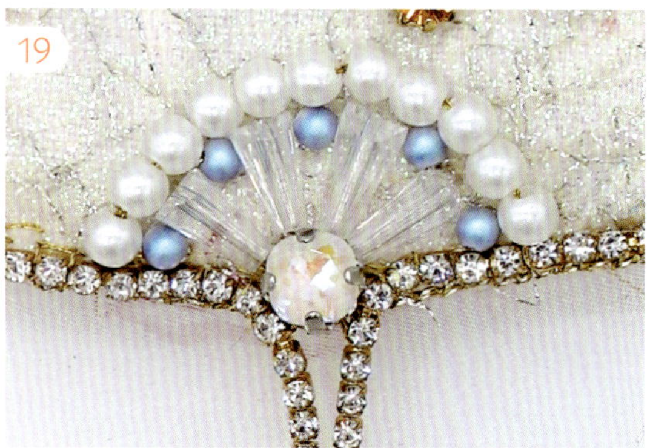

Apply the technique of stitching beads from the front side of the fabric using a hook needle and golden thread to sew 4 mm white pearls on top of the white trapezoidal crystals.

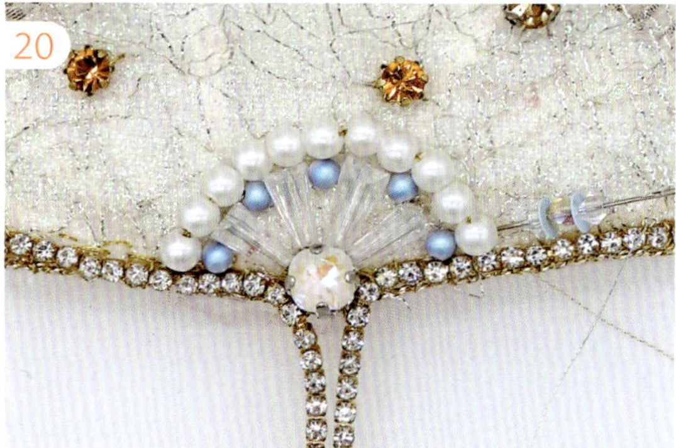

Apply the technique of embroidering beads groups using a hand sewing needle and silver thread. Thread in sequence a 2 mm white seed bead, a 4 mm light blue sequin, a 3 mm egg white gradient crystal, a 4 mm light blue sequin, and a 2 mm white seed bead. Sew them on top of the stitches completed in step 19.

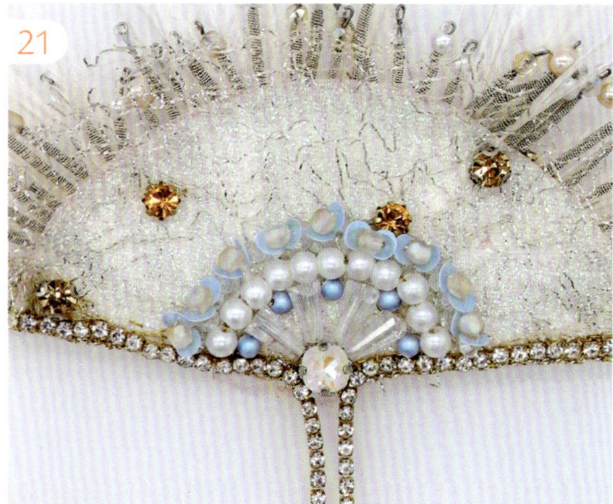

Using the same materials and technique as in step 20, complete the sewing of a row of patterns along the white pearls.

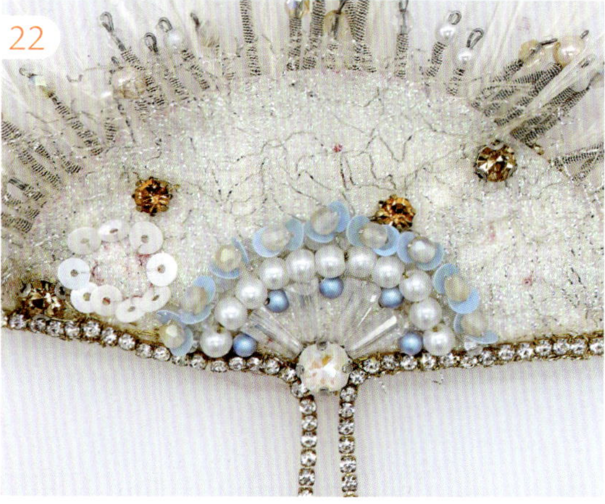

Sew sequins using a hand sewing needle, silver thread, and 4 mm white sequins to form the outer circle of the flower.

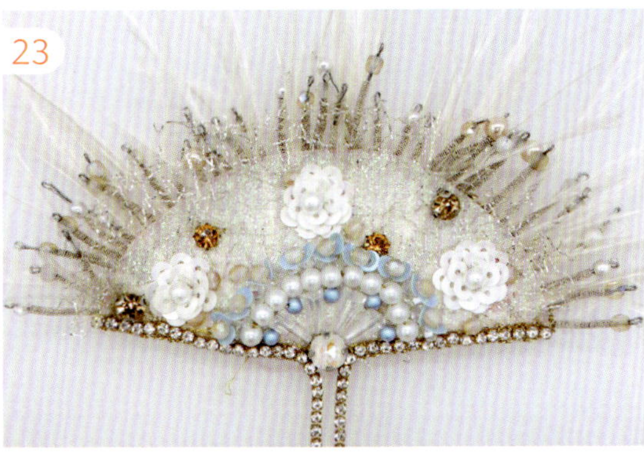

Using the same technique as step 22, complete the sewing of the white flower from the outside to the inside, and fix a 4 mm white pearl at the center of each flower with a hand sewing needle. Use the same method to complete two more white flowers. Fix several 3 mm egg white gradient crystals around the flowers.

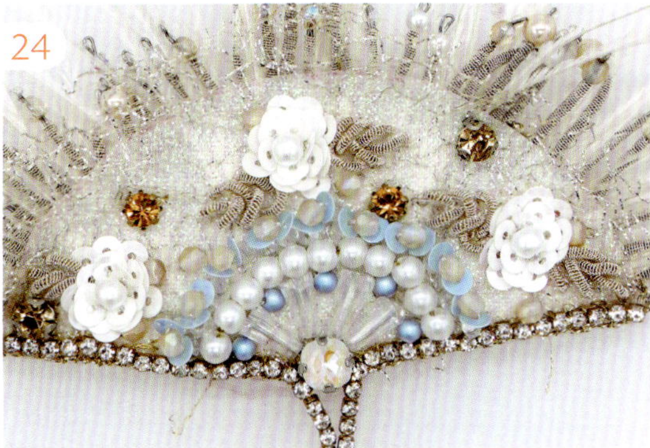

Cut out the light golden bullion wires into small pieces of about 8 mm each and fix them on both sides of the flowers using a hand sewing needle and golden thread to form leaves.

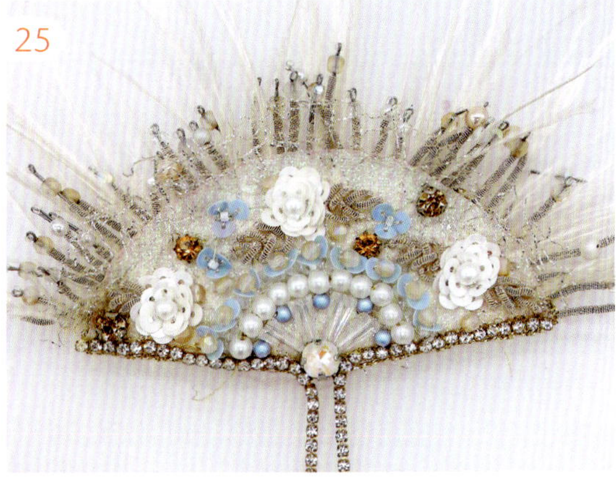

Sew sequins using a hand sewing needle and 4 mm light blue sequins to create blue flowers around the white flowers as ornaments. Next, fix a 2 mm white seed bead at the center of the blue flowers.

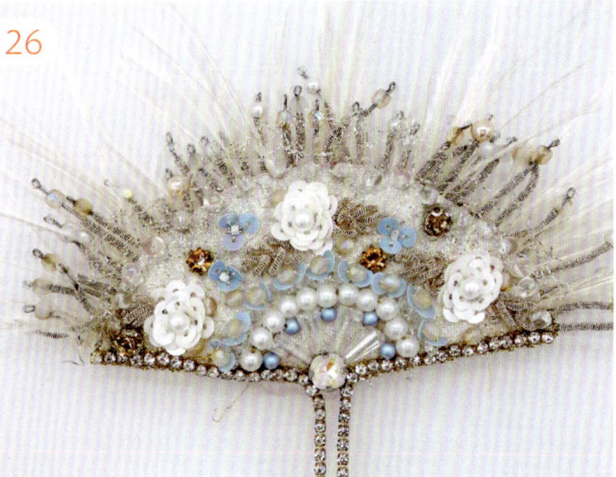

Sew a row of 3 mm white drop crystals at intervals along the upper outline of the fan. The embroidery is now complete.

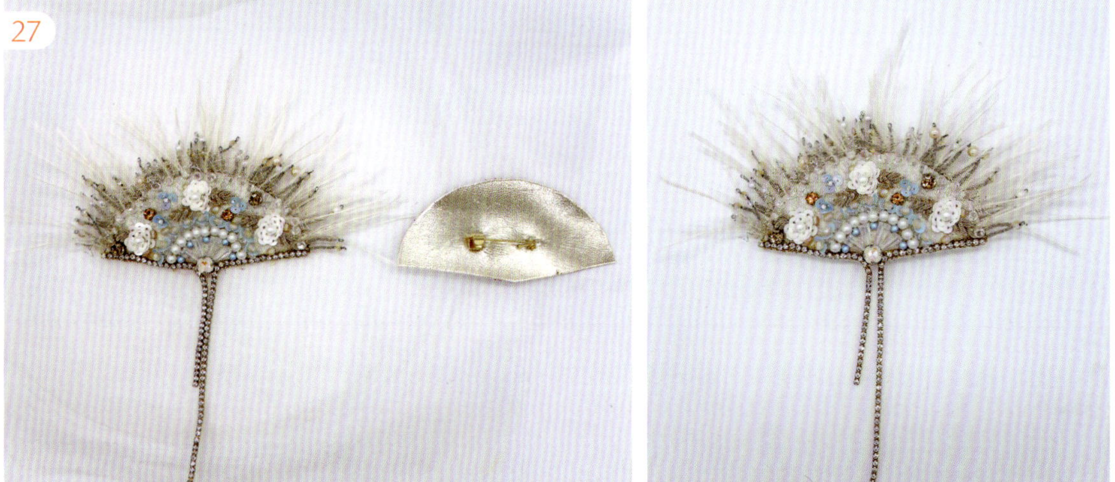

Cut out the embroidery piece and attach leather and bar pin on its back. Let it dry. The brooch is now complete.

Brooch 2

You Will Need

Threads	bullion wires	golden hard, light golden
	embroidery thread	white, golden, invisible
Beads	seed beads	1.5 mm white
	tube beads	2 mm translucent
	pearls	3 mm white, 4 mm white, 6 mm transparent, 6 mm white, 6 mm brown
	sequins	3 mm golden, 3 mm silver, 4 mm clear
	crystals	3 mm white, 4 mm white
	rhinestone chains	2 mm white
	sew-on rhinestones	10 × 15 mm yellow drop shape, 6 mm colorful round
Fabrics	3 mm beige plain ribbon, 3 mm golden glitter ribbon, 3mm silver glitter ribbon, glitter fabric, golden mesh fabric, white organza	
Tools	embroidery hoop, 70# hook needle, hand sewing needle, scissors, fabric glue, heat erasable marker, ball head pins, white goose feather, golden goose feather, 1 mm white artificial stamen, bar pin, 0.4 mm iron wire	

Embroidery Steps

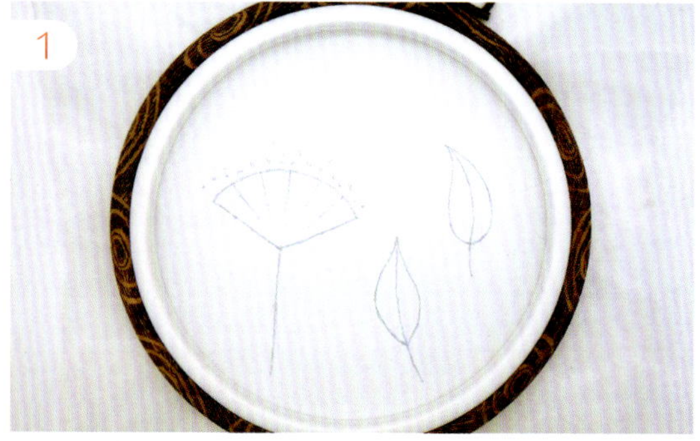

Stretch the white organza on the embroidery hoop and draw the patterns (see page 167) on the fabric with a heat erasable marker.

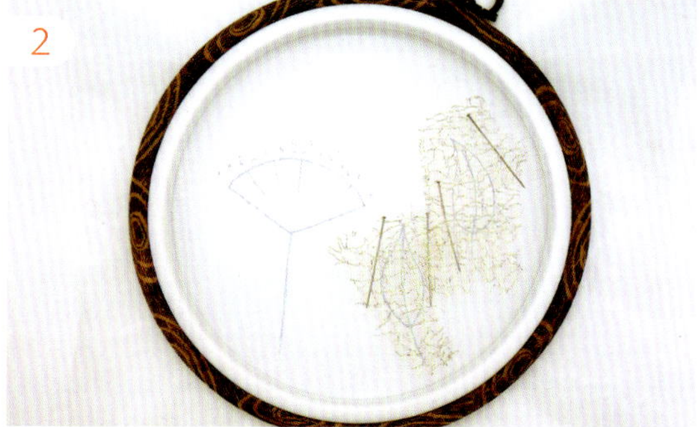

Cut two pieces of golden mesh fabric and pin them to the patterns of the two leaves with ball head pins.

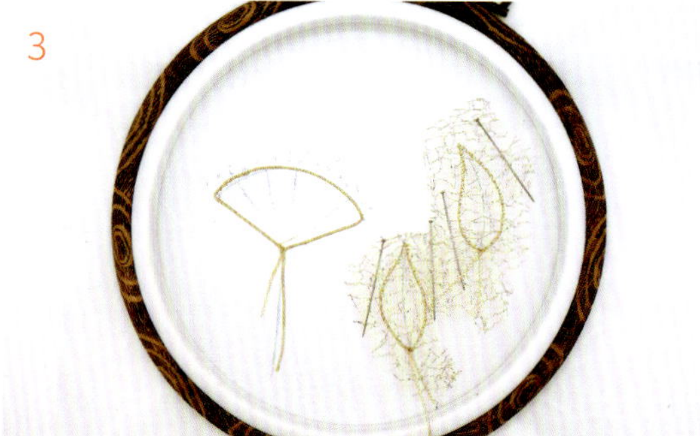

Pull the golden hard bullion wires slightly apart and then use a hand sewing needle and golden thread to fix it on the outline of the three patterns.

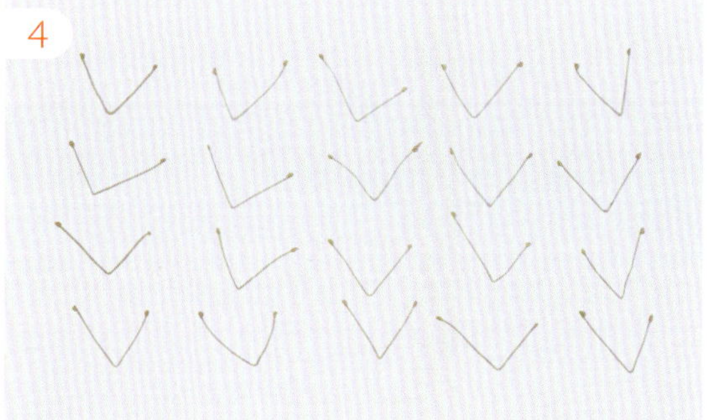

Fold about twenty 1 mm white artificial stamens in half for later use.

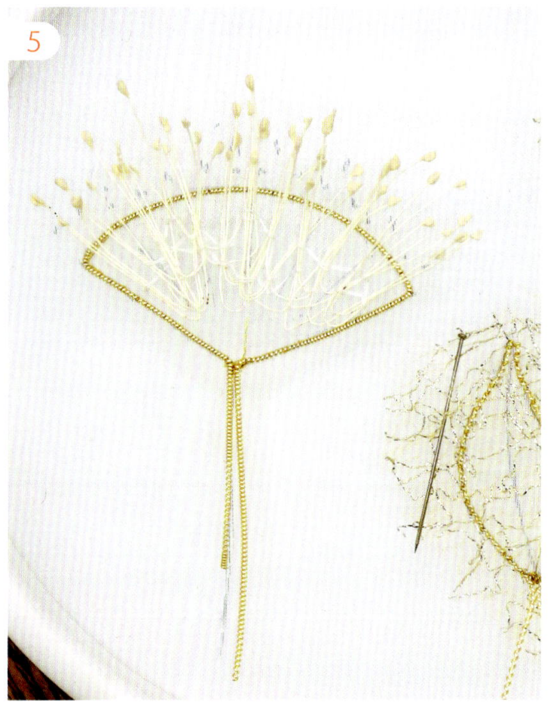

Use a hand sewing needle and white thread to sew the folded stamens on the inside of the fan shape, ensuring that the parts of the stamens protruding from the fan's outline are scattered.

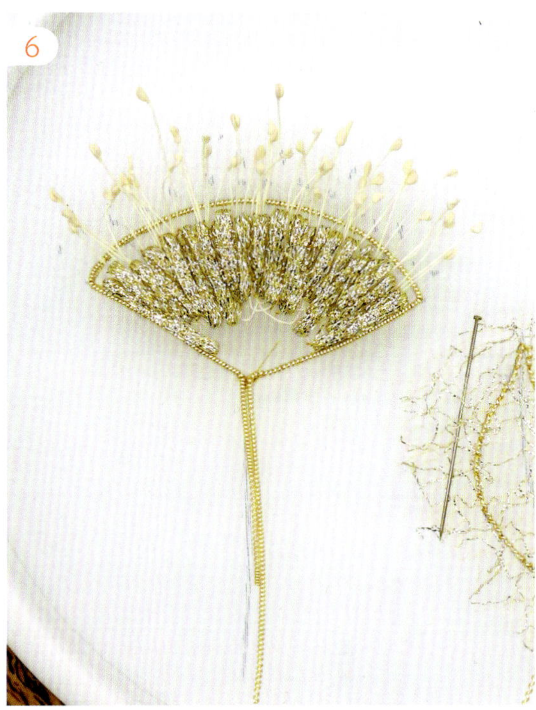

Use a hand sewing needle and 3 mm golden glitter ribbon to fill the upper half of the fan, leaving a 2 mm gap between the upper contours of glitter ribbon and bullion wire.

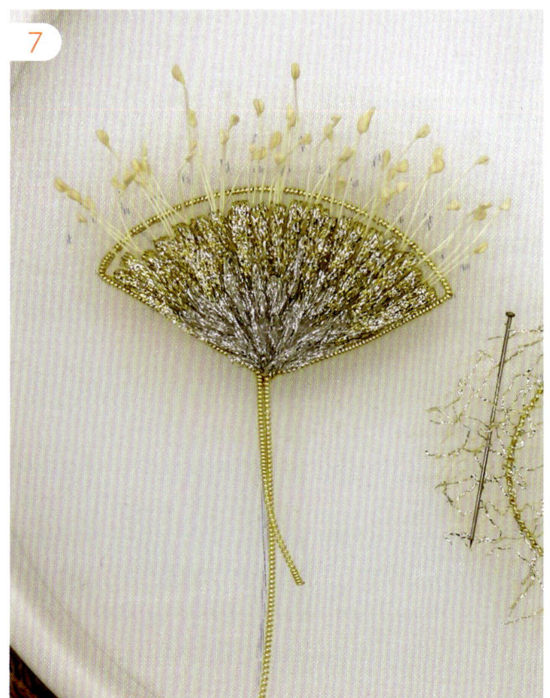

Use a hand sewing needle and 3 mm silver glitter ribbon to fill the lower half of the fan.

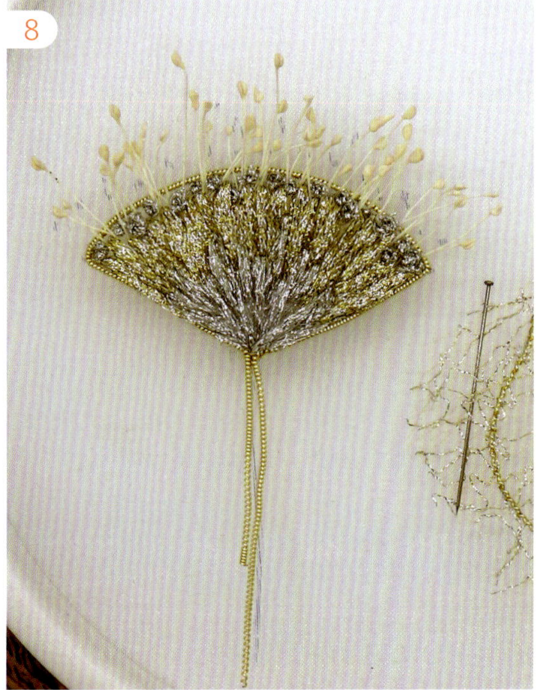

Use the French knot technique with a hand sewing needle and 3 mm silver glitter ribbon to fill the gap between the golden glitter ribbon and the upper outline of the fan shape.

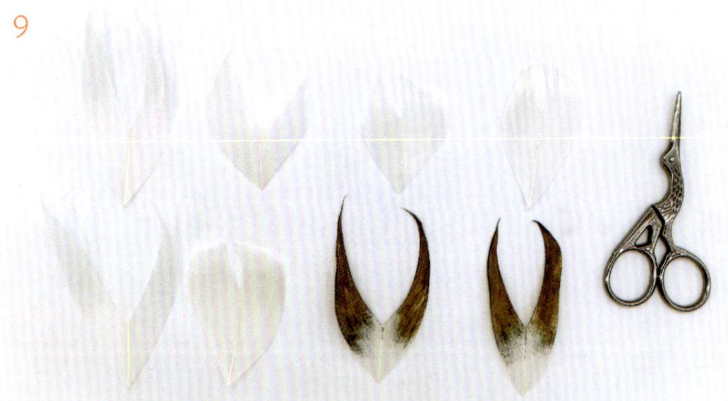

Prepare two pieces of golden goose feather, about six pieces of white goose feather, and a pair of scissors. Trim the goose feathers as shown in the picture.

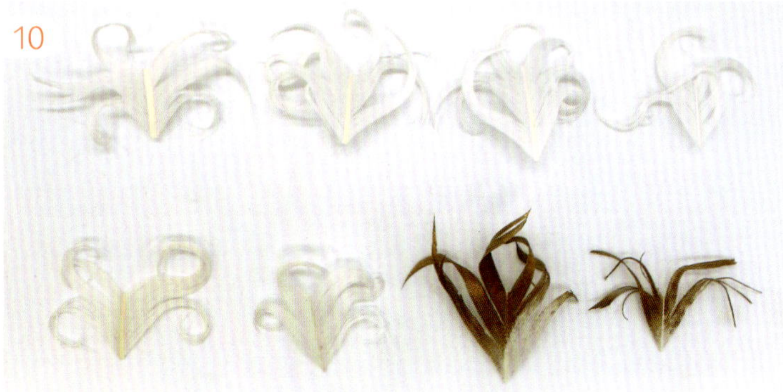

Use the scissors to curl the top of all the feathers.

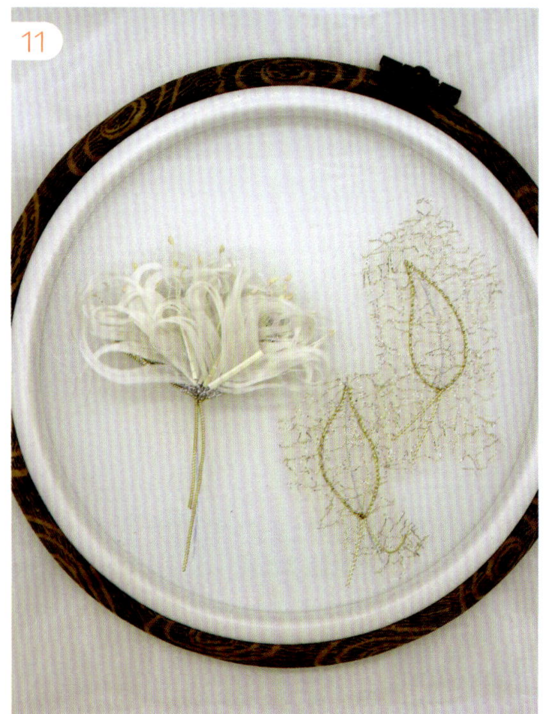

Use a hand sewing needle and white thread to fix the white goose feathers in a fan shape.

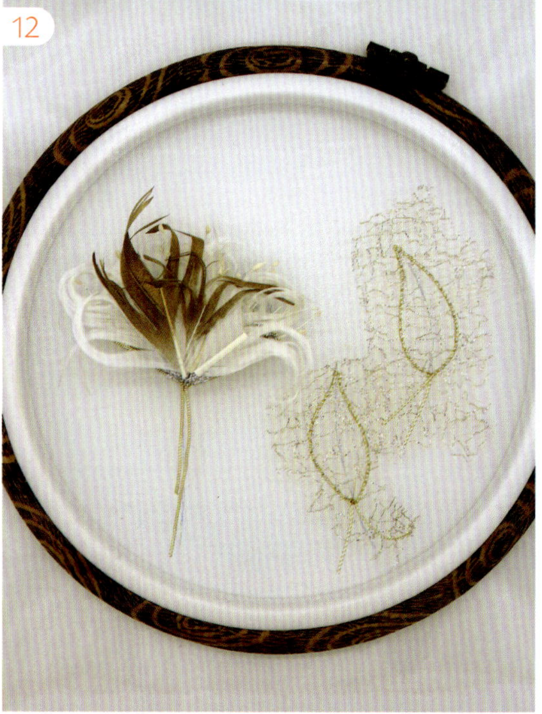

Use a hand sewing needle and white thread to fix the two golden goose feathers in the middle of the white goose feathers.

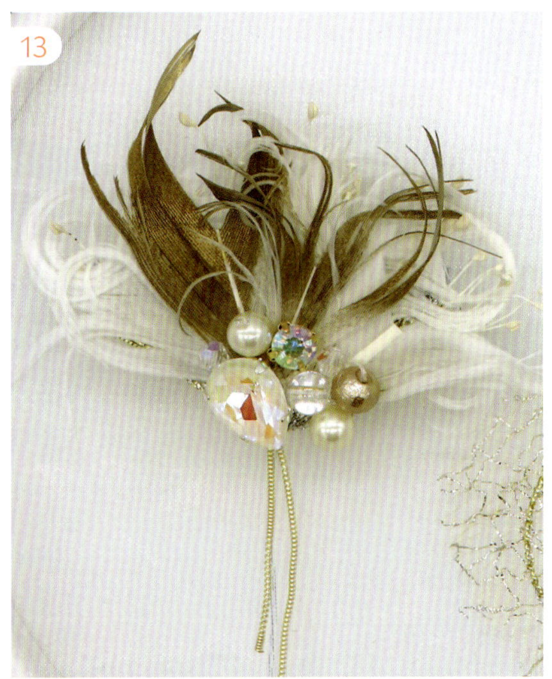

Use a hand sewing needle and white thread to fix the 4 mm white crystal, 10 × 15 mm yellow drop sew-on rhinestone, 6 mm colorful round sew-on rhinestone, 6 mm transparent pearl, 6 mm white pearls and 6 mm brown pearl at the base of the goose feathers.

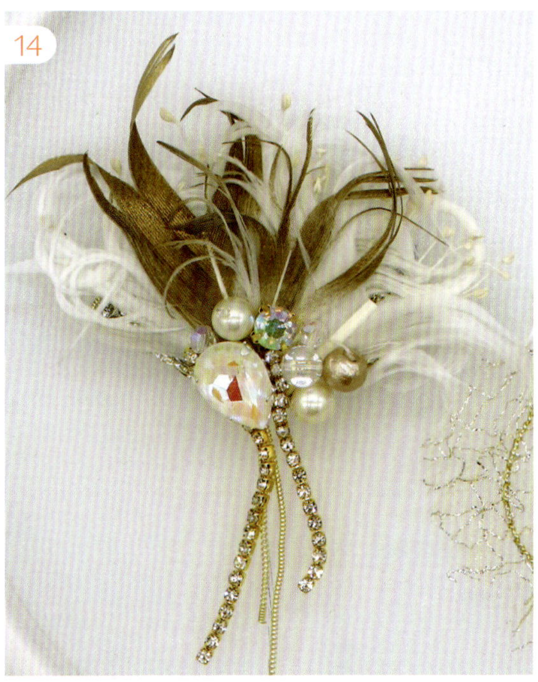

Fix two rhinestone chains of about 4 cm and 5 cm respectively along the lower contour of the pattern.

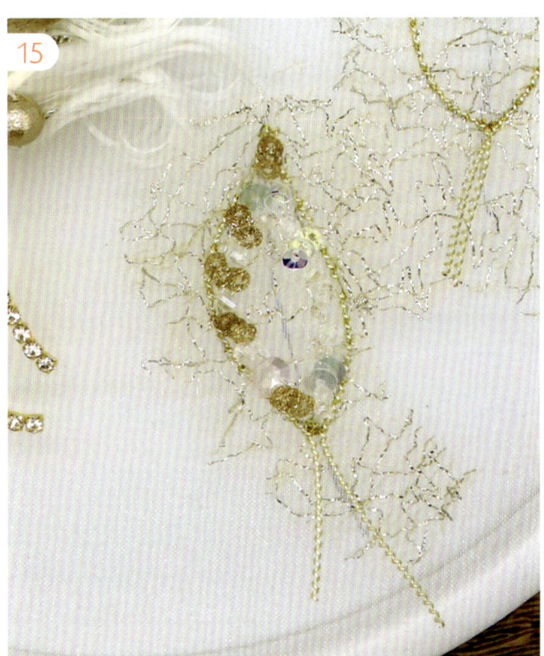

Use the technique of stitching beads and sequins from the front side of the fabric with a hook needle and invisible thread to sew alternate rows of 3 mm golden sequins, 3 mm silver sequins, 4 mm clear sequins, 3 mm white crystals, and 2 mm translucent tube beads inside the leaf blade.

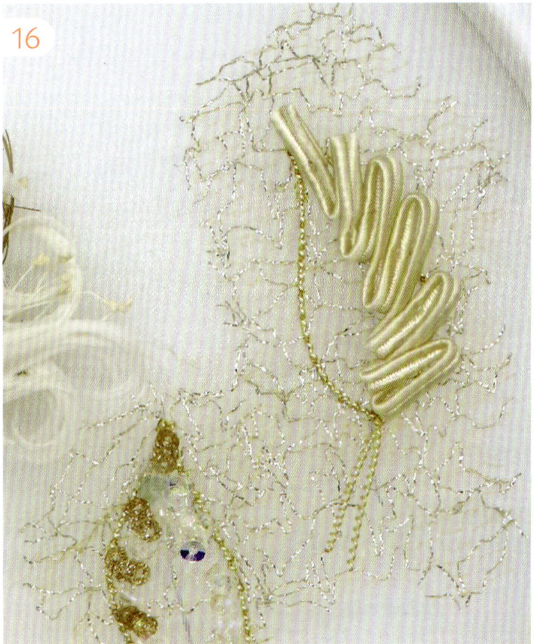

Use a hand sewing needle and white thread to fix the 3 mm beige plain ribbon in a bent shape at the position of the leaf blade as shown in the picture.

17

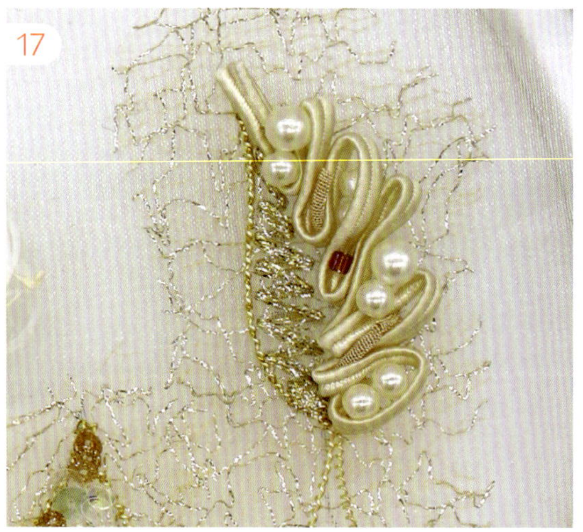

Use a hand sewing needle and white thread to sew 3 mm white pearls, 4 mm white pearls, and light golden bullion wire in the gaps of the beige plain ribbon, and fill the left half of the leaf with golden glitter ribbon.

18

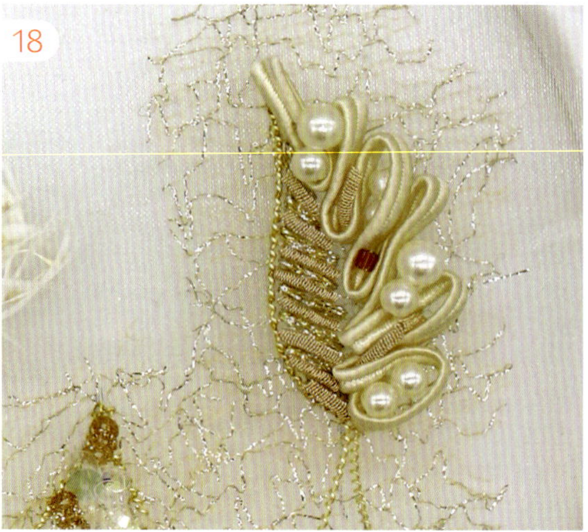

Use a hand sewing needle and white thread to sew light golden bullion wire pieces at the left half of the leaf along the golden glitter ribbons.

19

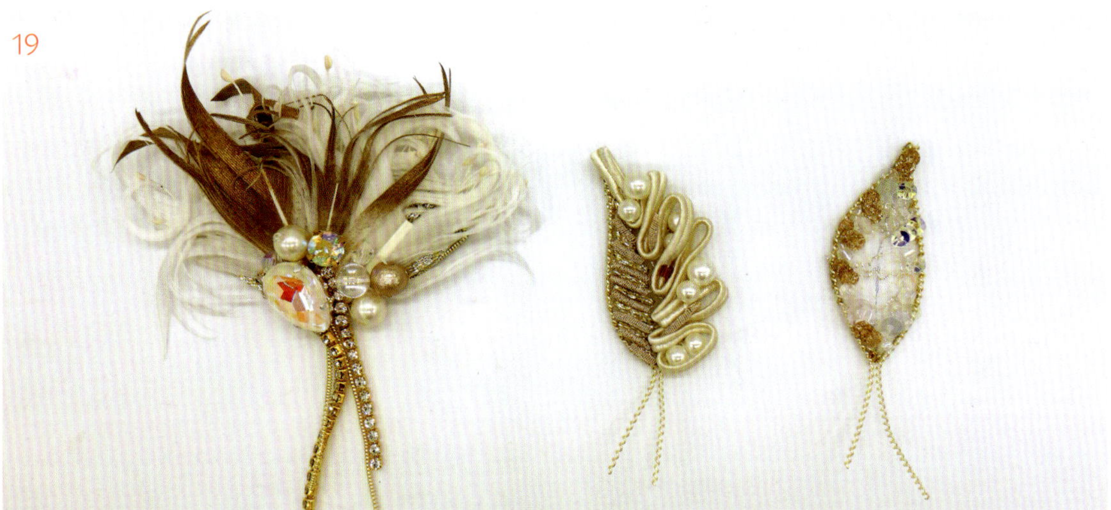

Apply some fabric glue to the back of the three embroidered patterns to make the edges of the embroidery pieces firmer, and prevent the bullion wire from breaking when the embroidery is cut. Cut out the patterns when the glue has dried.

20

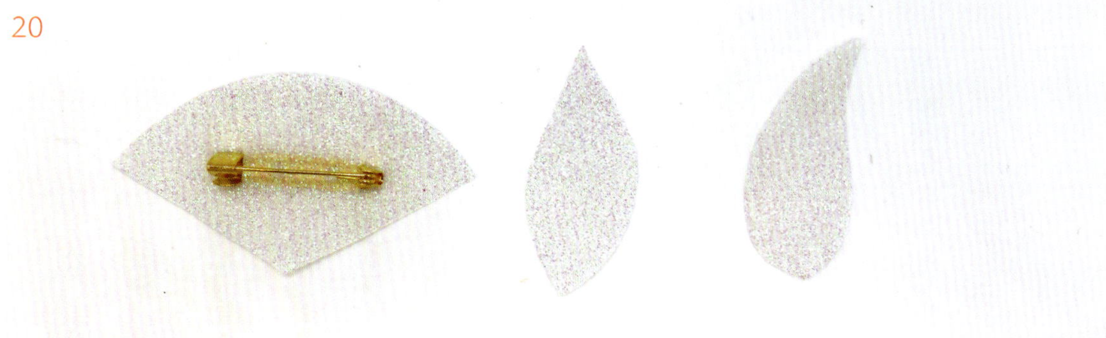

Cut three pieces of glitter fabric in the same shape as the embroidery pieces and attach a bar pin to the fan shape.

21

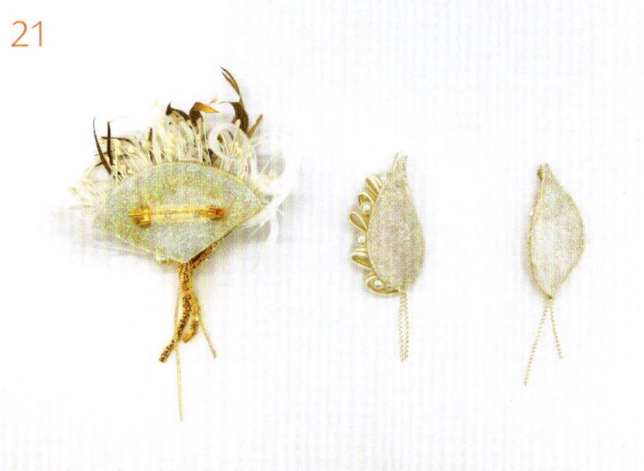

Use fabric glue to stick three suitable pieces of glitter fabric to the back of each embroidery piece. Allow the glue to dry.

22

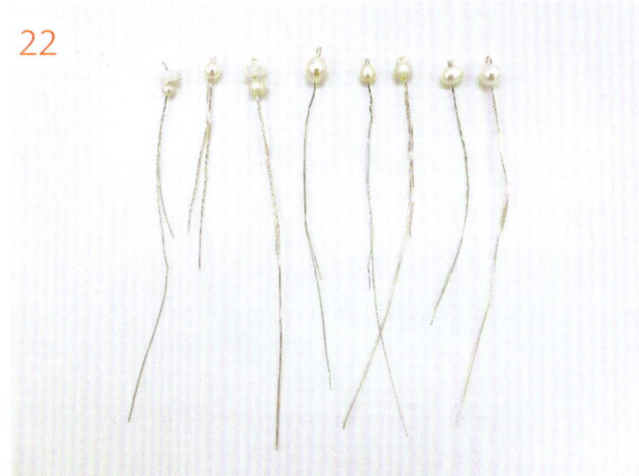

Take a piece of 0.4 mm iron wire. Thread a 1.5 mm white seed bead through it and fold it in half. Thread a 4 mm white pearl or any other crystals you prefer through it thereafter. Make eight groups of these. The length of the iron wire after it is folded in half should be about 2–8 cm.

23

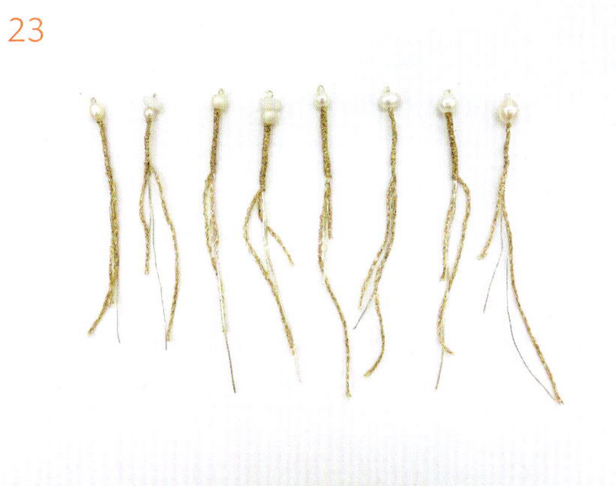

Wrap golden thread around the folded part of the wires.

24

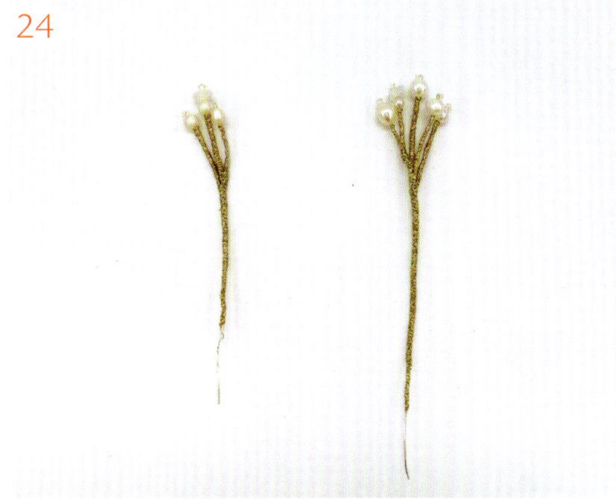

Divide the wrapped parts into two groups and wrap them with golden thread. The length of the iron wires are about 6 cm and 8 cm.

25

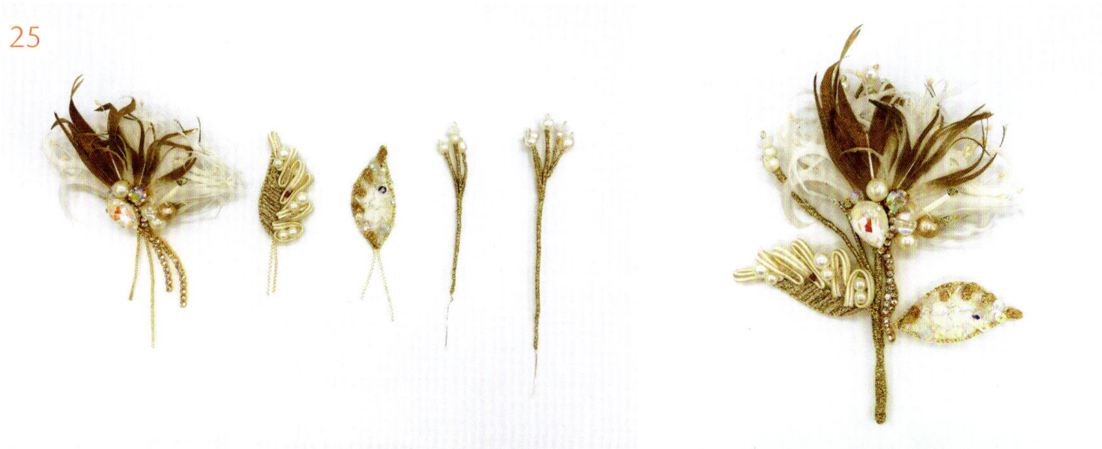

Use golden thread to wrap all the parts together. The second brooch is now complete.

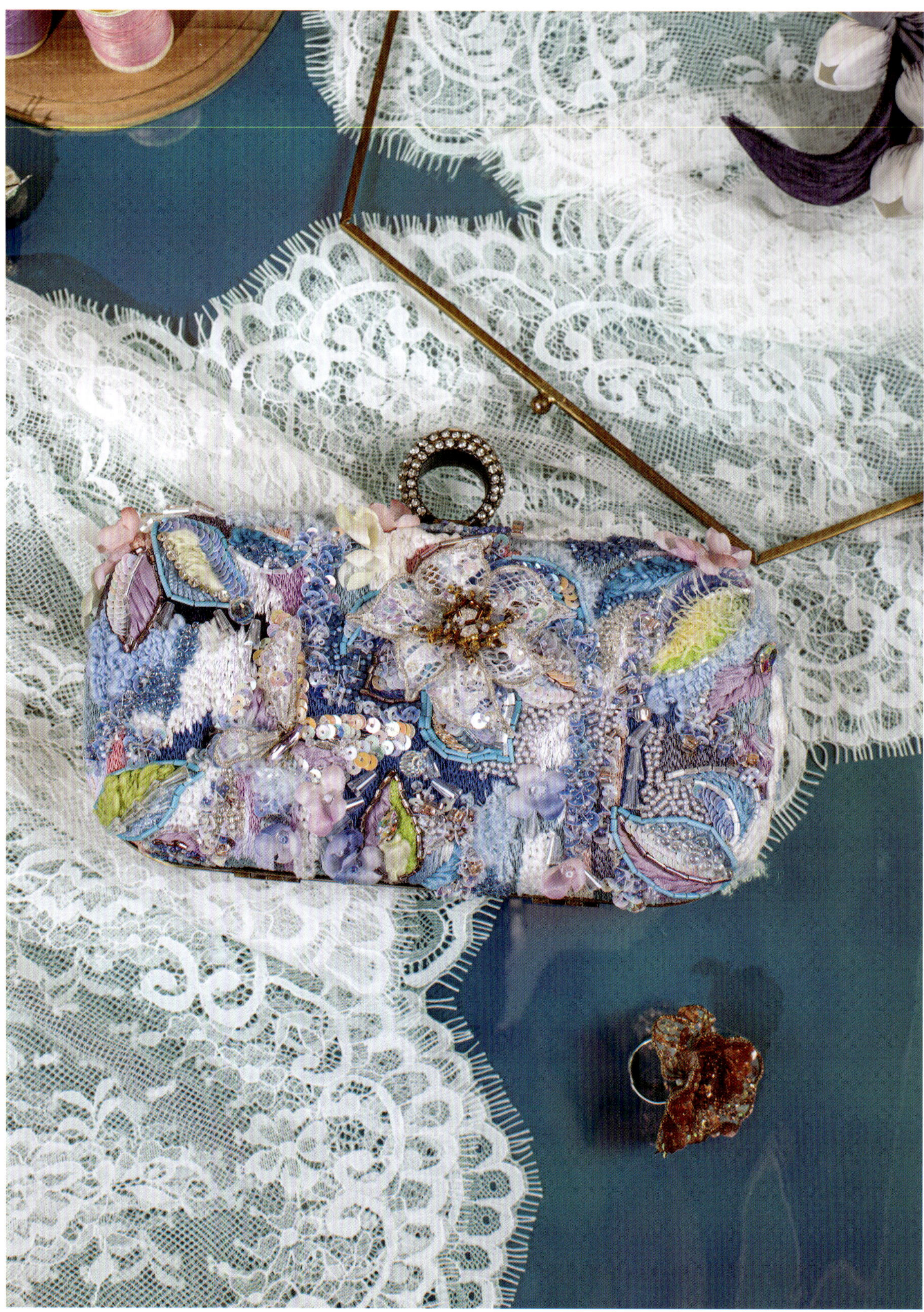

15. Lily Dinner Bag

The white lily, which is native to China, has jade-white flowers and is highly refined. In China, it carries the meaning of "a century of harmony," which explains why it is often selected as a gift to newlyweds, relatives, or friends to express good wishes. This gorgeous and dazzling piece features a three-dimensional lily made of lace, and the main body is decorated with colorful threads, beads, and sequins. It is the perfect accessory for an evening banquet.

You Will Need

Threads	embroidery thread	silver, blue shades, purple shades, pink shades, white
	yarn	blue shades, green shades, white shades, golden
	ribbon	35 mm light blue, 35 mm light purple
	soft bullion wire	golden
Beads	sequins	3 mm light blue, 3 mm white, 3 mm transparent, 4 mm light purple, 4 mm light blue, 4 mm blue, 4 mm transparent, 4 mm orange
	crystals	3 mm white, 3 mm golden coffee, 4 × 8 mm white trapezoidal
	sew-on rhinestones	5 × 10 mm colored horse eye shape, 4 × 15 mm purple horse eye shape, 6 mm white round
	tube beads	2 mm blue, 2 mm purple, 2 mm white, 3 mm golden coffee, 3 mm blue, 3 mm white, 6 mm blue, 6 mm transparent, 6 mm light purple, 6 mm golden coffee
	seed beads	1.5 mm transparent, 2 mm white, 2 mm purple, 2 mm blue, 2 mm golden
Fabrics	white organza, white lace, self-adhesive velvet	
Tools	embroidery frame, 70# hook needle, hand sewing needle, scissors, fabric glue, heat erasable marker, 26# iron wire, 19 × 10 cm clutch bag mold and a frame with clasp lock	

Embroidery Steps

◆ Three-Dimensional Portion

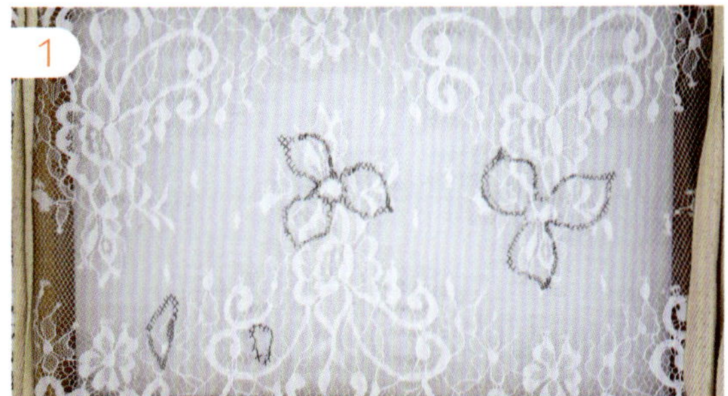

Stretch the lace fabric onto the embroidery frame, and draw the three-dimensional lilies and butterfly wing patterns (see page 170) onto it in a suitable position with a heat erasable marker.

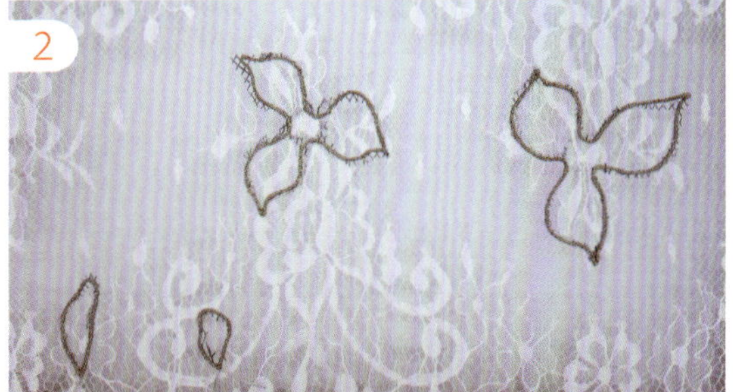

Apply the edging stitch technique using a hook needle, silver thread, and 26# wire to overlock the outlines of all the patterns.

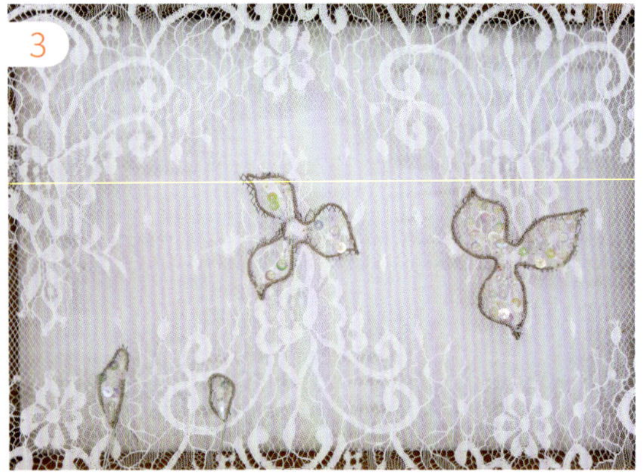

Apply the technique of embroidering sequin on single side using a hand sewing needle and silver thread to scatter and fix the 3 mm and 4 mm transparent sequins onto the patterns.

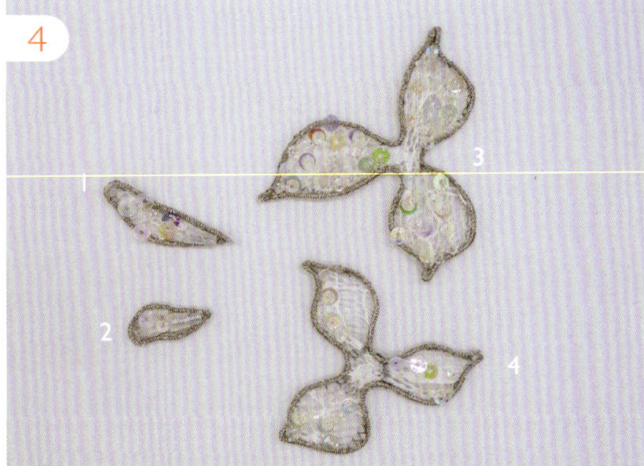

Cut out the embroidered patterns along the outer contour for later use. Parts 1 and 2 are butterfly wings, while parts 3 and 4 are petals.

◆ Background Patterns

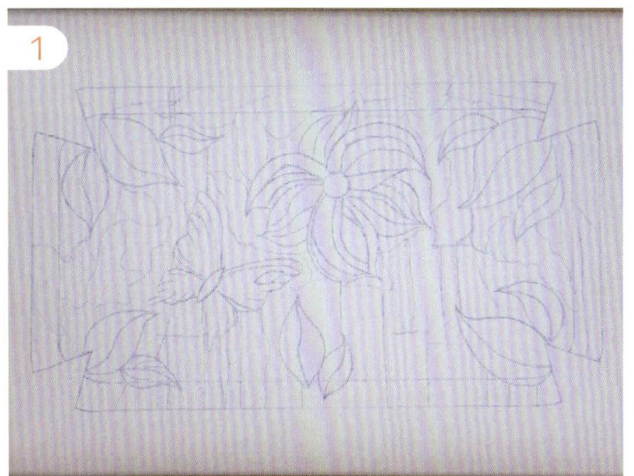

Stretch the white organza onto the embroidery frame, and use a heat erasable marker to draw the pattern (see page 170) on the fabric.

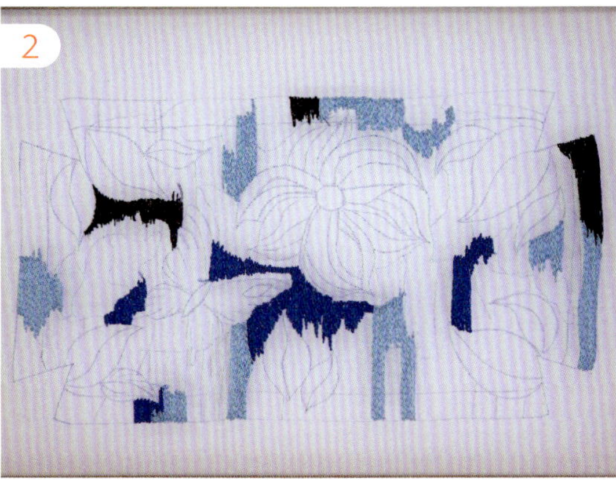

Apply the chain stitch technique using a hook needle and blue shades thread to fill parts of the pattern.

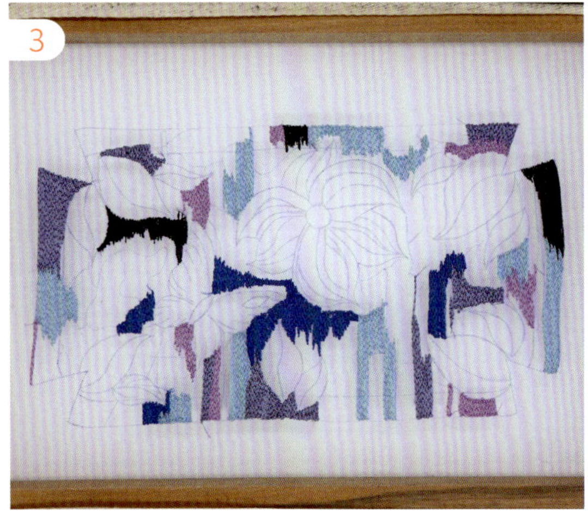

Apply the chain stitch technique using a hook needle and purple shades thread to fill parts of the pattern.

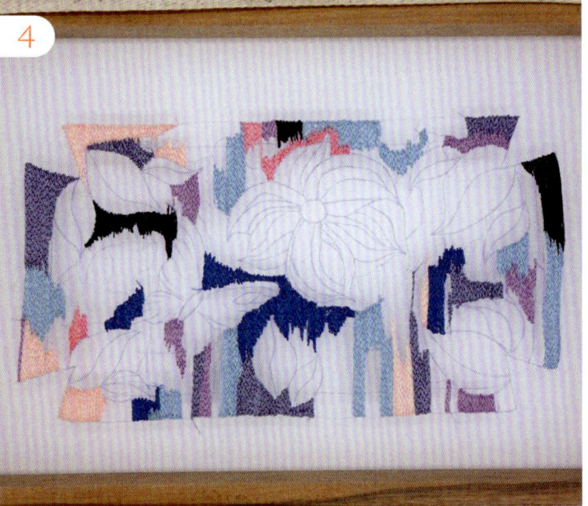

Apply the chain stitch technique using a hook needle and pink shades thread to fill parts of the pattern.

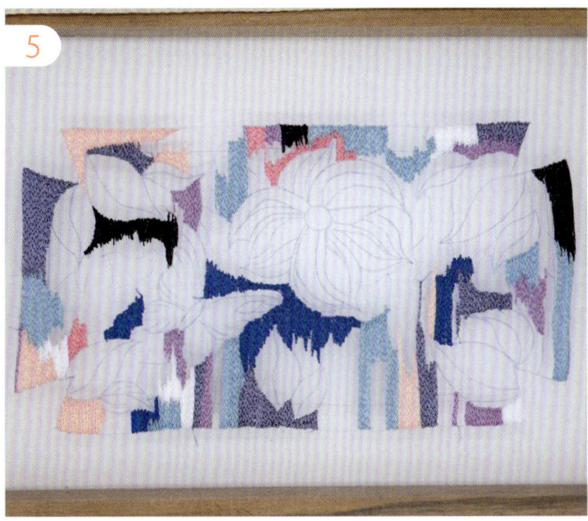

Apply the chain stitch technique using a hook needle and white thread to fill parts of the pattern.

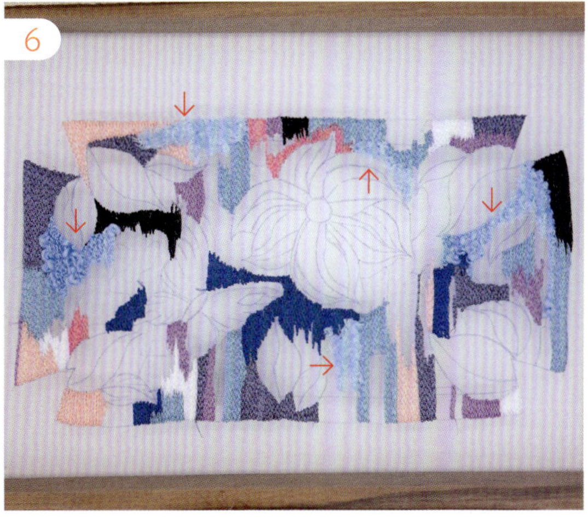

Use a large eye hand sewing needle to stitch the blue shades yarn in the areas shown in the picture.

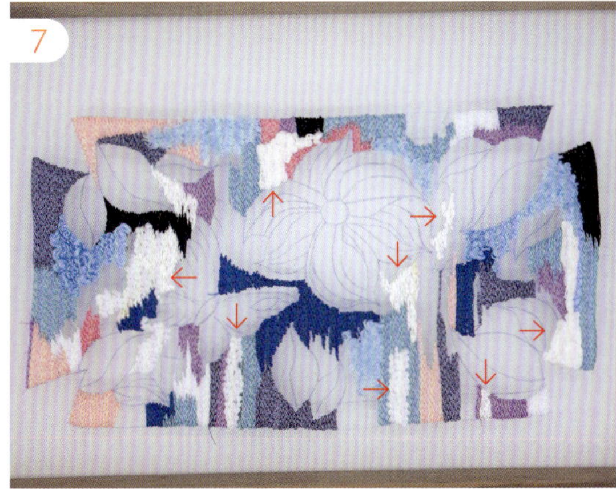

Use a large eye hand sewing needle to stitch the white shades yarn in the areas shown in the picture.

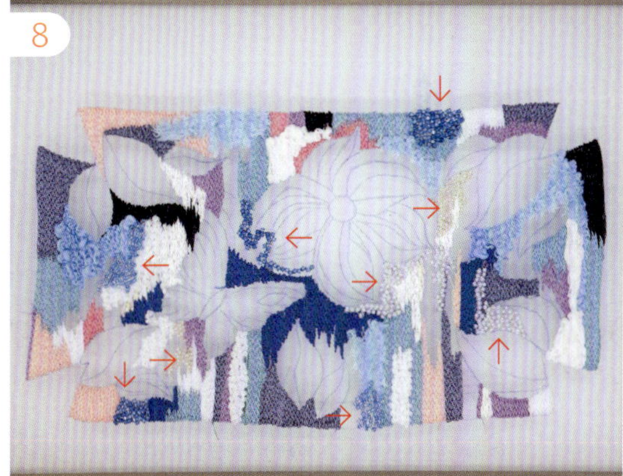

Apply the technique of stitching beads irregularly from the back side of the fabric using a hook needle, silver thread, 2 mm blue seed beads, 2 mm purple seed beads, and 1.5 mm transparent seed beads to fill parts of the pattern.

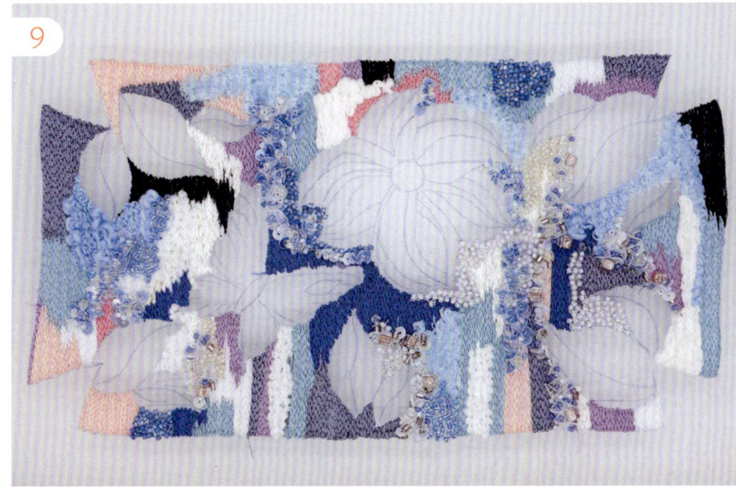

Apply the technique of stitching beads irregularly from the front side of the fabric using a hook needle, silver thread, 4 mm light purple sequins, 4 mm light blue sequins, 2 mm blue seed beads, 2 mm purple seed beads, 1.5 mm transparent seed beads, and 3 mm golden coffee tube beads to fill parts of the pattern. The embroidery of the background pattern is now complete.

◆ Leaves

1

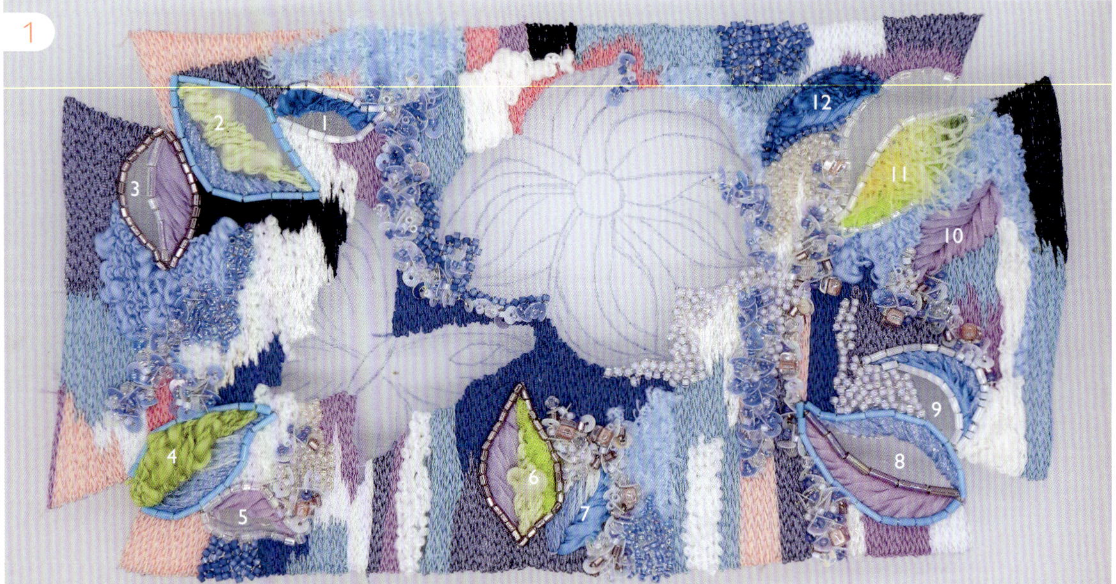

Use a hand sewing needle to sew the light blue and light purple ribbons on parts of the leaves 3, 5, 6, 7, 8, 9, 10, 12.

Use a hand sewing needle to sew the blue and green shades yarns on parts of the leaves 1, 2, 4, 6, 7, 8, 9, 11, 12.

Apply the technique of stitching beads from the front side of the fabric using a hook needle, silver thread, 3 mm blue tube beads, 3 mm white tube beads, 2 mm purple tube beads, 2 mm white tube beads, 6 mm blue tube beads, 6 mm transparent tube beads, 6 mm light purple tube beads and 2 mm white seed beads to sew the outer contours of leaves 1–6, 8–9, 11–12 and part of the veins.

2

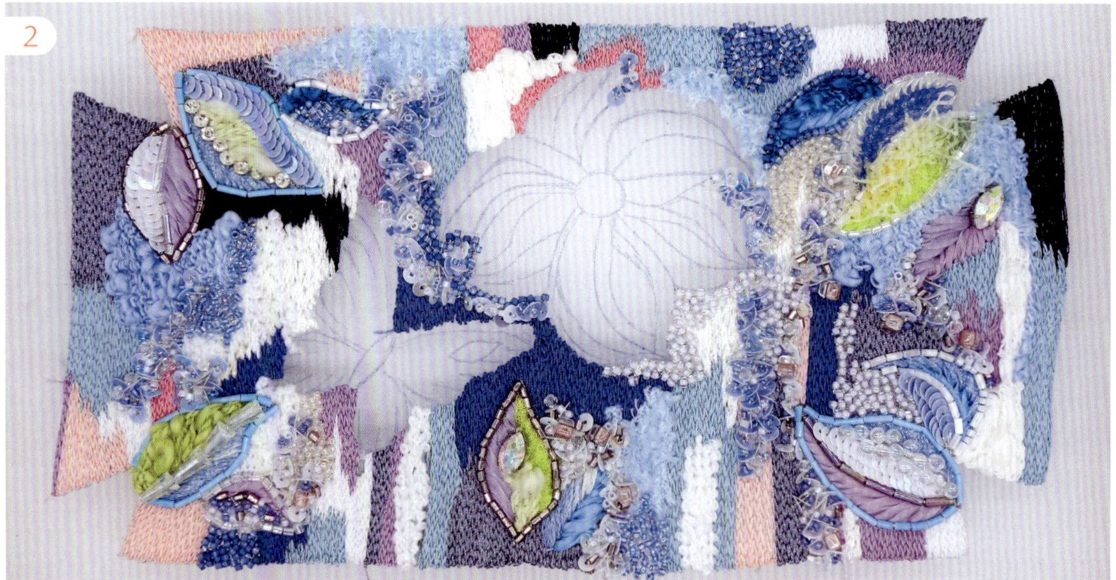

Apply the technique of stitching sequins from the front side of the fabric using a hook needle, silver thread, 4 mm light purple sequins, 4 mm light blue sequins, 4 mm blue sequins, and 4 × 8 mm white trapezoidal crystals to fill part of leaves 2, 3, 4, 8, 9, 11.

Apply the technique of stitching beads irregularly from the front side of the fabric using a hook needle, silver thread, 2 mm blue seed beads, 2 mm white seed beads, and 3 mm white crystals to fill the remaining areas of leaves 1, 5, 8.

Use a hand sewing needle and silver thread to fix two 5 × 10 mm colored horse eye shape sew-on rhinestones on leaves 6 and 10. The embroidery part of the leaves is now complete.

◆ Butterfly

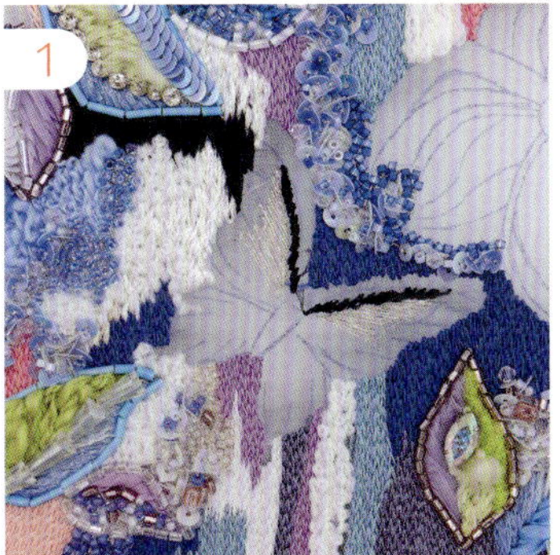

Apply the pulling stitch technique using a hook needle, dark blue thread and silver thread to sew part of the butterfly wings as shown in the figure.

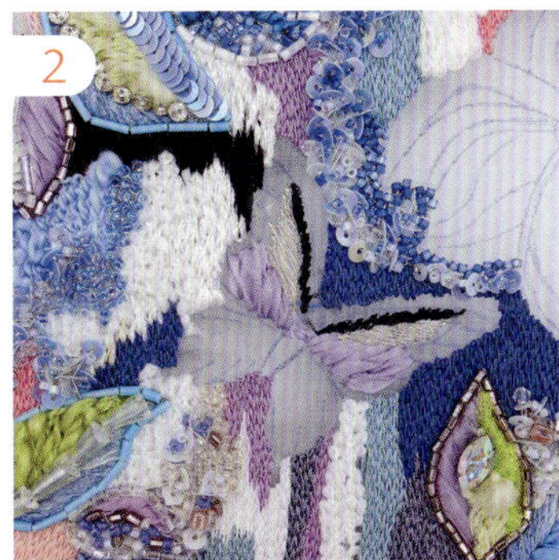

Use a hand sewing needle and light purple ribbon to fill parts of the butterfly wings.

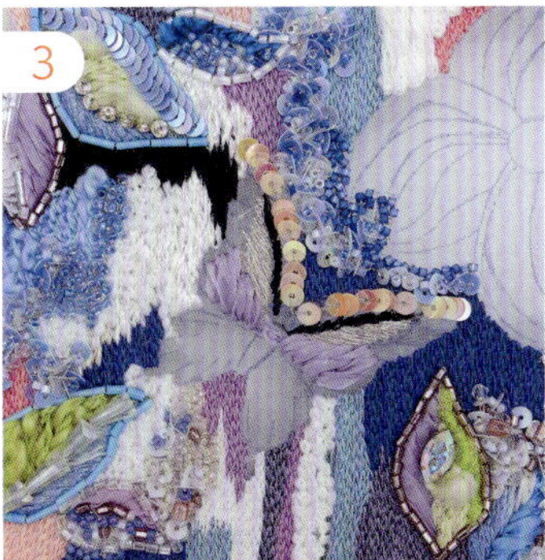

Apply the technique of stitching sequins from the front side of the fabric using a hook needle, silver thread, 4 mm orange sequins, and 4 mm transparent sequins to sew the outline of the butterfly's forewing.

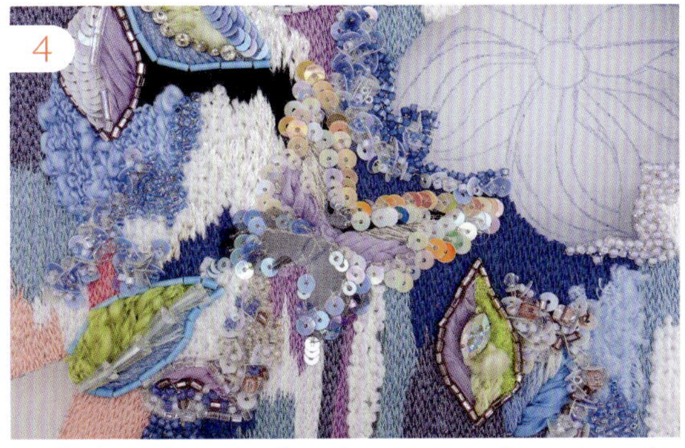

Apply the technique of stitching sequins discontinuously from the front side of the fabric using a hook needle and silver thread to combine 4 mm transparent sequins, 3 mm light blue sequins, 4 mm orange sequins, 4 mm light blue sequins, and 4 mm light purple sequins to sew the butterfly's silhouette.

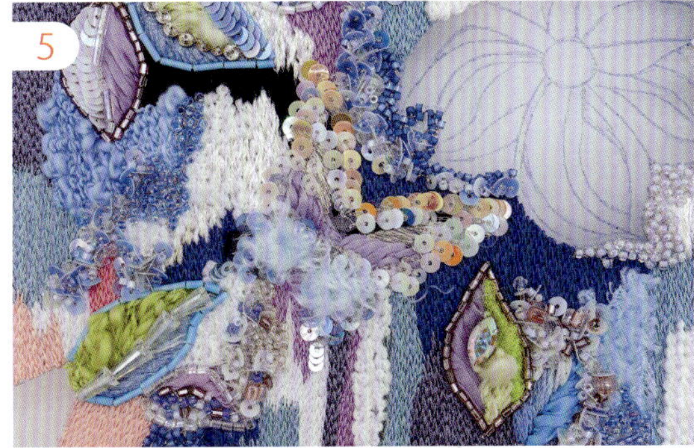

Use a hand sewing needle and blue shades yarn to fill the remaining parts of the butterfly wings.

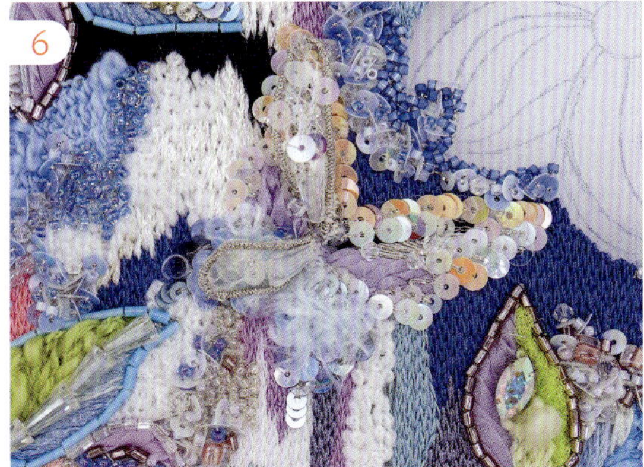

Use a hand sewing needle and silver thread to fix the three-dimensional parts 1 and 2 completed on page 144 to the left wings of the butterfly.

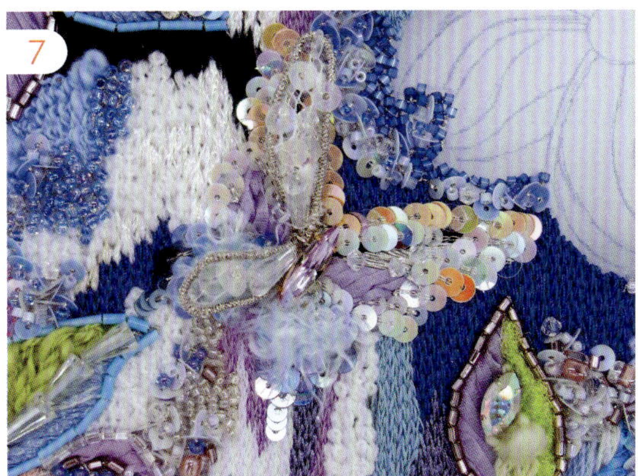

Use a hand sewing needle and silver thread to fix a 4 × 15 mm purple horse eye shape sew-on rhinestone as the body of the butterfly. The embroidery of the butterfly is now complete.

◆ Flower

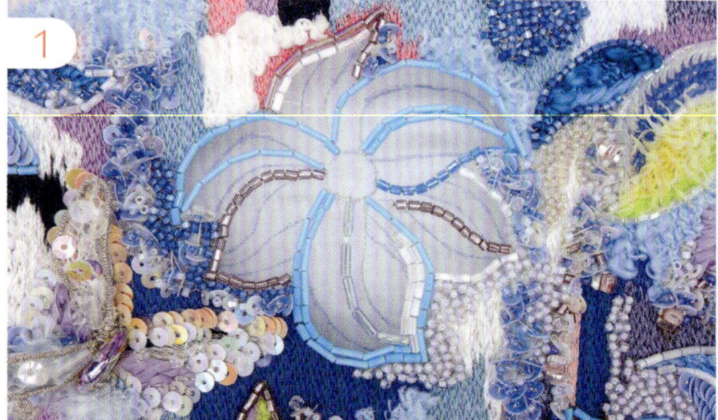

Apply the technique of stitching beads from the front side of the fabric using a hook needle, silver thread, 2 mm blue tube beads, 2 mm purple tube beads, 2 mm white tube beads, 3 mm white tube beads, 3 mm blue tube beads, 3 mm golden coffee tube beads, 6 mm transparent tube beads, and 6 mm blue tube beads to sew the outline of the petals.

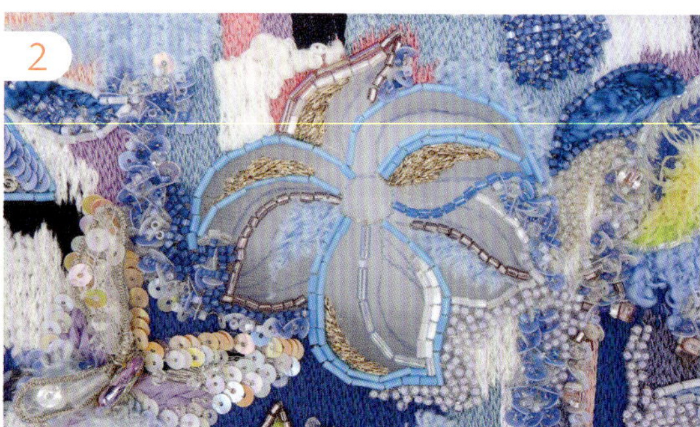

Use a hand sewing needle and golden and blue yarns to fill part of the petals.

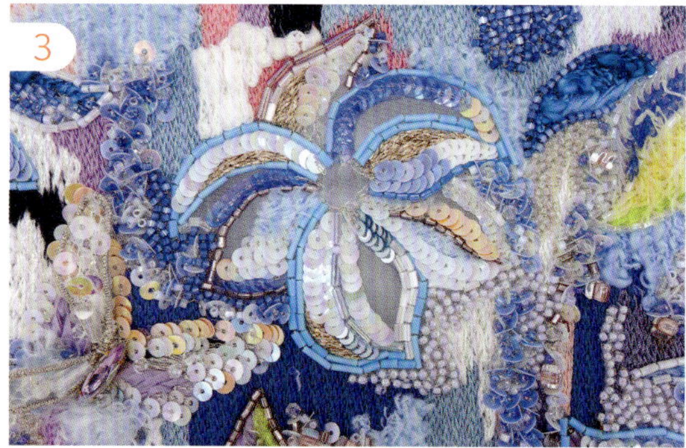

Apply the technique of stitching sequins from the front side of the fabric using a hand sewing needle, silver thread, 4 mm light purple sequins, 4 mm light blue sequins, 4 mm blue sequins, 4 mm orange sequins, 3 mm white sequins, and 3 mm transparent sequins to sew part of the inner lines of the petals.

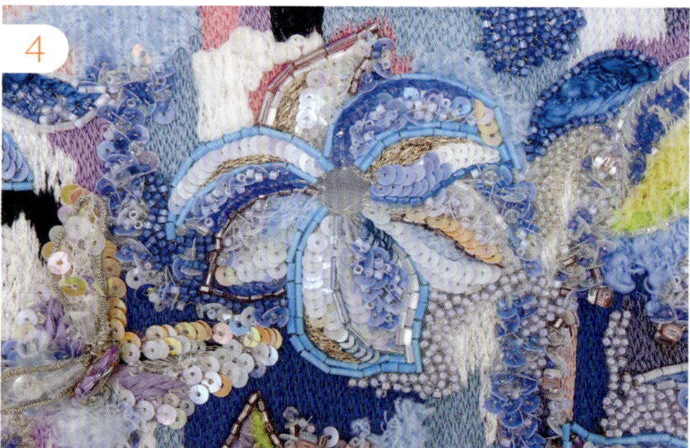

Apply the technique of stitching beads irregularly from the front side of the fabric using a hook needle, silver thread, 2 mm white seed beads, 4 mm light blue sequins, and 4 mm light purple sequins to fill the rest of the petals.

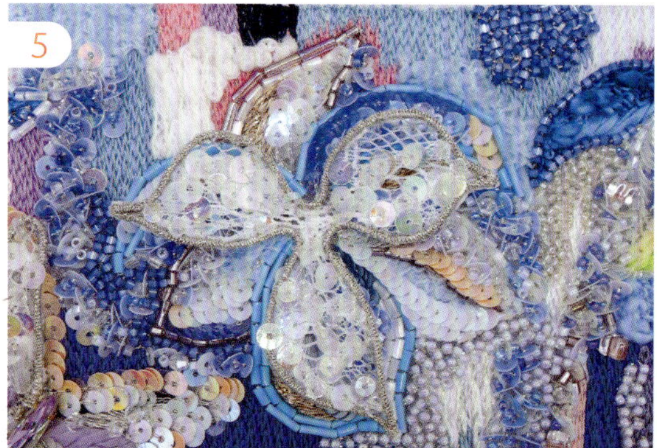

Use a hand sewing needle and silver thread to fix the larger three-dimensional petal 3 completed on page 144 to the center of the flower.

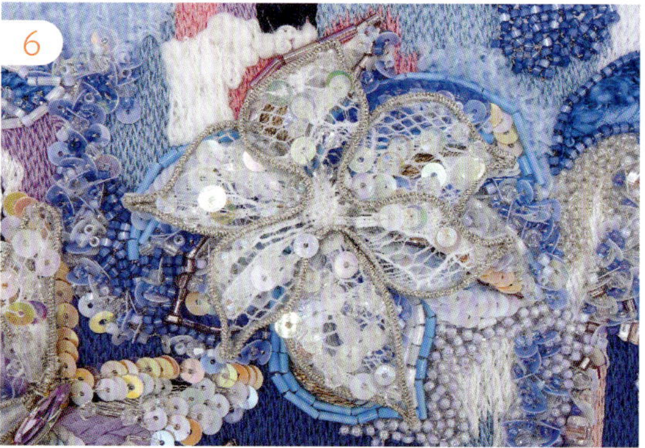

Use a hand sewing needle and silver thread to fix the smaller three-dimensional petal 4 completed on page 144 at the center of the flower. Ensure that its position is staggered from the larger three-dimensional petal beneath it.

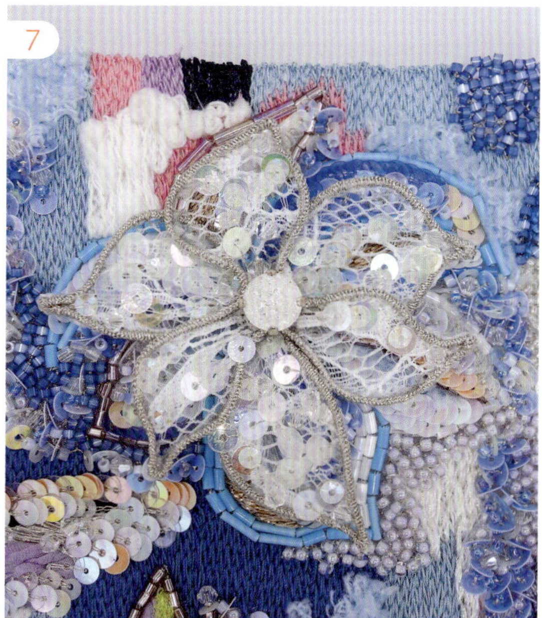

Use a hand sewing needle and silver thread to fix a 6 mm white round sew-on rhinestone at the center of the flower.

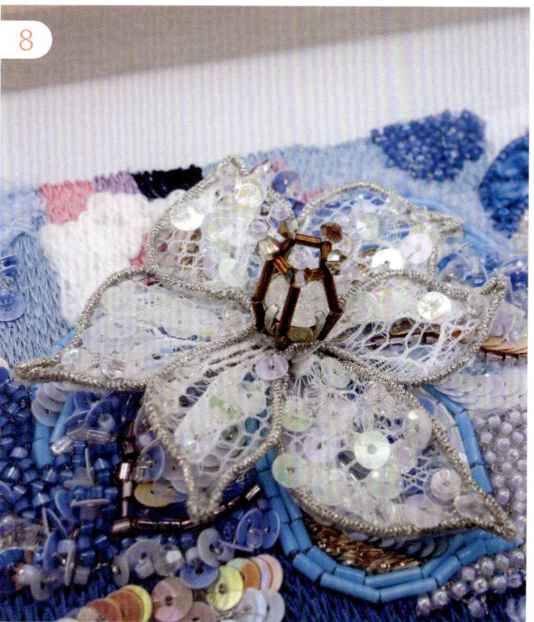

Apply the technique of embroidering a bead on top of a tube using a hand sewing needle, silver thread, 6 mm golden coffee tube beads, 3 mm golden coffee tube beads, 3 mm golden coffee crystals, and 2 mm white seed beads to sew a three-dimensional flower center as shown in the figure. See the box on page 150 for the specific steps.

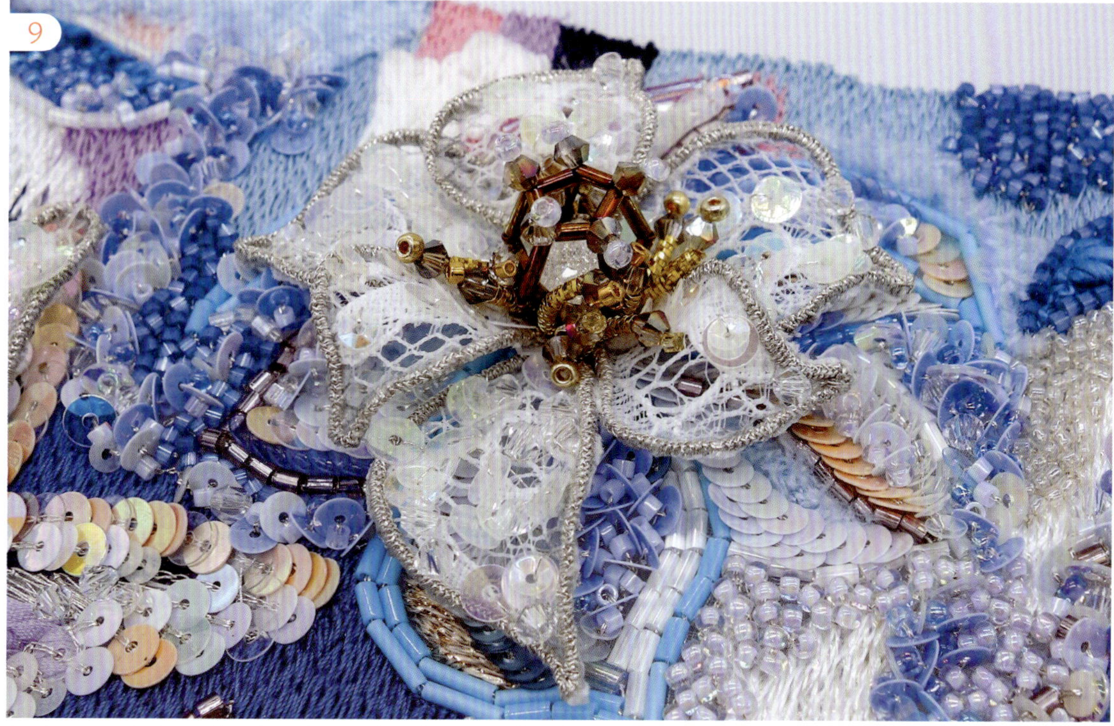

Apply the technique of embroidering a bead on top of a tube using a hand sewing needle, golden soft bullion wire, 3 mm golden coffee crystals, and 2 mm golden seed beads to sew stamens around the three-dimensional flower center. The embroidery of the flower and the front of the dinner bag is now complete.

Steps for the Three-Dimensional Flower Center

1

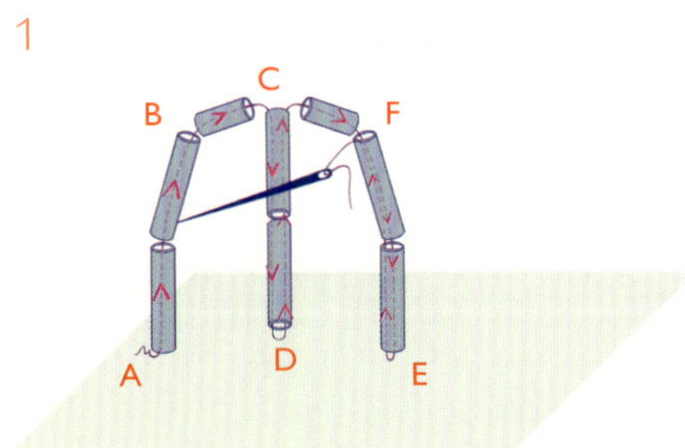

When embroidering the three-dimensional flower center, start sewing from point A. First, sew two 6 mm golden coffee tube beads vertically from A to B, followed by a 3 mm golden coffee tube bead horizontally from B to C, and two 6 mm golden coffee tube beads vertically from C to D. Place the needle and thread at the back of the cloth. Next, sew the thread from D to C through the tube beads, followed by from C to F horizontally through a 3 mm golden coffee tube bead, and from F to E vertically through two 6 mm golden coffee tube beads, before placing the needle and thread at the back of the cloth, and then pull the thread back again from E to F.

2

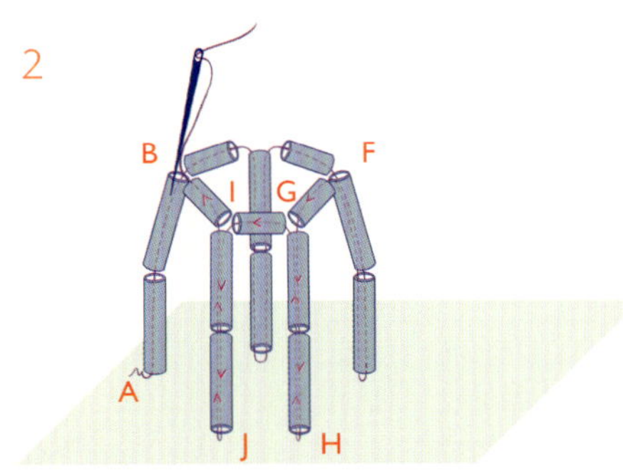

Using the same approach, follow the route of F–G–H–G–I–J–I–B–A to complete the beading, and return to point A to complete the frame construction.

3

The thread comes from point A to point J at the back of the cloth, then runs through the tube beads from J to I. Apply the technique of embroidering a bead on top of a tube with a 3 mm golden coffee crystal and a 2 mm white seed bead, then the needle and thread returns to point J to complete one vertical line.

4

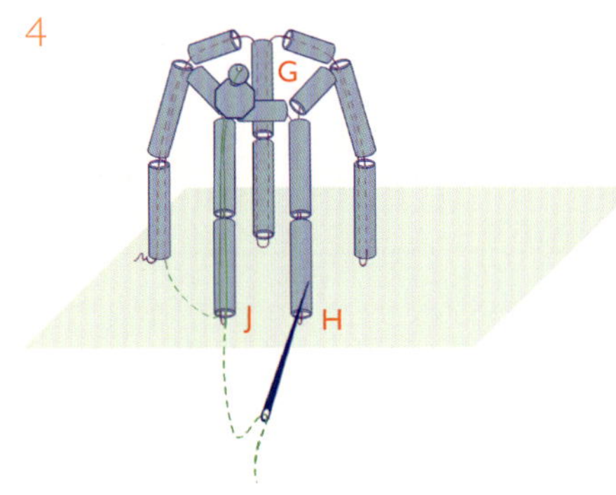

The thread comes from J to H at the back of the cloth, and complete embroidering a 3 mm golden coffee crystal and a 2 mm white seed bead from H to G with the same technique.

5

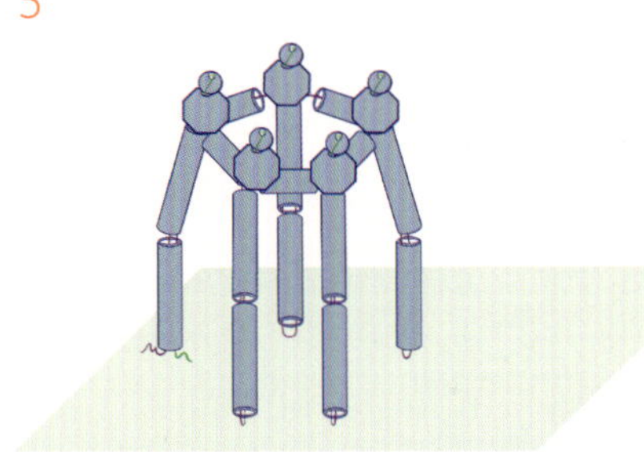

After embroidering the golden coffee crystal and white seed bead on all five vertical lines, the three-dimensional flower center is now complete.

◆ Putting the Pieces Together

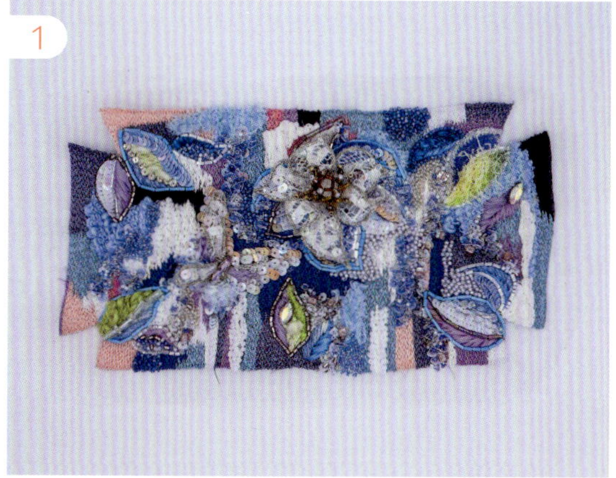

Cut out the embroidered piece, leaving an allowance of about 1 cm on the outer edge.

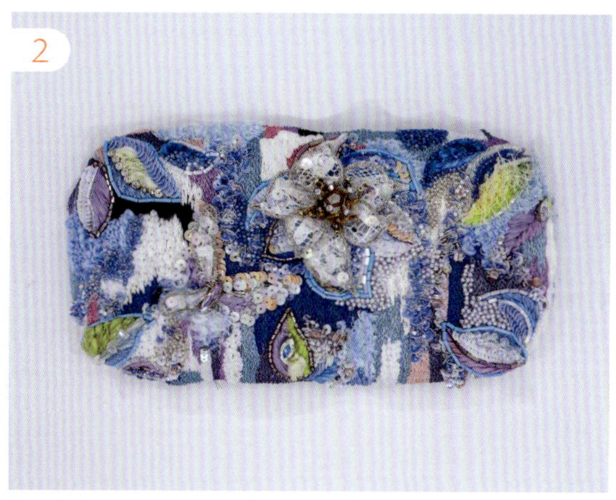

Apply fabric glue evenly on the front of the clutch bag mold, and paste the embroidery piece onto it. Ensure that the four corners are well aligned.

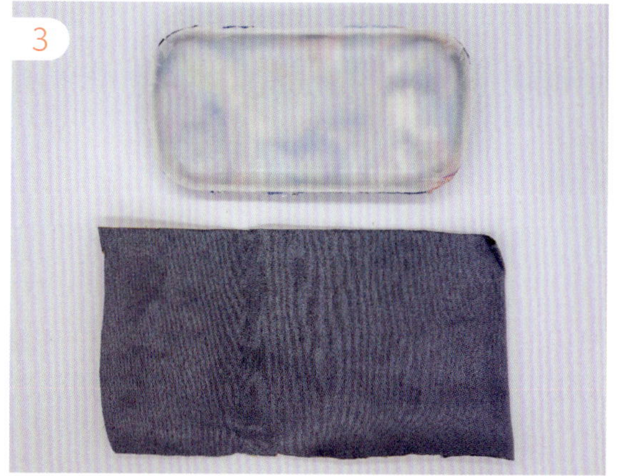

Fold the allowance of the embroidery piece inwards and use fabric glue to stick it onto the back of the mold. Prepare the self-adhesive velvet.

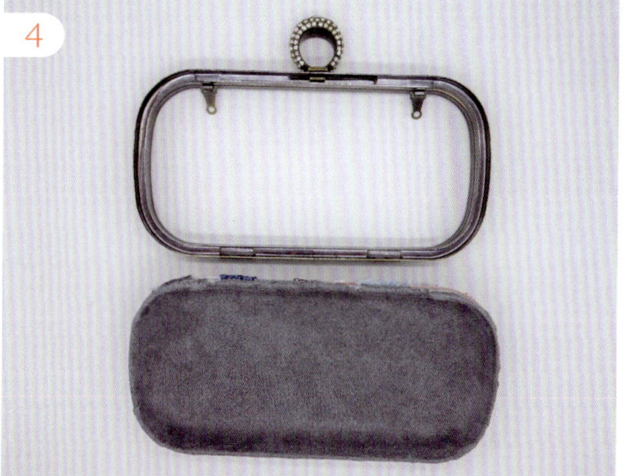

Stick the self-adhesive velvet onto the back of the mold and trim the edges neatly. Prepare a frame with clasp lock.

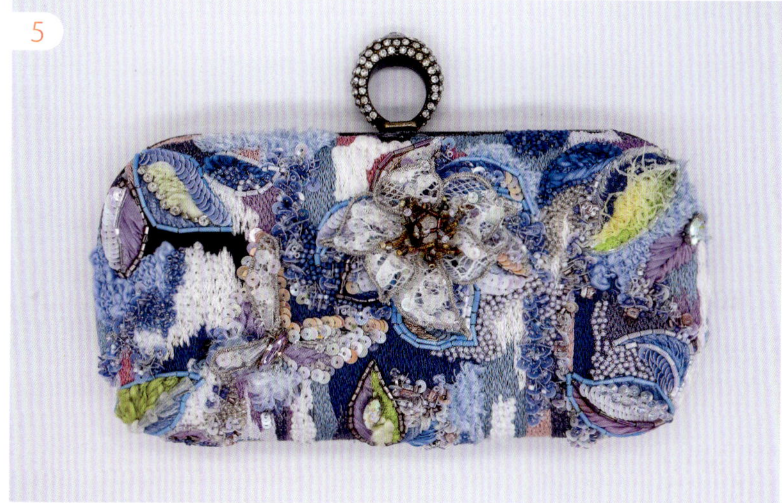

Apply fabric glue in the grooves of the frame and insert the mold into it. The front of the bag is now complete. The back of the bag can be produced using identical or similar patterns (see page 170 as a reference) and materials before inserting into the other side of the frame. The work is complete.

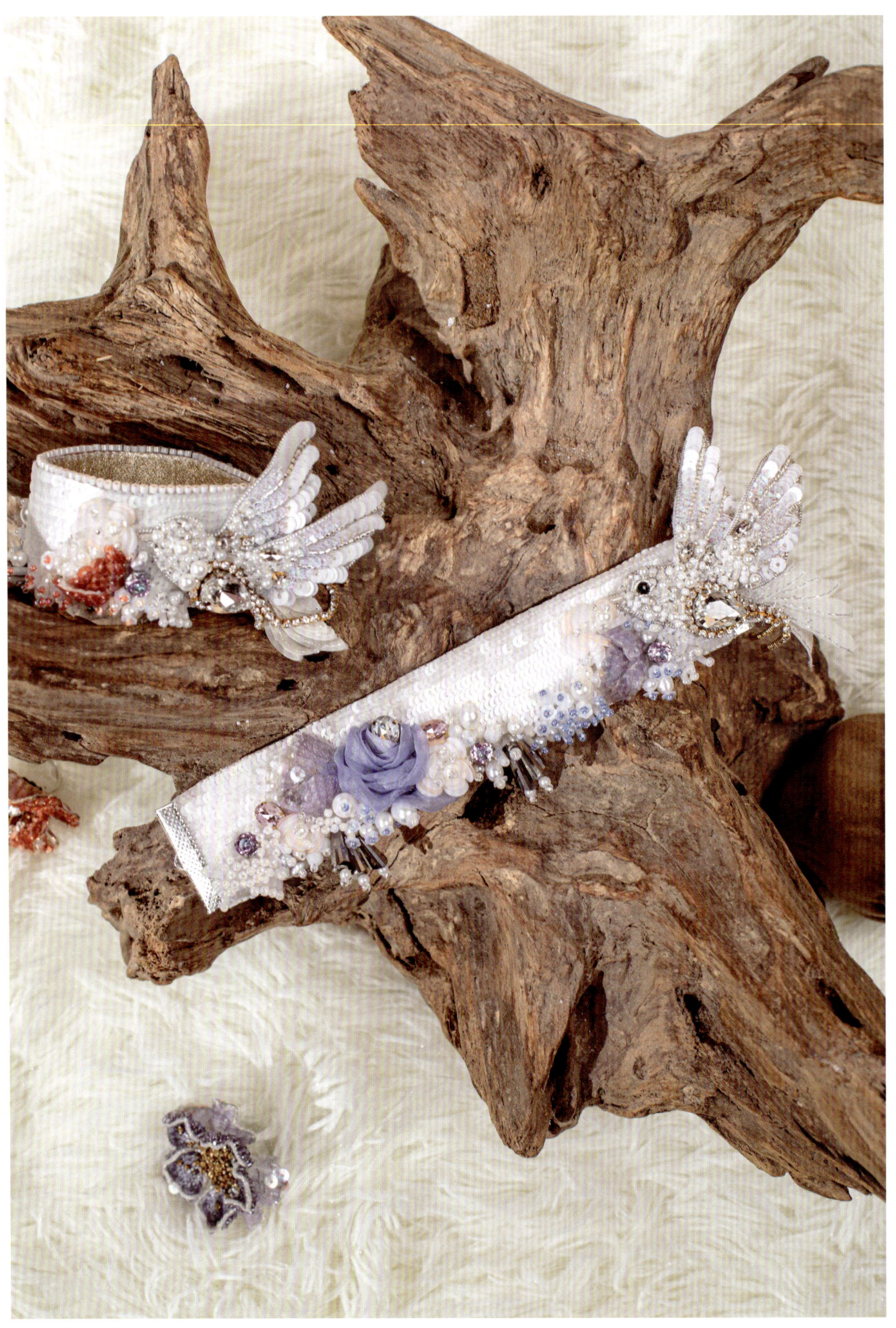

16. Flower and Bird Bracelet

Throughout thousands of years of Chinese history and culture, the "flower and bird" motif has been one of the three main themes in traditional painting. Also common as a decorative pattern in arts and crafts, flowers and birds have been used and interpreted by the great masters. This bead embroidery project features a white bird and a fragrant camellia—one of China's Ten Famous Traditional Flowers—as its main characters. A natural scene of white birds flying and dancing among the flowers is depicted with beads, as if the bird is fascinated by the beautiful flowers, plunging into the flowers and smelling their fragrance.

You Will Need

Threads	bullion wires	silver hard, silver soft
	thread	silver, white, black
Beads	seed beads	1.5 mm silver, 2 mm white, 2 mm silver, 2 mm purple, 2 mm pink
	pearls	3 mm white, 4 mm white, 4 mm light gray
	sequins	3 mm clear, 3 mm white, 4 mm white, 4 mm light purple, 4 mm white flower shape
	side hole sequins	4 mm white, 4 mm pink, 5 mm white, 5 mm pink
	tube beads	5 mm white, 6 mm white
	crystals	4 mm black, 6 × 12 mm silver trapezoidal
	sew-on rhinestones	3 mm white round, 3 × 6 mm white horse eye shape, 4 × 6 mm white drop shape, 6 × 8 mm pink oval, 6 mm purple, 10 × 15 mm white drop shape
	rhinestone chain	2 mm silver
Fabrics	white organza, blue-purple organza, white poplin, leather, self-adhesive velvet, regenerated leather	
Tools	embroidery hoop, 70# hook needle, hand sewing needle, scissors, fabric glue, heat erasable marker, ball head pins, 26# iron wire, 30 mm silver bracelet bookmark pinches, silver bracelet lobster clasp, silver chain extender, pliers	

Embroidery Steps

◆ Bird

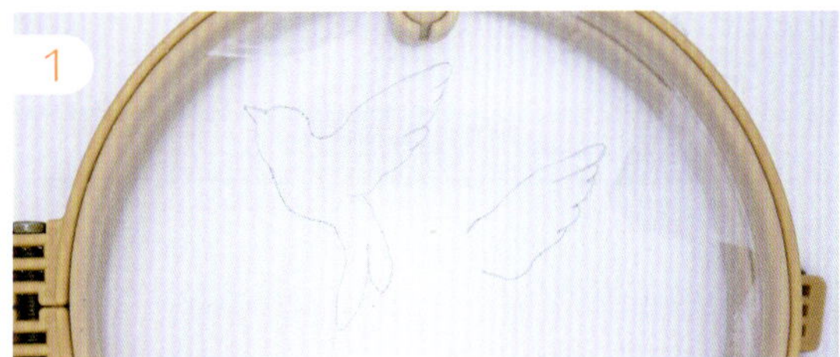

Stretch the white organza on the embroidery hoop and outline the bird (see page 168) on the fabric with a heat erasable marker.

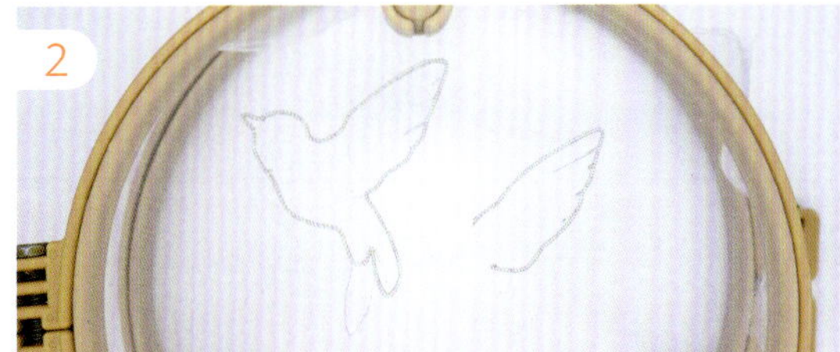

Pull the silver hard bullion wires slightly apart and fix it on the outline of the patterns with a hand sewing needle and silver thread.

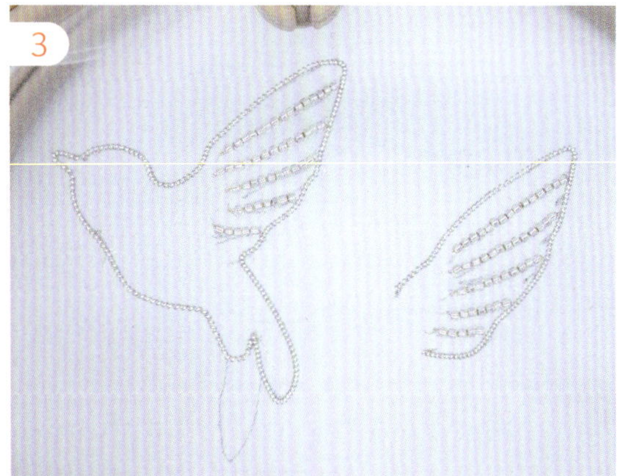

Apply the technique of stitching beads from the front side of the fabric using a hook needle, silver thread, and 1.5 mm silver seed beads to sew the lines inside the wings.

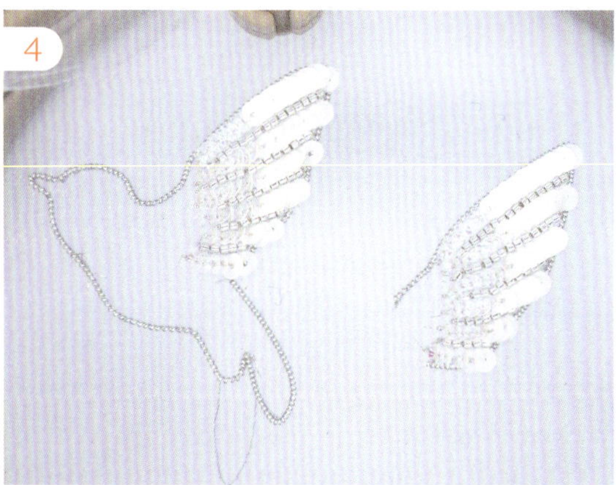

Apply the technique of stitching sequins from the front side of the fabric using a hook needle, silver thread, 4 mm white sequins, and 3 mm clear sequins to fill the wings from the outside in.

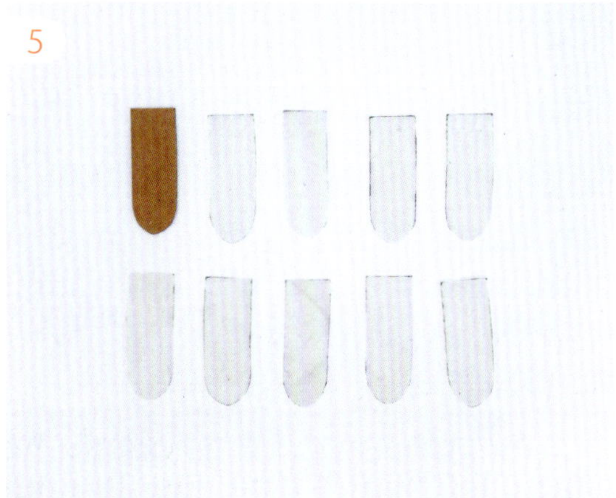

Cut out eight to ten pieces from white poplin according to the paper pattern.

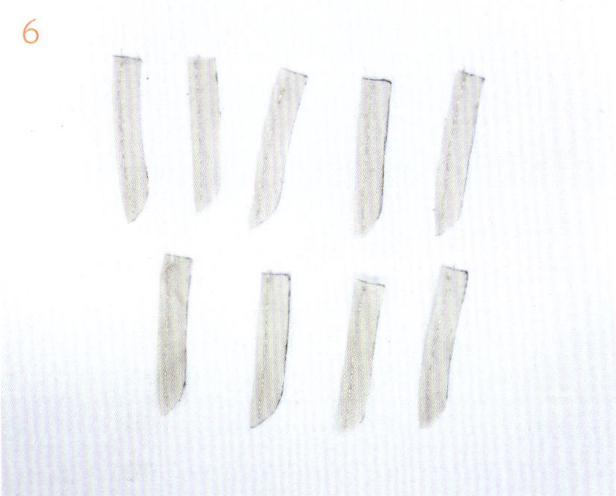

Fold the cut pieces in half and stitch them with a hand sewing needle and silver thread, approximately 1 mm away from the folding line.

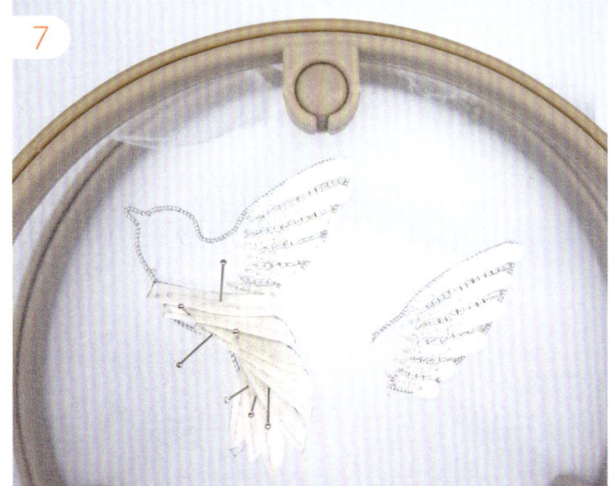

Use ball head pins to fasten the sewn pieces of step 6 to the bird's tail. Pay close attention to the shape of the tail.

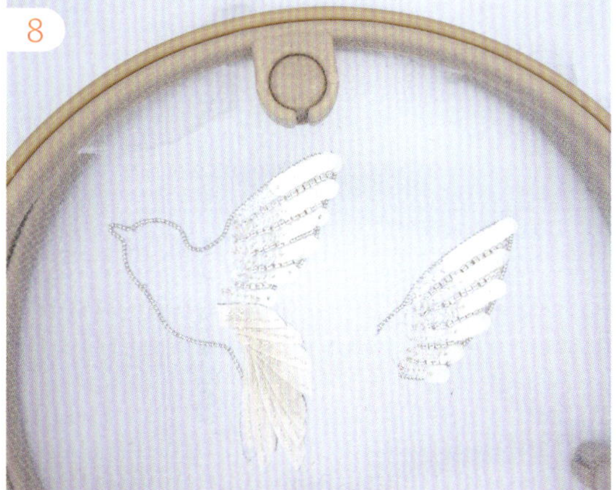

Fix the tail with a hand sewing needle and white thread. Next, trim off the excess along the contour of the tail.

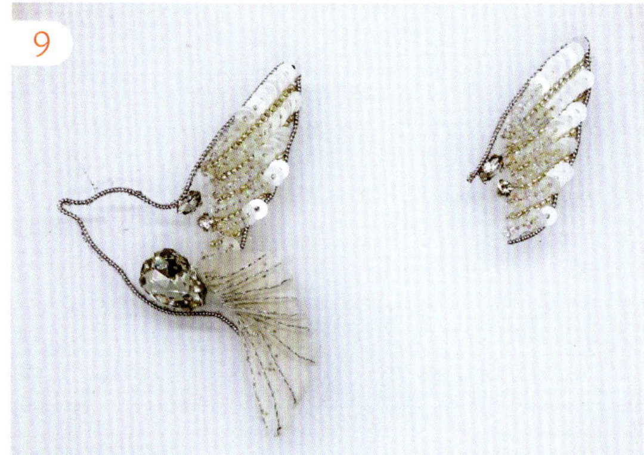
9

Use a hand sewing needle and white thread to fix the 3 mm white round sew-on rhinestone, 3 × 6 mm white horse eye sew-on rhinestone, and 10 × 15 mm white drop sew-on rhinestone, in their corresponding positions on the pattern.

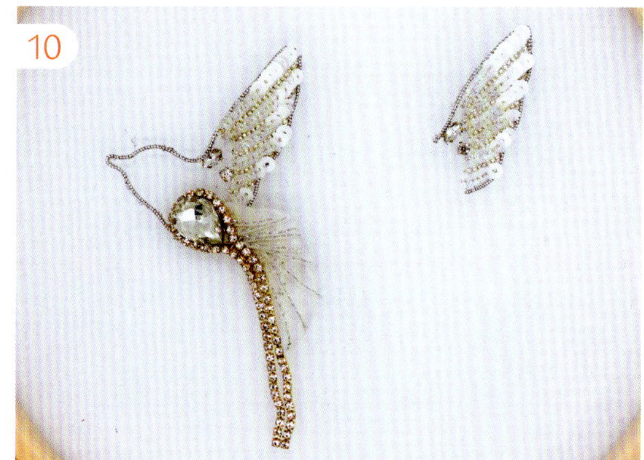
10

Fix the 2 mm silver rhinestone chain on the outer ring of the drop rhinestone and leave a length of about 40 mm beneath.

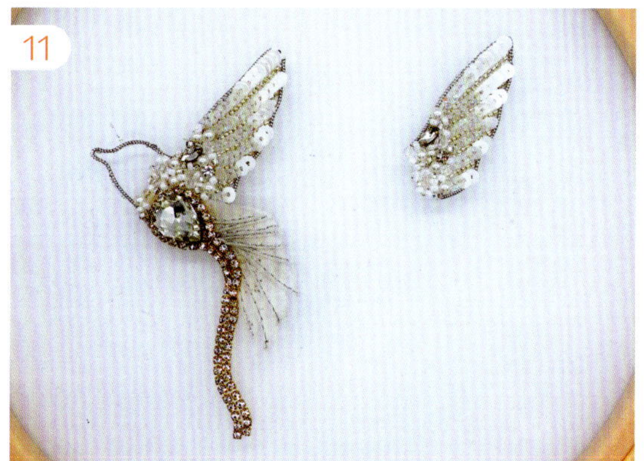
11

Apply the technique of stitching beads from the front side of the fabric using a hook needle, silver thread, 2 mm white seed beads, 2 mm silver seed beads, 5 mm white tube beads, and 3 mm white pearls to fill the remaining parts of the two wings in an irregular fashion.

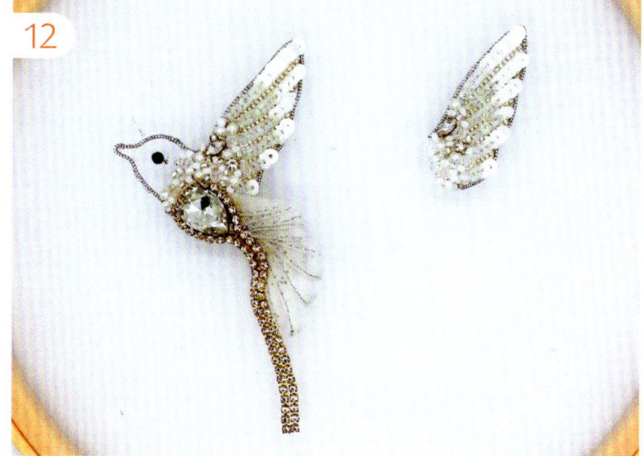
12

Use a hand sewing needle and black thread to fix a 4 mm black crystal as the bird's eye.

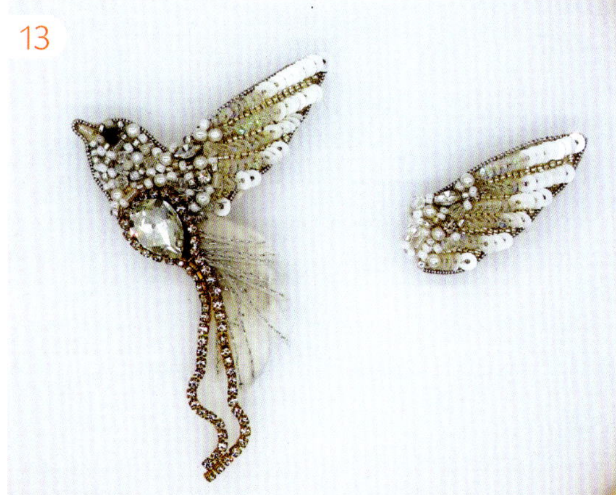
13

Using hand sewing needle and silver thread, sew 4 mm white sequins to fill the empty areas in the bird's head, and fix a 5 mm white tube bead at its beak.

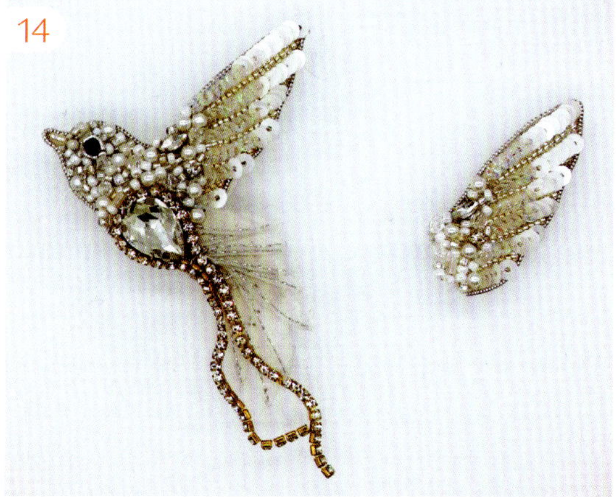
14

Use a hand sewing needle and silver thread to fix a piece of silver soft bullion wire along the upper and lower contours of the eye.

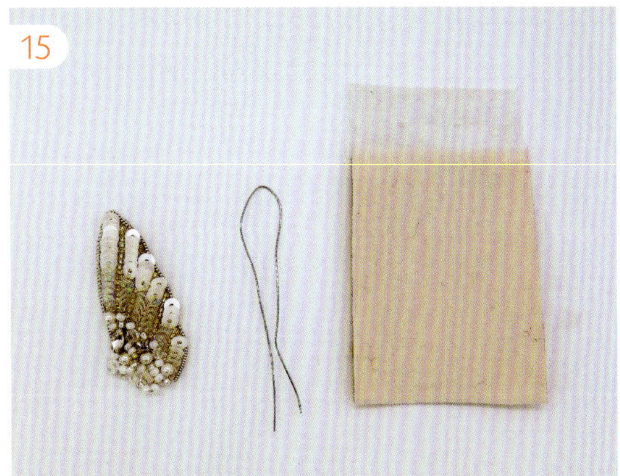

Cut off the single wing. Prepare a piece of self-adhesive velvet and a 26# iron wire. Bend the wire according to the outline of the wing.

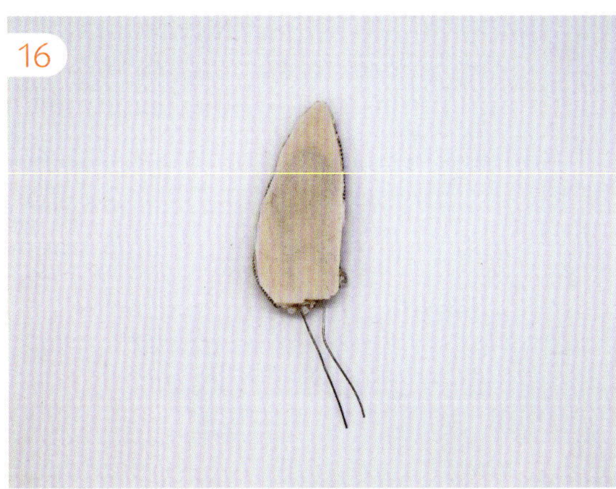

Using fabric glue, attach in order the iron wire and the self-adhesive velvet onto the wing, leaving a margin of about 5 cm for the iron wire. After it is dry, cut the excess velvet and set it aside.

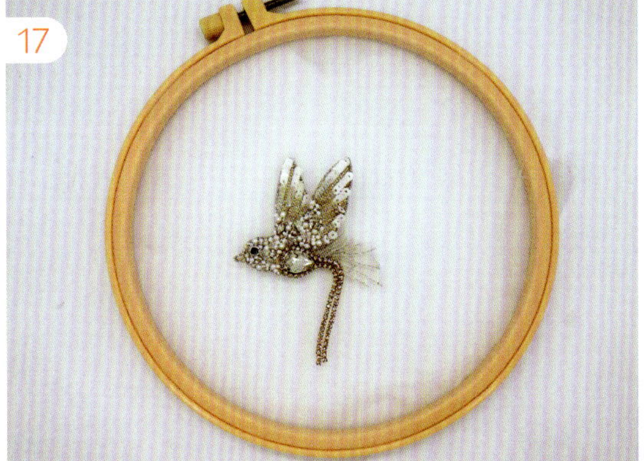

Insert the wire of the wing completed in the previous steps into the allocated position on the bird. Next, fix the joint between the embroidery pieces with a hand sewing needle and white thread to form a complete bird shape.

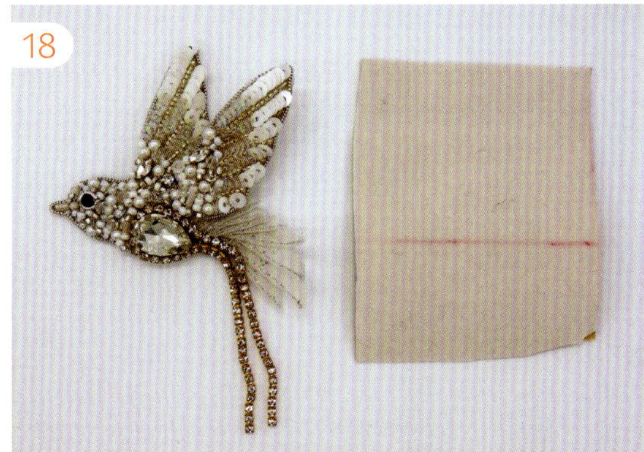

Cut out the embroidered pattern, leaving a margin of about 5 mm around the fabric. Prepare a piece of self-adhesive velvet.

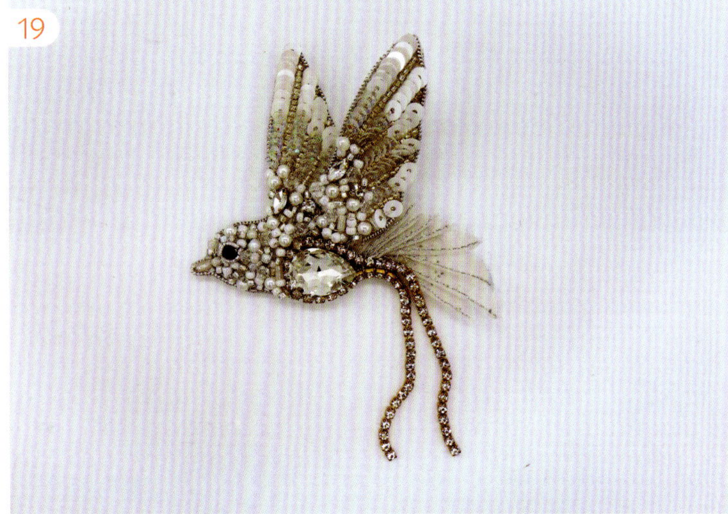

Stick the self-adhesive velvet onto the back of the embroidery piece and neatly trim off the excess fabric for later use.

◆ Camellia

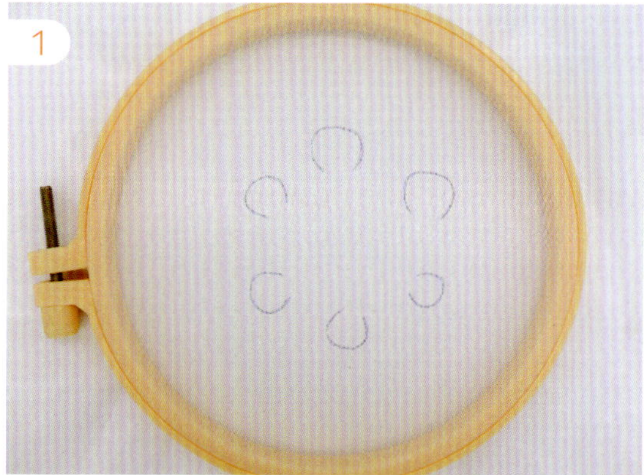

Re-stretch a piece of white organza and draw the petals (see page 168) with a heat erasable marker.

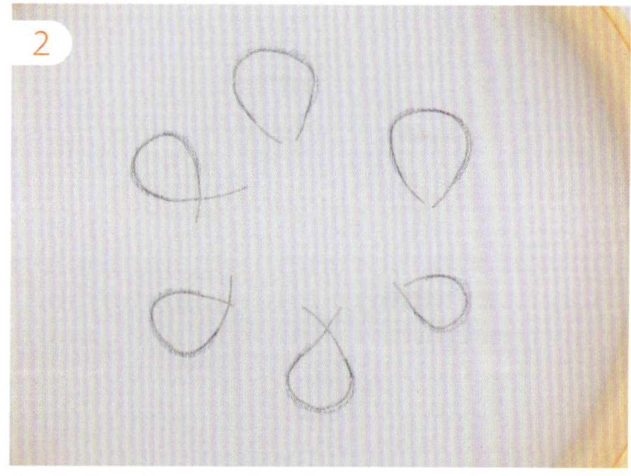

Apply the edging stitch technique using a hook needle and silver thread to sew 26# iron wire at about 1 mm along the inner contour of the patterns on the back side of the fabric.

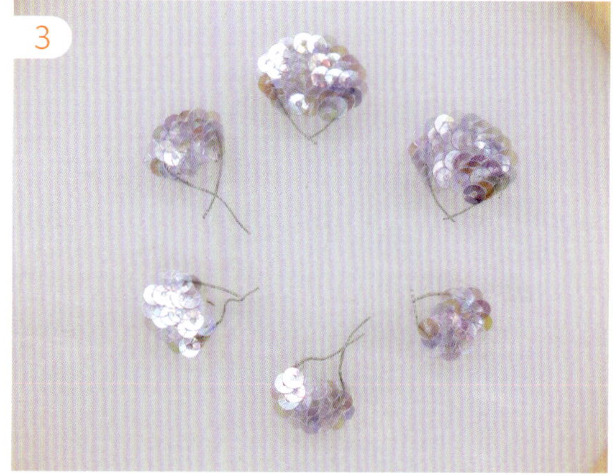

Apply the technique of stitching sequins from the front side of the fabric using a hook needle, silver thread, and 4 mm light purple sequins to fill the petals.

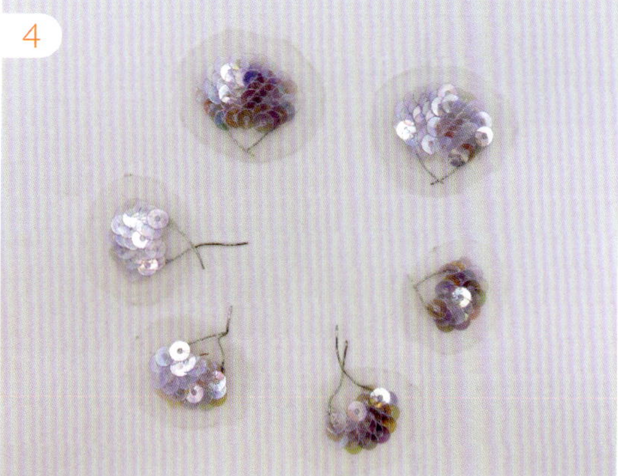

Cut out the embroidered petals and leave a margin of 5–8 mm on the edge of the fabric.

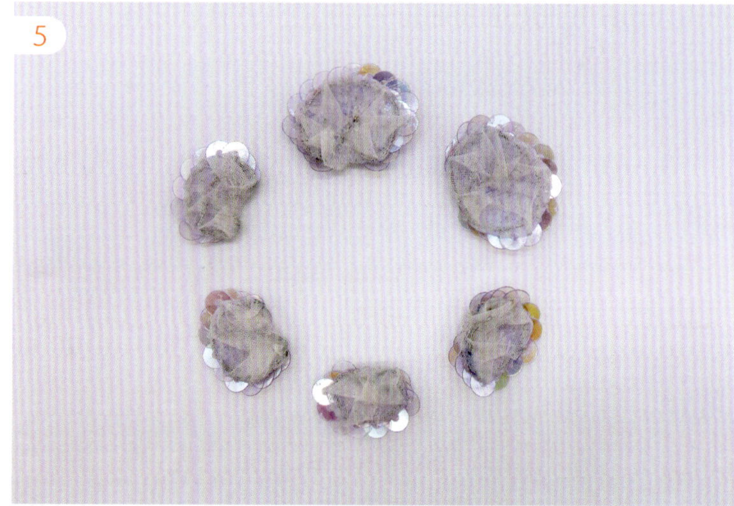

Fold the edge of the fabric inwards and fit it on the back of the embroidery pieces with fabric glue.

• Combination of the Bird and Flowers

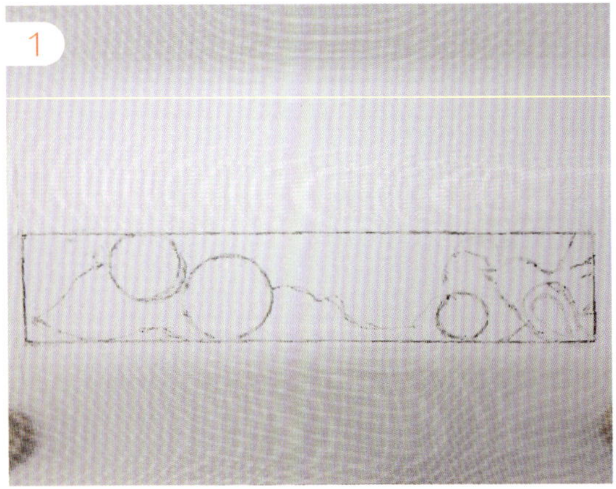

Re-stretch a piece of white organza and draw the main pattern (see page 168) of the bracelet with a heat erasable marker.

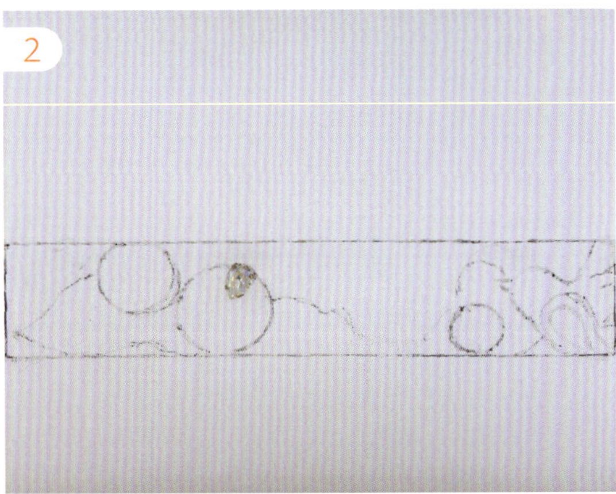

Use a hand sewing needle and white thread to fix a 4 × 6 mm white drop rhinestone at the position shown in the figure.

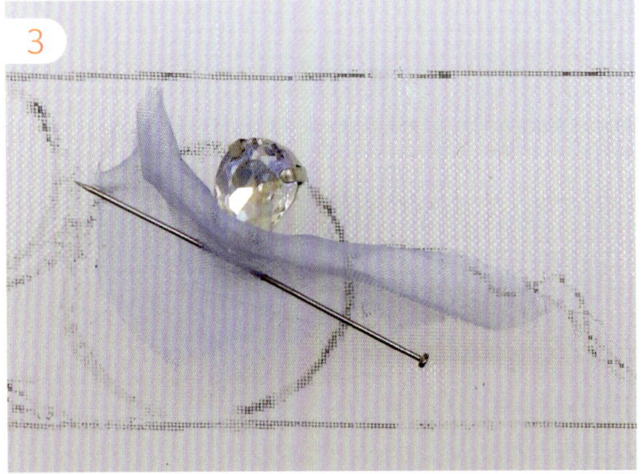

Take a piece of blue-purple organza and fold it in half along the diagonal texture. Next, fix it diagonally with a ball head pin beside the rhinestone completed in the previous step.

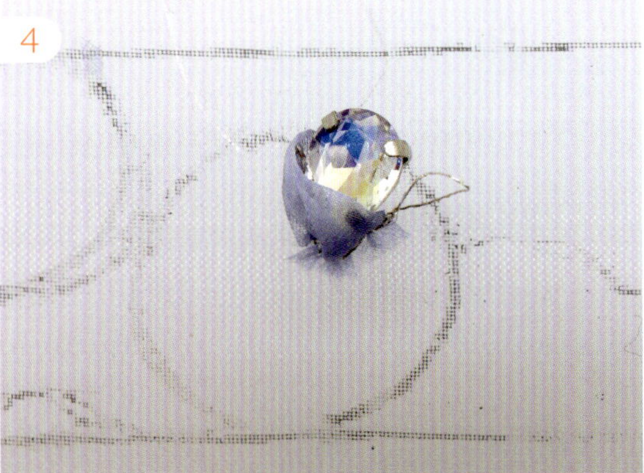

Apply the chain stitch technique from the front side of the fabric using a hook needle and silver thread to sew a petal as shown. Trim off the excess fabric.

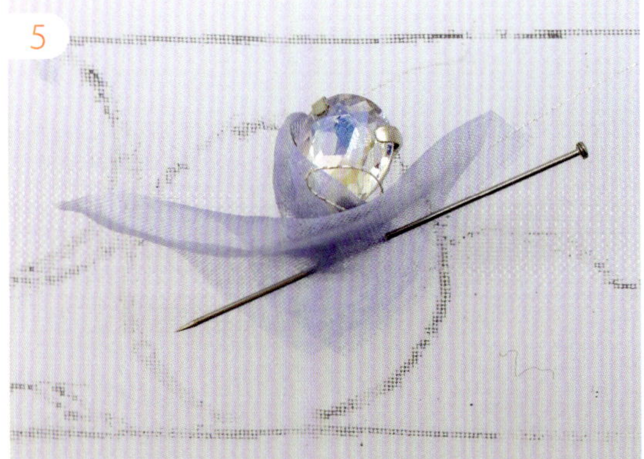

Take another piece of blue-purple organza, fold it in half along the diagonal texture, and fix it with a ball head pin on the opposite side of the previous petal. Cover the previous stitches.

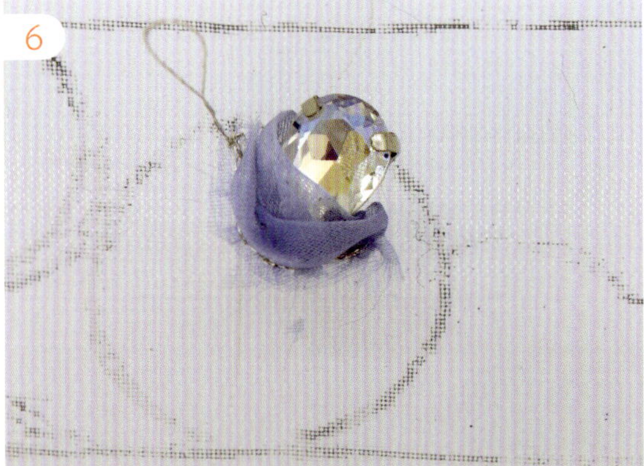

Apply the chain stitch technique from the front side of the fabric using a hook needle and silver thread to fix the petal. Trim off the excess fabric.

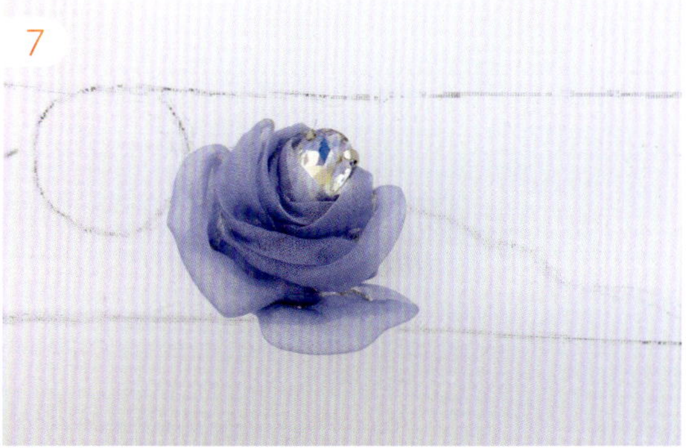

Apply the same technique used in steps 3–6 to sew the remaining petals. Make sure the arrangement of the petals looks natural.

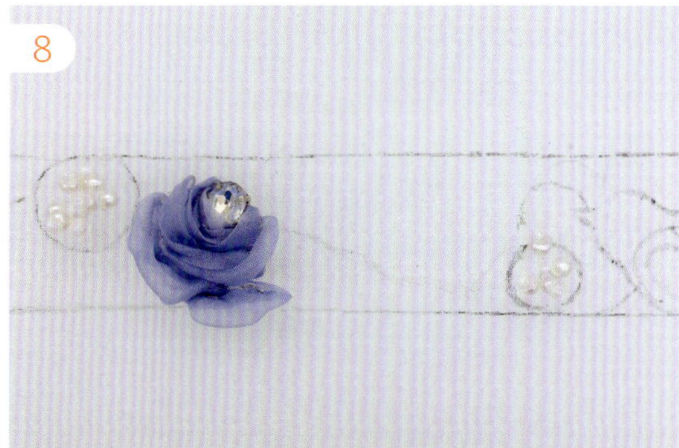

Apply the technique of embroidering a bead on top of a tube with a hand sewing needle, white thread, 2 mm white seed beads, 3 mm white pearls, 4 mm white pearls, and 4 mm white flower shape sequins to create the stamens of the other two flowers.

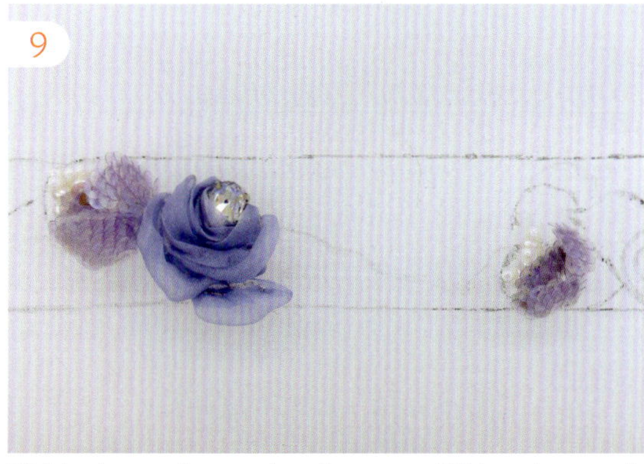

Divide the petals completed on page 157 into large and small groups. Fix them around the stamens from the previous step to form two flowers (one large and one small).

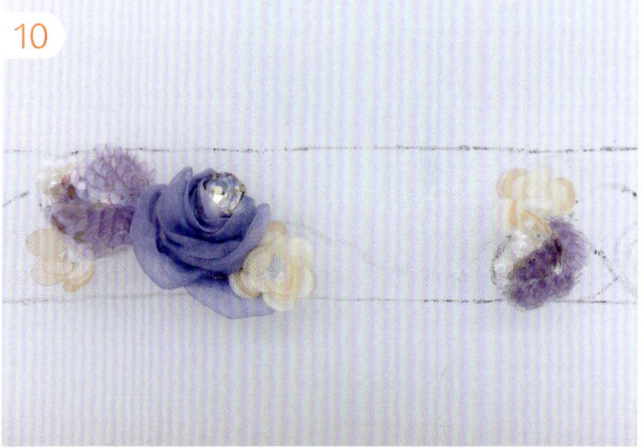

Use a hand sewing needle, white thread, 4 mm white side hole sequins, 4 mm pink side hole sequins, 5 mm white side hole sequins, and 5 mm pink side hole sequins to sew three small flowers as ornaments.

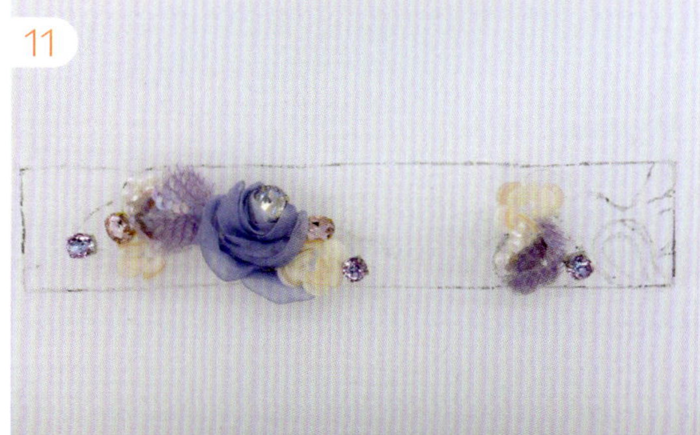

Use a hand sewing needle and white thread to fix 6 × 8 mm pink oval sew-on rhinestones and 6 mm purple sew-on rhinestones on the positions as shown in the figure.

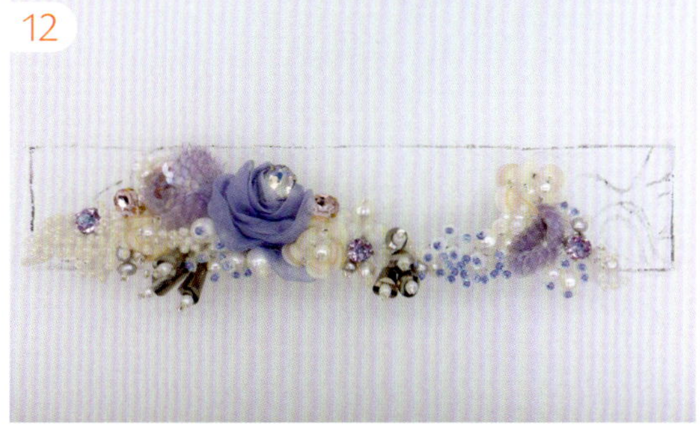

Apply the technique of embroidering a bead on top of a sequin (or a tube) with a hand sewing needle, white thread, 2 mm white seed beads, 2 mm silver seed beads, 2 mm purple seed beads, 2 mm pink seed beads, 4 mm light gray pearls, 6 mm white tube beads, 4 mm white flower sequins, 3 mm white pearls, and 6 × 12 mm silver trapezoidal crystals to irregularly fill in part of the area around the flowers, during which you can flexibly mix and match materials to create variation while also paying attention to the cohesion of the overall effect.

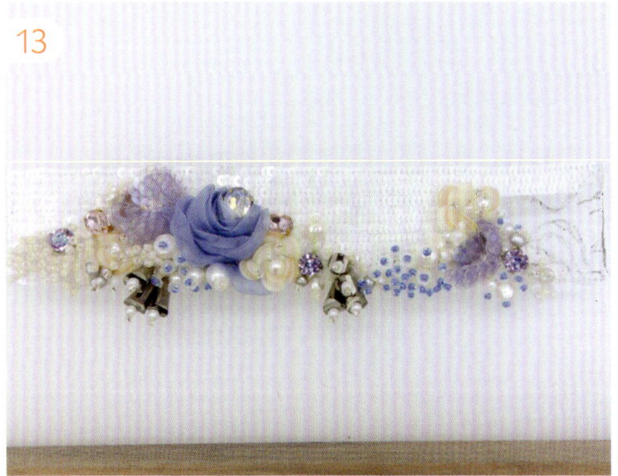

13

Apply the technique of stitching sequins from the back side of the fabric using a hook needle, white thread, and 3 mm white sequins to fill the rest of the pattern, apart from the space where the bird will be.

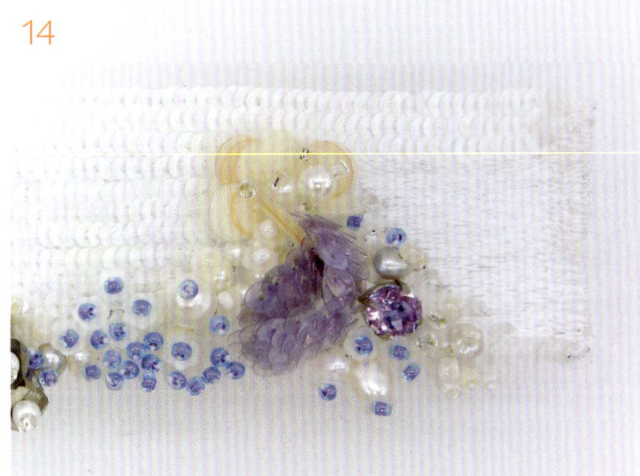

14

Apply the chain stitch technique using a hook needle and white thread to fill in the space where the bird will be. Ensure that there are no gaps at the point where they connect with the sequins.

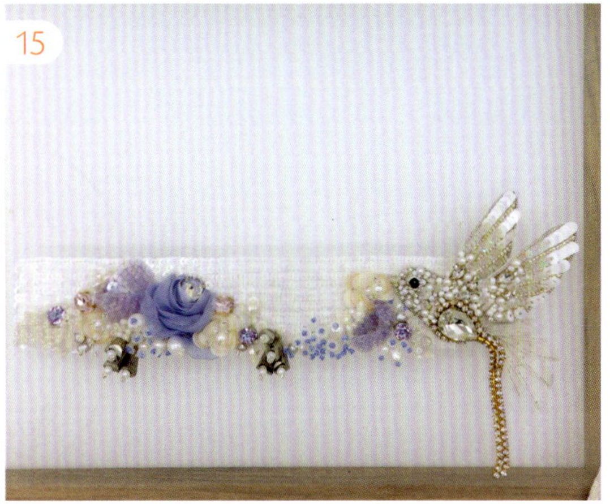

15

Use a hand sewing needle and white thread to sew the bird completed on page 156 into the pre-allocated position.

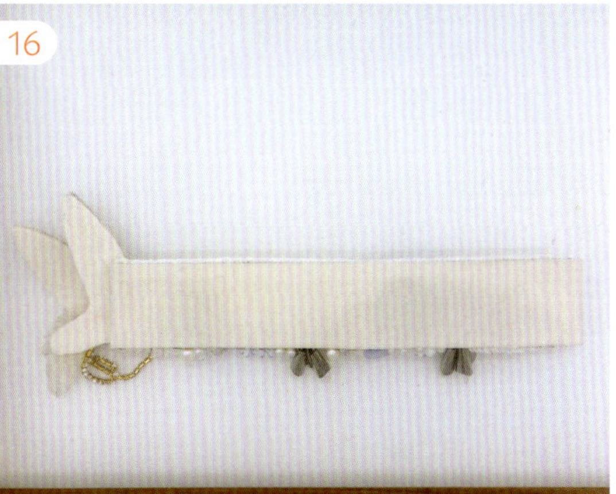

16

Stick a piece of self-adhesive velvet as large as the embroidery piece onto the back of it.

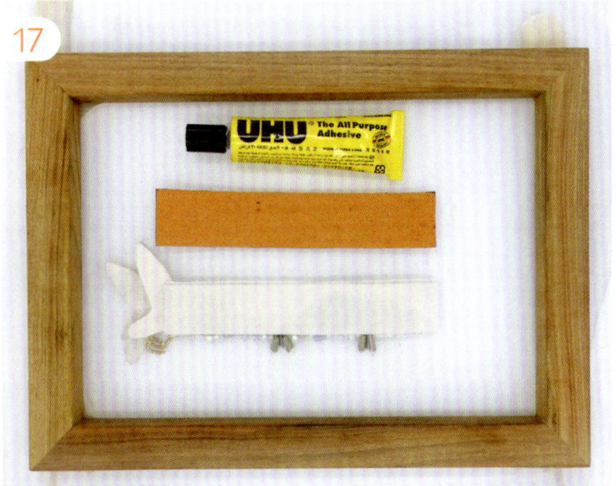

17

Prepare a piece of regenerated leather the same size as the back of the embroidery piece. Stick it onto the self-adhesive velvet with fabric glue.

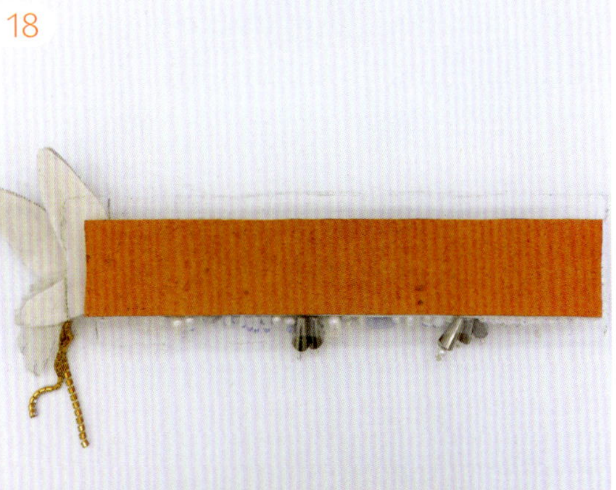

18

Cut out the embroidery piece and leave a margin of 5–8 mm at the edges.

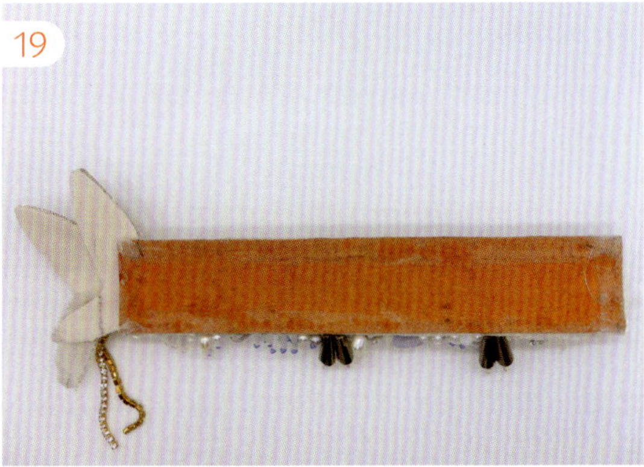

Fold the edges of the fabric inwards and stick it onto the regenerated leather on the back of the embroidery piece with fabric glue.

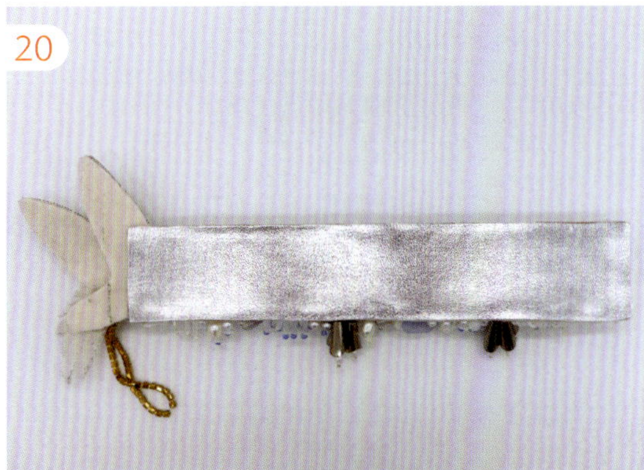

Apply fabric glue to the regenerated leather and stick a piece of silver leather of the same size onto it. Let it dry thoroughly.

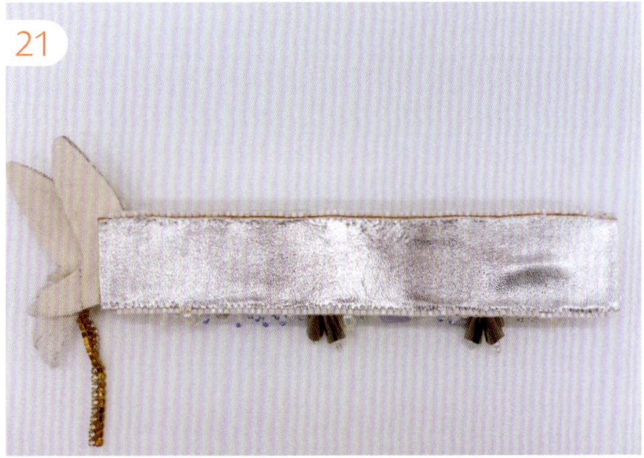

Use a hand sewing needle, silver thread, and 2 mm white seed beads to overlock the upper and lower edges of the bracelet.

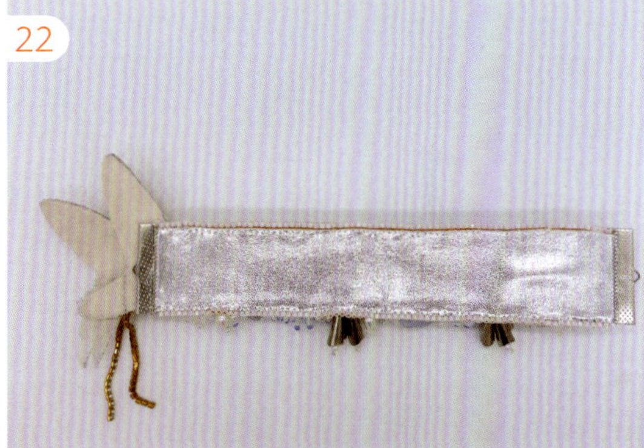

Apply a little fabric glue to both ends of the bracelet. Next, put the 30 mm silver bracelet bookmark pinches onto both ends of the bracelet and clamp them with pliers.

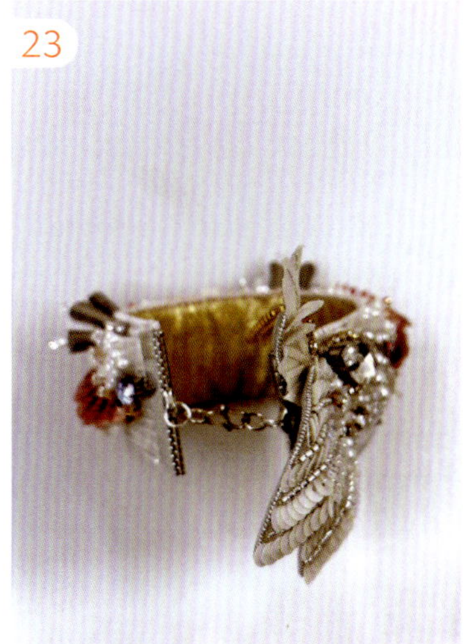

Attach the silver bracelet lobster clasp and chain extender to the bracelet bookmark pinches.

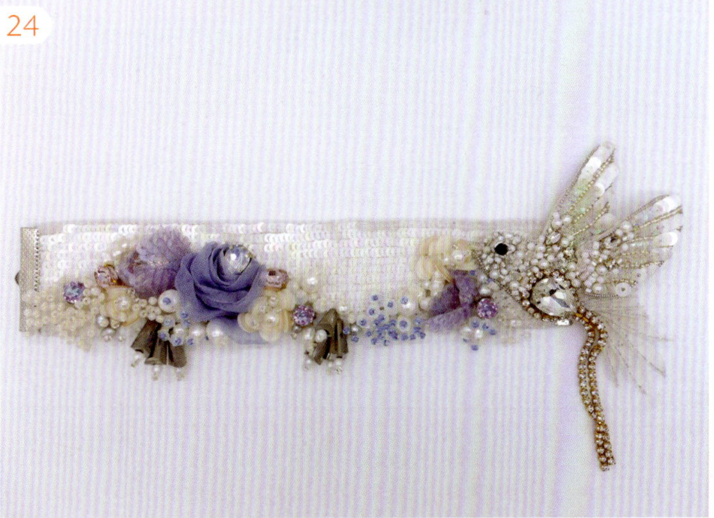

Allow the glue to dry thoroughly, then arrange the bird's wings into shape. The piece is now complete.

Appendix

Patterns

Wild Pansy Headband

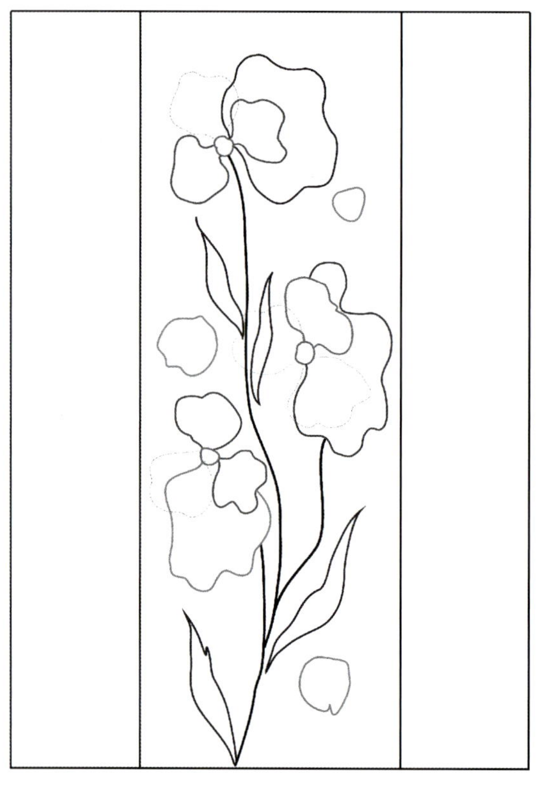

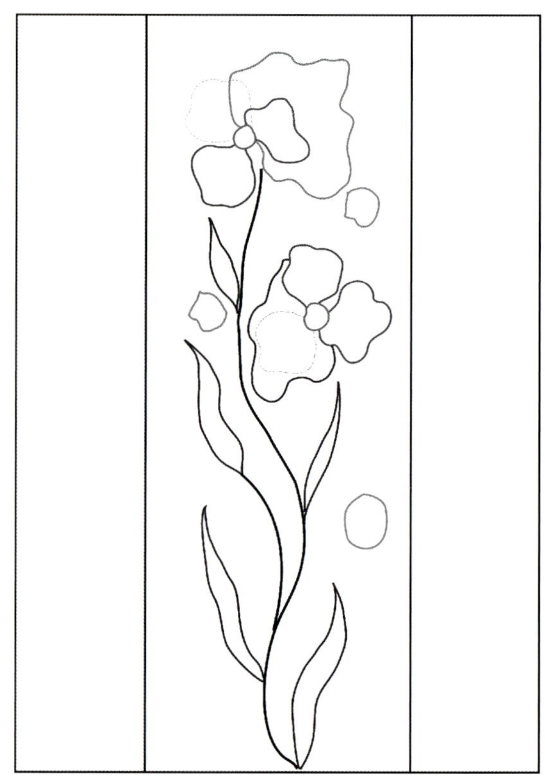

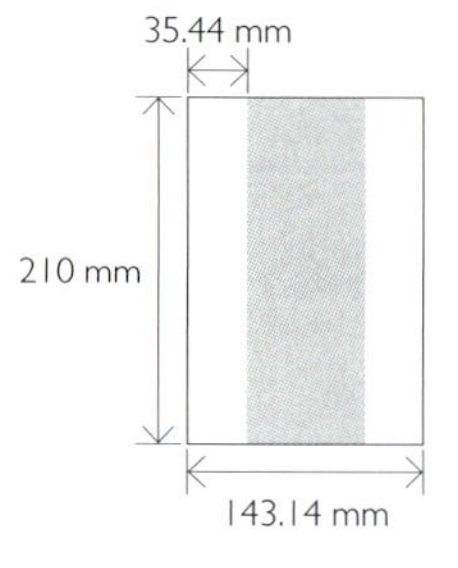

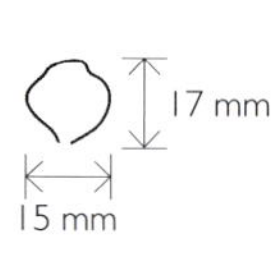

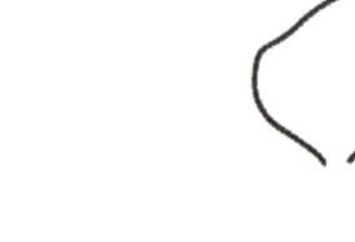

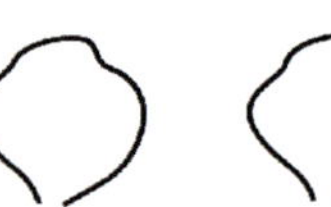

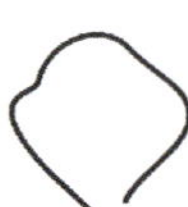

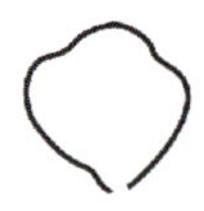

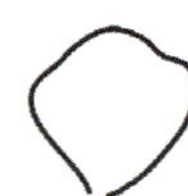

Lily of the Valley Cuff Bracelets

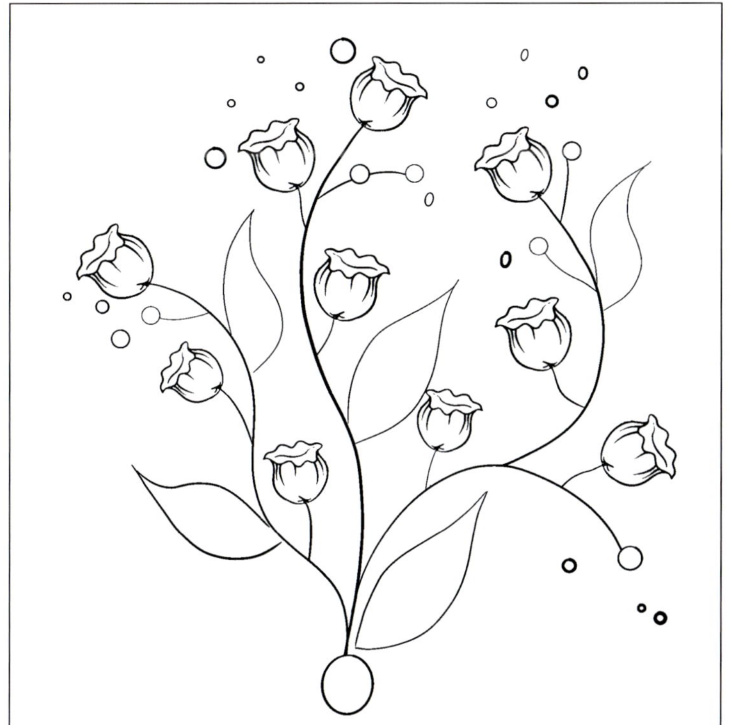

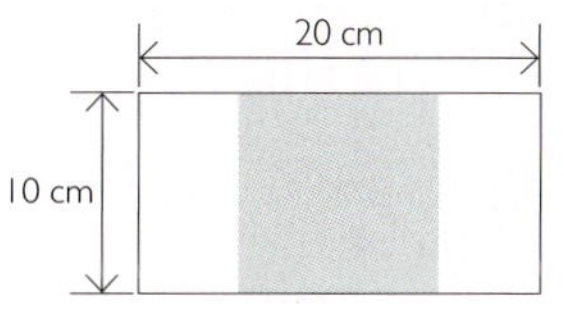

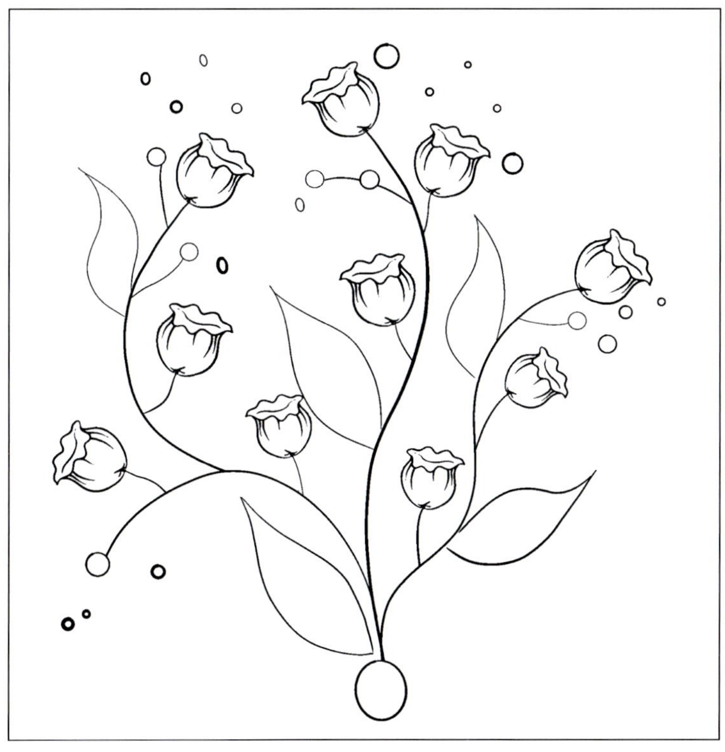

Iris Hair Accessory

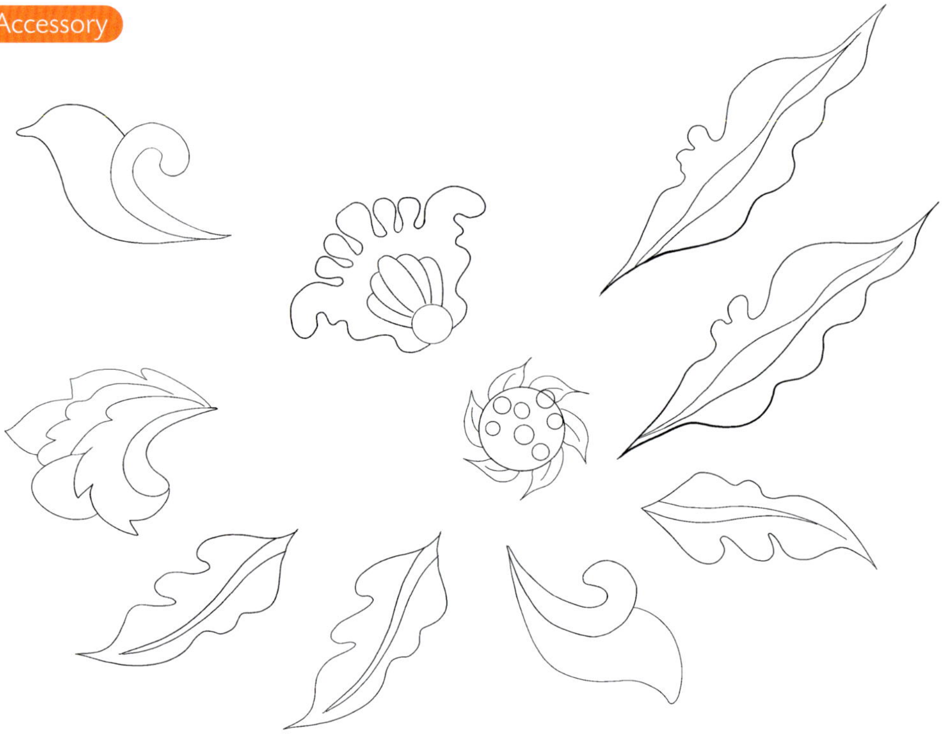

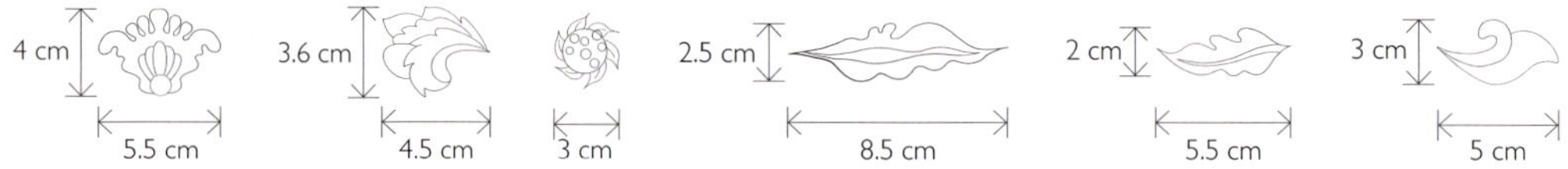

4 cm 5.5 cm
3.6 cm 4.5 cm
3 cm
2.5 cm 8.5 cm
2 cm 5.5 cm
3 cm 5 cm

Chinese Flowering Crabapple Ring

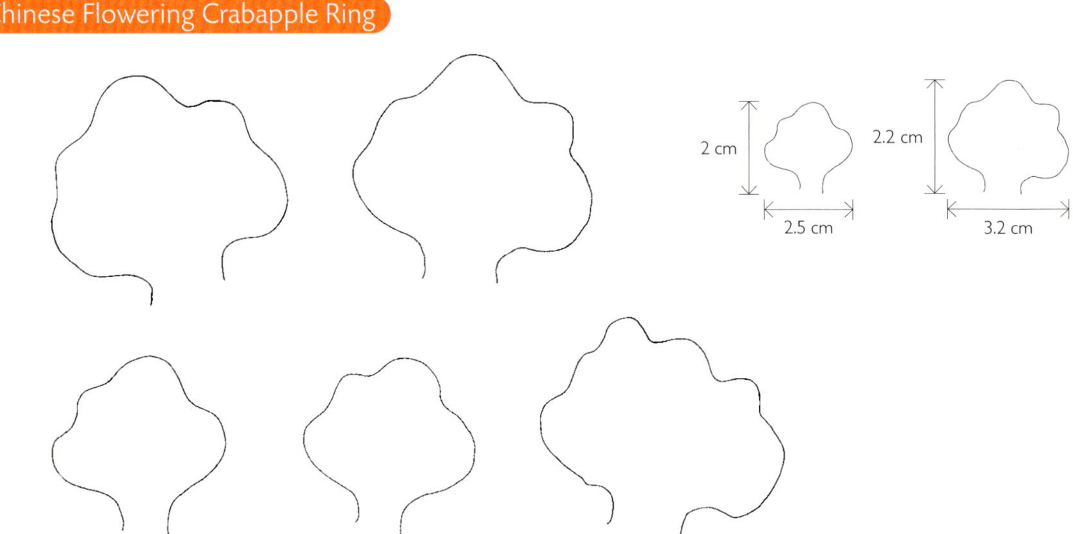

Bauhinia Ring

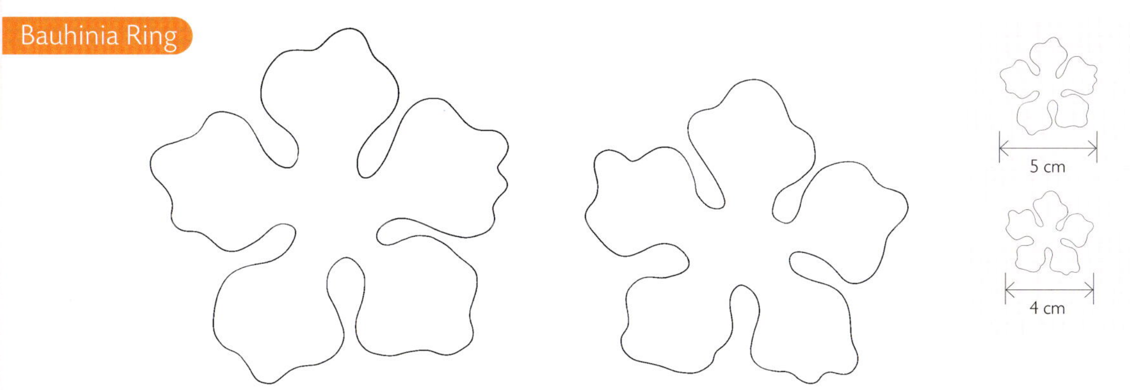

Mini Chinese Enkianthus Bag

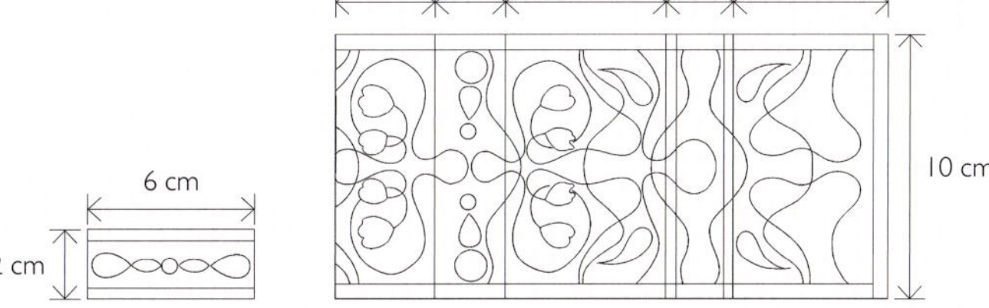

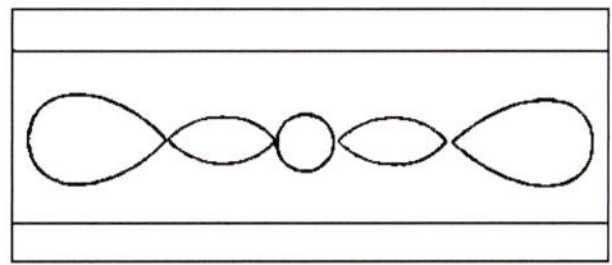

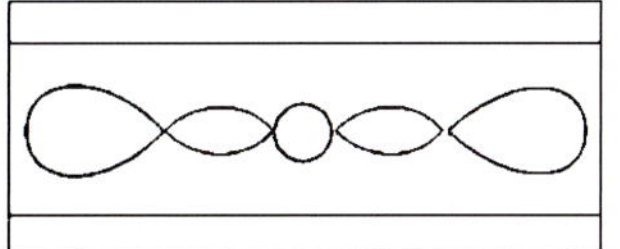

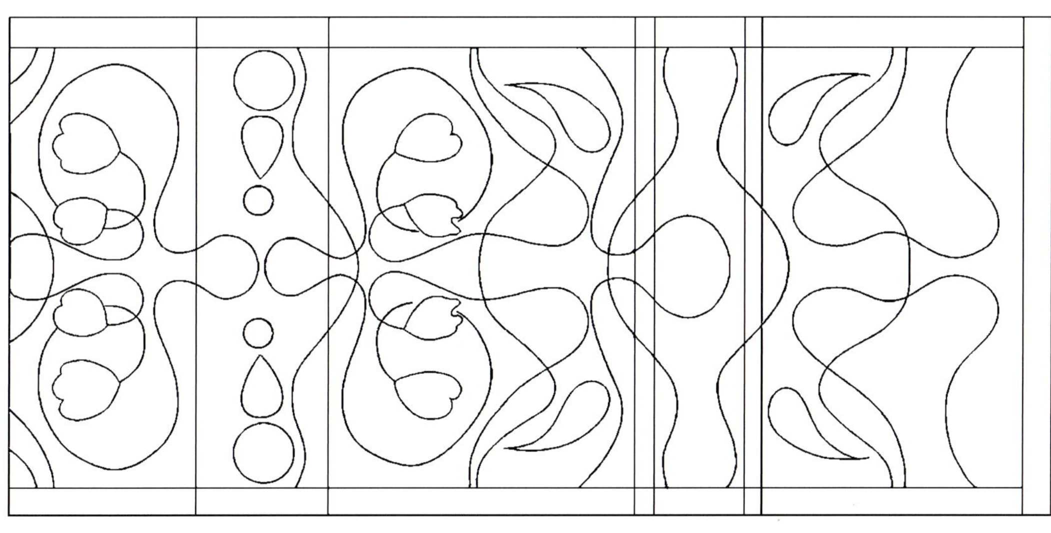

Canterbury Bells Earrings

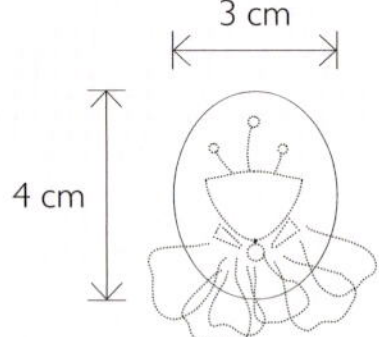

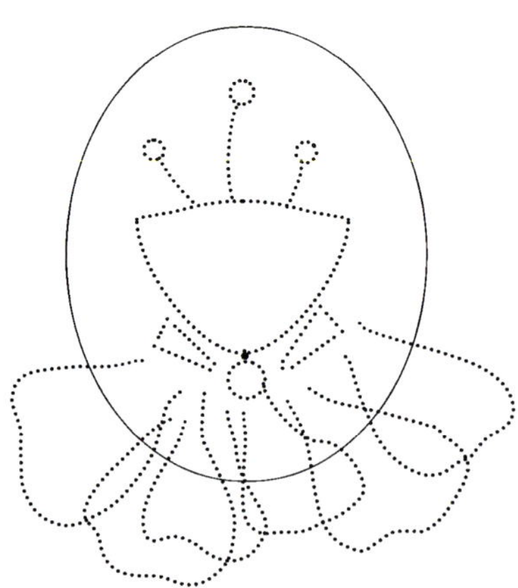

Twin Lotus Brooch

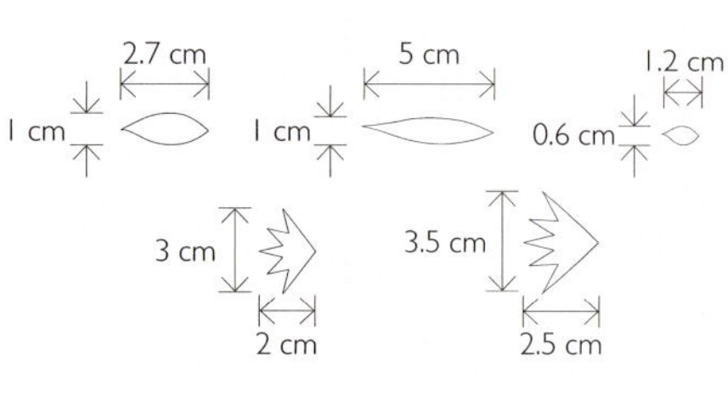

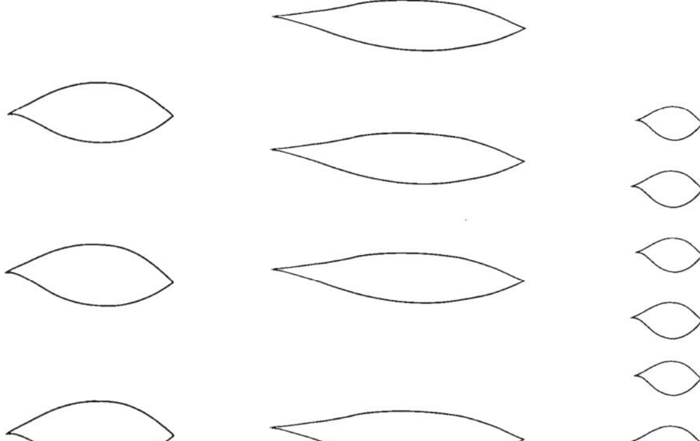

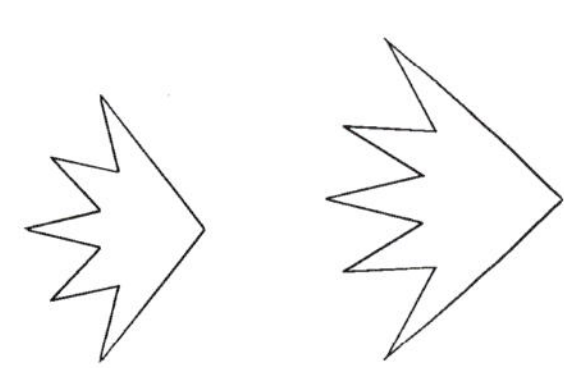

Balloon Flower Earrings

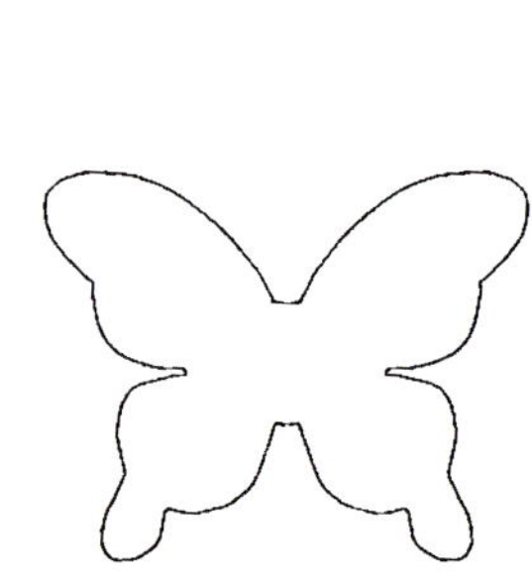

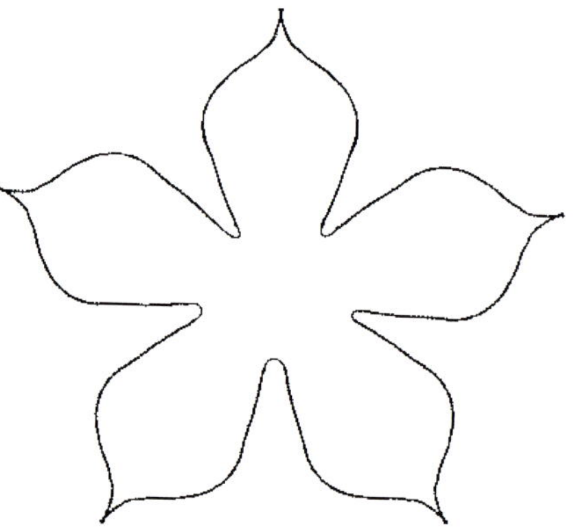

3 cm

2.5 cm

2.5 cm

5 cm

Rose Brooch

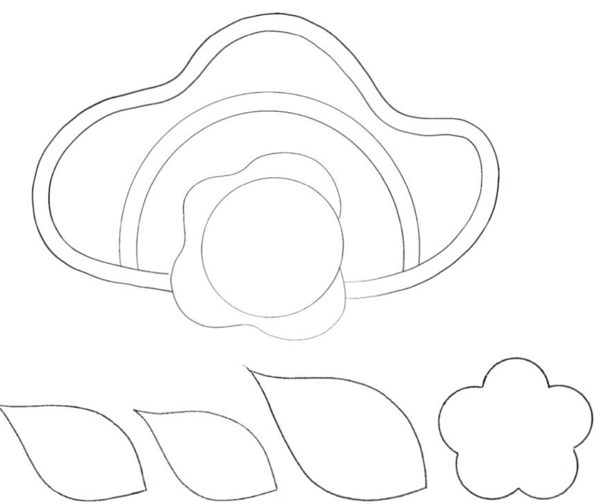

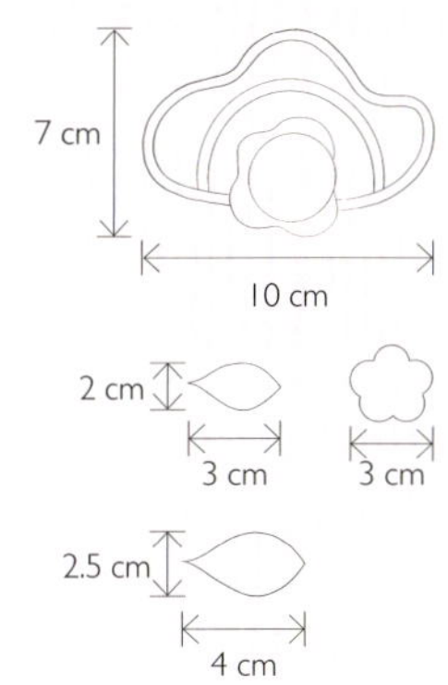

Silk Tree Flower Brooches

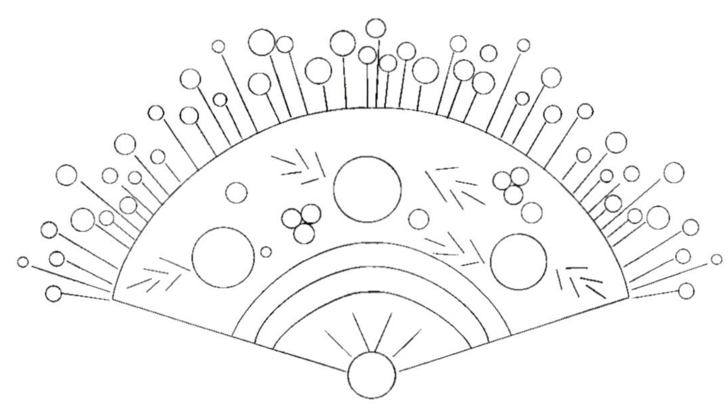

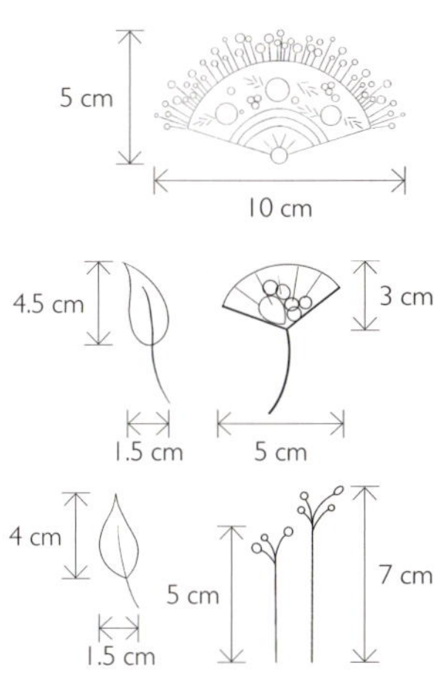

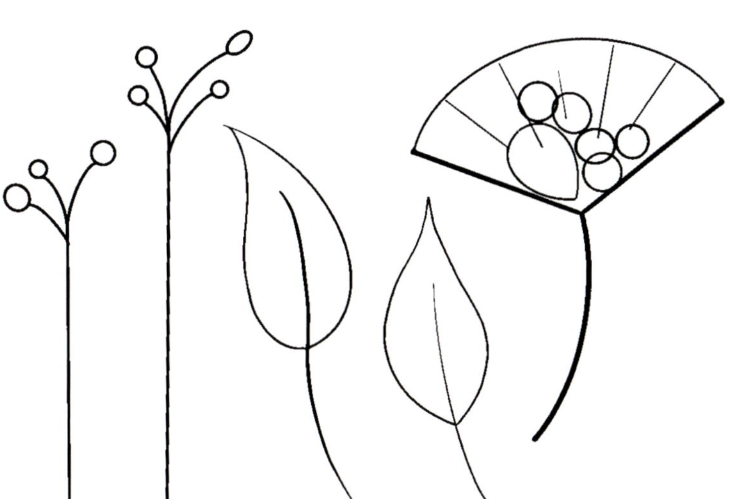

Peacock Flower Hair Band

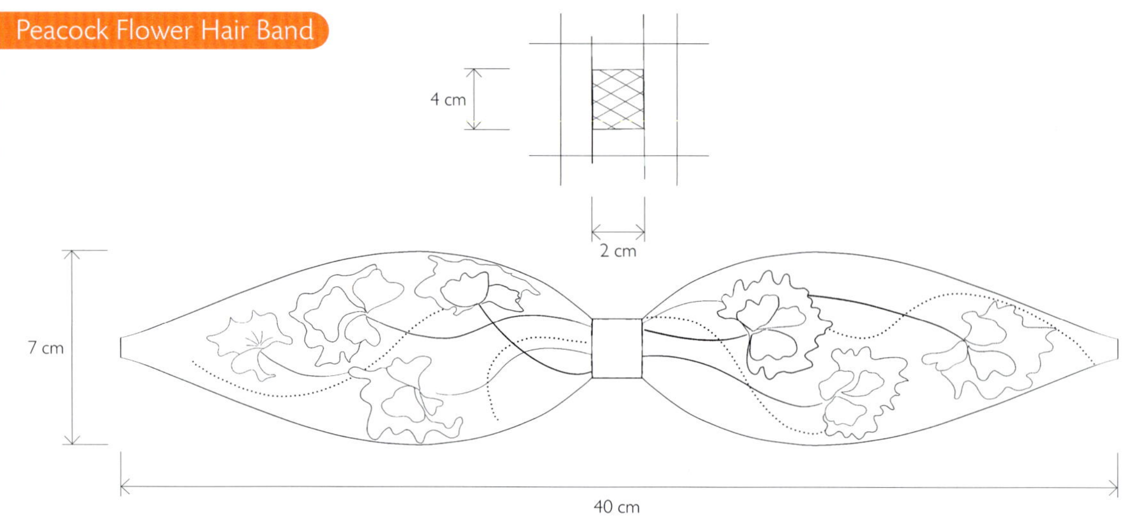

Flower and Bird Bracelet

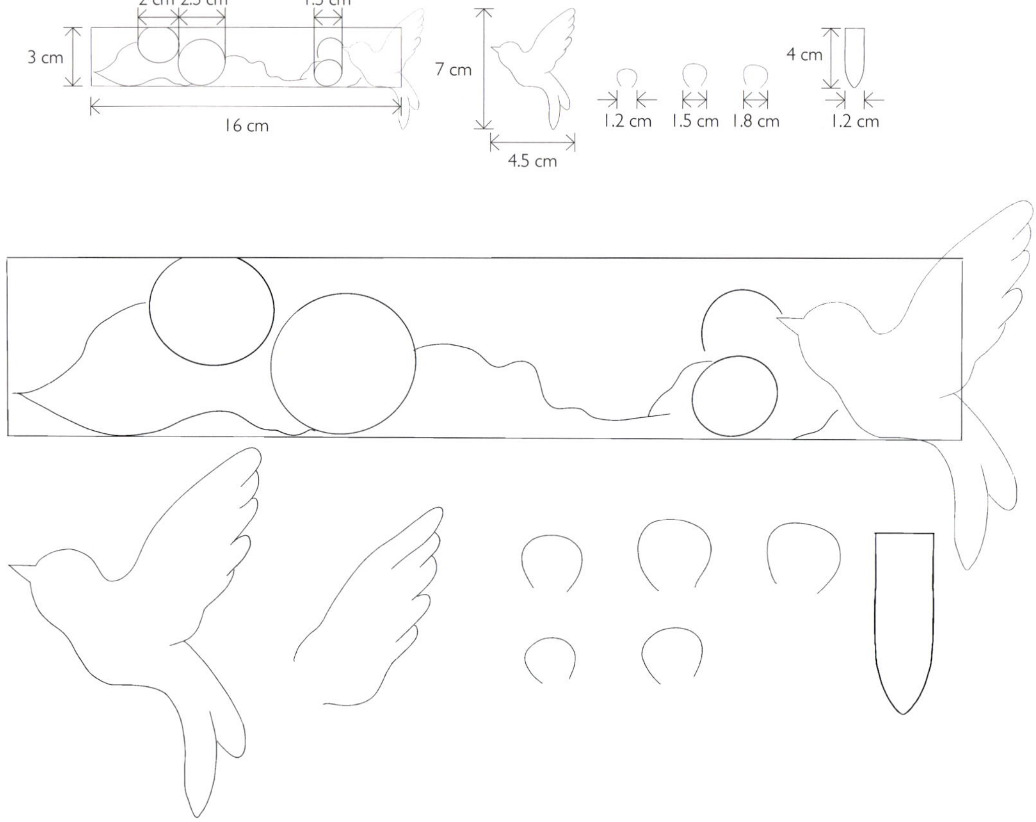

Dandelion Bridal Hair Ornament

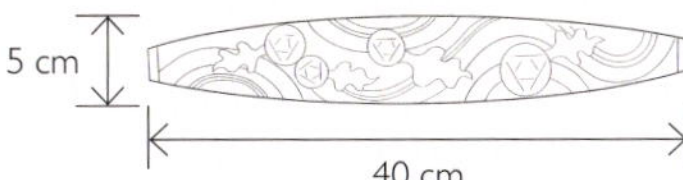

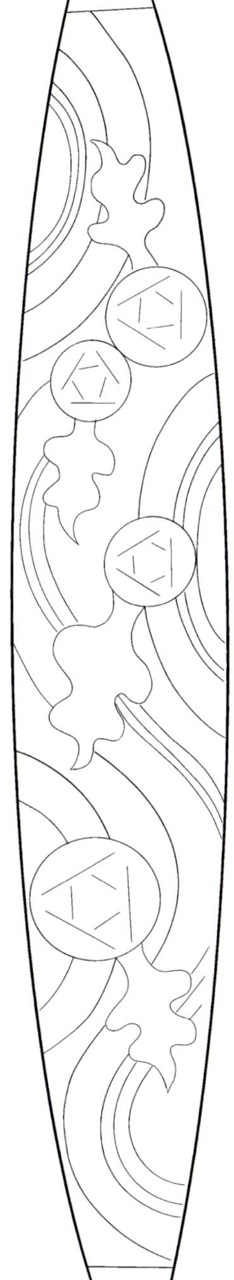

Plum Blossom Belt

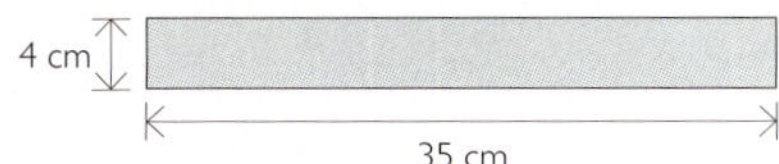

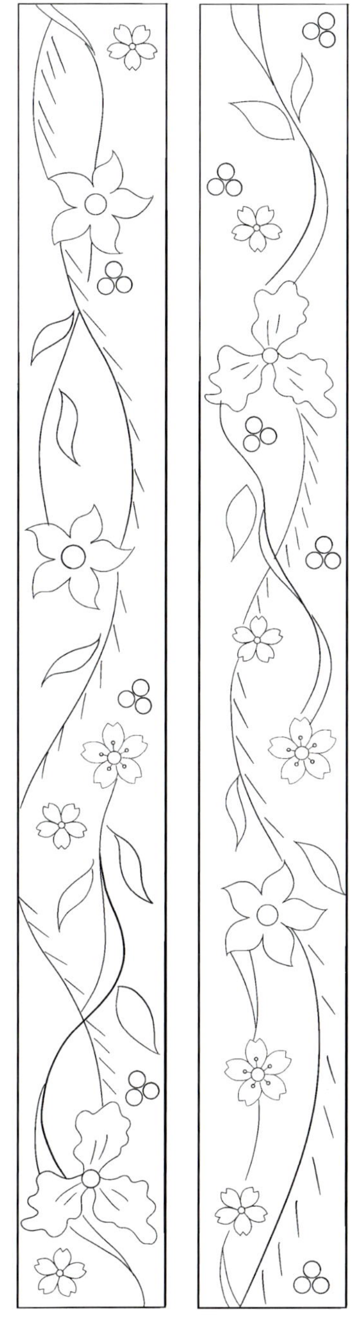

Lily Dinner Bag

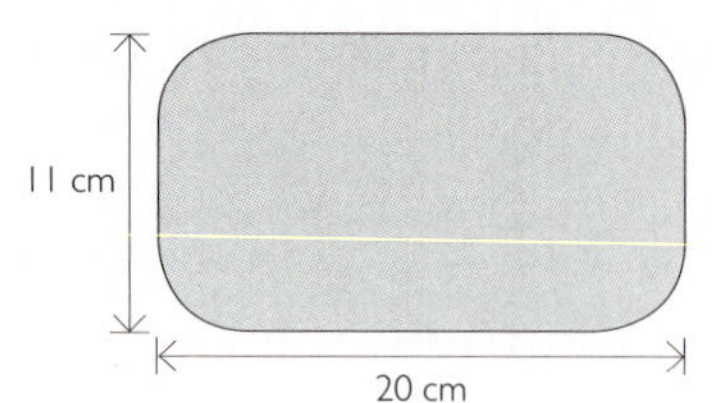

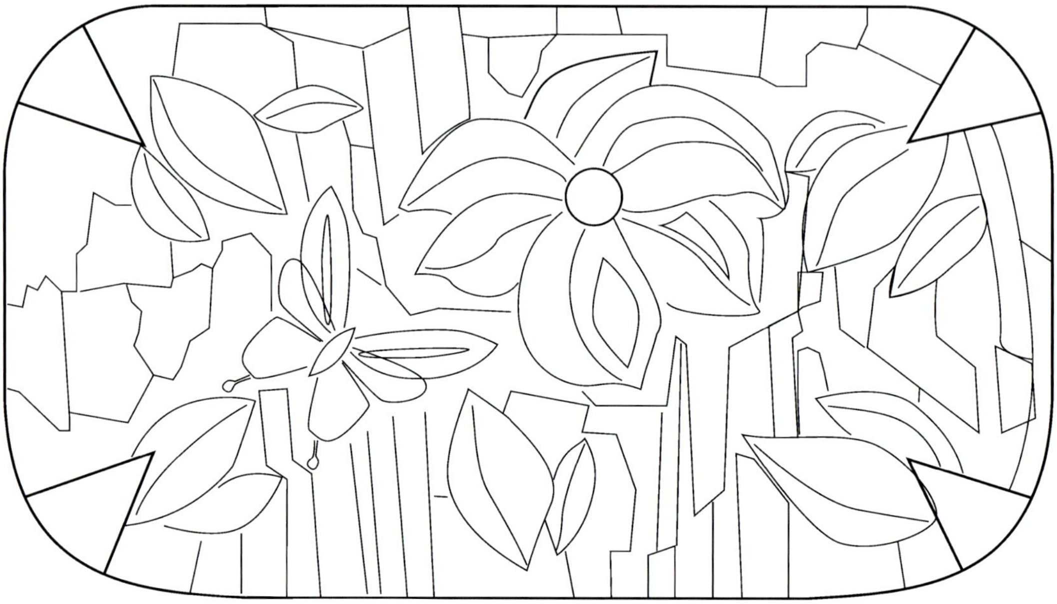

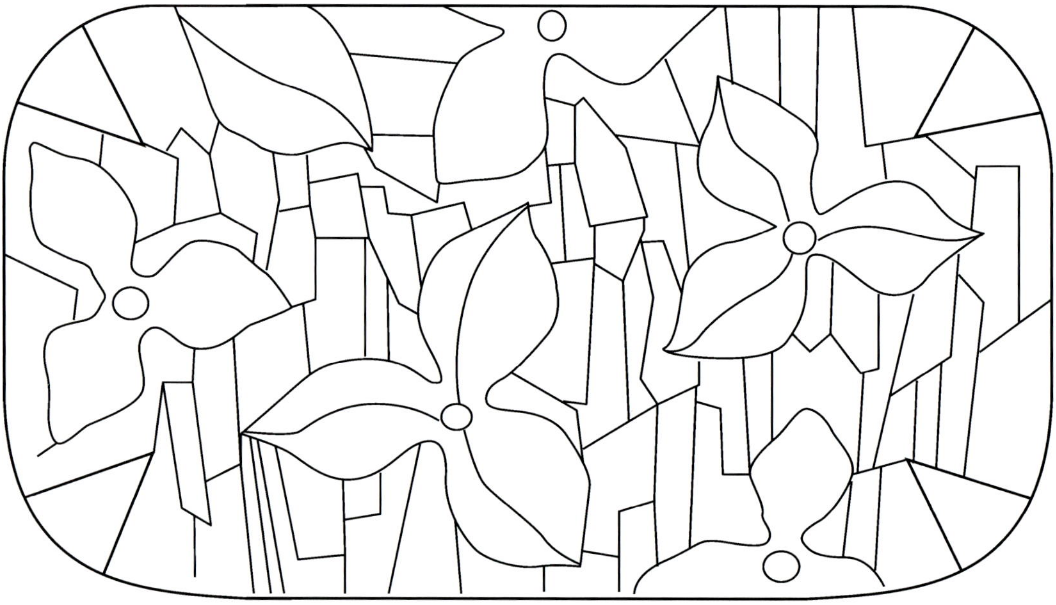